MAKING SENSE
OF THE
DOCTRINE & COVENANTS

MAKING SENSE
OF THE
DOCTRINE & COVENANTS

A Guided Tour through
MODERN REVELATIONS

STEVEN C. HARPER

DESERET BOOK
SALT LAKE CITY, UTAH

All photos courtesy Intellectual Reserve, Inc., except as noted individually.

Page 22, Angel Moroni: Courtesy Kendra and Allan Daniel Collection. All rights reserved. Used by permission.

Page 88, Emma Hale Smith in later life: Courtesy Community of Christ Archives, Independence, Missouri.

Page 128, Lucy Mack Smith: Courtesy Community of Christ Archives, Independence, Missouri.

© 2008 Steven C. Harper

All rights reserved. No part of this book may be reproduced in any form or by any means without permission in writing from the publisher, Deseret Book Company, at permissions@deseretbook.com or PO Box 30178, Salt Lake City, Utah 84130. This work is not an official publication of The Church of Jesus Christ of Latter-day Saints. The views expressed herein are the responsibility of the author and do not necessarily represent the position of the Church or of Deseret Book Company.

DESERET BOOK is a registered trademark of Deseret Book Company.

Visit us at deseretbook.com

First printing in hardbound 2008
First printing in paperbound 2020

Library of Congress Cataloging-in-Publication Data
Harper, Steven Craig, 1970–
  Making sense of the Doctrine & Covenants : a guided tour through modern revelations / Steven C. Harper.
       p.   cm.
  Includes bibliographical references and index.
  ISBN 978-1-59038-921-8 (hardcover); ISBN 978-1-62972-826-1 (paperbound)
  1. Doctrine and Covenants—Criticism, interpretation, etc.   I. Title.
  BX8628.H29 2008
  289.3'2—dc22   2008023952

Printed in the United States of America
Publishers Printing, Salt Lake City, UT

10   9   8   7   6   5   4   3   2

*For those who love the Doctrine and Covenants
and all who seek so to do*

Search these commandments, for they are true and faithful, and the prophecies and promises which are in them shall all be fulfilled.

Doctrine & Covenants 1:37

Contents

Preface xvii
Acknowledgments xxi
A Brief History of the Doctrine & Covenants 1
Explanatory Introduction 11
Doctrine & Covenants 1 18
    Hiram, Ohio, 1 November 1831
Doctrine & Covenants 2 21
    Manchester, New York, 21–22 September 1823
Doctrine & Covenants 3 24
    Harmony (now Oakland), Pennsylvania, July 1828
Doctrine & Covenants 4 29
    Harmony (now Oakland), Pennsylvania, February 1829
Doctrine & Covenants 5 31
    Harmony (now Oakland), Pennsylvania, March 1829
Doctrine & Covenants 6 36
    Harmony (now Oakland), Pennsylvania, April 1829
Doctrine & Covenants 7 40
    Harmony (now Oakland), Pennsylvania, April 1829
Doctrine & Covenants 8 42
    Harmony (now Oakland), Pennsylvania, April 1829
Doctrine & Covenants 9 44
    Harmony (now Oakland), Pennsylvania, April 1829
Doctrine & Covenants 10 46
    Harmony (now Oakland), Pennsylvania, Spring 1829
Doctrine & Covenants 11 51
    Harmony (now Oakland), Pennsylvania, May 1829

Doctrine & Covenants 12 54
  Harmony (now Oakland), Pennsylvania, May 1829

Doctrine & Covenants 13 56
  Susquehanna Riverbank near Harmony (now Oakland), Pennsylvania, 15 May 1829

Doctrine & Covenants 14 59
  Fayette, New York, June 1829

Doctrine & Covenants 15 59
  Fayette, New York, June 1829

Doctrine & Covenants 16 59
  Fayette, New York, June 1829

Doctrine & Covenants 17 62
  Fayette, New York, June 1829

Doctrine & Covenants 18 65
  Fayette, New York, early June 1829

Doctrine & Covenants 19 68
  Manchester, New York, March 1830

Doctrine & Covenants 20 73
  Fayette, New York, 10 April 1830

Doctrine & Covenants 21 76
  Fayette, New York, 6 April 1830

Doctrine & Covenants 22 79
  Manchester, New York, 16 April 1830

Doctrine & Covenants 23 81
  Manchester, New York, April 1830

Doctrine & Covenants 24 83
  Harmony (now Oakland), Pennsylvania, July 1830

Doctrine & Covenants 25 86
  Harmony (now Oakland), Pennsylvania, about August 1830

Doctrine & Covenants 26 90
  Harmony (now Oakland), Pennsylvania, July 1830

Doctrine & Covenants 27 92
  Harmony (now Oakland), Pennsylvania, August and September 1830

Doctrine & Covenants 28 95
  Fayette, New York, September 1830

Doctrine & Covenants 29 97
  Fayette, New York, September 1830

Doctrine & Covenants 30 101
  Fayette, New York, September 1830

Doctrine & Covenants 31 104
   Fayette, New York, September 1830

Doctrine & Covenants 32 107
   Fayette, New York, October 1830

Doctrine & Covenants 33 110
   Fayette, New York, October 1830

Doctrine & Covenants 34 113
   Fayette, New York, November 1830

Doctrine & Covenants 35 116
   Fayette, New York, 7 December 1830

Doctrine & Covenants 36 119
   Fayette, New York, 9 December 1830

Doctrine & Covenants 37 121
   Fayette, New York, 30 December 1830

Doctrine & Covenants 38 123
   Fayette, New York, 2 January 1831

Doctrine & Covenants 39 132
   Fayette, New York, 5 January 1831

Doctrine & Covenants 40 132
   Fayette, New York, 6 January 1831

Doctrine & Covenants 41 136
   Kirtland, Ohio, 4 February 1831

Doctrine & Covenants 42 139
   Kirtland, Ohio, 9 February 1831, vv. 1–72;
   23 February 1831, vv. 74–93

Doctrine & Covenants 43 147
   Kirtland, Ohio, February 1831

Doctrine & Covenants 44 152
   Kirtland, Ohio, February 1831

Doctrine & Covenants 45 154
   Kirtland, Ohio, about 7 March 1831

Doctrine & Covenants 46 159
   Kirtland, Ohio, about 8 March 1831

Doctrine & Covenants 47 162
   Kirtland, Ohio, about 8 March 1831

Doctrine & Covenants 48 164
   Kirtland, Ohio, 10 March 1831

Doctrine & Covenants 49 166
   Kirtland, Ohio, 7 May 1831

Doctrine & Covenants 50 172
   Kirtland, Ohio, 9 May 1831

Doctrine & Covenants 51 181
   Thompson, Ohio, 20 May 1831

Doctrine & Covenants 52 186
   Kirtland, Ohio, 6 June 1831

Doctrine & Covenants 53 190
   Kirtland, Ohio, 8 June 1831

Doctrine & Covenants 54 192
   Kirtland, Ohio, 10 June 1831

Doctrine & Covenants 55 194
   Kirtland, Ohio, 14 June 1831

Doctrine & Covenants 56 196
   Kirtland, Ohio, 15 June 1831

Doctrine & Covenants 57 199
   Jackson County, Missouri, 20 July 1831

Doctrine & Covenants 58 202
   Jackson County, Missouri, 1 August 1831

Doctrine & Covenants 59 207
   Jackson County, Missouri, 7 August 1831

Doctrine & Covenants 60 210
   Jackson County, Missouri, 8 August 1831

Doctrine & Covenants 61 212
   Missouri Riverbank, Missouri, 12 August 1831

Doctrine & Covenants 62 216
   Chariton, Missouri, 13 August 1831

Doctrine & Covenants 63 218
   Kirtland, Ohio, 30 August 1831

Doctrine & Covenants 64 223
   Kirtland, Ohio, 11 September 1831

Doctrine & Covenants 65 226
   Hiram, Ohio, 30 October 1831

Doctrine & Covenants 66 229
   Hiram, Ohio, 29 October 1831

Doctrine & Covenants 67 233
   Hiram, Ohio, 2 November 1831

Doctrine & Covenants 68 237
   Hiram, Ohio, 1 November 1831

Doctrine & Covenants 69 241
    Hiram, Ohio, 11 November 1831

Doctrine & Covenants 70 243
    Kirtland, Ohio, 12 November 1831

Doctrine & Covenants 71 247
    Hiram, Ohio, 1 December 1831

Doctrine & Covenants 72 250
    Kirtland, Ohio, 4 December 1831

Doctrine & Covenants 73 254
    Hiram, Ohio, 10 January 1832

Doctrine & Covenants 74 255
    Hiram, Ohio, January 1832

Doctrine & Covenants 75 258
    Amherst, Ohio, 25 January 1832

Doctrine & Covenants 76 262
    Hiram, Ohio, 16 February 1832

Doctrine & Covenants 77 273
    Hiram, Ohio, March 1832

Doctrine & Covenants 78 277
    Hiram, Ohio, 1 March 1832

Doctrine & Covenants 79 282
    Hiram, Ohio, 12 March 1832

Doctrine & Covenants 80 284
    Hiram, Ohio, 7 March 1832

Doctrine & Covenants 81 286
    Hiram, Ohio, 15 March 1832

Doctrine & Covenants 82 288
    Jackson County, Missouri, 26 April 1832

Doctrine & Covenants 83 292
    Jackson County, Missouri, 30 April 1832

Doctrine & Covenants 84 294
    Kirtland, Ohio, 22–23 September 1832

Doctrine & Covenants 85 304
    Kirtland, Ohio, 27 November 1832

Doctrine & Covenants 86 307
    Kirtland, Ohio, 6 December 1832

Doctrine & Covenants 87 310
    At or near Kirtland, Ohio, 25 December 1832

Doctrine & Covenants 88 313
   Kirtland, Ohio, 27–28 December 1832, vv. 1–126;
   3 January 1833, vv. 127–41

Doctrine & Covenants 89 322
   Kirtland, Ohio, 27 February 1833

Doctrine & Covenants 90 336
   Kirtland, Ohio, 8 March 1833

Doctrine & Covenants 91 340
   Kirtland, Ohio, 9 March 1833

Doctrine & Covenants 92 343
   Kirtland, Ohio, 15 March 1833

Doctrine & Covenants 93 345
   Kirtland, Ohio, 6 May 1833

Doctrine & Covenants 94 350
   Kirtland, Ohio, 2 August 1833

Doctrine & Covenants 95 352
   Kirtland, Ohio, 1 June 1833

Doctrine & Covenants 96 355
   Kirtland, Ohio, 4 June 1833

Doctrine & Covenants 97 357
   Kirtland, Ohio, 2 August 1833

Doctrine & Covenants 98 360
   Kirtland, Ohio, 6 August 1833

Doctrine & Covenants 99 364
   Hiram, Ohio, 29 August 1832

Doctrine & Covenants 100 367
   Perrysburg, New York, 12 October 1833

Doctrine & Covenants 101 370
   Kirtland, Ohio, 16–17 December 1833

Doctrine & Covenants 102 375
   Kirtland, Ohio, 17 February 1834

Doctrine & Covenants 103 379
   Kirtland, Ohio, 24 February 1834

Doctrine & Covenants 104 382
   At or near Kirtland, Ohio, 23 April 1834

Doctrine & Covenants 105 389
   Fishing River, Clay County, Missouri, 22 June 1834

Doctrine & Covenants 106 393
   Kirtland, Ohio, November 1834

Doctrine & Covenants 107 395
   Kirtland, Ohio, late April 1835 and November 1831

Doctrine & Covenants 108 400
   Kirtland, Ohio, December 1835

Doctrine & Covenants 109 402
   Kirtland, Ohio, 26 March 1836

Doctrine & Covenants 110 407
   Kirtland, Ohio, 3 April 1836

Doctrine & Covenants 111 412
   Salem, Massachusetts, 6 August 1836

Doctrine & Covenants 112 414
   Kirtland, Ohio, 23 July 1837

Doctrine & Covenants 113 418
   Near Far West, Missouri, March 1838

Doctrine & Covenants 114 421
   Far West, Missouri, 17 April 1838

Doctrine & Covenants 115 423
   Far West, Missouri, 26 April 1838

Doctrine & Covenants 116 427
   Spring Hill, Daviess County, Missouri, 19 May 1838

Doctrine & Covenants 117 430
   Far West, Missouri, 8 July 1838

Doctrine & Covenants 118 435
   Far West, Missouri, 8 July 1838

Doctrine & Covenants 119 440
   Far West, Missouri, 8 July 1838

Doctrine & Covenants 120 444
   Far West, Missouri, 8 July 1838

Doctrine & Covenants 121 446
   Liberty, Missouri, 20 March 1839

Doctrine & Covenants 122 446
   Liberty, Missouri, 20 March 1839

Doctrine & Covenants 123 446
   Liberty, Missouri, 20 March 1839

Doctrine & Covenants 124 455
   Nauvoo, Illinois, 19 January 1841

Doctrine & Covenants 125 462
   Nauvoo, Illinois, March 1841

Doctrine & Covenants 126 464
    Nauvoo, Illinois, 9 July 1841

Doctrine & Covenants 127 466
    Nauvoo, Illinois, 1 September 1842

Doctrine & Covenants 128 466
    Nauvoo, Illinois, 6 September 1842

Doctrine & Covenants 129 472
    Nauvoo, Illinois, 9 February 1843

Doctrine & Covenants 130 474
    Ramus (now Webster), Illinois, 2 April 1843

Doctrine & Covenants 131 477
    Ramus (now Webster), Illinois, 16–17 May 1843

Doctrine & Covenants 132 480
    Nauvoo, Illinois, 12 July 1843

Doctrine & Covenants 133 490
    Hiram, Ohio, 3 November 1831

Doctrine & Covenants 134 493
    Kirtland, Ohio, August 1835

Doctrine & Covenants 135 495
    Nauvoo, Illinois, after June 1844

Doctrine & Covenants 136 499
    Winter Quarters, west bank of Missouri River, near what is now Florence, Nebraska, 14 January 1847

Doctrine & Covenants 137 504
    Kirtland, Ohio, 21 January 1836

Doctrine & Covenants 138 508
    Salt Lake City, Utah, 3 October 1918

Official Declaration–1 514
    Salt Lake City, Utah, September 1890; read in general conference October 6, 1890

Official Declaration–2 521
    Salt Lake City, Utah, June 1978; read in general conference September 30, 1978

Epilogue 531
Notes 533
Index 579

Preface

It was very early one morning when I felt I finally understood Doctrine and Covenants 66. I had long been intimate with its thirteen verses, studied related documents in the LDS Church History Library and the Community of Christ (formerly RLDS) Archives, and painstakingly read the original journals of William McLellin, the man to whom the Lord spoke in section 66. But I wrestled with the revelation for a long time. Then, in an instant, it opened to me. The epiphany was well worth the price paid in study. I understood William McLellin, I comprehended the Savior's highly personalized words to him, and because of that, I felt empowered to apply them to myself as well.

As a professor of Church history, I have studied the Doctrine and Covenants this way for many years. I earned graduate degrees in history to better understand the period in which most of the revelations were given. I learned to read the handwriting of those who wrote the early manuscripts, so I could pore over them often. I continue to study the records left by the people through whom and to whom the Lord spoke His revelations, and it is my privilege to assist in editing revelation manuscripts for publication in the Joseph Smith Papers. I have spent countless hours reading and thinking about the texts of the revelations. All this is the beginning, not the end of my inquiry, and I invite readers to join me in the endlessly interesting and deeply satisfying quest.

Not long ago I had a candid conversation with a scholar of American religious history. "Reading the Doctrine and Covenants is like reading a dictionary," he confessed. He was frustrated, as many readers seem to be, by the challenges of making sense of the isolated sections. Most are freestanding texts, unconnected to those surrounding it. In comparison, the Book of Mormon contains dozens of revelations, but narrators, beginning with Nephi's introduction to readers in the book's very first words, do the work of creating connective tissue. Nephi and others lead readers through the revelations, seeing them safely from one to the next and explaining their significance in between. With few exceptions, there is little of that kind of narrative in the Doctrine and Covenants.

Each revelation is the heart of a story with no beginning or end in the book of scripture itself but which the Savior deemed important enough to address from heaven. Reading the sections is akin to joining a conversation that is well underway. Paying careful attention enables readers to make judgments about what they missed, but conclusions based on such judgments may be erroneous and hard to correct. Such mistaken conclusions have been perpetuated by influential commentaries or reinforced through generations of retelling. In such cases, the revealed texts may become casualties to traditional interpretations, some of which hold onto life tenaciously.

But deeper and inspiring understanding can be ours when we come to know the background questions or problems the text was revealed to resolve. In most cases the story of each revelation can be recovered from the historical record. Returning to the analogy of joining a conversation already underway, each of the sections is an answer or set of answers to a specific question. The "revelations were received in answer to prayer, in times of need," says the Explanatory Introduction, "and came out of real-life situations involving real people." The more we learn about those situations and people, the better we understand the Doctrine and Covenants. Knowing the questions that started the conversation makes the answers dramatically more understandable and interesting. Consider how much richer a conversation would be for someone briefed in advance about the personalities and issues in the discussion. This book describes the questions, problems, and personalities that shape the texts, helping us to understand more fully why the revelations say what they say in the way that they say it.

What we sometimes call *context*—for example, that a conversation took place in 1830 in Ohio in so-and-so's house and that one of the participants was John Johnson—is less illuminating than discovering specific information about the relevance of that place and person to the conversation. Why there? Why then? Why that individual?

The *text* of each revelation is even more important. Even if we join a conversation without context, much can be gained by listening carefully. Thus, the revelations themselves deserve our deepest attention. What do they say? How do they say it? What doctrines do they declare? What covenants do they make? What do they command, prophesy, and promise? Each revelation is coherent, with an internal logic that teaches us the Lord's mind and will. We sometimes cut the revelations into little pieces and comment on each slice. That can help, but it can also hinder our efforts to listen to the Lord. We can perhaps be too quick to comment and too slow to listen or hearken, as the revelations repeatedly command. Then-Elder Gordon B. Hinckley urged the Saints to "let the Lord speak for Himself to you."[1] That can be done in many ways, including through the study of each revelation as a whole. The Lord's logic, the rationale by which he communicates his mind and will, may be lost when the revelations are cut into pieces.

Assessing the outcomes of each revelation comes next. It is one thing to learn what each revelation says, and another to learn what each one does. For example, in section 66 the Lord gave William McLellin more than twenty commandments and promised specific outcomes if he obeyed. Did the commandments and promises motivate McLellin to obey? If so, did he receive the promised blessings? Assessing the fruits of a revelation is a profound way to appreciate its power—the difference that it did and can make. The revelations in the Doctrine and Covenants bore fruit when they were given and continue to do so. They change the eternal destinies of families—of worlds without end. They are powerful.

Imagine that each revelation is a work of art in a museum gallery. We can appreciate the works of art on their own, to be sure, but walking through the gallery with a guide enriches the experience. The guide can direct our attention to the composition, colors, and design of the art works, note how each piece was influenced by the period in which it was created, and make suggestions for interpretation. If the revelations recorded in the Doctrine and Covenants are the masterpieces, this book may be considered a guide to those masterpieces. It was written by a student of the scriptures who loves the revelations and longs to help others appreciate them more fully.

Each chapter explores one section, or in some cases, a few closely related sections, of the Doctrine and Covenants. First is a description, drawing on research in original sources, of why the Lord gave the revelation. The focus is sharp so as not to burden readers with context that does not answer the primary question the revelation speaks to. The purpose of this part of the chapter is to explain precisely the origin of each revelation, insofar as a thorough scouring of the historical record allows.

The second part of the chapter guides readers through the content of each revelation—the doctrines, covenants, commandments, prophecies, and promises it contains—so that readers may hear the Lord's voice more clearly and understand his words more fully.

The final part of the chapter assesses the fruits of the revelation—what it does. The purpose is to highlight and testify of the moving power of the revelations by discovering what happened because the Lord spoke those words then. This book avoids likening or applying the revelations to modern readers and situations. That is important work, but it is best done by individuals in the light of the Holy Spirit. A guide can help viewers appreciate a masterpiece, but it is best left to individual viewers to decide finally what significance they will discover in the master's work. Instead, each chapter ends by assessing what the revelation's original recipients did with it and implies an invitation for readers to answer the same question for themselves.

A note about information in the table of contents of this volume: Dates and places that differ from those in the Chronological Order of Contents given in the 1981 edition of the Doctrine and Covenants are based on the latest research associated with the *Joseph Smith Papers,* especially the *Revelations and Translations* series, volume 1, and *Documents,* volumes 1–4.

Acknowledgments

A book like this requires many minds and favors to compose, more than I can remember or adequately acknowledge. I owe my love for the Doctrine and Covenants to my parents, Carolyn and John Harper, in whose voices I first heard it read and in whose home its doctrine is believed and its covenants are kept. My brother David listened to me think through the book aloud and gave profound advice. I have great confidence in his judgment.

I have drawn liberally on the work of Robert Woodford, the foremost scholar of the Doctrine and Covenants. Patty Smith and her staff in the Religious Education Faculty Support Center at Brigham Young University, especially Stephen Haskin, did yeoman work in copying and checking sources. Robert Millet advised and encouraged me all along. Arnold Garr and Richard Bennett were extraordinarily supportive. Ronald Esplin at the Joseph Smith Papers was likewise, together with the host of talented and diligent scholars at work on the Prophet's papers. Among these, Robin Jensen, Rachel Osborne, and Richard Jensen made key contributions to my understanding and appreciation of Joseph's revelations.

At a critical point I appealed to Terryl Givens for help. His thoughtful critique changed the way I composed the content sections of each chapter, resulting in a much better book. Though blameless for its remaining defects, Terryl deserves credit for redeeming the book. So does Martha Parker, my editor. She reworked the manuscript repeatedly with efficiency, skill, and good cheer. Cory Maxwell and Suzanne Brady at Deseret Book saw it through the publication process.

My daughter Hannah typed some of the book and proofread some of the manuscript. Even more, she and her siblings have caused me to think much about how to better apply the Doctrine and Covenants, especially Doctrine and Covenants 121:34–46. I tell Hannah that she must not marry a man who cannot quote those verses to me (and, I should add, act on them with greater consistency than I do). Last and most of all I thank Jennifer Elizabeth. The Doctrine and Covenants promises that if she and I remain faithful to the new and everlasting covenant of marriage, we will come forth in the resurrection to inherit together a fulness and continuation forever and ever. How could I not love such revelations?

A Brief History of the Doctrine & Covenants

There has not always been a Doctrine and Covenants. It has a history and can best be understood by those who know that history. Robert Woodford, a great scholar of the Doctrine and Covenants, described how we tend to think of it as a "tidily defined book, quietly resting with the other scriptures. But the story of how those revelations were written, prepared for publication, and moved through various states until they reached our present edition is the story of trying to keep up with a flood of revealed knowledge."[1]

The early Saints delighted in the Prophet Joseph's revelations. They read them over and over, committing some to memory. They copied the manuscripts of the most important or personal ones and then copied the copies. They treasured these documents.[2] The growing number of missionaries needed the revelations in their ministry, but copies could only be made by hand when the missionaries happened to be at Church headquarters or crossed paths with someone who had a hand-copied manuscript of an earlier manuscript. Access was limited, and the potential for errors great. The Saints needed to publish the revelations.

In November 1831 Joseph Smith gathered Church leaders to the home of John and Elsa Johnson in Hiram, Ohio, to discuss how best to publish the revelations he had received and written. Printing in America had recently boomed. Religious and political groups were publishing newspapers, pamphlets, and books, reaching wider audiences than ever before with the printed word. Should the Saints tap into that power? The Lord

Elsa and John Johnson home in Hiram, Ohio. The preface (D&C 1) and appendix (D&C 133) and several other sections of the Doctrine and Covenants were revealed to Joseph Smith and others in this home. In November 1831 Church leaders used the home as their headquarters while they made plans to publish the revelations in Independence, Missouri.

had already commanded the experienced editor William Phelps to be a printer for the Church (D&C 57:11). A committee of talented writers drafted a preface. But it was the Lord's book, and he revealed what he called "my preface unto the book of my commandments, which I have given them to publish unto you, O inhabitants of the earth" (D&C 1:6). Joseph spoke the words slowly, and Sidney Rigdon wrote them down, but they originated in the mind of Jesus Christ in response to specific circumstances, thus making the Doctrine and Covenants "the only book in the world that has a preface written by the Lord Himself."[3]

"In that preface," said President Ezra Taft Benson, "He declares to the world that His voice is unto all men (see D&C 1:2), that the coming of the Lord is nigh (see D&C 1:12), and that the truths found in the Doctrine and Covenants will all be fulfilled (see D&C 1:37–38)."[4] He also indicts the world in its present state. "They seek not the Lord to establish his righteousness," the revelation said in condemnation of the earth's inhabitants, "but every man walketh in his own way, and after the image of his own god, whose image is in the likeness of the world, and whose substance is that of an idol, which waxeth old and shall perish in Babylon, even Babylon the great, which shall fall" (D&C 1:16).

Alexis de Tocqueville, the French observer of American life, was touring the States when the Lord gave this revelation. He observed what the Lord decried and called it *individualism*. Writing a decade later, Ralph Waldo Emerson called it *self-reliance*. "No law can be sacred to me but that of my nature," Emerson wrote. "Good and bad are but names very readily transferable to that or this; the only right is what is after my constitution; the only wrong what is against it." He did not want to be told of what he called "my obligation to put all poor men in good situations. Are they *my* poor?" he asked. "I grudge the dollar, the dime, the cent I give to such men as do not belong to me and to whom I do not belong."[5]

Historians see in this period "the installation of ambition as the one common good." Public worship, according to Emerson, "lost its grasp on the affection of the good and the fear of the bad." Antagonism, partisanship, and aspiration to acquire property and power grew to become false gods. Religion too often assisted rather than checked these worldly ambitions. A popular 1836 tract was called *The Book of Wealth; in Which It Is Proved from the Bible, That It Is the Duty of Every Man to Become Rich.*[6] By the time Joseph and his brethren began making plans to publish the revelations, "pride of self, once the mark of the devil, was now not just a legitimate emotion but America's uncontested god. And since everyone had his own self, everyone had his own god."[7] That is just what the Lord indicted in his preface to the Doctrine and Covenants (D&C 1:16).

Such attitudes defied the living God who gave revelations to Joseph Smith. The Lord did not will poverty for the earth's inhabitants. On the contrary, he wanted to give his children "greater riches, even a land . . . flowing with milk and honey," and promised that "if ye seek the riches which it is the will of the Father to give unto you, ye shall be the richest of all people, for ye shall have the riches of eternity" (D&C 38:18, 39). The problem was not riches but reliance on the arm of flesh. The increasingly popular myths of the self-made man sounded arrogant in the ears of the Lord, whose children seemed adamant to do things their "own way" (D&C 1:16). "The riches of the earth are mine to give," he said to the Saints in a variety of ways, "but beware of pride, lest ye become as the Nephites of old" (D&C 38:39). As creator and owner of the earth and its fulness, it was contrary to the Lord's will that one person should possess his wealth in excess of any other (D&C 49:20). All were to look to the poor and administer to their relief (D&C 38:34–35), acknowledging that all their wants and needs were generously supplied by his bountiful hand (D&C 59:15–21). It was selfishness that the revelations rejected. Instead, the Lord offered an alternative he called Zion, and the work of building Zion became the work of the revelations.

With Zion on their minds Joseph Smith gathered Church leaders at the Johnson home in Hiram, Ohio, in November 1831 to advance the plan for publishing the revelations. Oliver Cowdery asked how many copies the Lord wanted in the first edition of the Book of Commandments. The brethren voted for ten thousand, an extraordinarily large print run for such a project, and twice as many as the first printing of the Book of Mormon. They were willing to impoverish themselves to make the revelations widely available.

"Inasmuch as the Lord has bestowed a great blessing upon us in giving commandments and revelations," Joseph asked his brethren, "what testimony they were willing to attach to these commandments which should shortly be sent into the world."[8] He invited them to obtain a testimony for themselves that the revelations were divine, perhaps something similar to the ministering angel and heavenly voice experienced by the Three Witnesses of the Book of Mormon. There was hope among the brethren for such a witness but also fear. The testimony they received, therefore, came another way. Speaking through Joseph, the Lord exposed their secret thoughts and intents. "Your eyes have been upon my servant Joseph Smith, Jun., and his language you have known, and his imperfections you have known; and you have sought in your hearts knowledge that you might express beyond his language; this you also know" (D&C 67:5). He invited the brethren to choose the wisest among them to duplicate the simplest revelation. Joseph's history says that William McLellin "endeavored to write a commandment like unto one of the least of the Lord's, but failed."[9] This experience, this hands-on attempt to compose in the Lord's voice, proved much to the brethren present. They signed their names to a statement that the revelations were true.

It may be hard for modern readers to fully appreciate their actions. A poorly educated, twenty-six-year-old farmer was planning to publish ten thousand copies of his revelations that called his neighbors idolatrous, commanded them to repent, and foretold calamities upon those who continued in wickedness. Joseph was, by his own admission, no writer. He felt imprisoned by what he called the "total darkness of paper, pen, and Ink and a crooked, broken, scattered, and imperfect Language."[10] He thus considered it "an awful responsibility to write in the name of the Lord."[11] Yet the Lord had given him that responsibility. He had "called upon my servant Joseph Smith, Jun., and spake unto him from heaven, and gave him commandments" and declared to Joseph that "this generation shall have my word through you" (D&C 1:17; 5:10). Joseph hoped that his brethren would help shoulder the burden. Would they testify to the truthfulness of the revelations? Their initial fears were replaced by faith as the Lord demonstrated again that he spoke through Joseph.

These men based their conviction on the manuscript Book of Commandments lying before them. They knew Joseph's language. They knew his imperfections. And they knew that in his written revelations they heard the voice of God.[12] They were willing to testify to the world that they knew the revelations came from God. These men were going all the way to Zion. As the conference continued, "the brethren arose in turn and bore witness to the truth of the Book of Commandments. After which br. Joseph Smith jr arose & expressed his feelings and gratitude."[13] He loved the friends who sustained him in his heavy responsibility.

That responsibility included editing the revelations for publication. Joseph dictated a revelation in December 1832, and Sidney Rigdon wrote it down. Frederick Williams then transcribed it. Orson Hyde copied this transcription. John Whitmer then recorded Hyde's copy. Only a few of the revelations made their journeys to publication so circuitously, but not one of them was a pristine production. The Lord spoke in Joseph's imperfect language (D&C 1:24). And then Joseph usually spoke to a scribe, who wrote the words, which were then copied into books and then edited before being published. Not only were changes, both intentional and unintentional, made at every step, but Joseph did not suppose that he could receive the revelations perfectly, nor did the Lord ever set that standard. Joseph and his appointed brethren (see D&C 70:1–4) edited the revelations repeatedly based on the same premise that governed their original receipt, namely that Joseph represented the voice of God as He condescended to speak in what Joseph called his own crooked, broken, scattered, and imperfect language.[14]

Noting that some critics present the editorial changes made to the revelations as evidence that they are not true, then-Elder Boyd K. Packer observed: "They cite these changes, of which there are many examples, as though they themselves were announcing revelation, as though they were the only ones who knew of them. Of course there have been changes and corrections. Anyone who has done even limited research knows that. When properly reviewed, such corrections become a testimony for, not against the truth of the books."[15] The scholars editing the *Joseph Smith Papers* are intimately acquainted with all the known manuscript versions of the revelations and their printed history. Each of these scholars believes in the revelations and delights in their truths.[16]

Though some less-informed critics claim and others assume that the revelations cannot be true because they have been edited,[17] their logic is faulty. If it were not, then the Bible would have to be abandoned, too. It is important that the revelations are true, not that they are flawless.[18] After the Lord explained that distinction in section 67 at the November 1831 conference, none of Joseph's brethren were upset that the revelations were at once both true and in need of improvement. They simply resolved that Joseph "correct those errors or mistakes which he may discover by the holy Spirit" and bore their solemn testimonies that they knew the revelations were true.[19]

Meanwhile, William Phelps established the Church's press across from the courthouse in Independence, Missouri. Oliver Cowdery and John Whitmer took him the manuscript of the Book of Commandments, a few other revelations, and money to print them, and they stayed on to assist him. The Church's limited resources meant that they had to scale back the projected print run of the revelations to three thousand. But they never had a chance to get that far. In July 1833, antagonistic settlers of Jackson

County, Missouri, demanded that William Phelps cease printing what they called "pretended revelations from heaven" and destroyed the press and Phelps's home.[20] Brave Saints preserved some uncut pages, which were later bound. Thus only a few incomplete copies of A Book of Commandments were actually published.

The revelations kept coming, however, and the Saints bought a new press and set it up in Kirtland, Ohio. There, in September 1834, the Church appointed Joseph to head a committee to prepare his revelations for publication in an expanded form.[21] The committee worked hard to prepare the Doctrine and Covenants. Joseph was away in Michigan in August 1835 when other members of the committee appeared before a general Church assembly to seek the Saints' common consent for the book to become canonical scripture.

Oliver Cowdery held up a printed but not yet bound copy of the Doctrine and Covenants and asked the Saints for their consent to publish it. William Phelps said "that he had examined it carefully, that it was well arranged and calculated to govern the church in righteousness, if followed [it] would bring the members to see eye to eye. And further that he had received the testimony from God, that the Revelations and commandments contained therein are true, wherefore, he knew assuredly for himself having received witness from Heaven & not from men." John Whitmer, who transcribed many of the revelations for Joseph, followed with a similar expression of certainty, adding "that he was present when some of the revelations contained therein were given, and was satisfied they come from God." Others followed. Levi Jackman "arose and said that he had examined as many of the revelations contained in the book as were printed in Zion, & as firmly believes them as he does the Book of Mormon or the Bible and also the whole contents of the Book, he then called for the vote of the High Council from Zion, which they gave in favor of the Book and also of the committee." Newel Whitney rose and testified that he knew the revelations "were true, for God had testified to him by his holy Spirit, for many of them were given under his roof & in his presence through President Joseph Smith Junr."[22] This process of consent continued, endowing Joseph's revelations with canonical status.[23] It culminated with a consensus "of all the members present, both male & female, & They gave a decided voice in favor of it."[24] A testimony of the Twelve Apostles that the revelations came from God for the benefit of mankind was published in the 1835 Doctrine and Covenants, which was sent to Cleveland for binding. This testimony is included in the Explanatory Introduction to the current edition.

In 1844, the First Presidency announced plans to publish a second edition of the Doctrine and Covenants, adding seven revelations to the 1835 edition, including today's sections 103, 105, 112, 119, 124, 127, and 128. For years they had been raising money to procure the paper and skilled printers. Joseph had proofread the revelations. The *Nauvoo Neighbor* newspaper announced that the new edition would be off the press in about a month. That was two weeks before Joseph was murdered, and the tragedy, in which publisher and apostle John Taylor was severely wounded, delayed publication until later that year. By then the 1844 edition of the Doctrine and Covenants included the stirring eulogy to Joseph that is now section 135.

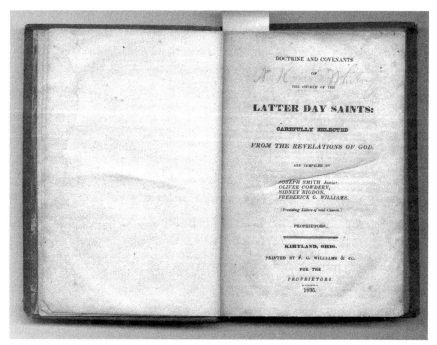

Many of Joseph's revelations were published in the 1833 Book of Commandments. The 1835 Doctrine and Covenants expanded on that project and added seven theological lectures on faith.

The next several editions were published in England, the first of those by Wilford Woodruff in 1845 during his second apostolic mission to Great Britain. Because some dissident Saints designed to publish first in Great Britain, Wilford rushed the book to press in order to beat them and secure the copyright. That became an important advantage for the Church, as the printing used for the first British edition was duplicated several times, including for shipments to the Saints in Utah, before a new edition of the Doctrine and Covenants was finally typeset in 1876.[25]

Orson Pratt of the Quorum of the Twelve Apostles edited the 1876 edition of the Doctrine and Covenants. Under President Brigham Young's direction, Elder Pratt made extensive changes that dramatically influence how we read the book today. He added several of Joseph's revelations and one of Brigham Young's, amounting to twenty-six new sections, including 2, 13, 77, 85, 87, 108, 109, 110, 111, 113, 114, 115, 116, 117, 118, 120, 121, 122, 123, 125, 126, 129, 130, 131, 132, and 136. Elder Pratt rearranged the order of the sections and divided them into verses. In 1879 he published another edition in England, adding footnotes but no new sections. Using Elder Pratt's 1879 typesetting, the Church published the Doctrine and Covenants in Utah in 1880 as part of the celebration of its fiftieth anniversary. The Church reprinted this edition at least twenty-eight times, adding in 1908 President Woodruff's declaration to end the practice of plural marriage (now Official Declaration–1). Orson Pratt's painstaking and inspired work on these editions is monumental. His editorial fingerprints are still found in the most recent edition of the Doctrine and Covenants.

In 1920 President Heber J. Grant appointed several of the apostles to arrange a new edition, which was published in 1921. They revised the footnotes and set the type in double columns on each page. They also removed seven lectures on faith that had been included since the 1835 edition. These examples of systematic theology were originally delivered to Church leaders in Kirtland, Ohio, as they prepared their hearts and minds for the solemn assembly in the temple. The lectures never claimed the status of revelation. They are still available in a number of free-standing editions but are no longer part of the canonized scripture of the Church.[26]

Later, the First Presidency appointed a committee of apostles to direct the publication of a new edition of the Doctrine and Covenants that was published in 1981. Featuring an extensive critical apparatus, including completely revised footnotes and enhanced study aids, it included sections 137, 138, and Official Declaration–2. In one sense these three texts complete the Doctrine and Covenants. They reveal how the Lord has included every soul, living and dead, of every nation, kindred, tongue, and people, in his plan for the salvation and exaltation of all mankind. These three texts finish what section 1 announced the Doctrine and Covenants would do, that is, testify that the Lord's "eyes are upon all" and manifest his willingness "to make these things known unto all flesh" (D&C 1:1, 34).

But in an important sense the Doctrine and Covenants remains open. As a contemporary of Joseph put it, this book of scripture shows us "that God is, not was; that He speaketh, not spake."[27] The future of the Doctrine and Covenants is as exciting as its past.

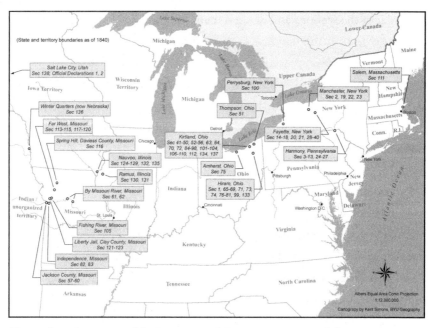

Places where the sections of the Doctrine and Covenants were revealed.

Explanatory Introduction

Directly after the title page of the 1981 edition of the Doctrine and Covenants is a useful Explanatory Introduction. It defines the Doctrine and Covenants as "a collection of divine revelations and inspired declarations" given to do the work of restoration and kingdom building. Joseph Smith himself marveled at these revelations. He considered them "so much beyond the narrow mindedness of men."[1]

The Explanatory Introduction makes the point early and often that the Doctrine and Covenants commands "all people everywhere to hear the voice of the Lord Jesus Christ" speaking the words of eternal life. Elder Neal A. Maxwell emphasized the point: "If asked which book of scripture provides the most frequent chance to 'listen' to the Lord talking, most individuals would at first think of the New Testament. The New Testament is a marvelous collection of the deeds and many of the doctrines of the Messiah," Elder Maxwell testified. "But in the Doctrine and Covenants we receive the voice as well as the word of the Lord. We can almost 'hear' him talking."[2]

Some versions of the New Testament print the first person voice of the Savior in red ink so readers can more easily discern when they are listening to the Lord himself. If all of the Latter-day Saint standard works were printed that way, the Doctrine and Covenants would be overwhelmingly the reddest. Historian Richard Lyman Bushman noted that "the striking feature of Joseph Smith's revelations is the purity of God's voice coming out of the heavens and demanding our attention."³ We can, if diligent and determined, listen to the Lord speak.

The Explanatory Introduction emphasizes that of all the standard works, only the Doctrine and Covenants is modern and not a translation from an ancient language. It points out that "in the revelations" received mainly by Joseph Smith but also his successors, "one hears the tender but firm voice of the Lord Jesus Christ, speaking anew in the dispensation of the fulness of times" and declaring just what is needed to prepare for his second coming.

Joseph's divine calling is emphasized in the fourth and fifth paragraphs of the Introduction, highlighting his credentials as a prolific revelator. He witnessed the Father and the Son and ministering angels. He received the holy priesthood and its keys, beheld visions, and dictated revelations by the power of the Holy Ghost. By this authority and through these experiences he restored and built the Church of Jesus Christ.

The Introduction gives us a key to understanding the book of Doctrine and Covenants: "These sacred revelations were received in answer to prayer, in times of need, and came out of real-life situations involving real people." The better we know the content of those prayers, the real world situations that shaped them, and the personalities that asked them, the better we will understand and therefore be able to apply the revelations. Such understanding will require much work, for the people and situations are highly varied and historically distant from us. Too often it seems easier to assume we already know what the revelations mean, and even easier to not care in the first place. But how tragic it would be for the Savior to have spoken and for us to treat his words casually.

Subsequent paragraphs of the Explanatory Introduction list a stunning array of doctrines and covenants as a sample of the contents of the revelations. The 138 sections and 2 Official Declarations include visions and revelations, angelic ministrations, Bible interpretations, ecclesiastical administration, economic organization, social and political principles, and policy statements.

A few of the revelations might be called strategic, meaning they are expansive in scope and doctrinal in orientation. They describe God's plans or strategies, his work and glory of exalting his children (see Moses 1).

These are the revelations that prompted one non-LDS scholar to observe that Joseph's revelations probe "realms of doctrine unimagined in traditional Christian theology."[4] Revelations of this kind describe the atonement of Jesus Christ; declare the laws of the gospel, sacrifice, and consecration; restore lost truths; map the heavens; define the nature of the Godhead; describe aspects of premortality, agency, the last days, the Savior's second coming, the Millennium, the various types of resurrection, and the postmortal spirit world.

Many other sections are better described as tactical, meaning the kind of revelation that calls on Saints to compile hymns, serve missions, move from one state to another, or to buy and sell specific pieces of real estate. These revelations are historically specific. Not all of their instructions are for us today, but the opportunity to listen to the Savior's voice is always instructive. What he reveals about himself and his principles is timeless.

Still other sections may be considered both strategic and tactical. Section 93 may be the finest example of this type. Its first thirty-nine verses contain some of the most profound revelation anywhere on the nature of God and Christ, the nature of man and individual agency, and the nature of truth itself. But all of that seems prologue to the specific tactical instructions the Lord gives in the last verses to each member of the First Presidency and to Bishop Newel K. Whitney. If "the glory of God is intelligence," the strategic part of the revelation says, then "bring up your children in light and truth" the tactical part commands (D&C 93:36, 40).

Some readers find the Doctrine and Covenants difficult to understand fully. This book of scripture presents several challenging characteristics, including the seeming irrelevance of some tactical revelations to present concerns as well as the separateness of its sections. They are not laced together with a narrative story. One reader acknowledged the challenge "to understand the significance of verses, longer passages, and even whole sections, many of which seemed dull, repetitive, and even uninspiring."[5]

If we look closely, however, we find several threads that sew the seemingly patchwork revelations together into remarkably coherent doctrines and covenants. These include the dualistic typology of the inescapable choice every person must make between Zion and Babylon; the nature of agency;

the doctrines and covenants of the temple; how to prevent deception; the order and organization of the Church; and the eternal law of consecration.

Sections 1 and 133 frame the book. They were designed by the Lord to preface and conclude the revelations. It is best to read them first, together. Doing so helps us understand from section 1 what we are supposed to learn from the book and from section 133 what we should have learned. These sections assert that because of apostasy, God's covenant with mankind is broken, and he has restored the gospel to renew that covenant and thus to save all who want to be saved. They declare a dualistic world in which Zion and Babylon are the only possibilities, and they are at odds with each other. They command all who will be saved to flee Babylon for Zion. This dualism, which is characteristic of much scripture, carries through many sections. They assert that one is either rebellious or repentant, a wise or a foolish virgin, wheat or tare. And Joseph Smith's revelations explicitly and emphatically declare that each of us has the agency to determine which category we will be in.

Agency may, in fact, be the Savior's most pervasive point in the revelations. He describes himself as the Savior of willing agents. Whereas many Christians have regarded God's elect as the ones God has arbitrarily chosen, the Lord's revelations to Joseph describe the elect as those who choose God of their own free will (D&C 29:7). Beginning in section 1, the Lord emphasizes his impartiality (D&C 1:11, 35). Whereas many Christians have believed in a limited atonement, in several sections the Lord declares himself mighty to save. The revelations repeatedly emphasize that he is both willing and capable of saving *all* who are willing to repent. One of the most beautiful doctrines is that of the Atonement set forth in section 18, which testifies that the Redeemer suffered the pain of *all* so that *all* might repent and come to him (D&C 18:11). The final sections of the Doctrine and Covenants testify that not even death can stop the Savior from saving all who are willing. Official Declaration–2 obliterates any artificial barriers and brings the Doctrine and Covenants full circle to the emphasis in section 1 concerning the Lord's willingness "to make these things known unto *all* flesh" so that "*all* that will hear may hear" (D&C 1:34, 11; emphasis added).

The Doctrine and Covenants includes some of the richest doctrinal descriptions in scripture of the nature of agency, especially in sections 29, 58, and 93. But even sections that do not specifically set forth agency as a doctrine assume it as part of the doctrinal basis of the plan of salvation. In other words, nearly every section sets forth the terms and conditions upon which we, as accountable agents, can claim specific blessings from God. Section 130 declares, "There is a law, irrevocably decreed in heaven before the foundations of this world, upon which all blessings are predicated—and when we obtain any blessing from God, it is by obedience to that law upon which it is predicated" (vv. 20–21). In section 58, the Lord explains that principle: "I command and men obey not; I revoke and they receive not the blessing" (v. 32). And in section 82 we hear, "I, the Lord, am bound when ye do what I say; but when ye do not what I say, ye have no promise" (v. 10).

In one sense, this way of locating agency in individuals is the *doctrine* and *covenants* of the book. Each section declares what we must choose to do in order to obtain specific blessings. Consider section 4 as an example. Its seven verses are packed with doctrine and covenants. Verse 2, for example, declares that *if* an individual chooses to obey the first great commandment, *then* that individual will be blameless before God. Verse 4 testifies that *if* a person labors to harvest souls, *then* salvation comes to that person's own soul. Verse 7 may be the most frequently stated covenant in scripture: *if* an individual chooses to ask, *then* God will answer. Readers who gain the most from the Doctrine and Covenants learn to see, hear, and then act on the doctrine and covenants that are embedded in every single section.

There are at least two common interpretive mistakes some readers make with this type of doctrine and covenants. First, some assume that by meeting the Lord's terms and conditions, they are *earning* the promised blessings. They are not. The revelations do not use the language of earning or of trading something of equal value for the Lord's blessings. The revelations are covenants, not contracts. By choosing to meet the terms of the covenants, individuals express their love for God and their desire to receive the promised blessings. They ask for his grace, forgiveness, answers, and, as section 95 testifies, even for his love to continue with them. We do not earn blessings; rather, we choose to meet the conditions upon which the Lord promises and provides them.

A second error some make is assuming they can set the terms and conditions of the covenants. The revelations do that. The Savior sets forth the covenantal terms on which receipt of his blessings depend. We do not. Twice Martin Harris approached the Lord with demands. Twice, in sections 5 and 19, the Lord responded with reminders about how covenants work. Agency is the power to choose whether to meet the Lord's terms and receive his blessings—or not. Because we are in need of redemption, it is the Lord's prerogative, not ours, to decide what the terms of the covenants of redemption will be. "I, the Lord, am bound when ye do what I say, but when ye do not what I say, ye have no promise" (D&C 82:10).

Another thread that ties the revelations together is their trajectory toward the ordinances of the holy temple. Section 2 was the first revelation, chronologically speaking. It tells Joseph Smith that he will receive priesthood keys to seal families together before the Savior's second coming. Subsequent sections help the Saints grow toward those blessings. Several sections contain prophecy about temple blessings, command the Saints to prepare for them, and command them to build temples and keep them holy, or rebuke them for failing to do so. Section 109 was the dedicatory prayer for the temple in Kirtland, Ohio, and then, as section 110 records, the Savior appeared and then sent ministering angels with the priesthood keys Joseph needed to seal families together in every temple built since. Joseph was overwhelmed with opposition after that, as if the hosts of hell could not abide the restoration of temple blessings. Undaunted, he sought and received more revelations to build more temples in which to perform the sacred, exalting ordinances. Section 132 is the culmination of several sections that set forth the Savior's terms and conditions for exaltation. Sections 137 and 138 further define the scope of temple doctrines and covenants. And Official Declaration–2 opens the temple doors to all who are willing to make and keep the sacred covenants the Lord offers. From beginning to end, the Doctrine and Covenants is about the temple and its profound, problem-solving blessings.

Section 50 declares that "Satan hath sought to deceive you" (D&C 50:3). It is one of several sections in which the Lord describes the devil and his deceptive schemes. The Doctrine and Covenants contains the most detailed and thorough descriptions of Satan in scripture. Moreover, several sections help the Saints understand deceptions including false revelations and impure motives. They set forth principles and patterns that empower those who know them to overcome Satan and his pervasive, sinister influences. These sections set forth the order in which revelation will come and to whom. They describe the gifts of the Spirit and command all to seek them as protection against deception.

Several sections build the Church. The organization restored by sections 20 and 21 was primitive in more ways than one. With two presiding elders and just a few members, the Church nevertheless had in those two revelations a clear statement of its authority, its core doctrines, and its order and organization. As the Church expanded, the Lord built it up with further revelations. He declared the law of the Church, called and gave responsibilities to bishops, established the First Presidency, Quorum of Twelve Apostles, Seventy, and other priesthood quorums and offices, and described their relationships to each other. He revealed the functions of stakes and explained how to conduct councils.

The law of consecration is a principal theme of the Doctrine and Covenants. Hugh Nibley went so far as to say that "the purpose of the Doctrine and Covenants, you will find, is to implement the Law of Consecration." It is "explained there not once but many times, so that there is no excuse for not understanding it."[6] Section 42 strategically sets forth the law, and section 51 begins to implement it tactically. Persecution and disobedience by individuals, together with Church growth, made it necessary to adapt the tactics for implementing the law. Subsequent revelations do that work. But the law itself is "still in effect," according to President Gordon B. Hinckley.[7] Elder Neal A. Maxwell taught that "many ignore consecration because it seems too abstract or too daunting. The conscientious among us, however, experience divine discontent."[8] Conscientious covenant keepers want to know the law. This guide helps explain the law as contained in the Doctrine and Covenants and embodied in present Church practices derived from the Doctrine and Covenants.

Doctrine & Covenants 1

ORIGIN

By 1831, widely varied religious and political groups were publishing newspapers and books, reaching through the power of print much wider audiences than ever before. The growing numbers of missionaries were to apply the revelations in their ministries, but copies could only be handwritten when a missionary happened to be at Church headquarters or crossed paths with someone who had a copy of an earlier copy. Already a revelation had assigned the experienced editor William Phelps to be a printer for the Church. Should he print the revelations? (D&C 57:11).

Joseph convened a council at John and Elsa Johnson's home in Hiram, Ohio, and laid the manuscript of the Book of Commandments on a table before the Church leaders. It was time for the revelations in it to be published.[1] Joseph testified that the revelations should "be prized by this Conference to be worth to the Church the riches of the whole Earth." Oliver Cowdery asked, "How many copies of the Book of commandments it was the will of the Lord should be published in the first edition of that work?" The council voted to publish ten thousand.[2]

A committee drafted a preface for the book, but then, through Joseph, the Lord revealed his own preface, recorded now as Doctrine and Covenants 1. Joseph spoke the words slowly as Sidney Rigdon wrote them down, but they are in the voice of Jesus Christ, who gave them to be what he called "*my* preface unto the book of *my* commandments" (v. 6; emphasis added).[3]

CONTENT

Doctrine and Covenants 1 is a preface to the Doctrine and Covenants (the appendix is section 133). The book is the Lord's book, and section 1, although not the first section revealed, outlines his purposes for all of it, both the sections given previously and those given subsequently.

Apocalyptic in nature, section 1 prophesies the imminent coming of the Savior and the just punishments awaiting the "unbelieving and rebellious" before and at the Savior's second coming (D&C 1:8). It separates mankind into two possible categories, the repentant and the unrepentant, and outlines the Lord's rationale for opening the last dispensation. The world was apostate, and the omniscient Lord has seen the devastating potential of such apostasy. He has provided a solution by calling a prophet, Joseph Smith, and giving him revelations, called "commandments," in section 1. Joseph's obedience to those commandments has resulted in the translation of the Book of Mormon and the restoration of the gospel, the only true and living Church, that is, the only one in which God still speaks, for as Wilford Woodruff taught, "the Church of God could not live twenty four hours without revelation."[4] Section 1 also leads men to serve missions and spread the restored gospel as the Lord's chosen way of fulfilling his promise to restore his covenant and offer the fulness of the gospel to mankind, enabling individuals to choose repentance or destruction of their own free will. Section 1 emphasizes the Lord's intention of making the gospel known throughout the world. No respecter of persons, the Lord does not play favorites or predetermine the destiny of souls. Instead he

Joseph Smith, by William Whittaker.

warns all of them, enabling each to choose. He speaks until every ear hears and every heart is penetrated. "The voice of the Lord is unto the ends of the earth, that all that will hear may hear" (v. 11).[5]

OUTCOMES

Doctrine and Covenants 1 introduces readers to the author of the Doctrine and Covenants, the Lord Jesus Christ, and acquaints them with his literary voice. He quickly frames the book in a typology of opposites: Babylon strays from God's order, breaks covenants, and does things its "own way" (v. 16). The restored Church is the vehicle out of Babylon. It reestablishes the broken covenants, facilitates repentance, increases faith, and proclaims the gospel to all mankind. The Lord is pleased with his restored Church, if not all of its members. He forgives and saves all the repentant. Babylon, meanwhile, is doomed to destruction (v. 16). The entire Doctrine and Covenants is framed by the contest between the type, Zion, and its antitype, Babylon. Section 1 informs mankind of the inevitable choice to be made between them to repent and be saved at the Lord's imminent coming, or rebel and be damned. It authoritatively establishes a repentant embrace of the Lord's covenant, available fully only in his restored Church, as the only alternative to impending calamities. "I am God and have spoken it," this revelation declares, "these commandments are of me" (v. 24). In the words of one theologian, such revelations bring us "face to face with the question: *does* God speak?"[6] Section 1 emphatically answers *yes* and from its first word commands all mankind to hearken.

Doctrine & Covenants 2

ORIGIN

"When I was about 17 years," Joseph Smith said, "I had another vision of angels; in the night season, after I had retired to bed; I had not been asleep, but was meditating on my past life and experience. I was well aware I had not kept the commandments, and I repented heartily for all my sins and transgressions, and humbled myself before him, whose eye surveys all things at a glance. All at once the room was illuminated above the brightness of the sun; an Angel appeared before me." He introduced himself as Moroni, saying, "I am a Messenger sent from God." He said that God had vital work for Joseph to do. There was a sacred book written on golden plates, buried in a nearby hillside. "He explained many of the prophecies to me," Joseph said, including "Malachi 4th chapter." Moroni appeared three times that night and again the next day, emphasizing and expounding the same message contained in Doctrine and Covenants 2. There was something vital in that message, something Joseph needed to know.[1]

CONTENT

When Joseph wrote his history in 1839, he recorded the words Moroni spoke regarding Malachi's prophecy of Elijah, also written in Doctrine and Covenants 2, noting the "little variation from the way it reads in our Bibles." Moroni "quoted the fifth verse thus, 'Behold I will reveal unto you the Priesthood by the hand of Elijah the prophet before the coming of the great and dreadful day of the Lord.' He also quoted the next verse differently.

Angel Moroni. Found in Palmyra, New York, this privately owned sculpture is seven feet tall and seven feet across. Carved wood with traces of gesso and gilt. Artist unknown, circa 1840.

'And he shall plant in the hearts of the children the promises made to their fathers, and the hearts of the children shall turn to the fathers, if it were not so the whole earth would be utterly wasted at his coming.'"[2]

Malachi foretold that Elijah, the Old Testament prophet, would return to the earth on a mission to unite the hearts of the first Israelites, with whom God had made covenants, with the hearts of their descendants, to whom Malachi wrote. The prophecy as recorded in the Old Testament is vague. All a Bible reader can surmise is that the Lord would send Elijah some time before the Second Coming. To do what? Moroni makes the prophecy directly relevant to Joseph and specifies that Elijah will reveal priesthood powerful enough to unite families forever.

OUTCOMES

Young Joseph sought forgiveness of personal sins, but in Doctrine and Covenants 2 an angel told him he had a role in fulfilling ancient prophecy, adding that "if it were not so, the whole earth would be utterly wasted." Moroni's words obviously made a deep impression on the teenaged seer. Whether Joseph understood them all that night is not clear, but they remained in his mind and heart until he witnessed their fulfillment nearly thirteen years later when Elijah fulfilled the prophecy by bringing to Joseph the priesthood keys needed to seal families together (see D&C 110). Joseph was called to receive and use those priesthood keys. He was to give every willing soul, living and dead, full access to the atonement of Jesus Christ and assist the Savior in offering eternal life. Elder Russell M. Nelson taught that "eternal life, made possible by the Atonement, is the supreme purpose of the Creation. To phrase that statement in its negative form, if families were not sealed in holy temples, the whole earth would be utterly wasted."[3] In Doctrine and Covenants 2, Moroni told Joseph Smith that his job was to save the earth.

Doctrine & Covenants 3

ORIGIN

Martin Harris, a prosperous farmer living near Palmyra, New York, traveled to Harmony (now Oakland), Pennsylvania, in the spring of 1828 to serve as scribe while Joseph translated the Book of Mormon. Martin's wife, Lucy, told neighbors that Joseph had tricked Martin into giving him money. She dramatically moved her favorite pieces of furniture out of the house, claiming she did not want Martin to give them away, too. Martin knew Joseph had a gift and that he translated the Book of Mormon by the power of God. Martin knew, but he wanted his family and friends to know. He resented that his wife's gossip had damaged his reputation and asked Joseph for the chance to take the manuscript home to Palmyra to prove to Lucy he was no fool.

Joseph faced great pressure. Martin was older than he and supportive of his mission. How could he say no? Who would write for him or provide needed money if Martin quit? Joseph asked the Lord for permission to send the manuscript pages with Martin. "The Lord said unto me that he must not take them," Joseph recalled, "and I spoke unto Martin the word of the Lord." Dissatisfied, Martin told Joseph to ask again. "I inquired again and also the third time," Joseph said, "and the Lord said unto me let him go with them."[1]

The Lord had declared his will. He knew what would happen if Martin took the translation home. But Martin was sure he knew better, and Joseph feared to disappoint him. He made Martin vow solemnly to show the pages only to his wife and her sister Abigail, his brother, and their parents. The Lord's answer made Joseph and Martin agents in the matter, but with agency came accountability. They could do their own will instead of God's, but making that choice meant that Joseph, at least for a time, could not be the seer chosen to bring forth the marvelous work. Moroni took away the plates and the interpreters. Sincere but unwise, Martin left for what was to be a brief trip to Palmyra with the translated manuscript. He failed to return.

On June 15, Emma gave birth to a son, whom she and Joseph called Alvin after Joseph's late brother. The babe did not live, and Emma also hovered near death for some time. As she slowly gained strength, Emma and Joseph worried about the manuscript. "I feel so uneasy," she finally said, "that I cannot rest and shall not be at ease until I know something about what Mr. Harris is doing with it." Perceiving that Joseph shared her concern, Emma urged him to visit Martin Harris. "Do you not think it would be advisable," she asked, "for you to go and inquire into the reason of his not writing or sending any word back to you since he left us?"[2]

Joseph protested, but Emma assured him that she would be all right. He caught a stagecoach headed north toward his parents' home in Manchester, New York. Hour after depressing hour he rode, reliving the extraordinary events of his life—the confusion and anxiety before the First Vision, his feelings of sinfulness in the following years, the repeated disappointments and rebukes before receiving the plates. Each of those setbacks recurred now, bringing an ominous feeling with them. Joseph neither ate nor slept as he traveled toward an uncertain encounter. He realized he had acted unwisely and with more concern for the will of Martin Harris than of his Heavenly Father. Joseph stepped off the stagecoach with twenty miles remaining between him and his parents' home. The hour was late, the sky dark, and he had no way to travel but walk. A stranger walked with him toward his destination, where he arrived with the dawn.[3]

Joseph wanted to see Martin Harris immediately, so the Smiths invited him for breakfast, assuming he would come quickly. "At eight o'clock we set the victuals on the table, looking for him every moment," Joseph's mother, Lucy, wrote. "We waited till nine, and he came not; till ten, and he was not there; till eleven, still he did not make his appearance. At half past twelve we saw him walking with a slow and measured tread toward the house, his eyes fixed thoughtfully upon the ground." Martin paused at the gate, then sat on the fence and drew his hat down over his sullen eyes.

When he finally entered, the house felt the same deep suspense it knew from September 22, 1827, the morning nearly a year earlier when Joseph returned after receiving the plates. Unlike that morning, however, there would be no joking on this summer day.

The Smiths and their guest began to eat, but Martin dropped his utensils. "Are you sick?" Hyrum asked. "I have lost my soul," Martin cried. "I have lost my soul." Unable to suppress his worst fears any longer, Joseph jumped up. "Oh! Martin, have you lost that manuscript? Have you broken your oath and brought down condemnation upon my head as well as your own?"

"Yes," Martin confessed. "It is gone and I know not where."

"Oh, my God, my God," Joseph uttered humbly, "all is lost! What shall I do? I have sinned. It is I who tempted the wrath of God by asking him for that which I had no right to ask." And he wept and groaned and paced the floor, forsaken.

Joseph told Martin to return home and find the manuscript.

"It is all in vain," Martin replied, "for I have looked every place in the house. I have even ripped open beds and pillows, and I know it is not there."

"Then must I return to my wife with such a tale as this?" Joseph asked. "I dare not do it lest I should kill her at once. And how shall I appear before the Lord? Of what rebuke am I not worthy from the angel of the Most High?" Still depressed, he left for home the next morning.[4] He received Doctrine and Covenants 3 in response to the situation.

CONTENT

Joseph goes into the Pennsylvania woods and prays mightily for redemption, pouring out sorrow, confessing weakness, beseeching the Lord for forgiveness. Moroni appears and returns the seer stones. Joseph looks and sees the strict words of a just God, now recorded in Doctrine and Covenants 3. "Remember, remember that it is not the work of God that is frustrated, but the work of men; for although a man may have many revelations, and have power to do many mighty works, yet if he boasts in his own strength, and sets at naught the counsels of God, and follows after the dictates of his own will and carnal desires, he must fall and incur the vengeance of a just God upon him" (D&C 3:3–4).

The Lord's words pierce Joseph's soul. "You have been entrusted with these things, but how strict were your commandments; and remember the promises which were made to you, if you did not transgress them" (v. 5). Joseph recalls Moroni's commission to be responsible for the sacred records and powers and the warning that "if I should let them go carelessly, or through any neglect of mine, I should be cut off; but that if I would use all my endeavors to preserve them . . . they should be protected" (Joseph Smith–History 1:59).

But Joseph has been persuaded to transgress. "How oft you have transgressed the commandments and the laws of God, and have gone on in the persuasions of men," the Lord continues firmly. "You should not have feared man more than God" (D&C 3:6–7). Martin Harris rejected the Lord's words, but Joseph knows better. By yielding to Martin, Joseph has turned his back on the Savior's will. "Thou wast chosen to do the work of the Lord," Jesus warns, "but because of transgression, if thou art not aware thou wilt fall" (v. 9). Historian Richard Bushman observed that these words "were hard for a young man who had just lost his firstborn son and nearly lost his wife, and whose chief error was to trust a friend, but there was comfort in the revelation."[5]

Then the tone of the heavenly message changes dramatically. "Remember," it says halfway through, "God is merciful" (v. 10). If he will repent, the Lord assures Joseph, he is still chosen to translate the Book of Mormon; otherwise, he is not. The manuscript is sacred; Joseph translated it by the power of God. Martin Harris pressured Joseph to give up the manuscript. Martin disregarded God's counsel and broke sacred promises. He depended on his own judgment, boasted in his mortal wisdom. Joseph lost the privilege to translate for a season because he listened to Martin. Indeed, the Lord declares, harking back to Joseph's teenage struggles to obey the commands he received, "Thou hast suffered the counsel of thy director to be trampled upon from the beginning" (v. 15). Still, God's work will go forward. Just as the world received knowledge of the Savior from the Jews in the Bible, the descendants of Lehi will know the Savior through the Book of Mormon. The plates were preserved so the Lord could keep this promise (Enos 1:15–18).

And by the Savior's keeping his promise to give Lehi's descendants their ancestors' knowledge of Him, "they may believe the gospel and rely upon the merits of Jesus Christ" (D&C 3:20), exercise faith, repent, and be saved.

OUTCOMES

Joseph received the words of Doctrine and Covenants 3 gladly, as if they were cool water for his thirsty soul. They illustrated God's perfectly harmonized justice and mercy. Repentance fully qualifies one for mercy, whereas stubborn willfulness leads to God's just vengeance. The revelation also strikes a crucial balance between Joseph's agency and the Lord's promises to the engravers of the Book of Mormon. Having assured them that their testimonies would be preserved and delivered to their descendants, the Lord must bring the Book of Mormon forth. That purpose will not be frustrated. But that does not mean Joseph has to bring it forth. He is free to disobey. He could have been disqualified had he not chosen to repent. This revelation demonstrates how the Lord preserves individual agency even as he guarantees that his works, designs, and purposes will not be frustrated.

The reception of section 3 also marked a turning point in the life of the young seer. It was likely the first time Joseph wrote one of his revelations. Only twenty-two years old, he had risen above the confines of his culture. He would no longer be bound by his youthful temptations. He was not perfect, but his eye was becoming single to God's glory. He had become a prophet, writing the words of Jesus Christ, foretelling the fulfillment of the Lord's promises to the house of Israel. He was the Seer chosen to bring forth the marvelous work that would eventually teach all nations to "rely upon the merits of Jesus Christ," as the revelation said, "and be glorified through faith in his name, and that through their repentance they might be saved" (v. 20).

Moroni took back the interpreters and the plates while Joseph acted on the revelation's command to repent. Then in September 1828, one year after Joseph first received them, the plates were again entrusted to him. By choosing to obey the revelation, Joseph was still chosen and was again called to the work.

Doctrine & Covenants 4

ORIGIN

The American Revolution made the world of Joseph Smith's father more free and also more uncertain. Unlike his Congregationalist ancestors, he did not belong to an established church. His best efforts to provide for his growing family failed repeatedly. When he went to bed at night, Joseph's father dreamed anxious dreams. In one dream he grew tired from walking a long distance in search of something. An angel showed him a beautiful garden, but Father Smith awoke before he could learn what the experience meant. In another dream he was going to be judged. He found himself locked out of a building. Fear overcame him, and he felt hopeless. As he cried out for help in the name of Jesus Christ, strength returned, the door opened, and Father Smith awoke. Shortly after moving his family yet again, this time to a new farm in Manchester, New York, he dreamed he met a peddler who promised to tell him the one thing he lacked. Father Smith jumped up to get some paper and awoke before learning the secret. Though he toiled hard and wanted badly to know God's will, Joseph Smith's father had a gnawing feeling that something vital was missing in his life.[1] As his understanding of Joseph's mission grew, Father Smith began to believe that his answers would come from his son. Early in 1829, Joseph Senior visited his son in Harmony (now Oakland), Pennsylvania, and received the anxiously anticipated answers he had sought for so long as Joseph "received the following revelation for him," recorded in Doctrine and Covenants 4.[2]

CONTENT

"A marvelous work is about to come forth," the Lord says in verse 1 of Doctrine and Covenants 4. Those who serve God wholeheartedly in the work will stand blameless before him. Those who have desires to serve God are called to help in the marvelous work. It is like a ripe field, ready for harvest, and all who help in the harvest bring salvation to their own souls. Faith, hope, charity, love, and an eye single to God's glory are the attributes that qualify harvesters for this work. They should also "remember faith, virtue, knowledge, temperance, patience, brotherly kindness, godliness, charity, humility, diligence" (v. 6). If they ask, they receive.

OUTCOMES

The revelation recorded in Doctrine and Covenants 4 is perfectly adapted to Joseph's father. A marvelous work about to come forth is the theme that characterized many of his dreams, yet here it is followed by empowering information missing from the frustrating dreams. The Lord gave Joseph Senior specific things he could do to become blameless, obtain salvation, and receive answers to his questions. The revelation gave him power to act in ways that would result in obtaining exactly what he most desired from God. Father Smith's deep spiritual longings helped him appreciate the Lord's penetrating, personal words. To Father Smith, the command to be temperate meant that he should not drink alcohol excessively, something, by his own admission, he struggled with at times.[3] The Lord's metaphor of a ripe field ready for harvesting made perfect sense to Father Smith, whose life as a farmer depended on reaping successful harvests and who knew exactly what it meant to thrust in his sickle and reap all day long. The revelation turned Father Smith into a harvester of souls. After the Book of Mormon came off the press and Joseph Smith organized the Church, Father Smith spent the harvest season visiting his parents and siblings. He found nearly all of them ripe, and he slept well.[4]

Doctrine & Covenants 5

ORIGIN

Joseph told Martin Harris that the Lord had identified him as one who would help Joseph translate and publish the Book of Mormon. "I retired to my bedroom," Martin said, "and prayed to God to show me concerning these things, and I covenanted that if it was his work and he would show me so, I would put forth my best ability to bring it before the world. He then showed me that it was his work, and that it was designed to bring in the fullness of his gospel to the gentiles to fulfill his word. . . . He showed me this by the still small voice spoken in the soul. Then I was satisfied that it was the Lord's work, and I was under a covenant to bring it forth."[1]

Martin gave Joseph money and scribed, but he later wavered in his faith. He broke his promises to Joseph and the Lord in June of 1828, resulting in the loss of the translation manuscript (see D&C 3). His testimony faded as he disobeyed, and the next spring Martin visited Joseph's home in Harmony (now Oakland), Pennsylvania, seeking more evidence. He told Joseph's father-in-law, Isaac Hale, that he "must have a *greater* witness, and said that he had talked with Joseph about it." The next day Isaac Hale walked in as Joseph and Martin were comparing manuscripts of a revelation, Doctrine and Covenants 5, that the Lord had just given. Emma's father remembered that "some of the words were, *'my servant seeketh a greater witness, but no greater witness can be given him.'*" He also remembered hearing something about three witnesses. "I enquired whose words they were," he said, "and was informed by Joseph or Emma . . . that they were the words of Jesus Christ."[2]

CONTENT

In Doctrine and Covenants 5 the Lord speaks to Joseph about Martin, not, as in other revelations, directly and intimately to the inquirer through Joseph. In many revelations Joseph disappears as the Lord speaks through him directly to the recipient(s). But in section 5 Joseph becomes the mediator between the Lord and Martin, as if they were no longer on speaking terms. Had Martin's covenant-breaking loss of the Book of Mormon manuscript created a gulf between him and his Lord? Or was the distance a result of Martin's lack of faith and humility? The Lord answers Martin's request for a greater witness by explaining the conditions of faith and humility and patience according to which that greater witness will be granted.

The Lord tells Joseph to remind Martin that Joseph is under covenant not to show the plates to anyone unless commanded, a stinging reminder to Martin. Joseph has the gift to translate the plates and will have no other gifts until he finishes that task. But soon Joseph will be ordained not only to translate but to deliver the Lord's words, to teach. The Lord curses those who will not believe then. If they will not believe the Lord's words, then showing them the plates will make no difference. "Oh, this unbelieving and stiffnecked generation," the Lord laments, "mine anger is kindled against them" (v. 8). He intends to select three witnesses to testify; he will show them the plates, and their witness will accompany his words to all mankind. He will bless those who believe, and they will be born again by water and by the Holy Spirit. He will condemn those who harden their hearts. This prophecy will be verified "even as I also told the people of the destruction of Jerusalem," the Lord says (v. 20).

The Lord commands Joseph to "repent and walk more

Martin Harris.

uprightly before me, and to yield to the persuasions of men no more," promising Joseph eternal life on the condition of obedience, intimating that Joseph's mortal life may be violently cut short (v. 21). Then the Lord speaks to Joseph specifically about Martin Harris, whom he refers to only as "the man that desires the witness" (v. 23). He is not humble. But if he will choose to become humble and pray in faith, he will be shown the things he wants to see. Then he must testify of their truthfulness. Otherwise he will break his covenant and be condemned. If Martin refuses to humble himself, confess his sins, covenant to keep the commandments, and exercise faith in the Savior, he will never get the witness he desires. The Lord will not give that witness to him on any other conditions, and he should stop asking. Joseph should stop translating soon and wait to resume until the Lord commands. Otherwise the Lord will take away his gift and confiscate the plates. The Lord foresees Martin's fall unless he chooses humility and obtains the witness that he seeks. And if Joseph is not careful to keep the commandments he is given in this revelation, he will fall prey to those seeking his destruction. The revelation will resolve those problems if Joseph and Martin choose to obey it.

OUTCOMES

Doctrine and Covenants 5 reorients Martin Harris. "Show me, and I'll believe," Martin essentially says. "Believe, and I'll show you," the Lord, in effect, replies, and in doing so exposes the mistaken idea that seeing is believing. The Lord instructs Joseph to tell Martin to seek humility and faith as prerequisites to receiving the witness he desires.

Martin received the greater witness he sought *after* he met the Lord's conditions of humility and faith. As the translation neared completion, Joseph gathered one morning with his family and friends for singing and prayer. Martin was there, having traveled from Palmyra to Fayette to see how the translation progressed. Joseph had recently read in the translated manuscript that the Lord would call three eyewitnesses of the plates and their translation. David Whitmer, Oliver Cowdery, and Martin Harris volunteered, hoping to be chosen. "They teased me so much," Joseph said, "almost without intermission for some time," that he finally asked the Lord for approval and received an exciting answer. Joseph rose from his knees and said to Martin, "You have got to humble yourself before God this day and obtain, if possible, a forgiveness of your sins. If you will do this, it is God's will that you and Oliver Cowdery and David Whitmer should look upon the plates."[3]

About noon, Joseph, David, Oliver, and Martin went into the woods near the Whitmer home. "Having knelt down," Joseph said, "we began to pray in much faith, to Almighty God, to bestow upon us a realization of those promises. According to previous arrangement, I commenced by vocal prayer to our Heavenly Father and was followed by each of the other three." Nothing happened. "We again observed the same order of prayer, each calling on and praying fervently to God in regular rotation, but with the same result as before." Finally Martin Harris confessed that he was responsible for the Lord's silence. He left the others humbly, disappearing deeper into the woods. "We knelt down again," Joseph stated, "and had not been many minutes engaged in prayer when presently we beheld a light above us in the air of exceeding brightness and behold an angel stood before us." He held out the plates for them to see, turning them over one by one. "We could see them," Joseph testified, "and discern the engravings thereon very distinctly." A heavenly voice declared, "These plates have been revealed by the power of God, the translation of them which you have seen is correct, and I command you to bear record of what you now see and hear."[4]

"I left David and Oliver," Joseph reported, "and went in pursuit of Martin Harris, whom I found at a considerable distance fervently engaged in prayer." Joseph knelt beside him, and their joined faith opened heaven. Joseph saw and heard the vision again while Martin cried out, "mine eyes have beheld, mine eyes have beheld," and was overcome with joy. Joseph helped him up and they returned to the Whitmer home, rejoicing.[5]

Martin Harris struggled with pride and doubt. In section 5, the Lord mercifully prescribes humility and faith. These are the same attributes that access grace sufficient to turn weakness into strength, as the Lord had revealed to Moroni (Ether 12:27). The revelation empowered Martin to choose the way he would go. He could choose faith and humility and consequently receive the greater witness he sought while the Lord turned his weakness into strength. Or he could choose pride and skepticism, fall into transgression, and be destroyed (D&C 5:32). In the course of his long life, Martin tried both approaches. Late in life, however, he humbled himself again and traveled to Utah. Reunited with his children and his second wife, Martin Harris bore his greater witness often. He was living proof not only of the Book of Mormon but of the truth that pride and unbelief make us weak, whereas the choice to kneel in faith and humility activates the power of the Atonement to turn weakness into strength.

Doctrine & Covenants 6

ORIGIN

Struggling to meet their temporal needs, Joseph and Emma Smith made little progress on the translation of the plates. Moreover, Joseph feared that Emma's father, Isaac Hale, who owned the property on which they lived, "was about to turn me out of doors." Joseph "cried unto the Lord that he would provide for me to accomplish the work whereunto he had commanded me."[1]

The sun was about to set on a spring Sabbath when the Lord answered Joseph's prayers with a full-time scribe. Joseph's younger brother Samuel arrived at the home of Joseph and Emma with a twenty-two-year-old school teacher named Oliver Cowdery. He had learned "the facts relative to the plates" from Joseph's parents and had prayerfully sought to know more. The following day, Oliver told Joseph's parents that he had decided what to do. "Samuel, I understand, is going down to Pennsylvania to spend the spring with Joseph; I shall make my arrangements to be ready to accompany him thither," Oliver declared, "for I have made it a subject of prayer, and I firmly believe that it is the will of the Lord that I should go. If there is a work for me to do in this thing, I am determined to attend to it." Sure that Oliver could know such things for himself, Joseph's parents urged him to seek confirmation. The Lord visited Oliver, showed him the plates in a vision, and told him of the translation Joseph had begun. Soon Oliver and Samuel set out for Pennsylvania, slogging through the spring mud.[2] On the second day after his arrival, Oliver began scribing as Joseph translated the Book of Mormon. Oliver brought with him a spiritual "gift" he may sometimes have doubted (D&C 6:10). It seems likely that one of Oliver's reasons to travel so far to see Joseph was the hope he could learn more and perhaps find a fellow believer in the gift and power of God.[3] If so, Oliver was not disappointed. Joseph "inquired of the Lord through the Urim and Thummim, and obtained" the revelation recorded as Doctrine and Covenants 6.[4]

CONTENT

In Doctrine and Covenants 6 the Lord speaks intimately to Oliver with words that are as precise and penetrating as a double-edged sword. If Oliver will ask, the Lord will answer, as illustrated by his own prior experiences and this very revelation. Oliver has asked. The Lord answers: Keep my commandments and seek to bring forth and establish Zion. Seek wisdom, not riches. Then God will reveal his mysteries, and Oliver will be rich and wise, "for he that hath eternal life is rich," while those who seek riches instead of eternal life are shortsighted fools (D&C 6:7). Whatever Oliver desires the Lord will grant, including the desire to be the means of doing much good. If so, Oliver should declare repentance, keep the commandments he has been given, and assist Joseph in publishing the Lord's words to the world. Oliver has a sacred gift from God. It works when Oliver asks and the Lord reveals great and marvelous mysteries, which Joseph and Oliver understood to be sublime truths God had kept hidden from the world.[5] The purpose for such mysteries is to help others discern between truth and error. But the gift of knowing mysteries is not a toy. It is not to be discussed with doubters or used for trifling purposes. If Oliver will do good to the end, he will receive an even greater gift—salvation, the

Oliver Cowdery.

greatest gift of all. Meanwhile, Oliver is blessed for taking his questions to the Lord. As often has he has done so, the Lord has responded with instructions. Consider, for example, the circumstances of Oliver's journeying to Pennsylvania to assist Joseph. Who else but the Lord can tell Oliver's thoughts and motives? Oliver knows that. The Lord reminds him as a way of testifying that the translated words Oliver has been scribing are true, which is the reason for Oliver to be a diligent scribe and to stand faithfully by Joseph through difficult circumstances. Oliver should counsel, advise, and even "admonish him in his faults" (v. 19).

The revelation proves to Oliver that the Lord knows him and responds to his heartfelt desires. "I am Jesus Christ, the son of God," the Lord declares (v. 21). If Oliver desires more evidence of that, he can reflect on the night that he prayed to know more about what Joseph's parents had told him. The memory of the Lord speaking peace to his mind is a powerful testimony, confirmed in Section 6. Oliver can have the gift to translate if he desires it. There are untold records kept hidden due to wickedness. The Lord now has two gifted seers, two witnesses to declare his words.

Though it foreshadows martyrdom, the revelation is remarkably encouraging and empowering. It is autobiographical. The Lord reveals much to Joseph and Oliver about himself. At one point it even seems visionary as he invites them to "look unto me in every thought; doubt not, fear not. Behold the wounds which pierced my side, and also the prints of the nails in my hands and feet" (vv. 36–37). Perhaps beholding the risen Christ gives Joseph and Oliver courage, as it had the apostle Peter.

OUTCOMES

Imagine what it was like to be Oliver Cowdery. He had interviewed Joseph's parents about the plates, received answers to his prayers about Joseph and the marvelous work, including a vision that changed the course of his life by giving him a determined resolve to assist Joseph. Oliver had great expectations. Then his toe froze on the cold trip to Pennsylvania.[6] There was no money to be made scribing. Could the painstaking scribing that went on "day after day," as Oliver put it, in a tiny house near the Susquehanna River have disillusioned him somewhat?[7] Would not doubts and fears come naturally? When they did, Oliver knew where to turn. He had successfully asked the Lord to grant his desires previously, and now he did again. According to Joseph's history, after the revelation in Doctrine and Covenants 6 came, Oliver confided to Joseph about his earlier answers to prayer. "He had kept the circumstance entirely secret, and had mentioned it to no one; so that after this revelation was given, he knew that the work was true, because no being living knew of the thing alluded to in the revelation, but God and himself."[8] Oliver wrote to David Whitmer in Fayette, New York, assuring him that Joseph "had told him secrets of his life that he knew could not be known to any person but himself, in any other way than by revelation from the Almighty."[9]

What we have in section 6, then, is a document of the Lord's lovingly employed omniscience. He is not the arbitrary sovereign many Christians imagined him to be.[10] He uses his limitless power to address the needs of those who desire and ask. He was answering Joseph's prayer for help before he voiced it. He came to Oliver's aid over and over, with experiences perfectly adapted to assure Oliver that He is Jesus Christ, the Son of God, and that if Oliver will choose to look unto Him in every thought, he need neither doubt nor fear. He proves to Oliver that Joseph Smith, whatever his "faults" (v. 19), is the Lord's chosen seer. The revelation not only says those things but by its perfect timing, its delivery through Joseph's mouth, and its personalized wording, it illustrates them.

Doctrine & Covenants 7

ORIGIN

While translating the Book of Mormon in April 1829, Joseph and Oliver discussed John 21:20–23. What was the meaning of the words "that disciple should not die"? Was John still alive? The biblical text is ambiguous, and Joseph and Oliver disagreed on its meaning. Rather than taking dogmatic positions without good evidence, they sought clarifying revelation through the interpreters Joseph used to translate the Book of Mormon. There they saw a parchment written and hidden away by John himself.[1] Doctrine and Covenants 7 is a translated version of this record.

CONTENT

In Doctrine and Covenants 7 the Lord asked John the apostle what he desired, assuring him if he would ask, the Lord would give. John asked for power over death so he could live and bring souls to Christ. The Lord granted John's desire and blessed him to live until the Second Coming, prophesying all over the world. The Lord asked Peter what difference it made to him if John lived to bring souls to Christ. Peter could have his desire to join the Lord in his kingdom as soon as possible. And John could have his desire to continue his ministry. Each had joy in his desire. Thus the Lord would make John as fire, a ministering angel to work for the salvation of men and women on earth. Peter would preside over James and John, the three to whom the Lord would give the priesthood and its keys until his second coming.

President Spencer W. Kimball (served 1973–1985) stood with apostles and local Church leaders in the Church of Our Lady in Copenhagen, Denmark, admiring Thorvaldsen's magnificent Christus *and his sculptures of the twelve apostles. "I stood with President Kimball before the statue of Peter," Elder Boyd K. Packer said. "In his hand, depicted in marble, is a heavy set of keys. President Kimball pointed to them and explained what they symbolized." He then charged Copenhagen stake president Johan Bentine: "Tell every prelate in Denmark that they do not hold the keys. I hold the keys!" As the party left the church, President Kimball shook hands with the caretaker, "expressed his appreciation, and explained earnestly, 'These statues are of dead apostles,'" and then, pointing to apostles Tanner, Monson, and Packer, added, "you are in the presence of living apostles."*[2]

OUTCOMES

The parchment John wrote and hid is apparently the original source for his New Testament Gospel. The revelation of the parchment to Joseph and Oliver restores much that was lost from the final few verses of John 21. The Lord did give John power. As the revelation now in Doctrine and Covenants 7 was first recorded, this was power to bring souls to Christ.[3] When Joseph reviewed the revelations for publication in 1835, he clarified that John asked the Lord for "power over death, that I may live and bring souls unto thee" (v. 2).[4] The Lord granted John's desire. This knowledge clarifies an ambiguous Bible passage and satisfied Joseph and Oliver's curiosity. But even that much pales in comparison to the rest of the work the revelation does. It restores to the Bible record the truth that Jesus gave keys of salvation to Peter, James, and John. The revelation confirms that the Bible is true, even as it confirms that the Bible is incomplete. Nor is it sufficient for salvation. Apostles with keys are required for that.

Doctrine & Covenants 8

ORIGIN

Translating by the gift and power of God was the most marvelous thing Oliver Cowdery had ever witnessed. He wanted to try. Joseph's history says that Oliver "became exceedingly anxious to have the power to translate bestowed upon him."[1] Could he? Joseph asked the Lord and received Doctrine and Covenants 8, a revelation to Oliver.

CONTENT

The Lord assures Oliver Cowdery in Doctrine and Covenants 8 that he will learn the knowledge of anciently engraved scriptures if he seeks it honestly, in faith, believing in the Lord's promise. The Lord will tell Oliver this knowledge in his heart by the power of the Holy Ghost. This spirit of revelation guided Moses in leading the children of Israel safely through the Red Sea. It is now Oliver's gift. "Apply unto it," the Lord commands him (v. 4). It can deliver Oliver from his enemies as powerfully as it did Moses from his. The Lord commands Oliver to remember these words, his commandments, this gift. And he reminds Oliver of his other gift: the gift possessed by Moses' brother, Aaron—the gift of working with a divining rod.[2] It has already told Oliver many things (D&C 6). Only God can cause it to bless Oliver. He should not doubt it. It is God's gift to him. He can hold it in his hands. He can do marvelous works with it. No power can take it from him, for it is God's work. Whatever Oliver asks by that means, the Lord will grant. But he must ask in faith. Without faith he can do nothing. The Lord commands Oliver not to trifle with the gift nor ask for things he ought not. What should he ask for? He should ask to know the mysteries of God. He should ask to translate and receive knowledge from ancient records that have been kept hidden. The Lord will grant these desires according to Oliver's faith, just as he has done for Oliver all along.

OUTCOMES

Gifts such as Oliver's rod, Lehi's "miraculous directors," the brother of Jared's Urim and Thummim, and Joseph Smith's interpreters may have been used more commonly in ancient times and in Joseph's day than in ours (D&C 17:1). By 1829, when Doctrine and Covenants 8 was given, such gifts were beginning to be questioned. Skepticism of "means," as the scriptures call such gifts, was part of the hostility of the Protestant Reformation and later of the Enlightenment to anything Joseph would have called "marvelous" (Alma 37:41).[3] Perhaps that is the reason Joseph revised the revelation before its 1835 publication, taking out the mention of Oliver's rod and referring to it more generally as "the gift of Aaron" (D&C 8:6).[4] What Bible believer could fault the legitimate use of a divining rod like Aaron's or Moses'? Far from discouraging Oliver from using his revelatory gifts, the revelation teaches him how to use them legitimately. The Lord legitimized, not criticized, these gifts (Moroni 10:8, 24). Neither Joseph nor Oliver denied his gifts. Oliver kept them sacred. As commanded, he did not trifle with his gift or make it known to unbelievers (D&C 6:12). As intended, little is known about it in our skeptical generation. Perhaps the equally marvelous, supernal gift of the Holy Ghost remains nearly as mysterious. It is remarkably available, yet few "apply unto it," as the revelation commands (D&C 8:4).

Doctrine & Covenants 9

ORIGIN

Given permission to translate in Doctrine and Covenants 8, Oliver Cowdery wanted to know the reason he could not, and the Lord explained with Doctrine and Covenants 9.

CONTENT

The Lord temporarily revokes the privilege of translating because Oliver has not continued as he began. Oliver is to return to scribing for Joseph until the Book of Mormon is translated. Other records will come to light later, and Oliver will have power to assist in their translation. "Be patient," the Lord tells Oliver. "Do not murmur, my son" (vv. 3, 6).

The Lord's dealings with Oliver in Doctrine and Covenants 9 help him learn the process of revelation, for he has not understood. Oliver thought that if he simply asked, the Lord would give him the translated words. "You must study it out in your mind," the Lord teaches, "then you must ask me if it be right" (v. 8). If so, the Lord will cause Oliver's bosom to burn. He will feel that it is right. Otherwise Oliver will have no such feelings. Instead, he will forget the mistaken thoughts. Thus, though Oliver's fallible mind must do much of the work, the Lord will prevent him from mistakenly writing what is not true. Oliver failed to "apply" the process of revelation and feared, and then the opportunity to translate passed. He could have translated as well as Joseph if he had worked for the revelation, but it is not important that he translate. It is important that he learn how to think in order to receive revelation. It was important for him to learn by experience. Condemning neither of them, the Lord asks Oliver to observe how He has given Joseph strength and ability in translating to make up for Oliver's weakness and the time spent experimenting, promising blessings to Oliver if he will be content for now to write. "Be faithful, and yield to no temptation," the Lord commands, promising to save him at the "last day" (vv. 13–14).

OUTCOMES

In Doctrine and Covenants 9 Oliver learned a lesson about revelation that is best understood through experience. Revelation is an active, not a passive, process requiring a combination of spiritual sensitivity and intellectual exertion. Joseph worked hard to translate, to tap the gift and power of God. As a result of Oliver's failure to "continue as you commenced, when you began to translate" and the Lord's explanation "that I have taken away this privilege from you" (v. 5), Oliver gained a respect for Joseph's gift he would never lose and a knowledge about the process of revelation he would never forget.[1]

Even so, this seems a lesson best learned by personal experience. The process of revelation is usually learned after wrestling with it for a while, gaining experience, and applying unto it, as the Lord told Oliver to do in section 8. Those unwilling to endure the struggle often arrive at the conclusion that because they did not receive revelation, no one does. But as an intimate witness of revelation flowing through Joseph, Oliver could not deny the gift and power of God.

Doctrine & Covenants 10

ORIGIN

Joseph did not begin translating the Book of Mormon where the book begins today. Martin Harris lost what he translated first, which included Mormon's abridgment of Lehi's writings. When Joseph resumed translating, he picked up where he left off and continued on through the book of Moroni. At some point, Joseph asked the Lord if he could retranslate what had been lost. In the spring of 1829, the Lord answered this question with the revelation recorded in Doctrine and Covenants 10, which led Joseph to translate the small plates of Nephi, beginning with 1 Nephi.[1]

CONTENT

Because Joseph disobediently delivered the Book of Mormon manuscript to a wicked man, his mind became dark and he lost the manuscript and the seer stones called the Urim and Thummin. The Lord labels Martin Harris *wicked* because he has taken what God entrusted to Joseph and nearly ruined Joseph's gift. As a result, the manuscript has fallen into evil, conspiring hands. Put simply, Joseph has allowed sacred things to be lost. Doctrine and Covenants 10 announces that his gift is restored, and Joseph is commanded to faithfully continue translating the rest of the Book of Mormon as diligently as he is able.

"Pray always," the Lord commands him, "that you may conquer Satan, and that you may escape the hands of the servants of Satan" (v. 5). The servants of Satan have tried to destroy Joseph. Even Martin Harris has served Satan in this way. Cunningly, Satan enticed his servants to alter the document so they could say that Joseph had only pretended to translate. The Lord will not allow Satan to accomplish this evil design. The Lord tells Joseph of the conspiracy and of the conspirators' intent to alter the original words if Joseph retranslates the portion of the plates he has already translated. They plot to "say that he has lied in his words, and that he has no gift, and that he has no power" (v. 18). They covet glory of the world and will destroy Joseph to get it. Satan holds their hearts and stirs them to sin against the good. With corrupt hearts, wicked and abominable, they love darkness. Their deeds are evil. They will not ask God but prefer to be led by Satan to destruction.

The Lord knows all about Satan's cunning conspiracy and will judge the conspirators accordingly. He knows Satan's tactics well, how he flatters his followers and assures them that lies and deceit are not sinful if used to catch another liar. Satan leads such servants to hell where the irony comes full circle as they are caught in the very trap they have laid for others. Unlike Satan, God does not justify those who lie because they suppose others are lying. He knows Satan's mind and thwarts his plan by commanding Joseph not to translate again what he lost. Instead, the Lord cautions Joseph not to reveal his knowledge of the conspiracy until the Book of Mormon is translated. He cannot always tell who to trust.

With that caution, the Lord unfolds to Joseph that the Book of Mormon plates contain a backup copy of what was lost. The Lord reminds him, "Remember it was said in those writings that a more particular account was given of these things upon the plates of Nephi" (v. 39). Joseph should therefore translate the small plates of Nephi until he gets to the reign of King Benjamin. The conspirators stole a translation of only part of Mormon's abridgment of the Nephite plates. Publishing the translation of Nephi's own small plates will derail Satan's conspiracy, demonstrating in the process that God's "wisdom is greater than the cunning of the devil" (v. 43). The writing on these plates expounds the gospel of Christ. It is wiser for Joseph to translate it than to retranslate what has been stolen. The Book of Mormon contains the gospel the prophets desired to preserve for the Lamanites and all peoples. The Lord promised them these desires would be granted according to their faith. They blessed the American continent to be free so that its inhabitants could believe the gospel and have eternal life. The Lord promised to bring the Book of Mormon in order to build upon what the land's inhabitants already knew of his gospel. This is the reason he promised to establish his church among Joseph's generation if they would not harden their hearts. He is building his church, not destroying it. True Christians need not fear. They will inherit the kingdom. But those who build up their own churches for personal gain should fear. It is they whom the Lord will disturb. He will cause the disobedient, the wicked, and the servants of the devil to tremble. "I am Jesus Christ, the Son of God" he testifies, who came to his own only to be rejected. "I am the light which shineth in darkness," though the darkness fails to apprehend or contain Christ's light (vv. 57–58). Christ teaches that his "other sheep" are also Israelites and that he will bring their miracles to light, along with the gospel they taught (v. 60). Once translated, the Book of Mormon will do this work. It will corroborate the doctrine Joseph has received from the Lord, who will use the Book of Mormon to establish his gospel and minimize the contention over doctrine that Satan stirs among those who twist the scriptures and do not understand them. The Lord will gather those who choose to believe his doctrine as a hen gathers her chicks. He will not coerce. If they will come of their own will, they may partake freely of the living water he offers. What is his doctrine? All who repent and come to Christ are his church. Those who preach their own doctrine are not his church. Christ establishes his church "upon my rock" and in safety (v. 69). Remember these words from "him who is the life and light of the world, your Redeemer, your Lord and your God" (v. 70).

OUTCOMES

Doctrine and Covenants 10 gives us Christ's embracing view of Christianity. Section 10 came well before the restoration of the Church of Jesus Christ, so what does the Lord mean by "my church" in verse 54? The answer is that the restoration of the Church of Jesus Christ is the redemption of all of Christianity. Someone who restores an old house preserves all that is good and wonderful in it while fixing and renewing what is broken or missing. Verse 55 is meant to ease the fears of all Christians concerning the restored Church. The only ones who need fear are those who build their own churches, those who are Christian in name but whose hearts are far from Christ. He restored the gospel to save his church, meaning all who will believe in him. He is not destroying the true church; he is building it. This is good news for all followers of Christ.

Section 10 illustrates that God is both omniscient and benevolent. Where Satan uses his influence to blind, to enslave, and to deceive, the Lord uses his power to bless, to save, and to preserve our agency. Theologians have long wrestled with the assumption that if God is all-knowing, there can be no such thing as individual agency. The whole script of human action must have been predetermined, this assumption goes, and therefore we have no power to stray from it. One alternative is to believe in a less than omniscient God. Section 10 presents a refreshing, completely different alternative. It reveals an omniscient Lord who uses his foreknowledge to preserve and protect individual agency.

Consider the immediate problem. The Lord promised the Book of Mormon engravers that their descendants would receive the Book of Mormon. He called fallible agents, Joseph Smith and Martin Harris, to keep that promise. Joseph and Martin chose to disregard his will and, as a result, have lost the manuscript. Can God keep his promise to the Lehite prophets and still allow Joseph and Martin freedom to obey or disobey his commands?

Section 10 answers yes and illustrates how. Knowing that Joseph and Martin would choose to disobey him and Satan would seize that opportunity to undermine the Book of Mormon's power to bring souls to Christ, the Lord commanded Nephi to prepare alternative plates, often called the small plates of Nephi. Nephi prepared them at the Lord's command, not knowing exactly why (1 Nephi 9). Nearly a thousand years later, Mormon, at the Lord's command, put Nephi's plates with his edition of the other Nephite plates. "I do not know all things," Mormon wrote, "but the Lord knoweth all things which are to come; wherefore, he worketh in me to do according to his will" (Words of Mormon 1:7). Joseph and Martin did not have to disobey the Lord, but if they did, the Lord was prepared to keep his promise without compromising their option to disobey.

How many permutations are in the intricate plan of salvation? How many backups has the Lord prepared? Who knows? But only an omniscient God could truthfully assure us in such absolute terms that "the works, and the designs, and the purposes of God cannot be frustrated, neither can they come to naught" (D&C 3:1). Section 10 not only restates that guarantee but illustrates how God uses his foresight to keep us free from Satan's oppressive tactics. Section 10 could have answered Joseph's questions in one word: No. Instead, the Lord proves that he knows the mind of Satan, for section 10 goes into great detail about Satan, his tactics, and his followers. The Lord explains in detail the whole conspiracy to undermine the Book of Mormon. He does not simply state that he benevolently uses his omniscience to deliver us from Satan. He shows us how he does it. "I will *show* unto them," he says to our delight, "that my wisdom is greater than the cunning of the devil" (v. 43; emphasis added). That is what section 10 does.

The plan of salvation did not grind to a halt when Adam and Eve obeyed Satan rather than God or when Joseph and Martin disobeyed Him and lost the manuscript. The Lord had planned for just such circumstances. In the first edition of the Book of Mormon, Joseph published a preface that quoted large passages of the revelation recorded in section 10, explaining the loss of the manuscript, the conspiracy to undermine the Book of Mormon, and the Lord's demonstration that we can put our complete confidence in Him.

Doctrine & Covenants 11

ORIGIN

Imagine Hyrum Smith's excitement at knowing his younger brother had been called to translate the Book of Mormon, receive the priesthood from ministering angels, and restore the gospel of Jesus Christ. He wanted to shout it from the housetops. Hyrum visited Joseph in Harmony (now Oakland), Pennsylvania, in the spring of 1829 as Joseph and Oliver Cowdery were translating the Book of Mormon. Hyrum's father had visited Harmony and received Doctrine and Covenants 4 through Joseph. Hyrum's younger brother Samuel had also visited and been baptized. Joseph's history says that after Hyrum made an "earnest request, I enquired of the Lord through the Urim and Thummin, and received for him the following,"[1] Doctrine and Covenants 11.

CONTENT

The revelation recorded now as Doctrine and Covenants 11 announces the forthcoming marvelous work and commands Hyrum to take part. This section, like other early ones, has formulaic elements, yet it is also highly personalized. Hyrum is told that if he will ask, the Lord will answer. And because he has asked about his role in the marvelous work, the Lord tells him to keep the commandments, work for Zion, and "seek not for riches but for wisdom" (v. 7). The Lord promises Hyrum that the mysteries of God will unfold before him and give him enduring riches as an heir of eternal life. Whatever Hyrum desires of the Lord will be granted.

Note the several specific commands from the Lord to Hyrum: say nothing but repentance, keep the commandments he has been given, assist with the marvelous work. The Lord makes these the conditions upon which he will grant Hyrum's desires. As with many others, the entire revelation follows this conditional formula. Hyrum has a spiritual gift to know whatever he righteously desires by faith and the power of the Holy Ghost. The Lord tells him to trust the Spirit and promises to enlighten his mind and fill him with joy.

Although anxious, Hyrum is not yet called to preach but rather to wait until he has the Book of Mormon and the restored Church. Then, as Hyrum desires, he will be a successful preacher of the gospel. But for now he should keep the Lord's commandments, be patient, appeal to the Spirit, and cleave unto Christ wholeheartedly in order to assist with the printing of the Book of Mormon. "Be patient until you shall accomplish it," Christ says to Hyrum (v. 19). That is Hyrum's work for now, simply to keep the commandments as best he can. He is not to declare the Lord's word but to obtain it. Then his tongue will be loosed and, if he desires, he will be full of the Spirit and the Lord's word, the power of God to convince many. So for now Hyrum should not preach but study the Lord's Bible and the Book of Mormon manuscript. Then he will receive more.

"Thou art Hyrum, my son," the Lord says affectionately, "seek the kingdom of God, and all things shall be added" (v. 23). Build upon the Lord's rock, the gospel. Do not deny revelation or prophecy, as so many do. Store up the precious words of Christ in anticipation for your call to serve. These commands are for all who desire, and have begun to harvest the ripened field. "I am Jesus Christ, the Son of God. I am the life and the light of the world," the Lord testifies (v. 28). He was rejected by his own people, but he offers himself again. All who choose to receive and believe him are endowed with his power to become the sons and daughters of God.

OUTCOMES

Doctrine and Covenants 11 channels Hyrum's zeal. Here the Lord bridles him, careful not to break his spirit but to train him. This revelation gives Hyrum and so many others the formula for becoming successful preachers of the gospel. Promised power to convince by the Spirit if he will first learn the gospel, Hyrum spends a year searching the scriptures and helping with the publication of the Book of Mormon. When the Lord speaks to him in April 1830, the Book of Mormon is printed, the Church is organized, the marvelous work has come forth, and Hyrum has the knowledge to match his desire to declare it. Promised in May 1829 that the Lord would loose his tongue if he would obtain the word, Hyrum learned in April 1830 that his heart was opened, his tongue loosed, and his calling was to exhortation (D&C 23:3).

Having acted on the commands received in section 11, Hyrum was ready when the call came. One of many examples illustrates that after he obeyed the revelation, he had the power of God to convince. In August 1831, William McLellin and Hyrum went into the woods and discussed the gospel for hours. McLellin had questions. Hyrum knew the answers. Later, McLellin asked God to confirm what Hyrum had taught and gained a testimony of the Book of Mormon and the Church. He asked Hyrum to baptize him and wrote in his journal that he "was immersed according to the commandments of Jesus Christ by HS."[2]

Doctrine & Covenants 12

ORIGIN

Joseph Knight lived in Colesville, New York, a long day's journey from Joseph's home in Harmony (now Oakland), Pennsylvania. Joseph fondly remembered how Father Knight repeatedly brought him food and other supplies so he could continue translating the Book of Mormon. During one of these visits in May 1829, Knight was "very anxious to know his duty as to this work." Joseph asked the Lord, who answered with the revelation recorded in Doctrine and Covenants 12.[1]

CONTENT

A great and marvelous work is about to be made known to mankind. In Doctrine and Covenants 12 God commands Joseph Knight to heed his powerful words. Like a sword that cuts both ways, his words can bless and curse, save and damn. It is vital to Father Knight to heed them. The figurative field is ready for harvest. Whoever desires to harvest should do so all day long, saving his soul in the process. God calls those who are willing to harvest. If Father Knight will ask, God will answer. Because he has asked his duty, the Lord tells him to keep the commandments and work for Zion. The Lord speaks to Father Knight and all who have desires to help with the marvelous work. They cannot help if they are not humble, faithful, charitable, and temperate in everything trusted to their stewardship. It is the Life and Light of the world who reveals this to Joseph Knight, who should therefore heed the words mightily. If he does so, he is called to the work.

OUTCOMES

One of the great souls who contributed much to the Restoration, Joseph Knight obeyed the revelation in Doctrine and Covenants 12. He did all in his power to bring forth the Book of Mormon. Joseph Smith traveled in Knight's wagon to organize the Church and in his sleigh when he moved to Ohio. Joseph recorded Father Knight's deeds in the Book of the Law of the Lord, noting "he is a righteous man."[2]

Doctrine & Covenants 13

ORIGIN

The Book of Mormon tells of the resurrected Savior's ministry among the Nephites, during which he said to Nephi and then others: "I give unto you power that ye shall baptize this people when I am again ascended into heaven" (3 Nephi 11:21). To settle disputations that had arisen, the Savior taught Nephi and others how to perform the ordinance, the words to say, and the requirements of those who could be worthily immersed (3 Nephi 11:22–30). And as Joseph read those words to Oliver in May 1829, it was as if the Savior were teaching them, too. They quickly realized that no one on earth in 1829 had the Lord's permission and power to baptize.[1] They went into the woods and prayed fervently to "inquire of the Lord respecting baptism for the remission of sins, that [they] found mentioned in the translation of the plates" (Joseph Smith–History 1:68).[2] Their ordination is recorded in Doctrine and Covenants 13.

CONTENT

Joseph's account continues: "While we were thus employed, praying and calling upon the Lord, a messenger from heaven descended in a cloud of light, and having laid his hands upon us, he ordained us, saying: *Upon you my fellow servants, in the name of Messiah, I confer the Priesthood of Aaron, which holds the keys of the ministering of angels, and of the gospel of repentance, and of baptism by immersion for the remission of sins; and this shall never be taken again from the earth until the sons of Levi do offer again an offering unto the Lord in righteousness*" (Joseph Smith–History 1:68–69).³ Their ordination in Doctrine and Covenants 13 restored the Aaronic Priesthood to the earth once more.

OUTCOMES

Only later in his narrative does Joseph reveal the messenger's identity: "The messenger who visited us . . . said that his name was John, the same that is called John the Baptist in the New Testament, and that he acted under the direction of Peter, James and John" (Joseph Smith–History 1:72).⁴ We should not let Joseph's plainness diminish the impact of his testimony. The messenger was John *the* Baptist, the man who baptized Jesus Christ in Jordan, the man who was ruthlessly beheaded in Judea. Now, standing in the Pennsylvania woods quite intact, he laid his hands on their heads and conferred upon them priesthood, under the direction of apostles ordained by Christ himself. John's appearance in Doctrine and Covenants 13 declares that Jesus is the Christ, that an apostasy from the gospel of repentance and baptism by immersion for the remission of sins had occurred, and that it was now ended. For the first time in a very long time, women and men could be baptized by immersion for the remission of their sins by men who could truly say, "Having authority given me of Jesus Christ, I baptize you in the name of the Father, and of the Son, and of the Holy Ghost. Amen" (3 Nephi 11:25). Oliver could barely contain himself when he wrote the story years later: "'Twas the voice of an angel from glory, 'twas a message from the Most High! . . . Where was room for doubt? Nowhere" (Joseph Smith–History 1:71, footnote).⁵

Joseph and Oliver followed John the Baptist's instructions and immersed each other in the

Sculpture of John the Baptist ordaining Joseph Smith and Oliver Cowdery.

Susquehanna River. "We were filled with the Holy Ghost," Joseph said, "and rejoiced in the God of our salvation" (Joseph Smith–History 1:73).[6] Soon Joseph's brother Samuel was baptized, then his parents and other siblings, and so on to each person who has received the gospel of repentance and baptism by immersion. And the restored priesthood of Aaron will remain on earth so that modern priests can continue to offer offerings to the Lord (D&C 84:31–34; 128:24).

And what of the Aaronic Priesthood keys of the ministering of angels? Shortly after John conferred the priesthood on Joseph and Oliver, another messenger met Joseph on the riverbank and taught him how to use these keys to identify the devil "when he appeared as an angel of light" (D&C 128:20). Joseph taught them to several of the apostles on June 27, 1839, five years to the day before he was murdered. He taught them to Parley P. Pratt in February 1843, resulting in the recording of the revelation now in Doctrine and Covenants 129.[7]

Doctrine & Covenants 14, 15, and 16

ORIGINS

Oliver Cowdery kept his acquaintance David Whitmer informed about the progress of the translation of the Book of Mormon. When antagonism against Joseph grew worse in Harmony (now Oakland), Pennsylvania, Oliver wrote to David to see if he and Joseph could translate at the Whitmer home in Fayette, New York. David himself went to Pennsylvania with a wagon to transport them, told them his parents would house and feed them while they were translating, and promised them all the help they might need. By early June 1829, the translation commenced in Fayette. The Whitmers and their neighbors were friendly and supportive. Whitmer sons David, Peter, and John were especially "zealous," Joseph said, "and being anxious to know their respective duties, and having desired with much earnestness that I should enquire of the Lord concerning them, I did so, through the means of the Urim and Thummim and obtained for them in succession the following Revelations," now recorded in Doctrine and Covenants 14, 15, and 16.[1]

CONTENT OF SECTION 14

A great and marvelous work is about to be made known to mankind. In Doctrine and Covenants 14 God commands David Whitmer to heed his powerful words. Like a sword that cuts both ways, his words can bless or curse, save or damn. It is vital that David heed the words of the Lord. The figurative field is ready for harvest. Whoever desires to harvest should do so all day long, saving his own soul in the process. God calls whoever will harvest. If David will ask, God will answer. He should work for Zion and keep God's commandments in all he does. If he does so and endures to the end, God will give him the greatest possible gift: eternal life. If David asks Heavenly Father in the name of Jesus Christ, faithfully believing that he will receive the Holy Ghost, he will. It will enable him to testify of things he will hear and see and to invite his contemporaries to repent. "I am Jesus Christ," the Lord says, "the Son of the living God" (v. 9). He created the heavens and the earth. He is a light that darkness cannot hide. He must give the fulness of his gospel to the Gentiles and then to the Israelites. He calls David to assist. If he does so faithfully, a great reward of blessings both spiritual and temporal await him.

OUTCOMES OF SECTION 14

Doctrine and Covenants 14 foreshadows David's role as one of the Three Witnesses of the Book of Mormon. David kept many of the commands given in the revelation. His testimony of the Book of Mormon, to which he remained faithful, is recorded in every copy. He assisted in the marvelous work. But in the case of David Whitmer, and others, the condition that he "endure to the end" (v. 7) is especially notable. David did not endure. Having served for almost four years as president of the Church in Missouri, he was cut off from the Church in 1838. He lived for another five decades as a respected citizen of Richmond, Missouri, and made a conscious effort to affirm the Book of Mormon while finding fault with Joseph Smith and The Church of Jesus Christ of Latter-day Saints.[2]

CONTENT OF SECTIONS 15 AND 16

John and Peter Whitmer receive the same revelation in Doctrine and Covenants 15 and 16. The Lord commands both servants to hearken to his words. He is their Lord and Redeemer. He speaks with sharpness and omnipotence to reveal what no one but these men and the Lord know: their secret desire to know what will be of most worth to them. He blesses them for this desire and for speaking his words. And he tells them the most valuable thing they can do: "Declare repentance unto this people, that you may bring souls unto me, that you may rest with them in the kingdom of my Father" (D&C 15:6; 16:6).

OUTCOMES OF SECTIONS 15 AND 16

Like all revelations, those recorded in Doctrine and Covenants 15 and 16 have an internal logic. Declaring repentance is the most valuable thing for John and Peter to do because that will enable them to rest with the repentant in Heavenly Father's kingdom. Later sections explain this logic further, but in these sections we are introduced to the idea that working for the salvation of others is eternally satisfying for ourselves.

Peter served with Oliver Cowdery and others on one of the Church's early formal missions and died of tuberculosis in 1836, firm in the faith, working for Zion in Missouri. John lived on for another forty-two years. Serving in the presidency of the Church in Missouri until he was excommunicated in 1838, John became increasingly selfish as the years went by. He acquired hundreds of acres of land in Caldwell County, Missouri, some by misusing Church funds, and had livestock and a fine home.[3] His neighbors regarded him as "a highly respected and law abiding citizen."[4] John died in 1878, bearing testimony of the Book of Mormon until his death.

Doctrine & Covenants 17

ORIGIN

In June 1829 as the translation of the Book of Mormon neared completion, Joseph gathered one morning with his family and friends for singing and prayer. Martin Harris was there, having come from Palmyra to see how the translation progressed. Joseph had learned while translating that the Lord would call three eyewitnesses of the plates and their translation. David Whitmer, Oliver Cowdery, and Martin Harris volunteered, hoping they could be chosen. "They teased me so much," Joseph said, "almost without intermission for some time," that he finally asked the Lord for approval and received the exciting answer recorded in Doctrine and Covenants 17. Joseph rose from his knees and said to Martin, "You have got to humble yourself before God this day and obtain, if possible, a forgiveness of your sins. If you will do this, it is God's will that you and Oliver Cowdery and David Whitmer should look upon the plates."[1]

CONTENT

The Lord covenants with Oliver, David, and Martin in Doctrine and Covenants 17 that if they will rely on his word wholeheartedly, he will show them the Book of Mormon plates, the breastplate, Laban's sword, the seer stones the Lord gave to the brother of Jared, and the Liahona, which directed Lehi and his family miraculously through the wilderness near the Red Sea. The witnesses will view these artifacts by faith like that of the brother of Jared or Lehi. Such evidence proves more than the fact that Joseph had plates.

Witnesses of Lehi's miraculous compass, Laban's sword, and the brother of Jared's seer stones know that the plates are inscribed with ancient writing about actual people who received revelations, knew the Lord, were directed to a promised land, and committed their testimonies of Christ to writing that has been translated by Joseph Smith. In exchange for such a witness, the Lord expects them to testify of the Book of Mormon to fulfill his purposes. Their witness will verify Joseph's, keep him from being overwhelmed, and accomplish the Lord's righteous purposes. On these conditions, the Lord covenants to lift up the witnesses "at the last day" (v. 8).

OUTCOMES

About noon on a late spring day in 1829, Joseph, David, Oliver, and Martin slipped into the woods near the Whitmer home. "Having knelt down," Joseph said, "we began to pray in much faith, to Almighty God, to bestow upon us a realization of those promises. According to previous arrangement, I commenced by vocal prayer to our Heavenly Father and was followed by each of the other three." Nothing happened. "We again observed the same order of prayer, each calling on and praying fervently to God in regular rotation, but with the same result as before." Finally Martin Harris confessed that he was responsible for the Lord's silence. He left the others humbly, disappearing deeper into the woods. "We knelt down again," Joseph stated, "and had not been many minutes engaged in prayer when presently we beheld a light above us in the air of exceeding brightness and behold an angel stood before us." He held out the plates for them to see, turning them over one by one. "We could see them," Joseph testified, "and discern the engravings thereon very distinctly." A heavenly voice declared, "These plates have been revealed by the power of God, the translation of them which you have seen is correct, and I command you to bear record of what you now see and hear."

"I left David and Oliver," Joseph reported, "and went in pursuit of Martin Harris, whom I found at a considerable distance fervently engaged in prayer." Joseph knelt beside him and their joined faith opened heaven. Joseph saw and heard the vision again while Martin cried out, "mine eyes have beheld, mine eyes have beheld," and was overcome with joy. Joseph helped him up and they returned to the Whitmer home, rejoicing.

Joseph entered the room where his parents and Mrs. Whitmer were visiting.

"Father! Mother! You do not know how happy I am. The Lord has caused the plates to be shown to three more besides me. They have also seen an angel and will have to testify to the truth of what I have said, for they know for themselves that I do not go about to deceive the people." The pressure of being the sole eyewitness had, Joseph said, become "almost too much for me to endure. But they will now have to bear a part, and it does rejoice my soul that I am not any longer to be entirely alone in the world."

Martin, Oliver, and David eagerly told what they had seen and heard. They wrote a statement of testimony to the whole world that they had seen the engraved plates and heard the voice of God state that they were translated correctly. "We declare with words of soberness," they affirmed, "that an angel of God came down from heaven, and he brought and laid before our eyes, that we beheld and saw the plates, and the engravings thereon." It happened just as all the witnesses said. "It is marvelous in our eyes," they declared together. "Nevertheless, the voice of the Lord commanded us that we should bear record of it; wherefore, to be obedient unto the commandments of God, we bear testimony of these things." David, Oliver, and Martin testified often of their experience. "I know that Joseph Smith was a true prophet of God," Martin said as an old man. "I know that the Book of Mormon was divinely translated. I saw the plates, I saw the angel. I heard the voice of God. I know that the Book of Mormon is true."[2]

As Doctrine and Covenants 17 emphasizes repeatedly, such witnesses fulfill the Lord's righteous purposes. They do not force people to believe, but they do make everyone able to accept or reject the testimony and accountable for their decision. Witnesses sift people into self-selected categories of believers or unbelievers. "Their testimony shall . . . go forth unto the condemnation of this generation if they harden their hearts," while those who believe will receive the testimony of the Spirit (D&C 5:18).

Doctrine & Covenants 18

ORIGIN

In June 1829, as the Book of Mormon translation was concluding, Joseph, Oliver, and David Whitmer sought revelation "relative to building up the church of Christ, according to the fullness of the Gospel."[1] Doctrine and Covenants 18 came in answer.

CONTENT

The Lord reveals Doctrine and Covenants 18 because Oliver Cowdery desires to know how to build the Church of Jesus Christ. The Lord tells him to rely on the Book of Mormon manuscript he has penned as Joseph translated. The Spirit has confirmed its verity to Oliver repeatedly. He can use it to compose a foundational document for the Church that is soon to be restored. If they build the Church on this foundation, "hell shall not prevail against" them (v. 5).

Meanwhile, mankind is increasingly wicked and needs to repent and be baptized, just as Joseph recently obeyed the Lord's command to baptize Oliver. The Lord commands Oliver not to marvel that Joseph has been called. Oliver may not know the answer to the question "Why Joseph?" but the Lord does.

The Lord teaches apostles Oliver Cowdery and David Whitmer the value of a soul and thus the importance of repentance. Apostles are to remember the value God gives to each soul. The Redeemer suffered death for each and every soul so that each one could repent and come to him.

The revelation sounds like an equation: The value of each soul is directly proportionate to the infinite atonement of Jesus Christ. He conquered death to bring the repentant to him. He feels great joy in repentant souls. For this reason Oliver and David are to cry repentance. If they spend their whole lives and only a single soul repents, their joy with that soul will be great in Heavenly Father's kingdom. How much greater joy, then, to help many repent? They are to follow the Book of Mormon in preaching the law of the gospel with faith, hope, and charity by inviting all mankind to come to Christ and assume his name, becoming his.

Section 18 promises the calling of twelve apostles in the restored Church. The Lord speaks to them, promising grace sufficient to save them if they choose to meet the conditions on which he offers it: Walk uprightly and do not sin. He will ordain them to ordain others to declare the gospel by the power of the Holy Ghost, according to the will of God. Jesus Christ has so declared. These are his words, and the apostles can therefore testify they have heard his voice. Without his power they would not have the revelation to read. They do have it, and so they can testify that they know his words. Oliver and David are to select these apostles, who will be known by their desires, manifest in their works.

OUTCOMES

After nearly two millennia, Doctrine and Covenants 18 commissions new apostles. A quorum of twelve would not be called for nearly six more years, but in section 18 the Lord calls apostles Oliver Cowdery and David Whitmer to select the members of that quorum and then speaks to them directly.

What does the Lord emphasize when he commissions apostles, when he gives them their job description, their marching orders? He teaches them that the Atonement, the price paid, makes each soul of infinite worth in God's sight. Based on that truth, he commissions the apostles to tell every soul to repent, to obey the law of the gospel, to become one with Christ by assuming his name. Truman Madsen drew on the doctrine of section 18 with these words: "If souls are of value in direct proportion to the concern and sacrifice of our Redeemer, then we know that in the eyes of the Father and the Son, your soul—even yours—and mine—even mine—is of infinite worth."[2]

Based on their commission in section 18, modern apostles emphasize how the Savior's atonement gives infinite value to each soul. "If we could truly understand the Atonement of the Lord Jesus Christ," said Elder M. Russell Ballard, "we would realize how precious is *one* son or daughter of God. . . . We would strive to emulate the Savior and would never be unkind, indifferent, disrespectful, or insensitive to others." Elder Ballard concluded: "It was Jesus who said, 'If . . . you should labor all your days in crying repentance unto this people, and bring, save it be *one* soul unto me, how great shall be your joy with him in the kingdom of my Father!' (D&C 18:15). Not only that, but great shall be the *Lord's joy* in the soul that repenteth! For precious unto Him is the *one*."[3]

Doctrine & Covenants 19

ORIGIN

Martin Harris was a respected farmer in Wayne County, New York, a prosperous, property-owning Palmyra resident since 1808 and a benefactor of Joseph Smith.[1] Early in June 1829, Joseph and Martin asked Palmyra printer Egbert Grandin to publish the Book of Mormon. Grandin reluctantly agreed to the controversial project only after learning that a printer in Rochester would do the publishing. They worked out an agreement with Grandin for him to print and bind five thousand copies of the Book of Mormon for three thousand dollars, with Martin putting up more than 150 acres of land as collateral. Martin mortgaged the land on August 25. He had eighteen months to repay the debt, hopefully with proceeds from book sales, or else Grandin could sell the property.[2] Once the financial arrangements were concluded, Grandin's employees began printing.

In January 1830, Joseph and Martin agreed to share profits from the Book of Mormon until Martin's mortgage was paid. In March, as the first copies came from the press, Martin became alarmed. He met Joseph on the road as he was traveling from his Pennsylvania home to Palmyra to check on the printing. Arms full of books, a distraught Martin Harris told Joseph, "The books will not sell for nobody wants them."

"I think they will sell well," Joseph responded.

"I want a commandment," Martin demanded, seeking a reassuring revelation.

"Fulfill what you have got," replied Joseph, referring to Doctrine and Covenants 5.

"I must have a commandment," Martin said, increasingly anxious.³

Martin stayed that night with Joseph at the Smith home. Restless, he had an anxious dream that an enormous dog was pouncing on him. He rose in the morning, again demanded a revelation, and left for home. That afternoon Joseph received the revelation recorded now in Doctrine and Covenants 19 as Oliver Cowdery scribed.⁴

CONTENT

In Doctrine and Covenants 19 Christ declares himself Redeemer and Judge of the world. Having accomplished the Atonement, he retains all power, including power over Satan at the end of the world. Christ will judge all mankind according to their deeds. Everyone must, therefore, repent or suffer, for none can outlive the endless Christ. He has become like his Father. He does not revoke his judgments and therefore the unrepentant will weep, wail, and gnash their teeth. Still, it is not written that their torment never ends. The scriptures that speak of endless damnation are not well understood. Christ explains this mystery in section 19. His punishment is endless in the sense that it comes from him. The eternal Christ gives eternal punishment, not necessarily punishment that lasts forever. The purposes, effects, and outcomes of his punishment last forever, though the punishment itself may not. The Atonement did not last forever, yet it is aptly described as "infinite and eternal" in its scope (Alma 34:10).

With that understood, Christ gives Martin Harris the commandment he had demanded. "I command you again to repent," the Lord says, "repent lest I smite you by the rod of my mouth, and by my wrath, and by my anger, and your sufferings be sore—how sore you know not, how exquisite you know not, yea, how hard to bear you know not" (D&C 19:15). Christ knows. He suffered exquisitely for all so that they would not have to suffer if they would choose to repent. If not, they must suffer as Christ did. The pain caused him, a God, to tremble, to bleed at every pore, to suffer both bodily and spiritually until he desired not to drink the bitterness any longer. Even so, he endured to the end and finished preparing the way for mankind to repent. He gives the glory for this atonement to his Father.

Because Christ atoned for Martin, he commands Martin to repent or else be humbled by Christ's almighty power. He commands Martin to confess his sins or suffer the punishments described. The Lord gave Martin a tiny foretaste of such suffering by withdrawing the Spirit from him.

The Lord commands Martin to preach only repentance and not show this revelation to the world until the Lord in his wisdom directs, for it deals with the mysteries of godliness, and the world needs more basic principles first. The Lord commands Martin to learn of him, listen to him, walk in his Spirit, and promises him peace. "I am Jesus Christ," the Lord declares in summary, "I came by the will of the Father, and I do his will" (v. 24).

The revelation becomes less urgent as it proceeds, and only late in the section does the Lord speak to Martin's concern about the mortgage on his land. The Lord commands Martin again not to covet his neighbor's wife or lifestyle, nor even to covet his own property but to give it freely to pay for the publication of the Book of Mormon, which contains the truth and the word of God. It is the Lord's word to the Gentiles and to all the Israelites, including Lamanites and Jews. It is designed to help them believe the gospel and realize that Christ, the Messiah, has already come. The Lord gives Martin a series of commands sufficient to guide him for the rest of his life and assures him misery if he disregards them. But if Martin will pray always, the Lord will pour out his Spirit upon him, resulting in far greater blessings than Martin could obtain if he amassed earthly treasures with their inherently short shelf lives. Can Martin read this without rejoicing? Or will he continue counseling others though blind himself? Can he be humble, meek, and wise? The Lord thinks he can. "Come unto me thy Savior," the revelation concludes (v. 41).

OUTCOMES

Doctrine and Covenants 19 restores doctrine related to the Atonement, emphasizing that there is no repentance without suffering, especially the exquisite suffering of Christ. It unfolds the mystery of divine punishment. It confirms a literal reading of the account in the Gospel of Luke of Christ sweating blood as he suffered in Gethsemane, adding that the Atonement caused Christ to "bleed at every pore" (v. 18). Thus, where other Christians cite the crucifixion, Latter-day Saints consider Christ's suffering in the garden as commencing the crucible of his Atonement.

Martin Harris got his commandment. Over and over the Lord commanded him to repent. Section 19 is unique in the standard works; it is the only text in which Christ describes his atonement so vividly. It is an extremely compelling revelation on the nature of the Atonement and the related doctrines of repentance or punishment. While it may sound harsh, this is a merciful text. Christ has already suffered for the sins of all mankind, but his unfathomably exquisite vicarious suffering does not negate the free will of those who choose not to repent. Christ's emphatic, repeated demand that Martin repent is love. Does Martin love him, the revelation asks? If so, he will repent.

Section 19 is a reorienting revelation. That is, Martin sees things from a narrow, materialist, mortal perspective and needs to be turned, to see things differently. The revelation opens his eyes, for he has been blind (v. 40). It reorients Martin by asserting priorities different from his. He is most concerned about his financial security. The Lord is most concerned about the welfare of his soul. Note the Lord's intense, sustained emphasis, beginning about verse 15. The consuming priority is Martin's soul, for which Christ suffered exquisitely. Note that late in the revelation the Lord answers Martin's consuming question. What about the mortgage? How can I keep my security intact and still fund the Book of Mormon? In answer to that question the Lord says to Martin, "Pay the debt" (v. 35).

Martin Harris did as section 19 commanded. He did not care for the counsel of Joseph the farmer to obey an earlier revelation, sound as it was. But he followed at significant cost the commandment he received in section 19 through Joseph the Prophet. Such behavior is a testimony to this revelation and the others. Martin knew Joseph well. He knew the difference between Joseph's voice and the Lord's. Whatever his weaknesses, Martin Harris believed in Joseph's calling and tried to obey his revelations. Similarly, Elder David B. Haight taught, "if we could feel or were sensitive even in the slightest to the matchless love of our Savior and his willingness to suffer for our individual sins, we would cease procrastination and 'clean the slate,' and repent of all our transgressions. This would mean keeping God's commandments and setting our lives in order, searching our souls, and repenting of our sins, large or small."[5]

Doctrine & Covenants 20

ORIGIN

In summer 1828, the Lord promised in Doctrine and Covenants 10 that he would reestablish his church if people were openhearted. A year later in section 18 the Lord commanded Oliver Cowdery to use the Book of Mormon manuscript as his source to draft a document on which to found the restored Church. Oliver wrote "Articles of the Church of Christ" by putting together doctrines and ordinances from the unpublished Book of Mormon, passages from Joseph's revelations, and some commentary.[1] But on April 10, 1830, just a few days after the restored Church was organized on April 6, the Lord revealed the Articles and Covenants of the Church, Doctrine and Covenants 20, to apostles Joseph and Oliver by the gift and power of God.[2]

CONTENT

Doctrine and Covenants 20 documents the rise of the Church of Christ in the latter days, specifically April 6, 1830, according to both human law and the will of God. Moreover, for the inexperienced presiding elders of the Church of Christ, this section answers the question: How do we build the Church?

The answer is threefold. The first thing needed to build the Church of Christ is his authority to do so. The first sixteen verses of section 20 declare that the Lord has called Joseph Smith and Oliver Cowdery and made them apostles. The two presiding elders testify of this as the first part of the revelation closes with verse 16.

The second thing needed to build the Church of Christ is <u>a foundation of fundamental doctrine</u>. Verses 17–36 declare this doctrine, beginning with the reality of Almighty God, his creation and plan of salvation, the Fall, and Heavenly Father's plan to send his Only Begotten Son to atone for sin and redeem all willing children of God from the Fall. This section sets forth obedience to the law of the gospel as the condition on which God saves his fallen children through the atonement of Jesus Christ. This expression of belief counters Calvinism, a common Christian theology. Section 20 and Calvinism agree that salvation comes as Jesus Christ justifies and then sanctifies fallen souls, but Calvinism's articles of faith declared that once God had predestined a soul for salvation, nothing that soul could do would change the inevitable outcome. Known as the perseverance of the Saints, this doctrine is refuted by section 20. Verses 17–36 clarify true theology, declaring that salvation does come through the grace of Jesus Christ but that we can fall from that grace if we choose to depart from the living God. Thus we have the need to pray always to overcome temptations that would carry us away from God. The two presiding elders of the Church end this section with their testimonies of the true doctrine taught by the restored Church of Christ.

One who wonders, "Is Mormonism Christian?" need only look at how these verses "concentrate on the reality of Christ's mission and how one gains the benefits of the atonement." Indeed, section 20 closely aligns with early Christian doctrine and "then sets out to wash away the later sediments that formed on the bedrock of Christ's saving work."[3]

<u>The final thing</u> needed to build the Church of Christ is practical knowledge of its basic procedures, sacraments, and duties of its officers and members. This knowledge is set forth in verses 37–84. The last and longest section of the revelation, these verses tell who can be baptized and how, instructs how to administer the sacrament, and relates the duties of priesthood holders and other Church members.

Oliver Cowdery did not initially like the detailed qualifications for baptism given in verse 37. His 1829 draft had specified only that "whosoever repenteth & humbleth himself before me & desireth to be baptized in my name shall ye baptize them."[4] By comparison, verse 37 adds the requirements of a broken heart and contrite spirit, evidence of true repentance and willingness to assume the name of Jesus Christ with determination to serve him to the end, and a godly life (see Moroni 6:1–4). Oliver demanded "in the name of God" that Joseph delete the requirement that baptismal candidates should "manifest by their works that they have received the Spirit of Christ unto the remission of their sins."[5] Joseph asked Oliver "by what authority he took upon him to command me to . . . add or diminish to or from a revelation or commandment from Almighty God."[6] Joseph finally convinced Oliver, who read section 20 to the Church's second conference in September 1830.[7]

OUTCOMES

Doctrine and Covenants 20 is a constitution for the Church. It establishes the Church's authority, core doctrines, and practical organization and procedures. At the first conference of the Church Joseph read section 20 and asked the Saints to accept it. They unanimously did, making it the first of Joseph's revelations to receive the common consent of the Saints.[8]

Much of what the Church does stems from section 20, including administering the ordinances of baptism and the sacrament. But sometimes the growing Church has wandered from the specific instructions in verses 37 and 68, leading to people being baptized and confirmed before meeting the Lord's requirements. Church leaders have repeatedly reminded local leaders of the need to apply those verses. Section 20 thus continues to guide and order the basic teaching, ordinances, and record keeping of the Church.

It has been that way from the beginning. Section 20 was the first revelation the Church published in its newspaper, and it was often copied by missionaries who needed to know how to build the Church in their ministries far from headquarters.

Doctrine & Covenants 21

ORIGIN

In spring 1830, Joseph Knight hitched his team to his wagon, picked up the Prophet in Pennsylvania, and headed for Fayette, New York. Joseph confided to Father Knight the purpose of the trip: "There must be a Church formed." Father Knight remembered that "on the sixth Day of April 1830 he [Joseph] Begun the Church with six members and received the following Revelation," now recorded as Doctrine and Covenants 21.[1]

CONTENT

The Lord commands Joseph to keep records that document his callings as seer, translator, prophet, apostle of Jesus Christ, and elder of the Church by the will of God and the grace of Christ. Inspired by the Holy Ghost to found the Church on April 6, 1830, Joseph will build it into the most holy faith. Doctrine and Covenants 21 establishes the Church and its distinctive order. The Lord addresses the Saints through Joseph, commanding them to patiently receive and obey all of the words and commandments Joseph receives from him and to walk in holiness. The Lord promises the Saints redemption for obedience to this command.

He has seen Joseph's diligence, heard his prayers, and counted the tears he has shed for Zion. Joseph is not flawless, but he is the Lord's choice for a mortal mouthpiece. The Lord will magnify him, for his words and his life testify that Jesus was crucified by sinners for sinners and that his atonement absolves the sins of the contrite.

To put his Church in order, the Lord tells Oliver Cowdery, an apostle, to ordain Joseph as the presiding elder of the Church. Joseph will preside over Oliver, and Oliver over the Church of Christ. Oliver will be the primary preacher to the restored Church and on behalf of the Church to all mankind.

OUTCOMES

As a result of Doctrine and Covenants 21, Joseph kept records, wrote histories, and collected documents that testify to his callings as seer, translator, prophet, and apostle of Jesus Christ. The Church continues to obey this mandate, not least by sponsoring the massive and painstaking process of collecting, editing, and publishing the papers of Joseph Smith. No church has ever had a greater sense of its history and destiny than the restored Church of Jesus Christ. This inspires record keeping.

Section 21 restored the Church of Jesus Christ. After nearly two millennia, duly authorized apostles are ordained and assigned by Jesus Christ to lead his Church. Many men and women have "wished," as one wrote, "I had lived in the days of the prophets or apostles, that I could have sure guides." Others looked forward, waiting for the Lord to send new apostles.[2] Those hopes were realized on April 6, 1830. In sum, as Joseph put it, "The Church of Jesus Christ of Latter-day Saints was founded upon direct revelation, as the true church of God has ever been, according to the scriptures."[3]

Section 21 gives order to the Church of Jesus Christ, who gives commandments to Joseph and makes Joseph responsible to give them to the Saints. The Lord appoints Oliver to preside over the Saints, Joseph over Oliver, and himself over Joseph. The Saints' role in the Church is to "give heed" (v. 4) to his apostles as they give heed to him, and to "labor in my vineyard" (v. 9). This is the order of the Church established in section 21. Having implemented it, Joseph said that afterward he and the others present enjoyed "a happy time spent in witnessing and feeling for ourselves the powers and the blessings of the Holy Ghost, through the grace of God bestowed upon us." For the first time in more than a millennium, a meeting of Saints "dismissed with the pleasing knowledge that we were now individually, members of, and acknowledged of God, 'The Church of Jesus Christ,' organized in accordance with commandments and revelations, given by him to ourselves, in these last days, as well as according to the order of the Church as recorded in the New Testament."[4]

A decade had passed since Joseph, distressed by his family's religious divisions, went into the grove, where he saw Heavenly Father and Christ and asked them which church he should join. "None of them," came the answer. They all denied God's power to speak, to call new apostles, to guide his church by revelation. The evening after he organized the Church, having witnessed his father's baptism, Joseph went into the woods to pray alone. Overwhelmed, Joseph poured out his heart to his Heavenly Father. A literal fulfillment of verse 8 followed. "His joy seemed to be full," wrote Father Knight. "I think he saw the grate work he had Begun and was Desirus to Carry it out."[5]

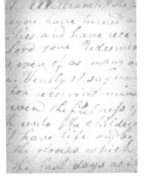

Doctrine & Covenants 22

ORIGIN

Joseph's history says Doctrine and Covenants 22 came "in consequence of some desiring to unite with the Church without re-baptism, who had previously been baptized."[1] Joseph asked the Lord and received section 22. Orson Pratt later explained that at least some of these people were Baptists, "very moral and no doubt as good people as you could find anywhere, who came, saying they believed in the Book of Mormon, and that they had been baptized into the Baptist Church, and that they wished to come into our Church. The Prophet Joseph had not, at that time, particularly inquired in relation to this matter, but he did inquire, and received a revelation from the Lord."[2]

CONTENT

In Doctrine and Covenants 22 the Lord declares that "old covenants" are "done away" because he has restored "a new and an everlasting covenant, even that which was from the beginning" (v. 1). So even a man baptized a hundred times will not enter the "strait gate" by obeying an irrelevant law, or "dead works" (v. 2). The Lord has given the new covenant and restored the Church because of these dead works, and he commands all to enter his gate according to his gospel and no other.

OUTCOMES

Doctrine and Covenants 22 answers the question whether persons already baptized by immersion for the remission of sins—and there were many who converted to the Church from a variety of denominations—needed to be baptized again. Sixteenth-century reformers were pejoratively called *Anabaptists* (rebaptizers) when they followed the biblical practice of immersing accountable believers, including people already baptized as infants. The American Baptist leader Francis Wayland defended this practice. "We consider ourselves not to *baptize again,*" he wrote, "but to baptize those who have never yet submitted to this ordinance."[3] Section 22 follows this logic and takes it a step further.

Doctrine & Covenants 23

ORIGIN

Soon after the Church was organized, Joseph's father and brothers Hyrum and Samuel, Oliver Cowdery, and Joseph Knight were "anxious to know of the Lord what might be their respective duties, in relation to this work." Joseph's history says, "I enquired of the Lord and received for them the following," the revelation now recorded as Doctrine and Covenants 23.[1]

CONTENT

The Lord speaks to each of the men in turn, offering blessings and warnings, prophecies and promises. Note especially the conditions on which the promised blessings depend. Note, too, how Doctrine and Covenants 23 declares the fulfillment of a promise in section 11. There the Lord tells Hyrum Smith that if he will obtain the word, then his tongue will be loosed for preaching it. Evidently Hyrum studied the scriptures for much of the year between the two revelations, for this one announces that his tongue is loosed. The Lord reveals that Joseph Knight needs to pray aloud publicly and privately, in his family and among his friends—indeed, everywhere.

OUTCOMES

The Lord's simple instructions and warnings in Doctrine and Covenants 23 inform these five men of his will for them, empowering them to obey or not. They can now act. Hyrum, for example, can preach powerfully and does. Joseph's father and his brother Samuel also became effective missionaries and Church leaders in response to this revelation. As for Joseph Knight, he had done so much for Joseph—provided money, paper for translating the Book of Mormon, food, transportation, and moral support. All of that was easy for Father Knight. He was comfortable behind the scenes. What this revelation commanded was more difficult for him: to join the Church and preach the gospel. Father Knight wrote that he wrestled with the decision to be baptized but decided not to. He said he wanted to read the Book of Mormon first. "I should a felt Better if I had a gone forward," he realized, and a few weeks later he and his wife, Polly Peck Knight, were baptized.[2]

The revelation also shows how well the Lord knows them. Pride plagued Oliver Cowdery, as it does so many others. He arrogantly withdrew from the Church in 1838, humbly returning a decade later. During that period he wrote defensively about his own importance in the Restoration. Afterward he testified meekly of the Book of Mormon and of receiving the priesthood from ministering angels along with Joseph Smith. Just as the revelation said, whenever Oliver humbly made his calling known, the Lord opened his heart to preach the truth.

Doctrine & Covenants 24

ORIGIN

Joseph had a rough month between the Church's Spirit-filled June conference in Fayette, New York, and this July revelation. He returned to his home in Pennsylvania and then visited the Saints in nearby Colesville, New York. Reverend John Sherer, who was losing some of his Presbyterian followers to the restored gospel, stirred prejudice against Joseph. Sherer's followers interrupted baptismal services, and Sherer himself kidnapped Emily Coburn in an attempt to prevent her baptism. Just when several who had been baptized, including Emma Smith, were to be confirmed, a constable arrested Joseph "on charge of being a disorderly person; of setting the country in an uproar by preaching the Book of Mormon." The constable protected Joseph from a mob determined to injure him and accompanied him to trial the following day. Josiah Stowell and his daughters testified of Joseph's upright character. Joseph was acquitted, but a constable from the neighboring county arrested him then and hauled him over the county line. "The next day I was brought before the Magistrate's Court of Colesville, Broom County," says Joseph's history, "and put on trial. My former faithful friends and lawyers were again at my side, my former persecutors were arrayed against me." All the antagonistic witnesses could offer was hearsay. Newel Knight embarrassed the prosecution with his testimony. Public opinion began to turn in Joseph's favor. The court again acquitted him as his persecutors threatened to tar and feather him. The formerly hostile constable helped Joseph escape to Emma's sister's house, where Emma anxiously waited. She and Joseph finally returned to their home in Harmony (now Oakland), Pennsylvania, the next day. He returned to Colesville a few days later with Oliver Cowdery to confirm the new converts, only to be chased all night by the same enemies. "Shortly after our return home," Joseph wrote, "we received the following commandments," referring to Doctrine and Covenants 24 and 25.[1]

CONTENT

The revelation recorded now in Doctrine and Covenants 24 is one of several revelations in which the Lord meets Joseph where he is. Though he has become larger than life to many Latter-day Saints, Joseph, like Nephi, was aware of his sins and his need for redemption through the atonement of Jesus Christ. In section 24 the Lord acknowledges both Joseph's accomplishments and his sins, commanding him to sin no more. Joseph must also have been concerned about providing for his family's physical needs and doing the Lord's work, because section 24 counsels him how to do both and assures him that the Saints whom he serves bear the responsibility to provide for his family. The Lord will curse them if they do not. The Lord commands Joseph to be fully devoted to Zion, for he will not be strong in temporal labors. That is not his calling. Joseph will have strength in his calling, and the Lord promises to be with him "even unto the end of [his] days" (v. 8). Oliver's calling is to continue preaching to the Saints and the world. If Oliver declares the gospel of Jesus Christ at all times and in all places, the Lord will give him extraordinary strength.

The Saints should not require miracles unless commanded, except casting out devils, healing the sick, and overcoming poisons. These miracles are not to be volunteered but performed when requested, as the scriptures say. When Joseph and Oliver are not received in the name of the Lord, they should curse rather than bless by dusting and cleaning their feet as a testimony that they offered the good news of the restored gospel. Joseph and Oliver should command anyone who uses violence against them to be smitten in the name of the Lord. He will then smite when he sees fit. Whoever prosecutes Joseph and Oliver through ostensibly legal methods will be cursed by the law. Joseph and Oliver are to take no money, no staves, nor even extra clothes. The Church is responsible to provide for their physical needs while they and those they have ordained prune the Lord's vineyard mightily for the last time.

OUTCOMES

Doctrine and Covenants 24 addresses Joseph's concern about finances and how to provide for his family. It does not promise wealth, only that Joseph will have sufficient if he attends to his calling: "Thou shalt devote all thy service in Zion" (v. 7). And because Joseph devotes all his service to the Saints, the Saints are responsible to see that his family's needs are met.

Oliver, too, is encouraged to give his all to the kingdom. Both presiding elders of the Church are promised plenty of afflictions to endure. The Lord does promise, however, to smite anyone who uses violence against them. And those who use the law to persecute the Prophet will find themselves cursed by the law. In sum, the two young apostles are now in the full-time service of the Lord. He promises to look after them as they trust him and take up his cross and follow him, devoting their lives wholly to his service.

Doctrine & Covenants 25

ORIGIN

Emma Hale's parents opposed her 1827 marriage to Joseph. Despite that opposition and knowing that controversy followed him, she married him anyway. Their abiding love and spirituality is evident in their surviving letters. Emma believed her husband and believed in him. She assisted and sustained him in translating the Book of Mormon. She was baptized in June 1830, but a wave of intense persecution battered Joseph, keeping him from attending to her confirmation (see D&C 24). She felt her "very heart strings would be broken with grief" as she witnessed her neighbors' hatred toward her husband.[1]

Joseph's receipt of the revelation recorded in Doctrine and Covenants 24 might have troubled Emma somewhat. Given her tumultuous married life thus far, she couldn't help but be concerned about her financial future. In section 24 the Lord essentially guaranteed Joseph and Emma a modest living dependent on the faithfulness of the Saints. If the Saints would support them, Joseph and Emma would have enough to enable him to devote his life to the Church, but there was no guarantee of "the things of this world" (D&C 25:10). Section 24 seems to assure Emma a life of hardship with a husband whose efforts belonged principally to the Church. In a remarkably affectionate yet straightforward revelation, Doctrine and Covenants 25, the Lord let Emma know that he could see through her eyes and gave her an opportunity to see through his.

CONTENT

The Lord speaks intimately to Emma in Doctrine and Covenants 25, even more so in the manuscripts than the later canonized revelation. "My daughter," he calls her, and continues speaking like a father speaks to a favored, or in Emma's case, "elect" daughter (vv. 1, 3). He reveals his will, promising to preserve her life and her place in Zion if she will be faithful and virtuous. "Murmur not," he commands her, "because of the things which thou hast not seen," which the Lord has withheld from her and from the world (v. 4). Emma's calling is to comfort Joseph. Perhaps the most compelling part of the revelation is verse 5's positioning of Joseph between the Lord and Emma: "The office of thy calling shall be for a comfort unto *my servant,* Joseph Smith, Jun., *thy husband*" (v. 5; emphasis added). As this sentence suggests, at times Emma might have felt she was in a tug-of-war with the Lord for Joseph's attention, which gave her daily opportunities to willingly submit herself to the Lord's will for her, or, as section 25 puts it, to "continue in the spirit of meekness, and beware of pride" (v. 14). Rarely did Emma fail to fulfill that difficult command.

Emma is to be Joseph's partner, his confidant, his strength; and he hers. The Lord commands her to go with Joseph when he goes, scribe for him when he has no other scribe (freeing Oliver Cowdery for other duties), and be ordained to expound scripture and exhort the Church by the Spirit. Joseph will lay his hands upon Emma to bestow the Holy Ghost, and she is to spend her time scribing and learning much in the process. She need not fear. Joseph will support her in her calling. His calling is to the Church, and by fulfilling it Joseph reveals whatever the Lord wills, according to the Saints' faith. Emma can see where this is leading. "Lay aside the things of this world and seek for the things of a better," the Lord invites (v.10).

The Lord chooses Emma to select sacred hymns for the Church. He delights in the heartfelt song of the righteous. Thus Emma may be encouraged and rejoice and cleave to her covenants. Continue to be meek, the Lord commands her, and beware of pride. "Let thy soul delight in thy husband, and the glory which shall come upon him" (v. 14). A crown of righteousness awaits Emma if she keeps these commandments continually. Otherwise, where the Lord is she cannot go.

OUTCOMES

Emma was confirmed a member of the Church and compiled the Church's first two hymnals in response to the instruction given in Doctrine and Covenants 25, but the revelation is significant far beyond those accomplishments, for it addresses Emma's deepest fears and fondest hopes. This is the only revelation in the Doctrine and Covenants addressed to a woman (D&C 90:28–31 was given for Vienna Jaques). Section 25 shows that the Lord knew his daughter Emma. He encourages her to be meek and warns her against pride. He counseled her not to murmur because she had not seen the marvelous things her husband had seen. He invited her to sacrifice the things of this world for infinitely better things. He knew before she knew that she was capable of scribing for Joseph, of learning much, and of teaching the Saints by the power of the Holy Ghost. Perhaps because these callings could cause Emma anxiety, the Lord assured her that Joseph would support her. She needed Joseph and Joseph needed her, and he called her to comfort and sustain her husband.

Emma Hale Smith in later life.

Section 25 oriented Emma's life. Expecting twins, she left her parents to obey the Lord's command to go with Joseph to Ohio (see D&C 37), and she never saw them again. In 1842 Joseph reflected on his life with Emma and wrote his feelings for her in his Book of the Law of the Lord (see D&C 85). "Again she is here," Joseph noted, "even in the seventh trouble, undaunted, firm and unwavering, unchangeable, affectionate Emma."² In September 1843 Joseph sealed on Emma's head the "crown of righteousness" the Lord promised her in section 25. Then, just days before his death in 1844, Joseph invited Emma to write her own blessing. She thought of section 25 and penned her hopes that she would be able to obey its commands and receive its promised blessings.³ She "cleave[d] unto [her] covenants" through Abrahamic tests (v. 13). Emma understandably could have considered herself in competition with the Lord for Joseph's time and attention. Section 25 assured her that however that might be, she was the Lord's highly favored daughter, that he expected more of her than she might have thought she could give, and that he would finally give her all she ultimately wanted.

Doctrine & Covenants 26

ORIGIN

Joseph and the Saints in southern New York endured a blast of persecution in the summer of 1830 (see D&C 24). Members of the Knight family in Colesville were understandably anxious. Back home in the nearby but comparatively peaceful setting of Harmony (now Oakland), Pennsylvania, Joseph received a series of revelations, including Doctrine and Covenants 26. The Lord gave instructions to Joseph, Oliver Cowdery, and John Whitmer about what to do until the conference scheduled for September in Fayette, New York.

CONTENT

In Doctrine and Covenants 26 Joseph and his brethren are asked to devote their time to scripture study, preaching, confirming the Saints at Colesville, New York, and farming until the conference later in the summer, when the Lord will direct them further. Everything in the Church should be done by common consent, by much prayer, and by faith.

OUTCOMES

Newel Knight said Doctrine and Covenants 26 provided "great consolation to the little band of Brethren and Sisters at Colesville after having been abandoned from time to time by the servants of God in consequence of the wicked who were constantly seeking to destroy the work of God from the earth. It showed us that the Lord took cognizance of us and also that he knew the acts of the wicked. So we resolved to continue steadfast in the faith and were diligent in our prayers and assembling ourselves together, waiting with patience until we should have the pleasure of again seeing Brother Joseph and others of the Servants of the Lord who had become dear to us by the ties of the gospel, and of being confirmed members of the Church of Jesus Christ by the laying on of hands of the Apostles."[1]

Though the Saints had followed the principle of common consent since organizing the church, this is the first revelation to prescribe that practice, which is a hallmark of the restored church. Even so, common consent is not well understood. Its purpose is to preserve agency. The *common* part means that all are to make their own individual choice, to speak for themselves. "Everyone is perfectly free. . . . There is no compulsion whatsoever in this voting." The *consent* part means to agree to what is proposed by someone else, "a yielding of the mind or will to that which is proposed," according to Webster's 1828 dictionary. We do not vote in the Church as we do in elections, hoping that our will can win out. We exercise our agency to consent to or dissent from what is proposed. "When you vote affirmatively, you make a solemn covenant with the Lord that you will sustain, that is, give your full loyalty and support, without equivocation or reservation, to the officer for whom you vote."[2]

Doctrine & Covenants 27

ORIGIN

In August 1830, anticipating the confirmation meeting at which the sacrament was to be administered and Emma Smith and Sally Knight were to receive the gift of the Holy Ghost by the laying on of hands, Joseph Smith "set out to procure some wine for the occasion but he had gone only a short distance when he was met by a heavenly messenger."[1] The angel gave Joseph part of Doctrine and Covenants 27, including the first four and a half verses and parts of verses 14 and 18. According to Newel Knight, the rest of verses 5–18 were revealed a few weeks later, but the later verses are not in the earliest manuscript or the first published version of section 27.[2] They were first published in the 1835 Doctrine and Covenants.

CONTENT

Speaking for the Savior, the angel informs Joseph in Doctrine and Covenants 27 that it does not matter what the Saints eat or drink for the sacrament. What matters is that they partake with an eye single to the Lord's glory, signifying to God that they remember the Savior's body sacrificed and blood shed for the remission of their sins. So the angel commands Joseph not to purchase wine or distilled drinks from his enemies but to drink in the Church only what they make themselves.

The revelation prophesies a future sacrament meeting on earth in which the Lord will drink wine with Joseph and with Moroni, who holds the keys of the Book of Mormon.[3] Elias will be there with the keys of restoration.

Another forerunner, John the Baptist, will be there with the preparatory Aaronic priesthood keys he conferred on Joseph and Oliver in May 1829 (see D&C 13). Elijah will be there with sealing keys (see D&C 2; 110). The patriarchs of Israel will be there. Through them God made covenant promises with Joseph and all who embrace the restored gospel. Adam will be there. Peter, James, and John will be there. They committed to Joseph the apostolic keys that authorize his ministry and revelations. All these restored keys constitute a dispensation of gospel fulness, the last dispensation before the Lord's coming, in which the Lord will finish his work of saving and exalting God's children and gather out of the fallen world those whom Heavenly Father gave him.

Rejoice, the revelation tells Joseph, and prepare to work and fight. Put on the armor of God described by Paul in his epistle to the Ephesian Saints.[4]

OUTCOMES

Newel Knight remembered how he, Joseph, and their wives obeyed this revelation. They "prepared some wine at our own make, and held our meeting. . . . We partook of the sacrament, after which we confirmed the two sisters into the church, and spent the evening in a glorious manner. The Spirit of the Lord was poured out upon us. We praised the God of Israel, and rejoiced exceedingly."[5]

Doctrine and Covenants 27 penetrates to the heart of the sacrament. If one's eye is not single to God's glory in that ordinance, tradition can transcend substance. It does not matter what the Saints eat or what they drink in that ordinance. What matters is what the emblems signify, namely, Jesus' body laid down for us and his blood shed to remit our sins. As a result of section 27, according to Brigham Young, "we use water as though it were wine; for we are commanded to drink not of wine for this sacred purpose unless it be made by our own hands."[6] In some places the Saints continued to use homemade wine for the sacrament until 1906.[7]

The 1835 text of section 27 adds considerable detail to the earlier prophecy that Christ would partake of sacramental wine with Joseph Smith and others. It emphasizes priesthood keys—rights associated with priesthood—and the transmission of those keys to Joseph by biblical prophets.

It is the earliest document we have confirming that Peter, James, and John ordained Joseph an apostle. It confirms that Joseph received priesthood keys from Peter, James, and John. Indeed, the 1835 version of section 27 adds considerable detail to the angel's prophecy that Christ would partake of sacramental wine with Joseph and others in the future. The revelation identifies the archangel Michael as Adam and Adam as the Ancient of Days referred to in the book of Daniel.[8]

Section 27 applies to Latter-day Saints the counsel Paul gave the Ephesian Saints to arm themselves spiritually.

Doctrine & Covenants 28

ORIGIN

As the Church's second conference approached in September 1830, Hiram Page, one of the Eight Witnesses of the Book of Mormon plates, began receiving revelations through a stone "concerning the upbuilding of Zion the order of the Church and so forth, but which were entirely at variance with the order of Gods House, as it is laid down in the scriptures and our own late revelations."[1] Newel Knight wrote that Hiram "had quite a roll of papers full of these revelations, and many in the Church were led astray by them," including Oliver Cowdery and many of the Whitmer family. Joseph was perplexed.[2] How could he help the Saints understand that each of them was entitled to direct revelation but that the order of revelation for the Church had been given in April when it was organized (D&C 21), namely, that Joseph would receive commandments from the Lord's own mouth? Joseph spent most of a sleepless night prayerfully seeking and receiving the revelation recorded now in Doctrine and Covenants 28.

CONTENT

The Lord speaks to Oliver Cowdery, the second elder of the Church, clarifying that his role is to teach the revelations given to Joseph. Likening Joseph to Moses and Oliver to Aaron, the Lord reminds Oliver of his position in Doctrine and Covenants 28. He is to "speak or teach" but not to write revelations for the Church or to command Joseph (v. 4). The Lord directs Oliver to go on a mission to the Lamanites, or Native Americans, in the West, hinting that Page's predictions for the location of Zion are wrong: "it shall be on the borders by the Lamanites" (v. 9). But first Cowdery is to assist in settling the controversy, in part by visiting Page privately to "tell him that those things which he hath written from that stone are not of me and that Satan deceiveth him" (v. 11). The Lord reminds Cowdery that Page has not been appointed to receive commandments on Church government and is therefore out of order. "For all things must be done in order, and by common consent in the church, by the prayer of faith" (v. 13).

OUTCOMES

In speaking through Joseph to Oliver, the Lord illustrated the order in which revelation flows for the Church. By commanding Oliver (through Joseph) to teach Hiram Page true principles, the Lord reinforced them in Oliver's mind and illustrated the order of the Church at work at a critical moment. By countering the information in Page's revelation with accurate details about Zion in Doctrine and Covenants 28, the Lord led Oliver to the conclusion that Joseph was the true revelator. Oliver obeyed the revelation and "after much labor with these brethren they were convinced of their error, and confessed the same, renouncing the revelations as not being of God, but acknowledged that Satan had conspired to overthrow their belief in the true plan of salvation."[3]

Doctrine & Covenants 29

ORIGIN

Quarterly conferences gave the early Saints opportunities to unite in their hunger and thirst for more light and knowledge. The September 1830 conference hosted by the Whitmers in their Fayette, New York, home became the setting for the sublime doctrinal revelation recorded in Doctrine and Covenants 29.

CONTENT

Many of the revelations begin with a command to listen to Jesus Christ, followed by a rationale for doing so. But none is more beautiful than Doctrine and Covenants 29. To listen to the Savior in this section is to hear a merciful voice of gladness offering forgiveness at the expense of his own atoning blood. He promises to give whatever the Saints at conference ask for in faith.

Section 29 hinges on agency—a mixture of power to act, commandments that determine good and evil, knowledge of the commandments to act upon, and Satan's opposition to our acting in obedience. Calvinist theology taught that the elect were the relative few God chose arbitrarily to passively receive his grace. But in section 29 the Lord defines the elect as those who actively choose to hear his voice (the commandments that activate agency) and harden not their hearts. The chicks he promises to gather like a hen are those who decide to humble *themselves*. That language is theologically significant and frames the entire revelation. Agency: Who has it, how did they get it, and what are the outcomes of using it to obey or disobey?

Several of the revelations are eschatological, meaning they deal with the last days, the end of time as we know it at the Lord's second coming. None is more vividly eschatological than section 29. It paints a horrifying picture of those who exercise their agency not to repent. "I will burn them up, saith the Lord of Hosts, that wickedness shall not be upon the earth" (v. 9). Note the way the revelation locates cause and effect in the eschatological verses. "Because of the wickedness of the world . . . I will take vengeance upon the wicked, for they will not repent; . . . my blood shall not cleanse them if they hear me not" (v. 17).

The Lord never specifies the timing of his second coming in the scriptures. He says only that it will be "soon," but as Elder Neal A. Maxwell suggested, wristwatch-wearing mortals are not well positioned to determine what *soon* means to "Him who oversees cosmic clocks and calendars."[1] But even if they are purposefully vague about precise dates, eschatological revelations such as section 29 are chronological. They tell the order of events that will lead up to and compose the Savior's return and reign. They are characterized by such words as *before* and *when:* "before this great day shall come" (v. 14), "when the thousand years are ended" (v. 22), and "before the earth shall pass away" (v. 26).

Section 29 sets forth the logic of gathering the elect because the unrepentant will soon suffer the Lord's just vengeance at his second coming. "The righteous shall be gathered on my right hand unto eternal life; and the wicked on my left hand will I be ashamed to own before the Father" (v. 27). The Lord explains that the wicked will be powerless to come where he is and then transitions into a passage on the importance, therefore, of being endowed with power. Section 29 thus prefigures the endowment of power restored later and received in temples today. It begins with a discussion of God's continuing work of creation. We tend to think of creation as something that happened at the beginning, but section 29 (and Moses 1) speak of creation as a process still very much underway. We are being created in God's image, accountable agents who choose to obey the laws of God and are being endowed with his power by degrees. Note how verses 30–33 outline this creation process in abstract terms. First we are created spiritually and then our spirit bodies are clothed in temporal bodies at birth. That is the first phase of God's creative work. Then fallen, temporal bodies are raised to become spirit filled, gloriously resurrected in God's image. That culminates his work of creating us in his image. That is his work and his glory (Moses 1).

How does this endowment of power work? Using Adam and Eve as examples, the Lord walks us through the process in the last part of the revelation. As the earliest known revelation to Joseph to describe premortal life, section 29 explains Satan's lust for power and how he led away a third of heaven's inhabitants "because of their agency" (v. 36). We too easily assume that Satan conspired to undermine agency by coercing his followers. Brigham Young taught that he intended, rather, to negate the consequences of exercising their agency to do evil. Section 29 emphasizes Heavenly Father's more excellent way. When Adam and Eve chose of their own free will to become subject to Satan by obeying him, they were cast out of God's presence "because" they transgressed the law (v. 41). They thus died spiritually. In other words, they were first spiritual and then temporal. Their fall made them carnal, mortal, natural. But that was only "the beginning of my work," the Lord says (v. 32). God began the "last" phase of creating Adam and Eve in his image by lengthening their mortal lives to enable them to exercise agency. He sent angels to teach them the law of the gospel, namely "repentance and redemption through faith on the name of mine Only Begotten Son" (v. 42). This plan safeguards agency, justice, and mercy. It guarantees redemption to all who choose to believe and "eternal damnation" to all who choose not to believe or repent (v. 44). Both get just what they want, what they choose.

Section 29 ends as it began, with emphasis on agency. Until His children are capable of acting for themselves, Heavenly Father restricts Satan's power to tempt them. In other words, we grow into our agency gradually and "begin to become accountable" (v. 47) in direct proportion to our ability to act of our own free will on our knowledge of the Lord's commands.

OUTCOMES

Doctrine and Covenants 29 sets forth the plan of redemption with clarity that belies its theological sophistication. The greatest teachers strive to similarly set forth the gospel accessibly without diminishing its depths and vast dimensions.

Two lessons are in order as section 29 concludes. First, the Lord expects earthly fathers to pattern their parenting after his, to rise to the responsibility described in section 29 of providing the children with agency by teaching them the laws of God, holding them accountable to the degree that they act knowingly to transgress the laws, and mercifully providing them opportunities for repentance and redemption, even at great personal sacrifice. Second, God requires repentance from every accountable agent, that is, from everyone to whom he has given "knowledge" of good and evil (v. 49). Every agent sins knowingly. The Lord sets willful, conscious repentance as the term and condition of redeeming his children "through faith on the name of mine Only Begotten Son" (v. 42).

This empowering revelation is a primer on parenting. It illustrates how Heavenly Father (note that the revelation begins in the voice of Jesus Christ, but the last part on raising children is in the voice of Heavenly Father) raises children. He begins by informing the children about the dangers of their world, telling them to gather for their own safety. Similar to the methods we might use to teach small children to stay out of the road or not to touch the stove, the revelation vividly pictures outcomes of forbidden behaviors. The Lord explains the different destinies awaiting the powerless and the empowered, encouraging children to qualify for the endowment of his power they can receive if they want it. How do they get it? By repentance and obedience. As with God, the best parents endow their children with agency. They teach the gospel, command, sacrifice, and extend opportunities for redemption. Their greatest work is the creation of fully developed children who have grown into their agency and become accountable for themselves. Parents are learning how to be like God. They, too, are being created in his image.

Doctrine & Covenants 30

ORIGIN

Revelation often flows to reward righteous desire, and during the second quarterly conference of the young Church of Christ, held in September 1830 at the Whitmer home in Fayette, New York, several of the elders showed "a great desire" to take the gospel to the Native Americans in the West. The Book of Mormon title page declared one of its primary audiences to be "the Lamanites, who are a remnant of the House of Israel." Doctrine and Covenants 3 helped him understand further that the plates were preserved so the Lamanites could know the Lord's promises to them, repent, and rely on Jesus Christ for salvation. Oliver Cowdery had just been called to lead a mission to the Lamanites, and at conference the desire to take the Book of Mormon to the Native Americans became "so great that it was agreed upon we should enquire of the Lord respecting the propriety of sending some of the Elders among them."[1] Joseph asked for and received a revelation calling Peter Whitmer Jr. to join Oliver. Peter's brothers David and John were assigned closer to home. Doctrine and Covenants 30 was first published as three revelations, one to each Whitmer brother.

CONTENT FOR DAVID WHITMER

The Lord chastens David Whitmer in Doctrine and Covenants 30 for fearing man and failing to serve faithfully in the ministry to which the Lord has called him. David has allowed his mind to dwell more on the things of the earth than on his Creator or his callings. He has refused to listen to the

Spirit and to Joseph, relying instead on Hiram Page for direction (D&C 28), resulting in his temporary separation from the Spirit. Left to reconsider his recent actions, David is instructed to remain home, serve in the Church, and proselyte locally until the Lord commands him otherwise.

OUTCOMES FOR DAVID WHITMER

David misplaced his devotion and his faith. Rather than loving God with all his mind, he became preoccupied with the things of the earth. The Lord is probably not accusing David of being worldly. The Lord uses the word *earth* in Doctrine and Covenants 30:2, not *world,* as in Doctrine and Covenants 1:16, where he describes the fallen earth to suggest evil or what we might call *worldliness.* He nearly always uses the word *earth* more positively, as he does in Doctrine and Covenants 30:2. The world (worldliness) is bad; the earth is good. What, then, is the problem? David's priorities. He is a farmer. It is harvest time. He is preoccupied with soil and crops instead of their Maker. David is looking down rather than up. His earthly cares have led him to neglect his commission to harvest souls (D&C 14; 17; 18).

CONTENT FOR PETER WHITMER

Regarding Doctrine and Covenants 30 Peter Whitmer Jr. writes in his journal, "The word of the Lord came unto me by the Prophet Joseph Smith . . . saying Peter thou shalt go with Brother Oliver to the Lamanites."[2] The Lord knows that declaring the gospel could be a fearful undertaking, and he reassures Peter, saying, "Fear not, but give heed to the words and advice of your brother, which he shall give unto you." The Lord has given Peter an able senior companion. Oliver holds sufficient authority to build up the Church among the Lamanites, and only Joseph is appointed to counsel him in Church matters. The Lord counsels Peter to listen to Oliver's instructions and endure whatever afflictions he endures, ever praying in faith for his companion and himself. The Lord promises Peter eternal life if he will obey the revelation and diligently keep the commandments.

OUTCOMES FOR PETER WHITMER

These revelations recorded in Doctrine and Covenants 30 moved people to inconvenient action. In a statement based on the revealed commands to Peter Whitmer, he and other companions covenanted to go with Oliver. And Peter went. They traveled nearly a thousand miles, trudging much of it through deep snow, to do as they were commanded. As with so many missionaries, they did not succeed as *they* hoped. Missionaries of other faiths and government agents opposed their efforts, and they eventually returned east without converting any Native Americans. Taking the Book of Mormon to them would have to wait.

Meanwhile, the missionaries had great success with another intended audience of the Book of Mormon. "Strange as it may appear," a northern Ohio newspaper reported, "it is an unquestionable fact, that this singular sect have, within three or four weeks, made many proselytes in this county. The number of believers in the faith, in three or four of the northern townships, is said to exceed one hundred—among whom are many intelligent and respectable individuals."[3]

CONTENT FOR JOHN WHITMER

In Doctrine and Covenants 30 the Lord issues John Whitmer his lifelong call to labor in Zion. Using the home of the friendly Philip Burroughs as a headquarters, John is called to preach with his whole soul, not fearing man, for he has the support of the Lord.

OUTCOMES FOR JOHN WHITMER

Early missionaries had success preaching the gospel from the Burroughs home in Seneca Falls, New York.[4] John Whitmer apparently preached for about six months, from this September 1830 calling recorded in Doctrine and Covenants 30 until his March 1831 calling to keep a history and transcribe for Joseph (D&C 47).

Doctrine & Covenants 31

ORIGIN

Thomas Marsh ran away from his New England home when he was fourteen years old. Working odd jobs, he made his way to New York City and then to Boston, where he found steady work in a foundry, making type for printing presses. Later, Thomas and his wife, Elizabeth, joined Methodism, which satisfied her but not him. He "expected a new church would arise, which would have the truth in its purity." In 1829 Thomas headed west, led by the Holy Spirit in search of this new church. In Lyonstown, New York, a woman asked Thomas "if I had heard of the Golden Book found by a youth named Joseph Smith. I informed her I never heard anything about it, and became very anxious to know concerning the matter," he wrote. "She told me I could learn more about it from Martin Harris, in Palmyra." He continued, "I returned back westward and found Martin Harris at the printing office, in Palmyra, where the first sixteen pages of the Book of Mormon had just been struck off, the proof sheet of which I obtained from the printer and took with me. As soon as Martin Harris found out my intentions he took me to the house of Joseph Smith, Sen. . . . Here I found Oliver Cowdery, who gave me all the information concerning the book I desired." Thomas headed home to tell Elizabeth. "I showed my wife the sixteen pages of the Book of Mormon," he wrote, "with which she was well pleased, believing it to be the work of God." Thomas kept in touch with Joseph and Oliver and prepared to move west. He moved his family to New York in September 1830, and was baptized in connection with the conference in Fayette that month.[1]

Doctrine and Covenants 31 calls Thomas to the ministry. It answers his questions, including how he should provide for his family and how he could best serve the Lord.

CONTENT

The Lord speaks affectionately to Thomas Marsh, blessing him for his faith and acknowledging the afflictions he experienced as a runaway. The Lord promises Thomas in Doctrine and Covenants 31 that one day his children will come to know the truth and join him in the Church. But just as joyful is the Lord's call to labor in preaching the gospel. "The hour of your mission is come; and your tongue shall be loosed, and you shall declare glad tidings of great joy unto this generation" (D&C 31:3). The Lord commands Thomas to thrust in his sickle mightily, forgiving his sins for doing so, and promising him a bountiful harvest of both souls and provisions. He allays any fears Thomas has for the support of his family while he is thus engaged. Laborers in the Lord's kingdom are worthy of temporal support (D&C 75:24–26), and while Thomas serves, the Lord will look after his family and open the hearts of those with whom Thomas shares the gospel. He is called to build a branch of the Church, strengthen the new Saints, and prepare them to join with the body of the Saints. The Holy Spirit will direct his path. Urging Thomas to be patient in his afflictions, resist the impulse to argue, and be kind to his wife and children, the Lord also commands him to "pray always, lest you enter into temptation and lose your reward" (D&C 31:12). The Lord promises to remain with Thomas as long as he chooses to remain faithful.

OUTCOMES

Doctrine and Covenants 31 marked a turning point for Thomas Marsh. His years of seeking the gospel were over. His years of declaring it were about to begin. The revelation's rich metaphors spoke to him. He served Saints who were sick, but at least as important was his work of prescribing the gospel of repentance.[2] He was also to be a harvester of souls, to cut and bundle wheat all day long before it grew too late.

Thomas obeyed this revelation falteringly. He helped build the local branch of the Church, and when it was time to gather he led them from Fayette, New York, to Ohio. The New York Saints converged at Buffalo, where the harbor was frozen. Places to stay while the migrants waited for a sufficient thaw were at a premium. Prices were high, supplies low. Conditions tested Marsh's willingness to declare the gospel and tried his patience and meekness. "You will be mobbed before morning," Thomas Marsh told Joseph's mother, Lucy, when she refused to keep her faith secret. "Mob it is, then," she shot back, "for we shall sing and attend to prayers before sunset, mob or no mob."[3]

Thomas presided unevenly over the Quorum of the Twelve Apostles from 1835 until 1838. He led them on a mission to the eastern United States and tried to heal wounds created by widespread dissent and apostasy in 1837 (D&C 112). But then Thomas himself came out against Joseph Smith late in 1838 and spent almost two decades outside the Church before he wrote to Church leaders in 1857, seeking "reconciliation with the 12 [apostles] and the Church whom I have injured." He lamented his poor choices and humbly acknowledged, as he wrote, "the Lord could get along very well without me and He has lost nothing by my falling out of the ranks; But O what have I lost?"[4] Reconciled to the Redeemer who gave him section 31, Thomas died in the faith in 1866.

Doctrine & Covenants 32

ORIGIN

Inspired by the Spirit, Parley Parker Pratt left his Ohio homestead in the summer of 1830 and learned of the Book of Mormon while preaching in western New York. He devoured it, became converted, and went in search of Joseph Smith. He first met Joseph around the time of the September 1830 Church conference. During that conference, several of the elders desired to know how they could best take the Book of Mormon to the Lamanites. They agreed to ask the Lord whether some of them should go to the Native Americans.[1] Oliver Cowdery had already been called to lead such a mission, and Peter Whitmer Jr. had been assigned to join him (D&C 28; 30). Parley wrote that Joseph "inquired of the Lord, and received a revelation appointing me a mission to the west, in company with Oliver Cowdery, Peter Whitmer, Jr., and Ziba Peterson. We started this mission in October, 1830."[2] The revelation is recorded in Doctrine and Covenants 32.

Emma Smith and others acted on the revelations that called missionaries to the West (D&C 28; 30; 32). Joseph's mother, Lucy, remembered Emma's service and sacrifices in response to these revelations. In 1853 Lucy shared them and paid tribute to her daughter-in-law: "As soon as this revelation was received, Emma Smith, and several other sisters, began to make arrangements to furnish those who were set apart for this mission, with the necessary clothing, which was no easy task, as the most of it had to be manufactured out of the raw material.

"Emma's health at this time was quite delicate, yet she did not favor herself on this account, but whatever her hands found to do, she did with her might, until she went so far beyond her strength, that she brought upon herself a heavy fit of sickness that lasted four weeks. And, although her strength was exhausted, still her spirits were the same, which, in fact, was always the case with her, even under the most trying circumstances. I have never seen a woman in my life, who would endure every species of fatigue and hardship, from month to month, and from year to year, with that unflinching courage, zeal, and patience, which she has ever done; for I know that which she has had to endure."[3]

CONTENT

In Doctrine and Covenants 32, the Lord calls Parley P. Pratt, a convert of less than two months, and Ziba Peterson to join with Oliver Cowdery and Peter Whitmer Jr. in declaring his gospel to the Lamanites in what is now Kansas. They will not be alone in the mission. "I myself will go with them and be in their midst; and I am their advocate with the Father, and nothing shall prevail against them" (v. 3). The Lord assures the brethren that they have enough revelation to fulfill this mission and commands them to teach from the scriptures and recently received revelations, promising to teach them the meaning of the revelations if they will pray always.

Parley P. Pratt.

OUTCOMES

Parley and Ziba took Doctrine and Covenants 32 seriously and worked hard to obey it. On October 17, 1830, they signed a statement that said the following: "Being called and commanded of the Lord God, to accompany our brother Oliver Cowdery to go the Lamanites and to assist in the . . . glorious work and business, we do, therefore, most solemnly covenant before God, that we will assist him faithfully in this thing, by giving heed to all his words and advise, which is, or shall be given him by the spirit of truth, ever praying with all prayer and supplication, for his and our prosperity, and our deliverance from bonds, and imprisonments and whatsoever may come upon us, with all patience and faith."[4] Joseph's mother remembered that "as soon as those men designated in the revelation were prepared to leave home, they started on their mission, preaching and baptizing on their way, wherever an opportunity afforded."[5] They walked nearly a thousand miles to obey this revelation.

Opposed by missionaries of other faiths and government agents, the Latter-day Saint missionaries were frustrated in their efforts to share the gospel with Native Americans. Instead, they found their greatest success in northeastern Ohio, where Parley had a homestead he had recently left to search for the gospel. Whole congregations of Parley's friends and associates were waiting for the restored gospel, and in less than one month he and his companions doubled the size of the young Church.[6] Historian Richard Anderson noted, "One assesses the impact of four men in four weeks with a certain awe. The fields were ripe, and the hands of the harvesters sure." They carried out the revelations precisely or, as one of their converts put it, "they brought the Book of Mormon to bear upon us."[7]

Doctrine & Covenants 33

ORIGIN

Ezra Thayre built bridges, dams, and mills in western New York, and he hired Joseph Smith to work for him. He had only praise for the Smith family until he heard prejudiced reports against the Book of Mormon. Finally he went himself to hear Hyrum Smith preach in October 1830. "Every word touched me to the inmost soul," Ezra testified. "I thought every word was pointed to me. God punished me and riveted me to the spot. I could not help myself. The tears rolled down my cheeks, I was very proud and stubborn. There were many there who knew me, I dare not look up. I sat until I recovered myself before I dare look up. They sung some hymns and that filled me with the Spirit. When Hyrum got through, he picked up a book and said, 'here is the Book of Mormon.'

"I said, 'let me see it.' I then opened the book, and I received a shock with such exquisite joy that no pen can write and no tongue can express. I shut the book and said, 'what is the price of it?'

"'Fourteen shillings' was the reply.

"I said, 'I'll take the book.' I opened it again, and I felt a double portion of the Spirit, that I did not know whether I was in the world or not. I felt as though I was truly in heaven. Martin Harris rushed to me to tell me that the book was true. I told him that he need not tell me that, for I knew that it is true as well as he."

Later, at home, Ezra had a memorable vision in which a man brought him a roll of paper and a trumpet, telling him to blow it. Ezra visited Joseph a week after he heard Hyrum preach. "I told him what had happened, and how I knew the book was true." Ezra wrote. "He then asked me what hindered me from going into the water."[1]

Parley Pratt baptized Ezra Thayre and two others that day, including a man named Northrop Sweet, husband to a niece of Martin Harris. Soon thereafter, Joseph received Doctrine and Covenants 33 for these two converts.

CONTENT

Through Doctrine and Covenants 33 the Lord calls Ezra Thayre and Northrup Sweet to lift their voices as trumpets declaring the piercing words of Jesus Christ to a dishonest and obstinately wayward people in a perverse and immoral world filled with priestcraft. Only a few good remain, erring because of apostasy, so the Lord calls his true Church out of hiding to gather his elect, the ones who will believe in him and obey his voice, from all over the world. Ezra and Northrop are called to open their mouths and teach the law of the gospel, saying, "Repent and be baptized, every one of you, for a remission of your sins; yea, be baptized even by water, and then cometh the baptism of fire and of the Holy Ghost" (v. 11). They are to confirm the faithful by the laying on of hands, but the Lord himself will bestow the gift of the Holy Ghost. They are further told to teach that there is no salvation without faith in Christ. The Lord has given the Book of Mormon and other scriptures to instruct Ezra and Northrop, and he gives the Spirit to help them understand. If the men will be faithful and open their mouths, the Lord promises to fill them and to make them like Nephi in their callings. He urges the men to pray always and prepare for the second coming of the Lord.

OUTCOMES

Oliver Cowdery delivered the contents of Doctrine and Covenants 33 to Ezra, who realized then how his own vision had foreshadowed it. The roll of paper in his vision "was the revelation on me and Northrop Sweet." Oliver handed it to him and said, "Here is a revelation from God for you, now blow your trumpet." Ezra protested, "I never blowed a trumpet." Oliver assured him, "You can."[2]

Would Ezra and Northrop blow their trumpets as the revelation commanded? Would they let their fears keep them from boldly opening their mouths as Nephi did? The revelation's reference to Nephi, with whom Ezra and Northrop had just become familiar as they studied the Book of Mormon, must have helped them understand that they were being asked to speak the truth boldly to an antagonistic audience—but that they would have success. They could speak as powerfully as Nephi, the Lord assured them, on the condition that they would simply be willing to preach the gospel.

Northrop Sweet chose not to become as Nephi. He did not endure long in his calling. He sought a greater one and thought he received a revelation that he should be a prophet. He left the Church and started his own. This is one of several revelations whose promises went unfulfilled because the individuals to whom the Lord declared his will exercised their God-given agency to choose to disregard it. Opposed by his wife and others, Ezra Thayre preached the Book of Mormon powerfully but only briefly. He maintained his faith in Joseph Smith, though after Joseph's death he left the Church. He was often distracted by business and economic concerns. A revelation one cannot obey is God's responsibility. A revelation the recipients choose not to obey is their responsibility. "I never blowed a trumpet," said Ezra in response to the Lord's command to lift up his voice like a trumpet in declaring the gospel. "You can," replied Oliver Cowdery.

Doctrine & Covenants 34

ORIGIN

"The greatest desire of my heart," wrote Orson Pratt of his youth, "was for the Lord to manifest his will concerning me." In the fall of 1829, eighteen-year-old Orson "began to pray very fervently, repenting of every sin." Soon two elders, including his older brother Parley, visited his upstate New York region with the restored gospel and baptized Orson on his nineteenth birthday. "I traveled westward over two hundred miles to see Joseph Smith, the Prophet," Orson recounted. "I found him in Fayette, Seneca County, N.Y., residing at the house of Mr. Whitmer. I soon became intimately acquainted with this good man. . . . By my request, on the 4th of Nov. [1830], the Prophet Joseph inquired of the Lord for me, and received the revelation" recorded in Doctrine and Covenants 34.[1]

CONTENT

Jesus Christ addresses Orson as his son in Doctrine and Covenants 34, commanding him to hear his Redeemer, who loves the world so much that he gave his life so that all who would embrace him could overcome the Fall and be born again as children of God. Orson is one of those who have received Christ, thereby becoming his son. Christ blesses Orson for believing and blesses him further to preach the gospel, calling a dishonest and willfully wicked generation to repentance. Orson is to prepare the world for the second coming of Jesus Christ, sparing no one in his rebuke. "Therefore prophesy," the Lord commands, "and it shall be given by the power of the Holy Ghost" (v. 10).

OUTCOMES

Nearly half a century after Doctrine and Covenants 34 was received, Orson Pratt reflected on it. "I well recollect the feelings of my heart at the time," he said. Joseph "inquired of the Lord and obtained a revelation for your humble servant. He retired into the chamber of old Father Whitmer, in the house where this Church was organized in 1830. John Whitmer acted as his scribe, and I accompanied him into the chamber, for he had told me that it was my privilege to have the word of the Lord; and the Lord in that revelation, which is published here in the Book of Doctrine and Covenants, made a promise which to me, when I was in my youth, seemed to be almost too great for a person of as humble origin as myself ever to attain to. After telling in the revelation that the great day of the Lord was at hand, and calling upon me to lift up my voice among the people, to call upon them to repent and prepare the way of the Lord, and that the time was near when the heavens should be shaken, when the earth should tremble, when the stars should refuse their shining, and when great destructions awaited the wicked, the Lord said to your humble servant—'Lift up your voice and prophesy, and it shall be given by the power of the Holy Ghost.' This was a particular point in the revelation that seemed to me too great for me ever to attain to, and yet there was a positive command that I should do it."[2]

Orson Pratt.

The Lord chose Orson as an apostle in 1835 at age twenty-three. As commanded in his youth in section 34, he lifted up his voice long and loud and cried repentance to a crooked generation until he died an old man in 1881. Brigham Young said of Orson, "If you were to chop up Elder Pratt into inch-square pieces, each piece would cry out, 'Mormonism is true.'"[3]

Doctrine & Covenants 35

ORIGIN

Church historian John Whitmer told the story of Doctrine and Covenants 35, beginning with an account of how Parley P. Pratt led his companions to northeastern Ohio, where "there was a man whose name was Sidney Rigdon, he having been an instrument in the hand of the Lord of doing much good. He was in search of truth, consequently he received the fullness of the gospel with gladness of heart, even the Book of Mormon, it being what he was in search after, notwithstanding it was some days before he obtained a witness from the Lord, of the truth of his work. After several days the Lord heard his cries, and answered his prayers, and by vision showed to him that this emanated from Him and must remain, it being the fullness of the gospel of Jesus Christ, first unto the Gentiles and then unto the Jews."[1] Whitmer continued, in the style of the Book of Mormon: "Now it came to pass, after Sidney Rigdon, was received into this Church, that he was ordained an elder, under the hands of Oliver Cowdery. He having much anxiety to see Joseph Smith, Jr., the Seer whom the Lord had raised up in these last days. Therefore he took his journey to the state of New York, where Joseph resided.

"There was another man whose name is Edward Partridge who was also desirous, to see the Seer, therefore, he accompanied Sidney, and journeyed with him, to behold this man of God, even Joseph Smith, Jr." Sidney arrived in Waterloo, New York, in time to hear Joseph conclude a sermon.[2]

John Whitmer wrote that Sidney desired "to have the Seer enquire of the Lord, to know what the will of the Lord was concerning him.

Accordingly Joseph enquired of the Lord, and these are the words that were spoken to him."[3] The revelation recorded in Doctrine and Covenants 35 followed.

CONTENT

"Listen to the voice of the Lord your God," the Savior tells Sidney as Doctrine and Covenants 35 opens (v. 1). He testifies of himself, saying he was crucified for "the sins of the world" so that they who believe on his name might become his children, unified with him as he is unified with his Father. The Lord assures Sidney that he has been watching him, listening to his prayers, and preparing him for a greater work. Like John the Baptist, Sidney has prepared people for the fulness of the Savior's gospel, baptizing the repentant "by water unto repentance, but they received not the Holy Ghost" (v. 5). Jesus commands Sidney to continue his work, but now those repentant who have been baptized by immersion can be baptized under divine authority and also receive the Holy Ghost by the laying on of hands, just as the apostles ministered in the New Testament. As he did in his mortal ministry, the Lord will continue to work miracles among those who believe him. He will ensure, in other words, that his servants preach his gospel to the poor and the meek who will be looking for his imminent coming.

The Savior sends forth the fulness of the gospel through the weak, unschooled, and unpopular Joseph Smith, to whom He has also given the keys of revelation. As long as he remains faithful, Joseph will retain these keys. If he does not remain faithful, the Lord will replace him. Sidney is to sustain and encourage Joseph as he receives revelations by the power of the Holy Ghost.

The Lord commands Sidney to scribe for Joseph as he revises the Bible. If Sidney will live and travel with Joseph and "forsake him not" (v. 22), the Lord promises to make them a potent companionship: Joseph will be given the spirit of prophecy, and Sidney will preach the gospel and prove Joseph's prophecies by using the holy scriptures. "Keep all the commandments and covenants by which ye are bound," the Lord directs Sidney, "and I will cause the heavens to shake for your good, and Satan shall tremble and Zion shall rejoice upon the hills and flourish" (v. 24).

OUTCOMES

John Whitmer wrote that "after the Lord had made known, what he wanted that his servant Sidney should do, he went to writing the things which the Lord showed unto his servant the Seer."[4] Joseph revised the Bible as Sidney scribed, giving us some of the most precious scripture ever revealed, including much of the book of Moses in the Pearl of Great Price.

Joseph and Sidney obeyed the command of the revelation in Doctrine and Covenants 35 to form a powerful companionship, with Joseph prophesying and Sidney teaching from the scriptures. They "went to the several churches preaching and prophesying wherever they went," wrote John Whitmer, "and greatly strengthened the churches that were built unto the Lord. Joseph prophesied saying: God is about to destroy this generation, and Christ will descend from heaven in power and great glory, with all the holy angels with him, to take vengeance upon the wicked, and they that know not God. Sidney preached the gospel and proved [Joseph's] words from the holy prophets."[5]

Doctrine & Covenants 36

ORIGIN

Edward Partridge grew up in New England. He spent four years apprenticed to a hatmaker before becoming a journeyman hatter with ambitions to go west to open his own factory. He married Lydia Clisbee, and they moved to Painesville, Ohio, where they succeeded according to their plans. But something was missing. Respected and prosperous, still Edward and Lydia lacked spiritual fulfillment. They began to worship with Sidney Rigdon in 1828 and were prepared to hear the restored gospel from Oliver Cowdery, Parley Pratt, and their companions in the fall of 1830. When Edward was offered a copy of the Book of Mormon, he refused but soon reconsidered.[1] Soon he "partly believed," as his wife put it, "but he had to take a journey to New York and see the Prophet."[2]

Joseph's mother, Lucy, continued the story. Joseph, she said, was preaching in Waterloo, New York, when Sidney Rigdon and Edward Partridge arrived. Joseph invited remarks after his sermon, and Edward "arose and stated that he had been to Manchester, with the view of obtaining further information respecting the doctrine which we preached; but, not finding us, he had made some inquiry of our neighbors concerning our characters, which they stated had been unimpeachable, until Joseph deceived us relative to the Book of Mormon. He also said, that he had walked over our farm, and observed the good order and industry which it exhibited; and, having seen what we had sacrificed for the sake of our faith, and having heard that our veracity was not questioned upon any other point than that of our religion, he believed our testimony and was ready to be baptized, 'if, said he, 'brother Joseph will baptize me.'"³ Joseph baptized Edward the next day and received for him the revelation recorded now in Doctrine and Covenants 36, perhaps even before Edward was confirmed by Sidney Rigdon.

CONTENT

In Doctrine and Covenants 36 the Lord blesses Edward Partridge and forgives his sins before calling him to preach the gospel. Before beginning that preaching, Edward will receive the Holy Ghost from the Lord by the hand of Sidney Rigdon. The Lord then extends the calling and commandment to all men. As many as embrace the call shall be ordained and sent to preach the gospel of repentance among all nations. The commandment is given to all the elders of the Church, commissioning all who willingly heed the voice of the Lord to take the gospel blessings to others.

OUTCOMES

This revelation shares a theme common to many others. It calls for urgency in declaring repentance to a perverted generation because the Lord is coming soon to burn the wicked.

Doctrine and Covenants 36 not only calls Edward Partridge to preach the gospel but sets forth the doctrine that every ordained man is a missionary, not so much in the formal sense but as a duty of holding the priesthood. Those who hold the priesthood are responsible to preach the gospel.

Edward Partridge obeyed this revelation. He was confirmed by the Lord's hand—that is, by Sidney Rigdon acting for the Lord—and he spent his life declaring repentance and serving as a bishop. In 1835 he traveled roughly two thousand miles, held fifty meetings, visited nearly thirty branches of the Church, preached the gospel, and baptized three persons. On November 7, 1835, Joseph received a revelation in which the Lord praised Edward and his companion for "the integrity of their harts in laboring in my vinyard for the salvation of the souls of men."[4]

Doctrine & Covenants 37

ORIGIN

Joseph received the book of Moses by revelation as part of his New Translation of the Bible. Late in 1830, with Sidney Rigdon as scribe, Joseph received the prophecy of Enoch, now Moses 6–8 in the Pearl of Great Price. Church historian John Whitmer noted that "after they had written this prophecy, the Lord spoke to them again and gave further directions,"[1] namely the revelation recorded in Doctrine and Covenants 37.

Joseph's mother, Lucy, recalled that Joseph received section 37 after receiving a letter from John Whitmer, who had gone to Ohio to preside over the Saints there when Oliver Cowdery and his companions headed further west to fulfill their mission call (D&C 28; 30; 32). Remembering nearly fifteen years after the fact, Lucy may have mixed up the sequence of events. Doctrine and Covenants 37 was given in December 1830. John Whitmer did not go to Ohio to preside over the Church there until January 1831. But Lucy may have remembered correctly the reason the revelation was given. She said it was that Joseph had received word from Ohio that leadership was sorely needed there.[2] The hundred or so converts had quickly multiplied to around three hundred, and Oliver Cowdery had left for the West. Satan was about to prey on the zeal of the young Church while it lacked experienced leadership and lead many astray with all kinds of counterfeit spiritual experiences.[3]

Joseph and Sidney received section 37 after leaving the Whitmers' home near Fayette, New York, and traveling to Canandaigua to work on their revision of the Bible.

CONTENT

In Doctrine and Covenants 37 the Lord tells Joseph that under present circumstances it is not expedient for him to continue revising the Bible until after he has strengthened the Saints in western New York, particularly those in Colesville, who have been praying to the Lord in great faith. The Lord commands the Saints to gather to Ohio, but as individuals with agency, each member is left to choose whether to obey, and each is accountable to the Lord for that choice.

OUTCOMES

Joseph and Sidney did exactly what the Lord told them to do in Doctrine and Covenants 37. John Whitmer's history says that after the "directions were received, Joseph and Sidney went to the several churches preaching and prophesying wherever they went, and greatly strengthened the churches." Specifically, as the revelation directed, "Joseph and Sidney went to Colesville to do the will of the Lord in that part of the land and to strengthen the disciples in that part of the vineyard." Joseph sent John Whitmer to Ohio to preside and to take a copy of the revelations to teach the Saints there. Whitmer reported what he found: "The enemy of all righteousness had got hold of some of those who professed to be his followers, because they had not sufficient knowledge to detect him in all of his devices."[4]

Back in New York the generally prosperous and longer-settled Saints struggled to come to terms with the revelation. John Whitmer blamed worldliness and false traditions for the Saints' hesitance to "believe the commandments that came forth in these last days for the upbuilding of the kingdom of God, and the salvation of those who believe."[5] They dragged their feet, and section 38 was revealed before they did what section 37 commanded them to do, namely to choose to obey or disobey.

Doctrine & Covenants 38

ORIGIN

Joseph Smith gathered the fledgling Church of Christ, not yet a year old, for general conference in Fayette, New York. It was January 1831. Newel Knight remembered that "it was at this conference that we were instructed as a people, to begin the gathering of Israel, and a revelation was given to the prophet on this subject."[1]

"Joseph the seer addressed the congregation," John Whitmer wrote. He noted that "having previously received a revelation to go to Ohio, they desired to know somewhat more concerning this matter. Therefore, the Seer enquired of the Lord in the presence of the whole congregation, and thus came the word of the Lord,"[2] now contained in Doctrine and Covenants 38.

CONTENT

In Doctrine and Covenants 38 the Lord introduces himself to the New York Saints as the creator of the world and as their advocate with the Father. He reminds them that "all things are present" before his eyes, and though they cannot not see him, he is continually in their midst [among]. He warns them to prepare for his second coming, the day wherein they will at last see their Savior and the wicked will be destroyed. It is an ominous warning, for he then reminds them that they too are unclean—all mankind is—and the enemy is continuing to combine.

The Lord reveals to the New York Saints a secret plan hatched for their destruction, a conspiracy they did not know about. He blesses them by revealing it, not because they deserve it (many lacked faith, and some were deemed guilty) but because he is merciful concerning their weakness. He loves all of his children, rich and poor, equally, and he covenants to give them and their posterity the earth—his own creation and an abundant promised land—as an inheritance for time and eternity, if they will seek it wholeheartedly. Twice the Lord commands the Saints to esteem one another as themselves. He is no respecter of persons, and he would have his children be likewise. Again, he commands the Saints to be one. "If ye are not one ye are not mine" (v. 27).

The Lord returns to his warning. The enemy is secretly seeking their lives, and though the Saints may be able to hear rumors and predict wars in distant countries, they do not know the hearts of their own countrymen. In section 37 the Lord has already given the Saints the means of escaping their enemy. By moving to Ohio they could gather as a righteous people, protected from the enemy's power. That is why he commands the move.

More blessings beyond escaping from their enemy await the Saints in Ohio. There the Lord will give unto them his law, there he will endow them with divine power, and from there he will send missionaries to all nations to gather Israelites scattered across the globe and bring them to Zion.

The Saints are commanded to appoint leaders by common consent to relieve their poverty and equip the Saints to make the move to Ohio. These leaders will govern the care of the Church's property. Those who have farms in New York are commanded to sell them. If they cannot find a buyer, they are commanded to leave or rent their property as they wish. The Lord promises the Saints that if they seek for the eternal riches Heavenly Father wants to give them, they will be the richest of all people. The riches of the earth are the Lord's to give, and he warns the Saints of the pride that led to the destruction of the Nephites. He commands them to meekly warn their neighbors to leave the wicked behind. "Save yourselves," he commands in conclusion. Then, likening the Saints to the Israelite priesthood holders who were responsible to preserve and carry the temple's sacred furniture from place to place as they wandered in the wilderness, the Lord commands, "Be ye clean that bear the vessels of the Lord" (v. 42; see Numbers 4).

OUTCOMES

Unlike the terse command in section 37 to move to Ohio, in Doctrine and Covenants 38 the Lord gives a detailed rationale for the commandment. The situation is bleak. "All flesh is corrupted . . . ; the powers of darkness prevail," and "eternity is pained" (D&C 38:11–12). The enemy, presumably Satan, plots the Saints' destruction. The Lord paints a vivid, apocalyptic picture of the different destinies awaiting those who believe and obey the revelation compared to those who "will not hear my voice but harden their hearts, and wo, wo, wo, is their doom" (v. 6). The January 1831 revelation caused the Saints to decide whether to serve themselves or the Lord. It provided them a way out of the world. It envisioned an alternative society. It came in the voice of the Lord who took "the Zion of Enoch into mine own bosom; and . . . by the virtue of the blood which I have spilt, have I pleaded before the Father for them" (v. 4). It foretold evil designs to destroy the Saints "in process of time" (v. 13). Those were the exact words that had recently been revealed to Joseph to describe how Enoch's Zion made it safely out of this world (Moses 7:21). The similarity to the New York Saints living in "Babylon" suggests that a creeping, cultural evil posed a great threat to the spiritual welfare of the New York Saints, though, like the proverbially slow-boiled frog, they could hardly discern it themselves. As John Whitmer put it, "Because of the abominations that are abroad in the world, it is hard for those who receive the fullness of the gospel, and come into the new and everlasting covenant, to get clear of the traditions of their forefathers."[3]

The revelation brought the crisis to the Saints' attention, compelling them to choose, for it described an either/or proposition: Begin the "process" of becoming like Enoch's Zion or continue the "process" toward "destruction" (v. 13). To be saved, the New York Saints must move to Ohio.

The choice to escape was also a choice to acknowledge the Lord as the source of authority, the maker of worlds as well as laws, and Joseph Smith as his spokesman (D&C 21:1–8). "Hear my voice and follow me," the Lord commanded unequivocally (D&C 38:22). The revelation required the Saints to relieve poverty, esteem everyone equally, and to "be one" (v. 27). To those at the conference, the revelation shouted objections to the cultural messages they received every day to be partisan, to be covetous, and to "possess that which is above another," "as the Nephites of old" (D&C 49:20; 38:39). It seemed calculated to test the integrity of covenant makers by compelling them to choose either "the things of this world" or "the things of a better" (D&C 25:10; see 38:17–20, 25–26, 39). The Lord shows little regard for the Saints' carnal security. "They that have farms that cannot be sold, let them be left or rented as seemeth them good" (v. 37). The irrelevance of property contrasts sharply with the revelation's emphasis on the welfare of souls. There is a sense of urgency that the Saints might make it safely out of a fallen world. "That ye might escape the power of the enemy, and be gathered unto me a righteous people, without spot and blameless—wherefore for this cause I gave unto you the commandment that ye should go to the Ohio" (vv. 31–32).

The revelation caused an initial shock. Some who were comfortable in New York did not want to obey it. Church historian John Whitmer said the revelation caused "some divisions among the congregation, some would not receive [section 38] as the word of the Lord." Some projected their own selfishness onto the Prophet. They said "Joseph had invented it himself to deceive the people that in the end he might get gain. Now this was because, their hearts were not right in the sight of the Lord, for they wanted to serve God and man; but our Savior has declared that it was impossible to do so."[4]

Even so, given the individualistic attitude of the society in which these Saints lived, the remarkable fact is not that "one or two" chafed at the "monumental sacrifice" of the command to gather in Ohio but that the Saints obeyed.[5] Whitmer wrote that "the Lord had manifested his will to his people. Therefore they made preparations to Journey to the Ohio, with their wives, and children and all that they possessed, to obey the commandment of the Lord."[6] Newel Knight wrote, "As might be expected, we were obliged to make great sacrifices of our property."[7] They were submitting to the process Elder Neal A. Maxwell called becoming "less possessed" by temporal possessions.[8] By keeping the command to pull up telestial roots and forsake telestial concerns, the New York Saints were yielding up themselves to God.[9] They were making a bold, counter-cultural declaration.[10] By so doing they prepared themselves to receive the law of consecration the Lord promised to give them when they gathered to Ohio. They were presenting themselves willing to be "endowed with power from on high" (v. 32).

Newel Knight remembered that "the Saints manifested unshaken confidence in the great work in which they were engaged."¹¹ Established families who were prospering in New York left for Ohio shortly after the January 1831 conference.¹² Expecting twins, Emma Smith bade her parents farewell and went with Joseph "at the time of his going" (D&C 25:6) in late January. She never saw her parents again. She was cleaving to covenants and laying aside the things of this world in lieu of incorruptible treasures in a better one (D&C 25:10; 38:17–20). Polly and Joseph Knight fled persecutors near Colesville, New York, and left their farms and mills there to be sold. Along the way they provided Emma and Joseph means for their trip to Ohio. The remaining sixty-seven Saints from Colesville helped each other prepare and determined "to travel together in one company" under the leadership of Newel Knight. They left in April in a wagon train bound for Cayuga Lake and thence by canals to Lake Erie. In a journey toward Zion both geographical and cultural, they braved persecution, injuries, and seasickness together. Enemies subpoenaed Newel Knight, who had to return to Colesville. "The whole company," he wrote, "declined traveling until I should return." Meanwhile his aunt, Electa Peck, "fell and broke her shoulder in a most shocking manner." When Newel returned she expressed her faith in the priesthood he held and bade him bless her: "O, Brother Newel, if you will lay your hands upon me, I shall be well and able to go on the journey with you." He did, and "the next morning she arose, dressed herself, and pursued the journey with us." For two weeks the company was detained at Buffalo, New York, their boat to Fairport, Ohio, held hostage by ice.¹³

From Ohio Joseph sent for his father and his brother Hyrum, and they came quickly in March. That left his capable mother, Lucy Mack Smith, to lead the rest of her family and others, about fifty in all, from Waterloo, New York, as soon as "the brethren considered the spring sufficiently open for traveling on the water."¹⁴ Having recently joined the Saints in New York from his home in Boston, Thomas Marsh led a group of about thirty, including the Whitmers, from Fayette. Martin Harris led perhaps fifty more from Palmyra to Kirtland in May. The Saints from Colesville,

Waterloo, and Fayette all converged at Buffalo, where the harbor was frozen. Places to stay while waiting for a sufficient thaw were at a premium. Prices were high, supplies low. Conditions tested the patience, faith, and will of the covenant makers.

Lucy Mack Smith had wanted the oldest man, a Brother Humphreys, to lead her group, but he declined, and "the whole company responded together, 'we will do just as Mother Smith says.'" An Esquire Chamberlain gave her funds to feed the sizable group, money sorely needed as the trip wore on. Lucy compared her little band to Lehi's. She was frustrated that some of the Saints "did not seem to consider that the revelation that they should help each other was binding upon them" (see vv. 24–27). There was, for her taste, too much worldliness among them. She found "several of the brethren and sisters engaged in warm debate, others murmuring and grumbling, and a number of young ladies were flirting, giggling, and laughing with gentlemen passengers who were entire strangers to them, whilst hundreds of people on shore and on other boats were witnessing this scene of clamor and vanity among our brethren." She reproved them: "We call ourselves Saints and profess to have come out of the world for the purpose of serving God at the expense of all earthly things; and will you, at the very onset, subject the cause of Christ to ridicule by your own unwise and improper conduct?"[15]

While waiting for the ice to clear so the boat could move, Lucy went ashore in search of a room in which the sisters could rest and tend sick children. She found only selfishness, "human nature," she called it, until "a fine, cheerful old lady" gave her board in exchange for the gospel. Lucy taught the good woman restored truth until two o'clock in the morning. She considered herself an ambassador

Lucy Mack Smith, mother of Joseph Smith.

of the Lord Jesus Christ. She was frustrated by Saints who feared to let others know they were Latter-day Saints.[16]

"You will be mobbed before morning," Thomas Marsh told Lucy when she refused to keep her faith secret. "Mob it is, then," she shot back, "for we shall sing and attend to prayers before sunset, mob or no mob." Lucy opened her mouth and it was filled with song, with the good word of God, and with reproof in season. She left boat captains and deckhands, the woman at the boarding house, and a man on the shore all wanting more of the testimony that flowed freely from her. Over and over Mother Smith acted in faith. She led and served her fellow Saints while she extended the glad tidings to those they passed on the way.[17]

Lucy seized her agency to obtain power over the telestial world, rather than letting it have power over her. She predicted that if her company would unitedly call upon God to break the ice, "as sure as the Lord lives, it shall be done." It happened as she said, though the ice quickly "closed together again, and the Colesville brethren were left in Buffalo," she wrote, "unable to follow us." Rumors began immediately that the boat would sink, "so that when we arrived at Fairport, we read in the papers news of our own death."[18] Neither death, hell, or the devil could deter Mother Smith. She defied faithlessness and fear to obey section 38. Lucy's narrative demonstrates that she understood the principle and intent of leaving one's carnal security and starting over. She was like Lehi. She was being born again in a new land. She would not be tethered to her old self or afraid of completely forsaking a corrupt world.

Less faithful and more fearful, perhaps, but still determined to act on the command to gather to Ohio, the Colesville Saints continued. Only one of their number turned back. Having arrived in Buffalo a week earlier than Mother Smith's group, they followed her safely into Kirtland after "a rather disagreeable voyage."[19] A local newspaper, the *Painesville Telegraph*, noted the May 1831 arrivals of "about two hundred men, women and children of the deluded followers of Jo Smith's Bible speculation."[20] The immigrants from New York were embraced by the Ohio Saints. Caroline Crosby joined many other gathered Saints in foregoing comforts to house the immigrants. "The idea of accommodating friends," she wrote, "stimulated me to make the sacrifice."[21] Ann and Newel Whitney welcomed Emma and Joseph to their own hearth.

By fall 1831, antagonists ordered Joseph Smith and other Mormon families "immediately to depart the Township."[22] The Saints continued to gather anyway. Jesus Christ was their "lawgiver," and Joseph Smith was his spokesman (v. 22). Brigham Young "had traveled and preached until I had nothing left to gather with; but Joseph said 'come up;' and I went up the best I could," a widower, with two young children. Amasa Lyman received baptism in New Hampshire in 1832 and walked most of the seven hundred miles to gather with the Saints. Like her future husband, Wilford Woodruff, Phoebe Carter left loved ones to gather to Kirtland in 1835. "I left the beloved home of my childhood to link my life with the Saints of God," she later wrote. Joseph Smith Sr. asked Oliver Huntington, a convert from upstate New York, to sell his farm and gather to Kirtland in 1835. He sold it for "much less than it was really worth for the sake of living with the church and obeying the word of God as given to Joseph Smith." When the Church's financial situation looked particularly bleak in the mid 1830s, Joseph Smith and others joined in a solemn prayer meeting, asking the Lord to send them a benefactor who could pay the mortgage on the Peter French farm the Church had purchased for the temple, housing, and other buildings. On Christmas day, 1835, a wealthy owner of considerable property in eastern New York, John Tanner, left his home to gather. His family journeyed five hundred miles in the dead of winter. His timely arrival in Kirtland led to the first of many generous gifts to the Church and enabled the Saints to continue building the temple in anticipation of the promised endowment. "Kirtland history is filled with examples of Saints who willingly sacrificed their worldly possessions to gather to Kirtland."[23]

Why did they do it? Because sections 37 and 38 commanded them to. What did they get in return? Everything the revelation promised. As promised in verse 32, in February 1831 the Lord gave Joseph Smith the law (D&C 42), which included the law of consecration, a law that according to President Gordon B. Hinckley is "still in effect."[24] Year after year the converts streamed into Ohio until in the spring of 1836 they were endowed in the temple with power—priesthood keys and spiritual gifts—fulfilling the last promise of the gathering.

A revelation to Joseph Smith on January 12, 1838, similar in tone to the one that commanded the Saints to gather to Ohio, commanded them to move again. New enemies sought Joseph's life and prevented his important work. Gathering to Kirtland had served its purpose. The promised blessings were fulfilled. The law had been revealed, and obedience to it had relieved poverty, gathered converts, sent missionaries far afield, and built several buildings, including the house of the Lord. There the promised endowment had been received. In Kirtland the Saints gained invaluable "experience" and were "endowed with power from on high" (D&C 105:10–11). They still needed to choose to be separate from the world, and thus the January 1838 revelation sent them on: "Get out of this place," it said, "and gather . . . together unto Zion and be at peace among yourselves, O Ye inhabitants of Zion, or their shall be no safety for you."[25]

The Saints overwhelmingly obeyed Joseph's revelations to gather, regardless of the "great sacrifices" required.[26] Those who knew Joseph best "accepted the voice in the revelations as the voice of God, investing in the revelations the highest authority, even above Joseph Smith's counsel."[27] He was "even as Moses" (D&C 28:2). And if, as Mother Smith wrote, his followers could be "even more unreasonable than the children of Israel," they were hardly deluded.[28]

Doctrine & Covenants 39 and 40

ORIGIN OF SECTION 39

In Doctrine and Covenants 39, the Lord invited a man named James Covill to receive the gospel covenant. Within days another revelation came, explaining to Joseph and Sidney Rigdon why Covill "rejected the word of the Lord, and returned to his former principles and people."[1] These events took place before Joseph began keeping a journal and after Oliver Cowdery and John Whitmer, who served as the Church's earliest clerks and chroniclers, had left New York for Missouri and Ohio. In other words, the events were not documented until nearly a decade later as Joseph and his clerks compiled this part of his history from their fallible memories.

Joseph's history says that soon after the January 1831 Church conference at Fayette, New York, "a man came to me by the name of James Covill, who had been a Baptist minister for about forty years, and covenanted with the Lord that he would obey any command that the Lord would give to him through me, as His servant, and I received" section 39.[2]

These events happened as Joseph's history says—Covill had been a minister for forty years and then covenanted to obey the Lord's will as revealed to Joseph Smith—but he had been a Methodist, not a Baptist minister.[3] There is no sign of Covill in Baptist records, but a James Covel appears in Methodist records beginning in 1791, forty years before section 39 was received, when he was appointed as a traveling preacher on the Litchfield, Connecticut, circuit. He rode various Methodist circuits for four years as an itinerant preacher. In 1795 James married Sarah Gould, the daughter of a Methodist preacher, on October 28. James rode the Lynn,

Massachusetts, circuit for a year before he "located."[4] That is, he settled, raised a family, apparently practiced medicine, and largely dropped out of the Methodist records. Sarah and James had a son, James Jr., who followed his father into the Methodist ministry. The Covels moved to Maine and then to Poughkeepsie, New York, around 1808.[5] It is not clear where they were when they heard of Joseph Smith and the restored gospel about 1830, but most likely they were still somewhere in New York.

CONTENT OF SECTION 39

Doctrine and Covenants 39 declares that Jesus Christ is the light and the life of the world. He came to earth in the meridian of time but was rejected by many. As many as received him then were empowered to become his sons, and he will likewise empower any who receive him now. We receive Christ by receiving his gospel, which is repentance, baptism by water, and baptism by fire—the gift of the Holy Ghost.

The Lord reveals to James Covill how well he knows him. The great sorrow of James's past stemmed from his pride and worldly cares, which led him to reject Christ many times. Yet the Lord assures James that his heart is now right, and if James will hearken unto the voice of the Lord, the day of his deliverance has come. The Lord commands James to "arise and be baptized, and wash away your sins" (v. 10). Receipt of the Lord's Spirit will follow.

The Lord has a greater work for James to do, if he will obey God's law: preaching the fulness of the gospel, which Christ has sent forth as a covenant to recover the house of Israel. James is also promised divine guidance, great faith, and the Lord's companionship if he will obey. He is called to go west to Ohio—not east, where he has come from and may be most comfortable.

As he has commanded James, the Lord commands the Saints to labor in his vineyard for the last time—to baptize and prepare the world for his second coming. Those who receive the full gospel and become sanctified will be preserved from the judgments of the Lord, and he will gather those who receive him and his gospel in time and eternity.

OUTCOMES OF SECTION 39 AND ORIGIN OF SECTION 40

The result of James Covill's choosing what to do with Doctrine and Covenants 39 led to Joseph's receiving section 40. James Covill broke his covenant. Joseph's history says that James Covill "rejected the word of the Lord, and returned to his former principles and people."[6] The Lord gave section 40 to explain why.

CONTENT OF SECTION 40

The order of events in Doctrine and Covenants 40 is important. First, James Covill covenants with an honest heart to obey the word of the Lord. He sincerely receives the gospel. But then, right away, Satan tempts him to fear the persecution that will result and to worry about making a living as an unpaid minister. James chooses to heed those fears and cares, resulting in his breaking his covenant.

OUTCOMES OF SECTION 40

Doctrine and Covenants 40 highlights the doctrine of agency. Persons have agency, or power to act independently, when they know what God wants, Satan poses an alternative, and they are free to choose between the two. Given section 39, James Covill knew what the Lord wanted him to do. Then, as he always does, Satan countered the commandments. James was free to choose between the two, and he chose to break his covenant, making it null and void.

Critics cite sections 39 and 40 as evidence that Joseph Smith was a fraud. They contend that these sections prove that Joseph's God did not know that James Covill would not obey. Theirs is faulty logic. Such critics must imagine that when God speaks, a person has no choice but to obey him. Perhaps they envision a variation on a Calvinist God, one who already determined what James could do and has, as a perverse parent, locked him into a covenant-breaking course to damnation. Does anything happen that is not God's will? Some theologians thought not and concluded that God is the author of sin. Joseph Smith restored truth that dispelled that darkness. He distinguished between the sovereignty of God and the agency of individuals (D&C 93). Joseph knew too that "God sees the secret springs of human action, & knows the hearts of all living," but he did not make the erroneous assumption that knowing is the same as causing.[7] "I believe that God foreknew everything, but did not foreordain everything," Joseph taught profoundly. "I deny that foreordain and foreknow is the same thing."[8]

God did not make James Covill break his covenant. Rather, the Lord gave James power to make and keep his covenant and the agency to decide for himself whether to make and keep the covenant. Revelations give us knowledge of God's will. They make us free. God gives agency by telling us what he wants us to do, allowing Satan to tempt us otherwise, and enabling us to choose between them freely. Section 40 explains that James Covill made and broke his covenant of his own free will. It is a more significant revelation than its brevity might suggest, for few theological works are as profound and efficient as this one.

Doctrine & Covenants 41

ORIGIN

Leman Copley became interested in the Church after missionaries passed through his northern Ohio neighborhood. He invited Joseph Smith and Sidney Rigdon to live on his large farm in Thompson Township and promised to furnish them houses and provisions. Joseph asked the Lord about the invitation and received Doctrine and Covenants 41, which answered Joseph's question and called Edward Partridge as a bishop.

Edward had apprenticed four years for a hatmaker in New England before venturing west to Ohio to open his own factory with his bride, Lydia Clisbee. They succeeded economically but remained unsettled spiritually. They could see a great need for God to "again reveal himself to man and confer authority upon some one, or more, before his church could be built up in the last days."[1]

Oliver Cowdery was just such a man. When he and his companions brought the Book of Mormon to Painesville, Ohio, Edward initially reacted with disbelief. Knowingly, and perhaps with a smile, Oliver thanked God for honest-hearted souls and departed. Before long Edward sent one of his employees to fetch a copy of the Book of Mormon from Oliver and his fellow missionaries.[2] Hungering for truth, Edward set out for New York to interview Joseph Smith and returned to Ohio having been baptized by the Prophet himself.[3] Lydia, meanwhile, had been baptized by Parley Pratt. "I saw the Gospel in its plainness as it was in the New Testament," she testified, "and I also knew that none of the sects of the day taught these things."4 Edward returned to New England to declare the good news to his parents and siblings.

Joseph, meanwhile, received sections 37 and 38, commanding the New York Saints to move to Ohio. Joseph and Emma traveled to Ohio by sleigh with the returning Edward Partridge and Sidney Rigdon. Section 41 is the first revelation Joseph received in Ohio, very soon after his arrival.

CONTENT

The Lord commands all his people to hearken to his voice in Doctrine and Covenants 41. He delights to bless with the greatest of blessings all those who hear his words, yet those who profess his name and hear not will he curse with the heaviest curses. He commands the elders to assemble to agree on his word. Receiving his law, which will give them the knowledge to govern his church as he wills, depends upon their asking in faithful prayer. The Lord reveals that he will be their ruler when he comes again. Those who receive the law and obey it are disciples of Christ, but those who say they have received it and choose not to obey it are not his disciples and should be cast out of the Church. The resources reserved for the obedient cannot be spared for the unworthy. The Lord commands the Church to appoint Edward Partridge to be their bishop, and he commands Edward to leave his hat factory and store to spend all of his time working for the Church, attending to the responsibilities the forthcoming law of consecration will give him. Like Nathanael in the Bible, Edward is without guile, that is, duplicity or deceit. The Lord has chosen him to serve as bishop for many reasons, including the purity of his heart.

Edward Partridge, the first man called as a bishop in the restored Church.

OUTCOMES

Church historian B. H. Roberts called the revelation in Doctrine and Covenants 41 an unexpected development in Church organization. "There was nothing in the preceding revelations that intimated that bishops would constitute any part of the church organization and government."[5] It also highlights the cultural differences between the kingdom of God and the world in which Joseph Smith lived. The revelation declares that the Lord, not the people, are sovereign. It does not separate legislative, judicial, and executive powers. The Lord exercises them all. He assumes both the power and the prerogative to bless and curse, to include and to cast out, to make and declare law, and to bring lawbreakers to judgment. He repeatedly refers to "my law" (v. 3), and calls for an assembly not to debate and create law but "to agree upon" (v. 2) law dictated by revelation. Moreover, he commands specific action, most notably for Edward Partridge, to "leave his merchandise" (v. 9) and spend his whole effort executing the divine law. Section 41 is a revelation from a King with instructions about how to build his kingdom. As section 38 declared, this King of kings gives laws that make us free (vv. 21–22). He retains sovereignty, including the prerogative to make the laws, but grants agency—the power to decide whether or not to obey them.

"Bishop Partridge had been a member of the Church for less than two months when he was asked to sacrifice everything he had worked for in his life and devote his time completely to his new Church." How did he choose to act on the revelation? He fed and clothed the Saints, left hat making and factory owning to others, and faithfully acted on the commands in this revelation and others for the rest of his life. It was the Lord's way. Edward Partridge was called to model and then implement the law of consecration (see D&C 42). His daughter remembered that he did both. Her father was "called to leave his business," she wrote, "which was in a most flourishing condition, and go to Missouri to attend to the business of the Church. He went and left his family to get along as best they could. I was at that time very sick, and he had no expectation of seeing me again, but the Lord had called, and he must obey. He showed his faith by his works."[6]

Doctrine & Covenants 42

ORIGIN

Twelve elders gathered in Kirtland, Ohio, on February 9, 1831, to hear the word of the Lord. He had promised a month earlier that if the Saints would gather in Ohio, he would give them his law (D&C 38:32). They had gathered, and he gave them his law. Doctrine and Covenants 42 contains the law of the Church of Jesus Christ.

The Saints in Kirtland were all recent converts. They knew the Bible, were determined to obey the scriptures, and had been looking forward to the restoration of apostolic authority. Joseph's history says they "were striving to do the will of God, so far as they knew it, though some strange notions and false spirits had crept in among them."[1] Many of the Ohio Saints belonged to a communal "family," as they called it, in which they pooled their property in an effort to emulate the Christians described in the New Testament, who "were of one heart and of one soul: neither said any of them that ought of the things which he possessed was his own; but they had all things common" (Acts 4:32).

In section 42, the Lord restored his law, including the law of consecration, to these Saints who were willing to act but lacked the knowledge upon which to do so. Joseph's history says they "readily abandoned" their errors "for the more perfect law of the Lord."[2]

Careful students of section 42 will notice that it is a series of revelations, most of which end with an Amen. *Each revelation answers a specific question asked by the elders who assembled to learn the will of the Lord. The questions are recorded and crossed out in an early manuscript, presumably as an indication that they were not part of the revealed text to be printed. We can profit from knowing the questions that were asked. They give us the background we need to better understand the revealed texts. The first ten verses answer the question, "Shall the Church come together into one place or remain as they are in separate bodies?" Verses 11–69 answer the question, "[What is] the Law regulating the Church in her present situation till the time of her gathering?" Verses 70–73 tell the priesthood holders the obligations the Church owes to their families while they are fulfilling their obligations to the Church. Verses 74–93 were given two weeks after the preceding verses and answer specifically how the elders are to act according to some parts of the revealed law.*[3]

CONTENT

Concerned with how best to administer to the needs of the Saints, the elders inquire whether the Saints should gather together in one location or remain scattered in various branches. In Doctrine and Covenants 42:1–10, the Lord answers by commanding that all the elders hearing the revelation, except Joseph Smith and Sidney Rigdon, should form companionships and serve short missions as led by the Holy Spirit. They are to go west and build local branches of the Church until the Lord reveals when the holy city New Jerusalem, the building of which was prophesied in both the Bible and the Book of Mormon, will be prepared. Then, the Lord commands, the Saints should gather there as God's people.

In verses 11–69 the Lord declares the law that will regulate his Church until the Saints gather in New Jerusalem. No one, then or now, shall preach the Lord's gospel or build his church unless he has first been ordained to do so by the leaders of the Church. Such an ordination must be common knowledge within the Church. There are to be no secret ordinations.

The Lord commands the elders and Aaronic Priesthood holders to teach the fulness of the gospel as contained in the Bible and the Book of Mormon. They are commanded to strictly follow the instructions given in section 20 regarding what to teach, whom to baptize, and how to baptize. They are to teach only as directed by the Holy Spirit, and they will receive the Spirit after praying in faith. Christ commands them not to teach if they do not have the Spirit. He also assures them that so long as they teach by the Spirit, he will approve of their teaching. The elders are to follow these instructions until Joseph finishes revising the Bible and, possibly, revealing other sacred scripture.

The law goes on to encompass the Ten Commandments, forbidding murder, stealing, lying, adultery (including lust), and gossip. Unrepentant lawbreakers are to be "cast out," or excommunicated, from the Church (D&C 42:28). Love for the Lord is the incentive for obedience. "If thou lovest me," the Lord taught, "thou shalt serve me and keep all my commandments" (v. 29), including the law of consecration, which followed immediately, beginning in verse 30.

The law of consecration requires the Saints to remember the poor and make a solemn covenant to use their temporal properties for relieving poverty, thus consecrating their possessions. This is to be done by making free will offerings to Christ's bishop, Edward Partridge, and his counselors. After consecration, the property belongs to the Church, but the law of consecration is about *receiving* as much as giving. Saints are in turn to receive property from the bishop and be accountable to Christ for the sacred stewardship they have received, which will amply supply the needs of their families.

The law requires the Saints to continually consecrate their surplus property to the bishop, whose stewardship is to use the property to fill the needs of the poor. Thus everyone in need, or *want,* as Joseph Smith used that word, can be provided for. As part of that same law, the high council and bishopric are commanded to establish a storehouse for the surplus property, all of which will be used not only to relieve poverty but also to purchase land for the Church, build houses of worship, and build the holy city New Jerusalem. The Lord's ultimate purpose for the law of consecration is to enable his covenant people to build up and gather to his temple and receive saving ordinances in anticipation of his coming. The Lord again warns that those who break the law and do not repent will be excommunicated from the Church, and they will not receive back any property that they have consecrated to the poor.

The Lord promises to fulfill prophecies by consecrating the riches of the Gentiles who embrace the gospel to the poor among the covenant people of Israel. He commands the Saints to "not be proud" (v. 40) in their hearts and to manifest their humility outwardly by dressing plainly in garments made beautiful by the workmanship of their own hands. He commands them to be clean and anxiously engaged rather than idle, for the idle are not consecrating the time or talent their Lord has given them as a stewardship, and therefore they "shall not eat the bread nor wear the garments of the laborer" (v. 42).

The law continues as the Lord commands that the sick among the Saints who lack faith to be healed, yet still believe, should be nourished tenderly by their brothers and sisters, using herbs and mild food. Two or more of the elders shall be called to lay hands upon them in the name of Christ and bless them, and whether the sick are healed or then die, it will be according to the will of the Lord. Those who have faith to be healed will be healed unless they are appointed to die. Death will be sweet to the repentant but bitter to the unrepentant. Those who have faith to see, hear, or leap will do so, and those without such faith who still choose to believe have power to become sons and daughters of Jesus Christ if they do not break his laws.

Christ warns against abuse of the law of consecration. He forbids taking what belongs to others without just compensation. "If thou obtainest more than that which would be for thy support," he commands, "thou shalt give it into my storehouse, that all things may be done according to that which I have said" (v. 55).

Once the fulness of the scriptures is received, the elders are to teach it to all mankind. The revelations of the Lord provide the law by which the Church should be governed. Those who obey the revelations will be saved.

Those who disobey them and do not repent will be damned. Missionaries are commanded to go forth in all directions, teaching their converts to move west to escape secret combinations and prophesied calamities. Any lacking wisdom may ask the Lord, and he will give unto them liberally and kindly. In conclusion to his answer about the law that should govern the Church in its youthful situation, the Lord says, "Lift up your hearts and rejoice, for unto you the kingdom, or in other words, the keys of the church have been given" (v. 69).

In answer to the query about how the families of the elders should be provided for while the elders are proclaiming repentance or otherwise serving the Lord, he gives verses 70–73.

Aaronic Priesthood holders assisting the bishop in meeting the Saints' temporal needs are to receive stewardships, meaning property for use in sustaining the material needs of their own families. Melchizedek Priesthood holders in the bishopric will receive support as needed from the property consecrated to the bishop's storehouse. They are commanded to counsel together about how best to meet the needs of their families while fulfilling their obligations to the Church.

Two weeks after receiving verses 1–73, Joseph and several elders gathered again to seek clarification about how the elders were "to act upon the points of the Law,"[4] particularly those regarding marriage and such sinful actions as adultery, divorce, and murder. The remainder of section 42 gives detailed answers.

When a chaste spouse testifies truly and humbly that he or she seeks a divorce from an adulterous spouse, the virtuous spouse is justified and not subject to Church discipline. Adulterous men and women are to be tried by two or more elders of the Church, and the charges against them established by at least two credible witnesses who are not antagonistic toward the accused. After hearing the witnesses, the elders are to present the case to the Church to ensure any action taken is in accordance with the law set forth in section 42. Adulterous spouses are to be excommunicated. The Lord commands the elders to carefully interview candidates for baptism to prevent adulterous men and women from being baptized. Fornicators who completely repent can join the Church.

If any Saints murder, they should be tried and punished according to the law of the land. Persons charged with robbery, stealing, or lying should likewise be tried and punished according to the law of the land. Other kinds of iniquity are to be handled by the law of God. When Saints offend each other, the law commands the offended party to approach the offender privately. If the offender confesses, the parties should be reconciled and the matter closed. If not, the offended party may tell the elders of the offense in a private meeting. Those who offend many or who offend openly should be corrected publicly and ashamed. Private offenses should be rebuked privately, giving the offender an opportunity to confess to the offended and to God without public humiliation.

OUTCOMES

The revelation in Doctrine and Covenants 42 motivated the early Saints to action. John Whitmer wrote that "after the above law or Revelation was received, the elders went forth to proclaim repentance according to commandment, and there were numbers added to the church."[5]

Section 42 does significant theological work. Without knowledge of God's law, no one can act independently as an accountable agent. Knowledge of good and evil is prerequisite to agency. Divine law differentiates what is good from what is evil. As part of his plan to create fully developed accountable agents in his image, Heavenly Father gives his children knowledge of good and evil by revealing his laws. Then the Saints have agency or power to act for themselves. Accountability always follows.

Some misunderstand this doctrine. "You mean he makes me obey his rules," they object. No, he does not. Knowledge of the law, even covenanting to live the law of our own free will, does not compel us to do it. Obviously the Lord's law against adultery has not put an end to adultery. The Lord's laws do not smother choice; they guarantee it. The laws provide opportunity for each of us to choose for ourselves whether to obey. Then the Lord holds us accountable for our choices. We act exactly as we please. But the law is just, and we are accountable for what we do with it.

The law of consecration in section 42 is founded on the doctrines of agency and accountability but also on stewardship. Agency is the power to act, stewardship is what we have to act upon, and accountability inevitably follows our actions. As the revelation declares, Bishop Partridge had the job of assisting the Saints who were willing to live the law of consecration. He was determined to serve well, and that sometimes led him to encroach on individual agency. When the bishop showed a tendency to count every bean in the Saints' pantries, Joseph showed him that he was not to enforce the law; rather, the Saints were to live it or not, as they chose. "Don't condescend to very great particulars in taking inventories," Joseph wrote. "A man is bound by the law of the Church, to consecrate to the Bishop, before he can be considered a legal heir to the kingdom of Zion; and this, too, without constraint; and unless he does this, he cannot be acknowledged before the Lord on the Church Book. . . . Every man must be his own judge how much he should receive and how much he should suffer to remain in the hands of the Bishop."[6]

When the talented but prideful William W. Phelps forgot that he was steward, not owner, of the Church's printing press, Joseph gently counseled him as well. "You say 'my press, my types, &c.' Where, our brethren ask, did you get them & how came they to be '*yours?*' No hardness, but a caution, for you know that it is *We*, not *I*, and all things are the Lord's, and he opened the hearts of his Church to furnish these things, or *we* should not have been privileged with using them."[7] Phelps had forgotten the first premise of consecration, namely, that the faithful are always of "one heart and of one soul: neither said any of them that ought of the things which he possessed was his own" (Acts 4:32). Rather, all is the Lord's, and he commands that all of his children have equal claim on the abundance he has provided for their needs (D&C 49:20; 78; 104:18, 55–56).

The divine law set forth in section 42 is not hard to understand. It is hard to do. It runs completely counter to our selfish natures and the deeply ingrained ideas that tenaciously defend them. The law declares that "the earth is the Lord's, and the fulness thereof" (Psalm 24:1). There are no self-made men, only stewards. The possessions God allows us to control give us something to act upon. When we act according to the law, demonstrating that we can be trusted to use his resources for his purposes, he will give us all he has.

Finding the law hard to keep, we sometimes blame others or even the Lord. Whenever we hear ourselves saying that the early Saints *could not* live the law, we are saying that God gave them a law they had no power to keep. There is a great theological difference between *could* and *would*. Agency hangs in the balance. In consecration, the Lord did not give a law we cannot keep. Some Saints would not keep it, but some of them kept it very well. Some of them kept it less well. Some of them did not try or even care. Not much has changed. The law is still on the books and the variety of Saints' choices regarding it are about the same. President Gordon B. Hinckley reminded us that "the law of sacrifice and the law of consecration were not done away with and are still in effect."[8] No one has to keep the law, but those who love the Lord do. "If thou lovest me thou shalt serve me and keep all my commandments" he said, just before he set forth the law of consecration in the Doctrine and Covenants (D&C 42:29).

Doctrine & Covenants 43

ORIGIN

Revelation poses a problem. Joseph Smith's critics complained that God had ceased to speak. There would be no more revelations. They had come to that conclusion through a long history of challenges to their authority from women and men who claimed to receive revelation.

Joan of Arc, Saint Teresa of Avila, Thomas Müntzer, and many, many others saw visions and received revelations that upset the political and religious establishments of their day. Müntzer died for his declaration that "all true parsons must have revelations, so that they are certain of their cause."[1] Müntzer was a toddler when Columbus landed in the Americas. He later criticized the clergy of his day for denying what he called the "living word of God."[2] Speaking in Prague in 1521, Müntzer denounced those who denied a need for continuing revelation. "These villainous and treacherous parsons are of no use to the church in even the slightest matter," Müntzer wrote, "for they deny the voice of the bridegroom, which is a truly certain sign that they are a pack of devils. . . . For all true parsons must have revelations, so that they are certain of their cause."[3] To Müntzer this seemed like the direction in which Martin Luther was headed, but as Müntzer became more outspoken, Luther retreated from his own conversion experience. He "did not share Müntzer's belief that the Holy Spirit gave new revelations in the present."[4] Instead Luther called Müntzer a fanatic, though one scholar noted that Müntzer was more "akin to the disciples of the New Testament church."[5] Müntzer gained support even as opposition to him increased. "The conviction grew in him that God still spoke directly through his chosen prophets."[6] In a famous 1524 sermon on Daniel 2, Müntzer preached that "in such momentous and dangerous matters as those which true preachers, dukes, and princes have to deal with, it would never be possible to guard themselves securely against error on all sides, and to act blamelessly, if they did not rely on revelations from God."[7] Müntzer's teachings and their political implications made him threatening to the established church and state. He was beheaded in 1525 and his impaled head and body were displayed as a warning against others who might outspokenly hope for prophets and revelations.

The official rejection of revelation left a deep longing in many souls. Ralph Waldo Emerson urged Harvard graduates in 1838 "to show us that God is, not was; that He speaketh, not spake."[8] Such demands for revelation were widespread in the 1830s. Numerous would-be prophets arose to supply them, opening the can of worms that worried orthodox leaders so much.

So here is the problem of revelation: Critics of revelation complain that God no longer reveals his will to women and men on earth. Believers in revelation, meanwhile, receive revelations themselves, and many fall prey to counterfeits. Joseph, of all people, did not want to diminish faith in a revealing God. Like Moses, he wished "that all the Lord's people were prophets, and that the Lord would put his spirit upon them!" (Numbers 11:29). But how could he affirm that God continues to reveal his will while simultaneously maintaining order and authority?

The problem became acute for the young Church in early 1831 when "a female professing to be a prophetess," whom we know only by her surname, Hubble, "made her appearance in Kirtland, and so ingratiated herself into the esteem and favor of some of the Elders." Church historian John Whitmer said "she appeared very sanctimonious and deceived some," apparently including Sidney Rigdon. Joseph's history suggests that there was a debate among the Saints, some of whom believed Hubble's "great pretensions of revealing commandments, laws and other curious matters."

Some have assumed that the problem was Hubble's gender, that a female had no place telling the brethren what to do. But gender was not the issue. Hiram Page had created a similar problem by presuming to receive revelations (see D&C 28). To Emma Smith, meanwhile, the Lord had promised the power to expound scripture and exhort the Church by the spirit of revelation (see D&C 25:7). The question was not whether women could receive revelation. They could and did and do. The question was to whom the Lord would reveal his will for the Church. The confusion required clarification. Whitmer prefaced the revelation by saying that "the Lord gave Revelation that the Saints might not be deceived."[9] That revelation is recorded in Doctrine and Covenants 43.

CONTENT

After commanding the elders to hearken unto his words, the Lord declares in Doctrine and Covenants 43, "And this ye shall know assuredly—that there is none other appointed unto you to receive commandments and revelations" (v. 3). Joseph is appointed of the Lord to receive commandments. The Lord further declares that, unless he proves unfaithful, Joseph will remain the one to receive binding revelations. Even if the Lord decides to give the gift to another, Joseph will be the one to appoint his replacement. Thus, the law of the Lord is that the Saints should not receive anyone else's teachings as revelations or commandments. Anyone other than Joseph claiming to command or reveal for others is not called by the Lord, and those who believe them are deceived. Obedience to the Lord's law prevents such deception.

After establishing Joseph's singular calling to receive revelation for the Church, the Lord addresses the elders, commanding them to assemble together and edify one another regarding how to act upon the newly revealed law. He calls them to teach mankind as they are taught by the Spirit of the Lord. As he prophesies in section 38, the Savior promises to endow the elders with power if they sanctify themselves. "Hearken ye," he urges them, stressing that his second coming approaches (v. 17). He commands the elders to be ready themselves and to call everyone else to repentance, saying,

"Prepare yourselves for the great day of the Lord" (v. 20), and asking mankind what response they will have when, after they have denied the words of mortal men, nature itself demands they repent and prepare for the Lord's coming? The Lord is telling the elders what to say in his behalf. He wants the elders to ask people how they will respond when thunder and lightning calls them to repentance. The Lord himself will speak from heaven, commanding all nations to hear the words of their Creator. He has often called through the voices of servants, ministering angels, thunder and lightning, tempests and earthquakes, hailstorms, famines, pestilence of every kind, and by his own merciful voice all day long. He would have saved all mankind, but much of it refuses to be saved. "The day has come, when the cup of the wrath of mine indignation is full" (v. 26), he declares. The elders should exhaust themselves in one last effort to call the inhabitants of the earth to repentance. The repentant will be redeemed when the Lord comes in judgment. The Lord concludes by commanding the elders to seriously and solemnly hearken to his revealed words and obey all his commandments. "I am Jesus Christ, the Savior of the world," he says. "Treasure these things up in your hearts, and let the solemnities of eternity rest upon your minds" (v. 34).

OUTCOMES

John Whitmer noted that "after this commandment was received the Saints came to understanding on this subject, and unity and harmony prevailed throughout the church of God: and the Saints began to learn wisdom, and treasure up knowledge which they learned from the word of God, and by experience as they advanced in the way of eternal life."[10]

Literarily speaking, Doctrine and Covenants 43 is one of the loveliest, most poetic of Joseph's revelations. It is another eschatological text, meaning that it addresses the end of the world and the events that lead up to the Savior's return. But perhaps its most significant contribution is its solution to the old and perplexing problem of revelation. Avoiding the extremes of no revelation at all or a completely chaotic revelation free-for-all, this text gives order to revelation and enables the sincere to avoid deception. No one but Joseph Smith or the successors he appoints will receive commandments by revelation. This leaves open the door to personal revelation even as it sets boundaries for what such revelations will contain. Hallelujah for this profound, balanced solution, for history is marked by the extremes of regimes that deny revelation or deceivers whose claims to revelation prey on sincere souls hoping to hear from their Heavenly Father.

Through Joseph Smith, the Lord provides the solution. Joseph will reveal the commandments. All Saints are empowered to verify Joseph's revelations individually for themselves. Joseph's critics project upon him a tyrannical intent to jealously put down potential rivals. But revelations such as this one actually empower individuals. Joseph's power came from the truthfulness of his teachings. He combined God's revelations to him on behalf of mankind with God's revelations to them for their individual needs. "Search the revelations which we publish," the Church has always taught, "and ask your Heavenly Father, in the name of His Son Jesus Christ, to manifest the truth unto you, and if you do it with an eye single to His glory nothing doubting, He will answer you by the power of His Holy Spirit. You will then know for yourselves."[11] Tyrants strive to keep their subjects ignorant. Joseph's revelations open the heavens to all who want to know for themselves.

Doctrine & Covenants 44

ORIGIN

The gathering of the Saints in Ohio led prominent and powerful men, including Eber Howe and Grandison Newell, to oppose the Church economically, in the press, and in the courts. Foreseeing such antagonism, the Lord gave Doctrine and Covenants 44 to Joseph Smith and Sidney Rigdon late in February 1831 as a call to the elders of the Church.

CONTENT

In Doctrine and Covenants 44 the Lord commands the elders of the Church to gather together in conference and promises that if they are found both true to their covenants and faithful in Christ, he will pour out the Holy Ghost upon them while they are assembled. Then, he commands, they should return to the surrounding areas and publicly teach repentance. "Many shall be converted," the Lord promises, and the gathering of converts will make it possible to organize the Church in accordance with Ohio law, thus blocking any of the Church's enemies who might appeal to the laws of the land as a means to undermine the Church. Meanwhile, the Lord commands the brethren to "visit the poor" (v. 6) and relieve their needs until the Church can fully implement the law of consecration (D&C 42).

OUTCOMES

Joseph's history says that Doctrine and Covenants 44 "caused the church to appoint a conference." A special meeting of the elders of the

Church convened on June 6, 1831 when, according to Joseph's history, "the Lord displayed his power."[1] The Church had met the requirements of New York state law when six men organized it in April 1830, but the move to Ohio in 1831 required more. Ohio law demanded that twenty members of the Church meet to elect officers and have their organization recorded by the county clerk. That would give the Church legal recognition, including the right to own land.[2] Available records do not reveal for sure when the Church was incorporated in Ohio, but it was done in response to section 44.

In section 44, the Lord warns the Saints to comply with the law of the land for protection against their enemies and to obey the law of consecration for protection against his just punishment of those who do not keep it.

Doctrine & Covenants 45

ORIGIN

Joseph Smith bought a copy of the King James Version of the Bible at Egbert Grandin's bookstore in Palmyra, New York, while the Book of Mormon was being printed upstairs. Shortly after the Church was organized, Joseph's main task became revising the Bible. He called the revision his New Translation. He began with Genesis and received by revelation much restored scripture, including the book of Moses, which is now in the Pearl of Great Price. We learn more from that book than any other source about how, "in process of time," Enoch led his people to unity of heart and mind—Zion (Moses 7:21).

In March 1831 Joseph received the revelation recorded in Doctrine and Covenants 45, a remarkable, composite text in which Jesus reiterates his own sermon from Matthew 24, comments on it, and applies it to Latter-day Saints striving to replicate Enoch's Zion. The very next day Joseph began reading and revising the New Testament.

Matthew 24 says that Jesus' disciples went to him privately as he sat upon the Mount of Olives overlooking Jerusalem. He told them that before his second coming they would be afflicted, hated, and killed (Matthew 24:3–9). In Doctrine and Covenants 45, the Lord repeats these teachings and explains their significance to the Latter-day Saints. The ancient apostles were understandably curious about their deaths and especially about how long they would remain dead before the day of redemption, the day Jesus would resurrect them.

CONTENT

Again and again, the Lord commands the Saints to hear and obey his voice—he who is our advocate with the Father, pleading for mercy on our behalf by virtue of his own sinless sacrifice.

In Doctrine and Covenants 45 the Savior sends his everlasting covenant into the world as a light, a messenger "to prepare the way before [him]," an ensign for his covenant people, and an invitation for those not yet covenanted to become so (v. 9). Christ's restored covenant testifies of his imminent coming. For that reason, he tells the Saints to prepare wisely, as did the people of Enoch, about whom Joseph has recently received a revelation while revising the Bible (Moses 6–8). In that revelation, the Lord reveals to Joseph that Enoch and his people were separated from the earth and received into heaven until righteousness rather than wickedness covers the earth—in other words, until the Millennium. All the holy have longed for such a blessed day; wickedness has left them feeling like strangers and mere temporary residents in this wicked world. Still, these righteous souls procured God's promise that they would live in the day of righteousness. The Lord commands the Saints to listen as he promises them the same blessings he made to the righteous in ancient times.

During his mortal ministry, outside Jerusalem on the Mount of Olives Christ spoke of the signs of his second coming. His apostles had questioned him, desiring to know when he would fulfill his promises to those with whom he covenanted anciently. The apostles considered the time they would be dead as bondage, and they looked forward to a glorious resurrection. Jesus showed them the signs of his coming. As they looked down over the walls of Jerusalem, Christ pointed out the temple. Though the apostles' enemies had guaranteed the temple would stand forever, Jesus prophesied that within a generation it would be completely demolished and the inhabitants of Jerusalem scattered across the globe. This would happen quite unexpectedly, Jesus said, "as a thief in the night" (v. 19) and within the lifetime of some of those then living. The apostles asked about the coming end of the world. Jesus assured them that it would end but not until the scattered Israelites were gathered in fulfillment of prophecy and his covenant with them renewed. The intervening years would be violent and tumultuous, leaving people anxious, fearful, and without hope in Christ and his coming. Love would turn to indifference. Gross injustices would prevail. But as it becomes time to invite the Gentiles to embrace the gospel covenant, Christ will restore the fulness of his gospel. He knows that most will not receive it. They will reject him because of the philosophies of men. Some in that generation will live to see overwhelming punishment in the form of a desolating and widespread sickness. The Lord's disciples who have taken a stand for holiness will maintain their ground while some of the wicked curse God and die and some of them murder one another. Even earthquakes in various places and other desolations will not be enough to persuade everyone to repent.

The Lord tells the Saints that his prophecies on the Mount of Olives troubled the apostles. He therefore assured them that the coming events should be viewed optimistically. "Be not troubled," he told them, because "when all these things shall come to pass, ye may know that the promises which have been made unto you shall be fulfilled" (D&C 45:35).

Section 45 justifies optimism in the face of evil and tumult. Sister Patricia Holland told about her own fears during a fierce storm that raged through her neighborhood. Just as she was "hearing news reports of semitrailer trucks—twenty of them—being blown over on the roadside," through her window she saw two trees crash to the ground. Truly fearful, she thought of the recent genocide in Kosovo, a school massacre in Colorado, murders in the Family History Library in Salt Lake City, and the pending dawn of the year 2000. She whispered to her apostle husband, "'Do you think this is the end? Is it all over—or about to be?'" He replied, "'No, but wouldn't it be wonderful if it were?'"[1]

Jesus then resumed his Olivet discourse, likening the restoration of the gospel to the parable of the fig tree with which the ancient apostles were so familiar. Just as the leaves of the fig tree sprout when summer has nearly arrived, so will the faithful anticipate his second coming when the signs Jesus has spoken of begin to appear. They will see signs and wonders in heaven and on earth. Some of the covenant people will return to Jerusalem, looking for a savior, a messiah. An angel will announce his coming with a trumpet, and he will appear in power and glory. The righteous dead will be resurrected, rising from their graves to join the returning Christ.

Though the time between death and resurrection can be seen as temporary bondage, the apostles and the righteous who die can be at peace. They will be perfectly redeemed in a gloriously resurrected body as surely as they can then see Christ before them and know that he exists. Then the Lord will judge the nations. Everyone will hear him as he speaks. Nations will mourn, and those who taunted the righteous will recognize their error. Mockers will be covered by calamity, and the filthy mowed down and burned. The Jews, looking on, will ask Christ how he received the wounds in his hands and feet. He will tell them that he is the very Jesus who was crucified, the very Son of God. Jews will weep as they recognize their sins and lament because they persecuted their promised Messiah. God's plan provides for the people who could not obey the gospel while they lived because they did not know it. They will be resurrected. With the wicked slain and death conquered by the righteous, Satan will lose his power and be kept bound by the righteousness of the people (Revelation 20:13; 1 Nephi 22:15, 26). This is the day when the Savior's parable about the five wise and the five foolish virgins will be realized. The wise who receive his truth are guided by the Holy Ghost and choose not to be deceived. They will survive the day. They will inherit the earth and have children who grow up sinless to be saved in the Lord's glory. He will reign in their midst as King and Lawgiver. The Lord tells the Saints he will reveal no more concerning this time until Joseph has revised the New Testament.

The Lord grants Joseph permission to begin translating the New Testament to prepare the Saints for the great things that await them. They have heard of foreign wars, yet they have not known that a few years will bring war to their own land. The Lord warns them and commands them to leave the eastern United States and move west, along the way calling on everyone to repent. He commands them to pool the wealth he has given them to buy land for the prophesied city New Jerusalem, a place of refuge for the Saints of God. People from all nations will gather there and be the only peaceful people on earth, causing the wicked to say, "Let us not go up to battle against Zion, for the inhabitants of Zion are terrible; wherefore we cannot stand" (D&C 45:70).

The Lord commands the Saints to keep these prophecies to themselves until they accomplish all he has commanded them to do. He commands them to conceal their intentions of purchasing property from "enemies" who would oppose the building of Zion. Zion must become powerful first, so that when its enemies learn of the Lord's designs, they will fear and tremble. All nations will fear the Lord.

OUTCOMES

Doctrine and Covenants 45 is an unusual revelation. It is a commentary on one of the most complicated and contested passages of the Bible. There is no shortage of interpreters of Jesus' Olivet discourse. Any number of commentaries on Matthew 24 provide all kinds of linguistic and cultural analyses. These may be helpful, perhaps, but section 45 is the only source on earth in which the Savior of the world interprets and applies his own Olivet discourse. It is the finest text in the world for understanding Matthew 24, Mark 13, and Luke 21. Section 45 cements a connection between the Old Testament, New Testament, and the restoration of the gospel through Joseph Smith. The Savior who reveals it is the "God of Enoch" (v. 11), about whom Joseph had recently learned so much in his revision of Genesis and his reception of the book of Moses. The Savior gave the discourse to his disciples on the Mount of Olives and in section 45 interprets and applies it to the Latter-day Saints.

Section 45 laces together the dispensations of Enoch, the Savior and his apostles, and the fulness of times. Overwhelming wickedness and pending calamities are common themes in each. Always the outnumbered righteous seek safety, peace, and refuge. They seek Zion. Section 45 gives coherence to the past, present, and future. We see in it the Lord's plans and purposes being accomplished. Without it the world might seem like a violent, purposeless mess. With it we need not be troubled, for we can see that Zion rises in contrast to the world and that calamities portend the fulfillment of Christ's promises that Zion is about to be established.

Doctrine & Covenants 46

ORIGIN

Missionary John Murdock and his companions were preaching in Cleveland, Ohio, when a deceiver came forward and knelt as if to pray, but actually he was giving "a sign to the banditry to begin their abuse." Immediately his cohorts blew out the candles and threw inkstands and books at the speaker.[1] Later, back in Kirtland, the brethren counseled about the situation. Some favored excluding from Church meetings all who were not firm in the faith. Others opposed this idea, citing the Book of Mormon passage in which the Lord commands the Church to "not forbid any man from coming unto you when ye shall meet together" for sacrament or confirmation meetings (3 Nephi 18:22). Both positions seemed justified. The Saints needed further light. "Therefore," wrote John Whitmer, "the Lord deigned to speak on this subject, that his people might come to understanding, and said, that he had always given to his Elders to conduct all meetings as they were led by the spirit."[2] That revelation is recorded in Doctrine and Covenants 46.

CONTENT

The Lord begins Doctrine and Covenants 46 by commanding the Saints to hearken to his words for their own improvement and instruction. The Lord then explains to the Saints a universal principle and its relationship to the teachings of the Book of Mormon about inclusive meetings (v. 2). The elders should *always* conduct *all* meetings by the power of the Holy Ghost.

There may be times when exceptions to what the Book of Mormon says are in order, and the Spirit will make those cases known.

The Lord then reiterates the policy from 3 Nephi 18. Under normal circumstances, do not remove anyone from public Church meetings. Do not exclude Church members from sacrament meeting, though sinners should not partake of the sacrament until they repent. Do not exclude investigators from sacrament or confirmation meetings. The Lord commands the Saints to ask should they have questions about these rules, and the Spirit will testify what to do case by case.

The Saints must prayerfully and gratefully seek the Spirit in holiness, with honest motives, a clear conscience, and concern about eternal consequences. Otherwise, they are likely to be seduced by evil spirits, doctrines of devils, or commandments of men. The Lord commands the Saints to beware of these deceptions and promises them they will not be deceived if they earnestly seek the gifts of the Holy Ghost, always remembering their intended purposes. The gifts are given for the benefit of those who love the Lord and keep all his commandments and those who seek to do so. They are given so that all who honestly seek the Lord's will may benefit, not so they can satisfy selfish lust. The Lord desires that all Saints always remember the spiritual gifts he has given to them and remember they are not given to a single person—they are given unto the Church. Not all Saints have every gift, but all have at least one gift that comes from the Holy Ghost. Some have one, some another, and thus by sharing, everyone gains access to all the gifts of the Spirit.

Section 46 reviews several of the gifts, echoing Paul's second epistle to the Corinthian Saints and Moroni's last words in the Book of Mormon. To some the Holy Ghost gives knowledge that Jesus Christ is the Son of God and that he was crucified for the sins of the world. To others the Holy Ghost gives the gift of believing the testimonies of those who know. This gift leads to eternal life for those who endure. To some the Holy Ghost gives understanding of the different yet acceptable ways in which the gifts may be used in a variety of circumstances (see Moroni 10:8). To some the Holy Ghost gives knowledge of different kinds of spiritual phenomena mentioned in this revelation—evil spirits, doctrines of devils, commandments of men, or authentic gifts of the Holy Ghost. Some are given wisdom; some, knowledge to teach others. Some are given faith to be healed; others, faith to heal. Some can work miracles. Others prophesy. Some discern true intentions and otherwise hidden motivations. Some speak in tongues; others interpret. All these gifts God gives to bless his children. Bishops and other presiding authorities cultivate the gift to discern and judge these gifts in those over whom they preside, guarding against those who testify and yet are not of God. Those who ask for gifts by the power of the Holy Ghost receive them by the same power. All things must be done by the Spirit and in the name Christ, which they have taken upon themselves by covenant. The Lord commands, "Give thanks unto God in the Spirit for whatsoever blessing ye are blessed with" (D&C 46:32).

OUTCOMES

As with so many of the revelations Joseph received shortly after arriving in Ohio, Doctrine and Covenants 46 deals with the problem of deception. The essential truth of this section is that we should seek the gifts of the Spirit so we will not be deceived. If Saints live in the light of the Holy Ghost, they will not be deceived. If they do not have the Spirit, they will be deceived. Joseph taught that a person "who has none of the gifts has not faith; and he deceives himself if he supposes he has."[3]

When asked by one skeptic whether an individual could be saved simply by repenting and being baptized but not seeking the Holy Ghost, Joseph gave an analogy. "Suppose I am traveling and am hungry, and meet with a man and tell him I am hungry; and he tells me to go yonder, there is a house for entertainment, go and knock and you must conform to all the rules of the house, or you cannot satisfy your hunger; knock, call for food, sit down and eat and I go and knock and ask for food and sit down to the table, but do not eat, shall I satisfy my hunger? No! I must eat: the gifts are the food."[4]

Doctrine & Covenants 47

ORIGIN

The revelation that organized the Church commanded the Saints to keep a written record of its activities (see D&C 21:1). Oliver Cowdery assumed the responsibility to do so, and then the Lord called him on a mission. John Whitmer, meanwhile, returned from a mission and "was appointed by the voice of the Elders to keep the Church record." Joseph asked him also to write and preserve a history of the Church. "I would rather not do it," John explained, "but observed that the will of the Lord be done, and if he desires it, I desire that he would manifest it through Joseph the Seer." Joseph asked, and the Lord answered with the revelation recorded in Doctrine and Covenants 47.[1]

CONTENT

It is expedient to the Lord that John write and preserve a history of the Church. In Doctrine and Covenants 47 he is called to assist Joseph in transcribing revelation until such time as the Lord assigns him more responsibilities. John is also given authority to preach to the Saints whenever necessary. The Lord repeats his will for a second time, saying that John should succeed Oliver Cowdery as the Church historian and recorder; the Lord needs Oliver elsewhere. The Lord promises that for as long as John is faithful, he will have the guidance of the Holy Ghost to direct him in fulfilling his calling.

OUTCOMES

Joseph's history says that John Whitmer was set apart "as a historian inasmuch as he was faithful."[2] He was sustained by the Church at a special conference in April 1831, a month after the revelation was received, and he began writing in June. "I shall proceed to continue this record," his first sentence says, "being commanded of the Lord and Savior Jesus Christ, to write the things that transpire in this church."[3] John was not nearly as good a historian as Oliver had been. His history is an important but sketchy source of early Church history that becomes quite cynical about the Church as John apostatized in 1838. John also transcribed revelations as Doctrine and Covenants 47 commanded. Many of the earliest existing revelation and Bible manuscripts are in his handwriting.

John Whitmer.

Joseph Smith had lived in John Whitmer's home, and John had scribed part of the Book of Mormon as Joseph translated. What does it tell us about Joseph Smith and the Restoration that someone who knew him as well as John did would resist obeying Joseph's personal counsel and then obey a revelation received through Joseph? Joseph's followers linked his authority to his revelations. The people who knew him best "accepted the voice in the revelations as the voice of God, investing in the revelations the highest authority, even above Joseph Smith's counsel. In the revelations, they believed, God himself spoke, not a man."[4]

Doctrine & Covenants 48

ORIGIN

Nearly two hundred Saints were on their way from New York to Ohio in obedience to the Lord's commands in Doctrine and Covenants 37 and 38. Very soon they would need a place to live. Bishop Edward Partridge, whose calling was to meet the Saints' needs, wondered how to accommodate the New York Saints. Because the Saints already knew that the "city Zion" was to be built "on the borders by the Lamanites" (D&C 28:9), should Bishop Partridge buy land in Ohio? Make long-term plans? "The Bishop being anxious to know something concerning the matter, therefore the Lord spoke unto Joseph Smith Jr."[1] in the revelation recorded in Doctrine and Covenants 48.

CONTENT

The Lord commands in Doctrine and Covenants 48 that for the present time the Saints should remain in Ohio. Saints with land should share it with the immigrating Saints from New York. If still more land is needed on which to live, the New York Saints should buy whatever is needed for the present time. The Lord commands the Saints to save all the money they can righteously earn in order to buy the land upon which the New Jerusalem, the holy city of Zion, should be built. Though the Lord has given the Saints a clue about where the city would be built (D&C 28), it is still not time to reveal its exact location. After the New York Saints arrive, the Lord will reveal the place to Joseph Smith. The Lord will appoint men to buy the land and begin the process of founding the city.

Then the Saints can begin to gather there with their families as long as their personal circumstances allow and as long as the leaders of the Church authorize the move. All of these changes depend on the Lord's past and future revelations.

OUTCOMES

Doctrine and Covenants 48 answered Bishop Partridge's questions and mapped out an orderly, step-by-step process for building and inhabiting New Jerusalem based on previous and future revelation. It also answers common questions related to the law of consecration. Is saving contrary to consecration? What about "obtaining" money? Section 48 clarifies that our motives matter very much when it comes to saving and obtaining. It commands the Saints to save all they can for righteous purposes. It commands them to earn all they can "in righteousness" so they can build Zion (v. 4). It is a restatement of the Lord's command to seek his kingdom first and foremost. Saving and earning to that end are not only justified but commanded.

Doctrine & Covenants 49

ORIGIN

In the 1700s a group of French Protestants known as Camisards fled to England to escape persecution. There they influenced a group of English Quakers. Both groups emphasized direct revelation to individuals, and the combination of their teachings gave rise to a new religion, the United Society of Believers in Christ's Second Appearing. An early history of the United Society says that "sometimes, after sitting awhile in silent meditation, they were seized with a mighty trembling, under which they would often express the indignation of God against all sin. At other times, they were exercised with singing, shouting, and leaping for joy, at the near prospect of salvation. They were often exercised with great agitation of body and limbs, shaking, running, and walking the floor, with a variety of other operations and signs, swiftly passing and repassing each other, like clouds agitated with a mighty wind. These exercises, so strange in the eyes of the beholders, brought upon them the appellation of Shakers, which has been their most common name of distinction ever since."[1]

Ann Lee and her family were early Shakers, or Believers, as they called themselves. At age twenty-two Ann believed she received a revelation that she was to be God's messenger. She became the leader of the group in 1772 and led her few followers to America two years later, settling near Albany, New York. They struggled during the Revolution but gradually gained momentum from the same series of spiritual awakenings that gave rise to the Restoration. Having lost all four of her children to death as infants before being abandoned by her adulterous husband, Lee died in 1784.

Shakerism continued to thrive in America, however, leading to the establishment of several communities, including one in North Union, Ohio, just a few miles from Kirtland. The Saints and the Believers traded with each other and were good neighbors.[2]

The Shakers believed that Christ instituted God's first church, which subsequently apostatized. They believed, therefore, that God would restore his church. Shakers acknowledged the goodness of "real reformers," but, asserting that both Catholic and Protestant Christianity were apostate from Christ's church, they held that "a true Church could have originated only by a new revelation from God to some one person." They believed that George Fox, the founder of Quakerism, prepared the world for God to establish his church again. And then "arose Ann Lee and her little company, to whom Christ appeared the second time." They held that Ann Lee, "by strictly obeying the light revealed within her, became righteous even as Jesus was righteous. She acknowledged Jesus Christ as her Head and Lord, and formed the same character as a spiritual woman that he formed as a spiritual man." She was, in a sense, "the second appearing of Christ."[3]

Shakers believed that marriage was a worldly, not a divine, institution (citing Matthew 22:30) and that sexual relations were ungodly. Thus, to choose to leave the world and live a celibate life was, in Shaker terms, to "take up the cross" (Mark 10:21). They rejected resurrection and looked forward to shedding their flesh at death to live a wholly spiritual afterlife. Shakers believed in individual moral agency, noting that only those who chose to obey the Lord would be saved and that coercion was wrong. They believed in confessing sin but not in the need for redeeming ordinances such as baptism. Shakers believed in temperance, including eating meat sparingly, if at all. Some preached vegetarianism. Shaker explanations for worshipping God by singing and dancing sounded like Doctrine and Covenants 136:28, in which the Lord acknowledges that repentant, forgiven souls long to sing and dance as forms of prayer and thanksgiving. Shakers believed in consecration and stewardship of property. They rejected all forms of exploitation—especially men of women, owners of laborers, and mankind of the physical environment. They envisioned God as both Father and Mother. They spoke of "our Eternal Heavenly Mother," citing

Genesis 1:26–27 thus: "Let *us* make man in *our* image, after *our* likeness. So God created man in his own image, *male* and *female*."[4]

Oliver Cowdery spent a few days among the North Union Believers and left several copies of the Book of Mormon with them in 1830, promising to return. Ashbel Kitchell, their impressive leader, kept thinking about Oliver's teachings. He decided that "if God had any hand in that work, he would inform me by some means, that I might know what to do, either by letting me have an interview with an angel, or by some other means give me knowledge of my duty."[5]

The Lord revealed Doctrine and Covenants 49 because it was not easy to discern exactly where Shaker beliefs and the restored gospel overlapped or diverged. A Believer named Leman Copley "embraced the fulness of the everlasting gospel." In May 1831 he went to Joseph, "apparently honest hearted, but still retained ideas that the Shakers were right in some particulars of their faith; and, in order to have a more perfect understanding on the subject," Joseph's history says, "I inquired of the Lord and received the following revelation."[6] Church historian John Whitmer added that Copley "was anxious that some of the elders should go to his former brethren and preach the gospel."[7]

CONTENT

Doctrine and Covenants 49 is a mission call to Sidney Rigdon, Parley P. Pratt, and Leman Copley. The Lord commands them to preach the gospel in its fulness to the nearby Believers, who desired to know the truth "in part, but not all" (v. 2). They are, therefore, not reconciled to the will of Christ and need to repent. The Lord sends missionaries to preach the gospel of repentance to them. He assigns Leman this call so he can reason with the Shakers based on what he will learn from Sidney and Parley. If Leman will learn the gospel, the Lord will bless him. Otherwise, Leman will not prosper.

"[I] have sent mine Only Begotten Son into the world for the redemption of the world, and have decreed that he that receiveth him shall be saved, and he that receiveth him not shall be damned" (v. 5), Heavenly Father says. The ungodly crucified God's Only Begotten Son, but Christ now reigns on his Father's right hand and will soon descend again to earth to vanquish his enemies. No mortal or even angel will know when the Lord comes until it happens. Mankind can be certain that rejecting Christ equals damnation and that he comes soon, but they cannot be certain exactly when. God wants everyone to repent, for everyone is sinful except those "holy men" whom he has reserved and of whom the world knows nothing (v. 8).

To facilitate the imperative need to repent, God has restored his everlasting covenant. The nations of the earth can submit to his law by humbling themselves or they will be compelled to be humble when the Savior comes. Willing submission is best, so first he commands three servants to go to the Shakers and tell them to believe on the name of Jesus Christ the Eternal God and repent and be baptized in his name as a requirement before receiving forgiveness. To those who accept this invitation, God will give the gift of the Holy Ghost by the laying on of hands through the elders of the Church.

Those who oppose or obstruct marriage are not God's servants, for he instituted the practice of marriage and made it sacred. It is right for a man to have a wife and for the two of them to unite, be a family, and have children so that the earth might accomplish the purpose of its creation, namely, to be part of God's work of creating and exalting his children (Moses 1:36–39).

Those who encourage others not to eat meat are not doing so because God appointed them to. He created animals for the use of mankind, so there is plenty of food and clothing for his children, but he did not grant that one man should own or occupy more than any other. The world lies in sin because inequality is so rampant. The Lord curses those who waste animal life when there is no need.

Christ will not come in the form of a woman or a man traveling on the earth. False Christs will. The Lord commands the Saints to look for the prophesied signs of the Second Coming. The Saints must watch, study, and be prayerful. Israel will be gathered to the restored Church and Zion built before Christ descends from heaven.

Sidney, Parley, and Leman are sent to convey these teachings to the Believers. The Lord commands, "Repent of all your sins" (v. 26), and he promises to answer their prayers and prepare the way before them. He will remain with them and ensure that they are not put to shame. "I am Jesus Christ," he emphasizes, "and I come quickly" (v. 28).

OUTCOMES

Doctrine and Covenants 49 clarifies errors and truths in Shaker doctrine. Is the Lord speaking to clarify the nature of the Godhead? Often in the Doctrine and Covenants we hear Christ speaking of himself as the Son of God. Section 49 ends that way, but most of the revelation is in Heavenly Father's voice. This is one of only two places in the Doctrine and Covenants where we hear the Father speak of Christ as his Only Begotten Son.

The revelation clarifies that Ann Lee was not Christ, nor is any man that comes claiming he is. Christ will come with power from heaven. Section 49 clarifies that the Shakers erred in thinking marriage is a temporary, human institution. Because the Shakers did not understand God's plan to embody his children on earth and make them immortal by resurrection and fully divine by exaltation, their opposition to marriage and procreation was counter to his plan. They were thwarting it, and section 49 tells them so. Similarly, Shakers erred in rejecting the ordinance of baptism and the laying on of hands for the gift of the Holy Ghost.

Section 49 affirms Shaker beliefs that were aligned with restored truths. Their beliefs were correct on the evils of inequality (v. 20) and exploiting the environment—"sheddeth blood" or "wasteth flesh"—for no need (v. 21).

Sidney and Leman left the day the revelation was given, a Saturday, and were in North Union in time to witness the Shakers' evening meeting. They visited with Kitchell afterward, discussing whether sexual relations, even in marriage, were Christian. The elders spent the night among the Shakers. Parley arrived in North Union early on the Sabbath and asked his companions how things were going. Sidney told him of the previous evening's discussion and that he (Sidney) and Kitchell had asked the missionaries not to debate doctrines but to join the Shakers for worship. Parley refused to sit by silently. "They had come with the authority of the Lord Jesus Christ," he contended, "and the people must hear it." The missionaries sat through the service respectfully. Afterwards Sidney rose and told them he had a message from the Lord Jesus Christ specifically for them.

"Could he have the privilege of delivering it? He was told he might." Sidney read Section 49 and asked the Shakers to receive it.[8]

Here was the answer to Ashbel Kitchell's desire that God would tell him whether Mormonism was true. He rejected it. He responded to the message of section 49, saying, "The Christ that dictated that I was well acquainted with, and had been from a boy, that I had been much troubled to get rid of his influence, and I wished to have nothing more to do with him; and as for any gift he had authorized them to exercise among us, I would release them & their Christ from any further burden about us, and take all the responsibility on myself."[9]

"You cannot," Sidney Rigdon protested. "I wish to hear the people speak." Kitchell told the Shakers to make their feelings known. They echoed their leader, and Sidney acceded to their will. Parley Pratt rose and shook his coat, signifying that responsibility had shifted from the elders to the Believers. Kitchell wrote that Parley "said he shook the dust from his garments as a testimony against us, that we had rejected the word of the Lord Jesus."[10]

"You filthy beast," Kitchell said to Parley. "Dare you presume to come in here, and try to imitate a man of God by shaking your filthy tail; confess your sins and purge your soul from your lusts, and your other abominations before you ever presume to do the like again."[11] What a scene that must have been. By Kitchell's account he cowed the missionaries with his forceful rebuke. Parley Pratt got back on his horse and went straight home to Kirtland. Sidney stayed for supper with the Shakers. Leman stayed overnight. Years later Parley summed up the whole episode with a single sentence: "We fulfilled this mission, as we were commanded, in a settlement of this strange people, near Cleveland, Ohio; but they utterly refused to hear or obey the gospel."[12]

Doctrine & Covenants 50

ORIGIN

"Have you heard the news?" Alvah Hancock asked his younger brother.

"What news?" asked twenty-seven-year-old Levi.

"Four men have come and have brought a book with them that they call history and a record of the people that once inhabited this land."

Levi wanted to know more.

"Do you not recollect of reading what the Savior said, how he had other sheep which were not of his fold at Jerusalem?" Alvah asked.

"I do," Levi said, increasingly anxious.

"Well, they were here," Alvah stated. Christ "came and taught them the same doctrine that he taught them at Jerusalem." The missionaries "baptized for the remission of sins and are building up the church as the apostles used to do in the days of Christ. Tomorrow they are to hold a meeting at Mr. Jackson's in Mayfield." Alvah continued, "They lay hands on those they baptize and bestow on them the Holy Ghost."

With these words Levi believed and felt "something pleasant and delightful. It seemed like a wash of something warm to me in the face and ran over my body which gave me a feeling I cannot describe."

"It is the truth. I can feel it," he told Alvah. "I will go and hear for myself tomorrow."

Levi arrived early that Sabbath morning to ensure a good seat. Finally Parley P. Pratt began to preach. "I sat with both ears open for the first word he spoke," Levi said. "I believed all he said." Parley invited the people to search the scriptures and know for themselves. He asked if anyone would like to respond. The former Reformed Baptist minister Sidney Rigdon arose "and advised the people not to contend against what they had heard." Then Oliver Cowdery, who was slightly younger than Levi, rose and testified that he was an eyewitness of the Book of Mormon. Parley invited those who believed to come and be baptized. Levi's father, sister, and others accepted. That afternoon "the Devil began to rage" as a neighbor to the Hancocks tried "every way he could to discourage us from believing."

Levi discerned between the Holy Spirit he had felt and the dark influence of this man. He set out the next morning to find Elder Pratt. "I dismounted my horse," Levi wrote, "and went and asked Parley P. Pratt if he would baptize me."

"I will if you believe," Parley replied. "I told him I believed that Jesus is the son of God, and felt within my heart that the things he had told us were the truth." Parley baptized Levi, who immediately began to spread the gospel. Within a week he was ordained an elder and began holding meetings himself. Oliver Cowdery, Parley Pratt, and their companions continued their mission west, leaving zealous, if inexperienced, elders to continue the work.

One night as Levi prayed, he envisioned a man who invited him (in the imagery of Matthew 11:29) to shoulder Christ's yoke. "I thought it was the Lord talking to me," Levi said, "and I felt willing to obey him." It seemed to Levi as if he could fly. "All my senses were perfect," he noted, "and I realized many things that I am not able to write or express with my tongue." The personage in the dream told him to "bear testimony to the world of the truth of the work."

Then one day three elders—Edson Fuller, Heman Bassett, and Burr Riggs—visited the home where Levi was working. He had not met them before. They preached and baptized in the area. Then the three elders began receiving revelations and seeing angels while falling down and foaming at the mouth. Burr Riggs jumped up and down, swung from the roof's crossbeams for a few minutes, and then fell down as if he were dead. After an hour or two he awoke and prophesied about what he had seen while unconscious. Edson Fuller fell down and Heman Bassett imitated a baboon. He testified that an angel had given him a revelation, and he read it to his companions.

Levi was confused. These things seemed ungodly to him, but he had never experienced such dramatic manifestations. He concluded that perhaps he was not as pure as the other elders. He didn't dare question them for fear that would be doubting the Holy Ghost.[1]

Similar experiences continued through the winter of 1830 and 1831. Oliver Cowdery had led his missionaries to Missouri. Joseph remained in New York. He had sent John Whitmer to preside over the hundreds of new converts in Ohio. Even so, they lacked experience and leadership, and it showed. Whitmer was bewildered at what he found: Saints pretending to fight with Laban's sword or sliding across the floor like snakes, saying they were on their way to preach the gospel to the Lamanites.[2] When he returned from Missouri, Parley Pratt visited the branches of Saints in Ohio and saw some swoon, fall into what he called "ecstasies," make unnatural gestures, and claim revelations and visions that did not teach anything sanctifying. "In short," Parley wrote, "a false and lying spirit seemed to be creeping into the church." He recognized that this infection had occurred while the Church in Ohio was without discerning leadership, between the time he and his companions left and Joseph arrived.[3]

Joseph Smith learned early in his life the difference between true and false spirits. As he walked briskly toward the hill after listening most of the night to Moroni, his mind turned to tales he had heard about buried treasure. He thought he would need to be courageous and strong so he could obtain the plates. His thoughts raced about the value of the gold, crowding out the angel's instructions. Near the top of the hill, Joseph found a large stone covering the box in which the plates were hidden. He pried it up, looked in, and beheld the plates and the seer stones, just as Moroni had said. He attempted to take them out of their hiding place but could not. "Why can I not obtain this book?" he cried out. "Because you have not kept the commandments of the Lord," Moroni replied to Joseph's surprise.

The angel seized the moment to teach Joseph. "I will show you the distance between light and darkness, and the operation of a good spirit and an evil one.

An evil spirit will try to crowd your mind with every evil and wicked thing to keep every good thought and feeling out of your mind, but you must keep your mind always staid upon God, that no evil may come into your heart." Just as Joseph had learned earlier in the grove, on the hillside he experienced both the power of the devil and the power of God. He began to discern the difference. But Satan remained a powerful influence. It was easy for Joseph to think of using the plates for his own gain. Moroni explained that it was not yet time for him to receive the plates. Still the experience had been important. Joseph now knew how powerfully Satan would work to ruin his gift. "I had been tempted of the advisary," Joseph said later, "and saught the Plates to obtain riches and kept not the commandment that I should have an eye single to the glory of God therefore I was chastened and saught diligently to obtain the plates."[4]

By the time he arrived in Kirtland, Joseph was ready to apply the lessons he had learned by encountering, discerning, and rejecting false spirits. Philo Dibble, one of the early Ohio converts, witnessed the "variety of false spirits" among the Ohio Saints, "such as caused jumping, shouting, [and] falling down." According to Dibble, as soon as Joseph arrived in Ohio and discerned the situation, he said, "God has sent me here, and the devil must leave here, or I will." Joseph stayed, and "those delusive spirits were not seen nor heard any more at that time."[5]

John Whitmer recognized that the new Saints were not familiar with the variety of spirits or influences that could be mistaken for the Holy Spirit. He wrote that the Saints' ungodly behaviors "grieved the servants of the Lord, and some conversed together on this subject." They consulted with Joseph to see what the Lord had to say, "for many would not turn from their folly," Whitmer wrote, "unless God would give a revelation."[6]

Parley Pratt described how the revelation came. "Feeling our weakness and inexperience, and lest we should err in judgment concerning these spiritual phenomena, myself, John Murdock, and several other elders, went to Joseph Smith, and asked him to inquire of the Lord concerning these spirits or manifestations.

"After we had joined in prayer in his translating room, he dictated in our presence the following revelation:—(Each sentence was uttered slowly and very distinctly, and with a pause between each, sufficiently long for it to be recorded by an ordinary writer, in long hand."[7] The revelation is recorded now in Doctrine and Covenants 50.

CONTENT

"Give ear to the voice of the living God," the Lord commands the elders of the Church in Doctrine and Covenants 50 and "attend to the words of wisdom which shall be given unto you" (v. 1).

The Lord explains the unusual phenomena the elders have been witnessing so much of recently. There are many false, deceptive influences. Satan himself is chief among them. He seeks to overthrow the elders and make evil good and vice versa. The Lord is watching the elders and has seen evil increasing in the Saints who covenanted to take his name upon them. He blesses the faithful Saints with eternal life and guarantees he will bring the hypocrites and deceivers to judgment. He knows very well that the Church is infected with people pretending to be what they are not. They have deceived some, thereby giving Satan power, but it will not last. The liars will be recalled, their hypocrisy detected, and their membership in the Church terminated either before or after they die, according to the Lord's will. He will choose when to expose them. He urges the Saints to beware of these deceptive influences or they are bound to go contrary to the will of the Lord.

The Lord invites the elders to reason with him. His goal is to help them understand the situation in which they now find themselves. He agrees to speak to them in terms they can understand. To reduce the perplexing problem to its basic principles, he begins a line of questioning: What were you ordained to do? He also gives the answer: To preach the gospel by the power of the Holy Ghost—the Comforter—whose role is to teach the truth. Then what happened? The elders were influenced by spirits they could not understand, yet they thought these were divine influences. Was such a conclusion justified? He lets them answer that question for themselves. His point is made. He has sent them to teach truth plainly through the comforting—not confusing—power of the Holy Ghost, but they have mistaken false influences for the Holy Spirit. His point made, the Lord promises to be merciful unto them (v. 16). Elders who were once easily deceived will now be discerning.

The Lord continues his teaching with another direct question. Do those who are ordained and sent to preach the gospel do it by the Holy Spirit or some other way? "If it be some other way it is not of God," the Lord says (v. 18). The Lord proceeds to his next point, this one about those who listen to the elders preach. Do they receive the teaching by the power of the Holy Ghost or some other way? "If it be some other way it is not of God," he repeats (v. 20). He has prepared the elders for his final question: Why do you not understand that the Holy Ghost mediates the communication between those who preach the gospel and those who receive it as truth, and that when the Holy Ghost mediates the communication, both preacher and receiver understand, and both are taught and experience joy together? Communication that does not teach and build is not of God. It is darkness. God communicates light. Those who receive God's light and persevere receive more and more. The Lord teaches the elders these principles so that they can know the truth and chase darkness from the Church.

The Lord reminds the elders that those he ordains, he calls to be the servants of all. They possess the priesthood by Heavenly Father's will and Jesus Christ's appointment. None of the elders could possess it, however, unless they were first purified and cleansed from all sin. Then their will becomes God's will, and they can therefore ask him in the name of Jesus Christ for whatever they want, and it will be done. They are exhorted to lead the Church by the power of the priesthood, and if they do so, false spirits will be subject to them. The Lord gives the elders precise, step-by-step instructions for dealing with false spirits in their ministries. If they see something happen that they do not understand, and they do not feel or experience the spirit of it themselves, they should ask Heavenly Father in the name of Jesus Christ for discernment. Then, as promised, He will answer their prayer. He promises to give them the Spirit if it is a true manifestation. If it is false, he will not send the Spirit, in which case they would know that it was a spirit of darkness and that God will give them power over it. The elders should then announce that the manifestation was darkness, being careful not to make accusations but to specifically identify the prevailing influence as ungodly. The elders must be especially careful at this point. As power to discern and subject false spirits flows through them, they can all too easily succumb to false spirits themselves—such as an adversarial or boastful attitude that compounds rather than solves a problem. To prevent this, the elders who exercise power over false spirits should acknowledge that the power is God's and be joyful that he found them worthy to receive it. By exercising the priesthood according to these principles, the elders will have power to overcome everything that is not of God.

The Lord blesses and forgives those who hear Joseph dictate this revelation. The Lord calls Joseph Wakefield, Parley P. Pratt, and John Corrill to visit the branches of the Church and strengthen them with sound teaching and encouragement. He commands that no one hinder them from fulfilling their callings, as Bishop Edward Partridge apparently has. The Lord promises to forgive Bishop Partridge if he repents.

"Ye are little children and ye cannot bear all things now," the Lord says lovingly. "Ye must grow in grace and in the knowledge of the truth" (v. 40). He commands the elders not to fear. "You are of them that my Father hath given me; and none of them that my Father hath given me shall be lost" (vv. 41–42). He testifies that he and Heavenly Father are one. He is in Heavenly Father, and Heavenly Father is in him, and to the extent that the elders have received Christ, they are in him, and he is in them. "I am in your midst," he assures them (v. 44). He is the Good Shepherd, the bedrock of Israel. All who build on him will never fall. The day will come when the elders will hear his voice, see him, and know that he exists. "Watch, therefore," he concludes, "that ye may be ready" (v. 46).

OUTCOMES

Doctrine and Covenants 50 is a masterpiece, perhaps the finest example of teaching anywhere. Christ speaks on the elders' intellectual level in order to be understood. He reaches them where they are and enlightens them. This kind of teaching has results beyond mastery of facts. As a result of it, the weak become strong, and the deceived become discerning. Though Satan had power over the deceived elders, those who "attend to the words" (v. 1) of this revelation are promised power over him. Christ assures them, "The spirits shall be subject unto you" (v. 30), on condition that they act on his instructions precisely. Do they?

Elder Jared Carter, who before the revelation had witnessed false spirits and debated with himself whether they were divine or not, learned the revelation and tried it. He was conducting a sacrament meeting in Amherst, Ohio, with his companion when a young woman fell to the floor. Jared, doubting that the Holy Spirit would interrupt the sacrament, thought a false spirit was at work. He suggested to his companion that they "try that Spirit according to the revelation that God had given." He explained how they followed verses 31–34 precisely. "We kneeled down and asked our Heavenly Father in the name of Christ, that if that spirit which the sister possessed was of him, he would give it to us. We prayed in faith, but we did not receive the Spirit." Jared's companion made a weak statement, "which was not proclaiming against the spirit" as verse 32 commands. "I arose and proclaimed against it with a loud voice," Jared wrote, reflecting his intimate knowledge of the revelation. Most of the congregation objected, sure that the young woman was full of the Holy Ghost, like the queen in Alma 19. But this was a counterfeit Jared discerned by the Holy Ghost and rebuked by the power of the priesthood. He lost much of his influence among that group of Saints but, as he wrote, "I received assurance that I had the approbation of my Heavenly Father, which was better than the good will of many deceived brethren."[8]

Section 50 puzzles some modern readers, who sometimes jump to the conclusion that anyone who sees a vision or falls to the floor unconscious or speaks in an unknown tongue is clearly not experiencing the Holy Ghost. If those were the criteria for discerning, we would have to reject large parts of the Book of Mormon and several sections of the Doctrine and Covenants along with much of our history. It is not that simple. Satan is abroad deceiving. As section 50 suggests, a knee-jerk reaction against false spirits can actually lead persons to be "seized" with a false spirit themselves. Ironically, a smug certainty that one would not be fool enough to fall for the kinds of things Levi Hancock did may indicate that one has already been deceived. Joseph taught, "It is that smooth, sophisticated influence of the Devil, by which he deceives the whole world."[9]

Discerning spirits takes a sound mind, but it is a spiritual process. To gain power over false spirits, we must obey the voice of Jesus Christ, be cleansed and purified by him, and learn the difference between light and darkness. For Joseph Smith, Levi Hancock, Jared Carter, and many others, that lesson has been learned by experiencing both kinds of spirits and learning to recognize the difference.

Like Jared Carter, several elders acted on the revelation and got the Church back in order. Parley Pratt told how he obeyed the Lord's command in verse 37: "Joseph Wakefield and myself visited the several branches of the Church, rebuking the wrong spirits which had crept in among them, setting in order things that were wanting."[10]

Doctrine & Covenants 51

ORIGIN

Prosperous New York families left for Ohio to obey Doctrine and Covenants 37 and 38.[1] Polly and Joseph Knight fled persecutors near Colesville, New York, leaving their farms and mills to be sold. The remaining sixty-seven Colesville Saints helped each other prepare for the journey, determined "to travel together in one company" under the leadership of Newel Knight. He remembered that "the Saints manifested unshaken confidence in the great work in which they were engaged." They left in April 1831 in a wagon train bound for Cayuga Lake and thence by canals to Lake Erie. In a journey toward Zion both geographical and metaphorical, together they braved persecution, injuries, and sickness. Only one turned back. For two weeks the company was detained at Buffalo, New York, their boat confined to the harbor by ice. After "a rather disagreeable voyage" they arrived in Ohio.[2] An antagonistic newspaper there reported the arrival of "about two hundred men, women and children of the deluded followers of Jo Smith's Bible speculation."[3]

Now Bishop Edward Partridge had a problem. It was his responsibility to organize and settle the immigrant Saints. Leman Copley had offered to let the Colesville Saints settle on some of his 759 acres in Thompson, Ohio.[4] Bishop Partridge asked Joseph how to organize the immigrant Saints and manage the Church's property. Joseph asked the Lord, who gave Doctrine and Covenants 51 at Thompson.

CONTENT

In Doctrine and Covenants 51 the Lord instructs Bishop Partridge to organize the Saints according to the law of consecration and warns that he will cut them off if they organize their social and economic affairs any other way. The Lord commands Bishop Partridge and his counselors to provide stewardships for the Saints. Each family's stewardship is to be relatively equal, depending on circumstances, needs, and wants.

The Lord uses the word wants *four times in section 51. He first used that word in section 42, when he gave the law of consecration, saying that the bishop should keep the Church's surplus property for use in relieving poverty, so that everyone in need "may be amply supplied and receive according to his wants" (D&C 42:33). That word no longer means what it did in those revelations and others.*

One linguist who specializes in translating the scriptures noted that the Church's official lexicon "concedes that some contexts are ambiguous and can take more than one meaning. [Nevertheless,] there is not one use of the noun 'want' anywhere in the D&C that has the meaning of 'desire.'

"The word 'want' has undergone a major sense change in our society in the last 100 years. We live in a time of instant gratification where advertising has shifted the synonyms 'need' and 'want' into antonyms. The word 'want' used to express the sense of 'lack or deficiency' is obscure today.

"Noah Webster published his great dictionary in 1828. In it we find the reverse of today's usage. The primary meaning he lists and the next three definitions all deal with 'lacking' or 'poverty' or 'deficiency' or 'necessity.' Only the fifth and most obscure general definition admits the sense of 'desire.' It would be a mistake to consider this last definition as a frequent sense intended in our scriptures."[5]

Joseph Smith used the words wants *and* needs *as synonyms. Perhaps by using both words in section 51, verse 3, the Lord means to emphasize them, or perhaps he intends to expand the idea of needs beyond mere necessities. It is most unlikely that he used* want *with today's definition, "something desired, demanded, or required."*

Along with the stewardship, the Lord tells Bishop Partridge to provide each family a written statement that the property belonged to them. If the stewards should be excommunicated, they would keep the property the bishop had deeded to them. They would have no claim, however, on the property they had consecrated to the bishop on behalf of the poor. Such a system would stand up in court. The Lord commands that the money consecrated by the Saints from Colesville, New York, be consecrated back to them and that an agent be appointed to use the money to provide them with food and clothing. The Lord commands all to deal honestly, be alike, and receive alike, so they can become one, as he commanded them in Doctrine and Covenants 38:27.

The money consecrated by the Colesville Saints is to be used for their needs, not given to Saints in another branch. If another branch of the Church is to receive money from the Colesville Saints, they must agree to pay it back and then keep their word. The bishop or the appointed agent for the Colesville Saints should arrange such loans. The bishop is also commanded to establish a storehouse for the Church in which to store surplus money and food. Because all his time is to be occupied caring for the Saints in these ways, the bishop is to receive a living for himself and his family from the Saints. Organizing themselves according to the law of consecration is a privilege given them from the Lord. He consecrates to them the land on which the Saints live until such time as he commands them to go to another place, a place the Lord will provide. Meanwhile, the Saints are to assume they will be in Ohio for years and act accordingly. The Lord gives these instructions as an example to Bishop Partridge. He should follow this model in other branches of the Church wherever they may be. The Lord covenants that faithful, wise, and just stewards will enter his joy. They will inherit eternal life.

OUTCOMES

This revelation begins to implement the law of consecration. As originally given, it instructed Bishop Partridge to obtain a deed from Leman Copley for his land, "if he harden not his heart."[6] But Copley did harden his heart and refused to sign over the land to the bishop. He forced the Colesville Saints off his land, and the Lord sent them to Missouri to establish Zion there (D&C 54).[7] Thus, when Doctrine and Covenants 51 was first published in 1835, the instructions about Bishop Partridge obtaining a deed to Copley's land were omitted.

Bishop Partridge tried to implement the revelation's other instructions in Missouri. He purchased hundreds of acres and established a storehouse to supply the needs of the Saints. He was sued by a man named Bates who had donated fifty dollars to purchase land and then decided he wanted it back.[8] Bates's suit was granted, apparently on the grounds that the bishop had done what section 51 originally said. He had purchased the land in his own name and then leased parts of it to individual stewards while he remained, on behalf of the Lord, the legal owner.

Bishop Partridge must have felt that the law of the land prohibited him from carrying out section 51. Joseph wrote to Bishop Partridge in Missouri in May 1833 to counsel him what to do, explaining much of section 51 in the process. Bates had expected something tangible in return for his fifty dollars.[9] Joseph assured the bishop that he remained bound by the law of the Lord to receive consecrated property to purchase inheritances for the poor. Joseph emphasized that such offerings were legal and in no way coerced: "Any man has a right . . . agreeable to all laws of our country, to donate, give or consecrate all that he feels disposed to give." Joseph counseled the bishop to ensure that all offerings were legal by making sure that donors understood they were giving money freely for the poor, not in exchange for anything temporal. "This way no man can take advantage of you in law [again]," Joseph wrote. He also counseled the bishop to apply section 51 by deeding pieces of land to Saints as their "individual property." Joseph called this "private stewardship," not ownership.[10] Bishop Partridge issued several such deeds based on section 51 (see commentary on

D&C 63). When section 51 was first published in 1835, much of verse 5 was added to keep individuals like Bates from suing the Church again. Joseph wrote Bishop Partridge that the doctrine in verse 5 was given so "that rich men cannot have power to disinherit the poor by obtaining again that which they have consecrated."[11]

Doctrine & Covenants 52

ORIGIN

Acting on the commandment in Doctrine and Covenants 44 to convene a conference, Joseph promised the priesthood leaders a blessing if they would come humbly and faithfully. "Therefore," John Whitmer wrote, "the elders assembled from the East, and the West, from the North and the South." Joseph presided over the series of priesthood meetings June 3–5, 1831. He and others prophesied at the conference, rebuked the devil, and ordained the first high priests in the Church. The next day he received Doctrine and Covenants 52 as directions to the elders.[1]

CONTENT

The Lord concludes the conference by giving the elders specific instructions regarding what they should accomplish before the next conference, which he commands them to hold in Missouri—the land that he will consecrate for his covenant people. The Lord commands Joseph and Sidney Rigdon to journey to Missouri as soon as possible. In Doctrine and Covenants 52 he promises that it will "be made known unto them what they shall do" (v. 4) as will "the land of your inheritance" (v. 5) if they remain faithful. If they do not, he will cut them off as he sees fit.

The Lord also calls Lyman Wight and John Corrill to go to Missouri. He calls John Murdock and Hyrum Smith to go to Missouri after detouring through Detroit. Along the way, they are to preach from the scriptures and from what they learn from the Holy Spirit in answer to their faithful prayers. The Lord commands these two companionships to preach, baptize by immersion, and confirm their converts immediately thereafter by the laying on of hands. He communicates his urgency, for he will soon end his redeeming work, judge mankind, and pronounce the repentant victorious over Satan. The Lord warns Lyman Wight to beware. Satan wants to separate him from the Lord, but the Lord promises to give power to those who are faithful to him.

The devil is at large, going about unobstructed and deceiving all nations. The Lord reveals a pattern the Saints can follow to avoid being deceived by false teachers. Those who pray and are humble and repentant are received by the Lord *if* they receive and obey his ordinances. Those who speak humble words that enlighten others are accepted by the Lord only *if* they obey his ordinances. Those whose voice or body trembles while speaking will become strong *if* it is the Lord's power that causes the trembling. They will speak wise, praiseworthy words that adhere to the revelations and restored truths. Those who are overwhelmed while speaking and do not regain their composure nor speak wisely according to restored truths are not speaking for God. This pattern provides the way to discern whether people are being influenced by the Holy Spirit or by some counterfeit influence. The Lord has restored the gifts of the Holy Ghost, and the Saints can receive them by faith. The elders are commanded to discern the difference between the Spirit of the Lord and Satan's deceptions.

The Lord calls twenty-four elders to serve as missionaries on their way to Missouri for the next conference, at which time the Lord will reveal to them the land he will consecrate for Zion. Except for those appointed to travel with Joseph, each pair is to take a different route and preach along the way. The Lord promises to bless the faithful with fruit or, in other words, rewards that grow from their labors.

The Lord calls Joseph Wakefield and Solomon Humphrey to proselyte in the East among their relatives, teaching the scriptures and backing them with personal testimony. Because Heman Bassett has sinned, his calling is revoked and given to Simonds Ryder. The Lord commands that Jared Carter and George James be ordained as priests. The elders remaining in Ohio are to watch over the Church in the absence of their brethren and preach the gospel locally, working for their living to keep them from idolatry and wickedness. They are commanded to meet the needs of the poor and sick. Those who fail to do so are not numbered as the Lord's disciples.

The Lord emphasizes again that if the brethren are faithful, they will assemble in Missouri—the land he will give them as his heirs, though at the time it belongs to their enemies. There is no need to worry, however, for the Lord promises to accelerate the construction of New Jerusalem when it is time, and he will crown the faithful with joy and rejoicing.

OUTCOMES

Doctrine and Covenants 52 gives the Saints knowledge and therefore power to discern devilish counterfeits from the Lord's power. Satan tried mightily to deceive the Saints from the time missionaries first arrived in Ohio through the priesthood meetings held just before section 52 was given. He mimicked spiritual gifts and convinced many people they were under the influence of the Holy Ghost.

Joseph taught that "some, by a long face and sanctimonious prayers, and very pious sermons, had power to lead the minds of the ignorant and unwary."[2] The fact that individuals speak well or are overwhelmed with emotion is not itself evidence that their actions are acceptable to God. Section 52 adds important criteria for discerning. Do those overcome with emotion regain their composure and teach wise, restored truth? Do those who pray, whose attitude seems Christian, obey the ordinances Jesus has established for his Church and kingdom? Do they follow the order of Jesus' Church? Do excellent speakers obey Christ's ordinances? Christ does not accept the sanctimonious prayers or pious sermons of those who are unwilling to obey his ordinances, and neither should the Saints. The knowledge in section 52 empowers the Saints to separate satanic imitations from the Lord's power.

Section 52 is exciting. This is the first revelation to identify Missouri as the location of Zion, the Saints' inheritance. It calls more than two dozen men to travel to Missouri for a conference at which the Lord will reveal more specifically the location for New Jerusalem. The Saints received section 52 with great anticipation, and many went to great lengths to obey its commands.

Joseph and those the Lord called to travel with him left Kirtland, Ohio, in mid-June and arrived in Independence, Missouri, about a month later. They were followed by most of the others who were called, taking different routes and making converts along the way, as section 52 commanded. The Lord fulfilled his promise to reveal more about Zion (D&C 57).

Section 52 draws the battle lines for a culture war. Missouri, it says, is the place the Lord has chosen for the Saints' inheritance. But in 1831 Missouri was inhabited by people the Lord called "enemies" (v. 42). The Lord's straightforwardness may make some a bit squeamish, but he sees things as they are and will be, and he knows his friends and his enemies.

Doctrine & Covenants 53

ORIGIN

A business partner of Newel Whitney, Sidney Gilbert was an entrepreneur in northern Ohio when the first missionaries to that area taught him the gospel in 1830. He was not named in Doctrine and Covenants 52 among the many brethren called by the Lord to journey to Missouri in the summer of 1831. He asked the Prophet what the Lord had in mind for him to do. As a preface to Doctrine and Covenants 53, Joseph's history says that he "inquired of the Lord and received the following" revelation calling Sidney Gilbert.[1]

CONTENT

The Lord assures Sidney Gilbert that He had heard his prayers concerning his duty in the Lord's Church. In Doctrine and Covenants 53 the Lord commands Sidney to forsake the world, to receive the priesthood, and to preach the law of the gospel—faith, repentance, baptism for remission of sins, and reception of the Holy Ghost by the laying on of hands. The Lord also appoints Sidney to be an agent for the Church in the soon-to-be-revealed Zion. Sidney is to journey to that place with Joseph Smith and Sidney Rigdon. The Lord calls these Sidney's "first ordinances" (v. 6) and he promises to reveal the rest later based on Sidney's work. Lastly, the Lord reminds Sidney that only those who endure to the end will be saved.

OUTCOMES

Sidney and his wife, Elizabeth, traveled to Missouri with Joseph Smith to obey Doctrine and Covenants 53. There, at the Lord's command (D&C 57), Sidney established a store to provide for the Saints. He helped Bishop Partridge purchase land for Zion. When the Saints were driven from Jackson County in 1833, Sidney was among the Church leaders who tried to pacify the mob and then obtain justice. Cholera claimed the life of Sidney in the summer of 1834. Until the end he was anxiously engaged in the cause of Zion.

Doctrine & Covenants 54

ORIGIN

Leman Copley had claimed land and was buying more than seven hundred acres in Thompson, Ohio. He "embraced the fulness of the everlasting gospel"[1] and preached the gospel to the Shakers, with whom he had affiliated before hearing the restored gospel (D&C 49). With the New York Saints migrating to Ohio to obey Doctrine and Covenants 37 and 38, Leman promised to let them settle on his farm in exchange for their labor.[2] Newel Knight led the New York Saints to Thompson, where they "commenced work in all good faith thinking to obtain a living by the sweat of the brow."[3] Then section 51 instructed Bishop Edward Partridge to obtain a deed from Leman for the land "if he harden not his heart."[4] But Leman did harden his heart. He didn't want consecration. He wanted exploitation.[5] He ordered the Saints off *his* land. Joseph Knight said they "had to leave his farm and pay sixty dollars damage for putting up his houses and planting his ground."[6] Where should they go and what should they do to provide for themselves?[7] Joseph Smith's history says that the Saints in Thompson, "not knowing what to do, sent in their elders for me to inquire of the Lord for them."[8] He did, and the Lord answered with Doctrine and Covenants 54.

CONTENT

The Lord addresses his words in Doctrine and Covenants 54 to Newel Knight, the presiding elder of the Saints in Thompson, Ohio. He commands Newel to "stand fast in the office" he has been appointed to (v. 2).

Repentance and humility are the conditions upon which the Saints in Thompson will escape their enemies. Leman Copley's covenant to consecrate land is now null and void, and the Lord curses Leman for breaking his covenant: "Wo to him by whom this offense cometh, for it had been better for him that he had been drowned in the depth of the sea" (v. 5). The Lord blesses the Saints who have kept the covenant. He will be merciful to them. He commands them to flee from their enemies by traveling to Missouri as a group, appointing a treasurer to pay fares and tolls along the way. They are to travel to western Missouri, which borders the territory recently set apart for Native Americans to settle. The Lord commands the Saints to make their own living until Zion can be established and land provided for them to inhabit. He commands them to "be patient in tribulation" until his coming. "They who have sought me early shall find rest to their souls" (v. 10).

OUTCOMES

As a result of receiving Doctrine and Covenants 54, the Saints from Colesville, New York, continued their trek as a group all the way to Missouri. Led ably by Newel Knight, they became the nucleus of the Church in Jackson County and gave their lives to building Zion.

Doctrine & Covenants 55

ORIGIN

William W. Phelps edited the *Ontario Phoenix* newspaper in Canandaigua, New York. He aspired to public office, could be arrogant and condescending, and yet became convinced of the truth of the Book of Mormon and bore a beautiful testimony of its truthfulness. In that spirit he went to Ohio to find Joseph just as the Prophet was leaving for Missouri. William told the Prophet that he had come "to do the will of the Lord." Joseph asked the Lord what that was, and the Lord answered with the revelation recorded in Doctrine and Covenants 55, calling both William Phelps and Joseph Coe to the work.[1]

CONTENT

William Phelps is called and chosen of the Lord in Doctrine and Covenants 55 to join in his work upon the earth. The Lord promises him forgiveness and the gift of the Holy Ghost by the laying on of hands on the condition that he is baptized with the pure motive of love for God. If William obeys that command, he will be ordained an elder by Joseph and called to preach the law of the gospel. Then William will have power to likewise bestow on the repentant the gift of the Holy Ghost by the laying on of hands. William is called to assist Oliver Cowdery as a printer, editor, and writer for the Church, including producing books for the education of children. This calling requires William to go to Missouri with Joseph and Sidney and to settle and work there. The Lord commands Joseph Coe to go with them also, and He promises to reveal more later according to His will.

OUTCOMES

William Phelps obeyed Doctrine and Covenants 55. He received the ordinances of baptism and confirmation. He traveled with Joseph to Missouri and became the Lord's printer there. He published the Church's first newspaper and hymnal and Joseph's revelations. Joseph Coe also responded to the Lord's commands and traveled to Missouri to obey section 55.

Doctrine & Covenants 56

ORIGIN

Ezra Thayre, an early convert who had come to Ohio from New York, consecrated his money to the Church and lived with Joseph's parents in the home of Frederick Williams while he was in Missouri on a mission. The Lord revealed that Ezra needed to "humble himself" and accept the calling and receive the priesthood. Everything depended on Ezra's agency, or, as the Lord put it, "if he be obedient unto my commandments."[1] But Ezra Thayre made selfish choices. The details are not clear, but apparently he wanted a deed for a part of the Williams farm in exchange for the money he had consecrated.

Meanwhile the Lord commanded Thomas Marsh to travel to Missouri with Ezra Thayre and Newel Knight to travel with Selah Griffin in the summer of 1831 (D&C 52:22, 32). Then, as often happens, complications arose. The Lord needed Newel Knight to preside over a whole group of Saints migrating to Missouri (D&C 54). Selah was therefore without a companion. Ezra refused to obey the commandments he had received, leaving Thomas without a companion. Finally Thomas approached Joseph "to inquire what he should do, as elder Ezra Thayre his yoke-fellow in the ministry, could not get ready for his mission to start." Joseph asked the Lord, who answered with Doctrine and Covenants 56.[2]

CONTENT

The Lord commands those who publicly declare that they have taken Christ's name upon themselves to hear and obey him. "Mine anger is kindled against the rebellious" (v. 1), he says in Doctrine and Covenants 56, and those choosing to resist his authority will shortly know his displeasure when he meets them at the judgment bar. Those who will not willingly suffer for the love of Christ, who will not follow him and do as he asks, will be damned. Those who choose to disobey the Lord's commandments will be severed from him when he sees fit—after he has given them the opportunity to exercise their agency to obey. The Lord may revoke commands that are not obeyed, and he holds the disobedient accountable. The Lord revokes the command for Thomas Marsh and Ezra Thayre to serve as companions on a mission to Missouri (D&C 52:22). Similarly, because Newel Knight was needed to lead the Saints in Thompson, Ohio, safely to Missouri (D&C 54), the Lord revokes the command for Newel to go with Selah Griffin to Missouri (D&C 52:32). The Lord then commands Selah Griffin to accompany Thomas Marsh. He commands Ezra Thayre to repent of his pride and selfishness and obey an earlier, uncanonized revelation in which the Lord commanded him not to seek to divide up the farm of Frederick Williams.[3] If Ezra will do as the Lord commands, his call to Missouri will still be in effect. If not, he will receive back the money he has paid to the Church, leave the farm, and be excommunicated.

The Lord then speaks to the Saints generally. They have much to accomplish and many sins to confess and forsake. He knows their sins and has not pardoned them because they seek their own will, not his. They are not content with what the Lord has granted them. The Lord curses the rich among them who will not share with the poor, their riches infecting their souls like a virus until Judgment Day, when they will realize it is too late to consecrate and thus they are damned. The Lord curses the poor who refuse to be humble and content, who lust and covet greedily and refuse to work with their own hands. The Lord blesses the humble and repentant poor. They will be delivered from sorrow and suffering at the Lord's second coming. In contrast to the cursed, unconsecrated rich who are consumed with regret, the righteous poor will be overwhelmed with joy as their children inherit the earth.

OUTCOMES

Thomas Marsh and Selah Griffin obeyed Doctrine and Covenants 56. As Thomas put it, they "journeyed to Missouri preaching by the way."[4] Little is known about Ezra Thayre's response. He did not go to Missouri on this mission, but he was not excommunicated, either. This is yet another revelation that wrestles with agency. The Lord called elders on missions, and some of them failed to act on their callings. The Lord revokes the refused callings and rearranges assignments so that the work is done without the help of the unwilling. The Lord does not coerce Ezra Thayre or anyone else to consecrate or serve. But if we suppose that this same Lord considers such disobedience unimportant, we have not read this revelation carefully. The Lord curses the rebellious and unconsecrated and promises undesirable futures for them. He blesses the obedient and promises a joyful eternity for them. This revelation allows Ezra to choose but outlines painful consequences for wrong choices.

Doctrine & Covenants 57

ORIGIN

Doctrine and Covenants 57 is the first revelation Joseph received in Missouri. After receiving the commandment in section 52 to travel to Missouri from Ohio, Joseph spent two weeks preparing and a month in making the long journey. He told the story in an 1835 church newspaper editorial:

"Having received, by an heavenly vision a commandment [D&C 52], in June [1831] . . . , to take my journey to the western boundaries of the State of Missouri, and there designate the very spot, which was to be the central spot, for the commencement of the gathering together of those who embrace the fulness of the everlasting gospel—I accordingly undertook the journey with certain ones of my brethren, and, after a long and tedious journey, suffering many privations and hardships, I arrived in Jackson county Missouri."[1]

Mindful of the prophecies of Isaiah, Joseph asked the Lord for details concerning their fulfillment: "When will the wilderness blossom as the rose; when will Zion be built up in her glory, and where will thy Temple stand unto which all nations shall come in the last days?"[2] Joseph described how the Lord answered with section 57 to have, among other Zion-building initiatives, Bishop Edward Partridge and Sidney Gilbert purchase land: "After viewing the country, seeking diligently at the hand of God, he manifested himself unto me, and designated to me and others, the very spot upon which he designed to commence the work of the gathering, and the upbuilding of an holy city, which should be called Zion:—Zion because it is to be a place of righteousness, and all who build thereon, are to worship the true and living God—and all believe in one doctrine even the doctrine of our Lord and Savior Jesus Christ."³

CONTENT

The Lord identifies Independence, Missouri, as the site for the city of Zion, the land he has appointed and consecrated for the gathering of the Saints in Doctrine and Covenants 57. It is the promised land. Indeed, the Lord specifies the very place he has chosen for the temple, directing Joseph to a spot just a few blocks west of the courthouse. He urges the Saints to purchase that land and every other tract they can in Independence and what is now Kansas City, Missouri, all the way to the territory created for Native Americans in 1831.

The Lord commands Bishop Edward Partridge to continue carrying out his duties as outlined in Doctrine and Covenants 41, 42, and 51. The Lord appoints Sidney Gilbert as the bishop's real estate agent, directing him to establish a store and use the revenue to buy land. Gilbert is also to obtain a license from the Indian agents that would permit him to sell supplies to the Native Americans. The idea is that he would receive government subsidies for that purpose, providing employment and resources for the Saints and opening opportunities for preaching the gospel to the Native Americans.

The Lord appoints William Phelps as the Church's printer, commanding him to set up shop in Independence and use his skills to obtain as much money as he righteously can to build Zion. Oliver Cowdery is to assist him. The Lord commands these four men to become "planted" (D&C 57:14) in Independence as soon as possible, along with their families, to begin building Zion. They are to prepare for the gathering of the Saints and to provide inheritances for them as they arrive. The Lord promises to provide further directions to that end.

OUTCOMES

Sidney Rigdon dedicated the land of Zion on August 2, 1831, and Joseph dedicated its temple site the following day. Bishop Partridge bought the sixty-three acres that included this site and accumulated more than two thousand acres in the area. These he technically owned, but he deeded them as stewardships to Latter-day Saints for their inheritances as Doctrine and Covenants 51 and 57 instructed him to do. Sidney Gilbert established a store across the street from the courthouse the Lord mentioned, and William Phelps established a printing office just down the street. These men and their families went to work to build New Jerusalem.

When part of the printing office was destroyed two years later and Bishop Partridge dragged from his home to be tarred and feathered on the courthouse square, it was not because a few Mormons had created hard feelings among the Missourians. It was because the men named in section 57 and their families were doing exactly what the revelation commanded them to do: printing the Lord's revelations, legally buying the Lord's land to provide inheritances for his people, and operating a store to facilitate the gathering of Israel. Having violently attacked the Saints, a group of antagonistic citizens drafted a "Memorandum of agreement" between them. It stipulated that the Saints stop doing what section 57 commanded them to do: "Remove with their families out of this county . . . to advise and try all means in their power to stop any more of their sect from moving to this county. . . . Gilbert may sell out his merchandise now on hand, but is to make no new importation.

"The *Star* [the Church's newspaper in which revelations and news were published] is not again to be published nor a press set up by any of the society in this county."[4]

The antagonistic Missourians hated Zion. No wonder the Lord had called them "enemies" (D&C 52:42).

Doctrine & Covenants 58

ORIGIN

With great expectations for Zion, the Prophet Joseph Smith, Bishop Edward Partridge, and others were disappointed on their arrival in Independence. They anticipated a thriving branch, but only a few converts awaited them, and Joseph thought the community was "nearly a century behind the times."[1] Independence was the geographical site for New Jerusalem, but culturally it was far from being the promised land. Bishop Partridge, whom the Lord had called upon to turn the place into Zion, despaired. The Lord asked Bishop Partridge for unconquerable optimism in the face of depressing circumstances.

A few days after Joseph's arrival in Independence, Sidney Rigdon, Isaac Morley, Ezra Booth, Sidney and Elizabeth Gilbert, and the Saints from Colesville, New York, arrived as well. Joseph received Doctrine and Covenants 58 to reveal to the Saints assembled in Missouri what they should do.

CONTENT

"The revelation implied that the enjoyment of Zion lay in the future."[2] Three times in its first four verses Doctrine and Covenants 58 warns of "tribulation" or "much tribulation" before the establishment of Zion. The revelation tempers the Saints' zeal even as it points to the promised land.

Indeed, the revelation launches into a grand vision of Zion's preparing a feast to which all nations should be invited. "First, the rich and the learned, the wise and the noble; and after that cometh the day of my power;

then shall the poor, the lame, and the blind, and the deaf, come in unto the marriage of the Lamb, and partake of the supper of the Lord, prepared for the great day to come" (vv. 10–11). These first few Saints called to Zion have the privilege of laying its foundation and testifying of its potential. Their calling is to pioneer.

Beginning at verse 14, the revelation gives specific instructions to the men called to build Zion. Bishop Edward Partridge questioned Joseph's expansive vision of Zion when there was so little evidence to support it. "I see it, and it will be so," Joseph replied.[3] Section 58 calls Bishop Partridge to repent of his skepticism and reiterates his commission to implement the law of consecration, divide the land, and give the Saints their inheritances. Doing so will not violate local laws (see D&C 51). In fact, by keeping the Lord's laws as set forth in section 42, the Saints will be living in accordance with the law of the land.

The Lord commands Bishop Partridge to move his family to Missouri and, to make the point that Bishop Partridge could do as he thought best, gives one of the most important scriptural texts on the nature of agency and accountability. God gives individuals agency—power to decide whether they will do God's will and obtain the promised reward or disobey God's will and be damned. The Lord fulfills his promises. If they are not fulfilled, it is not the Lord's fault but the fault of the agents who choose not to use their agency to keep the terms and conditions upon which his promises are predicated.

The Lord commands Martin Harris to be the first to consecrate his resources to the bishop for the establishment of Zion. Then the arrogant, talented William Phelps is commanded to repent of his self-centered striving, and the Lord gives the rules of repentance: He forgives the repentant and forgets their sins. "By this ye may know if a man repenteth of his sins—behold, he will confess them and forsake them" (D&C 58:43). Knowing that Ziba Peterson thought he could hide his sins and not confess them, the Lord commands that Ziba be stripped of his preaching license and his priesthood responsibilities until he repents according to these terms (v. 60).[4]

"The elders themselves were told not to move to Zion. Their assignment for now was to funnel people from the ends of the earth—and to do it cautiously."⁵ The Lord tells the elders it will be "many years" before they "receive their inheritance" in Zion (v. 44).

In the meantime, however, the Lord calls for an agent in Ohio to receive consecrated money with which to buy land in Missouri (v. 49); in a later revelation he calls Newel Whitney to this task (D&C 63:42–45). The Lord calls Sidney Rigdon to write a description of the land and a statement declaring the word of God concerning Zion, both of which are to be presented to the Saints to raise needed funds. Money will have to be raised and land obtained before the Saints gather to Missouri. The Lord calls for Sidney Rigdon to dedicate Zion and for a conference to be held, after which Joseph, Sidney, and Oliver Cowdery are to return to Ohio. The elders still en route from Ohio are to hold a conference after arriving. Bishop Partridge is to preside at the conference, and the elders are then to return home, "preaching the gospel by the way, bearing record of the things which [were] revealed unto them" (D&C 58:63). The revelation ends by focusing not on the site for Zion but on the elders' responsibility to "go forth from this place into all the world, and unto the uttermost parts of the earth—the gospel must be preached unto every creature, with signs following them that believe" (v. 64).

OUTCOMES

Doctrine and Covenants 58 is a map that shows how to get to Zion from where we are. It is a seldom used map, and some have wandered in the wilderness for years, not understanding the Lord's directions or preferring their "own way" (D&C 1:16). Those to whom the Lord spoke specifically in section 58 understood it and acted on it as commanded.

Bishop Partridge repented of his unbelief and blindness. Ezra Booth, by contrast, left the Church and criticized Edward Partridge for continuing to believe in Zion. It is not remarkable that Edward despaired that Zion would be established, given the evidence before his eyes. But the Lord called those eyes blind and invited him to see what Joseph could see. "I see it, and it will be so," Joseph said of Zion.⁶

The remarkable truth is that the intelligent, capable, prosperous Edward Partridge was willingly reoriented by section 58. He followed it precisely. He wrote to his wife, Lydia, that his great desire to return home was surpassed by his calling. He told her of the command that his family join him in Zion (D&C 57:14) and of the instructions to rely on personal revelation to arrange for the move as best they could (D&C 58:24–26).[7] Edward prepared Lydia for what she could expect when she joined him in Missouri: "We have to suffer and shall for some time, many privations here which you and I have not been much used to for years." He knew that his devotion to Zion would mean an eternal farewell to his extended family and friends, "unless they should be willing to forsake all for the sake of Christ, and be gathered with the saints of the most high God."[8]

Edward Partridge humbly acknowledged his calling, his shortcomings, and his inadequacies. "You know I stand in an important station," he confided to Lydia, "and as I am occasionally chastened I sometimes fear my station is above what I can perform to the acceptance of my Heavenly Father. I hope you and I may conduct ourselves as at last to land our souls in the heaven of eternal rest. Pray that I may not fall."[9] Lydia did pray, and she packed up their five daughters and made the difficult trek to Missouri to join Edward as commanded. Though faltering occasionally, perhaps, Edward and Lydia Partridge gave their all to Zion.

Elder Orson Pratt later observed: "Martin Harris was the first man that the Lord called by name to consecrate his money, and lay the same at the feet of the Bishop in Jackson County, Mo., according to the order of consecration [v. 35]. He willingly did it; he knew the work to be true; he knew that the word of the Lord through the Prophet Joseph was just as sacred as any word that ever came from the mouth of any Prophet from the foundation of the world. He consecrated his money and his substance, according to the word of the Lord. What for? As the revelation states, as an example to the rest of the Church."[10]

Sidney Rigdon dedicated Zion on August 2 as commanded in verse 57. He drafted the description of Zion as section 58 commanded, but the Lord rejected it and commanded him to try again (v. 50; D&C 63:55–56). The Saints held the conference called for in Doctrine and Covenants 58:58. Edward Partridge prayed, Sidney Rigdon charged the Saints to obey the law of consecration, Ziba Peterson confessed his sins, and Joseph exhorted the

Saints to obey the commands they had received and reaffirmed the promised blessings for doing so. The elders who had not yet arrived were shown section 58 when they did, and they obeyed verses 61–63 precisely.

Verse 64 continues to motivate Saints who live in the anxious space section 58 creates between the time-consuming requirements to preach the gospel globally and build Zion in the face of the imminent coming of Christ. If Joseph's question "When will Zion be built up in her glory?" is not yet fully answered,[11] the Church's history reveals how the revelation has worked itself out. The elders have gone forth to gather the righteous, including the wealthy, whose consecrations have put the Church on a firm financial footing Edward Partridge could only dream of. In the last century we began to see the gospel blessings extended even to remote, impoverished regions. Perhaps we are beginning to witness what the Lord called "the day of my power," the day when his resources are distributed evenly among his faithful, consecrated Saints, and all come to Zion to "partake of the supper of the Lord, prepared for the great day to come" (v. 11).

Doctrine and Covenants 58 puts Edward Partridge in charge of beginning to put the feast on the table and sends the elders to every nation under heaven to invite the Lord's children to come for supper.

Doctrine & Covenants 59

ORIGIN

Joseph attended the funeral of Polly Knight on August 7, 1831. The wife of Joseph Knight Sr., Polly was the matriarch of the Saints from Colesville, New York, the first group to gather to Zion. Though terminally ill, she had nonetheless made the journey to Missouri, hoping to be buried in Zion's blessed soil. She died shortly after her arrival in Zion, and Joseph's history noted that she "sleeps in Jesus till the resurrection."[1] After the funeral Joseph received Doctrine and Covenants 59, teaching the Saints to observe the Sabbath and how to fast and pray.

CONTENT

Doctrine and Covenants 59 begins by blessing those who have come to Zion to serve God with all they have and are. Those who live shall inherit the earth; those who die shall rest for the present and receive exaltation after the resurrection. The Lord is well pleased with the first Saints to gather obediently to Zion. He rewards them with the earth and its bounty.

The revelation reiterates the law of consecration, which, simply put, is the two great commandments: "Thou shalt love the Lord thy God with all thy heart, with all thy might, mind, and strength; and in the name of Jesus Christ thou shalt serve him" (v. 5). Then follows a review of the Decalogue, or the Ten Commandments, to which the Lord adds commandments to thank God in all things and to offer him a broken heart. He gives a specific purpose for observing the Sabbath day: "That thou mayest more fully keep thyself unspotted from the world, thou shalt go to the house of prayer and offer up thy sacraments upon my holy day" (v. 9). The Sabbath is for offering oblations—that is, time, talents, and material resources—for the establishment of Zion. It is a day of fasting and prayer (v. 14).

The Lord makes a covenant with the Saints in Zion: if they will keep the commandments thankfully and cheerfully yet soberly, he will give them the fullness of the earth—its plants and animals "for food and for raiment, for taste and for smell, to strengthen the body and to enliven the soul" (v. 19).

OUTCOMES

Obedience to Doctrine and Covenants 59 results in consecration: the exchange of all the Saints have for all God has. It is a countercultural revelation. When Joseph arrived in Independence, he saw Sabbath breaking and self-interest. Slave-owning speculators, traders, soldiers and a "sad lot of churchmen, untrained, uncouth, given to imbibing spirituous liquors," together with renegades all represented Babylon, in stark contrast to Zion.[2] Section 59 tells the Saints to behave completely differently from the world in which they are now living in order to keep themselves unsoiled by it.

President Gordon B. Hinckley applied this commandment to all Latter-day Saints. He noted how Latter-day Saints are forsaking the command to be Zion in the midst of Babylon by observing the Sabbath and keeping the other commandments. President Hinckley declared that "the Sabbath of the Lord is becoming the play day of the people. It is a day of golf and football on television, of buying and selling in our stores and markets. Are we moving to mainstream America as some observers believe? In this I fear we are. What a telling thing it is to see the parking lots of the markets filled on Sunday in communities that are predominately LDS. Our strength for the future, our resolution to grow the Church across the world, will be weakened if we violate the will of the Lord in this important matter. He has so very clearly spoken anciently and again in modern revelation. We cannot disregard with impunity that which He has said."[3]

The revelation reveals the Lord's aesthetics. Verses 17–20 rejoice in the created world, the "good things which come of the earth," freely given by the Lord to "please the eye and to gladden the heart . . . to strengthen the body and to enliven the soul." It pleases him "that he hath given all these things unto man" to use, to share, to enjoy. It displeases him when mortals ungratefully take his creation for granted, abuse his resources, and use creation "to excess." Section 59 reveals the owner of the created world and invites his heirs in Zion to see themselves as stewards into whose hands the creation has been trusted and who will be accountable to the Creator for what they do with it. "The land became beautiful in Joseph's eyes."[4] He later wrote about it in terms—beautiful, rich and fertile, fruitful, delightful, one of the most blessed places on the globe—that reflect the Lord's aesthetics revealed in section 59.[5]

Doctrine & Covenants 60

ORIGIN

Having dedicated western Missouri as Zion and a spot near the courthouse in Independence as the site for the temple in New Jerusalem, Joseph Smith and his companions sought to know what the Lord would have them do next. In response the Lord gave the revelation recorded in Doctrine and Covenants 60, instructing some of the elders to return home.[1]

CONTENT

In Doctrine and Covenants 60 the Lord tells the elders planning to return quickly to Ohio that he is pleased with their trek to Missouri, except for those whose fears kept them from preaching the gospel along the way: "Mine anger is kindled against them" (v. 2). Those elders will lose what the Lord has given them if they do not offer it freely to others.

The Lord commands the returning elders to speedily make or buy a boat to take them down the Missouri River toward St. Louis. Once there, Joseph, Sidney Ridgon, and Oliver Cowdery are to go to Cincinnati to declare the gospel with faith, not anger. Using a play on words based on his Old Testament title *I Am*—a variation on the name rendered in English as *Jehovah*—the Lord commands them to lift up "holy hands upon them. For I am able to make you holy, and your sins are forgiven you" (v. 7; see also Exodus 3:14; D&C 68:6).

The remaining elders should leave St. Louis in companionships and preach the gospel to those who have not yet repented until they arrive in

Ohio. The Lord issues this commandment as a way to benefit the branches of the Church.

The Lord then speaks concerning the elders who have left Ohio for Missouri but have not yet arrived because of their missionary work on the way among those who have not yet repented. He commands them: "Thou shalt not idle away thy time, neither shalt thou bury thy talent that it may not be known" (D&C 60:13). After arriving in Missouri, now Zion, and preaching there, they are to return to Ohio quickly, again preaching along the way. They are commanded to preach thoroughly, kindly, and without provoking the people. Rather than condemning those who choose not to receive the gospel openly, the elders are to signify that they have freely offered the gospel. They are to wash their feet privately as evidence on Judgment Day that they did not hide the good news from the unrepentant. This act transferred accountability from the missionaries to their hearers.

OUTCOMES

Joseph and his companions obeyed Doctrine and Covenants 60 and set out for home in Ohio as it directed. On August 9, Joseph and ten other brethren headed down the Missouri River on canoes bound for St. Louis.[2]

Doctrine & Covenants 61

ORIGIN

Joseph and the elders launched their canoes at the Missouri River landing just north of Independence, Missouri, to return home to Ohio. They camped at Fort Osage and "had an excellent wild turkey for supper."[1] But the good food did little to keep the men satisfied. By the second day "a spirit of animosity and discord" had infected the group. "The conduct of the Elders became very displeasing to Oliver Cowdery," who prophesied: "As the Lord God liveth, if you do not behave better, some accident will befall you."[2] At some point William Phelps "saw the Destroyer, in his most horrible power, ride upon the face of the waters," though what that means is not certain.[3]

Contention continued the next day. Joseph was frustrated. Some of the elders refused to paddle, and at least one of the canoes hit a submerged tree and nearly capsized. Joseph urged the frightened group to get off the river. Some of the men called him a coward. They landed on the north side of the river at McIlwaine's Bend (now Miami), Missouri, set up camp as best they could, and convened a council to address the contention. Some of the elders were critical of Oliver's rebuke. Some criticized Joseph for being "quite dictatorial." The council went on for some hours until, early in the morning, everyone reconciled.[4] Speaking of Doctrine and Covenants 61, Joseph's history says "the next morning, after prayer, I received the following."[5]

CONTENT

In Doctrine and Covenants 61 the Lord forgives the elders their sins; he continues to mercifully forgive the sins of all who humbly confess them. He tells the men it is no longer needful for the entire group to travel quickly down the river, for there are settlers on either side of it who need to be taught the gospel. The Lord has let the elders experience the river's terrors so they can testify of the "many dangers upon the waters" (v. 4) to others. In his anger, the Lord decreed "many destructions upon the waters" (v. 5), especially the Missouri River, but all flesh is in his hands, and he will preserve the faithful among this group of elders from drowning. The Lord has kept the group together this long so that they could be corrected, purified from their sins, and unified as a group, thus escaping punishment for their wickedness. The Lord commands them now to split up.

The Lord assigns Sidney Gilbert and William Phelps to travel on the river, so they can quickly accomplish the tasks he has assigned them by revelation (see D&C 55–56). If they remain faithful, the Lord promises they will overcome any problems that traveling on the Missouri River might cause. Sidney Gilbert is commanded to give the other elders enough money to buy necessary clothing and to take the rest of the Lord's money with him to Ohio. The Lord commands them to travel in these ways for their own good. He explains that he blessed the waters during the Creation but later cursed them through the apostle John (see Revelation 8:8–11). The day will come when only the honest-hearted will safely travel to Zion by water, and the Lord commands the elders to warn the other Saints not to travel on the dangerous Missouri without faith. After the Fall the Lord cursed the land for Adam's sake, but in the latter days he blessed it to be fertile for the Saints' sake. The Lord has determined that the destroyer cover the water, and He has not changed his mind. He was angry with the elders the day they nearly drowned, but his anger is turned away. He reminds Sidney Gilbert and William Phelps to get back quickly to Ohio. It does not matter whether they go by land or by water as long as they fulfill their assignments. They can judge for themselves the best way to travel. As for Joseph, Sidney Rigdon, and Oliver Cowdery, they are to stay off the rivers unless using the extensive, and comparatively safe, canal system. The Lord appointed the canals and overland travel as the best way for Saints migrating from the East to get to Zion in Missouri. This commandment is for all the Saints, though the Lord allows Joseph, and perhaps others, power to command the water. They are given the liberty to follow the Spirit in deciding how to travel.

The Lord tells Joseph, Sidney, and Oliver not to preach to the unrepentant until reaching Cincinnati. There they are to preach repentance to the people the Lord is angry with. They are wicked, "well-nigh ripened for destruction" (D&C 61:31). From Cincinnati, Joseph, Sidney, and Oliver are to return to the Saints in northeastern Ohio where they are sorely needed. The other elders present are commanded to preach the gospel to the unrepentant. If they will do so, they will not be accountable for the sins of the wicked on Judgment Day (see Jacob 1:19). He assigns them to go as companionships of their own choosing, specifying only that Reynolds Cahoon and Samuel Smith, with whom the Lord was well pleased, stay together all the way home. This pairing was "for a wise purpose in me," the Lord says (D&C 61:35). He tells Joseph, and by extension all the elders, to be cheerful, for He is with him. He affectionately calls them "little children," suggesting both immaturity and potential (v. 36). He has not forsaken them. If they will choose to be humble, he will bless them with his kingdom. "Pray always," the revelation concludes, "that you enter not into temptation, that you may abide the day of his coming, whether in life or in death" (v. 39).

OUTCOMES

William Phelps carried out the commandment in this revelation to tell all the Saints about the dangers of traveling to Zion on the Missouri River. He published Doctrine and Covenants 61 in the Church's newspaper, *The Evening and the Morning Star,* along with an editorial listing the most notable "risks and dangers." First, there were frequent disasters on the river. Second, there was cholera, a devastating water-borne illness "which the Lord has sent into the world, and which may, without repentance, ravage the large towns near the waters, many years, or, at least, till other judgments come."[6]

Phelps also wrote a short history of his stay in Missouri, in which he told how section 61 influenced his return to Ohio. "I, in company with

Joseph Smith, Oliver Cowdery and others started by water for Ohio, but being cautioned in a Revelation given at, McElwains bend, that Missouri River was cursed, all the company save myself and brother Gilbert left the river and proceeded by land. I was assured by revelation, to be safe by land or water."[7]

Doctrine & Covenants 62

ORIGIN

Leaving the Missouri River to travel by land, Joseph and the elders who had been to Missouri ran into a group of their brethren—Joseph's brother Hyrum, David Whitmer, John Murdock, and Harvey Whitlock—still en route to Zion. They had been preaching the gospel with great success along their way. The joyful meeting would not have occurred had Joseph's trip down the Missouri been tranquil. But the Lord had promised that the brethren would meet in Missouri to rejoice in the land of Zion. Joseph sought and received a revelation, now recorded in Doctrine and Covenants 62, concerning the elders who had not yet reached Independence.[1]

CONTENT

The Lord has been watching those elders who have not yet reached Missouri. Their missions are not complete. They are blessed for bearing testimony all along their journey. Their words are recorded in heaven for the angels to enjoy, and the Lord forgives their sins. He commands them to continue their journey to Independence—now Zion—and there rejoice and hold a sacrament meeting to commune with the Most High. They can then return to Ohio to testify of Zion. They are commanded to return together or two by two, whichever they please. The only thing that matters to the Lord is that they remain faithful and declare the gospel to the unrepentant. The Lord has brought the elders together in this fortuitous meeting to fulfill his promise to them that the faithful among them will safely arrive in Missouri and rejoice together there. "I, the Lord, promise the faithful and cannot lie," he says in Doctrine and Covenants 62 (v. 6). The Lord is willing that any who wished to ride horses or mules or in carriages could do so. If any do, they are to receive the blessing with thankful hearts, recognizing that the means come from his hand. The decisions are theirs to make under the influence of the Holy Spirit. "I am with the faithful always," he promised (v. 9).

OUTCOMES

Hyrum Smith, David Whitmer, Harvey Whitlock, John Murdock, and others who joined them obeyed this revelation. They pursued their journey to Independence and held a solemn meeting with the members of the bishopric there. They sang hymns, prayed, read scriptural prophecies about Zion and the Second Coming, and then turned around to return to Ohio.[2]

Doctrine and Covenants 62, like many others, is full of conditional clauses. It empowers the elders to control their own destiny by choosing to do the things that will bring the Lord's promised blessings.

The revelation is also richly autobiographical. The Lord tells us much about himself. He is our advocate. He knows our weakness. He knows how to run to our relief when we are tempted. He keeps his promises. He cannot lie. Who wouldn't gladly travel hundreds of miles to obey one of his revelations?

Doctrine & Covenants 63

ORIGIN

Joseph learned by revelation on his trip to Missouri the Lord's location for Zion, whose headquarters were to be in the holy city New Jerusalem. Satan hates Zion, and he was working hard to undermine it from every possible angle. Little wonder that "some apostatized" in Ohio while Joseph was in Missouri in the summer of 1831.[1]

Joseph's history says that when he returned from Missouri, the Saints were extraordinarily anxious to learn the Lord's will about Zion. When and how should they gather to Missouri? How should they fund Zion and the move there? What should they do with their property in Ohio, such as Whitney's store and the farms belonging to Isaac Morley and Frederick Williams? The revelations in Missouri commanded the Saints to purchase land there. How should they raise the money? Sidney Rigdon had been commanded to write an inspired description of Zion and God's will concerning it (D&C 58:50). What did the Lord think of his first draft? Isaac Morley had already moved to Missouri, and the several families living on his farm planned to follow as soon as the Lord directed. Because Joseph Smith and Sidney Rigdon and their families lived on Morley's farm, selling it would leave them homeless. Where should they live? Section 63 addresses the apostasy and pressing questions related to literally building Zion. Joseph summed them all up tersely in his history: "As the 'land of Zion' was now the most important temporal object in view, I inquired of the Lord for further information upon the gathering of the Saints and the purchase of the land and other matters."[2] The revelation he received is recorded in Doctrine and Covenants 63.

CONTENT

The Lord commands his people to hear his words in Doctrine and Covenants 63. His anger has been kindled against the wicked and rebellious. A day of wrath, wherein the Lord will preserve or destroy life as he pleases, is soon to come. He declares, "I, the Lord, utter my voice, and it shall be obeyed" (v. 5).

Sign-seeking Saints who demand miracles as proof will see miracles—but they will not be saved. Proof does not result in faith. Faith precedes miracles. Faith results in proof. Evidences of God are manifest in the lives of the faithful. Such signs come from God according to his will, not to satisfy the demands of mortals. God is displeased with those choosing to be faithless. Indeed, it makes him angry. He gives commandments, and many turn away and fail to keep them. Several Saints have been guilty of adultery or are still in adulterous relationships. The Lord warns them to repent, for if they do not, they will ultimately be exposed. God's judgment will trap them, their reputations will be spoiled, and their evils will become public knowledge. "He that looketh on a woman to lust after her, or if any shall commit adultery in their hearts, they shall not have the Spirit, but shall deny the faith and shall fear" (v. 16). The Lord states the punishment for disbelief, lying, unchastity, and calling on evil spirits: Those who commit these sins will suffer spiritual death—the second death, as described in Doctrine and Covenants 29:27–29. They will not be resurrected until the very end of the Millennium, having spent that time in hell. Some of the Saints are guilty of these sins. Still, the Lord promises that those who endure in faith and do the Lord's will rather than their own will overcome sin and inherit the earth when it is transfigured into a terrestrial kingdom during the Millennium and a celestial world after that. The Lord revealed this transfiguration to his ancient apostles, but the biblical account of it is incomplete.

The Lord has promised to reveal his will concerning the Saints, and now he begins to do so. He will not command them, for many will not keep his commandments. The Lord desires that the Saints in Ohio gather to Zion but not too quickly lest confusion and trouble follow. The Lord holds the land of Zion in his hands, yet, just as he did when living on earth, he chooses to obey the rules of earthly societies. Therefore, he commands the Saints to purchase lands in and around Independence, Missouri. This will give the Saints legal title to the lands. Satan will still persuade their enemies to be angry and violent, however, and the Lord forbids the Saints to attempt to take the land by force, warning that a bloodbath will ensue if their enemies respond violently. Purchasing the land is their only good option. The Lord is angry with the wicked. He keeps his Spirit from the people on earth. His anger has led him to decree wars upon the earth in which the wicked will kill the wicked and fear will possess everyone. Even the Saints will barely escape. But the Lord will soon come down from his Father's presence and consume the wicked with unquenchable fire. Knowing the gross wickedness of the world and the punishments he has planned for it, the Lord wants the Saints to leave the world and gather in Zion. Every one of them is to be clothed with faith and righteousness and warn others that the Lord is about to desolate the wicked.

The Lord commands the numerous Saints living on Isaac Morley's farm in Kirtland to prepare to move. He commands Titus Billings, whom Morley left in charge of the farm when he migrated to Missouri, to sell the farm and use the money to get himself and the others on the farm to Zion in the spring. The Lord will identify a few Saints to remain in Kirtland until they too are commanded to go. All the extra money, whether little or much, is to be sent to Bishop Edward Partridge in Zion. The Spirit will tell Joseph who should go to Zion and who should remain in Kirtland. Newel Whitney is to remain and keep his store running for a while longer. He is commanded to send all the money he can to Bishop Partridge in Zion. The Lord calls Newel Whitney to be an agent for the Saints remaining in Ohio.

The Lord commands Joseph and Oliver to visit the branches in the area, explain this revelation to them, and raise funds from them to purchase the land of Zion. Those who send money to Zion will inherit part of this earth and a reward in the one that will replace it. Their good works will be consecrated to their gain. The faithful dead will be resurrected when the Lord comes and renews the earth, and the Lord will give them an inheritance in New Jerusalem, the holy city. The faithful who are living when the Lord comes will grow old, die, and be resurrected instantaneously. Some

Saints will repent and prepare for Christ's second coming, and some will not. But at his coming, the Lord will send "angels to pluck out the wicked and cast them into unquenchable fire" (v. 54).

The Lord is displeased with Sidney Rigdon and his arrogance, unwillingness to be taught, and offensiveness to the Holy Ghost. His written description of the land of Zion is unacceptable. The Lord commands him to try again and warns that if he fails, he will no longer be assigned to write the description.

The Lord wants all Saints with a meek desire to warn sinners to repent to be ordained to do so. It is time to warn sinners to repent, not to become longwinded or get caught up in debates. The Lord will not be mocked for much longer. He warns the Saints to beware how they speak his holy name. Many Saints are guilty of acting in the Lord's name without authority. Those who repent will belong to Christ, but he will sever his relationship with the unrepentant.

The Lord urges the Saints to remember that revelations are sacred. They are to be spoken of reverently and only as the Spirit allows. The Spirit comes to the prayerful. All who are without the Spirit are guilty. The Lord counsels Joseph Smith and Sidney Rigdon, whose families have been living on Isaac Morley's farm, to prayerfully find new homes by the power of the Holy Ghost.

OUTCOMES

Doctrine and Covenants 63 motivated much action. Joseph began discerning by the Spirit those who should move to Zion.[3] As commanded, Titus Billings and several other Kirtland Saints moved to Missouri in the spring of 1832.[4] Sidney Rigdon humbled himself and wrote a description of the land of Zion based very much on this revelation and previous ones.[5] Oliver Cowdery and Newel Whitney used that description to carry out what the revelation commanded them to do. They wasted no time going "from place to place, and from Church to Church preaching and expounding the Scriptures and Commandments [that is, the recent revelations] and obtaining moneys of the disciples for the purpose of buying lands for the Saints according to commandments and the disciples truly opened their hearts."

Oliver Cowdery and John Whitmer took the money to Bishop Partridge and Sidney Gilbert in Missouri, "and thus there has been lands purchased, for the inheritance of the Saints."[6]

As commanded, Newel Whitney and Frederick Williams kept their property in Kirtland and consecrated it to the Church. Joseph, Sidney Rigdon, and their families moved south to Hiram, Ohio, in September 1831 where John and Elsa Johnson provided homes for them. Although there was some apostasy in Kirtland when the Lord gave section 63, many Saints responded to it with sacrifice and dedication.

Doctrine & Covenants 64

ORIGIN

Historical sources say little about the reasons why Doctrine and Covenants 64 was given. Joseph's history says simply that he was preparing to move from Kirtland to Hiram, Ohio, to work on his new translation of the Bible and that the Saints who had been commanded to move to Missouri (D&C 52; 57) were preparing to go.[1] Section 64 is perhaps best understood as directions to the elders.

CONTENT

The Lord speaks to the elders who have recently returned from Missouri, including those who are about to return there permanently to build Zion. The revelation commands them to forgive and repent, lest they be guilty of the "greater sin" (v. 9). Disciplinary councils concerning the unrepentant should be held as set forth in Doctrine and Covenants 42.

The Lord gives specific instructions regarding the consecration of property (he wants the Morley farms sold but the Williams farm and the Whitney store kept) as well as a general promise that all who tithe—which in Doctrine and Covenants 64 is the same as consecration—will not be burned at his second coming. Consecration is not as much about the giving of property or money as it is about keeping the great commandment to love God with all one's heart. He knows the location of individuals' hearts by noting where they choose to put their treasure.

Symbolically, only a day is left until the Lord's second coming, and that is a day for sacrifice and consecration. Those who obey the laws of sacrifice and consecration are the righteous who will escape the fire of the Lord's wrath at his second coming. He comes tomorrow, and the proud and wicked—those who do not obey the laws of sacrifice and consecration—will be burned like the stubble in a harvested grain field. "I will not spare any that remain in Babylon," the Lord declared unequivocally. "If ye believe me, ye will labor while it is called today" (vv. 24–25).

The Lord answers the Saints' specific questions about debt. Borrowing righteously is borrowing when the Lord commands them to do so. As his agents, they are justified in doing as he commands. The revelation continues with specific instructions for building Zion and disciplining her liars and hypocrites, namely, those who have not kept the law of consecration. All such unfaithful stewards, even the bishop, can be replaced. The Lord concludes in a positive, promising tone that murmurers and lawbreakers may hinder but will not ultimately ruin Zion. "For, behold, I say unto you that Zion shall flourish, and the glory of the Lord shall be upon her; and she shall be an ensign unto the people, and there shall come unto her out of every nation under heaven" (vv. 41–42).

OUTCOMES

The Lord was angry with Ezra Booth and Isaac Morley. They did not obey Doctrine and Covenants 42 or the commandment they had received to preach the gospel en route to Missouri in the summer of 1831 (D&C 52:23). They had evil desires and therefore lost the Holy Ghost. Then, as so often happens, they projected their own evil onto others who were innocent.[2] The Lord forgave the repentant Isaac Morley. Ezra Booth was disciplined by the Church as Doctrine and Covenants 64 directed, and he withdrew from membership.[3]

The Lord was also angry at Bishop Edward Partridge for quibbling with Joseph about the location of Zion (D&C 58).[4] Bishop Partridge repented as a result of section 64. Sidney Gilbert returned to Missouri and established a storehouse there and prepared to buy land for Zion. When he did so, Sidney could tell "that which he hath seen and heard" (v. 19) to the Missouri Saints to help them avoid sin.

Isaac Morley sold his farm and thus avoided the overwhelming temptations of materialism that the Lord knew could otherwise keep him from consecrating (see D&C 63:38–40). Frederick Williams consecrated his Kirtland farm to the Church for the Lord to use as a secure headquarters for five more years. Newel Whitney and Sidney Gilbert kept their Kirtland store and other properties for five years after this revelation.

Section 64 paints a vivid picture and makes a promise. It explains with clarity that the Saints must leave Babylon or perish, that the only place other than Babylon is Zion, and that the only way to get there is by obeying the law of consecration. The Lord's promise is that the willing and obedient will see Zion. It will come. They will get there. That is the promise, according to section 45, that all the holy have sought in ages past. They longed for Zion and never got there "but obtained a promise that they should find it and see it in their [resurrected] flesh" (D&C 45:14). Section 64 promises that those who obey the law of consecration will find Zion.

Doctrine & Covenants 65

ORIGIN

From Joseph's history we know only that the revelation recorded now in Doctrine and Covenants 65 was received in early October 1831 while he was living with the Johnsons in Hiram, Ohio, and that he regarded it as a prayer.[1] A manuscript copy of section 65 in the handwriting of William McLellin sheds some light on its origin and meaning. The revelation came in connection with Joseph's new translation of the Bible, especially the Lord's Prayer in Matthew 6, and particularly the meaning of verse 10: "Thy kingdom come. Thy will be done in earth, as it is in heaven."[2]

CONTENT

In Doctrine and Covenants 65 the Lord commands the Saints to listen to a voice of strength and power sent down from heaven to address the whole earth: "Prepare ye the way of the Lord, make his path straight" (D&C 65:1). The voice says that the keys of the kingdom of God are already on earth, and the gospel will spread over the globe like a grindstone rolling forward, growing larger and larger as it turns. The Lord urges the Saints to call upon him, asking for his kingdom to spread over the earth for all people to receive it and thus prepare them for the Savior's second coming.

OUTCOMES

Doctrine and Covenants 65 teaches us to pray for the ideal government. We look for a literal, earthly fulfillment of Isaiah's declaration: "The

Lord is our judge, the Lord is our lawgiver, the Lord is our king; he will save us" (Isaiah 33:22). This short revelation also reminds us how thoroughly biblical Joseph became as he read that sacred text by the light of the Holy Ghost. In the six verses of section 65 are clear references to Isaiah, Daniel, Matthew, and the Revelation of John.

Section 65 elaborates a prophecy of Daniel, who saw "the God of heaven set up a kingdom, which shall never be destroyed: and the kingdom shall not be left to other people, but it shall break in pieces and consume all these kingdoms, and it shall stand for ever" (Daniel 2:44). Daniel compared this kingdom to a stone that would eventually fill the earth. Some Saints envision a snowball effect, but Joseph clarified Daniel's meaning. The stone, Joseph said, "is stationary like a grind stone. It revolves." He taught that it grew as "the Elders went abroad to preach the gospel and the people became believers in the Book of Mormon and were baptized." In this way "they were added to the little stone. Thus they gathered around it so that it grew larger and larger." Joseph prophesied that in this way the stone, the kingdom of God, would fill the earth.[3]

In 1838, Judge Austin King charged Joseph Smith with treason and confined him in jail at Liberty, Missouri, for teaching the doctrines given in section 65. Parley P. Pratt wrote that Judge King "inquired diligently into our belief of the seventh chapter of Daniel concerning the kingdom of God, which should subdue all other kingdoms and stand forever." The Saints testified that they believed the prophecy, and Judge King instructed his clerk, "Write that down; it is a strong point for treason." The Saints' attorney objected. Is the Bible treason?[4] The next time he was charged with treason, Joseph did not escape. A month after "setting up the kingdom of Daniel by the word of the Lord" and declaring his intent to "revolutionize the whole world," Joseph Smith's life was ended abruptly by a lynch mob in Carthage, Illinois, on June 27, 1844.[5]

Daniel's prophecy of the kingdom was a favorite text for Church leaders in nineteenth-century Utah and continued to be among the most popular themes in twentieth-century conference addresses.[6] Introducing a twenty-first century general conference, President Gordon B. Hinckley evoked this text again, leaving little doubt that Latter-day Saints should desire deeply, as the Lord counseled us to pray in both Matthew 6:10 and Doctrine and Covenants 65, for the kingdom of heaven to come. When it does it will "stand forever" in contrast to all other, short-lived kingdoms. Said President Hinckley:

"It was said that at one time the sun never set on the British Empire. That empire has now been diminished. But it is true that the sun never sets on this work of the Lord as it is touching the lives of people across the earth.

"And this is only the beginning. We have scarcely scratched the surface. We are engaged in a work for the souls of men and women everywhere. Our work knows no boundaries. Under the providence of the Lord it will continue. Those nations now closed to us will someday be open. That is my faith. That is my belief. That is my testimony.

"The little stone which was cut out of the mountain without hands is rolling forth to fill the earth (see Dan. 2:31–45; D&C 65:2)."[7]

We can hear in such prophecies echoes of Joseph Smith's testimony that "the truth of God will go forth boldly, nobly, and independent till it has penetrated every continent, visited every clime, swept every country, and sounded in every ear."[8] May it be so, as we pray in section 65: "May the kingdom of God go forth, that the kingdom of heaven may come" (v. 6), that he who is entitled may reign as King of kings (Revelation 17:14).

Doctrine & Covenants 66

ORIGIN

For many years it appeared that the Lord gave the revelation in Doctrine and Covenants 66 on October 25, 1831, at a conference in Orange, Ohio, but the rediscovered journals of William McLellin indicate that the Lord gave this revelation to Joseph Smith in Hiram, Ohio, on October 29, 1831.[1]

After copying the revelation in his entry for that day, McLellin wrote that it "gave great joy to my heart because some important questions were answered which had dwelt upon my mind with anxiety and yet with uncertainty." Previous to meeting Joseph, McLellin secretly prayed that God would "reveal the answer to five questions through his prophet, and that too without his having any knowledge of my having made such request." In 1848, ten years after bitterly parting ways with Joseph Smith, McLellin wrote: "I now testify in the fear of God, that every question which I had thus lodged in the ears of the Lord of Sabbaoth, were answered to my full and entire satisfaction. I desired it for a testimony of Joseph's inspiration. And I to this day consider it to me an evidence which I cannot refute."[2]

McLellin's questions are unrecorded, but the revelation he wrote as Joseph dictated expresses the Lord's will for him (v. 4). The revelation therefore gave McLellin the choice of obeying or disobeying the Lord's will. His subsequent journal is an accountability report with the revelation in mind. It and related documents reveal his inconsistent effort to obey the revelation's several specific commands.

CONTENT

The Lord blesses McLellin for turning from his iniquities to truth and receiving the fulness of the gospel in Doctrine and Covenants 66. Still, he tells McLellin that he is not completely clean and needs to repent of his sins, in particular "adultery—a temptation with which thou hast been troubled" (v. 10). The Lord commands McLellin not to travel to Zion at that time but instead to serve a mission to the East with Samuel Smith until the Lord sends word for them to return. He commands McLellin to bear testimony to everyone everywhere he goes. "Lay your hands upon the sick, and they shall recover" (v. 9), the Lord promises. If McLellin continues obeying the word of the Lord, he will receive eternal life.

OUTCOMES

McLellin's journal testifies that he did set out on a mission in response to Doctrine and Covenants 66. He went about "reasoning with the people" (v. 7) while Samuel Smith bore his simple, powerful testimony as a witness

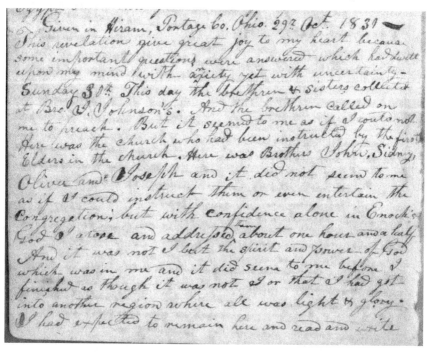

William E. McLellin journal, October 29, 1831.

of the Book of Mormon plates. McLellin also obeyed the commandment to heal the sick. He tried to "be patient in affliction" (v. 9), but as rejections mounted and winter approached, his resolve to obey the revelation faltered. He forsook Samuel Smith and returned to Kirtland in late December 1831 of his own volition. The Lord rebuked McLellin a few weeks later (see D&C 75:6–7).

Humbled, McLellin started on another mission but again forsook his companion and his calling, attributing his disobedience to poor health and lack of faith. He took a job to accumulate cash and married Emiline Miller, perhaps disobeying the command "seek not to be cumbered" with family obligations while called to serve as a missionary (D&C 66:10). The newlyweds set out for Zion in Jackson County, Missouri, where McLellin circumvented the law of consecration. Rather than meeting with Bishop Edward Partridge to consecrate his property and receive an inheritance, McLellin purchased two lots on Main Street, all in disobedience to specific commands that he "go not up unto the land of Zion as yet; but inasmuch as you can send, send; otherwise, think not of thy property" (v. 6).

William E. McLellin.

McLellin's disobedience to the revelation did not diminish his faith in it or its revelator. He wrote in August 1832 "that Joseph Smith is a true Prophet or Seer of the Lord and that he *has* power and *does* receive revelations from God, and that these revelations when received are of divine Authority in the church of Christ."[3] Upset by McLellin's actions in response to the revelations, Joseph wrote that his "Conduct merits the disapprobation of every true follower of Christ."[4]

Doctrine and Covenants 66 left McLellin's future in his hands. If he chose to do the Lord's will continually, he could "have a crown of eternal life" (v. 12). Instead McLellin chose to do his own will. On May 11, 1838, McLellin confessed that he had quit "praying and keeping the commandments of God and went his own way and indulged himself in his lustful desires."[5] The Church excommunicated him, and he spent the rest of his long life struggling to resolve the dissonance between his unshaken testimony and his unwillingness to repent.

Doctrine & Covenants 67

ORIGIN

Joseph convened a council at the Johnson home in Hiram, Ohio, and laid the manuscript Book of Commandments before the Church leaders. Joseph felt that "the Lord has bestowed a great blessing upon us in giving commandments and revelations."[1] He testified that the contents of the book should "be prized by this Conference to be worth to the Church the riches of the whole Earth." It was time to publish the revelations.[2] The council voted to print ten thousand copies.[3] The Lord revealed a preface for it in which he said, "These commandments are of me, and were given unto my servants in their weakness, after the manner of their language, that they might come to understanding" (D&C 1:24).

The question arose, "Was the simple language of Joseph Smith worthy of the voice of God?"[4] Joseph's history says that a discussion followed "'concerning Revelations and language.'"[5] Some fears went unspoken during the discussion. After all, everyone in the room must have recognized how their council might appear to an outsider. A poorly educated, twenty-six-year-old farmer planned to publish ten thousand copies of revelations that unequivocally declared themselves to be the words of Jesus Christ. They called the neighbors idolatrous and Missourians enemies, commanded them all to repent, and foretold calamities upon those who continued in wickedness. Moreover, the revelations were not properly punctuated, the orthography was haphazard, and the grammar was irregular.

Though lacking confidence in his own literary skills, or perhaps because of his limitations, Joseph was sure that his revelation texts were divine if imperfect productions. He promised the brethren present that they could know for themselves as well. Just a few days earlier Joseph had predicted that if the Saints could all "come together with one heart and one mind in perfect faith the vail might as well be rent to day as next week or any other time."⁶ Seeking confirmation of the revelations, the brethren tried to rend the veil, as had the brother of Jared in the Book of Mormon. They failed. Joseph asked why, and in answer he received Doctrine and Covenants 67.

CONTENT

The Lord speaks in Doctrine and Covenants 67 to the assembled Church leaders, noting that he has heard their prayers and knows the desires in their hearts. He knows they expected to receive a sure testimony of the revelations but were disappointed. "There were fears in your hearts," he tells them, "and verily this is the reason that ye did not receive" (v. 3). He gives them a testimony of the truthfulness of the book of revelations lying on the table before them. He assures them he has read their minds. They have been watching Joseph, listening to him, observing his imperfections, and have secretly wished, or perhaps even assumed, that they can do a better job than he. The Lord offers them the opportunity to try. He tells them to have the wisest man in the council (or any of them who cares to) duplicate the simplest revelation in the Book of Commandments. If he succeeds, they can all justifiably say they do not know the revelations are true. If he fails, the Lord will find them all guilty unless they testify of the truth of the revelations. The Lord knows that these men know that whatever imperfections the revelations show, they conform to God's law, are full of holy principles, and are just, virtuous, and good. They can conclude that such texts come from God.

The Lord covenants with the brethren that *if* they strip themselves of jealousy and fear and choose to be humble, *then* the veil between them and the Lord "shall be rent" (v. 10), and they will see him and know by their most reliable senses—their spiritual ones—that he exists. No mortal has ever seen God without the Holy Ghost activating their spiritual senses; otherwise, they are unable to endure his presence. Their fallen minds are incapable, and for these reasons the elders are unable to endure God's presence or even the presence of a ministering angel. "Continue in patience until ye are perfected. Let not your minds turn back," the Lord urges, "and when ye are worthy, in mine own due time, ye shall see and know that which was conferred upon you by the hands of my servant Joseph Smith" (vv. 13–14).

OUTCOMES

Doctrine and Covenants 67 challenges assumptions about what constitutes a revelation. Must it be literally lovely? Many revelations are, but not all. Nevertheless, any standard set by mortals will be subjective. God will never satisfy all his self-appointed editors. But the Lord seems unconcerned about the substance of the elders' literary fears. He does not ask whether Joseph dangled any of his participles or spelled everything just right. The Lord asks whether the revelations are righteous. He thus sets a standard for truthfulness that involves observations and experiments but in the end can only be known spiritually. The things of God are known only by communication from the Spirit of God (1 Corinthians 2:10–14).

Section 67 gave the brethren a certain testimony of the revelations, even if it was not the dramatic one they hoped for. In section 67, the Lord read their minds, provided them with a scientific, hands-on way of observing the properties of the revelations using a sample from them as a control in an experiment. The Lord gave the kind of testimony the brethren were suited to receive and gently urged them to become humble and spiritual enough to part the veil between him and them completely. The Lord invited the brethren to touch, feel, hear, see, taste, and testify of the revelations. He invited them to know him insofar as they were able and to "continue in patience" until they know him face to face (v. 13).

Joseph's history tells us how the brethren acted on the instructions in the revelation and became willing to testify before the world. William McLellin, who had the preceding week written as Joseph dictated a revelation, "endeavored to write a commandment like unto one of the least of the Lord's, but failed."[7] Joseph then asked the men present "what testimony they were willing to attach to these commandments which should shortly be sent to the world. A number of the brethren arose and said that they were willing to testify to the world that they knew that they were of the Lord," and they signed their names to a solemn statement as witnesses.[8]

Twelve more elders signed the statement in Missouri when the manuscript arrived there for printing. Joseph undoubtedly appreciated these witnesses. He was, by his own acknowledgment, no writer. He felt imprisoned by what he called the "total darkness of paper, pen, and Ink and a crooked, broken, scattered, and imperfect Language."[9] He considered it "an awful responsibility to write in the name of the Lord."[10] Yet he knew the responsibility was his. The revelations said God had "called upon my servant Joseph Smith, Jun., and spake unto him from heaven, and gave him commandments" and declared to him that "this generation shall have my word through you" (D&C 1:17; 5:10).

As section 67 acknowledged, the witnesses knew the limits of Joseph's imperfect language. It was a striking vote of confidence in Joseph and his revelations for eighteen men who knew him to declare their testimonies that the revelations were true. The discussion about revelations and language concluded as "the brethren arose in turn and bore witness to the truth of the Book of Commandments. After which br. Joseph Smith jr arose & expressed his feelings and gratitude."[11] The bold project of publishing the revelations required fearless believers to sustain Joseph in his awesome responsibility.

Doctrine & Covenants 68

ORIGIN

Some of the recently ordained high priests assembled for conference meetings in Hiram, Ohio, and "requested of the Lord to know his will concerning them." The Lord obliged them with the first twelve verses of Doctrine and Covenants 68. Then, anticipating that the revelation would soon be carried to the Saints in Missouri with the others, the Lord added an amendment to previous revelations, giving more instructions about the office of bishop and the responsibilities of parents in Zion.

CONTENT

New convert Orson Hyde, having recently been ordained a high priest, is therefore called to proclaim Christ's everlasting gospel by the power of the Holy Ghost (D&C 36). He is to go to the unrepentant everywhere, reasoning with them and explaining all scriptures to them. The Lord's instructions to Orson in Doctrine and Covenants 68 exemplify what he expects from the men who were ordained high priests at the recent conference.[1] All of them are to speak words inspired by the Holy Ghost. Such words are scripture—the mind, will, and word of the Lord. The Lord promises this gift of the Holy Ghost to these servants. The brethren have no need to fear. The Lord will stand beside them in their ministries as they testify that he is Jesus Christ, the son of the living God. The Lord commissions all faithful priesthood holders: "Go ye into all the world, preach the gospel to every creature, acting in the authority which I have given you, baptizing in the name of the Father, and of the Son, and of the Holy Ghost" (D&C 68:8). Christ will save those who choose to believe and receive baptism. He will damn those who do not.

The Lord adds to the constitution of the Church contained, essentially, in Doctrine and Covenants 20. There had been no bishops in the Church when section 20 was given in April 1830. Now, a year and a half later, the growing Church needs more revelation. The Lord tells the elders that he will call more bishops when he sees fit. The First Presidency will select them from the worthy high priests of the Church unless they are the first sons of literal descendants of Moses' brother Aaron. Such descendants have a legal right to preside over the Aaronic priesthood. No one else has that right, but high priests in the Melchizedek Priesthood have authority to officiate in all Aaronic Priesthood offices and therefore can serve as bishops when needed. Of course, both high priests and firstborn sons of literal descendants of Aaron must first be judged worthy, called, and set apart under the direction of the First Presidency.[2] Faithful firstborn sons of descendants of Aaron can claim their blessings if they prove their lineage or learn it by revelation from the First Presidency.

In the 1830s, the First Presidency judged all cases in which bishops were charged with transgressing the law of the Church. If they found a bishop guilty and he chose to repent, he would be forgiven according to the constitution of the Church in section 20 and to the law of the Church in section 42.

Parents in the Church who fail to teach their children the law of the gospel are accountable for their children's sins. Wherever the Church is organized, parents are responsible to teach their children the law of the gospel: faith in Jesus Christ, the Son of the living God, and the doctrines of repentance, baptism, and the gift of the Holy Ghost by the laying on of hands when eight years old. The Lord holds parents responsible for teaching their children to pray and live honestly. Those in Missouri are especially commanded to observe the Sabbath as a holy day. The Lord holds idle parents accountable for failing to build Zion. "I, the Lord, am not well pleased with the inhabitants of Zion," he said concerning the laziness, materialism, and misplaced priorities that resulted in children growing up in wickedness.

"They also seek not earnestly the riches of eternity, but their eyes are full of greediness. These things ought not to be, and must be done away from among them" (D&C 68:31–32). The Lord assigns Oliver Cowdery to take this revelation to the Saints in Missouri, so they can know and act on the Lord's will for them. He commands them to pray or be disciplined by Bishop Edward Partridge. The Lord wants this revelation read to and obeyed by the Saints in Missouri just as he has spoken it.

OUTCOMES

The Saints resolved to act on the instructions in Doctrine and Covenants 68 regarding bishops and Church discipline.[3] Oliver Cowdery took this revelation and others to the Saints in Missouri. The brethren who sought the Lord's will and received it acted on it fairly well in the short term. Orson Hyde, William McLellin, and the Johnson brothers were chosen as apostles in 1835, perhaps in part because of their faithfulness to the Lord's commission in this revelation to preach the gospel by his Holy Spirit. All of them struggled to endure in that commission and were at one time or another antagonistic to the Church.

Section 68 gives a unique definition of scripture as the voice of God communicated by his Holy Spirit to his authorized servants. In dictionaries of Joseph's day, the word *scripture* literally meant "what is written." Then and now the word denoted very old sacred writing. The sooner we get past that confining idea, the better. In 1838 Ralph Waldo Emerson urged Harvard graduates "to show us that God is, not was; that He speaketh, not spake."[4] Joseph Smith already had.

The Lord uses this revelation and others to give instruction on parenting. Children are born weak and helpless. Powerless to act for themselves but innately divine, children can be empowered to act for themselves if properly taught. Out of love, God empowers his children to act as he acts. He teaches them law, beginning with the law of the gospel. If children are not taught God's laws as they mature, they will never have agency or power to act for themselves. Teaching children the law of the gospel is a prerequisite to their gaining the ability to choose and act for themselves. Teaching children the laws of God does not guarantee they will keep them. It does guarantee that they will be able to choose for themselves whether to keep them. Parents who do not teach and therefore do not endow their children with agency will answer to God for deciding for their children rather than empowering them to choose for themselves. This revelation, together with sections 29 and 121, shows how the Lord both teaches and models how to endow children with power by giving them laws and, thus, agency.

Doctrine & Covenants 69

ORIGIN

Joseph spent the first two weeks of November 1831 in Hiram, Ohio, closely reviewing the revelations and counseling with his brethren about their publication. The Church's press was in Independence, Missouri. The handwritten copies of the revelations and the money to print them were in Ohio. The council contemplated sending Oliver Cowdery to Missouri with the revelations and commandments. "I also received a revelation to go with him," wrote John Whitmer, referring to Doctrine and Covenants 69.[1]

CONTENT

It is wisdom in the Lord that Oliver Cowdery not go to Missouri alone with the invaluable Book of Commandments and quite a bit of cash in his possession. He needs a companion. In Doctrine and Covenants 69 the Lord asks John Whitmer to go with Oliver as well as continue documenting the important history of the Church (D&C 47). He will be counseled and assisted as Church historian by Oliver, William Phelps, and perhaps others in Missouri who know important historical information or are good writers. Missionaries in the field should write about their experiences and send their accounts to Zion for John to use in keeping the Church history. Zion is the place for John to do this work and the place where the Saints should send him their documents. He should, however, travel often to the various Church branches to gather knowledge. He can then preach while he writes, copies, selects, and obtains historical information.

OUTCOMES

Joseph told the council that the revelations should be prized more than the riches of the earth and that he wanted to dedicate them, together with Oliver and John, to the Lord.[2] John went faithfully with Oliver to Missouri, carrying with them the revelation to parents in Zion (D&C 68), the priceless Book of Commandments to be published by William Phelps in Independence, Missouri, and considerable cash for printing and for Bishop Partridge to buy land in Missouri.[3]

Doctrine and Covenants 69, in combination with sections 21 and 47, records the Lord's commandments to document the history of the Church. In the restored Church of Jesus Christ, history functions much as theology does in other Christian traditions. Latter-day Saints know the nature of God and Christ not from the philosophical creeds of traditional Christianity but through records of historical experiences in which Joseph Smith saw and spoke with Them. We know, for example, that the priesthood needed to be restored because ministering angels brought it to Joseph Smith. We know of these experiences because they are described in documents. Thus, revelations such as section 69 are perhaps more important than they might at first seem.

John Whitmer wrote a history because of sections 47 and 69. It is an important, if sketchy, source of our knowledge of early Church events. As John's selfish interests overwhelmed him, he became bitter toward the Church in 1838. That attitude is reflected in the last chapters of his brief history.[4] When John stopped writing, Joseph started. With help from a host of assistants, Joseph compiled a much fuller history of the Church to document the Restoration.

Doctrine & Covenants 70

ORIGIN

In November 1831, the Church embarked on an ambitious and expensive publishing project. Church leaders had counseled about publishing Joseph's revelations. They had decided to send the manuscript record of the revelations with Oliver Cowdery and John Whitmer to Independence, Missouri, where Church printer William Phelps would print them on a press he was to purchase in Cincinnati. One issue remained unsettled. The Lord gave Doctrine and Covenants 70 to address it, and Joseph then discussed it with his brethren.

Joseph began by expressing gratitude for the brethren who had helped him with the Church's literary projects. He noted that Oliver Cowdery and Martin Harris had labored with him from the beginning to scribe and publish the Book of Mormon and that John Whitmer and Sidney Rigdon had long scribed and transcribed revelations and Joseph's new translation of the Bible. Joseph then raised the delicate issue: "As these sacred writings are now going to the Church for their benefit, that we may have claim on the Church for recompense." Joseph expressed his feeling that if the Saints valued the revelations enough to want them published, then those who gave their time and money to get them published deserved compensation. Likely referring to section 70, Joseph testified that the Spirit had put these sentiments into his heart.[1]

CONTENT

The Lord appoints Joseph Smith, Martin Harris, Oliver Cowdery, John Whitmer, Sidney Rigdon, and William Phelps to the business of managing the revelations from receipt through publication to sale. He proclaims to the Saints in Doctrine and Covenants 70: "I, the Lord, have appointed them, and ordained them to be stewards over the revelations and commandments which I have given unto them, and which I shall hereafter give unto them; and an account of this stewardship will I require of them in the day of judgment" (vv. 3–4). He commands the men not to give to the Church or to anyone else the challenge of publishing the revelations or the profits from selling the Book of Commandments. Rather, they are commanded to use the profits to provide for their families and consecrate anything left over by giving it to the storehouse for the Saints in Zion and their descendants who obey the laws of God. The Lord requires this of every steward he appoints.

No Latter-day Saints are exempt from the law of consecration—not Bishop Edward Partridge, nor his agent Sidney Gilbert, nor anyone the Lord appoints to do any job, whether the work is physical or spiritual. Those the Lord appoints as stewards over spiritual or physical matters are worthy to have their needs and wants supplied from the Lord's storehouse, although those who labor over spiritual things have the added benefit of working closely with the Spirit. The six brethren named are to willingly be equal, economically speaking, or they will not have the Spirit. The Lord gives these brethren such benefits as evidence of his blessings to them, as a reward for their diligence, and as a way to provide for them economically, so that they and their families can have food, clothes, homes, land, and an inheritance in Zion regardless of where the Lord may send them on his errands. The six brethren have been faithful and good stewards over the Lord's literary concerns. "I, the Lord, am merciful and will bless them," he says in conclusion, "and they shall enter into the joy of these things" (v. 18).

OUTCOMES

Doctrine and Covenants 70 creates what is often called the Literary Firm, a corporation assigned by the Lord to receive, write, revise, print, bind, and sell the revelations according to the law of consecration. The members of the firm were free to act on this revelation as they saw fit, knowing they would be accountable for their actions. They were stewards of the Lord's words and worthy to be supported out of the Lord's storehouse for the consecrated work they did. They anticipated that sales of the revelations would provide for their families.

Joseph modeled and taught his brethren the law of consecration as section 70 sets it forth. When William Phelps began acting as if he were the owner of the Lord's press rather than a steward "over the revelations" (v. 3), Joseph gently but directly sent him the following postscript. It penetrates to the heart of the principles of consecration and section 70: "Bro. William— You say 'my press, my types, &c.' Where, our brethren ask, did you get them, & how came they to be '*yours*'? No hardness, but a caution, for you know, that it is, *We,* not *I,* and all things are the Lord's, and he opened the hearts of his Church to furnish these things, or *we* should not have been privileged with using them."[2]

Most of the six brethren had already been deeply involved in this work and remained so through the 1833 publication of the Book of Commandments and, along with others, the 1835 publication of the Doctrine and Covenants. Martin Harris funded the publication of the Book of Mormon and perhaps the Firm's later projects. Sidney Rigdon served often as scribe of revelations and Joseph's new translation of the Bible and as a proofreader of the manuscript revelations. John Whitmer transcribed the texts. Oliver Cowdery assisted in all stages of receiving, editing, and printing. He and John Whitmer carried the revelations and money to print them to Missouri where the Lord's choice for an editor, William Phelps, printed the Book of Commandments.

Joseph received the revelations. He also edited and amended them as he saw fit. One of Joseph's stewardships in the Literary Firm was to "correct those errors or mistakes which he may discover by the holy Spirit."[3] Joseph believed in his revelations, but he never believed that any scripture was pristine.[4] He edited his own revelations because he regarded them as his best efforts to represent the voice of the Lord condescending to speak in what Joseph called "a crooked, broken, scattered, and imperfect Language."[5]

Most of the other members of the Firm were more literary than Joseph.

That was a blessing that occasionally annoyed him. After William Phelps criticized one revelation, Joseph responded defensively in behalf of himself and Oliver Cowdery. "We would say, by way of excuse, that we did not think so much of the orthography [spelling], or the manner, as we did of the subject matter; as the word of God means what it says; & it is the word of God, as much as Christ was God, although *he* was born in a stable, & was rejected by the manner of his birth, notwithstanding he was God." Joseph implicitly blamed the revelation's spelling and punctuation errors on his limited education and explicitly on the fatigue of his proofreader, Oliver, who had recently returned from Missouri and then New York, where he had purchased for the Church a new press amidst opposition. Frustrated, Joseph complained to his brethren that the Saints "are just like you—they will not receive anything but by revelation!"[6] And then, he implied, Phelps and perhaps others were critical of the revelation. Joseph confided to his history that "it was an awful responsibility to write in the name of the Lord."[7] Yet the Lord had made it his responsibility. In the revelations the Lord "called upon my servant Joseph Smith, Jun., and spake unto him from heaven, and gave him commandments" and declared to him that "this generation shall have my word through you" (D&C 1:17; 5:10).

The members of the Firm gave their best efforts to publish the revelations, impoverishing themselves in the process. Then, when Phelps had nearly finished printing the Book of Commandments, a mob of Missourians destroyed the press, his home and office, and as many copies of the revelations as they could. Some of the printed sheets were rescued by various Saints, and a few incomplete copies of the Book of Commandments were published. Today fewer than thirty known copies survive, and it is ironic that they can sell for millions. We should remember what the revelations originally cost. Joseph and the other members of the Literary Firm made themselves poor and persecuted by publishing them. They all voiced their conviction about the revelations before organizing the Literary Firm according to section 70. The brethren approved unanimously Joseph's motion that they should "prize the revelations to be worth to the Church the riches of the whole earth."[8]

Doctrine & Covenants 71

ORIGIN

Ezra Booth was a talented Methodist preacher who visited Joseph Smith at his home in Kirtland in 1831 with his wife, John and Elsa Johnson, and some others. An early history of Disciples of Christ in northern Ohio reported that "Mrs. Johnson had been afflicted for some time with a lame arm, and was not at the time of the visit able to lift her hand to her head. The party visited Smith partly out of curiosity, and partly to see for themselves what there might be in the new doctrine. During the interview, the conversation turned on the subject of supernatural gifts, such as were conferred in the days of the Apostles. Some one said, 'Here is Mrs. Johnson with a lame arm; has God given any power to men now on the earth to cure her?' A few moments later, when the conversation had turned in another direction, Smith rose, and walking across the room, taking Mrs. Johnson by the hand, said in the most solemn and impressive manner: *'Woman, in the name of the Lord Jesus Christ, I command thee to be whole,'* and immediately left the room."[1]

Ezra Booth and the Johnsons recognized that God had restored the New Testament gift of healing to Joseph Smith. They joined the Church. But a testimony of the truth is not necessarily conversion. Many people know in their minds but never receive the mighty change of their hearts. For many of these people, their witness of the truth is like a weight around their necks. They hate it, and they work hard to dislodge it. Ezra went with Joseph and many others to Missouri in the summer of 1831. He judged everything Joseph said and did with a jaundiced eye. He tried to undermine Joseph's authority by finding fault with his personality and prophecies. Then, casting himself in the role of a public servant, Ezra wrote nine letters against Joseph that were published in a local newspaper, the *Ohio Star*.[2] Joseph's cousin George A. Smith described this common phenomenon well. He said of Ezra Booth that "while he was in apostasy he searched his cranium for some means to justify himself and published a series of lying letters."[3]

Booth's letters claimed that Joseph's revelations were false and that Zion in Missouri was a scam upon the gullible. Booth justified his failure to do what the revelations commanded and persuaded himself and perhaps others that Joseph was "quite dictatorial" and no prophet after all. But what about that nagging miracle Ezra had witnessed? The fact that Elsa Johnson was healed could not be denied, even by Joseph's most outspoken antagonists. So a subsequent history explained that the "infinite presumption" of Joseph Smith gave Elsa Johnson a "sudden mental and moral shock—I know not how better to explain the well attested fact—electrified the rheumatic arm—Mrs. Johnson at once lifted it up with ease, and on her return home the next day she was able to do her washing without difficulty or pain."[4]

Booth's letters raised public consciousness of Joseph Smith and the Restoration.[5] In Doctrine and Covenants 71, the Lord called Joseph Smith and Sidney Rigdon to cease revising the Bible in order to take advantage of the opportunity Booth had given them to declare the gospel in the area and thus to set the record straight.

CONTENT

The Lord tells Joseph and Sidney Rigdon in Doctrine and Covenants 71 that it is time for them to proclaim his gospel and explain the mysteries of his kingdom by using the scriptures and following the inspiration of the Holy Ghost. The Savior commands Joseph and Sidney to preach the gospel to the Saints and their neighbors in the surrounding areas until he tells them otherwise. He commands them: "Labor ye in my vineyard. Call upon the inhabitants of the earth, and bear record" (v. 4). Their mission will prepare people to receive the Lord's wisdom in the revelations soon to be published as the Book of Commandments. Those who read it must choose whether to understand and receive the gospel it declares. To those who choose to receive, Christ gives more abundantly. He endows them with power. Christ commands Joseph and Sidney to confound their enemies—to invite them to meet in public and in private. As long as Joseph and Sidney remain faithful, their enemies will be openly shamed. "Let them bring forth their strong reasons against the Lord," he says, and then he renews the promise he made to Israel through the prophet Isaiah: "No weapon that is formed against you shall prosper" (vv. 8–9). The Lord promises to confound any who argue against Joseph and Sidney in his own due time.

OUTCOMES

Joseph and Sidney enjoyed obeying this revelation. "Knowing now the mind of the Lord," Joseph wrote, "that the time had come that the gospel should be proclaimed in power and demonstration to the world, from the scriptures, reasoning with men as in days of old, I took a journey to Kirtland, in company with Elder Rigdon, on the 3d day of December to fulfill the . . . Revelation."[6] Sidney Rigdon replied to Ezra Booth in the pages of the *Ohio Star* and invited him to meet publicly.[7] For nearly six weeks Joseph and Sidney "continued to preach in Shalersville, Ravenna, and other places, setting forth the truth; vindicating the cause of our Redeemer: shewing that the day of vengeance was coming upon this generation like a thief in the night: that prejudice, blindness, and darkness, filled the minds of many, and caused them to persecute the true church, and reject the true light: by which means we did much towards allaying the excited feelings which were growing out of the scandalous letters then being published in the 'Ohio Star,' at Ravenna, by the before mentioned Apostate Ezra Booth."[8]

Since Ezra Booth, many others have wielded weapons against the restored gospel. The Lord's policy, as stated in Doctrine and Covenants 71, is to "let them bring forth their strong reasons against the Lord" (v. 8). Such opposition facilitates agency and fulfills prophecy. It causes people to consciously choose whether or not to believe in Joseph Smith's testimony, and it honors Moroni's promise to the obscure, teenaged Joseph that his "name should be had for good and evil among all nations, . . . or that it should be both good and evil spoken of among all people" (Joseph Smith–History 1:33).

Doctrine & Covenants 72

ORIGIN

Kirtland was Joseph's first stop after he left his Hiram, Ohio, home for a local mission in obedience to Doctrine and Covenants 71. In Kirtland he counseled with the high priests "about our temporal and Spiritual welfare."[1] The Church was growing larger and more complicated to manage. Many of the ablest Saints, including Bishop Edward Partridge, had migrated to Missouri in obedience to earlier revelations, leaving a large number of Saints in Ohio without a bishop. In a revelation received a month earlier than Doctrine and Covenants 72, the Lord promised to call other bishops when he saw fit (D&C 68:14).

He saw fit in section 72, which is a series of three related revelations given to answer the questions Joseph and his brethren were asking. Verses 1–8 address whether the time is right for the appointment of a new bishop. And, if so, who should it be? One imagines that the new bishop wanted to know his duties. Verses 9–23 outline them. Joseph and his brethren were concerned about maintaining order in the process of gathering the Saints to Zion in Missouri. They could not wisely arrive faster than Bishop Partridge could have land available for them to inherit. Verses 24–26 are an amendment to earlier revelations, given to regulate the migration of Saints gathering to Zion. Section 72 can be summed up as the appointment of a bishop and a description of his duties in the early 1830s.

CONTENT

In Doctrine and Covenants 72 the Lord tells the elders that it is indeed time for him to call another bishop to serve the Saints in Ohio. They are wise, as stewards of the Church, in asking the Lord to appoint one. The Lord requires every steward to be accountable for his stewardship in both time and eternity. Stewards who act faithfully and wisely on earth become worthy to inherit heavenly mansions prepared by Heavenly Father. The elders in Ohio are to account to the bishop whom the Lord will appoint shortly. The new bishop will then record whether the elders are faithful and wise stewards and give those reports to Bishop Partridge in Missouri. The Lord has already revealed a bishop's duties in earlier revelations and in earlier proceedings of the conference. The Lord declares that Newel Kimball Whitney should be ordained as the bishop of the Saints in Ohio.

The Lord then outlines the bishop's specific duties. Bishop Whitney is to be the steward over the Lord's storehouse. He is to receive and take care of the Church's money in Ohio. As commanded in verse 5, he is to hear the accountability reports of the elders and ensure their physical wants are met. If able, the elders are to pay Bishop Whitney for what they receive from the storehouse. What they pay can then be consecrated to relieve poverty. Bishop Whitney is responsible to provide for those who cannot pay and to communicate his actions to Bishop Partridge, who will then pay the debts from the resources in the Missouri storehouse. Those who work for the Church will also receive their living from Bishop Partridge. According to the law of consecration, all Saints who gather

Newel K. Whitney, the second man called as a bishop in the restored Church.

to Zion are to consecrate all they possess. If the Saints obey this law, Bishop Partridge will have ample resources to satisfy the needs of the Saints who work for the Church.

Because every elder in Ohio is to account to Bishop Whitney, who is to send the accountability report to Bishop Partridge, the Lord directs Bishop Whitney to make certificates, or recommends, to send to Zion with each faithful servant. Bishop Partridge will accept them and grant an inheritance to those gathering to Zion with such a recommend from Bishop Whitney. "Otherwise," the Lord said, "he shall not be accepted of the bishop of Zion" (v. 18). Every elder in the East who desires to gather to Zion is commanded to furnish Bishop Whitney with recommendations from members of the branches of the Church where he has served. By accounting for their stewardships in this way, the elders can be approved by the Lord.

OUTCOMES

"I cannot see a Bishop in myself," Newel K. Whitney told Joseph after Doctrine and Covenants 72 was given, "but if you say it's the Lord's will, I'll try." Joseph replied that Newel "need not take my word alone. . . . Go and ask Father for yourself." Newel prayed privately for confirmation and "heard a voice from heaven [tell him,] 'Thy strength is in me.'" He found Joseph and told him he would accept the calling as the Lord's bishop.[2] He confided to his wife, Ann, "that it would require a vast amount of patience, of perseverance and of wisdom to magnify his calling."[3]

Early bishops such as Edward Partridge and Newel Whitney did not preside over wards as bishops do today. That began in the 1840s. Their primary duty was to implement the law of consecration. They managed the Lord's property and assets, relieved poverty, paid the Church's bills, and built Zion as best they could. Having received his calling and confirmation of it by revelation, Newel Whitney did his best to serve as a bishop for the rest of his life. Not only was he an experienced and able manager of properties, inventories, and accounts but he had a generous heart and, perhaps most important of all, he knew well that he was incapable of being a bishop unless he relied on the Lord for the patience, perseverance, and wisdom he needed.

The bishops were responsible to assist the members of the Literary

Firm (D&C 70) so they could concentrate on publishing the Lord's revelations and selling the Book of Commandments widely, thus raising funds to support their own families and, hopefully, generate a surplus to benefit the Church. In this way, assistance from the bishop would enable members of the Literary Firm to be faithful and wise stewards.

Section 72 is a blueprint for appointing bishops in all large branches of the Church to facilitate obedience to the law of consecration. Saints who act on this blueprint obey the law of consecration's principle of agency (acting of one's own will to obey God's will), stewardship (taking care of the Lord's property and business as commanded), and accountability (reporting to the Lord's appointed servant, the bishop).

The Saints struggled to obey the command in section 72 to gather to Zion only after receiving a recommend from the bishop to do so. Joseph wrote to Church leaders in Missouri that he rejoiced at the news that a group of Saints had arrived there safely, but "they left here under this displeasure of heaven." Why? For "making a mock of the profession of faith in the commandments by proceding contrary thereto in not complying . . . with the requirements of them in not obtaining recommends."[4] William W. Phelps reminded the Saints of the revelation. He wrote in the Church's newspaper that emigrating Saints would not be welcome in Zion "without regular recommends."[5] Slowly the Saints began to comply with the revelation by receiving recommends before moving to Missouri.[6]

Doctrine & Covenants 73

ORIGIN

After a month of preaching the gospel in the villages of northeastern Ohio in response to Ezra Booth's anti-Mormon letters (D&C 71), Joseph and Sidney Rigdon received Doctrine and Covenants 73.

CONTENT

The Lord says it will serve his purposes if the elders continue preaching the gospel and explaining it to the Saints in the local branches until their next conference, which is to be held in two weeks. At that time, the Lord will further command them in their duties. Joseph and Sidney, however, are commanded to continue revising the Bible. They may also preach locally until the next conference, but after that, they are to work on the Bible until it is finished. The elders can use Doctrine and Covenants 73 as a pattern in the future—a commandment to carry on in their assignments until instructed differently.

OUTCOMES

Joseph obeyed this revelation. He wrote that after receiving it, "I recommenced the translation of the scriptures." He wrote that he "labored diligently" until time for the conference mentioned in the revelation.[1] There, as Doctrine and Covenants 73 says, Joseph revealed new assignments to several of the elders (D&C 75).

Doctrine & Covenants 74

ORIGIN

As commanded in Doctrine and Covenants 73, Joseph and Sidney Rigdon resumed their revision of the Bible. Joseph's history says they "labored diligently" at the task.[1] While carefully studying the first letter of the apostle Paul to the Corinthian Saints, they received Doctrine and Covenants 74 as an explanation of 1 Corinthians 7:14. There Paul counseled Christian women who were married to Jewish men regarding the tension between their religions when it came to raising children. What did this verse mean?

CONTENT

The revelation in Doctrine and Covenants 74 begins by quoting the passage in question—1 Corinthians 7:14: "For the unbelieving husband is sanctified by the wife, and the unbelieving wife is sanctified by the husband: else were your children unclean; but now are they holy."

The Lord explains the religious context of this passage to Joseph. Jews in the first century after Christ continued to practice circumcision, cutting the foreskin from the penis. Though a widespread practice anciently, circumcision for the covenant people of Israel gained religious significance after Jehovah made it a token of his covenant with Abraham and commanded that male children of the covenant be circumcised when eight days old (Genesis 17).[2] In Paul's day, controversy rose within the Church over whether Christians needed to be circumcised. Section 74 addresses part of the controversy. Jewish husbands wanted their sons circumcised as evidence of their being subject to the law of Moses. Christian wives believed that Christ's atonement satisfied the law of Moses and that baptism was the new token of the gospel covenant. Children who followed the law of Moses were missing out on the sanctifying blessings of the gospel. Paul, therefore, counseled the Saints to not marry Jews unless they agreed in advance that their children would be raised in the gospel of Jesus Christ. This would do away with the false tradition that had grown out of the practice of circumcision that children were unholy. "But little children are holy," the Lord teaches Joseph, "being sanctified through the atonement of Jesus Christ; and this is what the scriptures mean" (v. 7).

OUTCOMES

This remarkable revelation makes us think of Joseph's teenaged struggles to understand the Bible. "The teachers of religion of the different sects understood the same passages of scripture so differently as to destroy all confidence in settling the question by an appeal to the Bible" (Joseph Smith–History 1:12). Joseph had learned then to take his questions to the Lord himself. In Doctrine and Covenants 74, as in several others, the Lord himself interprets the Bible for Joseph. In doing so he subtly solves an important theological problem that often occurs to parents of young children concerning original sin. Are mortals sinful by nature, or not? Ask a group of Latter-day Saints if they believe that man is inherently evil and, all evidence from themselves and their own children aside, they will overwhelmingly answer no, of course not. But Book of Mormon prophets give a different answer. They knew and taught that mortals are evil, at least in part (2 Nephi 2:29; 4:17–20). As the brother of Jared put it, "Because of the fall our natures have become evil continually" (Ether 3:2). Merely by being born as mortals, we have inherited a sinful nature.

What? We just read in section 74 that little children are holy. They are. Note why. The revelation says they are "sanctified through the atonement of Jesus Christ" (v. 7). Section 74 teaches us one more of the profundities of Christ's infinite atonement. Because children inherit the Fall helplessly without having exercised any agency in the matter, Jesus Christ atones for them. He sanctifies them and sets them on a course to begin to become accountable agents at about age eight if properly taught the law of the gospel (D&C 29; 68). As long as children are not yet accountable agents, too helpless to understand or do much about the fallen part of their nature, Jesus sanctifies them according to his will. That is what section 74 means. This beautiful doctrine, restored through Joseph Smith, solves an important theological problem.

Doctrine & Covenants 75

ORIGIN

The Church convened quarterly conferences in its early years, and an important one was held in January 1832 in Amherst, Ohio, the home of several Latter-day Saint families about fifty miles east of Church headquarters in Kirtland. The Lord had recently revealed that at this conference the elders would learn what he wanted them to do next (D&C 73). Joseph's history says they "seemed anxious for me to enquire of the Lord, that they might know his will, or learn what would be most pleasing to him for them to do."[1] Joseph asked for and received two revelations, and Sidney Rigdon wrote them down.[2] Combined, they now compose Doctrine and Covenants 75.

CONTENT

The Lord begins Doctrine and Covenants 75 by speaking specifically to those who had volunteered to preach the gospel. He proclaims his will that they work hard, lifting their voices to declare the truthfulness of the gospel as if with a trumpet. If they do so faithfully, he promises them a bountiful harvest of souls and eternal life. The Lord rebukes William McLellin for failing to honorably serve for the duration of the mission call the Lord gave him in Doctrine and Covenants 66. The Lord punishes him by revoking it. But he forgives William and mercifully offers another opportunity for him to qualify for the promised blessings by serving a mission to the South with Luke Johnson. If the two pray always without giving in to rejection, depression, or a lack of energy, the Holy Ghost will teach them everything they need to know, and the Lord will be with them to the end.

The Lord calls Orson Hyde to replace William McLellin as Samuel Smith's companion and to go east to preach the gospel. The Lord will likewise be with them to the end if they remain faithful in doing what he asks. The Lord then issues several mission calls, promising the elders that, if faithful, they will overcome all things and be caught up into heaven to meet the returning Christ at his second coming. He instructs all the elders to tract from house to house, village to village, city to city. He commands them to leave blessings on the homes of those who receive them. He tells them to quickly leave the homes of those who choose not to receive them and to shake the dust off their feet as a testimony that the elders offered the law of the gospel but the people rejected it. That testimony will be condemning. Those who have never heard the gospel and, therefore, are not accountable to act upon it, will be better off on Judgment Day than those who are offered it but reject it.

The Lord again speaks to those who expressed their desire to know his will. He tells them it is the duty of Church members to assist the families of missionaries sent to proclaim the gospel. The Lord commands the elders to find places for their families to live among the willing Saints. All who can find places for their families are to preach the gospel. If they ask, the Holy Ghost will direct them to where they should serve. Those who cannot find another way to provide for their families are to stay home and provide. They will not lose eternal life for doing so. The Lord commands them to work in the Church. Those unwilling to work are not welcome in the Church unless they repent and correct their behavior.

OUTCOMES

Many early elders kept journals of their missions or wrote letters to the Church newspaper to report on their service. They intended to document their obedience to the revelations, or, in some cases, to justify their disobedience. Their records tell whether they obeyed Doctrine and Covenants 75.

When they did obey, the Lord unfailingly granted them the blessings he promised on condition of their obedience.

William McLellin started his mission to the South with Luke Johnson but was soon overwhelmed with doubts. The Lord promised him that continual prayer would sustain him, that if William and Luke would pray, then "I will be with them even unto the end." William said he could not bring himself to pray in faith. He had his eyes on a young woman named Emiline Miller. He quit his mission and took a job so he could marry her, noting, meanwhile, that he was too sick for missionary work.[3] "Preferring not to proceed alone," Luke returned to Hiram, Ohio, where Joseph called Seymour Brunson to replace William. Luke and Seymour fulfilled their call and enjoyed the Lord's promised blessings on their mission in the "south countries," Virginia and Kentucky.[4]

Orson Hyde noted that he and companion Samuel Smith did "one of the most arduous and toilsome missions ever performed in the Church."[5] For eleven months they walked from Ohio to Maine and back. Samuel wrote that they followed the revelation as they "went from house to house" and shook the dust from their feet as a testimony against those who rejected the gospel of Jesus Christ.[6]

Lyman Johnson and Orson Pratt went east, as commanded, ending up in New England. They baptized many, including a future apostle (Amasa M. Lyman), and at Charleston, Vermont, twenty-two-year-old Orson Pratt pronounced a priesthood blessing that raised Olive Farr from the bed where she had lain an invalid for seven years. "Thank God," she wept. "I'm healed!" Such evidence that the Lord was with the elders, as he said in the revelation he would be, greatly increased their success. They baptized 104 sons and daughters of God for the remission of their sins and organized them into branches before returning to Ohio, after walking nearly four hundred miles.[7]

No known records tell whether Asa Dodds, Calves Wilson, Major N. Ashley, and Burr Riggs obeyed Doctrine and Covenants 75. Simeon Carter and Emer Harris did obey and achieved great success, though they each served with their brothers as companions.[8] Ezra Thayre and Thomas Marsh apparently served their mission. Hyrum Smith and Reynolds Cahoon obediently served together, and on his return home Hyrum set out to obey other instructions in the revelation. He noted that he "went to work with mine hands for the support of my family."[9] Seymour Brunson reported his mission with both Daniel Stanton and Luke Johnson. They baptized fifty-three and organized them into a branch.[10] Sylvester Smith and Gideon Carter obeyed the revelation. Sylvester had it in mind the next summer, too, when he went out again "resolved to blow the trumpet of the Gospel." He knew that if he would, the revelation promised that the Lord would be with him. "I trust I shall continue to receive the grace of God to support me even to the end."[11] No known evidence tells whether Ruggles Eames and Stephen Burnett obeyed the revelation. Micah Welton and Eden Smith obeyed. Eden's journal shows that he was especially mindful of the revelation's instructions to preach and provide for his family as best he could. "Preachd and then returned home and Laboured for the support of my family," he wrote, echoing the revelation's instructions.[12]

Doctrine & Covenants 76

ORIGIN

Joseph Smith grew up with some understanding of soteriology—the aspect of theology that deals with salvation. Many of his ancestors were practicing Calvinists. They believed that God saved and damned according to his "sovereign pleasure, his arbitrary will."[1] Joseph's paternal grandfather, Asael Smith, broke with this tradition. He and his son Joseph, the Prophet's father, affiliated with a Universalist society, whose members believed that God would save everyone. Although quite opposed in their views of who would be saved, Calvinists and Universalists agreed that God made all the decisions about salvation. Individual agency had no place in these soteriologies. Of the churches Joseph Smith sampled, Methodism was the one that took individual agency seriously. Methodists believed that Christ was mighty to save but that he would respect an individual's will to be saved or not. Which, if any, of these competing teachings was right?

Later, from the confines of Liberty Jail, Joseph described the requirements for understanding salvation. "The things of God are of deep import," he wrote, "and time and experience and careful and ponderous and solemn thoughts can only find them out. Thy mind, O Man, if thou wilt lead a soul unto salvation must stretch as high as the utmost heavens, and search into and contemplate the lowest considerations of the darkest abyss, and expand upon the broad considerations of eternal expanse; he must commune with God."[2]

The earliest manuscript of section 76 is the first revelation recorded in Revelation Book 2, called the Kirtland Revelation Book. Joseph probably purchased this book soon after he sent the manuscript Book of Commandments to Missouri for publication. The receipt of section 76 and the repeated command to write it while still in the Spirit may have been the catalyst for purchasing this book and recording The Vision in it. The few lines of heavy ink in the middle of this page are thought to be in Joseph Smith's handwriting.

Earlier, in February 1832 while carefully studying the Gospel of John, Joseph communed with God. Joseph and Sidney Rigdon saw a series of sublime visions that probed "realms of doctrine unimagined in traditional Christian theology."[3] The two seers described the visions in a self-contained text, meaning that Doctrine and Covenants 76, unlike other sections, tells its own story. It narrates the series of events that led to and composed the revelation, and it describes what was envisioned (D&C 138).

CONTENT

Doctrine and Covenants 76 begins with a preface that poetically invites us to listen to the Lord, the only Savior. It is not clear whether the Lord or Joseph or, perhaps, Sidney Rigdon is the author of the first four verses, but by verse 5 we hear the Lord's voice distinctly. He declares himself merciful. He gives grace to all who fear him. He loves to honor those who serve him righteously to the end. He promises them a great reward and eternal glory. He promises to reveal to them all mysteries, all the knowledge—past and future—he has not revealed. He will reveal his kingdom. He will show them the wonders of eternity. Their wisdom will reach to heaven. The worldly-wise will pale by comparison. The Lord will enlighten the faithful with his Spirit. He will reveal secrets never seen, heard, or even conceived before.

On February 16, 1832, Joseph Smith and Sidney Rigdon read John 5:29, in which Jesus testifies to some antagonistic Jews that he will raise the dead who "shall come forth; they that have done good, unto the resurrection of life; and they that have done evil, unto the resurrection of damnation." Joseph and Sidney marveled at Christ's power and the mystery of resurrection. They "meditated upon these things" (D&C 76:19), and the Lord touched their eyes so that they understood. They testify together of Jesus Christ. They declare that they saw and understood God's plans for salvation. They testify of the fulness of the gospel of Jesus Christ, whom they saw and with whom they spoke. They saw him at his Father's right hand and partook of his fulness. They saw holy angels and those Christ had sanctified, worshipping God and Christ forever. After all the testimonies given of Christ, they give the ultimate testimony: "He lives! For we saw him, even on the right hand of God; and we heard the voice bearing record that he is the Only Begotten of the Father—that by him, and through him, and of him, the worlds are and were created, and the inhabitants thereof are begotten sons and daughters unto God" (vv. 22–24).

Another vision is opened to Joseph and Sidney. They see and testify that an angel, one of God's spirit children, held authority from God but rebelled against Jesus Christ. Heavenly Father loved Christ and had chosen him. Heavenly Father banished the other son from his presence as a consequence of his rebellion. Heavenly Father wept, for this promising son was utterly lost and damned forever. His name is Lucifer. Joseph and Sidney thus see Satan, known in scripture as a serpent or the devil, rebel against God in an effort to steal the kingdom from his Father and His rightful heir, Jesus Christ. The Lord commands Joseph and Sidney to write what they saw about Satan.

Having been punished for his rebellion, Satan chooses to attack the Saints by surrounding them with evil. Joseph and Sidney envision the suffering of those who fall under Satan's onslaught. The Lord tells them that all who know his gospel and then choose to follow the devil and become subject to his power, denying the truth and defying Christ's power, become Satan's sons rather than Christ's. They are sons of the utterly lost. It would have been better for them not to have been born. They suffer God's justified anger with the devil and the spirits who rebelled with him. The Lord has said they are not and will not be forgiven. They deny the Holy Spirit after they receive it. They deny Christ. It is as if, knowing the power of his gospel, they openly crucify him themselves. They are sent to hell—a lake of fire and brimstone—with the devil and the spirits who rebelled with him. Though resurrected, they remain spiritually dead forever, cut off from the Godhead, the only ones unredeemed by Christ. Christ, whom Heavenly Father chose to fulfill the plan of salvation even before the Creation, saves everyone else. He resurrects them all as he, though once slain, is now resurrected.

A heavenly voice testifies to Joseph and Sidney that this is the good news, the glad tidings of Jesus Christ: He came into the world to be crucified, to endure the sins of the world, to sanctify and cleanse the world from all unrighteousness for the express purpose of saving every one of Heavenly Father's children who exercise their God-given agency to be saved. By saving all his children except the few who "defect to perdition," Jesus Christ glorifies his Heavenly Father.[4] He saves every one of his Father's children who have any desire to be saved. The few who do not so desire go the way their desires inevitably lead. God punishes them. They reign with the devil and the spirits that followed him, tormented by the toll of their terrible choices. The Lord gives a glimpse of this suffering to many, but no one knows the location or duration of such suffering except those who experience perdition—the unredeemed. A heavenly voice tells Joseph and Sidney to write their vision of this suffering.

Juxtaposed powerfully against the suffering of the damned, Joseph and Sidney testify of seeing and hearing about the resurrection of the just. The just are those who receive the testimony of Jesus Christ, believe and are baptized by immersion, signifying burial and rebirth as Christ commanded. Christ cleanses from sin all who choose to keep these commandments. They receive the Holy Spirit when an authorized priesthood holder lays on hands. The just overcome Satan by exercising faith in Christ. The Holy Ghost, in his role as the Holy Spirit of Promise, seals them by testifying that they have been faithful to their covenants. Heavenly Father sheds the Holy Spirit of Promise on all who are keeping their covenants. Covenant keepers belong to the church of the Firstborn. Heavenly Father gives them everything, including the fulness of temple blessings. They are priests and kings, priestesses and queens. They are the children of God who fully inherit his glory. They are thus gods themselves. Everything is theirs. Death cannot stop them. Their future is limitless. They belong to Christ, and he belongs to Heavenly Father. Nothing can damn them or hem them in. There is no reason to rejoice in fallen mortals, but fallen mortals should rejoice in God, for his plan of salvation solves the problems of sin and death and redeems fallen mortals so they can dwell with him and the Savior forever. The just are resurrected first and come with Christ at his second coming to reign on earth. They dwell in the heavenly Zion, the city of God. They commune with angels and the people of Enoch's Zion and the other Saints throughout time who have received the fulness of temple ordinances and been faithful to their covenants. Their names are written in heaven, where God and Christ judge everything. They have kept their covenant promises to obey the laws of God, and Christ therefore keeps his covenant promise to resurrect and perfect them by the power of his perfect atonement in which he shed his own blood. They are resurrected with celestial bodies as glorious as the sun, which is typical of God's glory.

Joseph and Sidney then envision the terrestrial world, which differs from the celestial as the moon differs from the sun. The celestial church of the Firstborn receives all Heavenly Father has. Inhabitants of the terrestrial glory do not. They died without fully obeying the laws of God. Christ arranges for the gospel to be preached to them in the spirit world. They receive the testimony of Jesus Christ there but would not receive it while alive on earth. They were honorable but deceived while on earth, blinded by crafty men. They receive only a portion of God's glory. They receive the Savior's presence but not the Father's. They are resurrected with terrestrial bodies, differing from celestial bodies as the moon differs from the sun, incapable of creating and sustaining life. They did not act strongly or courageously on their testimonies of Christ. They were promised the blessing to become kings and queens if they would obey the laws of God, but they did not, and thus they forfeit their crowns. The Lord commands Joseph and Sidney to write this vision before the Holy Spirit leaves them.

Joseph and Sidney then envision the telestial glory, which is less glorious than the terrestrial as the stars pale in comparison to the moon.

One Latter-day Saint student became distraught upon learning that an idea taught in an earlier discussion of Doctrine and Covenants 76 was inaccurate. The teacher had interpreted verse 89—"the glory of the telestial, which surpasses all understanding"—by telling the students that Joseph Smith taught that one would commit suicide to inherit the telestial kingdom. That is not what the revelation says, nor what Joseph Smith apparently said, nor is it consistent with the scriptures or Joseph's other teachings.

How do such popular folk doctrines develop and gain widespread acceptance? In this case, Lorin Farr reported in 1900 that some sixty years earlier he had heard Joseph say something like "If we knew the condition of the spirits in the spirit world, thousands would commit suicide to get there."[5] *Similarly, Charles Lowell Walker heard Wilford Woodruff refer to Joseph's teaching "that if the People knew what was behind the vail, they would try by every means to commit suicide that they might get there, but the Lord in his wisdom had implanted the fear of death in every person that they might cling to life and thus accomplish the designs of their creator."*[6]

As best we can tell from these accounts, Joseph said nothing at all about the telestial kingdom. He spoke about "spirits in the spirit world." He was explaining why humans have an innate fear of death. It is a gift from God that helps us remain on earth to finish our mortal probations. Otherwise we would move on to the next stage the first time things got tough. Fragments of Joseph's teaching were captured, like a puzzle missing some of its key pieces. Then the incomplete teachings were paraphrased. Then these corrupted versions were introduced out of context until many Latter-day Saints have heard from someone somewhere and are pretty sure it was Joseph Smith who said the telestial world is so great we would commit suicide to get there.

We need not impute meaning to verse 89. Let us be content to know, for now, that even the world in which we live surpasses our present understanding.

⸺

Heirs of telestial glory do not deny the Holy Ghost, but they do not receive it when it is offered to them. They do not want the gospel of Jesus Christ. They are thrust down to hell and remain there in Satan's power until the end of the Millennium. They are not resurrected until the very end of time, after Christ has finished his work. Heirs of telestial glory receive only a portion of what Christ offers them in heaven. The Holy Ghost ministers to them through the higher kingdoms of glory. But angels minister for the heirs of telestial glory, for they "shall be heirs of salvation" (v. 88). Joseph and Sidney testify that the telestial world exceeds our ability to comprehend without revelation from God.

Joseph and Sidney testify that the terrestrial world excels the telestial in glory, power, might, and extent. They testify, too, that the celestial world far excels everything else. There Heavenly Father sits on his throne forever and all bow humbly before him, reverently acknowledging his intelligence forever. Those who dwell in his presence belong to the church of the Firstborn. They have become like God, having been fully endowed with his power. He has created them in his image and made them his equals in power, might, and dominion. Celestial glory is like the sun. Terrestrial glory is like the moon. Telestial glory is like the stars, and the inhabitants thereof are as different as the stars in the heavens. They went their own way, and they did not submit their will to Christ by willingly receiving his gospel, his testimony, his prophets, or his everlasting covenant. They remain separate and single for all eternity, for they are not gathered with the Saints into the church of the Firstborn. They were liars and loved it. They trusted the devil. They were not chaste but adulterous. "These are they who are cast down to hell and suffer the wrath of Almighty God" (v. 106) until the end of the Millennium when Christ finishes his work of redeeming mankind and presents his kingdom to his Heavenly Father saying, "I have overcome and have trodden the wine-press alone, even the wine-press of the fierceness of the wrath of Almighty God" (v. 107). Then Heavenly Father will crown Christ, whose role encompasses reigning over the celestial earth forever.

Joseph and Sidney see that the heirs of telestial glory are as numerous as the stars or as the sand on the beach, and they hear the Lord say about them, "These all shall bow the knee, and every tongue shall confess to him who sits upon the throne forever and ever" (v. 110). Christ judges them by their actions and rewards them accordingly with a highly individualized dominion. The telestial heirs will serve God, "but where God and Christ dwell they cannot come" forever and ever (v. 112).

The visions end, and the Lord commands Joseph and Sidney to write them before the Holy Ghost leaves them. They marvel at the Lord's work and the mysteries. They acknowledge their inability to conceive of or communicate the glory, power, and extent of the Lord's kingdom, though he revealed it to them. The Lord commands them not to write all they saw. Only the Holy Spirit can enable mortals to see and understand such visions. Heavenly Father bestows the Holy Ghost on those who love him and purify themselves for him. To those who make these choices, Heavenly Father grants the privilege of seeing and knowing for themselves what Joseph and Sidney saw by the power of the Holy Ghost. In awe, Joseph and Sidney acknowledge that glory, honor, and dominion belong to Heavenly Father and Jesus Christ forever.

OUTCOMES

Doctrine and Covenants 76 testifies. Two eyewitnesses repeatedly declare what they saw, heard, and understood. "I know God," Sidney Rigdon testified in conference in April 1844. "I have gazed upon the glory of God, the throne, the visions, and glories of God."[7] Such testimony can be rejected but not discredited. It is powerful evidence.

Section 76 restores an enormous amount of truth that is available in no other place. Apostasy came because men without revelation floundered to conceive of God and eternity from their finite perspectives. Heaven and hell were reduced to simplistic concepts. Most Christians regarded heaven as tiny and hell as very big. They knew of no other possibilities. They debated the relative sizes of heaven and hell, and what, if anything, individuals could do to influence which they would inherit. But at the time of these visions, mankind knew nothing in the sensory way that Joseph saw and heard and to some degree experienced heaven and hell.

One of the ways in which section 76 restores lost knowledge is the way it blurs the dualistic line between heaven and hell. John 5:29, the text in the New Testament that led Joseph to seek further knowledge, mentions two resurrections, one of those who do good and another of those who do evil. Section 76 adds nuances, layers, and degrees of resurrection and salvation. We search section 76 in vain for a clear marker between the resurrection of the just and the unjust. Verse 50 introduces the vision of "them who shall come forth in the resurrection of the just," but where that category ends and that of the unjust begins is not explicit. We read of terrestrial heirs (vv. 71–80) and then the clearly unjust telestial heirs (vv. 81–86) before realizing that the answer to Joseph's question about the resurrection of just and unjust is that John 5:29 is an introductory text on salvation and resurrection, whereas section 76 is more advanced, like the difference in ways parents teach principles to a toddler compared to how they teach the same principles to a teenager. Salvation is sophisticated.

Some Christians demand to be left at the kindergarten level of understanding. They assume that because they have learned basic lessons about God's plans for salvation, he must not have any more. They are not interested in advancing beyond basic knowledge. Not so with Wilford Woodruff. He read section 76 before he ever met Joseph. "It had given me more light and more knowledge with regard to the dealings of God with men than all the revelation I had ever read in the Bible or anywhere else," he said. Wilford "had been taught that there was one heaven and one hell," and that those who were baptized would go to heaven, and those who were not would go to hell. Personal righteousness made no difference. "That was the kind of teaching I heard in my boyhood," he noted. "I did not believe one word of it then." But that left him without a church that taught the truth. He said section 76 "opened my eyes. It showed me the power of God and the righteousness of God in dealing with the human family. Before I saw Joseph I said I did not care how old he was, or how young he was; I did not care how he looked." Only one thing mattered about Joseph: "The man that advanced that revelation was a prophet of God," Wilford wrote. "I knew it for myself."[8]

Section 76 restored expansive truth inseparably linking salvation and individual agency. God is sovereign but not arbitrary. He loves mankind universally but does not save them unconditionally. Rather, as section 76 demonstrates, God endows his children with power to choose how they wish to be saved by Christ, if at all.

Rather than welcoming this restoration, traditional Christianity rejects it. Brigham Young described how his upbringing nearly kept him from receiving the testimonies of Joseph and Sidney. "My traditions were such, that when the Vision first came to me, it was so directly contrary and opposed to my former education[,] I said, Wait a little. I did not reject it; but I could not understand it. I then could feel what incorrect tradition had done for me. Suppose all that I have ever heard from my priest and parents—the way they taught me to read the Bible—had been true, my understanding would be diametrically opposed to the doctrine revealed in the Vision. I used to think and pray, to read and think, until I knew and fully understood it for myself, by the visions of the Holy Spirit."[9] Brigham's receptive response—thinking, reading, and praying for understanding—was more open-minded than that of some Saints who were sure they already knew God's mind on the subject, and it matched theirs. Some chafed at the expansive idea that God would justly prepare a place for all, "according to the light they had received and their rejection of evil and practice of good . . . and would bless the honest and virtuous and truthful, whether they ever belonged to any church or not."[10]

As he often did, Joseph responded to critics of his vision by evoking the Bible they claimed was all-sufficient for salvation. Many hold up the Bible on one hand, Joseph observed, while believing in one heaven and one hell. But the Bible records the apostle Paul teaching Saints that he knew of three heavens. Joseph playfully made his point, asking Paul why he would tell such a lie when the whole Christian world knew better.[11]

Joseph rebuked Saints who taught contrary to what the vision revealed. When some of the Saints speculated about the destiny of Satan and the sons of perdition, the First Presidency evoked verses 45–47 of section 76, reminding the Saints that "their state of destiny was not revealed to man, is not revealed, nor ever shall be revealed, save to those who are made partakers thereof: consequently those who teach this doctrine have not received it of the Spirit of the Lord."[12]

Joseph marveled at the vision. "That document is a transcript from the records of the eternal world," he said. He knew better than anyone that he had just received his first revelation dealing with exaltation—with a quality of life beyond salvation, regarding which traditional Christianity has nothing to offer. Section 76 is fuller, richer, and deeper than any of the Christian soteriologies of Joseph's time or ours. He felt awe at "the sublimity of the ideas; the purity of the language; the scope for action; the continued duration for completion, in order that the heirs of salvation may confess the Lord and bow the knee." He thought that "the rewards for faithfulness, and the punishments for sins, are so much beyond the narrow-mindedness of men that every honest man is constrained to exclaim: 'It came from God.'"[13]

Doctrine & Covenants 77

ORIGIN

Having been treated to Doctrine and Covenants 76 for his efforts to understand and revise the Bible, Joseph continued his painstaking study of the scriptures. His history says that "about the first of March, in connection with the translation of the scriptures, I received the following explanation of the Revelations of Saint John."[1] The questions answered by this revelation are embedded in Doctrine and Covenants 77 itself.

CONTENT

Revelation 4:6

What is the sea of glass John sees? The sanctified, resurrected earth. What do the four beasts signify? Heaven, God's paradise, the happiness of mankind and animals. God created the forms of all his creations spiritually and then physically (D&C 29; Moses 3:5). Did John see just four beasts or many? Was he suggesting that the four were typical of many that he saw? He saw just four, but they represent different kinds of beings God created, enjoying their heavenly happiness. What do their eyes and wings represent? Their eyes signify light and knowledge. Their wings signify agency and liberty. They are endowed with power—light and knowledge—enabling them to move and act as they will.

Revelation 4:10

John writes about twenty-four elders. Who are they? They were early

Christian missionaries who belonged to branches of the Church in Asia. Having served faithfully, they are now in the spirit world.

Revelation 5

What does the sealed book mean? It is a book of revelations. God's will, his mysteries, and his works are in it. It explains God's plan for creating his children in his image—not simply the initial phase of creation but the entire work of God in raising his children to perfectly resurrected and then exalted bodies. The book tells especially about the purpose of the earth in Heavenly Father's plan.

What do the seven seals in the book mean? Each sealed portion tells about a thousand-year period of God's plan as it is being worked out on earth, beginning with the first thousand years and continuing through the seventh.

Revelation 7:1

What do the four angels signify? God gave each of them power over a quarter of the earth. They oversee the spread of the gospel to all nations. Life, both temporal and eternal, is in their hands. They have sealing power.

Revelation 7:2

What about the angel who appears to be rising in the east like the sun? He is a messenger to whom God has given priesthood power to govern those who make and keep gospel covenants. He directs the four angels not to destroy the earth until they have guaranteed eternal life to all who make and keep gospel covenants. He is Elias. That is, he comes before the Lord's second coming so he can prepare the way by restoring the gospel and gathering Israel.

When will these things happen? During the sixth seal.

Revelation 7:3–8

Who was John talking about when he wrote about sealing 144,000, including twelve thousand from each of the tribes of Israel? They are high priests in the Melchizedek Priesthood from all over the world who serve in the Church. The priesthood they hold directs the work of bringing souls to

Christ through the covenants and ordinances of the gospel, culminating in the highest ordinances of the temple.

Revelation 8

What is meant by the trumpets sounded by seven messengers? They signify a pattern that was established when God created the earth in six days, including the creation of mankind, and then finished his work and sanctified the Sabbath, making seven trumpets for seven days. Following this pattern, God will finish his work and sanctify the earth at the beginning of the seventh seal. He will complete his plan of salvation, make his final judgments, and redeem all who are endowed with power and sealed. The seven angels blow their trumpets to signify the beginning of the culmination of God's work of bringing to pass immortality and eternal life for mankind.

Revelation 9

John sees wars and plagues unleashed on the earth. When does that happen? They are part of God's judgments that precede the redemption of the world. They happen in the seventh seal before the second coming of Christ.

Revelation 10

John writes that the seventh angel gave him a book, and he ate it. What could that mean? It signifies the mission John has to perform in gathering and organizing the house of Israel. He is an Elias, one of the many whose role is to restore the gospel before the second coming of Jesus Christ.

Revelation 11

Who are the two witnesses John mentions? Two prophets raised up to the Jewish nation in the last days before Christ's second coming to prophesy to the Jews who have gathered to Israel and rebuilt Jerusalem.

OUTCOMES

Doctrine and Covenants 77 is a key to unlocking the meanings of chapters 4–11 of the Revelation of John. It is also a model of the right way to approach that famously complicated book. Joseph Smith studied the book carefully, formulated questions for the Lord, and then sought and received the Lord's answers to his specific questions.

Joseph rarely spoke of or taught from John's Revelation. One exception is an April 1843 sermon. The Nauvoo high council had recently convened a hearing to correct Pelatiah Brown's interpretation of Revelation 4–5. Joseph described Brother Brown as "one of the wisest old heads we have among us," though he had misunderstood the meanings of the beasts John saw in Revelation 4. Joseph was frustrated that John's Revelation was "a subject of great speculation" among Latter-day Saints and others. He knew that such speculation grew from ignorance about John's intended meanings. He decided to reveal some of John's meaning to combat the ignorance.

Joseph taught that with the exception of chapter 12, John's Revelation is about the future, not the past. Joseph taught that "John saw curious looking beasts in heaven, he saw every creature that was in heaven, all the beasts, fowls, & fish in heaven, actually there, giving glory to God. I suppose," Joseph continued, "John saw beings there, that had been saved from ten thousand times ten thousand earths like this, strange beasts of which we have no conception all might be seen in heaven. John learned that God glorified himself by saving all that his hands had made, whether beasts, fowl, fishes, or man." Because of section 77, Joseph knew what the beasts represented. He had a key to John's Revelation, and he was not hostage to rampant speculation. "We may spiritualize and express opinions to all eternity," Joseph told the Saints, "but that is no authority."[2] Section 77 is an authoritative key to understanding parts of John's Revelation. As a possessor of such keys, Joseph could say as perhaps no other person can, "Revelation is one of the plainest books God ever caused to be written."[3]

Doctrine & Covenants 78

ORIGIN

Doctrine and Covenants 78 deals with Church finances and assets. It addresses the problem of paying for the things the Lord has commanded, namely the building of Zion and publishing the Book of Commandments. Joseph, whose responsibility in the Literary Firm was to oversee the expensive publication of the Book of Commandments (D&C 70), sat in counsel with Bishop Whitney, whose responsibility was to meet the Church's needs from the storehouse, which was literally his store.

The precise questions that led to section 78 are not clear. Joseph's history gives no specific context for it. But the lack of specific knowledge for this revelation is itself revealing. Joseph purposefully veiled it. Where the published versions of verse 3 talk about "an organization of my people," the manuscript versions more specifically speak of "an organization of the literary and mercantile establishments of my church."[1] The Church had enemies who were also, sometimes, creditors. Joseph and his brethren kept the issues behind section 78 as confidential as possible to avoid giving enemies of the Church information they could use to cripple it financially and thus undermine Zion.

Twenty-four pseudonyms were used to disguise the names of men, places, and assignments in five revelations published in the 1835 Doctrine and Covenants (78; 82; 92; 96; 103) and two additional revelations in the 1844 edition (104; 105). The pseudonyms were not original to the revelations. The early manuscripts verify, as Orson Pratt wrote, that the actual names were originally given, and then ancient-sounding pseudonyms were inserted before printing.[2]

Joseph Smith received these revelations between March 1832 and June 1834, but they were not published in the 1833 Book of Commandments. Each of the seven revelations is concerned with the United Firm (called the united order in published versions of these revelations), the group of men who held and managed the Church's assets until 1834.

The Church had enemies who were also creditors. Thus, beginning with section 78, revelations that deal with purchasing land for Zion or otherwise managing the Church's properties use pseudonyms when speaking of specific Church leaders and the properties or tasks over which they were stewards. In section 78, for example, the name Ahashdah signified Bishop Newel Whitney, Gazelam or Enoch meant Joseph Smith, and Pelagoram indicated Sidney Rigdon.[3]

Section 82 directed the joining of these leaders in Kirtland, Ohio, with Church leaders in Independence, Missouri, forming a united firm, or order. Section 82 names the men who belonged to the United Firm. When it was first published in 1835, section 82 used pseudonyms rather than the men's actual names. Similarly, pseudonyms were used in other revelations that added new members to the firm (D&C 92; 96), discussed Zion (103; 105), or gave directions to members of the firm regarding the properties or tasks over which they were stewards (104).

Under the direction of President Brigham Young, Elder Orson Pratt publicized the actual names and the reasons for the pseudonyms. As part of his work on the 1876 edition of the Doctrine and Covenants, Elder Pratt inserted in parentheses after the pseudonyms all the original names he could remember. By the 1921 edition most of the remaining identities had been discovered, and the practice of inserting them in parentheses continued. In the 1981 edition the pseudonyms were removed from the text, with four exceptions in section 82.

Research by David Whittaker published in 1983 drew on Orson Pratt's memory and a previously unknown manuscript written about 1863 by William W. Phelps in which he identified the actual names associated with the pseudonyms and offered meanings for the mysterious words. The Phelps document made it possible to replace the remaining four pseudonyms in section 82 with the real names: Edward Partridge for Alam, Algernon Sidney Gilbert for Mahalaleel, John Whitmer for Horah, and Phelps himself for Shalemanasseh.[4] Those changes were made in subsequent printings of the Doctrine and Covenants.

By interpreting the pseudonyms, Phelps's document may imply that they belong to an actual language. Some, Enoch and Gazelem, for example, are in the Bible or the Book of Mormon. Some sound Hebraic, and it may be that Joseph's study of Hebrew influenced the selection of these names. Their origin remains uncertain, however. No known records reveal their source.

Essentially the revelation recorded in section 78 tells how the Church could use its profitable mercantile assets such as Whitney's store to finance such priorities as buying land in Missouri and publishing the scriptures.

CONTENT

In Doctrine and Covenants 78 the Lord commands the assembled Melchizedek Priesthood holders to hear and obey him. He commands them to listen to his counsel (for he ordained them) as he speaks into their ears a wise solution to their problem.

It is time to organize a corporation responsible for supplying and running the storehouses of the Church so poverty can be eliminated among the Saints in both Ohio and Missouri. This way of organizing can be a permanent feature of the Church to advance the cause of Zion, to save mankind, and glorify God so that all of the assembled brethren can have all he has. That will happen if the assembled brethren share equally all the Lord has given them on earth. If, however, they will not share what he has given them on earth, the Lord will not give them all he has. If they want to inherit their Father's celestial kingdom, his children must obey his laws here and now.

It serves the Lord's purposes for the brethren to do all they do for the right motives. In other words, the Lord's first requirement for those who will unite to form this new corporation is to love him and do everything for the single motive of giving him glory. To that end, he commands Bishop Newel K. Whitney, Joseph Smith, and Sidney Rigdon to go to Missouri to counsel with Church leaders there. Satan is trying to turn them away from the truth, blind them, and confuse them about what the Lord wants to give them. Knowing Satan's designs, the Lord commands the Church leaders in Ohio and Missouri to unite in a corporation by entering a covenant. Anyone who breaks that covenant will be released from his calling in the Church and left unprotected from Satan's attacks until he is resurrected.

If the brethren make this covenant and keep it, the corporation they form will enable them to accomplish the work of building Zion. Then, despite the odds and opposition they will certainly face, the Church will become financially independent. But even that goal is a means to a greater end. The earthly Zion leads to the heavenly Zion, where the Lord will crown the brethren who keep their covenants and make them kings as well as priests. So promises the Lord, the Holy One of Zion, who has already done what he is here promising to do again. He has established Zion before. He has made Michael, or Adam, a king and a priest under his eternal direction.

The brethren are like young children. They cannot understand the extent of Heavenly Father's plans for them, nor are they strong enough yet to cope with all of them. But he commands them to be cheerful meanwhile. "I will lead you along," he promises (v. 18). Heavenly Father's kingdom and eternal riches are theirs when they grow up. Those who thankfully receive everything the Lord offers will become as glorious as he is. They will inherit the earth he made for them and exponentially more. For this reason the Son of God commands the brethren to visit their brethren in Missouri and covenant to unite with them in a corporation that will enable the Church to become financially independent, eliminate poverty among the Saints, and prepare them for eternal inheritances. They belong to the church of the Firstborn. He, the Savior, will take them to heaven and give them their inheritances there. If they are faithful and wise stewards, they will inherit all things.

OUTCOMES

Joseph and the other members of the Literary Firm had covenanted to publish the Book of Commandments, but they lacked funds for the expensive project. The Lord had commanded Bishop Edward Partridge to buy land on which to build Zion in Missouri. Bishop Whitney owned a profitable store and other businesses in Ohio. Based on the principle of the law of consecration of using the surplus of some to meet the needs of others, Doctrine and Covenants 78 provides a solution to these problems. Section 78 begins the process of uniting the assets of Bishop Whitney in Kirtland, Ohio, with those of the Literary Firm and the Church's store in Missouri. In obedience to section 78, Joseph, Bishop Whitney, and Sidney Rigdon traveled to Missouri to counsel with Bishop Partridge and the members of the Literary Firm who were there printing the Book of Commandments.

Section 78 resulted in the formation of the United Firm, which is often called the united order. It is not the law of consecration. It was a corporation designed to support the Church according to the law of consecration. Technically, it was the joining of the Literary Firm with Bishop Whitney's Kirtland, Ohio, store and the Independence, Missouri, store operated by Whitney's business partner, Sidney Gilbert. By uniting these firms into one, money earned by Whitney's store in Ohio or donated to the Church there could be sent to Missouri to buy land and print the Book of Commandments.

Doctrine & Covenants 79

ORIGIN

Jared Carter returned from a successful mission that had taken him through parts of Pennsylvania and New York to Vermont and back. He continued preaching the gospel in northeastern Ohio after his return. Then in March 1832 he went to the Hiram, Ohio, home of Joseph "the seer to inquire the will of the Lord concerning my ministry the ensuing season. And the word of the Lord came forth."[1] The revelation is recorded in Doctrine and Covenants 79.

CONTENT

The Lord wants Jared Carter to serve another mission to the villages and cities of the northeastern United States. When he was ordained to the Melchizedek Priesthood, Jared was commissioned to proclaim the joyful message of the everlasting gospel. The Lord promises to send the Comforter upon Jared to teach him the truth and the way he should go on his mission. If he is faithful, the Lord will ensure him a great harvest of souls. Jared should have a glad heart and no fear. So says his Lord, even Jesus Christ.

OUTCOMES

Jared noted that April 25, 1832, marked "the commencement of a mission by Jared Carter, a servant of the Lord." He followed the revelation specifically, going from town to town in the power of his ordination, "which was to the high privilege of administering in the name of Jesus Christ." Jared went northeast along Lake Erie and continued on to Benson, Vermont, his birthplace, proclaiming the everlasting gospel in each location. He battled opposition and bouts of deep discouragement. He kept careful track of his obedience to the revelation and the fulfillment of the promised blessings. His records testify that, as promised, the Lord sent him the Comforter, the Holy Ghost, to teach him the truth and where he should go. And because Jared was faithful to section 79, the Lord crowned him again with a bountiful harvest. Jared summarized his service after returning in October. "I have been gone six months and two days. The Lord has permitted me to administer the Gospel to 79 souls and many others by my instrumentality have been convinced of this most glorious work." He rejoiced on the completion of his difficult yet successful mission. "God has blessed me according to the prophecy of Brother Joseph before I went from Ohio," Jared wrote. "He has blessed me with sheaves."[2]

Doctrine & Covenants 80

ORIGIN

John Murdock baptized and confirmed Stephen Burnett, who was filled with the Holy Ghost and a desire to take the gospel to his relatives. He led his parents to the Church and was called to preach in January 1832 (D&C 75:35). He was called again through Doctrine and Covenants 80.

CONTENT

The Lord calls Stephen to preach faith, repentance, baptism, and the reception of the Holy Ghost to everyone who hears him. The Lord commands Stephen to go any direction with Eden Smith as his companion. He cannot go wrong unless he does not go at all. Stephen's calling is to clearly teach the gospel John Murdock taught him and which the Holy Ghost confirmed to him. The revelation represents the will of Jesus Christ. Will Stephen Burnett do it?

OUTCOMES

Stephen Burnett and Eden Smith started on their mission on July 15, 1832, and spent a few days together declaring the gospel in villages south of Kirtland, Ohio.[1] Stephen also went east with success. He "was the first one that sounded the glad tidings of the everlasting gospel" in Dalton, New Hampshire.[2] But then he apostatized in the wave of disaffection from the Church in 1837 and 1838. Stephen allied himself with Warren Parrish and others who were finding fault with Joseph Smith. The Prophet attributed

Stephen's apostasy to materialism. His "heart was so set on money that he would at any time sell his soul for fifty dollars; and then think he had made an excellent bargain; and who had got wearied of the restraints of religion, and could not bear to have his purse taxed." When Stephen tried but failed to regain the Holy Spirit, he "proclaimed all revelation lies" and left the Church.[3]

Doctrine & Covenants 81

ORIGIN

The Lord began to organize his First Presidency in early 1832. A conference in Amherst, Ohio, sustained Joseph Smith as president of the High Priesthood in January. On March 8, 1832, Joseph chose and ordained Sidney Rigdon and Jesse Gause as his counselors.[1] A week later Joseph received Doctrine and Covenants 81, giving Gause instructions for fulfilling his calling.

CONTENTS

Doctrine and Covenants 81 announces that the keys of the kingdom belong to the Presidency of the High Priesthood. In calling Jesse Gause to be a counselor to Joseph in that presidency, the Lord promises to bless Joseph and also Jesse, on the specific condition that Jesse remain faithful, pray always, and proclaim the gospel. Indeed, the Lord commands him to "be faithful; stand in the office which I have appointed unto you; succor the weak, lift up the hands which hang down, and strengthen the feeble knees" (v. 5). The revelation closes with a reiteration of the Lord's covenant with Jesse: "If thou art faithful unto the end thou shalt have a crown of immortality, and eternal life in the mansions which I have prepared in the house of my Father" (v. 6).

OUTCOMES

Jesse Gause had left the Church by 1833, and the Lord appointed Frederick Williams to replace him. In an early manuscript of Doctrine and Covenants 81, Jesse's name is simply crossed out and Frederick's inserted in his own handwriting as he took over the calling. As an accountable agent, Jesse chose not to abide by the Lord's terms and conditions. But here, as elsewhere in the revelations, the Lord simply replaced him, and the kingdom rolled forward (D&C 56; 124:91–95).

Doctrine & Covenants 82

ORIGIN

Joseph Smith and Sidney Rigdon were dragged from their Hiram, Ohio, homes late on March 24, 1832. A mob of apostates and angry, alcohol-fortified neighbors strangled Joseph until he lost consciousness. Then they stripped him, beat and lacerated him, and coated him with tar and feathers. Sidney Rigdon received similar treatment, leaving him delirious for several days. Joseph's adopted son, already sick with measles, caught cold and died within days.[1]

A week after the violence, according to Joseph's history, he "started for Missouri in company with Newel K. Whitney, Peter Whitmer, and Jesse Gause to fulfill the revelation" they had been given in Doctrine and Covenants 78 to visit Church leaders in Missouri and with them unify the Church's economic organization. Sidney Rigdon, who had fled Hiram to avoid the mob, met the other brethren en route. "Fearing for the safety of my family, on account of the mob," Joseph said, he pressed on, stopping in Wheeling, Virginia (now West Virginia), to buy paper for printing the revelations. By steamships and stagecoach, the brethren reached Independence, Missouri, in less than three weeks.

Joseph noted with relief that the Missouri Saints were glad to see them and sustained him as President of the High Priesthood and that Bishop Edward Partridge extended "the right hand of fellowship" in a scene the Prophet called "solemn, impressive, and delightful." This was the desired but uncertain outcome of their arrival. Hard feelings had existed between the leaders in Missouri and Kirtland. Some in Missouri felt Joseph was power-hungry. And Sidney Rigdon was upset with Bishop Partridge for some reason. Joseph's history says that between meetings the "difficulty or hardness which had existed between Bishop Partridge and Elder Rigdon was amicably settled, and when we came together in the afternoon all hearts seemed to rejoice, and I received the following Revelation given April, 1832, shewing the order given to Enoch and the church in his day."[2]

CONTENT

In Doctrine and Covenants 82, after repeated warnings against backsliding and covenant breaking, the Lord commands the nine men named in verse 9 to covenant with each other to form a corporation unifying leaders in Ohio and Missouri to manage the Church's printing projects, storehouses, and bishops' responsibilities for buying land. The Lord named these men as stewards over his property, under covenant to obey the law of consecration "for the benefit of the church of the living God" (v. 18).

In a beautiful statement about the law of consecration, the Lord declares the reason he has consecrated Zion and its stake in Kirtland to the Saints and why he commands them to covenant with him to consecrate: "That every man may improve upon his talent, that every man may gain other talents, yea, even an hundred fold, to be cast into the Lord's storehouse, to become the common property of the whole church" (v. 18). *Talent* in these verses refers to the parable of the talents in Matthew 25, in which a *talent* is a Hebrew coin. This revelation is about economics. But by Joseph Smith's time the word *talent* has taken on the metaphorical meaning of a natural gift or endowment, which gives the Lord's usage of it here an enriched meaning.

The Lord emphasizes that he wants this order—government of the Church's economic interests by covenanted leaders committed to the law of consecration—to endure. And it will, he tells them, "inasmuch as you sin not" (v. 20). He warns of a just punishment for anyone who "sins against this covenant" (v. 21). He gives them the kingdom forever, "if you fall not from your steadfastness" (v. 24).

OUTCOMES

Doctrine and Covenants 82 resulted in the formation of the United Firm, known as the united order in published versions of the revelations.³ The brethren named by the Lord met the day after the revelation was given and "resolved, that the name of the Firm mentioned in the Commandments yesterday be Gilbert, Whitney & Company in Zion. And Newel K. Whitney & Company in Kirtland, Geauga Co. Ohio."⁴ In essence, they joined the Church's two storehouses and made them a parent company of the Church's printing projects. They "named the newly integrated mercantile establishment the United Firm."⁵

In subsequent days Bishop Partridge and Sidney Gilbert drafted the covenant called for in Section 82 to bind the brethren together as business partners according to the law of consecration. Bishop Whitney and Sidney Gilbert were appointed agents for the branches of the Firm—Gilbert in Missouri and Whitney in Ohio—and the Firm decided to borrow fifteen thousand dollars to build Zion.⁶ "Possessing managerial, financial, or publishing skills, members of the United Firm consecrated their time, money, property, and energy and pledged their cooperation to advance the business of the new joint stewardship."⁷ They each maintained private ownership of their own properties but pooled the resources these generated to advance the causes of Zion.⁸

The members of the United Firm were diligent. They acquired properties in Ohio and Missouri and published the revelations, two newspapers, and a hymnal. They operated two stores until antagonistic neighbors in Independence, Missouri, dragged Bishop Partridge from his home in July 1833 to tar and feather him, demanding that the Firm shut down its Independence businesses. Then the mob attacked the Firm's printing office and destroyed its press. In Ohio, meanwhile, the Firm struggled with credit problems and debt. Building Zion was expensive, and the Saints were often frustratingly stingy. The Lord accused them of saying, "We will not go up unto Zion, and will keep our moneys" (D&C 105:8).

In section 104 the Lord finally dismantled the United Firm because some of its members broke the covenant he commanded them to enter in section 82. "I, the Lord, am not to be mocked in these things," he told them in verse 6, after reminding them about the punishments he had promised in section 82 for covenant breakers (D&C 104:3–10). In April 1834, two years after it began, the United Firm ceased to function unitedly. Some Latter-day Saints mistakenly think that this process ended the law of consecration, but that is akin to saying that if NASA were to stop functioning, the laws of physics would cease to be.

The successor organizations to the United Firm continue to operate the Church's economic interests on the same principles. Joseph's work continues. "It was my endeavor," he wrote in response to Doctrine and Covenants 82, "to so organize the church, that the brethren might eventually be independent of every incumbrance beneath the celestial Kingdom, by bonds and covenants of mutual friendship, and mutual love."[9] After so many frustrating setbacks, Joseph must be pleased whenever he sees Latter-day Saints cast their talents "into the Lord's storehouse, to become the common property of the whole church—every [one] seeking the interest of his neighbor, and doing all things with an eye single to the glory of God" (vv. 18–19).

Doctrine & Covenants 83

ORIGIN

After organizing the United Firm, Joseph visited the Saints living in various parts of Jackson County, Missouri. "It is good to rejoice with the people of God," he noted in his history. The next day he again convened a council and received Doctrine and Covenants 83.[1]

CONTENT

Doctrine and Covenants 83 clarifies some ways to keep the law of consecration. "In addition to the laws" already given in earlier revelations, this one clarifies that husbands are responsible to provide for their wives and children until the children become capable of providing for themselves (v. 1). It also clarifies that Saints who apostatize after receiving land from the bishop nevertheless retain that land (see D&C 85). Consecrating Saints freely offer their surplus property to the bishop, who keeps a storehouse to supply the needy according to Doctrine and Covenants 42:33–34. Widows, orphans, and children whose parents cannot provide for them have access to the storehouse to supply their needs.

OUTCOMES

Doctrine and Covenants 83 resolved some of the legal problems Bishop Edward Partridge had been facing as he tried to implement the law of consecration (D&C 51). It leaves no doubt that fathers are to provide for their families, and when fathers are unable to do so, the Saints are to minister to the needs of sisters and brothers from the surplus stored for such eventualities. Generally speaking, Latter-day Saints past and present have practiced these principles.

Doctrine & Covenants 84

ORIGIN

A "beardless boy" named Evan Greene was an experienced missionary by the time he noted his eighteenth birthday near the end of his 1832 journal.[1] Fresh from the mission field, he was one of several elders who met with Joseph Smith to report their missions. "While together in these seasons of Joy," Joseph's history says, "I enquired of the Lord and received the following" revelation.[2] Evan rarely spoke of the sacred experience. When he did he emphasized the solemnity of uniting in prayer with Joseph and witnessing "the glory which shown upon his countenance" and hearing "the exquisite cadence of the voice in which he spoke. It was as if they beheld the face of the Lord Jesus. And they did hear his voice as He declared those sacred truths."[3]

The manuscripts of Doctrine and Covenants 84 say that the revelation was initially given to six elders on September 22, but by the time it says "this day" in verse 42 there were ten high priests present and it was September 23. It is not clear whether the text was revealed in pieces on consecutive days with different audiences or during a single sitting that spanned both days as more and more brethren gathered to witness the outpouring.[4]

It is clear that Joseph had the temple on his mind. The Lord had already revealed to him the site for a temple in Independence, Missouri. Joseph had dedicated the ground. This revelation tells the Saints to build the temple and forges the gospel links between their missionary work, the gathering of scattered Israel, the fulfillment of ancient prophecies, and the building of New Jerusalem, crowned with its holy temple.

Section 84 is a landmark revelation with a breathtaking scope. Joseph's history designates it a "Revelation . . . On Priesthood." It is certainly that and can just as accurately be described as a revelation on temple ordinances, covenants, the gathering of Israel, missionary work, the law of consecration, and the imminent coming of the Savior to "reign with my people," in Zion, as he says in closing (v. 119).

CONTENT

In Doctrine and Covenants 84 Jesus reveals himself to his servant Joseph Smith and six elders united in prayer. He tells them about his Church, restored in the last days to gather Israel to Zion, headquartered in the holy city New Jerusalem, as prophesied anciently in both the Bible and the Book of Mormon. That city will be built around the temple site the Lord revealed to Joseph Smith in Independence, Missouri. Joseph and others with whom the Lord was pleased visited that site and dedicated it in August 1831. The Lord wants New Jerusalem built by the Saints. He wants the Saints then living to gather to that site and build the temple. He tells them that they will build a temple to him, and he will fill it with his glory.

The Lord wants priesthood holders then living to offer him acceptable offerings in the temple that will be raised on the appointed site. Verse 7 marks the beginning of a long digression that ends in verse 31. It is an explanation of priesthood, which the Lord uses to reveal the importance of temple ordinances. In short, priesthood validates the ordinances to be performed in the prophesied temple.

Moses received the holy priesthood from his father-in-law, Jethro, whose line of authority the revelation traces back to God through Abraham, Enoch, and Adam. The priesthood is eternal and continues in the Church in all dispensations. Moses' older brother, Aaron, and his male descendants received the priesthood from the Lord. This Aaronic part of the priesthood also endures and is present along with the Melchizedek Priesthood, otherwise known as the holiest order of God. The Melchizedek Priesthood holds the key to knowing God. The endowment of power needed to know God is in the temple ordinances. Without the temple ordinances performed by the Melchizedek Priesthood, the power to know God is unavailable to mankind. Without the endowment of priesthood power, man cannot endure God's presence. Moses plainly taught this truth to the Israelites, but they did not want a priesthood endowment. They could not, therefore, endure God's presence. Heavenly Father was angry that his children who had covenanted with him were not really interested in regaining his presence. He swore that they would have to wait a long time. He took Moses and the Melchizedek Priesthood from them. They still had the Aaronic priesthood. It could not fully prepare them for his presence but could administer the preparatory gospel—faith, repentance, baptism, and the sacrament—to prepare them for Melchizedek Priesthood ordinances. With Aaronic Priesthood keys they could discern true from false messengers—the ministering of angels. Angry that they would not receive more, the Lord left the Israelites with the preparatory commandments he had given them until John the Baptist came to teach them the law of the gospel.

The Lord sent John the Baptist and filled him with the Holy Ghost. He was baptized sometime after turning eight and ordained by an angel when just eight days old. He was given priesthood power to begin a spiritual revolution—"to overthrow the kingdom of the Jews" (v. 28) and prepare the world for the coming of its rightful King, the Lord Jesus Christ, who has been endowed with all priesthood power. Elder and bishop are offices in the high priesthood. Teacher and deacon are offices in the priesthood conferred on Aaron and his sons.

Having concluded his digression, the Lord returns to his main theme, namely, how priesthood holders will serve in the temple to be built on the consecrated spot in Independence, Missouri. Bearers of the Melchizedek and Aaronic Priesthood—figurative sons of Moses and Aaron—will be filled with the Lord's glory in the temple. Those who faithfully *obtain* "these two priesthoods" and *magnify* their calling to serve are sanctified by the Holy Ghost until their bodies are finally resurrected (v. 33). They become the sons of Moses and Aaron, the descendants of Abraham, the church and kingdom and chosen of God. All who actively *receive* the priesthood, not simply sit passively by as it is conferred upon them, receive the Lord. Receiving the Lord's servants is receiving him. Receiving him is receiving his Heavenly Father. Receiving Heavenly Father is inheriting all he has. This, then, is the oath and covenant of the priesthood: Those who receive and obtain the priesthood and magnify it will inherit all Heavenly Father has. Therefore, all who receive the Melchizedek Priesthood make this covenant and receive this promise from God. He cannot break or annul it. There is no forgiveness here or hereafter for those who completely abandon their priesthood covenant after they have received it of their own free will.

The Lord pronounces a curse on all who do not obtain the priesthood received by the men to whom he is speaking. He confirms the priesthood on them by his own voice out of heaven. He has entrusted them to the care of his angels. Now he commands them to be aware of themselves. With the priesthood confirmed upon them, these brethren are accountable to choose diligently to live by the oath and covenant of the priesthood. They should live by every word of God. His words are truth, and truth is light, and light is spirit, even the Spirit of Jesus Christ. The Spirit enlightens every one in the world who obeys its voice. Everyone who obeys the Spirit returns to Heavenly Father. Through the Spirit, Heavenly Father will teach these brethren the priesthood covenant he restored and confirmed on them not only for their good but so the priesthood can bless all mankind.

Sin pollutes the whole world, which groans in darkness, a slave to sin. This is obvious because most people do not choose God. And all who do not are slaves to sin. Those who do not receive the Lord's voice do not know it. They are not his. They are the wicked and can be discerned from the righteous, who do what the Lord says. And because most people are wicked, the world groans in sin and darkness. Even the minds of these priesthood holders have been dark in the past because they lacked faith and because they were too careless about the priesthood they received. The entire Church is condemned because of such arrogance and unbelief. All the Saints are condemned until they repent and remember the Book of Mormon, the law of consecration, and the other commandments the Lord has recently given—not simply to make covenants but to keep them by doing what the scriptures say. For unless they actually obey the laws of God, the Saints cannot become legitimate heirs of their Heavenly Father's kingdom. Thus, if they do not obey their Heavenly Father's laws, the Saints can expect a just punishment. "For shall the children of the kingdom pollute my holy land?" (v. 59), the Lord asks. "Nay," he answers, unequivocally.

The Lord blesses the assembled priesthood holders on the condition that they act on this revelation. He will forgive them on one condition: "that you remain steadfast in your minds in solemnity and the spirit of prayer, in bearing testimony to all the world of those things which are communicated unto you." He commands them to go back into the field and send their testimonies to those places they cannot actually visit, so their testimonies can reach everyone. Just as he commissioned his apostles, Jesus commissions these new apostles, witnesses, these high priests whom Heavenly Father has provided to the Savior, to declare the good news. "Ye are my friends," the Lord tells them (v. 63). Just as he commissioned his original apostles to teach the law of the gospel to every creature, so he commissions these brethren that "every soul who believeth on your words, and is baptized by water for the remission of sins, shall receive the Holy Ghost" (v. 64). The Lord lists miraculous signs that will follow these believers: They will do marvelous things in his name, including casting out devils, healing the sick, restoring sight to the blind, hearing to the deaf, and speech to the mute. They will have power over poisons dispensed by an enemy or a snake. The Lord warns that these impressive blessings are not to be bragged about or even mentioned outside of sacred settings, for they are given to bless and save the Saints, not contribute to self-righteousness.

The Lord tells the brethren that all who do not believe and obey the law of the gospel will be damned. They will not return to live with God and Christ. The great commission is thus renewed (Matthew 28:19–20). Priesthood holders are responsible to take the gospel to all who have not received it. People with evil, unbelieving hearts are to be rebuked. The Church leaders in Missouri are to be rebuked for rebelling against Joseph when he visited them earlier in the year.

The Lord commissions the brethren to teach the gospel to all mankind in order to hasten his work. And now that they are fully invested in his work, they are his friends, like the early apostles with whom he traveled to preach the gospel by virtue of the priesthood. Jesus told those early friends to go without money or a wallet to put it in or to take more clothes than they could wear at a time. He sent them out this way to test whether people would provide for the needs of his worthy, deserving servants. Anyone who goes to preach the gospel and continues faithful will have an active, enlightened mind and a strong body. Not a hair of their heads will fall unnoticed by the Lord. The missionaries will not starve or go thirsty. Since he will provide for them, they are not to worry about tomorrow's groceries or clothing. Consider how the lilies grow so beautifully. God clothes them more gloriously than kings. And so he will provide for his servants, whose needs he knows very well. He commands those who are called to his service to rely on him to meet their physical needs. He commands them not to think specifically about what they should say but to prepare by studying and internalizing the scriptures. Then the minds of these missionaries' will be stocked with the words of eternal life as needed.

The Lord sends them out to declare the world guilty for its unjust acts and to warn of the impending judgment. Christ will be with them. His spirit will be in them. His angels will surround them and sustain them. Those who receive the Lord's servants receive him. They are his disciples because they feed, clothe, and give the missionaries money as needed and are rewarded for serving the Lord's servants. The Lord tells these missionaries to privately clean their feet with pure water and testify to Heavenly Father against those who choose not to receive them. They are not to return to that house but follow this pattern, searching diligently, painstakingly inviting all to hear the gospel. The Lord curses the house, the village, the city that rejects the elders' testimony of Jesus Christ. For he, being omnipotent, has decided to punish them because they choose to remain wicked rather than repent and embrace the gospel. He will send plagues that will continue until he finishes his work shortly, with perfect equity. Then all who remain on earth will know the Lord. They will sing this new hymn (D&C 84:99–102):

The Lord hath brought again Zion;
The Lord hath redeemed his people, Israel,
According to the election of grace,
Which was brought to pass by the faith
And covenant of their fathers.

The Lord hath redeemed his people;
And Satan is bound and time is no longer.
The Lord hath gathered all things in one.
The Lord hath brought down Zion from above.
The Lord hath brought up Zion from beneath.

The earth hath travailed and brought forth her strength;
And truth is established in her bowels;
And the heavens have smiled upon her;
And she is clothed with the glory of her God;
For he stands in the midst of his people.

Glory, and honor, and power, and might,
Be ascribed to our God; for he is full of mercy,
Justice, grace and truth, and peace,
Forever and ever, Amen.

It seems good to the Lord that when missionaries with families receive gifts of money, they should send money to their families or use it to benefit them as the Lord inspires them. When missionaries who do not have families receive monetary gifts, they should send the money to Bishop Edward Partridge in Missouri or Bishop Newel K. Whitney in Ohio so it can be consecrated for publishing the revelations or buying land for Zion. When the missionaries are given a new coat or a suit, they should offer their old one to the poor and carry on their ministry, rejoicing. Spiritually strong missionaries should be paired with weaker companions, who can be edified and become strong, too. Aaronic Priesthood holders should go before their companions who hold the Melchizedek Priesthood, making appointments and preaching when an elder is not able. Jesus' first apostles followed this pattern. So every man is needed. Like the parts of a body, each priesthood holder performs an important, complementary function in the great commission to take the gospel to all mankind. The Lord wants the high priests, elders, and priests to travel while the teachers and deacons watch over the branches of the Church as "standing ministers unto the church" (v. 111).

The Lord calls Bishop Whitney to visit the branches of the Church to identify the poor and the rich and then meet the needs of the poor by asking the rich and proud to consecrate their surplus. Bishop Whitney should also appoint a steward over his various businesses. The Lord directs Bishop Whitney to visit New York City, Albany, and Boston to loudly proclaim the gospel, warning the people that they will be destroyed and their houses left empty if they reject the gospel. If he trusts in the Lord, Bishop Whitney will not become discouraged and the Lord will preserve him. To the rest of the missionaries the Lord says to proclaim the gospel in the well-known cities and villages as much as circumstances allow. The missionaries are to convict the worldly of their unjust, ungodly deeds and clearly declare the penalty: God will destroy the abominable in the last days. "I will rend their kingdoms," the Lord declares. "I will not only shake the earth, but the starry heavens shall tremble. For I, the Lord, have put forth my hand to exert the powers of heaven; ye cannot see it now, yet a little while and ye shall see it, and know that I am, and that I will come and reign with my people" (vv. 118–19).

OUTCOMES

One would think the revelation recorded in Doctrine and Covenants 84 would have provided the Saints enough incentive to begin building a temple on the dedicated site in Independence, Missouri—Zion. But they did not. There are several complicated reasons why, and later revelations will address them.

The Lord condemned the Saints for treating lightly what he had given them, including the Book of Mormon and the law of consecration (see v. 57).

Temples and holy cities are not built by covenanting to consecrate. They are built by keeping the covenant to consecrate. As he participated in a later temple dedication, President Ezra Taft Benson "received the distinct impression that God is not pleased with our neglect of the Book of Mormon."[5] Thus, one result of section 84 is that the children of Zion voluntarily "remain under this condemnation until they repent and remember the new covenant, even the Book of Mormon and the former commandments which I have given them, not only to say, but to do according to that which I have written" (v. 57). This passage prompted President Benson to declare that "we not only need to *say* more about the Book of Mormon, but we need to *do* more with it. Why? The Lord answers: 'That they may bring forth fruit meet for their Father's kingdom; otherwise there remaineth a scourge and judgment to be poured out upon the children of Zion.' (D&C 84:58.) We have felt that scourge and judgment!"[6]

If the Saints have been scourged for their part of the failure to fulfill the instruction in section 84 to build the temple in Independence, Missouri, they have worked to fulfill many of its commands and have received many of its promised blessings. Temples were built by Saints who were present when section 84 was revealed. They received the priesthood endowment section 84 describes.

The Saints obeyed section 84 in other specific ways. A council of high priests assigned Orson Hyde and Hyrum Smith to write a rebuke of the Church leaders in Missouri as verse 76 commanded.[7] As instructed in verses 112–114, Bishop Whitney and Joseph Smith left Kirtland "to fulfill the Revelation," making important contacts in New York City, visiting Albany, and prophesying in Boston.[9]

Evan Greene went over and over again into the mission field, as have so many since, in response to the instructions in section 84 to preach the gospel to "all who have not received it" (v. 75) and "to teach them of a judgment which is to come" (v. 87). Many have made the covenant of the priesthood—to receive, obtain, and magnify it according to the oath and covenant outlined in section 84. Many if not all have obeyed the law of consecration as instructed in verses 103–6.

Perhaps the most important result of section 84 is that it taught Joseph more about the fundamental importance of priesthood and, inseparably, the temple. He had listened attentively at age seventeen as Moroni explained the imperative need to obtain the restored priesthood and seal the human family together before the Savior's coming, and the doctrine of the priesthood distilled on Joseph like dew from heaven (D&C 121:45). Much of this knowledge was given September 22–23, 1832, as Doctrine and Covenants 84 explained the priesthood's past and projected its future use in temples.[9]

Doctrine & Covenants 85

ORIGIN

Joseph Smith wrote to William Phelps in Missouri in November 1832, and Doctrine and Covenants 85 is a portion of the letter. The call to migrate to Missouri and build Zion according to the law of consecration and stewardship created a need to keep accurate records. Some Saints moved to Missouri before being commanded and without recommends (D&C 78). Some refused to keep the law of consecration. William McLellin, for instance, failed to meet with Bishop Edward Partridge to give and receive by consecration as commanded in section 42. Instead he bought two lots on Main Street in his own name.[1] Church leaders in Missouri wondered "what shall become of those who are assaying to come up unto Zion in order to keep the commandments of God, and yet receive not their inheritance by consecration by order or deed from the bishop, the man that God has appointed in a legal way agreeable to the law given to organize and regulate the church." Far away in Ohio, Joseph Smith discerned this question by "the still small voice" and wrote the revealed answers. Though Frederick G. Williams scribed the first part of the letter, most of what is now Doctrine and Covenants 85 was originally in the handwriting of Joseph Smith.[2]

CONTENT

We hear a mixture of Joseph's voice and the Lord's in Doctrine and Covenants 85, which clarifies the duty of the Lord's clerk to keep a history of righteousness and unrighteousness in Zion. Accurate records are to be kept "of all those who consecrate properties, and receive inheritances legally from the bishop" (v. 1). Those that do not receive their inheritance by living the law of consecration, together with their ancestors and descendants, are to be excluded from the Church record referred to as the "book of the law of God" (v. 5). Verse 7 promises that the Lord will send someone to arrange inheritances for those whose names are recorded in the book, but those who are not in the book will receive no inheritance in Zion. Verse 8 warns that those who steady the ark (go beyond their assigned role in building Zion) will be smitten.

The prophecy in verse 7 about the "one mighty and strong" had "given rise to so much speculation" that in 1905 the First Presidency wrote an official explanation. They gave two possible readings. Either Edward Partridge, as bishop in Zion in 1832, was the Lord's choice to implement the law of consecration, or the prophecy is to be fulfilled in the future. In the latter case, "let the Latter-day Saints know that he will be a future bishop of the church who will be with the Saints in Zion. . . . He will be designated by the inspiration of the Lord, and will be accepted and sustained by the whole Church."[3]

Oliver Cowdery sought clarification from Joseph Smith on the prophecy in verse 8 that the man who steadied the ark would be smitten. Joseph told him that the prophecy "does not mean that any had" steadied the ark "at the time, but it was given as a caution to those in high standing to beware, lest they should fall by the vivid shaft of death as the Lord had said."[4] Church leaders in Missouri failed to fully heed the warning. Joseph subsequently wrote to them that "men should not attempt to steady the ark of God!"[5] Edward Partridge repented. The First Presidency stated in 1905 that the Lord "forgave his sins, and withheld the execution of the judgment pronounced against him."[6]

OUTCOMES

Joseph purchased his first journal on the very day this revelation was given, "for the purpose," he wrote, "to keep a minute account of all things that come under my observation."[7] At about this same time, Joseph began writing his history and recording his letters and minutes of Church council meetings. He knew, as John the Revelator had prophesied, that mankind would be judged by records of their works kept on earth (Revelation 20:12; D&C 128:6–8), and Joseph tried to document his own "manner of life" (D&C 85:2).

Later, in 1841, Joseph began another journal, the Book of the Law of the Lord, a title he derived from section 85. Joseph appointed Willard Richards as "Recorder for the Temple, and the Scribe for the private office of the President." Willard became what section 85 calls the "Lord's clerk," filling the duties described in the revelation (v. 1). He recorded historical entries and donations in the Book of the Law of the Lord.[8] In 1842, while preparing to leave for the East, Richards gave the book to William Clayton, whom Joseph appointed as temple recorder, with a commission to fulfill the duties named in section 85.[9]

These recorders carefully kept track of consecrations. They recorded the deeds and donations of property by those who freely offered their whole souls to the Lord's work. Joseph recorded a tribute to his wife Emma, to Bishop Newel Whitney, to his brother Hyrum, and to many others. "The names of the faithful are what I wish to record in this place." He recorded "the virtues and the good qualifications and characteristics of the faithful few," as he called them, but also noted that "there are a numerous host of faithful souls, whose names I could wish to record in the Book of the Law of the Lord."[10]

Consecration is never coerced. Section 85 clarifies that Church leaders are to keep track of who consecrates but are not to encroach on individual agency to obey or disobey. The Lord will bring judgment according to the records kept. The law will be kept quietly, and the names of those who live it recorded in appropriate places. The faithful whose names and deeds are documented will receive inheritances in Zion. But those "whose names are not found written in the book of the law . . . shall not find an inheritance among the saints of the Most High" (v. 11).

Doctrine & Covenants 86

ORIGIN

Joseph worked diligently on what he always called his new translation of the Bible. He had been over the parables in Matthew 13 in the spring of 1831, and he revised his own revision a year and a half later. His journal for December 6, 1832, says he spent the day "translating and received a revelation explaining the Parable [of] the wheat and the tares."[1] That revelation is recorded in Doctrine and Covenants 86.

"Another parable put he forth unto them, saying, The kingdom of heaven is likened unto a man which sowed good seed in his field: But while men slept, his enemy came and sowed tares among the wheat, and went his way. But when the blade was sprung up, and brought forth fruit, then appeared the tares also. So the servants of the householder came and said unto him, Sir, didst not thou sow good seed in thy field? from whence then hath it tares? He said unto them, An enemy hath done this. The servants said unto him, Wilt thou then that we go and gather them up? But he said, Nay; lest while ye gather up the tares, ye root up also the wheat with them. Let both grow together until the harvest: and in the time of harvest I will say to the reapers, Gather ye together first the tares, and bind them in bundles to burn them: but gather the wheat into my barn" (Matthew 13:24–30).

CONTENT

Doctrine and Covenants 86 defines and evokes powerful symbols to explain a parable about how the gospel spread, how apostasy followed and "[drove] the church into the wilderness" (v. 3), and how the Lord nevertheless protected and preserved his people and will cause the gospel to flourish again. The main metaphor of the parable is a field in which the apostles have planted wheat but Satan has sown weeds or tares. The question for Joseph Smith and Latter-day Saints is, How should the field be harvested? The version in Matthew 13 says to let the wheat and the tares "grow together until the harvest: and in the time of harvest I will say to the reapers, Gather ye together first the tares, and bind them in bundles to burn them: but gather the wheat into my barn" (Matthew 13:30). Importantly, section 86 reverses the order of the harvest recorded in Matthew: "Let the wheat and the tares grow together until the harvest is fully ripe; then ye shall *first* gather out the wheat from among the tares, and after the gathering of the wheat, behold and lo, the tares are bound in bundles, and the field remaineth to be burned" (v. 7; emphasis added; see also D&C 64:24). In his new translation, Joseph revised Matthew 13 according to what he had learned from the revelation (JST Matthew 13:29).

All of that is preliminary to the Lord's main point in section 86, which is to explain how, despite apostasy, the priesthood has been returned to its lawful heirs, and they are commissioned to harvest the wheat planted by the original apostles. Notice how the Lord develops this point with the four consecutive *therefore*s that begin verses 7, 8, 10, and 11.

OUTCOMES

With Christianity in apostasy and no living prophets, Protestant reformers retreated to the relative safety of the Bible, the known word of God. Some went so far as to declare, though the Bible itself never does, that it was all-sufficient and alone sufficient for salvation. Joseph faced the same fears and frustrations resulting from apostasy, but he took a different approach to the Bible. He "reflected . . . again and again" on its often repeated injunction to ask and receive, seek and find, knock and the door will open (Joseph Smith–History 1:12).

The difference between these ways of reading the Bible is fundamental. For most Christians the Bible is "a sealed book," as a popular Methodist preacher of Joseph's day described it, lamenting that he did not live "in the days of the prophets or apostles, that I could have sure guides."[2] Joseph's revelations open the Bible. Consider how profound it is that in section 86 the Lord explains his own parable. Is there any reason why he would not? Could not?

Doctrine and Covenants 86 revises and expands the biblical record. The fact that it came as Joseph was revising his previous revision is, itself, revealing. Joseph never felt finished with his new translation. One of his greatest contributions to us is his example of asking for and receiving revelations.

Doctrine & Covenants 87

ORIGIN

Doctrine and Covenants 87 resulted from a Constitutional crisis. Congress passed tax laws in 1828 and again in 1832 that favored Northern factories over Southern planters. A South Carolina convention "unilaterally nullified the tariff and forbade its collection. President Andrew Jackson, refusing to acknowledge this assertion of state power, called out troops. By Christmas 1832, a military confrontation appeared imminent."[1]

An article in the Church's newspaper about these events and a description of them in Joseph's later history shows that the Saints viewed these events, along with a plague in India and a nearly global outbreak of cholera, in millennial terms. Joseph's history notes that South Carolina had appointed a day of prayer "to implore Almighty God to vouchsafe His blessings, and restore liberty and happiness within their borders." Meanwhile, "President Jackson issued his proclamation against this rebellion . . . and implored the blessings of God to assist the nation to extricate itself from the horrors of the approaching and solemn crisis." No doubt wondering what God thought of the situation, Joseph received what his history calls a "revelation and prophecy on war" on Christmas day, 1832.[2]

CONTENT

Doctrine and Covenants 87 prophesies wars (plural), "beginning at the rebellion of South Carolina" (v. 1) and unfolding until they become global and result in "a full end of all nations" (v. 6). It foresees slave rebellions and the uprising of "remnants" (v. 5) angry at the Gentiles, which Joseph and the early Saints would have interpreted in Book of Mormon terms as descendants of Lehi vexing the unrepentant (see Mormon 7:1–10; 3 Nephi 10; D&C 19:27).

Section 87 is no text for the squeamish. It describes unfathomable violence by which the inhabitants of the earth "feel the wrath, and indignation, and chastening hand of an Almighty God" (v. 6), whom they have rejected. It describes how the Lord will avenge the "blood of the saints" (v. 7), a reference to, among others, the murder of the prophet who prophesied these events. It commands action. The *wherefore* in verse 8 links the prophecies of violence with a course of action for the Saints: a command to stand in holy places. That is not a command to be passive—to stand by. It is a command to take an immovable stand for holiness in a world descending into self-destruction. The otherwise depressing revelation ends with wonderfully good news for those who take their stand on the side of the Almighty God.

OUTCOMES

The revelation recorded in Doctrine and Covenants 87 is best known for the fulfillment of its remarkable prophecy of the American Civil War, which began in South Carolina over slavery, without which the war would not have happened. But the revelation is most significant for its millennialism. It "linked the 'appearances of troubles among the nations' to prophecies of the last days."[3] Though by no means the first millennial-minded of Joseph's revelations, section 87 was the first "to correlate political events with the millenarian calendar" as it charted the events that would lead the Lord of Hosts to come and avenge himself on his enemies.[4] It paints an expansive, violent, and depressing picture before concluding with comforting promises.

Joseph Smith cited this revelation at least once but did not publish it during his lifetime (D&C 130). It rose to the forefront of Latter-day Saint consciousness in the 1850s as the Civil War loomed. Then, in 1861 when it began to be fulfilled to the letter, with the Civil War beginning in South Carolina over the slavery crisis, a Philadelphia newspaper reprinted the revelation and asked, "Have we not had a prophet among us?"[5]

After a devastating defeat of the Union army in 1862, President Abraham Lincoln surmised that "in the present civil war it is quite possible that God's purpose is something quite different from the purpose of either party—and yet the human instrumentality, working just as they do, are of the best adaptation to effect his purpose."[6] Lincoln realized solemnly that both sides "pray to the same God, and each invokes His aid against the other. . . . The prayers of both could not be answered. That of neither has been answered fully. The Almighty has His own purposes."[7] The Almighty set forth some of those purposes with frightening clarity in section 87. With Lincoln, our concern should be not to ask God to join our side but rather to take our stand on his side.

Doctrine & Covenants 88

ORIGIN

Three months after receiving a revelation on priesthood that included a command to build a temple in Missouri (D&C 84), Joseph and a group of nine high priests "assembled in the translating room in Kirtland, Ohio." They prayed, and then Joseph rose and taught them that "to receive revelation and the blessing of Heaven, it was necessary to have our minds on God and exercise faith and become of one heart and one mind." He asked them each to pray in turn that the Lord would "reveal His will to us concerning the upbuilding of Zion and for the benefit of the Saints and for the duty . . . of the elders." Each man "bowed down before the Lord, after which each one arose and spoke in his turn his feelings and determination to keep the commandments of God."

The revelation began to flow, and by nine o'clock that night it had not ended. The brethren retired but returned the next morning and received most of the revelation. That is, they received the first 126 verses of Doctrine and Covenants 88. The remainder came a week later on January 3.[1]

Samuel Smith, Joseph's younger brother and one of those present when section 88 was received, wrote briefly about the revelation in his journal. He did not like to write, and what he chose to put down tells us what he thought was important about the revelation. Like Joseph, he focused on what the Lord told him to *do*. "Some of the elders assembled together & the word of the Lord was given through Joseph & the Lord declared that those Elders who were the first labourers in this last vineyard should assemble themselves together that they should call a solemn assembly &

every man call upon the name of the Lord & continue in prayer that they should sanctify themselves & wash their hands and feet for a testimony that their garments were clean from the blood of all men & the Lord commanded we the first elders to establish a school & appoint a teacher among them & get learning by study & by faith get a knowledge of countries, languages &c. Thus the School of the Prophets was established."[2]

CONTENT

Like section 84, Doctrine and Covenants 88 is thoroughly a temple revelation. Beginning with a promise of eternal life through Jesus Christ to the faithful, the revelation describes the purposeful creation of the earth and then tells how to obey divine law to advance by degrees of light or glory through a perfect resurrection and into the presence of God.

Doctrine and Covenants 88:15 is restored doctrine, defining a soul as the combination of spirit and body. Based on that doctrine, Elder Jeffrey R. Holland declared: "When one toys with the God-given—and satanically coveted—body of another, he or she toys with the very soul of that individual, toys with the central purpose and product of life. . . . In trivializing the soul of another (please include the word body *there) we trivialize the atonement, which saved that soul and guaranteed its continued existence. And when one toys with the Son of Righteousness, the Day Star Himself, one toys with white heat and a flame hotter and holier than the noonday sun. You cannot do so and not be burned. You cannot with impunity 'crucify . . . the Son of God afresh' [Hebrews 6:6]. Exploitation of the body (please include the word* soul *there) is, in the last analysis, exploitation of Him who is the Light and the Life of the world."*[3]

Historian Richard Bushman summarized section 88: It "runs from the cosmological to the practical, from a description of angels blowing their trumpets to instructions for starting a school. Yet the pieces blend together into a cohesive compound of cosmology and eschatology united by the attempt to link the quotidian world of the now to the world beyond. The revelation offers sketches of the order of heaven, reprises the three degrees of glory, delivers a discourse on divine law, offers a summary of the metahistory of the end times, and then brings it all to bear on what the Saints should do now."[4]

Section 88 is expansive. It maps the universe. Its concepts stretch the mind, inviting inquiry and awe. "Truth shineth" (v. 7), it says, introducing a series of related, if not synonymous, concepts that include truth, light, power, life, spirit, and even law (v. 7). Condescending from the revelation's lofty heights, the Lord simplifies its vastness in a metaphor suited for the Saints: "I will liken these kingdoms unto a man having a field, and he sent forth his servants into the field to dig" (v. 51). "My friends," the Lord says lovingly, "I leave these sayings with you to ponder in your hearts, with this commandment which I give unto you, that ye shall call upon me while I am near—draw near unto me and I will draw near unto you" (vv. 62–63). The revelation both commands and invites solemnity and action.

As do several other revelations, section 88 instructs the brethren to proclaim the gospel and connects this commandment to the imminent end of the world and impending judgment. Indeed, the passage dealing with the final events in the history of the world is the most detailed in the Doctrine and Covenants. "For not many days hence," it begins (v. 87), before describing the end of the world, the resurrections, and the judgments and triumphs announced by angels, all culminating in a final battle between good and evil, "the battle of the great God," in which the archangel Michael leads the armies of heaven against "the devil and his armies," resulting in the final conquest of death, hell, and the devil (v. 114). Concepts revealed in section 88 pervade other scriptural texts about the temple, as biblical temple scholar Margaret Barker noted: "Light and life . . . are linked and set in opposition to darkness and death. The presence of God is light; coming into the presence of God transforms whatever is dead and gives it life."[5]

The *therefore* in verse 117 marks the beginning of the Lord's final point in the initial, two-day revelation (vv. 117–26). This concluding segment reviews the instructions in the revelation as a kind of temple preparation class: "Therefore, sanctify yourselves that your minds become single to God, and the days will come that you shall see him" (v. 68).

Verses 126–41 were given on January 3, 1833, to implement the instructions in section 88 to teach and learn as part of the sanctifying preparation for temple attendance (vv. 77–78). Historian Richard L. Bushman wrote as follows about the school's meaning and significance:

"The practical point of the 'Olive Leaf' revelation of December 1832 was the organization of a school for training the elders for the next spring's missionary work. They were to study doctrine, history, politics, and more, in classes with instructors and books. Besides suggesting a curriculum and school regulations, the revelation set the school in a broad framework of history and metaphysics that focused the powers of heaven on the elders at their studies.

"The school has been represented as an early adult education effort, but the name 'the School of the Prophets' indicated a higher purpose. By alluding to the bands of prophets who received instruction under Samuel, Elijah, and Elisha, it implied preparation for a holy work. Missionaries had been going into the field without instruction; in the school, they were to teach one another the 'doctrine of the kingdom,' and virtually everything else—'things both in heaven, and in earth, and under the earth; things which have been; things which are; things which must shortly come to pass.' They were to study 'languages, tongues and people' and 'wars and the perplexities of the nations.' There seems to have been no limit on the knowledge needed to take the Gospel to the ends of the earth.

"The 'Olive Leaf' placed as much emphasis on spiritual preparation as on subject matter. 'Sanctify yourselves; yea, purify your hearts, and cleanse your hands and your feet before me, that I may make you clean.' They were told to be careful about idle thoughts and excessive laughter. They were to cease to be idle and stop sleeping longer than was needful. Lustful desires, pride and light-mindedness, and all 'wicked doings' had to be abandoned. The school required spiritual and moral discipline along with study out of the 'best books.' Learning and sanctification went together.

"Little was said about engaging a teacher. The pupils were to instruct one another, pooling their knowledge, taking care that only 'one speak at a time' while all listened 'that all may be edified of all, and that every man may have an equal privilege.' The revelation envisioned egalitarian rather than authoritarian instruction. To that end, the revelations concluded with instructions on how to mold the elders into a brotherhood. 'Above all things, clothe yourselves with the bond of charity,' they were told, and, to give that injunction form, a ritual was established for welding the students together. The president was to enter the schoolroom first and pray. As the students came in, he was to greet them with uplifted hand and the words 'Art thou a brother or brethren? I salute you in the name of the Lord Jesus Christ, in token, or remembrance of the everlasting covenant, in which covenant I receive you to fellowship in a determination that is fixed, immovable and unchangeable, to be your friend and brother through the grace of God, in the bonds of love.' The brethren in turn were to lift up their hands and repeat the covenant or say amen.

"The School of the Prophets tells more about the desired texture of Joseph's holy society—and more of what he was up against. The directions to quell excessive laughter and all light-mindedness implicitly reflect the rough-hewn characters who had joined him in the great cause. Few were polished—and he would never teach them gentility—but he wanted order, peace, and virtue. One verse said to organize 'a house of prayer, a house of fasting, a house of faith, a house of learning, a house of glory, a house of order, a house of God.' That succession of words captured his hopes for the whole society he was attempting to create. Zion was to be orderly, godly, and brotherly. At the center was learning—about God, creation, and the world. One verse in the 'Olive Leaf' was repeated later in other of Joseph's scriptures: 'Seek ye diligently and teach one another words of wisdom; yea, seek ye out of the best books words of wisdom: seek learning even by study, and also by faith.' The School of the Prophets was the prototype for the good society, a fraternity united by study and faith."[6]

OUTCOMES

The Latter-day Saints built their first temple as a result of receiving Doctrine and Covenants 88 and came into the presence of the Lord.

A few days after the revelations recorded in section 88 were completed, Joseph sent a copy of it with a rebuke to Church leaders in Missouri. Hard feelings continued to fester there, and the Missouri Saints had not acted on the command in section 84 to build a temple in Zion. "I send you the . . . Lord's message of peace to us," Joseph wrote, "for though our Brethren in Zion, indulge in feelings towards us, which are not according to the requirements of the new covenant yet we have the satisfaction of knowing that the Lord approves of us & has accepted us, & established his name in Kirtland for the salvation of the nations, for the Lord will have a place from whence his word will go forth in these last days in purity, for if Zion, will not purify herself so as to be approved of in all things in his sight he will seek another people for his work will go on until Israel is gathered & they who will not hear his voice must expect to feel his wrath."[7]

Joseph drew on section 84 to remind the Missouri Saints that, like the children of Israel, they were in danger of losing their temple blessings. "Seek to purify yourselves, & also all the inhabitants of Zion," he wrote, "lest the Lord's anger be kindled to fierceness. Repent, repent, is the voice of God, to Zion, and yet strange as it may appear, yet it is true mankind will persist in self-justification until all their iniquity is exposed and their character past being redeemed, and that which is treasured up in their hearts be exposed to the gaze of mankind. I say to you (and what I say to you, I say to all), hear the warning voice of God lest Zion fall, and the Lord swear in his wrath the inhabitants of Zion shall not enter into my rest" (see D&C 84:23–25). Joseph assured the Saints in Zion that "the Brethren in Kirtland pray for you unceasingly, for knowing the terrors of the Lord, they greatly fear for you." Referring to the copy of section 88 he had sent, Joseph observed, "You will see that the Lord commanded us in Kirtland to build an house of God, and establish a school for the Prophets. This is the word of the Lord to us, and we must, yea, the Lord helping us, we will obey, as on conditions of our obedience, he has promised us great things, yea even a visit from the heavens to honor us with his own presence." Joseph had learned from section 84 that the only way into the presence of God was through the temple. Nothing, therefore, should be more important. Yet, like Moses, he worried that Latter-day Saints would harden their hearts and provoke the Lord's wrath (see v. 24). "We greatly fear before the Lord lest we should fail of this great honor which our master proposes to confer on us, we are seeking for humility & great faith lest we be ashamed in his presence." He concluded his letter to the Missouri Saints by saying that "if the fountain of our tears are not dried up we will still weep for Zion, this from your brother who trembles greatly for Zion, and for the wrath of heaven which awaits her if she repent not."[8]

Joseph was driven by the command in section 88 to build a temple and the promise that the Lord would honor them with his presence (v. 68). He urged the Saints forward, at enormous sacrifice, to build the House of the Lord in Kirtland, Ohio. Joseph established schools and convened priesthood meetings to train and motivate the brethren, for the promise that the Savior would "visit from the heavens" was predicated not only on building the temple, but on his command to "sanctify yourselves" (v. 68).[9]

The Saints in Kirtland began building the house of the Lord in the summer of 1833 and, after some interruptions and a rebuke that reminded them of instructions in section 88 (see D&C 95), they dedicated it in 1836. Joseph, meanwhile, instructed the Saints to purify themselves and prepare for an outpouring of the Lord's power—an endowment. In November 1835 he met with the newly called apostles. He confessed his own shortcomings and then taught them section 88, or, as he called it, "how to prepare your selves for the . . . great things that God is about to bring to pass."[10]

Joseph told them he had assumed the Church was fully organized but that the Lord had taught him more, including "the ordinance of the washing of feet" mentioned in section 88 (v. 139). "This we have not done as yet," Joseph taught the apostles, "but it is necessary now as much as it was in the days of the Saviour, and we must have a place prepared, that we may attend to this ordinance, aside from the world." He continued to emphasize the need for the temple. "We must have all things prepared and call our solemn assembly as the Lord has commanded us [see D&C 88:70], that we may be able to accomplish his great work: and it must be done in

God's own way, the house of the Lord must be prepared, and the solemn assembly called and organized in it according to the order of the house of God, and in it we must attend to the ordinance of washing of feet; it was never intended for any but official members, it is calculated to unite our hearts, that we may be one in feeling and sentiment and that our faith may be strong, so that Satan cannot overthrow us, nor have any power over us—the endowment you are so anxious about you cannot comprehend now, nor could Gabriel explain it to the understanding of your dark minds, but strive to be prepared in your hearts, be faithful in all things that when we meet in the solemn assembly, that is, such as God shall name out of all the official members, will meet, and we must be clean every whit."[11]

Echoing the counsel of section 88 in verses 123–26, Joseph urged the brethren, "Do not watch for iniquity in each other. If you do, you will not get an endowment, for God will not bestow it on such; but if we are faithful and live by every word that procedes forth from the mouth of God, I will venture to prophesy that we shall get a . . . blessing that will be worth remembering if we should live as long as John the Revelator; our blessings will be such as we have not realized before, nor in this generation. The order of the house of God has and ever will be the same, even after Christ comes, and after the termination of the thousand years it will be the same, and we shall finally roll into the celestial Kingdom of God and enjoy it forever [see vv. 96–117]:—you need an endowment, brethren, in order that you may be prepared and able to overcome all things."[12]

Joseph helped them understand the relationship between the power with which God intended to endow them and their calling to preach the gospel (vv. 80–82). Then he concluded his teaching by reaffirming what section 88 twice calls the "great and last promise": "I feel disposed to speak a few words more to you my brethren concerning the endowment, all who are prepared and are sufficiently pure to abide the presence of the Saviour will see him in the solem assembly" (see vv. 69, 75).[13]

When the temple was finished and the solemn assembly convened, Joseph dedicated it with an inspired prayer that drew liberally on section 88 (D&C 109.) Joseph worked hard to get the Saints to see the importance of section 88, to understand the temple and its ultimate blessings. Like Moses, he wanted to usher his sometimes shortsighted people into the presence of the Lord. This revelation occupied Joseph's attention. He wanted its promised blessings, and he worked to explain them to the Saints. Section 88 caused the Saints to build a temple and establish schools. It motivated (and continues to motivate) Saints to learn by study and faith, helping many Saints to sanctify their lives and lay hold on the great and last promise of entering the Lord's presence.

Doctrine & Covenants 89

ORIGIN

Joseph Smith's mother said he preferred his father's embrace over liquor to numb the pain of a leg operation when he was seven years old, but neither Joseph or his family were strangers to alcohol, which was common in the 1820s and 1830s.[1] Distillers in the Smiths' region of upstate New York made corn whiskey and sent 65,277 gallons of it and sixty-nine tons of beer to market on the Erie Canal the year after Joseph's first vision.[2] Newspapers in the towns near Joseph's home advertised cheap alcohol, printed recipes for making beer, and sold the ingredients. One scholar described Joseph's America as "the alcoholic republic."[3] Joseph's father confessed in 1834 that he had, in the past, been "out of the way through wine," but "Joseph Sr.'s drinking was not excessive for that time and place."[4] Regardless of social class, nearly all men drank alcohol, and many women and children did too. There were only a few outspoken opponents of alcohol consumption, and their warnings fell largely on deaf ears as consumption rates rose between 1790 and 1830.

In the 1830s, America pulsed with evils and reformers determined to combat them. By the time Joseph Smith moved to Kirtland, Ohio, in 1831, more Americans were becoming concerned with social vices generally and alcohol abuse especially. "The thing has arrived to such a height," one widely quoted temperance advocate noted, "that we are actually threatened with becoming a nation of drunkards."[5]

America's desire for alcohol and the rise of temperance, the moderate use of alcohol, generated diverse opinions that led Joseph Smith to ask questions. Some activists advocated temperate use, but between 1831 and 1836, the cry for abstinence gained momentum. In 1833, in the middle of this controversy, the Lord clarified in the Word of Wisdom where the Saints should stand relative to this controversy.

Christopher Columbus introduced tobacco to Europe after Native Americans introduced it to him. In Europe, tobacco gained a reputation as a miracle drug, and by the 1500s it was prescribed as a cure for cancer, gout, asthma, ulcers, arrow wounds, flatulence, toothaches, bad breath, warts, deafness, constipation, tonsillitis, nose bleeds, epilepsy, and a host of other afflictions. Smoking quickly caught on among European elites, though by the seventeenth century, they were adopting a French practice of sniffing powdered tobacco—snuff—while the practice of smoking tobacco spread to working class people. A new method for delivering the powerfully addictive nicotine found in tobacco—the cigarette—was just about to spread across the globe when Joseph Smith received the Word of Wisdom in 1833.

Outspoken temperance crusaders added tobacco to their list of noxious substances in the 1830s. Opponents of tobacco use regarded it as akin to liquor. One called tobacco poison.

Was tobacco a powerful medicine capable of curing all kinds of afflictions or a noxious weed loathsome to the lungs? Was using tobacco a filthy habit or a socially acceptable pastime?

Uncertainty about these questions may have contributed to Joseph Smith's reception of the Word of Wisdom. He organized classes for men of the Church in an upstairs room of Newel K. Whitney's store in Kirtland, Ohio. When the brethren gathered for class, according to Brigham Young, "the first thing they did was to light their pipes, and, while smoking, talk about the great things of the kingdom, and spit all over the room, and as soon as the pipe was out of their mouths a large chew of tobacco would then be taken. Often when the Prophet entered the room to give the school instructions he would find himself in a cloud of tobacco smoke. This, and the complaints of his wife at having to clean so filthy a floor, made the Prophet think upon the matter, and he inquired of the Lord relating to the conduct of the Elders in using tobacco, and the revelation known as the Word of Wisdom was the result."[6]

There was no consensus of medical opinion in the nineteenth century. The prevailing medical theory held that diseases or disorders were caused by an imbalance in a person's inner energy source. Overstimulation, it was thought, resulted in fevers or infections. Treatments were aimed at releasing the excess energy through bleeding or purging or changing one's diet. Coffee and tea were often used as stimulants by those struggling with a lack of energy. Some herbs, spices, and fruits served the same purpose. Though medical professionals disagreed about how much of these substances could be safely consumed, all authorities agreed that excessive use of any stimulant, in which they included herbs, meats, coffee, and tea, could lead to overstimulation and therefore disease.[7]

The world into which the Lord revealed the Word of Wisdom was quite different from our own. Advances in medical science have provided more certainty about the dangers of consuming many of the substances that were thought by many in Joseph Smith's world to have medicinal value. Moreover, his contemporaries were in the process of reconsidering their certainty about the value of alcohol, tobacco, coffee, tea, meats, fruits, and some herbs. There was no prevailing view to which everyone subscribed, even among Church members. There were more questions than answers.

Nearly two dozen men gathered for school in a second-story room of Newel and Ann Whitney's Kirtland, Ohio, store on February 27, 1833. With one of them acting as his scribe and perhaps one or two others present, Joseph Smith, in a nearby room, received the revelation known as the Word of Wisdom. Besides answering the immediate question of whether the brethren should smoke or chew tobacco, or "the filthy weed and their disgusting slobbering and spitting," as one colorful account put it, the revelation clarified several other issues that were being debated by Joseph's contemporaries.[8]

CONTENT

The revelation recorded in Doctrine and Covenants 89 is introduced as a word of wisdom to benefit the high priests and Saints in Kirtland, Ohio, where Joseph Smith lives, and in Independence, Missouri, which the Lord has designated as Zion, and to be sent to these believers not as a commandment but as a revelation of wisdom, showing the will of God for the "temporal salvation" of all Latter-day Saints, given with a promise and adapted to the capacity of the weakest Saint (v. 2). The Lord gives this wisdom to warn against conspiracies that did, do, and will exist.

It is clear that Joseph Smith sought the revelation because of questions his circumstances generated, but the revelation itself does something far beyond answering questions then current. The Word of Wisdom states that it was given because "of evils and designs which do and will exist in the hearts of conspiring men in the last days" (v. 4). It is hard to overstate how remarkably prophetic the revelation is in forewarning Saints how to act wisely in the midst of conspiracies designed to harm them. Some of those conspiracies have come to light in the last generation. Saints who wisely heeded the warning escaped the evil designs against them.

The health benefits of obeying all aspects of the Word of Wisdom have become increasingly clear. Most obviously, tobacco was linked to lung cancer in the 1950s, and since then numerous other health problems have been linked to smoking, including heart disease and birth defects. Mounting scientific evidence has slowly persuaded governments to regulate the manufacture and marketing of tobacco products, causing tobacco companies to move their efforts to vulnerable populations in countries ill-equipped to combat them. One tactic of the conspirators is to smuggle millions of cigarettes into such countries and then persuade national leaders that they are losing tax revenue, so why not legalize and then tax the cigarettes?[9] Tobacco companies purchase influence while causing a public health crisis that has become a global pandemic.[10]

Shortly after scientific evidence linked cigarette smoking with lung cancer, fiercely competitive executives of America's largest tobacco companies met at the Plaza Hotel in New York City to become allies. They employed a public relations firm to sell the idea that public health was their primary concern. If cigarettes were as harmful as science indicated, their pitch declared, then obviously the tobacco companies would stop selling them. One non-Mormon analyst said that this "meeting marked the beginning of the conspiracy."[11]

In the 1960s, scientists began officially stating that smoking caused lung cancer. The tobacco conspiracy countered by organizing themselves and spending millions on advertising in what one professor called a "scheme to defraud" that differed little from organized crime. They also sponsored what has been called "scientific subversion" by hiring scientists to produce findings consistent with tobacco company aims.[12]

In the 1990s, with the evils and designs in the hearts of conspiring men clearly evident, several states filed suit against tobacco companies. In 1997, Mississippi attorney general Michael Moore visited Salt Lake City, where he was hosted by General Authorities of The Church of Jesus Christ of Latter-day Saints, W. Eugene Hansen and Marlin K. Jensen. All three men were lawyers, and their conversation naturally turned to the legal action Mississippi, Utah, and other states were then taking against tobacco companies. Moore explained that his legal strategy was to prove a "conspiracy" on the part of tobacco companies, using the overwhelming evidence that had come to light in the internal documents that revealed their intentions. Elder Jensen drew Moore's attention to the fourth verse of the Word of Wisdom. "We listened attentively," Elder Jensen said, "as he slowly and deliberately read that verse out loud in his appealing southern accent: 'Behold, verily, thus saith the Lord unto you: In consequence of evils and designs which do and will exist in the hearts of conspiring men in the last days, I have warned you, and forewarn you, by giving unto you this word of wisdom by revelation.'" Elder Jensen noted that "the scriptural reference to 'conspiring men' was not lost on Mr. Moore. As he finished reading verse 4, a broad smile came across his face, and with a twinkle in his eye he said, 'I never dreamed in visiting Utah I might find 10 million people who would agree with my conspiracy theories!'"[13]

Elder Jensen testified: "My heart burned within me that day and has many times since as I have thought about Joseph Smith's gift as a prophet and seer. There is really no other explanation for the origin of that 1833 revelation. It waited until nearly the end of the twentieth century for an almost literal verification of one of its key passages. In the hearts of the faithful Saints who have heeded its message for nearly 170 years, however, there has never been any doubt about its authenticity or relevance."[14]

⁓

The Lord forbids drinking both distilled and fermented drinks except wine in the sacrament, in which case it should be pure wine the Saints make themselves. Distilled, or "strong," drinks are for washing the body. Tobacco is not to be ingested but used with judgment and skill in treating bruises and sick cattle. Hot drinks are not to be ingested, either. God made wholesome herbs for human consumption, each in season, "to be used with prudence and thanksgiving" (v. 11). God created animals and birds to be used thankfully and sparingly by mankind. It displeases him if such are used unless circumstances of winter, cold, or famine dictate. God ordained all grains to be the staff of life for man, domesticated animals, fowls, and wild animals. Wild animals he made for mankind to use in times of excessive hunger. All grains, fruits, and vegetables are good food for mankind, particularly wheat for man, corn for oxen, oats for horses, and rye for fowls and pigs and other domesticated animals. Barley and other grains are good for useful animals and for mild drinks. All Saints who remember to keep and do the behaviors outlined in this revelation will receive health, wisdom, and "great treasures of knowledge" as a result. They can "run and not be weary, . . . walk and not faint." The Lord promises them protection against "the destroying angel," from which he preserved the Israelites (vv. 19–21).[15]

Much more is going on in the revelation than simply a ban on alcohol, tobacco, coffee, and tea. One of the first things to notice is the doctrinal basis for the revelation. It assumes, as an earlier revelation had declared, that "the spirit and the body are the soul of man" (D&C 88:15). Whereas some Christians think of the body as evil and look forward to leaving it behind at death, Latter-day Saints regard the body as godly and look forward to a literal, glorious resurrection. They believe God and Christ are perfectly embodied and that through the process of birth, earth life, death, and resurrection, men and women are being created in the image of God.

For these reasons, practical wisdom on the care of the body is no less religious to Latter-day Saints than is prayer.

The Word of Wisdom rests on three other important doctrines, namely, agency, stewardship, and accountability. These doctrines are everywhere in the revelations given to Joseph Smith. Agency is the power to act independently. Stewardship is what one has to act on. Accountability is the result. Agents ultimately account to God for what they do with the stewardship he gives them. The Word of Wisdom assumes that mankind has agency. Not all Christians believe that God has given mankind this power, but the revelations to Joseph Smith demonstrate that God has given to mankind this wonderful power to act, to choose. This agency needs to be understood. It is not freedom from making choices; it is the freedom and power to make choices. Agents must act. They have to choose, and there are inevitable consequences for each choice.

We can see agency in the Word of Wisdom as God declares his will. By communicating this knowledge, God makes us free to act. Some think that revelations, commandments, and laws curtail freedom, but that is not so. Knowing God's will does not coerce anyone to do it. Knowing God's will enables persons to knowingly, of their own free will, obey or disobey it. Not knowing God's will means persons remain ignorant and cannot act in ways that please God except by accident—not by free will. Thus, there is no agency until a person knows God's will. Notice that the Word of Wisdom declares God's will for the temporal or bodily salvation of all Saints in the last days. It is adapted to the weakest Saint, and thus is not beyond the power of individuals to obey or disobey as they please. God is not determining destinies but rather giving agency by giving knowledge and thus the power to choose.

The Church's official position on the Word of Wisdom is quite simple, but new products or changing circumstances lead Saints to ask new questions and Church leaders to clarify. In 1917, an article by Frederick Pack in the Church's Improvement Era *posed the question, "Should LDS Drink Coca-Cola?" He* argued no, given that it contained caffeine, as did tea and coffee. Coca-Cola representatives contacted President Heber J. Grant with concerns that the Church was against their product. President Grant refused to take an official position one way or the other, leaving the issue to principle. Church leaders since have followed his lead. "We teach the principle together with the promised blessings," Elder Boyd K. Packer declared. What is the principle? The list of prohibitions includes alcohol, tobacco, coffee, and tea. Together with these, all other habit-forming substances should be avoided. Obedience to this principle preserves individual agency. The obedient qualify for the promised blessings.[16]

Ever since the Word of Wisdom was given, some Saints have read it very closely in order to justify their own habits. They are sometimes the best experts on the technical wording of the revelation, including the placement of punctuation. This type of person reads the revelation as a legal code, determining precisely what they can get away with, not necessarily what is best for their temporal salvation. President Brigham Young noted that "many try to excuse themselves because tea and coffee are not mentioned, arguing that it refers to hot drinks only. What did we drink when that Word of Wisdom was given? Tea and coffee."[17] President Boyd K. Packer stated: "There are many habit-forming, addictive things that one can drink or chew or inhale or inject which injure both body and spirit which are not mentioned in the revelation. Everything harmful is not specifically listed; arsenic, for instance—certainly bad, but not habit-forming! He who must be commanded in all things, the Lord said, 'is a slothful and not a wise servant' (D&C 58:26)."[18]

President Gordon B. Hinckley and others have noted the terrible toll of drug abuse and have urged Saints to abstain completely from illicit drugs. President Hinckley noted that some have excused drug abuse by arguing that the Word of Wisdom does not prohibit it. "What a miserable excuse," he declared. "There is likewise no mention of the hazards of diving into an empty swimming pool or of jumping from an overpass onto the freeway. But who doubts the deadly consequences of such? Common sense would dictate against such behavior."[19]

Joseph Smith urged intemperate Saints to be temperate and teetotaling ones to be tolerant. Modern prophets and apostles urge addicted Saints to gain *control of their habits and all Saints to beware of "stretch[ing] the Word of Wisdom to conform with our own opinions."*[20]

Stewardship is what we have to act on. The most notable stewardship in the Word of Wisdom is our own body, but there are several others. The revelation gives instructions about how to act relative to distilled and fermented beverages, domesticated and wild animals, tobacco, hot drinks, and all kinds of grain, herbs, fruits, and vegetables.

These are all things God has made and given mankind to use. The revelation tells us how to use them in ways that please God. "All these to be used with prudence and thanksgiving," for example, speaking of herbs and fruits (D&C 89:11), or "they are to be used sparingly," speaking of meat and poultry (v. 12). A seldom noted aspect of stewardship in the Word of Wisdom is the repeated command to use what God has provided "with prudence and thanksgiving" (v. 11). In the Word of Wisdom, God is clearly the owner. Evidence is seen in such phrases as "all wholesome herbs God hath ordained for the constitution, nature, and *use* of man" or "flesh also of beasts and of the fowls of the air, I, the Lord, have ordained for the *use* of man," or "and these hath God made for the *use* of man" (vv. 10, 12, 15; emphasis added). The repeated emphasis is on *use*, not *abuse*. God created this earth and its life-sustaining abundance to be used by wise stewards who thankfully acknowledge him, not to be abused by the ungrateful or the gluttonous.

The doctrine of accountability is also evident in the Word of Wisdom. Good stewards recognize that they are not the owner of the stewardship but that they are accountable to the owner for the way they act in regard to what the owner provides. The last four verses of the revelation describe the promised blessings granted to those who act wisely on the stewardship God has provided. Note the powerful verbs: "All Saints who *remember* to *keep* and *do* these sayings, *walking* in obedience to the commandments, shall receive health in their navel and marrow to their bones; and shall find wisdom and great treasures of knowledge, even hidden treasures; and shall run and not be weary, and shall walk and not faint. And I, the Lord, give unto them a promise, that the destroying angel shall pass by them, as the children of Israel, and not slay them" (vv. 18–21; emphasis added). The promise of preservation from death or the destroying angel is conditional. It is guaranteed to those who remember, keep, do, and walk in obedience to the commandments in the Word of Wisdom. No one has to remember, keep, do, or obey those commandments. The commands themselves make us free to obey or disobey of our own free will, but we do not escape accountability for the way we act, and only if we choose to act wisely can we expect the promised wisdom, knowledge, health, and deliverance.

Summed up, the doctrines of agency, stewardship, and accountability make the Word of Wisdom "a principle with promise," as it describes itself (v. 3). It is an if-then contract. If Saints choose to obey God's will as described in the revelation (the principle), then he preserves their lives and endows them with wisdom (the promise). This is not the fountain of youth. It is a very specific principle with a very specific promise: those who obey all the commands in the revelation can expect to be delivered from death "as the children of Israel" (v. 21).

Moses revealed God's specific instructions to the elders of the Israelites enslaved in Egypt for how the children of Israel could be delivered. They were to take a lamb and kill it, dip a handful of twigs and leaves in the blood, and smear the blood above and beside the doors of their homes, and then stay inside the door until morning. The Lord would not allow the destroyer to enter such houses. While the firstborn among the Egyptians were smitten, obedient Israelites were delivered from death and then from slavery (Exodus 12). The Word of Wisdom was revealed to Joseph Smith by the same Lord who spoke to Moses. The Savior's redeeming blood, signified by the blood of the Passover lamb, saves all mankind, not arbitrarily, but because we, as accountable agents, choose to be saved by obeying the terms and conditions on which the Lord predicates his saving grace. He communicates his will to mankind through such prophets as Moses and Joseph Smith. These revelations have the powerful effect of giving us wisdom and knowledge, which enables us to act for ourselves in ways that deliver us from all kinds of bondage and lead to salvation both temporal and eternal.

The Word of Wisdom is much, much more than a list of thou shalt nots. It is more than a simple health code. It is a covenant. President Boyd K. Packer testified that "while the Word of Wisdom requires strict obedience, in return it promises health, great treasures of knowledge, and that redemption bought for us by the Lamb of God, who was slain that we might be redeemed."[21]

OUTCOMES

Some critics of the Word of Wisdom assert that because it addressed the circumstances of Joseph Smith's world, it must not be real revelation. This logic is simplistic and flawed. Its first error is to assume that any revelation that answers timely questions is somehow suspect. What good is an irrelevant revelation? We seek, and the Lord gives, revelations that answer the questions and problems of the day, and because those questions and problems change with circumstances, revelations to Moses or Peter are not always adequate for our needs. It does not follow that the revelation did not come from the Lord. Another error critics make is the simplistic assumption that the Word of Wisdom mimicked the prevailing idea of Joseph's time. There was no prevailing idea, no single opinion. Then, as now, there were many competing ideas and debate rather than consensus. The Word of Wisdom sorts out and clarifies the strengths and weaknesses among the variety of opinions.

One contested issue of the early nineteenth century was whether alcohol consumption was appropriate, and if so, how much and by whom. The Word of Wisdom gave the Lord's will with regard to various types of alcoholic beverages. Strong or distilled drinks, such as brandy or whiskey, have the highest alcohol content. The revelation declared that these are useful for washing the outside of the body but are not for the belly. Fermented drinks, such as wine and beer, are not to be ingested, with the exception of wine the Saints made themselves for the sacrament. Familiar as they were with this range of beverages, Joseph Smith and his contemporaries knew that not all alcoholic beverages were created equal. It is useful to learn enough about them to understand the Word of Wisdom.

Other questions of Joseph's Smith contemporaries, including followers and his family members, dealt with tobacco, coffee, and tea. The revelation acknowledged medicinal value in tobacco but prescribed it for treating bruises and sick cattle. It was not to be ingested, whether by smoking, sniffing, or chewing. The revelation declared hot drinks unfit for ingestion. Soon thereafter Joseph Smith clarified that tea and coffee "are what the Lord meant when He said Hot drinks."[22] Speaking before the Saints in 1842, Hyrum Smith quoted the Word of Wisdom passage on hot drinks and then interpreted it as Joseph had a decade earlier: "I say it does refer to tea, and coffee."[23] Considerable evidence testifies that Saints in the 1830s understood hot drinks to include tea and coffee and that they struggled to act on this wisdom.[24]

Other nineteenth-century debates concerned meats, herbs, fruits, and vegetables. By declaring that herbs and fruits should be used in season with prudence and thanksgiving, the Word of Wisdom approved the moderate position of the medical profession of the time, as did the declaration in the revelation that meat be eaten sparingly and especially in winter was healthful. These aspects of the revelation ran counter to the advice of such extremists as Sylvester Graham, an advocate of dietary reform, who had less in common with the Word of Wisdom than is sometimes thought.

In sum, the Word of Wisdom answered questions of the day in unpredictable ways. Forbidding the ingestion of nearly all alcoholic beverages as well as coffee, tea, and tobacco, the revelation ran counter to the mainstream culture, but it was also consistent with the emerging medical opinion regarding meats, herbs, fruits, and vegetables. Many Saints consumed more meat than was needful.[25] The revelation may not have been what they wanted to hear, but it was wisdom they needed to hear.

Latter-day Saints today are counseled not to drink anything alcoholic and to abstain from tobacco, coffee and tea, harmful drugs, and to eat moderately according to the principles of the Word of Wisdom. Fellowship in the Church is not dependent on keeping this counsel, but no one is knowingly baptized into the Church or recommended for admittance to Latter-day Saint temples for the highest forms of worship if they choose not to meet these basic requirements. Clearly there is a history of transition between the way Saints originally acted on the revelation and the way it is applied today.

A year after the Word of Wisdom was given, a question arose that led the Church to make a policy regarding it. Missionaries in Pennsylvania had refused to take the sacrament when they believed that the elder administering it did not obey the Word of Wisdom. When reports reached Kirtland, Ohio, the high council met to decide "whether disobedience to the Word of Wisdom was a transgression sufficient to deprive an official member from holding an office in the Church, after having it sufficiently taught him." Joseph Smith presided. Six counselors gave their views on the subject, and Joseph decided "that no official member in this Church is worthy to hold an office after having the Words of Wisdom properly taught to him, and he, the official member, neglecting to comply with, or obey them." The council sustained this decision.[26]

The decision meant that one who chose to disobey the Word of Wisdom could not be an officer of the Church—that is, hold an official calling. Obedience in the 1830s meant abstaining generally if not absolutely from using alcohol, coffee and tea, and tobacco. The policy did not mean that those who chose to disobey could not belong to the Church, just that they could not represent the Church or officiate in its ordinances if they had been properly taught the Word of Wisdom and chose to disobey it. The Saints were accountable agents. Once they had knowledge to act upon, they were accountable for the choice they made. A choice to disobey resulted in losing the privilege to represent the Savior. This policy has remained in effect, though the years have seen several attempts to apply the Word of Wisdom more strictly.

When exactly did the Word of Wisdom become a commandment? The answer depends on what one means by *commandment*. If one means, when did the Lord express his will that Saints obey the Word of Wisdom, then the answer is, the day He gave it, February 27, 1833. The Lord revealed wisdom to the Saints and expected them to obey it, from the beginning, as best they could. Some claim the Word of Wisdom became binding in 1851, when Brigham Young asked for and received the Saints' sustaining vote to obey it. President Young himself sometimes chewed tobacco to dull the pain of broken teeth. Some claim the Word of Wisdom became binding in the 1880s, when President John Taylor re-emphasized obedience. Still others claim the Word of Wisdom finally became binding when

President Heber J. Grant made obedience to it a requirement for obtaining a temple recommend.[27]

If no single date can be established when the Lord made obedience to the Word of Wisdom binding upon Latter-day Saints, his merciful forewarning and longsuffering with weakness is clear. The Lord's prophets have consistently applied the principle of agency, always urging obedience yet making allowances for those who were acted upon by powerful substances before they had enough knowledge to act intelligently for themselves. President Grant taught that obedience to the Word of Wisdom resulted from love for God: "If you love God with all your heart, might, mind and strength, does he need to command?"[28]

Doctrine & Covenants 90

ORIGIN

Joseph's history says almost nothing about the circumstances that called forth Doctrine and Covenants 90. It is full of instructions about finances, so we may assume that Joseph was concerned about his and the Church's precarious financial situation, given the expensive projects the Lord had commanded them to accomplish. Moreover, the revelation answered, at least in part, Joseph's prayers for forgiveness (v. 1). Prayers of Joseph's brethren have also reached the Lord's ears. It seems likely that those brethren were Sidney Rigdon, who had been serving as Joseph's counselor, and Frederick Williams, who just a few weeks earlier received a revelation through Joseph that he was to be a counselor and scribe to Joseph.[1] The Lord refers again to these brethren by name in verse 6.

CONTENT

Doctrine and Covenants 90 blesses those who bear the keys of the kingdom, the authority to exercise the priesthood to govern the Church of Jesus Christ. It grants them the oracles—the revelations to govern the Church—and commands the Saints not to take them lightly.

The Lord forgives Sidney Rigdon and Frederick Williams and makes them equal with Joseph in holding the keys of the kingdom. Verse 9 nevertheless clarifies that Joseph presides over his counselors, who preside over the earth and are commanded by the Lord to spread the gospel and gather Israel in anticipation of his coming.

Beginning in verse 13, the Lord gives the Presidency their day-to-day duties: to finish revising the Old Testament, to preside over the Church and the school of the prophets (D&C 88), to receive revelations as needed, to study and learn all they can, and to preside over and set the Church in order.

Verses 13 through the end include the kind of revelation needed to set the Church in order. Here the Lord gives specific instructions about a variety of people, property, and finances. Joseph and his counselors are reproved for their pride and told to set in order their own homes and lives. The Church is to provide a home for Frederick Williams, who has consecrated his farm in obedience to the same revelation that called him to be a counselor to Joseph. Joseph's parents are to live on Frederick's farm, Sidney to remain where he lives, and the bishop to find an agent both faithful and of means to help pay the Church's debts. The Lord refers to the covenant of the United Firm in verse 24, which is itself a covenant (see D&C 82). In verse 25 he counsels Joseph's father to conserve his financial resources by not assuming responsibility for more people than he can afford in his advancing years. Vienna Jaques, a Bostonian convert who had gathered with the Saints and consecrated her considerable wealth, is promised an inheritance in Zion for her faithfulness.

In July 1833, a few months after section 90 was received, the Saints in Jackson County, Missouri, were forced to give up their land, their temple site, and their efforts to build New Jerusalem. Vienna Jacques, who had moved from Kirtland to Missouri as a result of section 90, was an eyewitness on July 20 when a mob violently humiliated Bishop Edward Partridge with a coating of tar and feathers. Joseph wrote to Vienna after he heard the news a few weeks later. Part of his letter, now in the Church History Library in Salt Lake City, follows. It reflects Joseph's frustrations with the Saints but also his indomitable will to build Zion with them and his spontaneous, prayerful way of invoking the Lord's blessings.

"Kirtland Sept 4th 1833

"Dear Sister,

"Having a few leisure moments I sit down to communicate to you a few words which I know I am under obligation to improve for your satisfaction if it should be a satisfaction for you to receive a few words from your unworthy brother in Christ. I received your Letter some time since containing a history of your Journey and your safe arrival for which I bless the Lord. I have often felt a whispering since I received your letter, like this: Joseph, thou art indebted to thy God for the offering of thy Sister Vienna which proved a savior of life as pertaining to thy pecuniary concern; therefore she should not be forgotten of thee for the Lord hath done this and thou shouldst remember her in all thy prayers and also by letter for she oftentimes calleth on the Lord, saying, O Lord, inspire thy servant Joseph to communicate by letter some word to thine unworthy handmaid. Canst thou not speak peaceably unto thine handmaid and say all my sins are forgiven and art thou not content with the chastisement wherewith thou hast chastised thy handmaid? Yea, sister, this seems to be the whisperings of a spirit and Judge ye what spirit it is. I was sensible, when you left Kirtland, that the Lord would chasten you but I prayed fervently in the name of Jesus that you might live to receive your inheritance agreeable to the commandment which was given concerning you [D&C 90:28–31]. I am not at all astonished at what has happened to you, neither to what has happened to Zion, and I could tell all the whys & wherefores of all their calamities, but alas it is in vain to warn and give precepts, for all men are naturally disposed to walk in their own paths as they are pointed out by their own fingers and are not willing to consider and walk in the path which is pointed out by another, saying, this is the way walk ye in it, although he should be an unerring director and the Lord his God sent him; nevertheless, I do not feel disposed to cast any reflections but I feel to cry mightily unto the Lord that all things might work together for good which has happened; yea, I feel to say, O Lord, let Zion be comforted let her waste places be built up and established an hundred fold."[2]

The Lord rebukes William McLellin, who has forsaken two mission calls and circumvented the law of consecration to purchase two lots on Main Street in Independence, Missouri (D&C 66; 75; 85).[3] The Lord also reproves Church leaders in Zion who have been badgering Joseph to move to Missouri to live.

OUTCOMES

Joseph acted on the instructions in Doctrine and Covenants 90. Ten days after the revelation was received, he convened a council of high priests, at which he ordained Sidney Rigdon and Frederick Williams "by the laying on of hands to be equal with him in holding the Keys of the Kingdom and also to the Presidency of the high Priesthood."[4]

Section 90 reassured Joseph. The keys are his forever. He will have revelations as needed.

The pressures of building Zion were overwhelming. Because the Lord told Joseph how to cope, strategize, delegate, prepare, and press forward, we can read between the lines that Joseph did not know what to do in several pressing situations. Section 90 treated Joseph's anxiety, uncertainty, and stress. Zion, Joseph's overwhelming project and problem, "shall not be removed out of her place. I, the Lord, have spoken it" (v. 37). If the Lord was confident in Zion, Joseph could be too. He would need such reassurance, for just when Joseph was sure his hands were full, things in Zion were about to get much worse.

Doctrine & Covenants 91

ORIGIN

Joseph's copy of the King James Version of the Bible included fourteen books from the Greek Septuagint that are not in the Hebrew Bible. Together these books are known as the Apocrypha. Some early Christians considered the Apocrypha scripture, but because the books were not in the Hebrew Bible, St. Jerome left them out of his Latin translation, the Vulgate.

During the Reformation, Protestants generally rejected the Apocrypha as scriptural and either relegated it to a separate section between the Old and the New Testament, as in Joseph's King James Version, or eliminated it completely. Catholics responded at the Council of Trent that the Apocrypha might be deuterocanonical, or secondary, but was scripture nevertheless and left some of the Apocryphal books scattered throughout the Old Testament. Though they varied slightly in which books they considered canonical, Orthodox Christians also included much of the Apocrypha in their scriptures.

Because it was not clear whether the Apocrypha should be considered canonical, Joseph asked whether he should read the Apocrypha and revise it as part of his new translation. His history says, "Having come to that portion of the ancient writings called the Apocrypha, I received the following" revelation, recorded in Doctrine and Covenants 91.[1]

CONTENT

In Doctrine and Covenants 94 the Lord tells Joseph that he need not translate the Apocrypha, and he explains why. Much of it is true and already translated correctly. But much of it is not true, having been inserted into the texts by uninspired scribes. The revelation hinges on the *therefore* that begins verse 4. Because there is much truth and much else in the Apocrypha, let it be understood by the Spirit, which testifies of truth. That is the way to get the most from the Apocrypha.[2]

An example of an interpolation by the hands of men is 1 John 5:7–8, which in the King James Version reads: "For there are three that bear record in heaven, the Father, the Word, and the Holy Ghost: and these three are one. And there are three that bear witness in earth, the Spirit, and the water, and the blood: and these three agree in one."

The emphasized text above is known as the Comma Johanneum. It is not in ancient Greek, Syriac, or Coptic manuscripts, nor is it cited by early Christian philosophers who were defending trinitarianism and would presumably have cited the passage had it been available. It appears to have been introduced into Jerome's Latin translation of Greek manuscripts.

Writing in 1690, Isaac Newton noted that "in all the vehement universal and lasting controversy about the Trinity in Jerome's time and both before and long enough after it, this text of the 'three in heaven' was never once thought of. It is now in everybody's mouth and accounted the main text for the business and would assuredly have been so too with them, had it been in their books."[3] Newton believed that Christianity had decayed and that the interpolation of the Comma Johanneum reflected corruption of the scriptures.

Strangely, some ardent defenders of the King James text today believe that removing the interpolation would corrupt the infallible, inerrant text of the Bible. Because of revealed principles, such as the ones in Doctrine and Covenants 91, members of the Church do not need to be confused.

OUTCOMES

Doctrine and Covenants 91 helps us understand the essential nature of scripture and of revelation. Many historical arguments have been made and dogmatic positions taken relative to the Apocrypha. Section 91 is the revealed position and among the least dogmatic. Rather than declaring the highly varied books of the Apocrypha either true or false, the Lord focuses on truth and error within the texts. Nor does he seem worried about errors in or sufficiency of scripture, a term Latter-day Saints do not even use. He gives instead an infallible principle that can be applied to all fallible fields and texts, including apocryphal or pseudepigraphical literature as well as science or art. The principle is that the companionship of the infallible Holy Spirit will enlighten and benefit those who seek truth, wherever it may be.

Like section 68, section 91 expands traditional Christian definitions of scripture. And like section 68, this revelation places highest priority not on parsing ancient texts but on each individual's receptivity to the Godhead through the Holy Ghost.

Doctrine & Covenants 92

ORIGIN

In April 1832 Doctrine and Covenants 82 organized several Church leaders into a corporation called the United Firm (often known as the united order), to manage the Church's finances, properties, and publishing projects.¹ In January 1833, the Lord gave a revelation calling Frederick G. Williams to be a counselor and scribe to Joseph and to consecrate his substantial farm to the Church. "Let thy farm be consecrated for bringing forth of the revelations and tho[u] shalt be blessed," the Lord told Frederick.² Section 90 affirmed Frederick's calling as counselor to Joseph, and a few days later section 92 was received.

CONTENT

The Kirtland Minute Book says Doctrine and Covenants 92 revealed that Frederick "should be received into the United Firm in full partnership agreeable to the specification of the bond" mentioned in Doctrine and Covenants 78:11 and 82:11.³ It instructs the members of the United Firm (united order) to receive Frederick, instructs him to be a "lively member" (v. 2), and reaffirms the earlier revelation's blessing to Frederick on the condition of obedience.

OUTCOMES

Frederick joined the United Firm, consecrated his farm, was ordained a counselor to Joseph Smith, continued to serve as a scribe, and was "lively" in building Zion. Joseph wrote in his journal, "Brother Frederick . . . is one of those men in whom I place the greatest confidence and trust for I have found him ever full of love and Brotherly kindness. . . . He is perfectly honest and upright, and seeks with all his heart to magnify his presidency in the church."[4]

Doctrine & Covenants 93

ORIGIN

Historical records say nothing about why Doctrine and Covenants 93 was given, but the Lord tells us why in verse 19 of the text itself: "I give unto you these sayings that you may understand and know how to worship, and know what you worship, that you may come unto the Father in my name, and in due time receive of his fulness."

CONTENT

Doctrine and Covenants 93 adds *intelligence* to the impressive catalog of synonyms in section 88 that include light, life, law, power, and glory—most memorably in verse 36: "The glory of God is intelligence, or, in other words, light and truth."

The Lord's use of the word *fulness* tells us that section 93 is a revelation about exaltation. *Fulness* is used occasionally in the Book of Mormon and early revelations to describe the gospel, but in section 76, the first of the revelations to describe progress beyond simple salvation from sin and death, the word bursts onto the page nine times. In section 93 we hear it fifteen times, sometimes enriched as in "fulness of truth" (v. 26) or "fulness of joy" (v. 34). Section 93 is an introductory text on how to come into the Lord's presence and become like him.

From the beginning the revelation describes what we must do to see his face and know him. Critics of the Church argue that such revelations as section 93 emphasize works, what we must do to *earn* exaltation. They feel that such theology minimizes or negates the atonement of Jesus Christ. But there is not a more Christ-centered revelation than section 93. It says nothing about earning God's fulness. Rather, Christ himself describes what we must do to become like him, to grow in light as he did until we have been *given* God's fulness. The reception of grace is conditional. We must forsake sins, come to Christ, and call upon and obey him in order to see and know him face to face (v. 1).

Section 93 draws on otherwise lost writings of John. The revelation clearly echoes the New Testament Gospel of John (vv. 7–11), but it also recounts the testimony of John the Baptist (v. 15). Authorities have expressed different opinions about which John is the writer.[1] It is clear that the revelation restores tantalizing lost texts and promises that even more will be forthcoming (vv. 6, 18). By drawing on these lost sources, section 93 restores richness about the nature of God, Christ, and man that is lost from traditional Christianity. Indeed, it explains how and who to worship (v. 19).

We worship the Father, the organizer of eternal elements and intelligent beings whom he designs to inherit his attributes and with them his "fulness of joy" (v. 33). We worship a God who did not create us from nothing but rather from eternally existing element and intelligence (see vv. 33–35). We worship a God whose work is to frame worlds and inhabit them with his children to provide them a sphere in which they can act independently, truly free to do their Father's will or their own. And that is how we worship: by choosing of our own free will to receive the light he offers us, to keep his commandments and therefore receive more truth, more light, more intelligence, until we know all he knows and have become all he is. We worship our Heavenly Father by becoming like him. To emulate him is the highest worship we can offer him. Christ is the example: "He received not of the fulness at the first, but received grace for grace" (v. 12). He obeyed his Father and grew by degrees of glory "until he received a fulness" (v. 13). Christ declares that we have similar potential for growth and godliness (v. 20).

Critics reject the premise of section 93 that Christ became God, and they find especially blasphemous the idea that mortals can also aspire to "grow up" (D&C 109:15) to become like their Heavenly Father. But such critics offer nothing as compelling as the description in section 93 of the nature of a Heavenly Father (in every sense of those words), of his firstborn Son (see vv. 4, 21), and of mankind as uncreated and therefore agents under a Heavenly Father's care but not compulsion.

Perhaps the most interesting aspect of section 93 is the transition at verse 40 to practical instructions. The final verses "descend from the heavens into the everyday concerns of Joseph and his friends. The Lord scolds them for not keeping order in their families."[2] The Lord singles out and names all the members of the First Presidency and Bishop Newel K. Whitney for failures in their most important responsibilities—their family responsibilities. This part of the revelation is not disconnected from the lofty verses preceding it. All of them tell how to raise children and why. God organizes life and provides his children a setting in which they can act freely. He endows them with light, truth, or knowledge to act upon independently, leaving them free to choose to obey or disobey when "that wicked one cometh and taketh away light and truth, through disobedience, from the children of men, and because of the tradition of their fathers" (v. 39). Section 93 is a masterpiece of parenting from a most concerned Father and a commandment to go and do likewise (v. 40). Moreover, since the glory of God is intelligence, he adds a commandment to worship by learning, by obtaining knowledge as a means to the end of exaltation. Exalting knowledge comes by obedience to God's light and truth. "He that keepeth his commandments receiveth truth and light, until he is glorified in truth and knoweth all things" (v. 28).

OUTCOMES

It may be true that Doctrine and Covenants 93 "suggests more than it precisely defines," but it also affirms good Bible teaching. The apostle Paul admonished the Philippians: "Let this mind be in you, which was also in Christ Jesus: who, being in the form of God, thought it not robbery to be equal with God: but made himself of no reputation, and took upon him the form of a servant, and was made in the likeness of men: and being found in fashion as a man, he humbled himself, and became obedient unto death, even the death of the cross. Wherefore God also hath highly exalted him, and given him a name which is above every name: that at the name of Jesus every knee should bow, of things in heaven, and things in earth, and things under the earth; and that every tongue should confess that Jesus Christ is Lord, to the glory of God the Father. Wherefore, my beloved, as ye have always obeyed, not as in my presence only, but now much more in my absence, work out your own salvation with fear and trembling" (Philippians 2:5–12). If Joseph Smith blasphemed, then so did Paul. More likely, both revealed sublime truth about the nature of God and man that was lost in the intervening years.

In his classic reflections on Joseph Smith, Harvard-educated scholar Truman Madsen cited section 93 as evidence that Joseph Smith provided more profound answers to philosophical questions than did Plato. One of Brother Madsen's footnotes expounds his point and increases our appreciation for the depth of section 93: "The *Timaeus,* one of Plato's last dialogues, deals with cosmology, the relationship of *nous,* or mind, to the soul and the soul to the body. It also presupposes complex theories of the nature of truth, and of universals (ultimate ideas) in abstraction. Section 93 was received in May, 1833, when Joseph was twenty-seven years old. It defines beginningless beginnings, the interrelationships of truth, of light, of intelligence, of agency, of element, of embodiment, of joy. Every sentence, every word, is freighted with meaning. In one fell swoop it cuts many Gordian knots. For example: How can something come from nothing? Answer: The universe was not created from nothing. 'The elements are eternal.' How can Christ have been both absolutely human and absolutely divine at the same time? Answer: He was not both at the same time. Christ 'received not of the fulness at the first, but continued . . . until he received a fulness.' If man is totally the creation of God, how can he be anything or do anything that he was not divinely pre-caused to do? Answer: Man is not totally the creation of God. 'Intelligence . . . was not created or made, neither indeed can be. . . . Behold, here is the agency of man.' How can man be a divine creation and yet be 'totally depraved'? Answer: Man is not totally depraved. 'Every spirit of man was innocent in the beginning; and God having redeemed man from the fall, men became again, in their infant state, innocent before God.' What is the relationship of being and beings, the one and the many? Answer: 'Being' is only the collective name of beings, of whom God is one.

Truth is knowledge of things (plural), and not, as Plato would have it, of Thinghood. 'Truth is knowledge of things as they are, and as they were, and as they are to come.' How can spirit relate to gross matter? Answer: 'The elements are the tabernacle of God.' Why should man be embodied? Answer: 'Spirit and element, inseparably connected, receive a fulness of joy.' If we begin susceptible to light and truth, how is it that people err and abuse the light? Answer: People are free; they can be persuaded only if they choose to be. They cannot be compelled. The Socratic thesis that knowledge is virtue (that if you really know the good you will seek it and do it) is mistaken. It is through disobedience and because of the traditions of the fathers that light is taken away from mankind."[3]

During a presentation at the Yale Divinity School, Brother Madsen told of a conversation with some Catholic priests, learned Jesuits, who expressed their inability to conceive of God as an intimate father intent on raising mankind to share in his glory and status. Brother Madsen offered to them how hard it is for Latter-day Saints to conceive of God as anything other than a concerned father whose work and glory is to glorify and exalt all of his willing children in the ways outlined by section 93.

Doctrine & Covenants 94

ORIGIN

Early manuscripts show that Doctrine and Covenants 94 is the last part of the revelation recorded in section 97.[1] Those manuscripts indicate that the revelation was given August 2, 1833; the May 1833 date in Joseph's history appears to be in error. Section 94 makes the most sense when read as an extension of section 97. Addressing similar concerns, it says that the Lord had already revealed the pattern for the house of the Lord in Kirtland, which he did in section 95. Moreover, on August 6, 1833, the First Presidency wrote to Church leaders in Missouri and included in the letter the revelation now recorded in sections 97 and 94. They explained that having received letters from the leaders in Missouri, "according to your request we inquired of the Lord and send in this letter the communication which we received from the Lord concerning the school in Zion. It was obtained August 2nd."[2]

CONTENT

In Doctrine and Covenants 97 the Lord requires the Saints in Zion (Missouri) to build a temple. In section 94 he commands the Saints in Ohio to build a stake of Zion, beginning with a temple in Ohio, as commanded in section 88 and again in section 95. Just south of the temple the Lord wants an office for the First Presidency. He specifies its design and the conditions on which he will abide there. On the next lot south the Lord wants a printing office, perhaps to replace the Church's press destroyed by a mob just a few days earlier in Missouri (reports of that event had not yet reached Joseph). The members of the Church's building committee, Hyrum Smith, Reynolds Cahoon, and Jared Carter, are appointed lots, or "inheritances" (v. 14), near the building sites. Verse 16 is not in the early manuscripts. Joseph may have added it as clarification before the revelation was published in the 1835 Doctrine and Covenants.

OUTCOMES

In the letter to Missouri Church leaders that included Doctrine and Covenants 94, the First Presidency explained that the Saints in Zion should build similar buildings for meetings and printing the scriptures.[3] But the Saints in Zion were already being forced from their land and homes and those in Kirtland struggled to muster the resources to build, besides the temple already underway, the two buildings called for in section 94. They scaled down the revealed instructions and on the west side of the temple built one building that was used as a printing office, a school, and office space for the First Presidency.

Doctrine & Covenants 95

ORIGIN

"A conference of High Priests assembled in Kirtland" to discuss how to keep the commandment in Doctrine and Covenants 88 to establish a house of the Lord, including a school for prophets.[1] The brethren appointed Jared Carter, Hyrum Smith, and Reynolds Cahoon as a committee to oversee fundraising and construction. They went to work and drafted a letter to the Saints, inviting them to contribute: "Unless we fulfill this command, namely establish an house, and prepare all things necessary whereby the elders may gather into a school, called the School of the Prophets, and receive that instruction which the Lord designs they should receive, we may all despair of obtaining the great blessing that God has promised to the faithful of the Church of Christ; therefore it is as important as our salvation that we obey."[2]

It is not clear whether Doctrine and Covenants 95 came before or after the building committee drafted this letter, but it came the same day to rebuke the Saints for procrastinating in their building the temple.

CONTENT

Doctrine and Covenants 95 is a revelation concerning God's love. He revealed in section 88 the conditions on which he would welcome the Saints into his light, his presence. The conditions included sanctifying their lives, building a house for the Lord, and assembling solemnly in it to worship him. But nearly a year later there was still no progress toward a temple. "Thus saith the Lord unto you whom I love, and whom I love

I also chasten that their sins may be forgiven, for with the chastisement I prepare a way for their deliverance in all things out of temptation, and I have loved you" (D&C 95:1). Given the premises that God loves the Saints and chastens those he loves as a means to their forgiveness, the next passage of the revelation is, predictably, a rebuke for what the Lord calls the "very grievous sin" of not building the temple (v. 3).

Then he emphasizes again the importance of the temple. It is the school for prophets, the way to "pour out my Spirit upon all flesh" (v. 4), the way out of darkness, the venue for receiving an endowment of heavenly power. The Lord wanted the elders to remain in Kirtland to receive this endowment, but they were contentious, and he sent them into the field to be chastened—because he loved them.

Beginning in verse 11, the Lord promises the Saints power to build the temple *if* they keep his commandments. "If you keep not my commandments," he emphasizes, "the love of the Father shall not continue with you, therefore you shall walk in darkness" (v. 12). The revelation does not say that the love of God will not continue, only that it will not continue with those who choose to reject it, who "love darkness rather than light" (D&C 29:45). By juxtaposing his love with darkness, the Lord equates his love with light and the synonyms for it described in sections 88 and 93, including *truth, glory, intelligence, power,* and *life.* Why, the Lord seems to lament in section 95, would Saints choose to walk in darkness at noonday when God's loving light shines for all who choose to obey the conditions on which he offers it?

So what would be the wise course? "Let the house be built," the Lord says, and gives the dimensions and a promise to reveal it to "three" (vv. 13–14).

OUTCOMES

The Saints in Kirtland got the point. They went to work at enormous cost. It appears that they finally understood that no price was too great for the blessings the Lord had promised, and perhaps they realized that their sacrifices would be sanctifying preparation for their temple worship.

The Lord promised in Doctrine and Covenants 95 to show three of the Saints how to build the temple (v. 14). Joseph and his counselors knelt in prayer to seek a fulfillment of this promise, and the Lord revealed the building in a vision.³

Hyrum Smith broke ground on June 5, 1833, in a wheat field on the bluffs above the Chagrin River. Everyone helped. Saints consecrated funds, labor, and expertise, but "the project was far out of proportion to the Church's pitiful resources." They had to rely on the Lord's promise of power to build it if they kept his commandments. "The economic realities gave Joseph no pause."⁴ He borrowed money to finance the construction. He understood "the great and last promise" better than anyone (D&C 88:69). He had tried to get the Saints to understand. A few months before the rebuke given in section 95 Joseph had written of the imperative in section 88 to build the temple: "The Lord commanded us in Kirtland to build an house of God, & establish a school for the Prophets, this is the word of the Lord to us, & we must—yea the Lord helping us we will obey, as on conditions of our obedience, he has promised us great things, yea even a visit from the heavens to honor us with his own presence, we greatly fear before the Lord lest we should fail of this great honor which our master proposes to confer on us, we are seeking for humility & great faith lest we be ashamed in his presence."⁵

Section 95 motivated the Saints in Kirtland to action. After receiving it they no longer walked in darkness at noon. They saw the light available in the temple. "Beginning in Kirtland," wrote historian Richard Bushman, "temples became an obsession. For the rest of his life, no matter the cost of the temple to himself and his people, [Joseph] made plans, raised money, mobilized workers, and required sacrifice."⁶

Doctrine & Covenants 96

ORIGIN

In the spring of 1833, high priests in Kirtland met to plan how to acquire several farms in the area, particularly a farm and tavern owned by an early settler named Peter French. The Saints hoped to build a stake of Zion surrounding the house of the Lord, which they intended to build on French's farm. They sent a committee to ask the farm owners the terms on which they would be willing to sell. The committee returned with news that the farms could be bought for around eleven thousand dollars, and the council decided to buy, appointed agents to negotiate the sale, and called the elders out of the school to raise funds among the Saints.[1] The funds were raised, and the farms purchased, leading to another council on June 4. This council disagreed about who should be the steward of the French farm, "but all agreed to inquire of the Lord."[2] Doctrine and Covenants 96 was the result.

CONTENT

The Lord appoints Bishop Newel K. Whitney as the steward of the farm and says that John Johnson should become a member of the United Firm and use his financial resources and skills to pay the Church's debts (D&C 78; 82; 92).

In Doctrine and Covenants 96 the Lord speaks as the owner of the farm, "the place . . . upon which I design to build mine holy house" (v. 2). He begins the revelation by stating the rationale for buying the farm: "It is expedient in me that this stake that I have set for the strength of Zion should be made strong" (v. 1). Bishop Whitney is to "take charge of the place" as a good steward (v. 2), but the Lord, the owner, gives Whitney and others instructions on how to act relative to the land, by dividing it among the Saints and using the proceeds to fund the United Firm (called "the order" in vv. 4 and 8 but "the Firm" in early manuscripts), especially in its priority of funding the Literary Firm's commission to publish the revelations (D&C 70; 78; 82; 92).

OUTCOMES

After Doctrine and Covenants 96 was received, Bishop Whitney became steward of the farm and acted on the instructions in the revelation to divide it and to finance the Church's publications with it. John Johnson moved from Hiram to Kirtland, joined the United Firm, became steward of the tavern, and worked to obey the revelation by paying the Firm's debts.[3]

Doctrine & Covenants 97

ORIGIN

Less than two weeks before Doctrine and Covenants 97 was received, the Saints in Jackson County, Missouri, having been pressured by mob violence and threats, agreed to an ultimatum that required them to leave the county.

Parley P. Pratt described Zion during the summer of 1833 as the opposition escalated. "Immigration had poured into the County of Jackson in great numbers; and the Church in that county now numbered upwards of one thousand souls." He described how the Saints industriously improved their situations by building homes and cultivating farms. He said that they observed the Sabbath according to section 59 but made no mention of building the temple described in section 84. "I devoted almost my entire time in ministering among the churches," Parley wrote, "holding meetings; visiting the sick; comforting the afflicted, and giving counsel. A school of Elders was also organized, over which I was called to preside. This class, to the number of about sixty, met for instruction once a week. The place of meeting was in the open air, under some tall trees, in a retired place in the wilderness, where we prayed, preached and prophesied, and exercised ourselves in the gifts of the Holy Spirit. Here great blessings were poured out, and many great and marvelous things were manifested and taught. . . . To attend this school I had to travel on foot, and sometimes with bare feet at that, about six miles. This I did once a week, besides visiting and preaching in five or six branches a week."[1]

Parley and his brethren wrote to Joseph, seeking the Lord's will concerning their school. "While thus engaged," Parley wrote, "and in answer to our correspondence with the Prophet, Joseph Smith, at Kirtland, Ohio, the following revelation was sent to us by him, dated August, 1833."[2]

CONTENT

The Saints in Zion have just received an ultimatum from their antagonistic neighbors: Stop obeying the revelations, or we will force you to. In Doctrine and Covenants 97, the Lord issues a counter ultimatum. "The ax is laid at the root of the trees," he says, "and every tree that bringeth not forth good fruit shall be hewn down and cast into the fire. I, the Lord, have spoken it" (v. 7).

Section 97 highlights the Lord's priorities for Zion. "I, the Lord, am well pleased that there should be a school in Zion, and also with my servant Parley P. Pratt, for he abideth in me" (v. 3). But the Lord requires a temple in Zion to "be built speedily, by the tithing of my people" (v. 11), by obedience to the law of sacrifice set forth in verses 8–12. The temple—or, rather, the keeping of covenants required to build and worship in the temple—will be the salvation of Zion. Thus, section 97 is conspicuously full of if-then constructions. It promises conditionally that *if* the Saints obey the commandment to sacrifice to build a temple in Independence, *then* Zion will prosper and become great and immovable. She will escape her enemies *if* she observes to do all things whatsoever I have commanded her. If not, *then* Zion will be visited with sore afflictions. The future of Zion is in the hands of the Latter-day Saints. *If* the Saints want Zion as their first priority, *then* they will sacrifice to build it and keep it holy. In verse 27, the Lord gives Zion a second chance. If Zion has since been, at least temporarily, "moved out of her place," it is because too few Latter-day Saints share the Lord's priorities set forth in section 97 (v. 19).

OUTCOMES

Parley Pratt testified that the Lord poured forth the blessings promised in Doctrine and Covenants 97 when he did as the revelation commanded regarding the school for the elders. "The Lord gave me great wisdom," Parley wrote, "and enabled me to teach and edify the Elders, and comfort and encourage them in their preparations for the great work which lay before us. I was also much edified and strengthened." But Parley also noted that "this revelation was not complied with by the leaders and Church in Missouri, as a whole." As section 97 itself shows, the Saints in Zion were not unified, not all committed to keeping their covenants. Thus, "notwithstanding many were humble and faithful," Parley noted, "the threatened judgment was poured out to the uttermost."[3] The Saints were driven from Zion, and we still weep for her.

Doctrine & Covenants 98

ORIGIN

Oliver Cowdery wrote from Independence, Missouri, to Church leaders in Kirtland, Ohio, informing them that opposition from the Saints' Missouri neighbors was rising. By the time the letter arrived in Ohio, in Missouri Bishop Edward Partridge had been tarred and feathered, the Church's press destroyed, and the Saints given an ultimatum to leave Jackson County or face continued oppression. Joseph had not received reports about the full extent of this persecution when he received Doctrine and Covenants 98, but the Lord braced the Saints with a revelation on how to respond when attacked.

CONTENT

Foreseeing the Saints' emotional reactions to the violence, in Doctrine and Covenants 98 the Lord prescribes "be comforted," "rejoice," "give thanks," and wait "patiently" for him, the Lord of Hosts, the defender of his people, to answer their prayers, for he has sworn to do so (vv. 1–2). This is his covenant with them. He promises that "all things wherewith you have been afflicted shall work together for your good, and to my name's glory" (v. 3).

The revelation upholds the rule of constitutional law applied without bias. The principle of freedom "belongs to all mankind," and it comes from God (v. 5). The Saints should therefore do all that lies in their power to preserve freedom for themselves and everyone else.

Section 98 reiterates the law of sacrifice described in section 97. The

Saints are being tried and proven to see "whether you will abide in my covenant," the Lord says, "even unto death" (v. 14; see also Mosiah 18:8–10). He commands the Saints to "renounce war and proclaim peace" (v. 16). The Saints' work is proclaiming peace, the good news of the gospel, and the binding and sealing of hearts and families.

At verse 19 the revelation turns attention to materialistic Saints in Kirtland. "I, the Lord, am not well pleased with many who are in the church at Kirtland; for they do not forsake their sins, and their wicked ways, the pride of their hearts, and their covetousness, and all their detestable things, and observe the words of wisdom and eternal life which I have given unto them" (vv. 19–20). He then repeats the terms and conditions on which he will save or damn them.

Beginning in verse 23 the Lord reveals his law of just war, the same law on which Nephi and the Israelite patriarchs acted and which is applicable to all (vv. 32, 38). Simply put, it is to bear attacks "patiently and revile not . . . neither seek revenge" (v. 23). After three offenses, patiently endured, the Saints are to warn their attackers in the name of the Lord to stop. If they do not, the Lord says, "I have delivered thine enemy into thine hands" (v. 29). At that point the Saints can opt to spare the transgressor or deliver justice. "If he has sought thy life, and thy life is endangered by him, thine enemy is in thine hands and thou art justified" (v. 31).

The Lord's law of just war includes the commandment that his people "should not go out unto battle against any nation, kindred, tongue, or people, save I, the Lord, commanded them" (v. 33). When an enemy declares war, the Saints "should first lift a standard of peace" (v. 34). If that gesture is rejected three times, the Saints should testify to the Lord of their good faith efforts. "Then I, the Lord, would give unto them a commandment, and justify them in going out to battle against that nation," and then the Lord would be on the Saints' side (v. 36).

Beginning in verse 39, the Lord adds another dimension to the law. Enemies are to be forgiven as often as they truly repent. "If he do this, thou shalt forgive him with all thine heart," the Lord says, "and if he do not this, I, the Lord, will avenge thee of thine enemy an hundred-fold" (v. 45). The

Lord's vengeance is just and sure but it evaporates as soon as there is repentance (vv. 46–48).

OUTCOMES

Oliver Cowdery arrived in Kirtland with news of the violent persecution in Missouri and the Saints' pending expulsion from Jackson County. Joseph was passionate about Zion and responded to the crisis with emotion. He wrote a long letter in his own hand to the Church leaders in Missouri, beginning with a brokenhearted prayer that the Lord would comfort the Saints and curse their enemies before concluding, "O Lord glorify thyself thy will be done and not mine."[1]

Joseph's first reaction was to curse the Saints' enemies, but he believed the promises of Doctrine and Covenants 98 and bowed to its moderating instructions in responding to the crisis. For example, he urged the Saints to "wait patiently until the Lord comes and restores unto us all things and build the waste places again for he will do it in his time." He wrote to Zion, "there is no safety only in the arm of Jehovah none else can deliver and he will not deliver unless we do prove ourselves faithful to him in the severest trouble for he that will have his robes washed in the blood of the Lamb must come up through great tribulation even the greatest of all affliction but know this when men thus deal with you and speak all manner of evil of you falsely for the sake of Christ that he is your friend and I verily know that he will speedily deliver Zion for I have his immutable covenant that this shall be the case but God is pleased to keep it hid from mine eyes the means how exactly the thing will be done." Joseph concluded his letter "by telling you that we wait the Command of God to do whatever he please and if he shall say go up to Zion and defend thy Brethren by the sword we fly and we count not our lives dear to us."[2]

Section 98 was the first of Joseph's revelations to acknowledge earthly government. Zion had been considered independent, soon to govern the world as nations fell before the millennial reign of Christ (D&C 87). By acknowledging the rule of constitutional law, section 98 got Joseph thinking in new ways. He wrote to Zion, "'we are all friends to the Constitution yea true friends to that Country for which our fathers bled.'" As a result of section 98, the Church befriended constitutional law and principles as allies in seeking redress for the violations of the Saints' civil and religious liberties and property rights. "From then on," wrote historian Richard Bushman, "Joseph was never far removed from politics. For a decade, he sought protection from the government, usually without success, until finally, frustrated by his inability to rally government to the Saints' side, he ran for president."[3]

The command in section 98 for the Saints to befriend the rule of law and to provide evidence or testimonies of the abuses of the lawless seems to have shaped the way the Saints presented their story. Joseph and his followers obeyed section 98 in part by writing the history of these events as a law-abiding and unlawfully persecuted minority. In telling the expulsion from Jackson County, Joseph's history says that the Saints were driven by a mob led by civic and religious leaders "while there was not a *solitary* offence on record; or proof that a Saint had broken the law of the land."[4]

Doctrine & Covenants 99

ORIGIN

John Murdock spent years seeking for the gospel of Jesus Christ. He carefully observed, read, and studied the scriptures and other religious literature. He believed there were many forms of godliness, but he wanted the Holy Spirit to teach him which church possessed the power of God. In the fall of 1830, Oliver Cowdery and other missionaries passed through the area of John's northern Ohio residence, carrying with them the Book of Mormon (D&C 28). John read it, and observed Oliver's preaching. "The spirit of the Lord rested on me," he wrote, "witnessing to me of the truth." John's wife, Julia, believed. He wrote that he "was filled with the spirit as I read" to her. He asked Oliver and his companions to baptize him in the cold Chagrin River. He was immersed, confirmed, and ordained an elder by the power of the Holy Priesthood. "It was truly a time of the outpouring of the spirit," John wrote. "I know the spirit rested on me as it never did before."[1]

With the succession of sacred ordinances—baptism, confirmation, ordination—John Murdock went from investigator to missionary. His autobiography (based on his journal) documents his extensive missionary work. Many families received the good news of the gospel from John Murdock as he consecrated himself and his family to the Church. In April 1831 Julia died hours after giving birth to twins, leaving John to care for the two newborns and three other children. Then section 52 called John to preach and travel to Missouri in the summer of 1831. John shouldered and balanced his priesthood responsibilities to nurture the children and preach the gospel the best he could. He made a selfless decision to ask Joseph and Emma Smith, whose twins had just died, to adopt his. John left his other children in the care of relatives and fellow Saints and endured a long, sickly, and extremely successful mission to Missouri and back, where he found his children well with the exception of little Joseph, who had measles and died as a result of being exposed to the cold night air when the Prophet was mobbed in March 1832 (see D&C 71).

John nurtured his children, regained his health, and served in the Church in Ohio until August 1832, when Doctrine and Covenants 99 called him back to the mission field.

CONTENT

Doctrine and Covenants 99 is a mission call. The Lord calls John to go east "to proclaim mine everlasting gospel unto the inhabitants thereof, in the midst of persecution and wickedness" (v. 1). John's job is to activate the agency of everyone he can. By proclaiming the gospel, in other words, John will give his hearers the power to choose either to *receive* or to *reject* the Lord (note his careful wording of vv. 2–4). When John's offering is rejected, the Lord instructs him to cleanse his feet privately to signify that with the transmission of the gospel, agency shifted. When missionaries adequately impart the law of the gospel, their hearers know enough to act for themselves. They must then choose. Section 99 calls John Murdock to help people choose for themselves. This is an urgent part of the Lord's plan of salvation, for "I come quickly to judgment," He declares (v. 5).

The Lord reveals his intimate acquaintance with John's family situation and tells him how to both provide for his motherless children and perform his mission. John, meanwhile, has the choice to inherit Zion in a few years or continue his missionary labors for the rest of his life.

OUTCOMES

John wrote that having received Doctrine and Covenants 99, "I immediately commenced to arrange my business and provide for my children and send them up to the Bishop in Zion," Edward Partridge. Then John set out to preach the gospel. Some received him as the revelation predicted. Others, including his in-laws, rejected him. John "met with a Dr. Matthews, a very wicked man" who rejected his offering. John documented how he and his companion applied section 99: "We bore testimony according to the commandment and the Lord helped us in tending to the ordinance" of cleansing their feet.[2]

Doctrine & Covenants 100

ORIGIN

The Saints in Zion were not the only ones besieged in late 1833. Joseph wrote from Kirtland, Ohio, that "we are suffering great persecution on account of one man." Philastus Hurlbut had been excommunicated for adultery and responded with a concerted effort to undermine Joseph. "He is lying in a wonderful manner," Joseph wrote, "and the people are running after him and giving him money to break down Mormonism which much endangers our lives at present but God will put a stop to his career soon and all will be well."[1] Hurlbut threatened to wash his hands in Joseph's blood, before Joseph and Sidney Rigdon left for New York and Ontario, Canada, to preach.[2] Joseph's journal does not mention the revelation being given, but the entry for October 12 may allude to it and certainly to some of the concerns that led to it: "I feel very well in my mind the Lord is with us but have much anxiety about my family."[3]

CONTENT

Doctrine and Covenants 100 addresses Joseph's mission with Sidney Rigdon and the two concerns that occupy his anxious mind: Zion and the safety of his family and other Saints. The revelation begins with the Lord's omnipotent assurance that Joseph and Sidney's families are well. "They are in mine hands, and I will do with them as seemeth me good" (v. 1).

The Lord gives Joseph and Sidney specific, omniscient counsel to ensure the success of their mission. The Lord's instructions take the form of covenants. *If* Joseph and Sidney speak the thoughts the Lord puts into their hearts, they will not be confounded. *If* they solemnly, meekly declare the gospel in the Lord's name, he promises that the Holy Ghost will testify of their words. He promises Joseph a powerful testimony and Sidney the ability to expound scripture, and he makes Joseph a revelator for Sidney and Sidney a spokesman for Joseph.

Beginning in verse 13 the Lord offers "a word concerning Zion." He promises protection and salvation to the brethren Joseph sent to Missouri with messages. "Zion shall be redeemed," the Lord promises, after she is chastened and becomes pure and willing to serve the Lord. He declares the terms on which he will save souls.

OUTCOMES

Joseph Smith possessed a dogged tenacity. He did not want to give up on Zion or on New Jerusalem being built around a holy temple in Jackson County, Missouri. Oliver Cowdery had recently suggested that the Saints could start again somewhere else. Joseph rejected that thought. He told the Saints in Missouri that the Lord wanted them to hold on to their land, refuse to sell it, refuse to give up on Zion. He promised them that Zion would flourish in spite of hell, though he did not pretend to know how or when.[4]

Joseph described himself as praying fervently and often in these months. He could not understand why Zion had been forsaken. He even said that he murmured, though he knew better.[5] Doctrine and Covenants 100 comforted Joseph. It reinforced his faith in Zion, though it did not answer his questions about how or when the Lord would bring the Saints back to the promised land. After receiving section 100, Joseph wrote, "I know that Zion, in the own due time of the Lord will be redeemed, but how many will be the days of her purification, tribulation, and affliction, the Lord has kept hid from my eyes; and when I enquire concerning this subject the voice of the Lord is, Be still, and know that I am God! all those who suffer for my name shall reign with me, and he that layeth down his life for my sake shall find it again."[6]

Section 100 eased Joseph's anxieties about his family's safety in the hostile environment of Kirtland, Ohio. On returning from his month-long mission, he dictated the following journal entry: "Found my family all well according to the promise of the Lord for which blessings I feel to thank his holy name."[7]

Doctrine & Covenants 101

ORIGIN

On December 10, 1833, Joseph Smith opened letters from Church leaders in Missouri. They were full of what Joseph called "the melancholy intelligence of your flight from the land of your inheritance having been driven before the face of your enemies in that place."[1] He had learned from earlier reports that prominent citizens had led a mob in destroying the Church's press and printing office, that the Saints had been forced to agree to an ultimatum to leave Jackson County, and that at least one Saint had died in the violence. Joseph hoped, however, that the rule of law would prevail, that the Saints could get redress for the illegal acts against them, and that they would not have to leave the land they had legally purchased and occupied. The December 10 letters from Liberty, north of the Missouri River, where many Saints had fled for safety, dashed that hope.

The news depressed and bewildered Joseph. The Saints had been driven from the promised land. Why? Would they return? If so, how? The Lord had told him to consecrate Zion as a refuge and gathering place for the Saints and promised that no other place would be appointed for the holy city. "Therefore I ask thee," Joseph prayed, "in the name of Jesus Christ, to return thy people unto their homes . . . [and] that all the enemies of thy people, who will not repent and return unto thee be destroyed from off the face of that Land."[2]

Doctrine and Covenants 101 came a week later to answer these questions and Joseph's prayer. Oliver Cowdery announced the revelation: "Good morning Brethren, we have just received news from heaven."[3]

CONTENT

"Like biblical accounts of Israel's defeats, the revelation blamed the losses in Missouri on Zion's own sins. God suffered affliction to come upon the Saints 'in consequence of their transgressions.' But, again like Israel, the Saints were not cast off. 'Yet, I will own them, and they shall be mine in that day when I come to make up my jewels.' They were not to give up Zion but to purchase even more land in Jackson County."[4]

In Doctrine and Covenants 101 the Lord reveals himself to be both strict and compassionate. The Saints must be chastened and tried like Abraham in order to become sanctified. They must stop being contentious, jealous, covetous, and lustful or there will be no Zion even if he comes to their rescue. Yet, he promises emphatically, he will come to their rescue. "Notwithstanding their sins, my bowels are filled with compassion towards them. I will not utterly cast them off; and in the day of wrath I will remember mercy" (v. 9).

Joseph had written a week before Doctrine and Covenants 101 was received that he murmured because "those who are innocent are compelled to suffer for the iniquities of the guilty; and I cannot account for this."[5] The Lord acknowledges in verse 41 the perceived injustice and has his own "wisdom" in allowing it.

From the Lord's perspective, a potent dose of "trouble" can be useful. When the Saints were well and good, they treated lightly the revelations to gather, to consecrate, to buy land and to build a temple. Now, all of a sudden, "of necessity they feel after me," the Lord says (v. 8).

Section 101 reaffirms that Zion will be built in Jackson County, despite the Saints having been driven out. It prophesies the millennial day when the pure in heart will inherit Zion, enmity will cease, Satan will become powerless, the Lord will reveal all things, and death, like sorrow, will depart. The persecuted faithful will inherit these blessings, the Lord promises, so from that perspective they should "fear not even unto death; for in this world your joy is not full, but in me your joy is full" (v. 36).

Beginning in verse 43, the Lord relates a parable to explain his will concerning how to get Zion back. In it he implies that unfaithful Saints in Zion were bad stewards. Rather than building the temple as commanded, they second-guessed the Lord, used his money selfishly, and opened themselves to attacks that could have been prevented by obedience. "Ought ye not to have done even as I commanded you . . . ?" the nobleman of the parable asks the disobedient servants (v. 53).

The nobleman's plans for reclaiming his vineyard from enemies include gathering an army of his servants, "the strength of mine house," to do battle (v. 55). The nobleman promises to redeem his overrun vineyard, and the servants ask when. He answers, "When I will; go ye straightway, and do all things whatsoever I have commanded you" (v. 60). The servants go and do as the nobleman commanded, "and after many days all things were fulfilled" (v. 62).

Immediately after giving the parable the Lord resumes giving his "will concerning the redemption of Zion" (v. 43), as if he were the nobleman commanding his servants what to do. He commands the Saints to obey sections 57, 63, and 86—that is, to continue the work of gathering by preaching the gospel, gaining converts, and gathering together to pool resources to systematically (not hastily or haphazardly) purchase land and build Zion legally. He calls for "wise men" to be sent to purchase the lands, to buy out the settlers of Jackson County, satisfying them for their land and eliminating the controversies between them (v. 73). There is no shortage of money among the Saints in the eastern branches, the Lord says. They have enough to buy the land if they are willing to consecrate it for Zion (v. 75).

In verse 76 the Lord calls for the Saints to continue to appeal to government for redress of their civil and property rights, like the biblical parable of the unjust judge who finally relented to an insistent woman's pleas for justice. Similarly, the Saints are to petition for justice at the feet of every government official, including the president. "And if the president heed them not, then will the Lord arise and come forth out of his hiding place, and in his fury vex the nation" (v. 89). The Saints are to pray for their government officials to be responsive and therefore escape the Lord's vengeance.

The revelation closes with a command that the Saints are not to sell the storehouse nor any of the land they legally own. Though driven unjustly, they must not surrender to their oppressors. They must not sell the promised land.

OUTCOMES

Doctrine and Covenants 101 explains in terms of individual agency the reasons Zion has fled. God is sovereign. He could stop every mobbing and prevent every Saint from being lustful, covetous, and contentious. He chooses instead to allow his individual children to have agency. He gives them power to act and commandments to act upon. When they or some of them disobey his commands, the blessings promised for obedience are not forthcoming. That is how some of the Saints and their enemies postponed Zion. It is the fault of the Saints, not of God, that there is no holy city in Jackson County, Missouri.

Agency is a theme in most of the revelations, but in section 101 it is particularly clear. The Lord is explicit about cause and effect and the nature of agency. In verses 77–80, for example, the Lord explains what Hugh Nibley called the ancient law of liberty, or, simply, the free exercise of conscience that is vital to God's plan of salvation.[6] Early Christians regarded the power to choose for oneself intrinsic to humanity, an endowment from God. But as soon as the Roman Empire became officially Christian, it began enforcing apostate faith by the sword. Not until the Constitution of the United States was established was the ancient law of liberty again enshrined, and even then inconsistently. For, as section 101 emphasizes, the Lord approves the "just and holy principles" of the Constitution "for the rights and protection of all flesh" (v. 77). The choice of words could hardly be more inclusive. It is important to understand the Lord's purpose in making *all flesh* free. Freedom is not for its own sake. Freedom facilitates agency, the means to which accountability before God is the end. Or, in the Lord's words, freedom is so "that every man may act in doctrine and principle pertaining to futurity, according to the moral agency which I have given unto him, that every man may be accountable for his own sins in the day of judgment. Therefore, it is not right that any man should be in bondage one to another" (vv. 78–79).

Section 101 promises an ultimate redemption of Zion, though its timing depends on the Saints' decisions. In several places the Lord guarantees that Zion will come. In just as many he speaks ambiguously about when in his timetable the holy city will be built. Meanwhile, section 101 portends the possibility of calling on an army of the Lord's servants to reclaim his land (D&C 103).

Joseph had the revelation printed immediately, circulated it among the Saints, and sent a copy to Missouri governor Daniel Dunklin.

Doctrine & Covenants 102

ORIGIN

Joseph Smith convened councils to arbitrate and adjudicate Church decisions, especially disciplinary decisions. Previous to the organization of a standing stake high council in February 1834, such councils were composed ad hoc, according to the law of the Church revealed in February 1831 (D&C 42). Experience and Church growth created a need for standing councils to deal with complex issues. On February 17, 1834, Joseph told an assembly of twenty-four priesthood brethren that he "would show the order of councils in ancient days as shown to him by vision."[1] The minutes of that meeting, recorded by Oliver Cowdery and Orson Hyde, revised by Joseph, and approved by a Church council, are Doctrine and Covenants 102.

CONTENT

The new council, which would help in governing the Church in administrative and judicial matters, is to be composed of a presidency of three high priests with twelve more high priests as counselors. While continuing as president of the Church, Joseph Smith and his counselors—Sidney Rigdon and Frederick G. Williams—are also to serve as the presidency of the new standing high council of the Church's first stake, headquartered in Kirtland, Ohio. Twelve high priests including Joseph's father, Joseph, and his uncle John Smith, together with Joseph Coe, John Johnson, Martin Harris, John S. Carter, Jared Carter, Oliver Cowdery, Samuel H. Smith, Orson Hyde, Sylvester Smith, and Luke Johnson are chosen as high councilors and unanimously sustained by the brethren present. "The above named councilors were then asked whether they accepted their appointments, and whether they would act in that office according to the law of heaven: to which they all answered, that they accepted their appointments, and would fill their offices according to the grace of God bestowed upon them."[2]

Joseph tells the brethren that he "would show the order of councils in ancient days . . . as shown to him by vision." He explains that "Jerusalem was the seat of the Church Council in ancient days" and that "the apostle, Peter, was the president of the Council and held the keys of the Kingdom of God on the earth [and] was appointed to this office by the voice of the Savior and acknowledged in it by the voice of the Church. He had two men appointed as Counselors with him, and in case Peter was absent, his counselors could also transact business alone." Joseph explains that Church councils operate on principles of jurisprudence different from those of secular courts. "It was not the order of heaven in ancient councils to plead for and against the guilty as in our judicial courts (so called) but that every councilor when he arose to speak, should speak precisely according to evidence and according to the teaching of the Spirit of the Lord."[3]

Clerks keep minutes of Joseph's teachings on how the council should be organized. They record that "many questions have been asked during the time of the organization of the Council and doubtless some errors have been committed, it was, therefore, voted by all present that Bro. Joseph should make all necessary corrections by the Spirit of inspiration hereafter."[4]

Joseph began that job the next day, February 18, and the following day an even larger gathering of priesthood holders and general members met to review and consent to the new "constitution of the high council of the Church of Christ."[5] The minutes Joseph refined were subsequently canonized and are currently found in Doctrine and Covenants 102.

OUTCOMES

At the February 19 meeting, Joseph laid hands on his two counselors and blessed them with "wisdom to magnify their office, and power over all the power of the adversary." He then laid hands on the twelve men called as high councilors and set them apart. He blessed them with "wisdom and power to counsel in righteousness upon all subjects that might be laid before them." He also prayed that they might be delivered from those evils to which they were most exposed and that their lives might be prolonged on the earth. Then, in the name of Jesus Christ, Joseph gave his counselors and the high council a charge to "do their duty in righteousness and in the fear of God." They signified their acceptance of Joseph's charge by raising their right hands. Joseph pronounced the council organized "according to the ancient order, and also according to the mind of the Lord."[6]

Doctrine and Covenants 102 restores the ancient order of Church councils. The organization of the high council also went far toward establishing a stake of Zion in Kirtland, an ecclesiastical jurisdiction drawn on imagery from Isaiah 33:20 and 54:2 and applied to the Church in a May 1833 revelation (D&C 94:1; 96:1). Moreover, the minutes provided for other standing high councils to be established as well as temporary councils to be organized beyond Zion and her stakes.

The first high council of the Church went to work immediately. As specified in the minutes, the counselors drew numbers 1–12, with even-numbered councilors responsible to prevent insult and injustice against the accused person and the odd numbered councilors responsible to ensure the interests of the Church. Ezra Thayre charged Curtis Hodges, an elder, with preaching too loudly and unclearly and claiming he was justified in doing so when corrected. Elder Hodges said he was not guilty. Witnesses confirmed "that bro. Hodges was guilty of hollowing so loud that he, in a measure, lost his voice." Oliver Cowdery, who had drawn number 1, summarized the case against Hodges. Joseph Coe, who had drawn number 2, summarized the case from Hodge's perspective "but could say but few words." Thayre restated his accusations, and Hodges restated his pleas.[7]

The case, which was not considered complicated, was conducted exactly as Section 102 specifies, including the ruling of Joseph Smith, president of the council. He announced "that the charges in the declaration had been fairly sustained by good witnesses, also, that bro. H[odges]. ought to have confessed when rebuked by bro Thayre also that if he had the spirit of the Lord at the meetings when he hollowed, he must have abused it, and grieved it away. All the council agreed with the decision." Brother Hodges then confessed, acknowledging that he could now see his error and would repent.[8]

Not all high council hearings are this straightforward, but the specific instructions set forth in section 102 continue to guide the standing high councils of the Church in every stake of Zion.

Doctrine & Covenants 103

ORIGIN

As 1834 dawned, the Saints in Missouri were "exiles in a land of liberty."[1] What should they do now? They sent Parley P. Pratt and Lyman Wight to Kirtland, Ohio, to seek counsel on their beleaguered situation. The messengers arrived in February, probably with a letter from William Phelps informing Joseph that Missouri governor Daniel Dunklin was willing to help restore the Saints to their Jackson County lands but that he would not maintain a militia to defend them indefinitely, and they were therefore afraid.[2] Would eastern Saints come to the aid of Zion? Joseph counseled with his brethren, resolved that "he was going to Missouri, to assist in redeeming it," and asked for volunteers to go with him. Joseph received Doctrine and Covenants 103 to answer the Missouri Saints and to organize his plans to march to their aid.[3]

CONTENT

Doctrine and Covenants 103 reiterates the emphasis on individual agency in section 101. Zion depended on the Latter-day Saints. They were driven by wicked individuals acting on their own free will. The Lord promises to punish them "in mine own time" (D&C 103:2). But they were driven "because they did not hearken altogether unto the precepts and commandments which I gave unto them" (v. 4). The Lord offers another chance at Zion by setting forth the conditions on which the Saints can prevail against their enemies. First he states these positively (what will happen if they do;

vv. 5–7) and then restates them negatively (what will happen if they do not; vv. 8–10).

Section 103 reaffirms the earlier revelations that promise Zion while it reminds the Saints of the repeated prophecy in section 58 of Zion "after much tribulation" (D&C 103:12). Even these promises, the Lord qualifies, are conditional. "If they pollute their inheritances," he says of the Saints again, "they shall be thrown down" (v. 14; see also D&C 84:59).

Beginning in verse 15, the Lord maps out the way Zion will be reclaimed "by power" (v. 15). Then the Lord evokes section 101, reminding the Saints of his promise to raise up a Moses to lead the modern Israelites and of the command to buy land and consecrate it in Missouri. He calls on Joseph to gather an army of Israel, to curse "mine enemies," the Lord says, "and ye shall avenge me of mine enemies" (vv. 24–25). It could become violent, the Lord suggests, perhaps as a test to see who is willing "to lay down his life for my sake" (v. 27). The Lord calls Sidney Rigdon to teach the eastern Saints the revelations that set forth how to build Zion by missionary work, consecration, and gathering. He appoints Parley and Lyman to help gather five hundred men to march to Zion, though he acknowledges that because they are agents, "men do not always do my will" (v. 31), and few may respond to the call. He forbids them to march unless they get at least one hundred who are willing to consecrate their lives to Zion. He commands them to pray that Joseph will be able to go and preside and organize the kingdom according to the law of consecration. He calls eight recruiters, including Joseph, to gather the men and means to make the march. As expected, the Lord leaves the outcome in the hands of accountable agents. "All victory and glory is brought to pass unto you through your diligence, faithfulness, and prayers of faith" (v. 36).

OUTCOMES

Heber Kimball described the action motivated by Doctrine and Covenants 103. "Brother Joseph received a revelation concerning the redemption of Zion. . . . He sent Messengers to the East and to the North, to the West and to the South to gather up the Elders and, He gathered together as many of the brethren as he conveniently could, with what means they could spare to go up to Zion and render all the assistance that we could to our afflicted brethren. We gathered clothing and other necessaries to carry up to our brethren and sisters who had been plundered; and putting our horses to the wagons and taking our firelocks and ammunition, we started on our journey."4

They were a faltering band, to be sure, but willing to give their lives for Zion. The most significant result of section 103 is the way it tested that resolve. The revelation seems purposefully ambiguous, leaving Joseph and his followers uncertain how Zion would be redeemed. "By power," they knew, but what kind of power? Were they to take the promised land by military power? Would the God of Israel lead them "with a stretched-out arm"? (v. 17). Would they lay down their lives? By providing no answers to these questions, the revelation accomplished the Lord's purpose of providing an Abrahamic test (D&C 101:4–5). The men of Zion's Camp, as it came to be known, walked in faith, the considerable faith required to kiss their families good-bye and march with a small, poorly-equipped band to an unknown encounter for the cause of Zion. As a result of section 103, the Lord let many, though not as many as he asked for, pledge their allegiance to him and his cause. Their lives were his. He let them march all the way there before explaining that the power to redeem Zion would come not from a confrontation in Missouri but from an endowment in the house of the Lord back in Kirtland (D&C 105).

Doctrine & Covenants 104

ORIGIN

Joseph Smith and other members of the United Firm in Kirtland were mired in debt. The members of the Firm in Missouri had been driven from their land, store, and printing office and, therefore, from the ability to make money to pay the Firm's bills. And as a result of receiving Doctrine and Covenants 103, Joseph was determined to aid them by making an expensive trip to Missouri. Joseph and others visited Saints in New York to raise money. At one council meeting he called on the able-bodied men to march with him to Missouri, "and for the Church to gather all their riches and send them to purchase land according to the commandment of the Lord. Also, to devise means, or obtain moneys for the relief of the brethren at Kirtland; say two thousand dollars, which sum will deliver Kirtland from debt for the present."[1] The brethren in the council pledged to raise the money and split up to visit the Saints in the region.

Joseph returned to Kirtland without the needed funds. He met with other members of the Firm for prayer and asked the Lord for a miracle. Otherwise, Joseph explained, he could not go to Missouri, "and if I do not go it will be impossible to get my brethren in Kirtland . . . to go and if we do not go it is in vain for our eastern brethren to think of going up to better themselves by obtaining so goodly a land which now can be obtained for one dollar and a quarter per acre and stand against that wicked mob for unless they do the will of God, God will not help them and if God does not help them all is vain."[2] Joseph was deeply frustrated that the Saints "will not help us when they can do it without sacrifice with those blessings which

God has bestowed upon them." He prophesied that unless the Saints willingly consecrated as he had done, "God shall . . . prevent them from ever obtaining a place of refuge or an inheritance upon the Land of Zion."[3]

Still too many of the Saints withheld the Lord's resources. Joseph and the members of the United Firm (united order) in Kirtland met on April 10 and reluctantly decided to dissolve the Firm and make its members individual stewards over its various properties.[4] Two weeks later the Lord revealed Doctrine and Covenants 104, affirming the decision to dissolve the United Firm and giving each of its members his respective stewardship.[5]

CONTENT

Doctrine and Covenants 104 is straightforward. It begins with a curse upon the members of the United Firm who had broken the covenant of section 82. "I, the Lord, am not to be mocked in these things," he says, meaning the mockery of making covenants with "feigned words" (vv. 6, 4). Covenants to consecrate are serious, and section 104 announces that those who break them cannot escape the Lord's wrath and the buffetings of Satan, as the Lord has warned in Doctrine and Covenants 82:21. In verse 10 the Lord offers the members of the United Firm an opportunity to repent and consecrate, after which he reviews the law of consecration in verses 11–18, before being very specific in verses 19–46 about the stewardships for which he will hold each member of the Firm accountable.

No revelation more emphatically sets forth the law of consecration than Doctrine and Covenants 104:13–18. The Lord declares the first principle of consecration—"the earth is the Lord's" (Exodus 9:29)—repeatedly and with clarity: "I, the Lord, stretched out the heavens, and built the earth, my very handiwork; and all things therein are mine" (D&C 104:14). Having made the earth, the Lord can decree the rules of stewardship and accountability over it. Indeed, he endowed mankind with agency to act on the ample, abundant earth as stewards. He also requires the rich to share with the poor (v. 16): "Therefore," the passage concludes, "if any man shall take of the abundance which I have made, and impart not his portion, according to the law of my gospel, unto the poor and the needy, he shall, with the wicked, *lift up his eyes in hell, being in torment*" (v. 18; emphasis added). *This passage is wonderfully potent, drawing on the New Testament story in Luke 16 of Lazarus and the rich man.*

The earliest manuscripts of this revelation link the Lord's point even more closely with the passage in the Gospel of Luke to which this revelation alludes. The Kirtland Revelation Book, for example, says that if a person does not share according to the Lord's law, "he shall with Dives *lift up his eyes in hell being in torment.*"[6] Dives *is the Latin word meaning "rich"; in the Middle Ages it was adopted as the name of the rich man in Christ's story of the rich man and Lazarus in Luke 16:19–31, a fact that was probably better known in the 1830s than it is today. In the Savior's story as recorded in Luke, the rich man had "fared sumptuously" in life while a "beggar named Lazarus" waited in vain for some of his table scraps. When the two men died, angels carried Lazarus into Abraham's bosom while the rich man went to hell. "And in hell he lift up his eyes, being in torments," ironically begging Lazarus to relieve his suffering. Doctrine and Covenants 104:18 evokes that story and applies it to Latter-day Saints. Before the Church published this revelation as section 98 in the 1835 Doctrine and Covenants, the name* Dives *was changed to "the wicked," perhaps because the Latin name* Dives *is not found in the New Testament but comes from later lore. Even so, the presence of* Dives *in the earliest manuscripts makes the essential meaning of this passage unmistakable, namely that the rich in Zion who do not impart of their substance to the poor will, like the rich man in Christ's story, regret that unrighteousness.*

Beginning in verse 47, the Lord dissolves the United Firm into two firms, one in Kirtland, Ohio, and the other in Missouri. He emphasizes that the United Firm, which was supposed to last and would have, according to the terms of the covenant in Doctrine and Covenants 82:20–21, has been undermined by the broken covenants of accountable agents, "the covenants being broken through transgression, by covetousness and feigned words" (v. 52).

102

the Lord hath decreed to provide for my Saints, that the poor shall be exalted in that the rich are made low: for the earth is full and there is enough and to spare; yea, I have prepared all things, and have given unto the children of men to be agents unto themselves: wherefore, if any man shall take of the abundance which I have made and impart not his portion according to the law of my Gospel unto the poor and the needy, he shall with the wicked lift up his eyes in hell being in torments.

And now, verily I say unto you concerning the properties of the Firm: let my servant Sidney have appointed unto him the place where he now resides, and the lot of the Tannery for his stewardship for his support while he is labouring in my vineyard, even as I will, when I shall command him; and let all things be done according to council of the Firm, and united consent or voice of the Firm which dwells in the land of Kirtland. And this stewardship and blessing, I the Lord confer upon my servant Sidney for a blessing upon him and upon his seed after him; and I will multiply blessings upon him and upon his seed after him inasmuch as he shall be humble before me.

And again, let my servant Martin have appointed unto him for his stewardship the lot of land which my servant John obtained in exchange for his farm, for him and his seed after him; and inasmuch as he is faithful, I will multiply a multiplicity of blessings upon him and his seed after him. And let my servant Martin devote his moneys for the printing of my word according as my servant Joseph shall direct.

And again, let my servant Frederick have the place upon which he now dwells; and let my servant Oliver have the lot which is set off joining the house which is to be for the printing office, which is lot number one, and also the lot upon which his father resides; and let my servants Frederick and Oliver have the printing office and all things that pertain unto it; and this shall be their stewardships which shall be appointed unto them, and inasmuch as they are faithful

Doctrine and Covenants 104 in Revelation Book 2, commonly called the Kirtland Revelation Book.

Beginning in verse 54, the Lord reviews the principle of stewardship with emphasis on how it relates to the specific stewardships he gave to the Literary Firm in section 70 (and the United Firm is responsible to support the Literary Firm, as revealed in sections 78 and 82). Verses 55 and 56 of Doctrine and Covenants 104 reaffirm the first premise of consecration—"the earth is the Lord's, and the fulness thereof" (Psalm 24:1)—with an inescapable logic that brings covenant-breaking Saints face to face with hypocrisy: If the Lord is not Creator and Owner of the earth, why worship him? If he is, why pretend to be "owners" of anything or to resent his prerogative to distribute his resources in what he calls "mine own way"? (D&C 104:16). In other words, to acknowledge the Lord at all is to accept the role of an accountable steward, not that of an unaccountable owner determined "to play-act just a little longer—risking righteousness and true happiness merely in order to be reassured about our independence."[7]

The Lord's new instructions for fulfilling the stewardship of the Literary Firm to print the scriptures begin in verse 60. There the Lord calls for the establishment of a consecrated treasury, an account designated for funding the publication of scriptures. Originally, this part of the revelation had more specific instructions for the members of the Literary Firm (see D&C 70) to reserve copyright for the Church's publications.[8] In subsequent verses, the Lord emphasizes that these funds are solely for printing the scriptures, or what he calls "sacred and holy purposes" (D&C 104:65). Beginning in Doctrine and Covenants 104:67, he authorizes a second account, a "treasury" for the members of the United Firm. They are to put all the money they obtain into this treasury and then, as long as they are in full fellowship with the Saints, draw out of it what they need by the common consent of the members of the Firm.

The last segment of section 104, beginning with verse 78, commands Joseph and his brethren to pay their debts and sets forth the conditions on which the Lord will enable them to do so. More than economic initiatives, they are to "humble yourselves before me, and obtain this blessing by your diligence and humility and the prayer of faith" (v. 79). He promises them deliverance if they choose to meet those conditions and gives them permission in this specific instance to borrow against the properties they own in

Kirtland in order to pay their debts. These words remind the brethren that they are dependent upon the Lord. They must choose humility, diligence, and faith in him, but the revelation makes him the ultimate problem solver. He is the agent who will soften the hearts of the creditors and provide Joseph and the others the needed means. "I will give you the victory," he declares (v. 82).

The revelation ends by reminding the brethren that the Lord is the sovereign God who has given them agency to act and stewardships to be acted upon, and he will continue to hold them accountable. He concludes with what must have been a wonderfully reassuring guarantee that his house will not be broken up (v. 86).

OUTCOMES

After the Lord revealed Doctrine and Covenants 104, Joseph and his brethren in the United Firm at Kirtland assumed control of the properties the Lord had assigned each individual as a stewardship.[9] They also forgave each other all debts they owed to the Firm. This relieved Joseph of paying $1,151.31, and the six men forgave debts they owed each other, totaling $3,635.35.[10] Still, the debts they owed to outside creditors remained unsatisfied.

Ever mindful of their obligations, Joseph and his brethren acted on this revelation. They did the specific things the Lord set forth as terms on which he promised to "soften the hearts of those to whom you are in debt, until I shall send forth means unto you for your deliverance" (v. 80). Joseph's journal records humility, diligent effort, and faithful prayers for this deliverance, and documents that it came as promised. On the day the revelation came, Joseph and other members of the Firm "united in asking the Lord" to bless Zebedee Coltrin and Jacob Myers in their efforts "to borrow for us." Meanwhile, donations began to pour in from consecrating Saints. Joseph and Oliver Cowdery "united in prayer" for such blessings to continue and covenanted that as the Lord was enabling them to pay their debts, they would return one-tenth of what they received "to be bestowed upon the poor of his Church, or as he shall command, and that we will be faithful over that which he has entrusted to our care."¹¹ They prayed and prayed, asking the Lord "to lift the mortgage on the farm upon which the temple was being built."¹²

One evening they received an impression "that in a short time the Lord would arrange his providences in a merciful manner and send us assistance to deliver us from debt and bondage."¹³ Two months later, as creditors were about to foreclose on the temple site, a prosperous hotel owner from New York, John Tanner, who had joined the Church, arrived in Kirtland with two thousand dollars, "with which amount the farm was redeemed."¹⁴ Good for his word, the Lord had sent forth the "means" he promised to deliver (v. 80). In the meantime, Joseph and his brethren learned to trust in the Lord, to pray in faith, and to be humble and diligent. The Saints in general also rose to the occasion and, though belatedly, consecrated to the building of Kirtland and its crowning temple. As a result of their offerings, the Lord poured out blessings in that temple that no amount of money could buy (see D&C 109–10).

Doctrine & Covenants 105

ORIGIN

Zion's Camp arrived in Clay County, Missouri, about June 19, 1834, having traveled some eight hundred miles in six weeks. In the meantime, as Missourians burned the Saints' buildings in Jackson County, Governor Daniel Dunklin backed away from his promise of an armed force to assist the Saints.[1] In mid-June, messengers Orson Hyde and Parley P. Pratt reported to the camp that Dunklin "refused to fulfill his promise of reinstating the brethren on their lands in Jackson County."[2] Joseph knew very well that the camp was "altogether too small for the accomplishment of such a great enterprise." He repeatedly urged the eastern Saints to provide men and means to reclaim Zion, but they offered too little too late.[3]

Preceded by exaggerated rumors of its size and intentions, the camp alarmed residents when it arrived. Several hundred from the surrounding area gathered, threatening attack. Violence seemed imminent, but a torrential spring storm prevented a battle on the day Zion's Camp arrived in Clay County.[4] On June 20, Zion's Camp moved four miles north to camp on land owned by fellow Saints. On June 21, the county sheriff and area militia officers met with the Saints to mediate the crisis. Joseph assured them that the camp came for defense, not to attack. "We are anxious for a settlement of the difficulties existing between us," Joseph assured them, "upon honorable and constitutional principles."[5]

Wondering when and how, not if, Zion would be reclaimed, Joseph sought revelation to know what the Lord wanted the camp to do next.

While encamped on Fishing River, he received the landmark revelation recorded in Doctrine and Covenants 105.

CONTENT

"I do not require at their hands to fight the battles of Zion," Doctrine and Covenants 105 says of the elders of Israel (v. 14). It assures them that their prayers have been heard, that their offering is accepted, and that they have been "brought thus far for a trial of their faith" (v. 19). Because an insufficient number of Saints has chosen to live the law of consecration and to respond to the Lord's will and Joseph's repeated invitations to send men and means to redeem Zion, the Lord postpones it (vv. 1–10). He says it has to wait until the elders can be endowed with the necessary power. That power will come through a priesthood endowment in the house of the Lord being built in Kirtland (vv. 11, 33).

The revelation, which is both pacifistic and militant, marks a turning point in Church history. It is a document of détente. It calls for a proclamation of peace now even as it foreshadows a future role for the army of Israel in redeeming Zion. It postpones Zion in Jackson County for an ambiguous "little season" (v. 9). It commands Saints in the meantime to receive the anticipated endowment of power to help them gain experience, to learn their duty and doctrine better, and to increase in number and holiness. They are to continue to purchase western Missouri lands but to avoid gathering in numbers perceived as threatening by non-Mormon settlers.

Doctrine and Covenants 105 gives Joseph and his army orders to retreat. They are instructed to seek redress lawfully. But the war is far from over. These tactics will buy time "until the army of Israel becomes very great" (v. 26) while more land in Jackson and adjoining counties can be legally purchased. Once it is, the revelation says, "I will hold the armies of Israel guiltless in taking possession of their own lands, which they have previously purchased with their moneys, and of throwing down the towers of mine enemies that may be upon them" (v. 30). First, however, "let my army become very great, and let it be sanctified before me, that it may become fair as the sun, and clear as the moon, and that her banners may be terrible unto all nations; that the kingdoms of this world may be constrained to acknowledge that the kingdom of Zion is in very deed the kingdom of our God and his Christ; therefore, let us become subject unto her laws" (vv. 31–32). Meanwhile, Latter-day Saints are to "sue for peace, not only to the people that have smitten you, but also to all people; and lift up an ensign of peace, and make a proclamation of peace unto the ends of the earth" (vv. 38–39).

OUTCOMES

Doctrine and Covenants 105 led Joseph to disband Zion's Camp and direct its members to return to their families or, if they had none, to remain in Missouri to assist the dispossessed Saints. The revelation powerfully refocused Joseph Smith and the Church. Zion remained the ultimate goal, but the revelation declared that Zion would not be redeemed until the Saints were endowed with power. All of a sudden, having submitted to the trial of their faith, the brethren could understand the promise of section 103 that Zion would be redeemed by power—by the power of righteousness, the might of an army of God both massive and moral. The brethren were to return to the house of the Lord in Kirtland, to be endowed with power on conditions of humility and faithfulness (v. 12), and then spread out over the globe to gather Israel. Then, when the army became very great both numerically and in obedience to the law of consecration, they would regain Zion.

Joseph organized the Saints in Missouri and appointed many of them to return to Ohio to participate in the solemn assembly. Back in Kirtland he urged the Saints to finish the house of the Lord, and he began holding sanctifying training meetings to prepare the brethren for the solemn assembly. He gathered the brethren of Zion's Camp in one of these meetings and told them, "God did not want you to fight. He could not organize his kingdom with twelve men to open the gospel door to the nations of the earth . . . Unless he took them from a body of men who had offered their lives, and who had made as great a sacrifice as did Abraham."[6] Most of the apostles and all of the First Quorum of the Seventy were chosen from veterans of the Camp.

Joseph and the Saints finished the temple, convened solemn assemblies, and received an endowment of priesthood power (see D&C 110). This was the way to establish Zion, and Joseph turned his attention back to regaining the promised land. He anticipated that the "little season" preceding Zion would end within three years, and it might have done so if the Saints had carried out the specific instructions listed in Doctrine and Covenants 105:10.[7] We remain in the little season, perhaps in part because we have not fully learned obedience to the law of consecration and gained experience obeying it. Some commentators have suggested that verse 34 rescinds, postpones, or suspends the law of consecration, but that is not what it says. It says that the specific commands for the bishop to give the Saints inheritances in the land in Zion and to establish a storehouse and print the scriptures there will need to wait until after the Saints reclaim the land on which to keep those commandments (see D&C 57).

Section 105 continues to guide the course of the Church. The Church works to grow in numbers and in holiness, to proclaim peace and cultivate positive public relations. "Wise men" were sent to purchase land in Jackson County and elsewhere, as commanded in Doctrine and Covenants 101:73 and reiterated in 105:28. The Church continues to quietly acquire land in obedience to commandment.[8] Most important, the Church works to accomplish the specific instructions in verse 10 concerning teaching, providing experience, and preparing Saints for Zion, all of which stem from the ordinances in the house of the Lord on which the Church continues to focus so much of its effort, as it has since Joseph received section 105.

Section 105 charts the way to Zion by obedience to the law of consecration. It declares that "Zion cannot be built up unless it is by the principles of the law of the celestial kingdom; otherwise I cannot receive her unto myself" (v. 5). Zion will be postponed as long as the Lord sees fit. Verse 34 cannot be to blame. President Gordon B. Hinckley taught that "the law of sacrifice and the law of consecration were not done away with and are still in effect."[9] But just as when section 105 was given, "there are many who will say: Where is their God? Behold, he will deliver them in time of trouble, otherwise we will not go up unto Zion, and will keep our moneys" (v. 8).

Doctrine & Covenants 106

ORIGIN

When Joseph and others went east in March 1834 to recruit volunteers to march to the aid of Saints who had been exiled from Zion in Missouri, he visited Warren A. Cowdery, an older brother of Oliver and a Church member living at Freedom, New York, where he practiced medicine. A leading citizen in his community, Warren housed and fed Joseph and his companions as they preached the gospel and gained converts.[1] In November, Joseph received Doctrine and Covenants 106 as a call for Warren Cowdery to preside over the growing number of Saints in his area.

CONTENT

Doctrine and Covenants 106 expresses the Lord's will, which is that Warren Cowdery devote all of his time to the high and holy calling of presiding over the Saints in and around Freedom, New York, and preaching the gospel in the area. In verse 3 the Lord promises Warren a living if he obeys the revelation and in verses 4–5 explains in eschatological terms why he should. In other words, Warren should preside and preach to prepare himself and his neighbors for the imminent coming of the Lord. Beginning in verse 6, the Lord reveals his joy when Warren joined the Church and blesses him. The language of this verse suggests that what pleased the Lord was Warren's willing submission to his divine authority, his kingly scepter. The Lord exposes Warren's vanity and promises to preserve him at the Second Coming on the condition that Warren will choose to be humble.

The last verse, too, is a conditional promise, a covenant between the Lord and Warren in which the Lord promises him his own kingly crown in heavenly mansions "if he continue to be a faithful witness and a light unto the church" (v. 8).

OUTCOMES

After receiving Doctrine and Covenants 106, Warren presided over his fellow Saints in New York until he and his family moved to Kirtland early in 1836. There he served the Church as a scribe and recorder, but by 1838 he became one of many who did not continue in their faithful witness as lights to the Church.[2]

Doctrine & Covenants 107

ORIGIN

The first Quorum of Twelve Apostles in this dispensation was called on February 14, 1835, and its members were ordained between February and April of that year. They met frequently to receive instructions from Joseph. In their March 12 council meeting, Joseph proposed that the apostles spend the summer traveling "through the Eastern States, to the Atlantic Ocean, and hold conferences in the vicinity of the several branches of the Church for the purpose of regulating all things necessary for their welfare."[1] As the time for their departure neared, the apostles made a written request asking Joseph "to inquire of God for us, and obtain a revelation" to help them fulfill their callings. "We have unitedly asked God our heavenly Father to grant unto us through His Seer," the apostles said, "a revelation of His mind and will concerning our duty this coming season, even a great revelation, that will enlarge our hearts, comfort us in adversity, and brighten our hopes amidst the powers of darkness."[2]

The Lord answered with the first 58 verses of Doctrine and Covenants 107. "One evening when we were assembled to receive instruction," according to Heber Kimball, the revelation "was given to Brother Joseph as he was instructing us, and we praised the Lord."[3] Joseph had received most of verses 59–100 earlier in November 1831.[4] When he was editing the revelations for publication in the 1835 Doctrine and Covenants, Joseph joined these two texts on priesthood organization and function into a single document and added passages describing duties of the bishop and the newly called quorum of seventy, forming a composite revelation on priesthood government and function.[5]

CONTENT

Doctrine and Covenants 107 begins with a clear description of the two divisions of priesthood and the names given to each—Aaronic and Melchizedek. In 1841 Joseph taught that "all Priesthod is Melchizedek; but there are different portions or degrees of it."[6] Verses 18–19 declare the exalting power of the Melchizedek Priesthood, and verse 20 declares the preparatory power of the Aaronic Priesthood. Several offices are described within these divisions of priesthood, as well as several quorums and councils composed of priesthood holders. Most notably the revelation describes the First Presidency as a quorum of three high priests who preside over all priesthood holders (vv. 21–22). "Twelve Apostles, or special witnesses of the name of Christ in all the world" (v. 23) form a quorum whose authority is equal to the First Presidency. The Seventy are called as missionaries to the Gentiles, and they form a quorum whose authority is equal to that of the quorum of apostles. These quorums are to arrive at their decisions by consensus and finally unanimity in order to be binding. And the decision-making process is to be characterized by the Christlike attributes listed in verse 30 because they are the condition on which the Lord will endow the presiding quorums with his "knowledge" (v. 31). Verse 32 provides an appellate process in case decisions are made "in unrighteousness."

Beginning in verse 33, section 107 describes the order and relationship of the quorums of twelve apostles, the seventy, and stake high councils. The apostles preside under the First Presidency and travel the globe to build and regulate the Church because they hold the keys to open doors through which the gospel is proclaimed (v. 35; D&C 112:16–19). The Seventy also travel the world to build and regulate the Church but under the direction of the apostles, who call on the Seventy for assistance. Verses 36–37 explain that the presidencies of the Church in Zion (Missouri) and the stake in Kirtland, Ohio, as well as future stakes with the twelve high priests in each location that serve as councilors to these presidencies, function with the same authority in their local jurisdictions as the General Authorities do worldwide.

Patriarchs, or what verse 39 calls "evangelical ministers," are to be identified by revelation to the apostles, who have the duty of ordaining them in any area where there is a large number of Saints, which, today, generally means a stake. Before section 107 describes the next duty of the apostles in verse 58, verses 40–57 explain the rich history and provenance of the patriarchal priesthood, as recorded in the book of Enoch, which was handed down from Adam to his posterity. They tell how Adam gathered his righteous posterity before his death for a patriarchal blessing. Adam, "notwithstanding he was bowed down with age, being full of the Holy Ghost, predicted whatsoever should befall his posterity unto the latest generation" (v. 56).

Verse 58 transitions between the two major segments of Section 107 and gives the apostles responsibility for implementing the November 1831 revelation by ordaining priesthood holders and setting the Church in order under their direction. Much of the subsequent verses were related to the first part of section 107 as well as section 68, including the nature of being a bishop and a provision for a "common council of the church" (v. 82) headed by what is now called the presiding bishop in case the president of the Church is tried for transgression (vv. 76–84).

Verses 85–88 describe the duties of presiding in Aaronic Priesthood quorums, and beginning in verse 89 the Lord sets forth the duties of presiding in Melchizedek Priesthood quorums both generally and locally. Having declared the duties of priesthood holders, quorums, and presidents clearly, the Lord finishes section 107 with a statement of accountability, a concise restatement of the oath and covenant of the priesthood that emphasizes learning and acting diligently in one's appointed office or else being judged unworthy of that office in the holy priesthood (vv. 99–100).

OUTCOMES

One immeasurable result of Doctrine and Covenants 107 is the way it gives meaning to men's lives. Section 132 emphasizes the priesthood's exalting power for women and men, but the particular power of section 107 gives ordinary, even inadequate men both duty and destiny that can motivate them to rise to far greater heights of service to God and family than they would if left to their natural inclinations. The revelation came at a time when American culture was beginning to erode fatherhood. Noting how the exalting priesthood principles of section 107 seemed to have a powerful influence on Joseph's own father, historian Richard Bushman went so far as to say that "in restoring priesthood, Joseph restored fatherhood."[7] That restoration continues. Section 107 has evoked a response from countless men to quit being "slothful" and instead learn their duty and act accordingly. It inspires many men to "stand" (vv. 99–100). It sounds like Heavenly Father's version of Lehi's admonition, "arise from the dust, my sons, and be men" (2 Nephi 1:21).

As if it were architectural drawings, section 107 built a Church that has not required much remodeling since. From its basic organization in 1830 with two presiding elders (D&C 21), the Church's structure and organization changed more in the five years before section 107 was given than it has since. That is a remarkable role for this anchoring revelation, for Christians have long argued whether the Church should be a rigid institution or a Spirit-filled body. Meanwhile, as the number of Latter-day Saints has multiplied into the millions and congregations grow apace, the Church is still built as section 107 described it. This longevity is due in part to the revelation's perfect balance of structure and flexibility.

Like modern buildings made of reinforced concrete and steel, designed to flex and sway rather than crumble, the Church is founded on institutional councils and quorums of revelators experienced in obtaining "the knowledge of the Lord" (v. 31). The entire Church is presided over by "a seer, a revelator, a translator, and a prophet, having all the gifts of God which he bestows upon the head of the church" (v. 92). Yet the responsibility for governing and building the Church is diffused widely among its members.

The revelation provided for growth in the Church that would necessitate more seventies, allowing for "seven times seventy, if the labor in the vineyard of necessity requires it" (v. 96). Moreover, it provided for other Church officers to be called as needed to hold "high and responsible offices in the church" (v. 98). Invoking this passage in April 1995, President Gordon B. Hinckley announced "the call of a new local officer to be known as an area authority. These will be high priests chosen from among past and present experienced Church leaders."[8]

Speaking at the Library of Congress in 2005, one scholar suggested that future growth of the Church could require it to decentralize and perhaps even divide into regionally or culturally distinct entities.[9] That assessment seems to underestimate the proven power of the Lord's revealed word in section 107 to govern a global Church that is both securely rooted and infinitely malleable.

Doctrine & Covenants 108

ORIGIN

Joseph Smith was studying his Hebrew lesson on December 26, 1835, when Lyman Sherman, who was serving in the quorum of the seventy, came to his home and said he had been "wrought upon to make known to you my feelings and desires, and was promised that I should have a revelation which should make known my duty." Joseph received Doctrine and Covenants 108 and recorded it in his journal.[1]

CONTENT

By exercising the faith to obey the Lord's revelation to him, Lyman obtains forgiveness and comforting counsel in Doctrine and Covenants 108 as well as instructions relative to his calling and future responsibilities in the Church. When Lyman said he was wrought upon, he meant that he was unsettled, even disturbed. "Let your soul be at rest," the Lord counsels him, and "wait patiently until the solemn assembly . . . of my servants," referring to the meetings in the house of the Lord in which Church leaders, including Sherman, were to receive sacred ordinances and blessings in 1836 (vv. 2, 4).

OUTCOMES

The way Doctrine and Covenants 108 came to Lyman Sherman reveals much about the order of revelation. Joseph Smith taught that revelations are universally available to mankind directly but also that there is order to receiving revelation. Lyman's role as a general authority and his invitation to the upcoming solemn assembly were matters to be revealed through Joseph Smith. In verse 1, the Lord forgave Lyman because he submissively acknowledged and followed this order. He was a loyal, devoted Saint. In January 1839, the First Presidency called Lyman as an apostle, but he died before he could fill the calling.[2]

Doctrine & Covenants 109

ORIGIN

The Saints put finishing touches on the house of the Lord in Kirtland, Ohio and prepared to assemble in it solemnly as they had been commanded (see D&C 88:70, 117). Joseph spent the day before with his counselors and secretaries "to make arrangements for the solemn assembly."[1] Oliver Cowdery's sketchbook adds the detail that he assisted Joseph "in writing a prayer for the dedication of the house."[2] The next morning the house of the Lord was filled to capacity with nearly a thousand Saints. An overflow meeting convened next door in the building housing the Church's printing office and First Presidency's office. The solemn assembly began at 9 a.m. with scripture readings, choir singing, prayer, a sermon, and the sustaining of Joseph Smith as prophet and seer. In the afternoon session the sustaining continued, with each quorum and the general body of the Church sustaining, in turn, the leaders of the Church.[3] Another hymn followed, "after which," Joseph's journal says, "I offered to God the following dedication prayer," Doctrine and Covenants 109.[4]

CONTENT

Doctrine and Covenants 109 is an inspired prayer. It begins with thanks to God, and then makes requests of him in the name of Jesus Christ. It is based heavily on the temple instructions in section 88 as well as other temple-related scriptural texts. It "sums up the Church's concerns in 1836, bringing before God each major project."[5] It is a temple prayer.

PRAYER.

At the Dedication of the Lord's House in Kirtland, Ohio, March 27, 1836.—By JOSEPH SMITH, jr.
President of the Church of the Latter Day Saints.

Thanks be to thy name, O Lord God of Israel, who keepest covenant and shewest mercy unto thy servants, who walk uprightly before thee with all their hearts: thou who hast commanded thy servants to build an house to thy name in this place. (Kirtland.) And now thou beholdest, O Lord, that so thy servants have done, according to thy commandment. And now we ask thee, holy Father, in the name of Jesus Christ, the Son of thy bosom, in whose name alone salvation can be administered to the children of men: we ask thee, O Lord, to accept of this house, the workmanship of the hands of us, thy servants, which thou didst command us to build; for thou knowest that we have done this work through great tribulation: and out of our poverty we have given of our substance to build a house to thy name, that the Son of Man might have a place to manifest himself to his people.

And as thou hast said, in a revelation given unto us, calling us thy friends, saying—"Call your solemn assembly, as I have commanded you; and as all have not faith, seek ye diligently and teach one another words of wisdom; yea, seek ye out of the best books words of wisdom: Seek learning, even by study, and also by faith."

"Organize yourselves; prepare every needful thing, and establish a house, even a house of prayer, a house of fasting, a house of faith, a house of learning, a house of glory, a house of order, a house of God: that your incomings may be in the name of the Lord; that your out goings may be in the name of the Lord; that all your salutations may be in the name of the Lord, with uplifted hands to the Most High."

And now, holy Father, we ask thee to assist us, thy people with thy grace in calling our solemn assembly, that it may be done to thy honor, and to thy divine acceptance, and in a manner that we may be found worthy, in thy sight, to secure a fulfilment of the promises which thou hast made unto us thy people, in the revelations given unto us: that thy glory may rest down upon thy people, and upon this thy house, which we now dedicate to thee, that it may be sanctified and consecrated to be holy, and that thy holy presence may be continually in this house; and that all people who shall enter upon the threshold of the Lord's house may feel thy power and be constrained to acknowledge that thou hast sanctified it, and that it is thy house, a place of thy holiness.

And do thou grant, holy Father, that all those who shall worship in this house, may be taught words of wisdom out of the best books, and that they may seek learning, even by study, and also by faith; as thou hast said; and that they may grow up in thee and receive a fulness of the Holy Ghost, and be organized according to thy laws, and be prepared to obtain every needful thing: and that this house may be a house of prayer, a house of fasting, a house of faith, a house of glory and of God, even thy house: that all the incomings of thy people, into this house, may be in the name of the Lord; that all their outgoings, from this house, may be in the name of the Lord; that all their salutations may be in the name of the Lord, with holy hands, uplifted to the Most High; and that no unclean thing shall be permitted to come into thy house to pollute it.

And when thy people transgress, any of them, they may speedily repent and return unto thee, and find favor in thy sight, and be restored to the blessings which thou hast ordained, to be poured out upon those who shall reverence thee in this thy house.

And we ask thee, holy Father, that thy servants may go forth from this house, armed with thy power, and that thy name may be upon them and thy glory be round about them, and thine angels have charge over them; and from this place they may bear exceeding great and glorious tidings, in truth, unto the ends of the earth, that they may know that this is thy work, and that thou hast put forth thy hand, to fulfil that which thou hast spoken by the mouths of thy prophets concerning the last days.

We ask thee, holy Father, to establish the people that shall worship and honorably hold a name and standing in this thy house, to all generations, and for eternity, that no weapon formed against them shall prosper; that he who diggeth a pit for them shall fall into the same himself; that no combination of wickedness shall have power to rise up and prevail over thy people, upon whom thy name shall be put in this house: and if any people shall rise against this people, that thine anger be kindled against them: and if they shall smite this people, thou wilt smite them—thou wilt fight for thy people as thou didst in the day of battle, that they may be delivered from the hands of all their enemies.

We ask thee, holy Father, to confound, and astonish, and bring to shame, and confusion, all those who have spread lying reports abroad over the world against thy servant, or servants, if they will not repent when the everlasting gospel shall be proclaimed in their ears, and that all their works may be brought to nought, and be swept away by the hail, and by the judgments, which thou wilt send upon them in thine anger, that there may be an end to lyings and slanders against thy people: for thou knowest, O Lord, that thy servants have been innocent before thee in bearing record of thy name for which they have suffered these things; therefore we plead before thee for a full and complete deliverance from under this yoke. Break it off O Lord: break it off from the necks of thy servants, by thy power, that we may rise up in the midst of this generation and do thy work!

O Jehovah, have mercy upon this people, and as all men sin, forgive the transgressions of thy people, and let them be blotted out forever. Let the anointing of thy ministers be sealed upon them with power from on high: let it be fulfilled upon them as upon those on the day of Pentecost: let the gift of tongues be poured out upon thy people, even cloven tongues as of fire, and the interpretation thereof. And let thy house be filled, as with a rushing mighty wind, with thy glory.

Put upon thy servants the testimony of the covenant, that when they go out and proclaim thy word, they may seal up the law, and prepare the hearts of thy saints for all those judgements thou art about to send, in thy wrath, upon the inhabitants of the earth, because of their transgressions, that thy people may not faint in the day of trouble.

And whatever city thy servants shall enter, and the people of that city receive their testimony, let thy peace and thy salvation be upon that city, that they may gather out of that city the righteous, that they may come forth to Zion, or to her stakes, the places of thine appointment, with songs of everlasting joy,—and until this be accomplished let not thy judgments fall upon that city.

Prayer at the dedication of the Lord's house in Kirtland, Ohio, March 27, 1836. Joseph may have read a printed version of section 109 like this one.

What does one pray for in such settings? Joseph begins by asking God to accept the temple on the terms He had given in section 88 and the Saints had worked to fulfill in order to obtain the promised blessing of entering the Lord's presence (D&C 88:68; 109:4–12). Joseph prays that all who worship in the temple will be endowed with God's power, that they will be taught by God "that they may grow up in thee, and receive a fulness of the Holy Ghost, and be organized according to thy laws, and be prepared to obtain every needful thing" (v. 15). Joseph prays, in other words, a temple prayer that the Saints will become like their Heavenly Father by degrees of glory as they obey his laws and prepare to enter his presence. He prays for what section 88 has taught him to pray for.

Joseph prays that the Saints, "armed" or endowed with priesthood power from the temple, can go to "the ends of the earth" with the "exceedingly great and glorious tidings" of the gospel to fulfill prophecies declaring that they would do so (vv. 22–23). He asks Heavenly Father to protect the Saints from their enemies (vv. 24–33). He asks Jehovah to have mercy upon the Saints and to seal the anointing ordinances that many of the priesthood brethren received in the weeks leading up to the solemn assembly. He asks for the gifts of the Spirit to be poured out as on the biblical day of Pentecost (Acts 2:2–3). He asks the Lord to protect and empower the missionaries and to postpone judgment until they have gathered the righteous. He prays that God's will be done "and not ours" (D&C 109:44).

Joseph prays that the Saints will be delivered from the prophesied calamities. He asks Heavenly Father to remember the Saints oppressed and driven from Jackson County, Missouri, and prays for their deliverance. He asks how long their afflictions would continue until avenged (v. 49). He asks for mercy "upon the wicked mob, who have driven thy people, that they may cease to spoil, that they may repent of their sins if repentance is to be found" (v. 50). He prays for Zion.

Joseph prays for mercy on all nations and political leaders, so that the principles of individual agency established in the Constitution of the United States will be established forever. He prays for "the great ones of the earth" and for "all the poor, the needy, and afflicted ones of the earth" (v. 55). He prays for an end to prejudices so that the missionaries "may gather out the righteous to build a holy city to thy name, as thou hast commanded them" (v. 58). He asks for more stakes to facilitate the gathering and growth of Zion. He asks for mercy for the Native Americans and for the Jews; indeed, he prays for "all the scattered remnants of Israel, who have been driven to the ends of the earth, [to] come to a knowledge of the truth, believe in the Messiah, and be redeemed from oppression" (v. 67).

Joseph prays for himself, reminding the Lord of his sincere effort to keep his covenants. He asks for mercy upon his family, praying that Emma and their children "may be exalted in thy presence" (v. 69). This is the first usage of *exalted* in the Doctrine and Covenants to refer to the fulness of salvation through temple blessings.[6] Joseph prays for his in-laws to be converted. He prays for the other presidents of the Church and their families. He prays for all the Saints and their families and their sick and afflicted. He prays, again, for "all the poor and meek of the earth" (v. 72) and for the glorious kingdom of God to fill the earth as prophesied.

Joseph prays that the Saints will rise in the first resurrection with pure garments, "robes of righteousness," and "crowns of glory upon our heads" to "reap eternal joy" (v. 76). Thrice repeating his petition, Joseph asks the Lord to "hear us" and accept the prayers and petitions and offerings of the Saints in building the house to His name (v. 78). He prays for grace to enable the Saints to join the choirs surrounding God's throne in the heavenly temple "singing Hosanna to God and the Lamb" (v. 79). "And let these, thine anointed, be clothed with salvation, and thy saints shout aloud for joy. Amen, and Amen" (v. 80).

OUTCOMES

Doctrine and Covenants 109 dedicated the first house of the Lord in the last dispensation and set the pattern for all subsequent solemn assemblies met for the same holy purpose. It teaches the Saints how to pray, including what to pray for and to ask according to the will of God. It teaches the doctrine and evokes the imagery of the temple, perhaps most poignantly in the idea that temple worshippers can "grow up" (v. 15) by degrees of glory until they become like their Heavenly Father (see D&C 93). This is what it means to be exalted in God's presence. The temple

Kirtland Temple and cemetery, 1907.

revelations call this "fulness," including fulness of joy. Section 109 continues the expansive work of the temple revelations in sections 76, 84, 88, and 93 and points us forward to the culminating revelation on exaltation, Doctrine and Covenants 132:1–20. Section 109 invites mortals who occupy a polluted telestial planet where they cannot think of more than one thing at a time and generally only in finite terms to receive power that will enable them to journey to the real world where God lives "enthroned, with glory, honor, power, majesty, might, dominion, truth, justice, judgment, mercy, and an *infinity of fulness,* from everlasting to everlasting" (v. 77; emphasis added).[7]

Doctrine & Covenants 110

ORIGIN

A week after dedicating the house of the Lord in Kirtland, Joseph attended meetings there, including an afternoon sacrament meeting. For Christians it was Easter Sunday; Jews were celebrating Passover.[1] Joseph and Oliver Cowdery retreated behind the heavy curtains used to divide the room. They bowed in what Joseph's journal describes as "solemn, but silent prayer to the Most High. After rising from prayer the following vision was opened to both of them."[2] That vision is recorded in Doctrine and Covenants 110.

CONTENT

In Doctrine and Covenants 110, the minds of Joseph Smith and Oliver Cowdery are unveiled as they see and hear the Lord standing before them. Four times, in a voice like rushing water, he declares, "I am," evoking Old Testament revelations in which he repeatedly identified himself, saying, "I am the Lord thy God" (Exodus 20:2; Leviticus 19:3). This is a play on the related words of the Hebrew verb meaning "to be" and the name transliterated in English as *Jehovah*. It is the Lord Jesus Christ declaring that he is the God who told Moses to tell the Israelites that "I AM hath sent me unto you" (Exodus 3:14). It is Christ testifying that he is the God of Israel, the promised Messiah.

In a powerful juxtaposition of present and past, the risen Savior declares himself the crucified Christ who conquered death. "I am he who liveth, I am he who was slain; I am your advocate with the Father" (D&C 110:4).

Though it was not published or widely known until the 1850s, the vision of the Savior and ministering angels documented in section 110 was recorded in Joseph Smith's journal entry for April 3, 1836, the last entry in that journal.

The Lord forgives Joseph and Oliver, pronounces them clean, and commands them and those who have built the temple to rejoice. He accepts the temple and makes conditional promises to manifest himself to his people there. He promises that as the temple's fame spreads to foreign lands, tens of thousands will rejoice in the endowment poured out on his servants in the temple, the beginning of the endowment to be poured out on the Lord's people.

The Lord disappears, and Moses appears and commits the keys of the gathering of Israel from all the earth, the permission to lead the lost tribes of Israel from the north. Next Elias appears and dispenses the gospel of Abraham, "saying that in us and our seed all generations after us should be blessed" (v. 12). Another glorious vision follows as Elijah, who went to heaven without tasting death, appears and says that it is time to fulfill Malachi's prophecy that Elijah would turn the hearts of the fathers to their children and vice versa before the dreadful day of the Lord, "lest the whole earth be smitten with a curse" (v. 15). Therefore, the keys of the kingdom are in the hands of Joseph Smith. This is evidence that the Lord's great and dreadful day is near.

OUTCOMES

Doctrine and Covenants 110 fulfills the Lord's conditional promise to the Saints that if they would move to Ohio and build him a holy house, he would endow them with power in it (D&C 38; 88; 95). It fulfills the great promise of section 88 that the sanctified would come into the presence of the Lord. Indeed, Joseph promised the Saints that "on conditions of our obedience," the Savior had promised "a visit from the heavens to honor us with his own presence."[3]

Section 110 also fulfills a multilayered prophecy. Through Malachi, the Lord prophesied, "I will send you Elijah the prophet before the coming of the great and dreadful day of the Lord" (Malachi 4:5). Moroni reiterated this prophecy to Joseph Smith in 1823 (D&C 2). Elijah fulfilled it nearly thirteen years later as recorded in section 110. Jews had long awaited Elijah's prophesied return and welcomed him during the Passover *Seder*.

On the very day that some Jews were celebrating the sacred meal with the hope that Elijah would return, he visited the house of the Lord.[4]

Moses' appearance is just as significant. "His appearance in company with Elijah offers another striking parallel between Mormon teachings and Jewish tradition, according to which Moses and Elijah would arrive together at the 'end of time.'"[5]

Section 110 reenacts the endowment received in the biblical account of events on the Mount of Transfiguration (Matthew 17:1–9). Joseph received priesthood keys from the heavenly messengers. He had received all the priesthood when he was ordained by Peter, James, and John years earlier (D&C 27:12), but he did not have all the keys he needed to exercise the priesthood until after he received section 110. In other words, Joseph had power but not permission to send missionaries globally or to perform temple ordinances until Moses, Elias, and Elijah gave him the keys—the permission to exercise the priesthood in those ways.

Few texts weld dispensations as thoroughly as does section 110. Given on Easter and during the Passover season, the revelation links Israel's Old Testament deliverance with Christ's New Testament resurrection and affirms that Joseph Smith and the temple-building Latter-day Saints are the heirs of God's promises to the Israelite patriarchs. Christ is the Passover lamb who "was slain" and then resurrected and now appears to Joseph in Kirtland, Ohio, to approve of the latter-day work and commission the Prophet to fulfill the work of Moses (the gathering of Israel), Elias (the gospel of Abraham), and Elijah (the sealing of families).

Joseph put the keys to use despite great opposition. Not long after receiving the keys to gather Israel from Moses, Joseph whispered in Heber Kimball's ear a mission call to Great Britain. Joseph had previously sent missionaries on short local or regional missions. Heber and his companions began the ongoing process of gathering Israel from the ends of the earth. Though oppressed by what seems like concerted opposition that included financial collapse, widespread apostasy, an executive order driving the Saints from Missouri, and then unjust imprisonment in Liberty, Missouri, Joseph began to teach and administer the ordinances of the temple. In sum, the endowment of priesthood keys he received in the house of the Lord in Kirtland authorized him to begin performing temple ordinances.

Section 110 communicated temple knowledge and power. It came in the temple, behind a veil, was recorded but not preached, and acted on but not publicly explained.[6] After the revelation, Joseph used the keys to gather, endow, and seal in anticipation of the Savior's second coming. Section 110 marks a restoration of temple-related power and knowledge that Moses possessed and "plainly taught" but which had been forfeited by the children of Israel (D&C 84:23).

Doctrine & Covenants 111

ORIGIN

Just as the Saints in Missouri were being forced from yet another county, (Clay County), Joseph and the Saints in Ohio finished the house of the Lord in Kirtland at great expense. The resulting blessings far surpassed the value of every penny, but the process left Joseph in debt approximately thirteen thousand dollars, with more expenses looming. Under these circumstances Joseph took a risk. "A convert named Burgess had persuaded Church leaders that a large sum of money was hidden in the cellar" of a house in Salem, Massachusetts. Joseph, his brother Hyrum, Oliver Cowdery, and Sidney Rigdon set out for Salem in July to meet Burgess and hopefully find the treasure. They searched in frustration for the house.[1] On August 6, 1836, the Lord gave Doctrine and Covenants 111.

CONTENT

The Lord says in Doctrine and Covenants 111 that he is not displeased with the Prophet, despite his follies, which meant "a weak or absurd act not highly criminal; an act which is inconsistent with the dictates of reason, or with the ordinary rules of prudence."[2]

In several of the revelations that result from Joseph or other Saints being in anxious, high-pressure situations, by contrast the Lord's responses seem cool and in control. Section 111 is like that. Joseph is overwhelmed with debt to the point of taking unsound risks. The Lord replies that he will gather Salem's treasures and souls for Zion in due time. He gives Joseph and his companions assignments to redeem their time in Salem:

make inspired contacts, seek out the place the Lord wants them to stay, and learn about Salem's early inhabitants. Joseph was concerned, anxious, eager to the point of making hasty, unwise decisions. Section 111 is soothing, reassuring, gentle, and patiently instructive.

OUTCOMES

Doctrine and Covenants 111 reoriented Joseph and his companions. They sought out the place where the Lord wanted them to stay, a house on Union Street not far from where Nathaniel Hawthorne was writing tales of buried treasure in Salem and the local newspaper was reporting similar rumors.[3] They visited from house to house and did some preaching. On August 19 they visited the East India Marine Society Museum. They were comparatively relaxed as they attempted to obey the revelation instructing them to stop being concerned with their debts and with things they could not control in Zion and to focus instead on souls both past and present.

These efforts led to some of the "treasures" the Lord mentioned in verse 10. Returning from another trip to Salem in 1841, Hyrum Smith met with Erastus Snow, gave him a copy of section 111 and urged him to go there and harvest the "many people" the Lord promised to gather in due time (v. 2). At great sacrifice to himself and his family, Elder Snow went. He and Benjamin Winchester started the harvest, and others followed. In 1841 the *Salem Gazette* announced that "a very worthy and respectable laboring man, and his wife, were baptized by immersion in the Mormon Faith." Six months later the *Salem Register* noted that "Mormonism is advancing with a perfect rush in this city."[4] The Church has inquired into Salem's early inhabitants, too. The early records of Salem and surrounding areas have been preserved and are accessible for genealogical research leading to the sacred ordinances of the house of the Lord.

With section 111, the Lord turned follies into treasures in his own due time.

Doctrine & Covenants 112

ORIGIN

As apostasy swept through the Church membership in Ohio in 1837, Thomas Marsh, president of the Quorum of Twelve Apostles, tried to reconcile the disaffected members of his quorum and solidify plans for the apostles to undertake a mission to Great Britain under his leadership. Thomas had scheduled a meeting of the apostles on July 24, 1837, in Kirtland. He arrived to find that Joseph had already called and sent apostles Heber Kimball and Orson Hyde to England.[1] After consulting with Quorum member Brigham Young, Thomas went to Joseph for counsel and reconciliation.[2] In that meeting, Thomas wrote Doctrine and Covenants 112 as Joseph dictated.[3]

CONTENT

Doctrine and Covenants 112 is notable for the penetrating way it addresses Thomas Marsh and the other apostles. Aspiring and full of potential, Marsh and some of the apostles found themselves divided and unfulfilled. The revelation acknowledges the apostles' receipt of priesthood keys handed down from prior dispensations and the greatness of their calling, but it simultaneously implies pride, even blasphemy and apostasy, among some, and it points out the need for Marsh and other Quorum members to repent and then preach repentance and baptism, in anticipation of apocalyptic punishments, beginning with the Latter-day Saints (vv. 23–26).

Characteristic of Joseph's revelations, this one outlines conditions for promised outcomes, both positive and negative, thus giving the recipients agency to act in the face of historical circumstances to influence a desired result. Perhaps the best known example is verse 10. Another poignant example is the admonition to the apostles to "exalt not yourselves; rebel not against my servant Joseph" (v. 15). Several of the apostles, including David Patten, John Boynton, Luke and Lyman Johnson, and William McLellin, were disaffected at the time of this revelation, and Parley and Orson Pratt had only recently reconciled with Joseph.[4] Thomas Marsh worked to reconcile those still disaffected, but by October 1838 he had himself become estranged from Joseph and accused him of treason.

OUTCOMES

Though he wrote the Lord's words as Joseph spoke them, Thomas Marsh heard Doctrine and Covenants 112 selectively. He took the revelation to Heber C. Kimball's wife, Vilate, and told her that Joseph had assured him that her husband would not be effective as a missionary until Thomas said so.[5] Heber and his companions enjoyed great success meanwhile and wrote back across the Atlantic their version of what Joseph had said, that "it was all right to prepare the way for brother Marsh."[6]

Thomas Marsh was arrogant. He heard and self-servingly interpreted the passages of the revelation that reminded him of his high position, the greatness of his calling, his possession of powerful priesthood keys, and his impressive role in spreading the gospel to the nations. But he did not hear the revelation's command to be humble (v. 10), to "exalt not yourselves," or to "rebel not against my servant Joseph" (v. 15).

Thomas returned to his home in Missouri, as commanded in verse 6, and continued under Joseph's direction to publish the *Elders' Journal* newspaper for the Church. But by the fall of 1838 he had begun to exalt himself and rebel against Joseph. He famously repudiated the decisions of Church councils to defend his wife in a dispute with another sister.[7] Then he signed an affidavit charging Joseph Smith with treason, which led to the Prophet's incarceration. "That affidavit brought from the government of Missouri an exterminating order, which drove some 15,000 Saints from their homes and habitations."[8] Thomas was excommunicated in March 1839 and remained estranged from the Church for nearly two decades.

President Gordon B. Hinckley recounted how, on a Sunday in September 1857, President Brigham Young presented to a congregation of Saints meeting in the Old Bowery on Temple Square "a man who appeared to be old and infirm and weary of life.

"Said President Brigham Young to the congregation:

"'Brother Thomas B. Marsh, formerly the President of the Quorum of the Twelve Apostles, has now come to us, after an absence of nearly nineteen years. He is on the stand to-day, and wishes to make a few remarks to the congregation. . . .

"'He came into my office and wished to know whether I could be reconciled to him, and whether there could be a reconciliation between himself and the Church of the living God. He reflected for a moment and said, I am reconciled to the Church, but I want to know whether the Church can be reconciled to me.

"'He is here,' said President Young, 'and I want him to say what he may wish to. . . . Brethren and sisters, I now introduce to you Brother Thomas B. Marsh. When the Quorum of the Twelve was first organized, he was appointed to be their President.'

"Brother Marsh rose to the pulpit. This man, who was named the first President of the Council of the Twelve Apostles and to whom the Lord had spoken in so marvelous a manner, as recorded in section 112 of the Doctrine and Covenants—which I wish you would read—said to the people:

"'I do not know that I can make all this vast congregation hear and understand me. My voice never was very strong, but it has been very much weakened of late years by the afflicting rod of Jehovah. He loved me too much to let me go without whipping. I have seen the hand of the Lord in the chastisement which I have received. I have seen and known that it has proved he loved me; for if he had not cared anything about me, he would not have taken me by the arm and given me such a shaking.

"'If there are any among this people who should ever apostatize and do as I have done, prepare your backs for a good whipping, if you are such as the Lord loves. But if you will take my advice, you will stand by the authorities; but if you go away and the Lord loves you as much as he did me, he will whip you back again.

"'Many have said to me,' he continued, '"How is it that a man like you, who understood so much of the revelations of God as recorded in the Book of Doctrine and Covenants, should fall away?" I told them not to feel too secure, but to take heed lest they also should fall; for I had no scruples in my mind as to the possibility of men falling away.'

"He continued, 'I can say, in reference to the Quorum of the Twelve, to which I belonged, that I did not consider myself a whit behind any of them, and I suppose that others had the same opinion; but, let no one feel too secure; for, before you think of it, your steps will slide. You will not then think nor feel for a moment as you did before you lost the Spirit of Christ; for when men apostatize, they are left to grovel in the dark.' (Journal of Discourses, 5:206)."[9]

In May 1857 Thomas Marsh wrote a humble letter to Heber C. Kimball, then serving in the First Presidency. "I deserve no place among you in the church as the lowest member," Thomas confessed, "but I cannot live without a reconciliation with the 12 and the Church whom I have injured." In the letter Marsh referred to his apostolic commission affirmed in section 112. "A mission was laid upon me & I have never filled it and now I fear it is too late but it is filled by another I see, the Lord could get along very well without me and He has lost nothing by my falling out of the ranks; but O what have I lost?"[10]

Doctrine & Covenants 113

ORIGIN

Persecution, apostasy, dissent, and bankruptcy plagued Joseph in 1837. A Church-sponsored joint stock company called the Kirtland Safety Society, which was designed to liquidate the Saints' real estate assets, failed. Several of Joseph's close associates turned against him. Most of the Saints sustained Joseph, but as many as three hundred were disfellowshipped or excommunicated. Among them were leading elders—apostles, seventies, Book of Mormon witnesses, Joseph's secretary.

Joseph's enemies pursued civil and criminal lawsuit actions. Joseph was tried and found guilty of violating Ohio's banking laws. He was charged with attempted murder and was acquitted. There was no peace, no rest, in Kirtland, Ohio. It seemed that with the bestowal of priesthood keys (D&C 110) concerted opposition overwhelmed the Saints. In January 1838 Joseph received a revelation that is not in the Doctrine and Covenants:

"Thus saith the Lord, let the presidency of my Church[1] take their families as soon as it is practicable and a door is open for them and move on to the west[2] as fast as the way is made plain before their faces and let their hearts be comforted, for I will be with them. Verily I say unto you the time [page damaged] to come that your labours are finished in this place, for a season. Therefore arise and get yourselves on to a land which I shall show unto you, even a land flowing with milk and honey.[3] You are clean from the blood of this people, and wo unto those who have become your enemies who have professed my name, saith the Lord, for their judgement lingereth not and their damnation slumbereth not. Let all your faithful friends arise with their families also and get out of this place and gather themselves together unto Zion and be at peace among yourselves, O ye inhabitants of Zion, or there shall be no safety for you."[4]

Joseph obeyed this revelation and left immediately for Missouri, arriving in the Mormon settlement of Far West on March 14.[5] He, Emma, and their children Julia, Joseph III, and Frederick lived with George and Lucinda Harris. Within just a few days of his arrival, probably during an informal meeting with Elias Higbee and others, Joseph clarified passages of the book of Isaiah. His explanations regarding verses of Isaiah 11 and 52 were noted in his Scriptory Book by secretary George Robinson and are recorded in Doctrine and Covenants 113.

CONTENT

In Doctrine and Covenants 113, the Lord identifies himself as the stem of Jesse, King David's father, mentioned in Isaiah 11. The rod or branch growing out of the stem is a servant of the Lord. Similarly, the root of Jesse in Isaiah 11:10 is an Israelite with priesthood and keys to establish the Church and gather Israel in the last days.

Joseph receives answers to Elias Higbee's questions about Isaiah 52, interpreting some of the symbolism in terms of Doctrine and Covenants 86 and what he has learned by revelation about priesthood, Zion, and the gathering of Israel.

OUTCOMES

Though Joseph never explicitly identified himself as the rod and root of Isaiah 11, Moroni quoted these passages to him repeatedly in 1823 and told him they were about to be fulfilled, meaning, given what Joseph tells us in Doctrine and Covenants 113, that the Lord was about to call a servant, an Israelite heir to the covenant blessings, and give him priesthood and keys to establish the Church and gather Israel in anticipation of the Lord's second coming. It must have been a sobering September night for Joseph, who had wondered only if he could be forgiven of some youthful sins (D&C 2; Joseph Smith–History 1:36–40.)[6]

The Book of Mormon identified Joseph as a descendant of Joseph of Egypt (2 Nephi 3:6–16). As he matured, the Prophet must have thought often of Moroni's repeating to him Isaiah's words and seen himself in them. When Joseph's father gave him a patriarchal blessing in 1834, it said: "I bless thee with the blessings of thy fathers Abraham, Isaac and Jacob; and even the blessings of thy father Joseph, the son of Jacob. Behold, he looked after his posterity in the last days, when they should be scattered and driven by the Gentiles, and wept before the Lord: he sought diligently to know from whence the son should come who should bring forth the word of the Lord, by which they might be enlightened, and brought back to the true fold, and his eyes beheld thee, my son: his heart rejoiced and his soul was satisfied."[7]

Imagine being an obscure, poorly educated "boy of no consequence," as Joseph described his teenage self (Joseph Smith–History 1:22), and then to learn from an angel standing in the air inside your bedroom that you are the fulfillment of Old Testament prophecies, that you will receive the priesthood and its keys to gather the scattered remnants of Israel "to return [them] to the Lord from whence they have fallen" (D&C 113:10) and "to bring again Zion" (v. 8).

It is not clear exactly when Joseph understood himself to be the fulfillment of Isaiah's prophecies of a servant of Christ who would establish a gathering place for Israel and bring again Zion. But the recording of Doctrine and Covenants 113 in his journal in early 1838 attests that these ideas were on his mind at that time. Given the upheaval the Church was experiencing, Joseph may have been seeking the Lord's direction about how to exercise the priesthood keys he had just received to loose the scattered Israelites from the bands around their necks and bring them to Zion (D&C 110; 113:8–10).

Doctrine & Covenants 114

ORIGIN

Elder David W. Patten was second in seniority in the Quorum of Twelve Apostles when he and his wife, Phoebe Ann Babcock, moved from Kirtland, Ohio, to Far West, Missouri, in late 1836 or early 1837. With his Quorum president Thomas Marsh, David led the Saints in Missouri as several Church leaders apostatized in the early months of 1838. On April 17, 1838, a month after Joseph Smith's arrival at Far West, Patten sought out the Prophet to request a revelation on his behalf. Doctrine and Covenants 114 was recorded in Joseph's Scriptory Book, his journal for 1838. The journal also records counsels in which several of the apostles as well as Oliver Cowdery and David Whitmer were disciplined or excommunicated from the Church.[1]

CONTENT

The revelation in Doctrine and Covenants 114 instructs Patten and the other members of the Twelve to prepare to embark on a collective mission the following spring (1839). Although the revelation does not mention where the Twelve will be sent, apostles Heber Kimball and Orson Hyde and their companions had sent reports of their success in Great Britain. Section 114 implies a call to the entire quorum to perform a follow-up mission to the British Isles the next year. And rather quietly, given the widespread apostasy of Church officials, the revelation says the apostates' "bishopric," or office, can be filled by others (v. 2).

OUTCOMES

David Patten did not live to fulfill the revelation. He was killed on October 25, 1838, after being wounded in a conflict between Saints and Missouri militiamen. But the apostles did go to Britain. On July 8, just over two months following the receipt of this revelation, Joseph received another with more details of their call (D&C 118).

The vacancies left by David Patten's death and the apostasy of Oliver Cowdery, the entire presidency of the Church in Missouri, and a third of the apostles, did not last long. Their positions were quickly, quietly, and efficiently filled. Doctrine and Covenants 114 shows how the Lord grants individuals their agency, including the potential for apostasy, without compromising the kingdom. Sad as the casualties are, the work rolls forward when individuals opt out. Replacements are ready. In this case men named John Taylor and Wilford Woodruff, among others, were called, and they continued the work of the Lord (D&C 118).

Doctrine & Covenants 115

ORIGIN

In December 1836, the Missouri state legislature created Caldwell County, allocating it for Mormon settlement, and named Far West its seat. As many as two thousand Saints gathered to Far West with a few thousand more in the surrounding area. On April 6, 1837, the seventh anniversary of the organization of the Church, they made plans to build a temple like the one in Kirtland, Ohio. They chose a site in the center of town and came together to break ground.[1] Then the work stopped. When Joseph visited Far West in November, a council decided that "the building of the House of the Lord be postponed until the Lord shall reveal it to be His will to have it commenced."[2] A few weeks after Joseph moved to Far West in March 1838, the Lord revealed in Doctrine and Covenants 115 his will concerning the temple.

CONTENT

The Lord names his Church in Doctrine and Covenants 115. At its organization on April 6, 1830, it bore the name the "Church of Christ" (D&C 20:1). Then, beginning on May 3, 1834, Church leaders officially adopted the title, "The Church of the Latter Day Saints."[3] Section 115 commands that the Church be called "The Church of Jesus Christ of Latter Day Saints," a designation Joseph had already begun using.[4]

Once named, the Church is commanded to rise and shine as a gathering place for the faithful in all nations who choose Zion over the wrath of God "when it shall be poured out without mixture upon the whole earth" (v. 6). The Lord commands Far West to be consecrated, to have a temple, and for the Saints to begin preparations on July 4 and to lay the foundation on April 26, 1839, a year from the date section 115 was revealed. Still indebted from building the temple in Kirtland, Ohio, Joseph and his counselors are forbidden to go deeper into debt for the temple in Far West. As with his instructions for the Kirtland Temple, in verse 16 the Lord covenants to accept this one if the Saints build it as he specifies (D&C 95).

Section 115 specifies Far West as the Saints' primary gathering place and commands Joseph to identify and establish other stakes in the region. In the midst of dissent and apostasy, the Lord ends section 115 with an emphatic declaration that he remains with Joseph and will sanctify him. "For unto him have I given the keys of this kingdom and ministry" (v. 19).

Shortly after the Lord revealed section 115, Thomas Marsh, president of the Quorum of the Twelve Apostles, wrote of its content to Wilford Woodruff. "Since Br. Joseph came to this place, we have been favored with a lengthy revelation in which many important items are shown forth. First, that the Church, shall hereafter be called. 'The Church of Jesus Christ of Latter-day Saints.' Second, it saith 'Let the City Far West be a holy and a consecrated land unto me, and it shall be called most holy, for the ground upon which thou standest is holy: Therefore, I command you to build a house unto me, for the gathering together of my Saints, that they may worship me.' It also teaches, that the foundation stone must be laid on the 4th of July next, and that a commencement must be made in this following season; and in one year from that time, to continue the work until it is finished. Thus we see that the Lord is more wise than men, for [some] thought to commence it long before this, but it was not the Lord's time, therefore, he overthrew it, and has appointed his own time. The plan is yet to be shown to the first presidency, and all the Saints, in all the world, are commanded to assist in building the house [of the Lord]."[5]

Section 115 is an optimistic declaration. In the face of overwhelming opposition, including indebtedness, persecution, and poverty, the Lord is building Zion. The temple is all important. Having recently received the priesthood keys to authorize temple ordinances (D&C 110), Joseph is the

Lord's choice to carry Zion forward, establish its stakes, oversee its temples, and gather the faithful of all nations to be endowed with power.

OUTCOMES

The Saints gathered on July 4, 1838, to obey the command in Doctrine and Covenants 115 to begin work on the temple. George Robinson, Joseph's secretary, reported, "We therefore met on this day in Far West Mo. To make our declaration of independence, and to lay the corner stones of the house of the Lord agreeably to the commandment of the Lord unto us given April 26th 1838."[6] The Saints then gathered building materials so that construction could proceed "in one year from this day," namely, April 26, 1839. Meanwhile, according to one Missouri historian, the walls had inched upwards to nearly three feet before the Saints were driven from the state by the governor's executive order in October 1838.[7]

In obedience to verse 18, Joseph led three expeditions in the spring of 1838, primarily in Daviess County, to search out locations for "stakes in the regions round about" (v. 18).[8] Additional explorations were conducted throughout the summer, and land surveys were conducted in anticipation of more Saints arriving in the fall. On June 28, 1838, at a small grove near the home of Lyman Wight near Spring Hill in Daviess County, Joseph Smith organized the Adam-ondi-Ahman Stake, the third stake organized in the Church.[9]

The name of the Church revealed in section 115 continues to identify the Church today (note the hyphen between *Latter* and *day*, with *day* not capitalized). A *New York Times* News Service article in February 2001 cited Elder Dallin H. Oaks as saying that the Church will increase efforts to discourage the use of the term Mormon Church and emphasize the name Jesus Christ in references to the Church. "It will urge that the church be called by its full name and then, in subsequent references, the Church of Jesus Christ." Elder Oaks explained this emphasis as "a 'deliberate reaffirmation' of a long effort in favor of wider use of the church's full title. 'We haven't adopted a new name of the church,' Elder Oaks said, noting that Mormons regard the full name as having been revealed by God to Mormonism's first prophet, Joseph Smith. 'We have adopted a shorthand reference to the church [Church of Jesus Christ] that we think is more accurate."[10]

Doctrine & Covenants 116

ORIGIN

In late 1836 the Missouri legislature created two new counties to effect a peaceful solution to what was commonly called the "Mormon problem," the anti-Mormon feelings among many settlers. The smaller county, created especially for settlement by the Saints, was named Caldwell. The northern county, called Daviess, had a few scattered occupants and was open for settlement.[1] Many Missourians anticipated that the Saints would confine themselves to Caldwell County, but less than a year later Church leaders were looking, as commanded, for more land on which to settle the gathering Saints (D&C 105:29–31).[2]

Daviess County appealed to the Latter-day Saints because of the pre-emption laws that applied. As federal land newly opened for settlement, northern Missouri could be settled by pioneers claiming up to 160 acres while postponing actual purchase of the land until the government had surveyed it and advertised it for sale.[3] Church leaders took advantage of these laws to obey the command to acquire land, including land in Daviess County. Lyman Wight purchased a preemption claim for land near the Grand River and Spring Hill in Daviess County.

Shortly after Joseph moved to Missouri in March 1838, the Lord commanded him that "other places should be appointed for stakes in the regions round about" (D&C 115:18). Anticipating that large numbers of Saints would gather to the area from Ohio, Canada, and elsewhere, Joseph and other leaders set off to explore Daviess County "for the purpose of . . . making locations &

laying claims for the gathering of the Saints for the benefit of the poor."[4] Near Lyman Wight's home, Joseph received Doctrine and Covenants 116.

CONTENT

Orson Pratt inserted the words "Spring Hill is named by the Lord Adam-ondi-Ahman" when he included this statement in section 116 of the 1876 edition of the Doctrine and Covenants. The entry in Joseph's journal, made by his secretary George Robinson, reads: "Spring Hill, a name appropriated by the brethren present, but afterwards named by the mouth of the Lord and was called Adam Ondi Ahman, because, said he, it is the place where Adam shall come to visit his people, or the Ancient of days shall sit as spoken of by Daniel the Prophet."[5]

OUTCOMES

Doctrine and Covenants 116 links the past with the future, sacred history with prophecy. Adam-ondi-Ahman is the place Adam and Eve went after being expelled from the Garden of Eden. They offered sacrifices and blessed their posterity. Joseph learned by revelation in 1831 that Adam, prior to his death, gathered his posterity in a valley called Adam-ondi-Ahman. The Lord appeared to them and promised Adam that he would preside over a multitude of nations. Adam rose and prophesied what would happen to his posterity (D&C 107:53–56; see also 78:15–16). Section 116 identifies the specific site of that impressive occasion and says that it has a future role as Adam, or the Ancient of Days, as Daniel called him, will again gather his righteous posterity there, for the sacrament and stewardship meeting prophesied in section 27.[6]

Approximately fifteen hundred Latter-day Saints settled at Adam-ondi-Ahman in 1838. They planned a temple. They laid out a stake in obedience to section 115. They obeyed the law of consecration in obedience to section 119.[7] But the Saints were driven from the land in November after Missouri governor Lilburn Boggs issued an executive order in October that effectively and purposefully enabled Missourians to steal the land by preventing the Saints from asserting their preemption rights.[8] Even so, the Church has regained its land and preserves the sacred site.

Doctrine & Covenants 117

ORIGIN

The year 1838 began grimly as dissent from within the Church and opposition from outside it pressured Joseph Smith. The Church's bank had failed. Joseph was mired in debt because of his efforts to turn Kirtland, Ohio, into a stake of Zion, including crowning it with a priceless but expensive temple. Creditors, some of whom were Joseph's avowed enemies, hounded him. Some filed suits against him. Some of his associates and friends rejected him as a prophet. Apostates started their own church.

Joseph sought counsel from the Lord and received a revelation on January 12 that is not canonized in the Doctrine and Covenants: "Thus saith the Lord: Let the presidency of my Church take their families as soon as it is practicable and a door is open for them, and move on to the west as fast as the way is made plain before their faces, and let their hearts be comforted, for I will be with them. Verily I say unto you, the time [page damaged] to come that your labours are finished in this place, for a season. Therefore, arise and get yourselves on to a land which I shall show unto you, even a land flowing with milk and honey.[1] You are clean from the blood of this people, and wo unto those who have become your enemies, who have professed my name, saith the Lord, for their judgment lingereth not and their damnation slumbereth not. Let all your faithful friends arise with their families also and get out of this place and gather themselves together unto Zion and be at peace among yourselves, O ye inhabitants of Zion, or there shall be no safety for you."[2]

Joseph left Kirtland immediately following this revelation. His family and remaining members of the First Presidency followed him. The question remained whether his "faithful friends" would "arise with their families also and get out of this place and gather themselves together unto Zion."

Joseph moved to Far West, Missouri, and received a series of revelations that relocated, reorganized, and reoriented the Church, whose headquarters had been in Kirtland, Ohio, since 1831. One of the new revelations, Doctrine and Covenants 115, declared Far West to be the new center of gathering for the Saints.

The First Presidency expected that William Marks, a bookseller who had remained in Kirtland to preside over the Saints there, and Newel K. Whitney, the bishop in Kirtland, would obey the revelations to leave Kirtland and come to Far West. Yet these men dragged their feet. Whitney was Kirtland's most prosperous merchant. He owned a store and a profitable ashery situated near the main intersection through town. He was torn between his material prosperity and the revelations.

Almost all the faithful Kirtland Saints had left for Missouri by May 1838. When neither Whitney nor Marks had arrived in Missouri by July, Joseph received a revelation about their situations and about what to do regarding his indebtedness and the bankruptcy of the First Presidency. The revelation is recorded in Doctrine and Covenants 117.

CONTENT

In direct and certain terms the Lord commands Newel Whitney and William Marks to relocate to Missouri before winter to continue serving in their respective callings, Marks to preside over the Saints in Far West and Whitney to serve as a bishop at Adam-ondi-Ahman, which entailed managing the Church's material assets for the building of Zion and relieving the poverty of the Saints.

There is a fascinating dynamic to Doctrine and Covenants 117. No other revelation—no other scripture, in fact—uses the words "saith the Lord" with the same frequency. Some Old Testament prophets use the phrase nearly as often, and sections 124 and 132 use it frequently too. But its unusually high frequency in section 117 may tell us something about Joseph's awkward position. Newel Whitney was his friend and benefactor. Newel and Elizabeth Ann Whitney had welcomed the homeless Joseph and Emma to their own hearth when they first moved to Ohio. The Whitneys repeatedly housed Joseph and Emma as well as Sidney Rigdon's family. Emma gave birth to Joseph III in the Whitney home. Emma and Elizabeth Ann Whitney were dear, close friends. Newel had served ably as a bishop and tried to implement the law of consecration. He largely financed the United Firm as one of its charter members (D&C 72; 78; 82; 104). He used his own connections and resources to set Joseph up as a rival storekeeper in Kirtland.[3] For all of that, Newel was beset by "covetous desires."[4]

The Lord speaks directly to those desires in section 117. He speaks as the Creator and Owner of the earth with whom Newel had covenanted to consecrate and serve as a bishop. He commands Newel and William to "repent of all their sins, and of all their covetous desires, before me" (v. 4). He directs a series of penetrating questions at the two men who are still deciding whether to serve God or mammon. The Lord paints a comparative picture, juxtaposing what Joseph called Newel's "narrow mindedness," his acquisition of a tiny telestial empire in Kirtland, Ohio, with the Lord's expansiveness as the Creator.[5] In verse 8 he uses terms from his own elevated "language" to describe northern Missouri, where Newel is commanded to relocate and serve the Saints (see D&C 116).

In verse 11 the Lord speaks of Newel Whitney in connection with a Nicolaitane band. Nicolaitanes were followers of Nicholas of Antioch, an early Christian called and ordained to look after the business of ministering to widows (Acts 6:1–6). Nicholas apostatized, however, and led a faction that justified their covetous and lustful impulses.[6] The allusion is the Lord's potent way of conveying to Newel how evil the Lord finds the Kirtland apostates and how near Newel is himself to committing their sins.

The Lord commends Oliver Granger and commissions him with redeeming the credit of the First Presidency in Ohio before returning to Missouri as a merchant for Zion (D&C 117:12–14). The Lord does not promise Oliver success in this labor, only that his repeated efforts and sacrifice will be sanctifying for him and that his name will be sacredly remembered (vv. 12–13).

On a final note, in verse 16 the Lord invites the Saints still in Kirtland to preserve the temple and keep it holy by overthrowing the money changers as he had done in his Father's house in Jerusalem (John 2:14–15; Matthew 21:12; Mark 11:15).

OUTCOMES

Oliver Granger returned from Missouri to Kirtland to obey his part of Doctrine and Covenants 117 by representing the First Presidency in selling some property and settling debts. One Saint on the scene noted Oliver's "strict integrity" and testified that his "management in the arrangement of the unfinished business of people that have moved to the Far West, in redeeming their pledges and thereby sustaining their integrity, has been truly praiseworthy, and has entitled him to my highest esteem and ever grateful recollection."[7] Still, "there was not much chance that he could succeed," President Boyd K. Packer said, "and, really, he did not succeed!" President Packer emphasized that section 117 does not praise Oliver for his success but rather for his efforts, for earnestly contending at personal sacrifice. Thus, for efforts with which Oliver himself may not have been entirely satisfied, his name and example have been remembered.[8]

When Oliver returned from Ohio ready to fulfill the instructions in verse 14, the First Presidency wrote him a letter of recommendation. "We have entrusted vast business concerns to him," the letter said, "which have been managed skillfully to the support of our characters and interest as well as that of the Church; and he is now authorized by a general conference to go forth and engage in vast and important concerns as an agent for the Church, that he may fill a station of usefulness in obedience to the commandment of God" (see vv. 13–14). The First Presidency's letter includes a short revelation in which the Lord promises to "lift up my servant Oliver . . . because of the integrity of his heart" and commands the Saints to be generous when Oliver solicits donations from them.[9]

Oliver Granger delivered a copy of section 117, together with a letter from the First Presidency, to Newel Whitney and William Marks. The revelation and the related letter put Newel and William in the position of the rich ruler of Luke 18 who kept all of the commandments except the full measure of consecration required to enter the kingdom of God. As Jesus counseled the rich man, so he counsels Newel and William in section 117 to sell what they have, distribute unto the poor, come literally to Missouri, and choose "treasure in heaven" instead of the comparatively tiny, if highly coveted, "drop" (Luke 18:22; D&C 117:8).

The First Presidency's letter explained to Newel and William that with section 117 "you will understand the will of the Lord concerning you & will doubtless act accordingly." The revelation compelled the brethren to act—whether in obedience or disobedience. They could not remain indecisive about obeying Jesus Christ. The First Presidency was confident that they would "doubtless act accordingly," and they did.[10] Newel Whitney and his family left Kirtland in the fall of 1838, too late to join with the Saints in Missouri who were being driven from the state but soon enough to continue serving as a bishop in Nauvoo, Illinois. William Marks obeyed also and became the Nauvoo stake president.

Section 117 powerfully motivated Newel Whitney, William Marks, and Oliver Granger. They believed the revelation was indeed from the Lord, and they acted at great personal sacrifice to obey it as best they could.

Doctrine & Covenants 118

ORIGIN

Doctrine and Covenants 117, 118, 119, and 120, as well as several uncanonized revelations, were given on July 8, 1838, a veritable flood of necessary information. Church headquarters had moved with Joseph to Missouri in March. One third of the apostles had been released or excommunicated for apostasy. The Church needed to be reoriented and reordered. A council including Joseph, his counselors, secretary, the bishopric in Missouri, and Thomas Marsh, president of the Quorum of Twelve Apostles, met to seek revelation. "Show unto us thy will O Lord concerning the Twelve," Joseph prayed, and Doctrine and Covenants 118 followed.[1]

CONTENT

In Doctrine and Covenants 118 the Lord calls for a conference to immediately reorganize and fill the vacancies in the Quorum of the Twelve Apostles. Thomas Marsh, who besides presiding over the quorum was the Church's publisher in Missouri, is to continue in that role. The other apostles are to continue preaching. The Lord covenants with them that if they endure in their ministries meekly and humbly, he will provide for their families and give them success. In verse 4 the Lord elaborates on a call spoken of in section 114 for the apostles to cross the Atlantic Ocean in the spring of 1839 on a mission to Great Britain. This time the call is very specific. "Let them take leave of my saints in the city of Far West, on the twenty-sixth day of April next, on the building-spot of my house, saith the

Lord" (v. 5). The Lord then names the men he chose to replace the fallen apostles and commands that they be officially notified.

OUTCOMES

The day after the revelation in Doctrine and Covenants 118 was received, the apostles who were in Far West met with the First Presidency and acted on the command to officially notify the new apostles. Sidney Ridgon wrote to Willard Richards, who was already serving in England. Willard was ordained there by Brigham Young in 1840. Wilford Woodruff was serving a mission in the islands off the coast of Maine in August 1838 when, according to his journal, "I received a letter from Thomas B. Marsh, informing me of my appointment to fill the place, in the Quorum of the Twelve, of one who had fallen, and I was requested to come to Far West as soon as possible, to prepare for a mission to England in the spring."[2]

Obedience to the rest of the revelation proved to be more problematic. In October 1838 the governor of Missouri issued an executive order to the state militia to drive the Saints from the state. The Saints lost their property and retreated east to the relative safety of Illinois. There, as April 1839 approached, the apostles and others counseled about the specific instructions in section 118 to leave for England from the temple site in Far West, Missouri, on April 26. Quorum president Thomas Marsh had been excommunicated for apostasy and apostle David Patten had been killed in the Missouri violence, leaving Brigham Young as the senior apostle.

Wilford Woodruff reported that "as the time drew nigh for the accomplishment of this work, the question arose, 'What is to be done?' Here is a revelation commanding the Twelve to be in Far West on the 26th day of April, to lay the corner stone of the Temple there; it had to be fulfilled. The Missourians had sworn by all the gods of eternity that if every other revelation given through Joseph Smith were fulfilled, that should not be, for the day and date being given they declared that it should fail. The general feeling in the Church, so far as I know, was that, under the circumstances, it was impossible to accomplish the work; and the Lord would accept the will for the deed."[3] But Brigham Young was presiding over the apostles, and the

Lord had commanded them to leave from the Far West temple site on April 26, 1839. Those who wondered whether the apostles would do so were not familiar with the iron resolve of Brigham Young.

Wilford Woodruff reported that on April 17 he got his family settled in Quincy, Illinois, and "prepared myself to accompany the twelve to fulfill a certain revelation & commandment of the Lord which required us to take our leave of the Saints at far west on the 26th day of April 1839 for the nations of the earth." He joined Brigham Young and others on a journey west over the Mississippi and into hostile Missouri. He noted that the roads were full of Saints heading east, "fleeing from Missouri to Illinois for they were driven from their houses & lands by the State." On April 25 Brigham, Wilford, and their party arrived at Far West at the abandoned home of Brother Morris Phelps, who remained in prison with apostle Parley P. Pratt in Columbia, Missouri.[4]

Wilford documented the historic significance of the next day in his journal: "April 26th 1839. The events of this day are worthy of record, for a revelation of God & commandment is this day fulfilled & that too under circumstances which to all human appearance could not have been done. The Lord had given a commandment to the Twelve to assemble upon the building spot of the house of the Lord in Far West, Caldwell Co., Mo., on the 26th day of April & there take the parting hand with the Saints to go to the nations of the earth. But persecution had arisen to such an height that about ten thousand souls of the Saints had been driven from the State, & the city Far West almost made desolate & laid waste while at the same time the Presidency Joseph & his council with other elders were in prison & they had been under the sentence of death several times because of their religion & they would have been put to death had not the Lord saved them, for their lives were in his hands & notwithstanding the lives of those men were preserved yet there were about thirty-five souls martyred & put to death. David W. Patten one of the Twelve Apostles were among the martyred. And not only so but the Missourians had sworn that the revelation above alluded to should not be fulfilled.

"It was in the midst of these embarrassments that we moved forward to the building spot of the house of the Lord in the City of Far West & held a

Council & fulfilled the revelation & Commandment." Wilford noted that they also fulfilled the command in section 115 to begin to lay the foundation for the temple on that day. "Elder [Alpheus] Cutler, the master workman of the house, then recommenced laying the foundation of the Lord's house agreeable to revelation by rolling up a large stone near the southeast corner" (see D&C 115:11). Wilford sat on that stone as the apostles led by Brigham Young ordained him an apostle. George A. Smith was also ordained to replace Thomas Marsh. Brethren recently freed from prison in Missouri were ordained seventies. Each of the apostles prayed, and Alpheus Cutler placed the cornerstone before, as Wilford put it, "in consequence of the peculiar situation of the Saints he thought it wisdom to adjourn until some future time when the Lord should open the way expressing his determination then proceed to with the building."[5]

Less than a week after Brigham Young led the apostles in obeying section 118, William W. Phelps, who had apostatized and remained behind in Missouri, reported the event to his wife in a mocking, critical tone. "One of the least of all the forcible tricks of the Mormons, was performed in the morning of the 26th April, in secret darkness about three o'clock in the morning. Probably seven shepherds and eight principal men, from Quincy and elsewhere assembled at the big house cellar, and laid *one* huge stone, in addition to those already there, to fulfill the revelation given the 26th of April one year ago. I think they strained at a camel and swallowed a gnat. . . . I have also learned that, at the sham meeting at the big house cellar, there not being a quorum of the old 'Twelve' present, they had recourse to 'shift,' and ordained Wilford Woodruff, and Geo. Smith as apostles, which with HC Kimball Orson Pratt, Brigham Young (old ones) and John E Page and John Taylor (new ones), made seven. They prayed (in vain) sung Adam ondi Ahmah, and closed. There were others there. This looks a little like choosing or loving *darkness* rather than light because their deeds are evil." Phelps continued with profound irony, "You know I think as much of pure religion as ever, but this foolish mocking disgusts me and all decent people. *Force* the fulfillment of Jo's revelation! You might as well damn the waters of Missouri River with a lime riddle. It was undoubtedly done to strengthen the faith of weak members, and for effect abroad: as I understand the Twelve are a going to try their luck again among the nations: It's really a pity they cannot get a looking glass large enough to see the saw log in their own eyes while they are endeavoring to pull the slab out of the neighboring nations. All I can say is 'Physician save thyself!' Whether you laugh or cry, I have one thing to confess, and that is: *I never was so lonesome before.*"[6]

Truly "fools mock, but they shall mourn" (Ether 12:26). While Phelps pitied himself and mocked the apostles, they turned east and continued to obey Section 118. They returned to Illinois to make final preparations for their mission to Great Britain. They left their families sick and destitute and, some of them suffering from malaria, struggled to make their way to England. There they experienced an unprecedented harvest, which over the next five years brought more than forty-five hundred converts to gather with the Saints.[7]

Doctrine & Covenants 119

ORIGIN

In early February 1831, Joseph Smith received the law of consecration. It commanded the Saints to freely offer the Lord what he had given to them. Then he would consecrate a stewardship to them. Thereafter, the Saints were to be stewards of what they needed to be "amply supplied" and return surplus to the bishop of the Church for his stewardship "to administer to the poor and the needy" (D&C 42:33–34).

The Lord revealed the law of consecration to relieve poverty, purchase land for the public benefit of the Saints, and to build temples and the New Jerusalem so that his covenant people could be saved by gathering to his temple (D&C 42:30–36). Joseph and the bishops of the Church worked to implement the law of consecration, but unwilling Saints and antagonistic neighbors in both Ohio and Missouri thwarted their efforts.

By mid-1837, the Church was in a desperate condition financially, and the United States had slumped into an economic depression that would last five years. Feeling the pressure keenly, Bishop Newel Whitney and his counselors in Ohio issued a letter proposing that the Saints be tithed. "It is the fixed purpose of our God," they wrote, "that the great work of the last days was to be accomplished by the tithing of His Saints." They invoked Malachi 3:10 to assert that "the Saints were required to bring their tithes into the storehouse, and after that, not before, they were to look for a blessing that there should not be room enough to receive it."[1] The bishopric in Missouri proposed and adopted a similar but more specific policy in December 1837, recommending that the Saints be tithed two percent annually after paying their debts.² Both bishoprics emphasized the voluntary nature of the offering based on the principle of individual agency.

Joseph moved from Ohio to Missouri early in 1838. There the city of Far West began to bustle with people and economic enterprise, the Saints planned and the Lord approved the construction of a temple (D&C 115), and hundreds of Saints gathered from the East, with more arriving all the time. By July the prospects of establishing an enduring stronghold in northern Missouri appeared both promising and daunting. The Church needed revenue to accomplish its divine mandates. Joseph prayed, "O! Lord, show unto thy servents how much thou requirest of the properties of thy people for a Tithing?"³ The revelation recorded now as Doctrine and Covenants 119 was the Lord's answer.

CONTENT

In his journal, Joseph's prayer is followed by the word "Answer" and then the text of Doctrine and Covenants 119. Though it is clearly worded and consistent with Joseph's earlier revelations, section 119 may be his most misunderstood revelation. It begins with a direct restatement of the law of consecration stated originally in Doctrine and Covenants 42:33 and section 54. Then verse 2 states the purposes for the consecration of surplus property, which are the same for the law of consecration and related revelations given in sections 51, 70, 72, 78, 82, 104, and 105. "This," the revelation says, "shall be the beginning of the tithing of my people" (D&C 119:3). That is the first of the three uses in the revelation of *tithing* or *tithed*. All of them refer to the voluntary offering of surplus. "And after that, those who have thus been tithed," says verse 4, "shall pay one-tenth of all their interest annually." This is not a lesser law to be replaced at some future point but "a standing law unto them forever" and applicable to all Saints everywhere (v. 4).

The Lord had previously given the law of consecration and stewardship, which all Latter-day Saints were to keep by covenant of their own free will

(D&C 42:30–36). Saints were expected, not coerced, to live this law. All could. Some would, and some would not (D&C 51; 66; 85; 90).

The covenant for all Latter-day Saints to keep the law of consecration is different from the covenant made by the leading elders to own and administer the Church's assets according to the law of consecration. That covenant led to the United Firm, often known as the united order, which involved a few Church leaders, never the general membership of the Church (D&C 78; 82; 104). In verses 4–9 of section 104 the Lord declared the covenant of the United Firm broken and therefore void. He then dismantled the United Firm but never repealed the law of consecration. President Gordon B. Hinckley taught that the law of consecration was not rescinded and is "still in effect."[4] Thus, section 119 may be best understood as part of, not instead of, the law of consecration. Section 119 is God's law and covenant to be kept or rejected according to the free will of each individual.

The revelation ends with a covenant. "If my people observe not this law, to keep it holy, and by this law sanctify the land of Zion unto me, that my statutes and my judgments may be kept thereon, that it may be most holy, behold, verily I say unto you, it shall not be a land of Zion unto you" (v. 6).

OUTCOMES

Brigham Young was present when the Lord revealed Doctrine and Covenants 119. He was assigned to go among the Saints "and find out what surplus property the people had, with which to forward the building of the Temple we were commencing at Far West." Before setting out he asked Joseph, "'Who shall be the judge of what is surplus property?' Said he, 'Let them be the judges themselves.'"[5] As a result, some Latter-day Saints offered all their surplus property. Some offered some of it. Some offered none. No one was coerced. And so it remains.

Section 119 is stunningly effective. When significant numbers of Saints have obeyed the instruction to offer a tenth of their annual increase, the Church has prospered and has been able to carry out some of its divine mandates. Temples dot the earth, and Israel is being gathered, educated, and prepared for Zion because of obedience to this revelation. The money the Saints offer is calculable. The resulting blessings are incalculable. The Lord has opened heaven's windows and poured out a blessing.

Doctrine & Covenants 120

ORIGIN

Joseph moved to Missouri in 1838 as the Church suffered dissent from within and persecution from without. The Church regained its footing in Far West, Missouri. On the same July day that Doctrine and Covenants 119 reaffirmed the law of consecration and defined tithing, the Lord gave Joseph Doctrine and Covenants 120, "making known the disposition of the properties tithed, as named in the preceding revelation."[1]

CONTENT

Doctrine and Covenants 120 is about timing and the Lord's omniscience. It says that the time has come for the Lord to appoint the First Presidency, bishopric, and high council as a standing council to dispose of the tithes "by mine own voice unto them, saith the Lord" (v. 1).

OUTCOMES

Less than a month passed before this newly revealed council met in Far West, Missouri, to obey the revelation, that is, to "take into consideration the disposing of the public properties in the hands of the Bishop, in Zion, for the people of Zion have commenced liberally to consecrate agreeably to the revelations, and commandments of the Great I Am of their surplus properties." The council agreed that the First Presidency should keep all the property they needed "and the remainder be put into the hands of the Bishop or Bishops, agreeably to the commandments, and revelations."[2]

Doctrine and Covenants 120 created the council that continues to guide the Church's financial and property management and declared the principle of revelation by which they do so. When section 120 was revealed, Far West served as Church headquarters, and its bishop and high council served with the First Presidency. The Quorum of the Twelve Apostles and the Presiding Bishopric replaced the local authorities as those quorums developed and matured and as Church headquarters moved. Today, in other words, the council is composed of the First Presidency, the Quorum of the Twelve Apostles, and the Presiding Bishopric.

Speaking from the vantage point of nearly two decades as a member of this council, Elder Robert D. Hales said: "It is remarkable to witness this council heed the Lord's voice. Each member is aware of and participates in all the council's decisions. No decision is made until the council is unanimous. All tithing funds are spent for the purposes of the Church." He continued: "I bear my testimony of the Council on the Disposition of the Tithes. . . . Without exception, the tithing funds of this Church have been used for His purposes."[3]

Doctrine & Covenants 121, 122, and 123

ORIGIN

After weeks of fighting between Missourians and Latter-day Saints in northern Missouri, the governor issued an executive order for the militia to remove Mormons from the state. General Samuel Lucas, an anti-Mormon from Jackson County, arrested Joseph and others in Far West, held a court martial, and sentenced them to execution. The actions were illegal because Joseph and others arrested were not members of the militia and were therefore subject to civil rather than military law. Cooler heads prevailed when General Alexander Doniphan, formerly a lawyer for the Saints, refused to obey the order and vowed to hold Lucas accountable if he carried out the executions.

As Latter-day Saint women were abused and men forced to sign over their property as citizen militia shot their livestock and pillaged their homes, General Lucas allowed Joseph and his brethren to return home for a few belongings. Clinging to Joseph, Emma and the children cried as a guard swore at six-year-old Joseph and ordered him to "get away you little rascal or I will run you through."[1] Joseph was carted off to Independence and then to Richmond, Missouri, where, as he wrote to Emma as positively as he could, he was shackled to five of his brethren "in chains as well as the cords of everlasting love."[2]

Joseph Smith and five of his brethren were jailed in Liberty, Missouri, having been charged with treason against the state in a preliminary hearing before Judge Austin A. King.[3] On December 1, 1838, a committee of the Missouri legislature who studied the hearing found that the evidence presented was one-sided "and not of the character which should be desired for the basis of a fair and candid investigation."⁴ Joseph's brother Hyrum, who had overheard Judge King say "that there was no law for us, nor for the 'Mormons' in the state of Missouri," called it a "pretended court."⁵ The case against Joseph was unfounded, and he was denied due process of law. Judge King was simply on a "quest for hostages."⁶

For four winter months and five days Joseph and his brethren languished in jail at Liberty, Missouri. In a cramped and filthy dungeon room without beds, bathroom, warmth, or adequate food, Joseph passed his darkest days. He was awaiting trial for a capital offense without hope for due process of law as his wife, children, and beloved followers were robbed of their property, stripped of their civil liberties, and driven midwinter by a mob acting under the guise of official orders from the governor, aided and abetted by a host of apostates. Indeed, many of Joseph's most trusted and stalwart brethren had forsaken him. Most of the Book of Mormon witnesses, still certain of their testimony, nevertheless turned against him. Several of the apostles were antagonistic, including Thomas Marsh and Orson Hyde, who accused Joseph of treason for advocating the fulfillment of Daniel's prophecy of the

Jail at Liberty, Missouri.

kingdom of God (see D&C 65). Apostle William E. McLellin, who had had no doubt that Joseph was a prophet (see D&C 66), joined Lucas's soldiers in plundering the Saints in Far West and expressed his desire to beat Joseph Smith.[7] William W. Phelps turned his powerful pen against Joseph. As historian Richard Bushman wrote, the trying events of 1838 pushed "faithful souls to the breaking point."[8]

Some of the Saints reviewed their history and found no evidence "that God has been our leader." They had not prospered or built Zion. Rather, they had been repeatedly driven "in hope of deliverance, but no deliverance came."[9] Even Sidney Rigdon, Joseph's counselor in the First Presidency and fellow sufferer in jail, began to resent God for the seemingly inexplicable treatment the Saints were receiving. "If ever there was a moment to give up the cause, this was it," wrote Bushman. "Joseph puzzled over the Saints' suffering in the cause of God. Why had they been defeated? He never questioned his own revelations, never doubted the validity of the commandments. He did not wonder if he had been mistaken in sending the Saints to Missouri or requiring them to gather."[10]

Joseph put these questions to the Lord in a long letter he dictated to the Saints on March 20, 1839, after nearly four months behind what he called "iron doors and screaking hinges."[11] It is a remarkable document. In a single stream of profound consciousness, "the words came rapidly from his lips without calculated organization. No paragraphs break up the flow; sentences merge; frequent misplaced and misspelled words show the rush in which the dictation was scribbled down. Yet parts of the letter rose to a level that merited later canonization in the Doctrine and Covenants."[12] Doctrine and Covenants 121, 122, and 123 come from this one profound letter, from which the otherwise undocumented quotations that follow are drawn to provide context.[13]

CONTENT OF SECTION 121

In Doctrine and Covenants 121, verses 1–6 come immediately after Joseph reviews the "hell surrounded with demons" of Liberty Jail and, what was more in his mind, the driven Saints, the widows and orphans of the men murdered at Haun's Mill, "the unrelenting hand" of oppression. It is about the duration of these injustices that Joseph inquires, "How long . . . ? Yea, O Lord, how long?" (vv. 2–3). *Sheol,* in verse 4, is a transliteration of the Hebrew word for the spirit world.

In the extended letter, Joseph recounts the opposition of apostates, judges, his own lawyers, the governor, "and the one-sided rascally proceedings of the Legislature" before noting his recent reception of letters from Emma, his brother Don Carlos, and Bishop Edward Partridge that softened his heart. "When the heart is sufficiently contrite," his letter says, "then the voice of inspiration steals along and whispers," followed by the answer to his prayer, verses 7–25.[14]

The Lord's answer to "how long?" is "a small moment" (v. 7), accompanied by a curse on Joseph's enemies and the identification of their real motive, personal sinfulness, in verse 17. The Lord severs them "from the ordinances of mine house" (v. 19) and promises just punishments for the severity of their sins.

Verses 26–33 are the promised blessings of a covenant, the terms and conditions of which precede the promises but were not included in the canonized part of Joseph's letter. "Let honesty and sobriety, and candor and solemnity, and virtue, and pureness, and meekness, and simplicity, crown our heads in every place, and in fine become as little children without malice, guile, or hypocrisy: and now, Brethren, after your tribulations *if* you do these things, and exercise fervent prayer, and faith in the sight of God," *then* God will grant the exalting blessings promised in verses 26–33.[15]

The context for verses 34–46 is consecration. In the part of the letter preceding these verses, Joseph cautions against "any among you who aspire after their own aggrandizement and seek their own opulence while their brethren are groaning in poverty and are under sore trials." Such covetous Saints "cannot be benefited by the intercessions of the Holy Spirit," Joseph writes. "We ought at all times to be very careful that such highmindedness never have place in our hearts but condescend to men of low estate and with all long-suffering bear the infirmities of the weak."[16]

It is immediately following those thoughts that Joseph explains why many are called but few are chosen: "Because their hearts are set so much upon the things of this world, and aspire to the honors of men, that they do not learn this one lesson" (v. 35), namely, that they cannot have power in the priesthood if they cover sins, gratify pride, have vain ambition, or exploit the weak and impoverished. In this light, these verses clearly resemble sections 85 and 104. There, too, the Lord explains that the choice to disobey the law of consecration is the choice to forfeit the priesthood and its exalting ordinances. Put another way, the covenant to consecrate is one of the conditions on which the temple blessings are granted.

Sadly, however, experience shows that most mortals choose not to submit to the power of the Atonement to change their human nature. "It is," in other words, "the nature and disposition of almost all men" to oppress their neighbors as soon as they are in a position to do so (v. 39). That is forbidden by section 121, and, beginning in verse 41, an antidote is prescribed in the Godlike qualities of persuasion, long-suffering, gentleness, meekness, pure love, and knowledge. Reproof should come at precisely the right time, which is "when moved upon by the Holy Ghost," and then to remove the problem with the sharpness of a surgeon's scalpel, leaving as little scar tissue and collateral damage as possible and "showing forth afterwards an increase of love toward him whom thou hast reproved, lest he esteem thee to be his enemy" (v. 43).

This is righteous dominion, God's way of governing, and with those who master it he makes a covenant in verses 45–46. Those who choose charity over covetousness, unceasing virtue over self-interestedness, will receive "an everlasting dominion" that will grow without compulsion forever (v. 46). They are the only ones whom God can trust with power. They are the only ones who have proven willing to share and not coerce as soon as they get a little authority.

CONTENT OF SECTION 122

Doctrine and Covenants 122 immediately follows the last part of section 121 in Joseph's long letter. Several of the statements in it refer to his experiences. Verses 6–7, for example, evoke the awful events in Far West, Missouri, the preceding fall as Joseph was wrenched from his family, sentenced to execution, later charged with treason, and confined in the "pit" of Liberty's jail.

Section 122 is a literary masterpiece. It compounds Joseph's suffering in potent *if* statements that build to an almost unbearable crescendo as if they were rocks being piled on his body or lashes across his bare back. All of that makes two profound points, communicated in what must have been, especially juxtaposed with what preceded it, an enormously comforting voice, the voice of the Savior himself. "Know thou, my son, that all these things shall give thee experience, and shall be for thy good" (v. 7) The revelation made the second point to Joseph by posing the profound question of verse 8: "The Son of Man hath descended below them all. Art thou greater than he?" Instruction follows as Joseph is encouraged to hold on and fear not. He is promised the priesthood forever and life until his work on earth is finished.

CONTENT OF SECTION 123

Doctrine and Covenants 123 comes toward the end of the letter amid other suggestions to the Saints. It contains valuable counsel from the Prophet for the Saints to document the injustices and atrocities they have endured in Missouri in order to assert their First Amendment rights to a redress of grievances. Joseph repeatedly tells the Saints to write what happened to them in Missouri. It is "an imperative duty" they owe to God, to angels, to each other, to those murdered in Missouri, to the rising generation, "and to all the pure in heart" (vv. 7, 9, 11). In powerful, metaphor-rich language, Joseph and his brethren urge the Saints to attend to this important matter. Joseph was not certain that the government would respond to the petitions, but he knew the Lord required the Saints to do all in their power, including this "last effort" to obtain justice, before He would "send forth the power of his mighty arm" (v. 6).

OUTCOMES OF SECTION 123

In response to Joseph's counsel, recorded now in Doctrine and Covenants 123, 678 Latter-day Saints wrote or dictated sworn statements documenting the abuses they had suffered and property they had lost in

Missouri. In the fall of 1839, having escaped from Missouri, Joseph took the documents to the president of the United States. He literally knocked on the door of the White House and asked to see President Martin Van Buren, whom Joseph had supported. Joseph presented the petitions, and Van Buren, facing an election year, responded, "What can I do? I can do nothing for you! If I do anything, I shall come in contact with the whole state of Missouri." President Van Buren pleaded impotence, based on the federalist doctrine of limited powers which held that he could not constitutionally intervene in a state matter. Joseph turned to the Congressional delegation from Illinois for help in appealing to Congress. The Senate referred the case to the Judiciary Committee, which, with pressure from Missouri, arrived at the same conclusion, knowing very well that the Saints had been driven for their religion. There would be no justice, no due process, no redress of grievances, and no guarantees of the free exercise of religion. But the documentation of abuse "did have a long term effect on Mormonism's public image. . . . The accounts of the persecutions turned the expulsion from Missouri into an asset in the battle for popular support."[17] The redress petitions were turned over to the Library of Congress, where they remain as a testimony "of diabolical rascality and nefarious and murderous impositions that have been practiced upon this people" (v. 5).

OUTCOMES OF SECTIONS 121 AND 122

Joseph wanted Emma to be first to read his long letter, and he pleaded with her in a letter the following day to have it copied immediately and circulated to the leaders of the Church and to his parents. Though the letter from which Doctrine and Covenants 121–23 derive demonstrates the limits of Joseph's formal schooling, he regarded it as the vessel of some of the most profound revelation and counsel ever given. The parts that became sections 121 and 122 reoriented and motivated Joseph and have had a similar effect on many others.

In a dark, confined space he was powerless to escape, Joseph pleaded "How long?" with an implied "Why?" From His timeless and infinite vantage, the Lord answered "a small moment" and because "all these things shall give thee experience" (D&C 121:7; 122:7). These words "turned the raw Missouri experience into a theology of suffering" that made sense when seen from God's perspective.[18] Liberty Jail illustrated a microcosm of life in a telestial world, a dog-eat-dog sphere of power-seeking, aspiration, materialism, and unrighteous dominion. There, in that hell, Joseph was powerless. Or was he? B. H. Roberts called the jail "more temple than prison, so long as the Prophet was there. It was a place of meditation and prayer. A temple, first of all, is a place of prayer; and prayer is communion with God. It is the 'infinite in man seeking the infinite in God.' Where they find each other, there is holy sanctuary—a temple. Joseph Smith sought God in this rude prison, and found him."[19]

As a result, sections 121 and 122 endowed Joseph with power. Though the bounds of his enemies were set, Joseph would always have the priesthood (see D&C 122:9). It would distill on him like dew from heaven until he obtained a kingly scepter and reigned over a never-ending dominion in the presence of God. Meanwhile, his oppressors, those who used their supposed power and influence to hurt, take, abuse, insult, misrepresent, and compel, would be cursed, lose their posterity, and be severed from the temple and thus confidence in the presence of God. It was they who were powerless "to hinder the Almighty from pouring down knowledge from heaven upon the heads of the Latter-day Saints" (D&C 121:33). The powerful on earth would, in a small moment, be made impotent while Joseph and the faithful would reign with gentleness, meekness, and love unfeigned forever and ever (D&C 121:41, 46).

These divine explanations helped Joseph see as if from God's eyes that things were not as they seemed. They made sense of suffering. Mankind was on earth to gain experience. Those who chose to be meek, gentle, and without guile would gain power in the priesthood as indiscernibly as dew from heaven. They could be trusted with God's power, whereas those who made their experience "sad" by choosing unrighteous dominion were testifying to God of their unwillingness to exercise His power as He does and therefore demonstrating their unworthiness to have that power (D&C 121:39).

"The word 'experience' suggested that life was a passage. The enduring human personality was being tested. Experience instructed. Life was not just a place to shed one's sins but a place to deepen comprehension by descending below them all." In sum, sections 121 and 122 taught Joseph that "the Missouri tribulations were a training ground" for godhood.[20]

A seeming hell could serve as a temple, a place to be endowed with God's heart and mind in anticipation of assuming his "everlasting dominion" (D&C 121:46). Joseph came to understand this truth because of his experience in Liberty Jail. He wrote from that stinking but sacred space, "It seems to me that my heart will always be more tender after this than ever it was before." He recognized that trials "give us that knowledge to understand the minds of the Ancients" like Abraham, who typified the Savior's unequaled unjust suffering. "For my part," Joseph wrote, "I think I never could have felt as I now do if I had not suffered the wrongs that I have suffered."[21]

Renewed certainty resulted from these revelations. The day after he dictated them, Joseph still did not know how long he would be in jail, but he wrote to Emma that since he knew "for a certainty of Eternal things if the heavens linger it is nothing to me." Hinting at his new eternal perspective, Joseph began signing his letters to Emma, "yours forever."[22] After he finally escaped from Missouri a few weeks later while being transported to Columbia for trial, Joseph seemed the most confident and determined soul on earth. His days were not only known but numbered, and with them he pursued a course to train the apostles, give them the priesthood keys he had received from ministering angels, and build a temple to begin offering the ordinances of exaltation to the faithful.

As a result of these revelations, Joseph emerged from his darkest hour not broken but renewed.

Doctrine & Covenants 124

ORIGIN

The Saints retreated from Zion in 1838. The state of Missouri drove the Latter-day Saints out while some of its leading citizens stole their land.¹ Joseph escaped from Missouri after being unjustly confined for more than five months. He emerged from the depressing days spent in Liberty Jail with an undaunted spirit. He knew from revelations received in jail that his days were numbered but that his work was not yet finished and the Lord would protect him until it was (D&C 122:9). Joseph was determined to give temple blessings to the Latter-day Saints.

He and the Saints invested in land along both sides of the Mississippi River in the state of Illinois and the newly created Iowa Territory. They began to build a city on the site of a town called Commerce. Joseph renamed it Nauvoo, the Hebrew word translated as *beautiful* in Isaiah 52:7.² In October 1839 he called for all Saints to gather and build a holy city. He lobbied the Illinois legislature for a city charter. The largest cities in Illinois were chartered, giving them constitutional controls independent of the state. Nauvoo's charter, for instance, created an independent militia, city courts, and city officers empowered to "pass ordinances that contradicted state law, as long as those ordinances did not conflict with the state or national constitution."³ Illinois legislators overwhelmingly approved the charter in December 1840, and it became effective with the election held the first Monday in February 1841.

Between those dates Joseph prayed for and received Doctrine and Covenants 124, a momentous revelation, the longest in the Doctrine and Covenants.

CONTENT

Coming shortly after a presidential election and just days before Nauvoo's first city election, Doctrine and Covenants 124 begins by expressing the Lord's approval of Joseph's efforts. Then, "that I might show forth my wisdom through the weak things of the earth" (v. 1), the Lord commands Joseph to immediately write a proclamation "to all the kings of the world, . . . to the honorable president-elect," William Harrison, "and the high-minded governors of the nation in which you live" (vv. 1, 3). Joseph is to write "in the spirit of meekness and by the power of the Holy Ghost" (v. 4) but to uncompromisingly declare the will of Christ to the world's political authorities. Inherent, then, in this revelation as in Joseph's earlier ones, is sovereign authority. The Lord says nothing of the will of the people but declares his will to "my people" (vv. 10, 11, 21, 40, 45, 84, 92, 104). In America generally, the voice of the people was considered the voice of God (*vox populi, vox Dei*). In Nauvoo, the Lord spoke to his people through his prophet, Joseph Smith.

The Lord describes in verses 3–6 what the proclamation should say, and in verses 7–10 why it should say it. The proclamation is to be in the prophetic voice, the voice of authority inviting all to come build Zion and the voice of warning declaring the impending judgments of God upon those who "reject my servants and my testimony which I have revealed unto them" (v. 8).

In verses 15–24 the Lord extends callings and commendations for service. Robert Thompson is to help Joseph write the proclamation, though he died before he was able to do so. The Lord blesses and expresses his love for Hyrum Smith for his integrity and love. John Bennett gets more qualified commendation. A skillful but self-serving strategist, Bennett is to help Joseph disseminate the proclamation and is promised wonderful blessings based on three conspicuous *if*s in verses 16–17. As it turned out, Bennett chose not to meet the revelation's conditions and therefore could not expect its promised blessings. Adulterous, he apostatized, profaned the temple ordinances, and campaigned for the death of Joseph Smith.

Apostle David Patten, Patriarch Joseph Smith Senior, and Bishop Edward Partridge have all passed away by the time of the revelation. The Lord relays to Joseph that they are with Him, even detailing that Joseph's father "sitteth with Abraham at his right hand" (v. 19).

Nauvoo Temple. Section 124 instructs the Saints to build a temple in Nauvoo and explains why.

George Miller, whom the Lord calls in verses 20–21 as a bishop in place of Edward Partridge, is appointed with John Snider, Lyman Wight, and Peter Haws to be trustees of the Nauvoo House Association. The revelation calls them to lead cooperative efforts to raise money, establish a joint-stock company, and build a boarding house (vv. 22–24, 56–82, 111–22).

The command for all the Saints to consecrate to the building of the temple begins with verse 25. The logic for doing so begins in verse 28: "For there is not a place found on earth that he may come to and restore again that which was lost unto you, or which he hath taken away, even the fulness of the priesthood." The Lord grants the Saints sufficient time to consecrate and build the temple as a sacred location for baptisms and the other sacred ordinances, after which he will not accept their ordinances, for in the temple "are the keys of the holy priesthood ordained, that you may receive honor and glory" (v. 34; see D&C 128). The Lord continues his rationale for building the temple. Verse 41 is a restatement of the promise to reveal fulness in the temple.

Some have misread verses 31–34. President Joseph Fielding Smith explained the condition of verse 32: "And if ye do not these things at the end of the appointment," that is, the period for building the temple. It "does not mean 'if ye do not build a temple at the *end* of the appointment,' as our critics infer it does, but it refers to the *ordinances* that were to be performed in the Temple." President Smith clarified that if the Saints fail to perform the temple ordinances for the dead, then they will be rejected by the Lord per Doctrine and Covenants 124:32.[4]

President Boyd K. Packer explained the references (in verses 37–39 of the revelation) to the ordinances of washing and anointing: "The ordinances of washing and anointing are referred to often in the temple as initiatory ordinances. It will be sufficient for our purposes to say only the following: Associated with the endowment are washings and anointings—mostly symbolic in nature, but promising definite, immediate blessings as well as future blessings. . . . In connection with these ordinances, in the temple you will be officially clothed in the garment and promised marvelous blessings in connection with it."[5]

Covenants and specific instructions follow the verses on temple ordinances, including the spot on which to build the temple and the terms and conditions on which the Lord will make it holy and on which the Saints will be able to remain in Nauvoo to see it finished. These covenants hinge on the inseparable doctrines of individual agency and accountability and culminate in verses 47–48: "If you build a house unto my name, and do not do the things that I say, I will not perform the oath which I make unto you, neither fulfil the promises which ye expect at my hands, saith the Lord. For instead of blessings, ye, by your own works, bring cursings, wrath, indignation, and judgments upon your own heads." In verses 49–54 the Lord explains accountability in terms of agency. That is, he holds accountable those who have power to determine the outcomes he commands. Following that principle, verse 55 is another statement of rationale for building the temple in Nauvoo.

The Lord returns to the boarding house in verses 56–82 and again in 111–22, specifying stock sales and the holding, naming, oversight, and construction of the Nauvoo House.

William Law, a recently converted Irish immigrant, was one of many who worried about Nauvoo's poor drainage and the resulting malaria. The Lord speaks of William in verses 82–83 and invites him to settle not in Kirtland, Ohio, but in Nauvoo. When section 124 was given, Almon Babbit was presiding over the Saints remaining in Kirtland, and he counseled them to stay there contrary to Joseph's counsel that all Saints should gather to Illinois to build the temple. The Lord rebukes Almon in verse 84, reaffirms his command to gather, and resumes in verse 87 his instructions and callings to William Law. Verse 91 calls William as a counselor to Joseph in the First Presidency to replace Hyrum Smith, who is to replace his deceased father as Church Patriarch and to replace Oliver Cowdery as assistant president of the Church with all the priesthood keys and prerogatives Oliver had as Joseph's companion when the priesthood and its keys were restored (see D&C 13; 27; 109). Oliver Cowdery and Hyrum Smith are the only ones to have held the office of assistant president of the Church.

Hyrum Smith.

Beginning at verse 97, the Lord returns to William Law. He commands Joseph to teach William the temple ordinances and William to live worthily of them, promising that he will have power in the priesthood if he does. Verse 102 closes this section of the revelation with a mission call for Hyrum and William; the details are not given now but are promised to them later.

Joseph's first counselor, Sidney Rigdon, suffered from what was likely recurrent malaria from 1839 to 1844, which may have been worsened by his exposure and malnutrition in Liberty Jail (see D&C 121). Sidney had been beaten, driven, imprisoned, and impoverished. Now in his weakened condition he was not enthusiastic about gathering again with the Saints, and he contemplated returning to the east, perhaps to his native Pittsburgh.

Verses 103–10 are a revelation to him that both gently and firmly counsels Sidney to gather to Nauvoo and assist Joseph with his work, promising health and wellness "if he will hearken unto my voice" (v. 110).

The rest of the revelation, beginning with verse 123, reconstitutes the priesthood quorums of the Church, beginning with the First Presidency (vv. 123–26). The Lord presents the reorganized quorums to the priesthood holders, giving them Hyrum Smith as a patriarch and sealer. The Lord gives Joseph as "presiding elder over all my church" (v. 125), as well as a translator, seer, and prophet. For counselors to Joseph, the Lord gives Sidney Rigdon and William Law. He gives the quorum of the First Presidency to receive the oracles or revelations for the whole church.

Verses 127–30 present the reorganized Quorum of the Twelve Apostles, with Brigham Young as president (see D&C 126). Verses 131–32 present the Nauvoo Stake high council (see D&C 102), and verses 133–36 present a presidency for a high priests quorum, from which to draw stake and mission presidents. The elders quorum presidency is presented in verse 137 (see D&C 107:89–90), the seven presidents of the seventies in verses 138–40 (see D&C 107:93–97). Aaronic Priesthood presidencies are presented in verses 141–42, and the Lord finishes the revelation by giving his rationale for giving these offices, together with their keys, followed by two commandments: First, at the coming April conference the Saints should sustain or reject the priesthood brethren the Lord calls. Second, the Saints should prepare offices for the priesthood quorums in the temple.

OUTCOMES

Nauvoo rose like a fortress on a hill, up from a swampy lowland along the Mississippi. Latter-day Saints streamed into Illinois from Upper Canada, the British Isles, and the Atlantic seaboard. The population of Nauvoo rose quickly to twelve thousand because of this revelation and Joseph's counsel to gather and build Zion. Joseph began a sacred record book, the Book of the Law of the Lord, with section 124. The revelation oriented his life and that of the Church. It gave Joseph the rest of his life's work, and he entered the names of those who consecrated to the temple in the Book. At April conference in 1841 the revelation was read, and then Joseph rose and urged the Saints to obey it by building the temple and the Nauvoo House.[6]

Doctrine and Covenants 124 set in order the Church's presiding priesthood quorums, replacing apostates and filling the vacancies left by brethren who had passed away. The Saints acted on the Lord's commands to sustain those called to the priesthood quorums, which they did at April conference in 1841, as well as building offices for them in the temple.

Section 124 reoriented the Church by giving it specific work to do, most importantly in building the Nauvoo Temple as a means to the end of receiving the ultimate blessings, the fulness of priesthood ordinances. Knowing that his days were numbered, Joseph began giving the ordinances in May 1842 to a select few, fifty-seven brothers and sisters in all, even before the temple was finished. He sealed couples and confirmed the fulness of priesthood ordinances on a few according to section 132. Joseph was killed in June 1844 before the temple was ready for ordinances, but in March of that year he had commissioned the apostles to carry on the work and had given them all the necessary priesthood keys to do so. Beginning in December 1845, the apostles and others who had been endowed by Joseph officiated in the temple ordinances for fifty-six hundred Saints.

The temple blessings thus resulting from section 124 are inestimable. Speaking of temples, President Gordon B. Hinckley declared, "These unique and wonderful buildings, and the ordinances administered therein, represent the ultimate in our worship. These ordinances become the most profound expressions of our theology."[7]

Doctrine & Covenants 125

ORIGIN

From the confines of a wretched jail cell in Liberty, Missouri, Joseph wrote to Bishop Edward Partridge in Illinois, where the Saints had fled after being driven from Missouri by the militia acting on the governor's orders. Joseph reminded the bishop that Isaac Galland, a land speculator in Iowa Territory, had invited the Saints to buy land for two dollars an acre over twenty years with no money down. "To an impoverished people," wrote historian Richard Bushman, "those terms seemed heaven-sent."[1] Joseph told Bishop Partridge he thought it would be wise for the Saints to contract with Galland for the land, which they did.[2]

Joseph escaped from Missouri and joined the Saints in Illinois a few weeks later. He purchased land on a peninsula across the Mississippi River from the Saints' Iowa tracts and named the site Nauvoo. The land in Illinois was comparatively expensive. Joseph hoped that the Church could buy it with consecrated funds and offer lots to the poor at prices they could afford, but the offerings were insufficient. As it became clear that the Church would have to sell lots in order to pay its mortgage, Joseph closed outlying stakes and urged all Saints to gather to Nauvoo and help pay for the land.[3] Did that policy apply to the Saints already in Iowa? Joseph received the answer to that question, which is recorded now in Doctrine and Covenants 125.

CONTENT

The Lord's will declared in Doctrine and Covenants 125 is for the Saints to build a city in Iowa across from Nauvoo and to call it Zarahemla, after the Nephite stronghold of the Book of Mormon. The Saints are to gather from everywhere else and settle there, or in nearby Nashville, Iowa, or in Nauvoo. As with many other revelations, the Lord tells why the Saints should do his will: "That they may be prepared for that which is in store for a time to come" (v. 2).

OUTCOMES

By declaring the Lord's will regarding approved gathering places, Doctrine and Covenants 125 made the Saints capable of acting to obey or disobey—once they knew it. At general conference on April 6, 1841, the revelation was read to the Saints. "Many of the brethren immediately made preparations for moving" and did so as soon as their planting was finished.[4] Saints moved as a result of section 125. Alanson Ripley reported that "Joseph said it was the will of the Lord the brethren in general . . . should move in and about the city Zarahemla with all convenient speed which the Saints are willing to do because it is the will of the Lord."[5]

Doctrine & Covenants 126

ORIGIN

Brigham Young answered the Lord's call to serve in England (see D&C 118). Both he and his family were sick and homeless when he left Nauvoo in the fall of 1839. While he was in England, Brigham's calling as president of the Quorum of the Twelve Apostles was formalized (see D&C 124:127). Having converted hundreds, he returned to Nauvoo in July 1841 and found his family living in a small, unfinished cabin. A week later the Lord gave Doctrine and Covenants 126 to Joseph.[1]

CONTENT

Joseph communicates the revelation to Brigham with his own affectionate introduction to his "Dear and well-beloved brother." In Doctrine and Covenants 126 the Lord, having accepted Brigham's offering in laborious missions away from home, requires him no longer to leave his family. Instead, the Lord commands Brigham to send the Lord's word abroad and look to the care of his family "henceforth and forever" (v. 3).

OUTCOME

Brigham set to work to care for his family. He chinked the cracks in the cabin, planted an orchard, built a cellar, and put in a garden to meet their needs. Joseph gave Brigham a few weeks and then assigned him to lead the apostles in taking care "of the business of the church in Nauvoo," including overseeing missionary work (in obedience to the command to "send my word abroad"), the gathering of converts, and consecration.[2] These assignments represented a shift in the apostles' responsibility. Joseph had often kept them at arm's length since their calling in 1835, testing them to see who could be trusted with apostolic assignments. During that time, while several of his fellow apostles apostatized, Brigham had done everything asked of him. He had marched into hostile Missouri to obey a revelation and, sick and impoverished, had forsaken everything dear to preach the gospel in England. As a result of Doctrine and Covenants 126, Brigham remained near Joseph for the Prophet's few remaining years, learning and receiving the keys conferred on Joseph. As a result of obedience to section 126, Brigham was ready to lead when Joseph's earthly mission was finished.

Doctrine & Covenants 127 and 128

ORIGIN

Early Christians believed that the Lord had planned a "rescue for the dead," as one scholar called it; only later, largely influenced by Augustine, did Christianity apostatize from the doctrine of redemption for the dead.[1] Put simply, early Christians baptized each other for their kindred dead, as the apostle Paul noted in 1 Corinthians 15:29.[2]

On a summer day in 1840, Joseph Smith chose to use the funeral sermon of Seymour Brunson to speak of the restoration of the doctrine of baptism for the dead. Joseph read most of 1 Corinthians 15, in which Paul speaks of the resurrection and mentions the early Christian practice of being baptized for the dead in anticipation of the resurrection. The Prophet "remarked that the Gospel of Jesus Christ brought glad tidings of great joy." Noticing a widow in the congregation, the mother of a child who had died before receiving baptism, Joseph gave the good news "that people could now act for their friends who had departed this life, and that the plan of salvation was calculated to save all who were willing to obey the requirements of the law of God." One witness called it "a very beautiful discourse."[3]

Joseph again taught the doctrine of baptism for the dead at October conference in 1840. The Saints eagerly performed the sacred ordinance in the Mississippi River because there was not yet a temple baptismal font.[4] One witness wrote that "during the conference there were some times from eight to ten elders in the river at a time baptizing."[5] But in their understandable zeal, they lacked knowledge: No one recorded the ordinances. A year later Joseph taught the doctrine in conference again and announced, as the Lord had declared in the meantime, that baptisms for the dead performed outside the temple were no longer acceptable (see D&C 124:29–36).[6] The Saints pushed harder to complete the temple, and just over a year later, in November 1841, performed the first baptisms for the dead in the unfinished but rising Nauvoo Temple.

In the midst of teaching the temple ordinances to the Saints, Joseph was charged with masterminding an attempted murder of former Missouri governor Lilburn Boggs. There was no evidence for the charge, and Joseph regarded it as another attempt by his enemies to get him to Missouri to lynch him. He went into hiding. Joseph was finally arrested in August 1842 but was released, and the charges were dismissed a few months later.

Meanwhile, as Joseph moved from house to house in and around Nauvoo, protected by friends, he pondered the newly restored doctrines of the temple. There was something missing. He sought revelation while he was in hiding and learned more about the nature of the ordinances. Then he looked for the first safe opportunity to teach the Saints. In August he taught the Relief Society that "all persons baptiz'd for the dead must have a Recorder present, that he may be an eye-witness to testify of it. It will be necessary in the grand Council, that these things be testified."[7]

The next day Joseph dictated a letter to the Saints, Doctrine and Covenants 127, in which he shared some of what he had recently learned. Less than a week later, Joseph dictated a much longer, more detailed explanation of the order of sacred ordinances, recorded now in Doctrine and Covenants 128. Baptism for the dead "seems to occupy my mind," he wrote (D&C 128:1).

CONTENT OF SECTION 127

Joseph was nostalgic and melancholy as he hid from extradition officers bent on delivering him to a state in which there was no due process of law for Latter-day Saints. In Doctrine and Covenants 127 he rehearses his eventful life, alternating between frustration at his enemies, the hostility that oppressed him, evidences of God's deliverance, and hope for a final triumph. Mixed in are two revelations, the first in verse 4 and the second in verses

6–9, before Joseph closes with a lament that he is unable to teach the Saints in person and offers a prayer for their salvation.

In the first revelation the Lord urges the Saints to finish the temple despite persecution. In the second he links recording the ordinances to their being sealed. That is, baptisms for the dead are not valid in heaven unless properly recorded by an eyewitness on earth. There is coherence in the two revelations. It is imperative that the Saints learn the conditions on which ordinances performed on earth are validated in heaven, for, as the Lord declares in verses 8–9, he is about to restore more that pertains to the priesthood ordinances of the temple and the records of all such ordinances are to be in order and preserved in the temple.

CONTENT OF SECTION 128

Doctrine and Covenants 128 adds practical instructions to the revelation recorded in section 127 that baptisms for the dead, to be valid, must be recorded by an eyewitness. Joseph proposes a recorder for each of Nauvoo's four wards, each of whom will account to a general Church recorder, who will be responsible to collect, certify, and keep the records.

Verse 5 uses three related words: *order, ordinance,* and *ordained.* President Boyd K. Packer cited the definition of *order* given in the *Oxford English Dictionary* as "'arrangement in sequence or proper relative position'" and noted how often the scriptures emphasize the importance of order. *Ordinance,* wrote President Packer, derives from *order.* He defined an ordinance as "the ceremony by which things are put in proper order." *Ordain,* "a close relative of the other two words," is the process of putting in order, including appropriately appointing someone to the ministry. "From all this dictionary work," said President Packer, "there comes the impression that an ordinance, to be valid, must be done in proper order."[8]

That is precisely Joseph's point in section 128. To be valid, an ordinance must be ordained of God, or, in other words, performed according to the order or procedure he dictates. Beginning in verse 6, Joseph traces the doctrine of recording earthly ordinances through the Bible to make his point and substantiate what he has previously taught. He begins with the book of Revelation, in which John saw that the dead would be judged by what is recorded on earth, which is mirrored in the book of life kept in heaven. "It may seem to some to be a very bold doctrine that we talk of," Joseph says in verse 9, speaking of the priesthood power to seal earthly ordinances in heaven. He then evokes the description in Matthew 16 of Jesus' promise to give Peter sealing keys to bind on earth and in heaven (D&C 128:9–10). Joseph turns to the symbolic significance of baptism and cites Paul's teaching in 1 Corinthians 15 and Hebrews 11:40. Joseph adds Malachi's prophecy of the mission of Elijah to unite generations before the Savior's second coming and elaborates on its meaning.

Interestingly, with the teaching of temple ordinances, Joseph remarks that the dispensation of the fulness of times "is now beginning to usher in, that a whole and complete and perfect union, and welding together" of generations, dispensations, and, indeed, of the human family can be accomplished (D&C 128:18). Joseph is exultant at this prospect. Beginning at verse 19 he celebrates the Restoration. Recounting the sources of his knowledge and priesthood power, Joseph lists a number of heavenly messengers he has seen—Moroni, Michael, Peter, James, John, Gabriel, Raphael, "all declaring their dispensation, their rights, their keys, their honors, their majesty and glory, and the power of their priesthood; giving line upon line, precept upon precept; here a little, and there a little; giving us consolation by holding forth that which is to come, confirming our hope" (v. 21). At least one of the events to which Joseph refers—Michael's teaching him how to detect false messengers (v. 20)—must have taken place before Joseph moved from the Susquehanna River to Ohio in 1831, yet this is his first known mention of it. These verses are at least a partial answer to the questions of when and by whom was Joseph endowed with priesthood power, becoming able to give the temple ordinances to the Saints.

In sum, Joseph had revelatory experiences and learned glorious truths that he did not readily share except in the right places at the right times to prepared people. That is exciting, and in a final burst of rhapsody, Joseph celebrated the profundity of the revealed solution to the terrible theological problem that has perplexed every thoughtful Christian: "What about those who never heard?"[9] The answer? "The King Immanuel . . . *ordained*, before the world was, that which would enable us to redeem them out of their prison; for the prisoners shall go free" (v. 22; emphasis added).

Joseph closes section 128 excited about these "glad tidings of great joy" (v. 19) and tells the Saints what to *do* with them: "Let us, therefore, as a church and a people, and as Latter-day Saints, offer unto the Lord an offering in righteousness; and let us present in his holy temple, when it is finished, a book [or, more recently, electronic files] containing the records of our dead, which shall be worthy of all acceptation" (v. 24). In other words, let us organize families in the order God ordained for the performance of the holy ordinances, ordinances that take families and put them into the holy order to which they belong.

OUTCOMES

Wilford Woodruff wrote that "Joseph has been deprived of the privilege of appearing openly & deprived of the society of his own family Because Sheriffs are hunting him to destroy him without cause Yet the Lord is with him.... Joseph has presented the Church of late with some glorious principles from the Lord concerning Baptism for the dead & other interesting subjects, he has appeared occasionally in the midst of the Saints which has been a great comfort."[10]

The Saints were thrilled with the restoration of the doctrine and practice of baptism for the dead for its perfect justice and its power to weld generations. "There is a chance for all. Is not this a glorious doctrine?" Vilate Kimball asked her missionary husband, Heber, then serving in England.[11] Wilford Woodruff remembered how, when the apostles returned from England, Joseph called them "together and told us that the Lord had revealed to him a principle whereby we could go forth and redeem our dead. It was like a shaft of light from the throne of God to our hearts. It opened a field wide as eternity to our minds."[12] Sally Carlisle wrote to her mother, "what a glorious thing it is that we believe and receive the fulness of the gospel as it is preached now and can be baptized for all our dead friends and save them as far back as we can get any knowledge of them.... O Mother, if we are so happy as to have a part in the first resurrection, we shall have our children just as we laid them down in their graves."¹³

Doctrine and Covenants 127 and 128 restored in part the order of sacred ordinances, without which they would not be valid. Joseph's role in restoring these truths can hardly be overstated. Having proven that baptism for the dead was practiced by the earliest Christians but not since, Hugh Nibley asked, "Where did Joseph Smith get his knowledge? Few if any of the sources [available to us] were available to him; the best of these have been discovered only in recent years, while the citations from the others are only to be found scattered at wide intervals through works so voluminous that even had they been available to the Prophet, he would, lacking modern aids, have had to spend a lifetime running them down. And even had he found such passages, how could they have meant more to him than they did to the most celebrated divines of a thousand years, who could make nothing of them? This is a region in which great theologians are lost and bemused; to have established a rational and satisfying doctrine and practice on grounds so dubious is indeed a tremendous achievement." In awe, Nibley summarized the significance of these sections of the Doctrine and Covenants: "Work for the dead is an all-important phase of Mormonism about which the world knows virtually nothing."¹⁴

It is impossible to estimate the outcomes of these revelations, these glad tidings. Because of them, innumerable spirit prisoners continue to go free (see D&C 138). "Shall we not go on in so great a cause?" (D&C 128:22).

Doctrine & Covenants 129

ORIGIN

Joseph escaped from his persecutors in Missouri in the spring of 1839. Knowing that his days were numbered and he had none to spare, Joseph gathered several of the apostles on June 27, 1839, exactly five years before his violent death at the hands of a murderous mob, and taught them what he had learned a decade earlier from Michael about "detecting the devil when he appeared as an angel of light" (D&C 128:20). Wilford Woodruff drew tiny, symbolic keys in his journal, where he wrote what he learned about the "keys of the Kingdom of God Joseph presented . . . in order to detect the devel when he transforms himself nigh unto an angel of light."[1]

In December 1840, Joseph taught these keys to William Clayton, a trusted convert recently arrived from England.[2] In April 1842 he introduced the principles recorded in Doctrine and Covenants 129 to the Relief Society. The following month he gave the Saints a temple preparation sermon, including the explanation that there are "certain signs & words by which false spirits & personages may be detected from true—which cannot be revealed to the Elders till the Temple is completed."[3] A few days later Joseph endowed a few Church leaders in a temporary temple in the second story of his Nauvoo store. Heber C. Kimball was there and subsequently wrote to fellow apostle Parley P. Pratt, who remained in England to preside over the mission: "We have received some precious things through the Prophet on the priesthood that would cause your soul to rejoice," Heber wrote. "I can not give them to you on paper for they are not to be written. So you must come and get them for your Self."[4]

Parley arrived in Nauvoo early in 1843, eager to be taught by Joseph. At a February 9 meeting, Joseph instructed him in the keys he had learned from Michael and had subsequently taught to Wilford, Heber, and a few others. The entry in Joseph's journal for that day is the source for Doctrine and Covenants 129.

CONTENT

Joseph's rough journal entry captures only some of the teaching that took place. It reads: "Parley Pratt & other come in—Joseph explained the following. There are 3 administrater: Angels, Spirits, Devils one class in heaven. Angels the spirits of just men made perfect—innumerable co of angels and spirits of Just men made perfect. An angel appears to you how will you prove him. Ask him to shake hands. If he has flesh & bones he is an Angel 'spirit hath not flesh and bones.' Spirit of a just man made perfect. Person in its tabernacle could hide its glory. If David Patten or the Devil come. How would you determine should you take hold of his hand you would not feel it. If it was a false adminestiter he would not do it. True spirit will not give his hand the Devil will. 3 keys."[5]

In its polished form, Doctrine and Covenants 129 is more clear. In heaven are resurrected beings and spirits who are not yet resurrected. Either kind can be sent as messengers. Satan or his angels can and will try to counterfeit this kind of revelation. But there are keys to discern such imposters, as explained in verses 5–9. It is not safe to conclude that Satan is ignorant of these keys. It seems more likely, as Joseph taught, that God sets boundaries to Satan's power to deceive. Otherwise "we could not be free agents."[6]

OUTCOMES

Doctrine and Covenants 129 contains esoteric knowledge. That is, it says much more to those who have been taught than to those who have not. It is a temple-related text. It gives those who understand it power to discern true from false messengers (see v. 8; see also D&C 128:20), for if Satan could appear in the guise of an angel without our having any ability to know better, "we could not be free agents."[7]

Doctrine & Covenants 130

ORIGIN

Joseph Smith presided over a stake conference in Ramus, Illinois, on April 2, 1843. Joseph's secretary, William Clayton, accompanied him, as did apostle Orson Hyde, who spoke at the Sunday morning session on New Testament passages, especially John 14:23 and 1 John 3:2, which prophesied Christ would come and reveal Heavenly Father. A Campbellite preacher before his conversion to the restored gospel, Elder Hyde mixed old ideas into his sermon. Between conference meetings Joseph and Orson dined at Joseph's sister's home, where Joseph told Orson, "I am going to offer some corrections to you." Wisely he replied, "They shall be thankfully received."[1] Joseph and the Saints were also aware of the prophecies of a contemporary named William Miller, who had predicted that the Savior's second coming would be April 3, 1843, the day after conference.

Joseph preached twice at the stake conference, offering corrections to Elder Hyde, answering William Clayton's question about time relativity and refuting Miller's prediction of the second coming.[2] William Clayton captured Joseph's teachings in his journal, and Willard Richards later copied them into Joseph's journal. Some of the teachings were clarified and prepared for publication in the Church's newspaper in the 1850s and then added to the 1876 edition of the Doctrine and Covenants, becoming section 130.

CONTENT

Doctrine and Covenants 130 begins by clarifying John 14:23, which prophesies that the Savior will appear and reveal his Heavenly Father.

Joseph emphasizes, contrary to what Orson Hyde suggested, that the appearance of the Father and Son are literal. They are exalted, embodied Gods; the designation Heavenly Father is literal, and the social relationship sealed here will endure into eternity only with "eternal glory, which glory we do not now enjoy" (D&C 130:2).

Beginning in verse 4, Joseph answers a question William Clayton posed about the relativity of time depending on one's proximity to God. Joseph declared that time is relative but that all angels who minister to our earth have themselves lived on this earth. The angels now reside with God "on a globe like a sea of glass and fire" where "past, present, and future . . . are continually before the Lord" (v. 7). Joseph taught that this earth will become a celestial kingdom, a great seer stone in which its inhabitants will be able to see inferior kingdoms. Even more exciting, each individual who enters this kingdom will get a personal "stone" as a means of learning and progressing eternally (v. 11).

Beginning in verse 12, Joseph prophesies the American Civil War based on his Christmas 1832 revelation (see D&C 87). He refuses to prophesy specifically about the date of the Savior's second coming, having learned his lesson from an earlier earnest prayer, which the Lord answered with intentional ambiguity, leaving Joseph unable to decide (see v. 16).

Verses 18–21 teach principles revealed in sections 51, 58, 88, 93 and elsewhere about the relationship between God's law, individual agency, and growth. Intelligence is gained by choosing to diligently obey God's laws. This is one of Joseph's most profound, exalting teachings.

The last two verses clarify the nature of the Godhead. Joseph's teachings at the conference focused on the Holy Ghost. "The Holy Ghost is a personage," he said, "and a person cannot have the personage of the H.G. in his heart. A man may receive the gifts of the H.G., and the H.G. may descend upon a man but not to tarry with him."[3] Church historians—apostles—amended the text in the 1850s to its current reading.[4]

OUTCOMES

One result of Doctrine and Covenants 130 is clarification of what we do not know: the timing of the Savior's second coming. But the section leaves no doubt that Joseph was a true prophet. He knew by revelation the nature of the American Civil War long before it came to pass. Elder Neal A. Maxwell wrote: "The Prophet Joseph and the revelations confirm that God lives in an 'eternal now,' where the past, present, and future are continually before Him. He is not constrained by the perspectives of time as we are."[5]

Section 130 captures glimpses of the expansive Nauvoo teachings of Joseph Smith. In the last years of his life Joseph was teaching temple ordinances to selected Saints, but he related principles to the general membership. Some of section 130 is simply fascinating answers to questions of curious inquirers. But it is laced with temple teachings, including the eternal nature of social relationships, the exaltation of man in the image of God, the heavenly temple, eternal progression, and growth by degrees of knowledge or intelligence based on obedience to the laws of God.

Doctrine & Covenants 131

ORIGIN OF SECTION 131:1–4

Joseph Smith spent the evening of May 16, 1843, at the Ramus, Illinois, home of Benjamin Johnson and his wife, Melissa. They were dear friends, but Joseph was not there simply to socialize. Benjamin wrote that Joseph "called me and my wife to come and sit down, for he wished to marry us according to the law of the Lord." Benjamin thought Joseph was joking and protested in jest that he would not marry his wife again "unless she courted me."

"He chided my levity," Benjamin said of Joseph, "told me he was in earnest, and so it proved, for we stood up and were sealed by the Holy Spirit of Promise."[1] Using his secretary, William Clayton, as an example of one who had taken the step the Johnsons were taking, Joseph taught them the doctrines of exaltation through faithfulness to covenants sealed by sacred ordinances.

CONTENT OF SECTION 131:1–4

William Clayton, who kept Joseph's journal and thus the source of the content of Doctrine and Covenants 131, wrote that Joseph "put his hand on my knee and says 'your life is hid up with Christ in God, and so is many others.'" Joseph turned to Benjamin and said, speaking of Clayton, "Nothing but the unpardonable sin can prevent him from inheriting eternal glory for he is sealed up by the power of the priesthood unto eternal life having taken the step necessary for that purpose." Joseph introduces the doctrine in verses 1–4 that unless a marriage is sealed before the resurrection, it would not endure in the resurrection, and, as Clayton noted, "they will not have children in the resurrection." Joseph warns the Johnsons not to commit the unpardonable sin against the Holy Ghost or of shedding innocent blood, and he expresses his deepest desire to be sealed to his own Emma ere long. Joseph then taught the Johnsons the doctrine contained in verses 1–4.[2]

OUTCOMES OF SECTION 131:1–4

There are many, many descendants of the Johnsons today, and there will be forever. But they are only the beginning of the beneficiaries of the knowledge contained in Doctrine and Covenants 131:1–4. Motivated by these truths, millions of couples have since been sealed, including Joseph and Emma Smith. Those who keep their covenants will, like the Claytons, the Johnsons, and the Smiths, will be sealed to eternal life by the power of the priesthood.

ORIGIN OF SECTION 131:5–6

The day after he sealed the Johnsons, Joseph preached a sermon on 2 Peter 1 about making one's eternal destination sure and included the information recorded now in Doctrine and Covenants 131:5–6.

CONTENT OF SECTION 131:5–6

William Clayton wrote that Joseph taught "that knowledge is power and the man who has the most knowledge has the greatest power. Also that salvation means a man's being placed beyond the powers of all his enemies. He said the more sure word of prophecy meant, a man's knowing that he was sealed up unto eternal life by revelation and the spirit of prophecy through the power of the Holy priesthood. He also showed that it was impossible for a man to be saved in ignorance."[3]

In speaking of *knowledge* and *ignorance* Joseph meant that unless we know for ourselves the fulness of temple ordinances and their promised blessings, we are not yet endowed with power over all enemies, including death, both spiritual and physical.

He had taught the same principle the preceding Sunday. He tried to help the Saints understand the difference between having a testimony that one *could be* saved if they obeyed the gospel and gaining the testimony that one *has been* saved because they obeyed the gospel. Step one is to gain a testimony of Christ and the possibility of salvation, Joseph taught. But that was just the beginning of the quest for knowledge of God, which to Joseph was the equivalent of power over sin and death. "They would then want that more sure word of Prophecy that they were sealed in the heavens & had the promise of eternal life in the Kingdom of God," Joseph taught. This is what he called *knowledge*, which is what he meant in section 131— and what the Lord meant all the way back in section 84:19–24.[4]

OUTCOMES OF SECTION 131:5–6

Doctrine and Covenants 131:5–6 leads willing Saints to the knowledge of God, the certainty of a future exaltation by virtue of sacred covenants sealed by priesthood. Ignorance of the knowledge of God leads to a less certain, or at least less celestial, future. One wants to be more sure in what the Prophet Joseph Smith called "matters that involve eternal consequences."[5]

ORIGIN, CONTENT, AND OUTCOMES OF SECTION 131:7–8

Samuel Prior, a Methodist, had listened to Joseph's sermon on 2 Peter 1 and come away unexpectedly impressed. Joseph returned the gesture in the evening by listening to Prior's sermon. Afterward Joseph "arose and begged leave to differ from me in some few points of doctrine," wrote Prior, "and this he did mildly, politely, and affectingly; like one who was more desirous to disseminate truth and expose error, than to love the malicious triumph of debate over me."

Drawing on Doctrines and Covenants 93:33, Joseph noted that matter endures eternally and added verses 7–8 to section 131. "I was truly edified with his remarks," Prior noted, "and felt less prejudiced against the Mormons than ever." Joseph invited Prior to visit him in Nauvoo, which he did.[6]

Doctrine & Covenants 132

ORIGIN

Doctrine and Covenants 132 was not written until July 1843, but parts of it were certainly revealed long before then. It answers two questions Joseph had about the Bible, one from the Old Testament, the other from the New. Joseph frequently asked the Lord questions as he revised the Bible, and it seems likely that Joseph had years earlier received some of section 132 in answer to the question the Lord restates in verse 1 about His rationale for the seemingly adulterous yet biblical practice of polygyny—simultaneously having more than one wife—by His servants Abraham, Isaac, Jacob, and others. The New Testament question comes from Matthew 22:30, Jesus' teaching that "in the resurrection they neither marry, nor are given in marriage, but are as the angels of God in heaven."

The answer to the New Testament question was wonderful news. But the answer to the Old Testament question was potentially scandalous. It was more than Joseph had anticipated. Though he began to obey it within a few years, he did not write the revelation on eternal marriage, including the practice of plural marriage, until events in the summer of 1843 persuaded him to do so.

The Book of Mormon forbade plural marriage unless the Lord commanded otherwise (Jacob 2:27–30). The revelations Joseph had received declared adultery an abomination and promised punishment. "With these prohibitions emblazoned in his own revelations, Joseph was torn by the command to take plural wives. What about the curses and the destruction promised adulterers? What about the heart of his tender wife?"[1] It tells us something about Joseph's certainty of the command that he acted on the revealed instructions. Joseph Smith entered a plural marriage in the 1830s, though it did not last. Then, between early 1841 and the fall of 1843, Joseph was sealed to approximately thirty women. As historian Richard Bushman observed, "What drove [Joseph Smith] to a practice that put his life and his work in jeopardy, not to mention his relationship with Emma?"[2]

Joseph's critics assume they know the answers to these questions. But their assumptions do not match up well with the historical Joseph. He acted on the Lord's commands to him, inviting opposition, ostracism, persecution, beatings, mockery in the press, imprisonment, extradition, and finally murder. The one commandment Joseph did not throw himself headlong into obeying was taking plural wives. Uncharacteristically reluctant, Joseph resisted for years and then waited several more years before trying again.[3] The Lord evidently gave Joseph an ultimatum he had no doubts about. The revelation of the new and everlasting covenant of marriage required an Abrahamic test, which for Joseph and Emma and other members of the Church was plural marriage. Helen Kimball, who became one of Joseph's plural wives, testified that "Joseph said that the practice of this principle would be the hardest trial the Saints would ever have to test their faith."[4]

Joseph knew and followed section 132 carefully. Two facts that may disturb some are that Joseph was sealed to women who were already married and that several of his plural marriages were performed without Emma's knowledge or consent. Section 132 gives precise instructions for both instances (vv. 41–45, 64–65). Joseph followed these as best he could.

It is clear from the historical record that Joseph married plural wives "to create a network of related wives, children, and kinsmen that would endure into the eternities. The revelation on marriage promised Joseph an 'hundred fold in this world, of fathers and mothers, brothers and sisters, houses and lands, wives and children, and crowns of eternal lives in the eternal worlds.' Like Abraham of old, Joseph yearned for familial plentitude."[5] He wanted to obey the commandment of the Lord, even as Abraham had.

Revelation governs and dictates the practice of plural marriage, not only generally but case by case. Indeed, even as the Lord exacts such extreme tests, he offers personal confirmation and an accompanying peace.

Joseph nearly always went through the father, uncle, or brother of a woman to ask for her hand in marriage, but in each documented case he promised the woman her own personal revelation to confirm what one of them, Zina Huntington, called "a greater sacrifice than to give my life." She wrote, "I searched the scripture & by humble prayer to my Heavenly Father I obtained a testimony for myself that God had required that order to be established in this church."[6]

Joseph's friend Benjamin Johnson described how Joseph taught him. Joseph visited Benjamin in Macedonia, Illinois. "Come Br. Bennie," Joseph said, "let us have a walk." Benjamin wrote, "I took his arm and he led the way into . . . the woods. . . . and here, we sat down upon a log he began to tell me that the Lord had revealed to him that plural or patriarchal marriage was according to his law; and that the Lord had not only revealed it to him but had commanded him to obey it; that he was required to take other wives; that he wanted my Sister Almira for one of them, and wished me to talk to her upon the subject. If a thunderbolt had fallen at my feet I could hardly have been more shocked or amazed. He saw the struggle in my mind and went on to explain. But the shock was too great for me [to] comprehend anything, and in almost an agony of feeling I looked him square in the eye, and said, while my heart gushed up before him, 'Brother Joseph, this is all new to me; it may be true,—you know, but I do not, to my education it is all wrong; but I am going, with the help of the Lord to do just what you say, with this promise to you—That if ever I know you do this to degrade my sister I will kill you, as the Lord lives.' He looked at me, oh, so calmly, and said, 'Br. Benjamin, you will never see that day, but you shall see the day you will know it is true." Joseph's prophecy was fulfilled as Benjamin acted in faith. He engaged his sister in a private conversation. Trembling, hardly knowing what to say, "I opened my mouth and my heart opened to the light of the Lord, my tongue was loosened and I was filled with the Holy Ghost. I preached a sermon that forever converted me and her also."[7]

Joseph proposed a plural marriage to Lucy Walker in 1842 with the words, "I have a message for you. I have been commanded of God to take another wife, and you are the woman." She wrote, "My astonishment knew no bounds. This announcement was indeed a thunderbolt to me. He asked me if I believed him to be a Prophet of God. 'Most assuredly I do' I replied. He fully explained to me the principle of plural . . . marriage. Said this principle was again to be restored for the benefit of the human family. That it would prove an everlasting blessing to my father's house, and form a chain that could never be broken, worlds without end. 'What have you to say?' he said. 'If you will pray sincerely for light and understanding in relation thereto, you shall receive a testimony of the correctness of these principles.'" Lucy wrote of her great struggle with the predicament. "I thought I prayed sincerely but was so unwilling to consider the matter favorably that I fear I did not pray in faith for light." She went through excruciating bouts of what she called "darkness," praying, like Christ, "Oh let this bitter cup pass. And thus I prayed in the agony of my soul." When Joseph gave Lucy a date by which she had to make a decision, she responded, "'although you are a Prophet of God, you could not induce me to take a step of so great importance unless I knew that God approved my course.'" Joseph "walked across the room, returned and stood before me with the most beautiful expression of countenance and said 'God Almighty bless you. You shall have a manifestation of the will of God concerning you; a testimony that you can never deny. I will tell you what it shall be. It shall be that peace and joy that you never knew.'" Lucy "prayed for these words to be fulfilled. It was near dawn after another sleepless night. While on my knees in fervent supplication, my room became filled with a holy influence. To me it was a comparison like the brilliant sunshine bursting through the darkest cloud. The words of the Prophet were indeed fulfilled. My soul was filled with a calm sweet peace that I never knew. Supreme happiness took possession of my whole being and I received a powerful and irresistible testimony."[8]

Helen Kimball wrote about the Abrahamic test her father, Heber, and her mother, Vilate, endured well when Joseph commanded Heber to take a plural wife without disclosing it to Vilate. Heber became sick and overwhelmed with anxiety. "Finally . . . his misery became so unbearable that it was impossible to control his feelings. He became sick in body, but his mental wretchedness was too great to allow of his retiring at night, and instead of going to bed he would walk the floor; and the agony of his mind was so terrible that he would wring his hands and weep, beseeching the

Lord with his whole soul to be merciful and reveal to his wife the cause of his great sorrow, for he himself could not break his vow of secrecy. His anguish and my mother's were indescribable and when unable to endure it longer, she retired to her room, where with a broken and contrite heart, she poured out her grief to [God]." Helen described her mother's revelation and its comforting, assuring power. "She returned to my father, saying, Heber, what you have kept from me the Lord has shown me. She related the scene to me and to many others, and told me she never saw so happy a man as father was, when she described the vision and told him she was satisfied and knew it was from God."[9]

Even so it was not easy to participate in plural marriages. Joseph's wife Emma understandably vacillated between accepting and resenting the practice. She and Joseph spent many hours discussing and struggling with the issues leading up to the July 12, 1843, writing of section 132. In those weeks Joseph had the undesirable task of convincing the two people closest to him—Emma and Hyrum, his brother—of the legitimacy of the revelation. Hyrum did not believe the first rumors he heard about the practice. He publicly spoke out against the idea of plural marriage but decided that he "needed to see Joseph about it, and if Joseph had a revelation on the subject, he would believe it."[10] Hyrum's heart softened as Joseph explained that he could be sealed to his deceased wife, Jerusha, as well as his living wife, Mary, who was subsequently sealed to Hyrum and also served as proxy for Jerusha.

At times Emma worked up the will to consent to some of the sealings, but then her will failed and her feelings overwhelmed her. She had forsaken her parents and siblings to marry and follow Joseph. She believed in him and had made monumental sacrifices for her faith. But this one was Abrahamic. All she had was Joseph, and that was enough to compensate for all she had laid aside, but now she was being asked to share him. She would not do it willingly, at least not consistently. During a period of her willingness, however, in May 1843 she and Joseph were sealed. By July Emma was struggling to be reconciled to the revelation, and Joseph decided to commit it to writing. Joseph and Hyrum counseled about what to do for her and decided to write the revelation and see if it would help. William Clayton, Joseph's secretary, wrote the revelation as Joseph dictated, with Hyrum present, in Joseph's upstairs office in his Nauvoo store. It took nearly three hours and ten pages to write, after which Clayton read it back to Joseph for accuracy. Hyrum optimistically took it to Emma, who rejected it. Clayton confided to his journal that Joseph "appears much troubled about E[mma]."[11]

By September Emma was again reconciled to the revelation, and she and Joseph received the crowning ordinances of exaltation that Doctrine and Covenants 132 describes.[12] Joseph was determined that if he was going to break Emma's heart to obey a commandment of the Lord, he would not lose her eternally. Despite their difficulties he was heard to say, "You must never speak evil of Emma."[13]

CONTENT

Doctrine and Covenants 132 is an extraordinarily complicated text. Not only does it intertwine the answers to two questions but it is the culmination of the Restoration, the most exalted of the exaltation revelations (see D&C 76; 84; 88; 93; 131). It sets forth gospel fulness in somewhat cryptic terms, as if some of its pearls were too precious to be cast more publicly. Moreover, though it contains much that was revealed to Joseph earlier, the actual text of section 132 was determined by events in the summer of 1843, including Emma's opposition to Joseph's plural marriages, an otherwise unknown test the Lord gave her, and her concerns about the economic security of herself and her children.

Section 132 begins by acknowledging Joseph's question about the polygynous relationships of Old Testament patriarchs, but in verse 4 it leaves that ultimately tangential question to set forth a fundamental premise: "For behold, I reveal unto you a new and an everlasting covenant." One must enter this covenant to obtain a fulness of God's glory, as verses 4–6 explain, but this covenant is not *plural* marriage. It is marriage according to the law of God—the law set forth in verses 7–8 and again in verses 15–21. In other words, the Lord leaves the discussion of plural marriage at verse 4 and does not return to it specifically again until verse 29. Meanwhile, he answers the question about whether there will be marriage after the resurrection and on what terms.

The answer, gloriously, is yes, and the terms and conditions are very specific. They are set forth in verse 7 in a three-step process where the word *and* connects the steps. It is one long *if-then* statement. It is a covenant. It says that any kind of marriage agreement is temporary unless a covenant is "made and entered into" as the first step, "sealed by the Holy Spirit of promise" as the second step, and "that too most holy, by revelation and commandment through the medium of mine anointed," the one man on earth at a time authorized to confirm the sealing. All three steps are required. "All contracts that are not made unto this end have an end when men are dead" (v. 7). That is the Lord's law. This world's legal codes do not endure past death. Marriages that do not meet these conditions do not endure eternally. People who desire to be married forever will sooner or later participate in the three steps of the new and everlasting covenant. Otherwise they will remain "separately and singly, without exaltation, in their saved condition, to all eternity" (v. 17).

Verses 19–20 restate the three-step process with even greater detail than verse 7, explicitly using the words *if* and *then* as they describe the terms and conditions of exaltation. Step 1: "*If* a man marry a wife by my word, which is my law, and by the new and everlasting covenant . . ." Step 2: "and it is sealed unto them by the Holy Spirit of promise," meaning the Holy Ghost in his role as verifier of faithfulness. Step 3: "and it shall be said unto them—Ye shall come forth in the first resurrection; and if it be after the first resurrection, in the next resurrection; and shall inherit thrones, kingdoms, principalities, and powers, dominions, all heights and depths—*then* shall it be written in the Lamb's Book of Life" that if the marriage partners do not commit the unpardonable sin explained best in verse 27, "it shall be done unto them in all things whatsoever my servant hath put upon them, in time, and through all eternity; and shall be of full force when they are out of the world; and they shall pass by the angels, and the gods, which are set there, to their exaltation and glory in all things, as hath been sealed upon their heads, which glory shall be a fulness and a continuation of the seeds forever and ever. Then shall they be gods, because they have no end" (vv. 19–20; emphasis added). Verses 21–28 restate the law and the unpardonable sin— "blasphemy against the Holy Ghost . . . in that ye commit murder wherein ye shed innocent blood, and assent unto my [Christ's] death after ye have received my new and everlasting covenant" (v. 27).

Having established the legal foundation of exaltation, the Lord returns in verse 29 to Joseph's concerns about plural marriage and apparent adultery, though plurality of wives is not addressed until verse 34. Before that the Lord says more about exaltation. The first premise is that Abraham received and obeyed revelation and is now exalted (v. 29). The second is that God promised him an endless posterity (v. 30). The third is that Joseph has the same promise. The last is that Joseph should do as Abraham did—that is, receive and obey revelation, whatever it may be (vv. 31–32).

Beginning in verse 34, the Lord justifies plural marriage in cases where he commands it. Indeed, the justification is that he commands it. If he does not command it, it is not justified. The Lord illustrates, citing David as one who entered plural marriage without justification and lost his exaltation as a result.

But isn't plural marriage adulterous, Joseph wonders? No, the Lord answers, very specifically, in verses 41–44 and 58–63. Adulterers will be destroyed. Will their adulterous choices ruin their innocent partner's potential for exaltation? No, the Lord explains in verse 44, where he describes the power Joseph has to seal the innocent wife of an adulterous husband to another man, including as a plural wife. This is part of the sealing power, as explained in verses 44–48.

Because of Joseph's willingness to sacrifice his life, in verse 49 the Lord seals him to exaltation, in verse 50 forgives his sins, and then promises to help him escape the awful predicament the commandment about plural marriage has put him in. Then the Lord addresses Emma's situation in verse 51 before speaking directly to her beginning in verse 52. It is hard doctrine to hear. The Lord requires Emma to receive Joseph's plural wives, to cleave to him, to "abide this commandment" (vv. 54, 55), and to obey the "law of Sarah," Abraham's wife, as set forth in verses 64–65, meaning that having been taught the doctrine, Emma is supposed to facilitate Joseph in taking plural wives as Sarah did Abraham.

OUTCOMES

Doctrine and Covenants 132 resulted in an Abrahamic test. "Plural marriage was the most difficult trial of 1843," wrote historian Richard Bushman, and he could just as accurately have said of Joseph and Emma's life and of the lives of many Latter-day Saints today.[14] It is hard to imagine a more wrenching test for Joseph, and it was incomparably difficult for Emma. The revelation forced them—and us—to find out whether we trust the God who gave it. That would not be an Abrahamic test if the circumstances were simple and made sense, as if the gospel could be summed up as "exaltation made effortless." The God of Abraham is all for all. Indeed, Abraham heard him saying that his plan for his children was to "prove them herewith, to see if they will do all things whatsoever the Lord their God shall command them" (Abraham 3:25). He asks all and gives everything, including his Only Begotten Son. He asked Joseph to accept plural marriage. He asked Emma to consent to it, even to sustain it, when it seemed to her more repugnant than anything else she could imagine.

Section 132 leads us to the conclusion that God requires all of our hearts first and foremost before he finishes the work of sealing them to each other and exalting them forever. The same revelation that requires such an extreme sacrifice of Emma, after all, sets forth the terms and conditions on which she will be exalted with Joseph. It seems that one of the main points of section 132 is to assure Joseph that he and Emma will be exalted together, that despite the wedge plural marriage has driven between them, the Lord will weld them eternally. Joseph had specifically prayed in the Kirtland Temple that Emma and their children would be exalted (D&C 109:68–69).

That would not require an exception to the law, for the law of exaltation is set forth in Doctrine and Covenants 132:7, 19–20, and the historical record shows that Joseph and Emma met its terms and conditions precisely. They made and entered the covenant on May 28, 1843, and received the confirming ordinance section 132 refers to as "most holy" on September 28, 1843 (v. 7).[15] Though neither Joseph nor Emma was flawless after meeting the conditions on which the Lord will exalt them, neither committed the unpardonable sin verse 27 describes. Emma was never excommunicated, her ordinances never voided. She gave her children faith in the Book of Mormon but blamed Brigham Young for plural marriage. It seems as if the Lord spoke verse 26 specifically to set Joseph's mind at ease about Emma's eternal destiny. Perhaps that knowledge was the "escape" Joseph needed in order to make the extreme "sacrifices" for plural marriage that contributed to his death (v. 50; see D&C 135).

As they parted for the last time on earth, Emma asked Joseph for a blessing. He was unable to minister to her then but bade her write the desires of her heart and he would seal it. She wrote of her desire "to honor and respect my husband as my head, ever to live in his confidence and by acting in unison with him retain the place which God has given me by his side."[16] She wrote, in other words, that she wanted the blessings promised to her in section 132 and that she desired to obey its challenging commands. The next time Emma saw Joseph he had been shot to death. But section 132 makes that a small matter, for it promises them, and all others who make and keep the same covenants, "Ye shall come forth in the first resurrection; and if it be after the first resurrection, in the next resurrection; and shall inherit thrones, kingdoms, principalities, and powers, dominions, all heights and depths" (v. 19). Those last three words sum up section 132, the highest and deepest of Joseph's revelations. Perhaps we are to understand that if we never plumb the depths, we will never ascend to the heights.

Doctrine & Covenants 133

ORIGIN

The November 1831 conference at Hiram, Ohio, sustained the decision to publish ten thousand copies of Joseph's revelations under the title of A Book of Commandments for the Government of the Church of Christ. Joseph began to edit the revelations, and Oliver Cowdery planned to take them to Independence, Missouri, for publication by William W. Phelps on the Church's press. Joseph's history says that "at this time there were many things which the elders desired to know relative to preaching the gospel to the inhabitants of the earth, and concerning the gathering: and, in order to walk by the true light, and be instructed from on high, on the 3d of November 1831 I inquired of the Lord and received the following revelation, which . . . has since been added to the Book of Doctrine and Covenants, and called the Appendix."[1] It is recorded now in Doctrine and Covenants 133.

CONTENT

Doctrine and Covenants 133 continues and even escalates the apocalyptic tone of section 1. Echoing themes of the Apocalypse, the Revelation of John, which concludes the Bible by prophesying a tumultuous future of merciful triumph for the repentant sealed believers and unavoidable justice for the unrepentant damned, section 133 tells readers what they should have learned from the Doctrine and Covenants. It announces that Christ will come soon, dramatically. He will come to judge all that forget God, including the ungodly Latter-day Saints. So the Saints should prepare for his coming by sanctifying their lives and becoming Zion. "Go ye out from Babylon," the Lord says again and again, reinforcing the dualistic typology of Zion versus Babylon that he used to frame the entire Doctrine and Covenants. Zion will be rescued when the Lord comes. Babylon will be destroyed. "Hearken and hear, O ye inhabitants of the earth. Listen, ye elders of my church together, and hear the voice of the Lord; for he calleth upon all men, and he commandeth all men everywhere to repent" (v. 16). The angels have already been sent to announce that the hour of his coming nears. Indeed, such ministering angels ushered in the Restoration. As section 133 explains, messengers commit the gospel to mortal prophets, who offer it to "some," who then go to "many" until "this gospel shall be preached unto every nation, and kindred, and tongue, and people" (vv. 36–37). Then the Lord answers the prayers of his people, who have long pled, "O that thou wouldst rend the heavens, that thou wouldst come down, that the mountains might flow down at thy presence" (v. 40). He will answer "as the melting fire that burneth, and as the fire which causeth the waters to boil" (v. 41). He comes soon to sanctify the repentant and to burn the unrepentant.

So how does the revelation answer the elders' questions about preaching the gospel and gathering Israel? With a distinctively Latter-day Saint approach. First, it emphasizes, the Saints must get themselves out of Babylon, and the only alternative the revelation envisions is to "flee unto Zion" (v. 12). Second, send the elders to rescue any who will repent. Send them first to the Gentiles and then to the Jews. They should "thrash the nations by the power of his Spirit" (v. 59) and invite those who repent to be endowed with priesthood power and the blessings promised to the house of Israel. That's why the revelations were given and why they are to be published to all mankind. "And unto him that repenteth and sanctifieth himself before the Lord shall be given eternal life. And upon them that hearken not to the voice of the Lord shall be fulfilled that which was written by the prophet Moses, that they should be cut off from among the people" (vv. 62–63).

OUTCOMES

Doctrine and Covenants 133 answers the elders' questions about preaching the gospel and gathering lost Israel. Other revelations give much more detailed instructions about how to do those things. This one emphasizes why and when. To a fledgling group of fallible Latter-day Saints gathered in a private home, it sets forth an audacious scope of covering the globe with the restored gospel. It reiterates Christ's great commission to take the gospel to every creature so that each can decide whether to repent or not. Moreover, there is no time to lose. The revelation's urgent tone emphasizes that Christ soon comes to judge an apostate world—Babylon. What results from this revelation? That small group of Latter-day Saints has grown exponentially and sent tens of thousands of its sons and daughters to the ends of the earth to preach the gospel and gather scattered Israel to Zion in anticipation of the Lord's second coming. It would be hard to overstate the motivating power of sections like 133. It is, as one early Saint declared, "fraught with so much heavenly intelligence."[2]

Doctrine & Covenants 134

ORIGIN

Mormonism has been dubbed the American religion, but in the beginning it struck its enemies as anything but American. Direct revelations to a prophet in which Christ reserved to himself ultimate executive, legislative, and judicial power seemed undemocratic to the Saints' neighbors.[1] Moreover, controversial statements made in a Church newspaper by editor William W. Phelps demanded that the Church clarify its position relative to slavery.[2]

A general assembly of priesthood leaders convened in Kirtland, Ohio, on August 17, 1835, to listen to Oliver Cowdery and Sidney Rigdon present the Doctrine and Covenants for their approval. Oliver introduced the book and its contents to the assembled councils, after which the priesthood leaders unanimously testified of their satisfaction with the work. Then Oliver Cowdery read a statement entitled "Of Governments and Laws in General," which is probably primarily if not exclusively the product of his mind and pen. The assembly "accepted and adopted" it for inclusion also, and thus section 134, though not a revelation, became canonized as part of the Doctrine and Covenants.[3]

CONTENT

Doctrine and Covenants 134 mixes republican principles of constitutional government and individual liberties, emphatically including the right of religious conscience, with the Church's concern for its ecclesiastical rights. Nothing in it was new or objectionable to Joseph. It informs a misled and sometimes hostile public that the Church is in harmony with mainstream American values at the time of its publication. It distances the Church from parties or causes other than sharing the gospel.

OUTCOMES

Joseph was in Michigan when the general assembly made these decisions. He did not write Doctrine and Covenants 134, but he endorsed it in April 1836.[4] The principles in section 134 continue to guide the Church's actions regarding political questions and controversies. The principles in verses 4–6 are more concisely expressed in Articles of Faith 1:11–12.

Doctrine & Covenants 135

ORIGIN

Unable to persuade government officials to redress the wrongs committed against the Latter-day Saints in Missouri, Joseph Smith ran for the office of president of the United States. His campaign platform circulated far and wide in the early months of 1844. Dozens of campaigning missionaries stumped across the country. "There is not a nation or dynasty, now occupying the earth, which acknowledges Almighty God as their lawgiver," Joseph declared. "I go emphatically, virtuously, and humanely for a THEO-DEMOCRACY, where God and the people hold the power to conduct the affairs of men in righteousness."[1] In Nauvoo, meanwhile, Joseph continued to offer the temple ordinances to a few prepared Saints, and in March he gave the apostles the priesthood keys to perform the ordinances and a commission to carry on after his death. He also secretly practiced plural marriage.

Joseph's growing political power ignited deep-seated resentment against him among non-Mormons, and a faction of alienated Mormons opposed the revelation on plural marriage. Apostates published a dissenting paper, the *Expositor,* on June 7, that publicized Joseph's private life and attacked his religious and political leadership. As mayor, Joseph led the Nauvoo city council to a decision to destroy the press as a public nuisance. The action seemed despotic to antagonists inside and outside of Nauvoo, and it gave Joseph's enemies an opportunity to denounce and prosecute him. As a result, Illinois governor Thomas Ford summoned Joseph to Carthage, the Hancock County seat, to answer charges of inciting a riot. Joseph appeared at the hearing and "entered into recognizance," promising to appear for trial at the next term of the circuit court. But a conspiracy was afoot, and before he could return to Nauvoo, Joseph and his brother Hyrum "were immediately arrested again on a charge of Treason against the state of Illinois." On that pretense they were "committed to Jail to await their examination," but many people knew they were jailed to facilitate their murders. There would be no trial, only a massacre.[2] Governor Ford promised to protect them, but the militiamen he provided as protectors were themselves complicit with the lynch mob who shot Joseph and Hyrum in the heat of June 27, 1844. It was "a deliberate political assassination, committed or condoned by some of the leading citizens in Hancock County."[3]

Apostles John Taylor and Willard Richards were voluntarily with Joseph and Hyrum in jail that day. They survived as witnesses of the restored gospel of Jesus Christ, of the Prophet Joseph Smith, who restored it, and of his brutal martyrdom. Their witness is declared in Doctrine and Covenants 135.

CONTENT

Doctrine and Covenants 135 is a eulogy of the Prophet and an indictment of the state and nation that allowed him and his brother to be slain. As such, its tone is a rich mixture of reverence and disdain, praise and contempt. Attributed to John Taylor, who was himself shot repeatedly in the massacre, the document has an apostolic air. It declares a witness in certain terms. It declares Joseph Smith's significance to mankind, his translation of the Book of Mormon and spreading of the gospel, his receipt of revelations, gathering of Israel, founding of Nauvoo, and, with Hyrum, the sealing of his testimony with the ultimate sacrifice of his life. Though critics have knowingly manipulated the language of verse 3 to make it sound as if Latter-day Saints value Joseph Smith more than Jesus Christ, the text does not say that, nor do Latter-day Saints believe it. Rather, they praise Joseph Smith because he revealed Jesus Christ, which no one had done for more than a millennium before him. Section 135 testifies that Joseph and Hyrum died innocent and that their deaths put their testaments in full force. It testifies that the Lord will avenge their deaths and that the honest hearted in all nations will be touched by their testimony of Jesus Christ.

OUTCOMES

Doctrine and Covenants 135 emphasizes the enduring significance of Joseph Smith and his testimony. Joseph regarded himself as "obscure," a "boy of no consequence" (Joseph Smith–History 1:22), but at age seventeen he received from an angel the improbable news that "my name should be had for good and evil among all nations" (Joseph Smith–History 1:33). In his own lifetime his name became known for good and evil in Missouri, in Illinois, in the United States, and now in the world. However unlikely, Moroni's prophecy continues to be fulfilled. Bostonian Josiah Quincy visited Joseph shortly before he went to Carthage. Quincy wrote that Joseph Smith was "born in the lowest ranks of poverty" and came of age "without book-learning and with the homeliest of all human names," and that by the end of his shortened life he had become "a power on earth."[4]

It is not remarkable that a flawed Joseph sought forgiveness in the Sacred Grove and on his knees at his bedside, nor that he had to grow into his demanding calling, nor that he often felt frustrated at both himself and the Saints, nor that his testimony deeply touched the hearts of some and antagonized others, nor that it continues to do so. The remarkable thing about Joseph Smith, as section 135 emphasizes, is what he did. Who else has brought forth the equivalent of the Book of Mormon or the Doctrine and Covenants? Who else restored the fulness of the gospel of Jesus Christ? He "left a fame and name that cannot be slain" (D&C 135:3). In every way he gave his life for the Lord's work. And what a life it was! Josiah Quincy, who was no fan of Joseph's, nevertheless recognized his enduring significance. "Fanatics and imposters are living and dying every day," Quincy wrote, "and their memory is buried with them; but the wonderful influence which this founder of a religion exerted and still exerts throws him into relief before us, not as a rogue to be criminated, but as a phenomenon to be explained. The most vital questions Americans are asking each other today have to do with this man and what he has left us."[5]

That is Joseph Smith's significance and his appeal: he revealed the answers to the ultimate questions Why am I here? Where did I come from? Where am I going? Is there purpose in life? What is the nature of the Fall?

Are individuals accountable agents or are their actions predetermined? What is the nature of Christ's atonement? What about those who do not hear the gospel in mortality? And perhaps above all, what is the nature of God? If "I am so fortunate as to comprehend and explain" that, Joseph taught a few weeks before his violent death, then "never lift your voice against the servants of God again."[6] Joseph answered these questions as a witness. He had beheld angels, translated scripture by the power of God, received visions and revelations. He knew God and Christ. He thus died as a testator—a witness—and Doctrine and Covenants 135 declares that though a testator can be killed, his testimony endures forever.

Doctrine & Covenants 136

ORIGIN

Joseph gathered most of the apostles three months before his death and said, "It may be that my enemies will kill me, and in case they should, and the keys and power which rest on me not be imparted to you, they will be lost from the earth; but if I can only succeed in placing them upon your heads, then let me fall a victim to murderous hands if God will suffer it, and I can go with all pleasure and satisfaction, knowing that my work is done, and the foundation laid on which the kingdom of God is to be reared in this dispensation of the fullness of times. Upon the shoulders of the Twelve must the responsibility of leading this church hence forth rest until you shall appoint others to succeed you. Your enemies cannot kill you all at once, and should any of you be killed, you can lay your hands upon others and fill up your quorum. Thus can this power and these keys be perpetuated in the Earth." Joseph then began to talk about the "sore trials await you" as if foreshadowing his own imminent death. "After they have killed you," he said, "they can harm you no more. Should you have to walk right into danger and the jaws of death, fear no evil; Jesus Christ has died before you."[1]

Joseph and his brother Hyrum then confirmed the ordinations of each of the apostles who were present, and Joseph gave them a final charge. "I roll the burthen and responsibility of leading this church off from my shoulders on to yours," he declared. "Now, round up your shoulders and stand under it like men; for the Lord is going to let me rest."[2]

As president of the Quorum of the Twelve Apostles, Brigham Young explained these principles to the Saints on August 8, 1844. Many, including

Martha Tuttle Gardner, received a confirming witness from the Lord. She testified that Brigham Young "told the people that although Joseph was dead, Joseph had left behind the keys of the Kingdom and had conferred the same power & authority that he himself possessed upon the Twelve Apostles and the Church would not be left without a leader and a guide. Truly the mantle of Joseph had fallen upon Brigham and he spoke with power even to the convincing of the Saints, assuring them they had nothing to worry about as all would be well if they would hearken to the Word of God & the council of his servants & keep his commandments." Martha had written reverently of witnessing the Prophet Joseph Smith and she now confidently transferred that designation to "the Prophet Brigham Young." She wrote that he "had the Nauvoo Temple finished" and endowed her with power there early in 1845. Then, under Brigham's leadership, she and many other Saints fled Nauvoo for peace and safety somewhere in the West.[3]

President Young led them across Iowa, and they camped for the winter on the banks of the Missouri River. There, in a January 1847 council meeting, the prophet Brigham Young asked the Lord to reveal "the best manner of organizing companies for emigration." He answered with Doctrine and Covenants 136, and "President Young commenced to give the Word and Will of God concerning the emigration of the Saints."[4]

Brigham Young.

CONTENT

Doctrine and Covenants 136 is concerned with three basic issues: "governing authority, camp organization," and individual behavior.[5]

The key words in the early verses of section 136 are *organized* and *covenant*. The Saints were to be organized into companies "under the direction of the Twelve Apostles" (v. 3). "And this shall be our covenant—that we will walk in all the ordinances of the Lord" (v. 4). Like Martha Gardner, hundreds of them had recently made sacred covenants as they received the ordinances of the temple in Nauvoo. They had covenanted to consecrate their lives to Zion. Section 136 tells them how to do so. It reiterates the principles of consecration that pervade so many of Joseph Smith's revelations.

The first principle is agency. Section 136 tells the Saints how to act relative to organization, preparation, property, contention, alcohol, fear, sorrow, ignorance, and the commandments not to covet or take the Lord's name in vain. The Lord prescribes specific behaviors for each of these.

The next principle is stewardship. Agents act upon stewardships, or what the Lord gives them to act upon. "Thou shalt be diligent in preserving what thou hast," he commands in verse 27, "that thou mayest be a wise steward; for it is the free gift of the Lord thy God, and thou art his steward." Section 136 tells the Saints how to act relative to stewardships that include draft animals, seeds, farming tools, widows, orphans, the families of the men who have joined the United States Army, houses, fields, and other Saints who will follow in later waves of migration. He adds instructions for the use of "influence and property" (v. 10) and even for borrowed and lost property.

The last principle of consecration is accountability. Verse 19 declares the consequence of failing to keep one's covenant to walk in the ordinances of the Lord: "And if any man shall seek to build up himself, and seeketh not my counsel, he shall have no *power,* and his folly shall be made manifest" (emphasis added), suggesting that a person's endowment of power is dependent on keeping the covenants made in the temple.

The motif of pilgrims in search of a promised land, of exodus as a sanctifying precondition to finding and becoming Zion, is common in scripture, and it is the backbone of section 136. It casts the Saints as a modern "Camp of Israel" (v. 1) following "the God of Abraham and of Isaac and of Jacob" as they are led through the wilderness by a modern Moses in search of a promised land (v. 21). They are wanderers, exiles even from the United States, upon which the Lord prophesies an imminent punishment for rejecting the Saints' testimony and killing the prophets "that were sent unto them" (v. 36). In these ways section 136 includes the Latter-day Saints with all the faithful of past dispensations, those whom section 45 describes as "pilgrims on the earth" who wandered in search of Zion and "obtained a promise that they should find it" (D&C 45:13–14).

Finally, section 136 explains Joseph Smith's martyrdom from the Lord's perspective. "Many have marveled because of his death," the Lord states, "but it was needful that he should seal his testimony with his blood, that he might be honored and the wicked might be condemned" (v. 39). From the Lord's vantage point, allowing Joseph to die as a testator left an enduring witness of His name even as it delivered the Saints, including Joseph, from their enemies (v. 40).

The revelation ends with a poetic covenant in verse 42, promising deliverance on the condition that the Saints choose to diligently keep his commandments.

OUTCOMES

Doctrine and Covenants 136 resulted in the best organized and executed overland emigration in American history. "It not only defined the authority of the exodus but also laid down a blueprint for action."[6] Even so, it may be more important for its other accomplishments. The Saints who followed Brigham Young, who were willing to see in him their Prophet, did so at great personal sacrifice and tremendous faith. Section 136 rewarded them. It confirmed the correctness of their choice. Others had and some still were outspokenly contending against Brigham Young when section 136 was received. "For a people accustomed to prophetic utterances—but who had been driven out of their homes after seeing their leaders martyred and who were witnessing opposing claimants from all sides seeking to lead the Church—the very fact that God would speak again brought redemption and vindication."[7] Apostle Heber C. Kimball noted in his journal that section 136 was the first revelation "penned since Joseph was killed. . . . The Lord has given it through the President for the good of this people as they are traveling to the west."[8] Jedediah Grant voiced what many Saints felt: "Since the death of Joseph, [I] have believed that the keys of revelation were in the Church. When I heard that [section 136] read I felt a light and joy and satisfied that the Holy Ghost had dictated the words within."[9]

Section 136 would sustain the Saints who had covenanted to "walk in all the ordinances of the Lord" up and over the Rocky Mountains as outcasts opposed by all kinds of influences. Joseph was gone, but the prophet Brigham Young would lead them onward according to the word and will of the Lord.

Doctrine & Covenants 137

ORIGIN

Joseph's older brother Alvin died painfully not long after Moroni appeared to Joseph and taught him of the Book of Mormon plates. Nearly twenty years later Joseph dictated an entry in the Book of the Law of the Lord, the blessing and record book he kept near the end of his life. "I remember well the pangs of sorrow that swelled my youthful bosom and almost burst my tender heart, when he died," Joseph said of Alvin. "He was the oldest, and the noblest of my father's family. He was one of the noblest of the sons of men."[1] Even so, at Alvin's funeral his mother's minister, Reverend Benjamin Stockton, "intimated very strongly that he had gone to hell, for Alvin was not a Church member." Joseph's father "did not like it."[2] He recognized what philosophers have called the "soteriological problem" of evil and others have termed a "scandal."[3] It is a dilemma between doctrines of salvation.

The problem seems to arise from three truths, any two of which can work together but not all three:

1. God desires the salvation of his children.

2. Salvation comes only through one's knowing acceptance of Christ's atonement.

3. Millions of God's children have lived and died without an opportunity to knowingly accept Christ's atonement.

Joseph translated the Book of Mormon, which clarified that unaccountable infants would not be damned, but it said nothing of accountable adults who died before accepting the gospel. He received the priesthood, restored the Church, worked to establish Zion, and built the temple in Kirtland, Ohio. But not until the temple was nearly finished did the Lord teach Joseph the solution to the problem of righteous accountable persons who die before accepting the gospel.

One evening Joseph met on the top floor of the nearly finished house of the Lord with the other members of the First Presidency, his father, who was the patriarch to the Church, Joseph's secretary, and the bishoprics from Missouri and Ohio. The brethren came to the meeting freshly bathed, symbolizing their efforts to repent and present themselves in the temple clean before the Lord. The First Presidency consecrated oil and then anointed and blessed Father Smith, who in turn anointed and blessed Joseph. Oliver Cowdery wrote that "the glorious scene is too great to be described. . . . I only say, that the heavens were opened to many, and great and marvelous things were shown." Bishop Edward Partridge affirmed that some of the brethren "saw visions & others were blessed with the outpouring of the Holy Ghost."[4]

Joseph was the only one present to describe in detail some of what he experienced. Doctrine and Covenants 137 is a passage from his journal entry for January 21, 1836.

CONTENT

The point of Doctrine and Covenants 137 is to teach Joseph the revelation in verses 7–10, but first the Lord shows Joseph a future celestial kingdom. Joseph sees the Father and the Son on their heavenly throne, Adam and Abraham, his own parents, and his brother Alvin. Joseph did not expect to see Alvin, for he had died before the restoration of the gospel and had never been baptized. The vision causes Joseph to marvel that Alvin could be an heir of celestial glory. The Lord speaks the answer not just for Alvin but for "all who have died without a knowledge of this gospel, who would have received it if they had been permitted to tarry" (v. 7). They will inherit celestial glory. Indeed, anyone who dies without knowing the gospel but who would have received it otherwise, will. Death is not a deadline that determines salvation, "for I, the Lord, will judge all men according to their works, according to the desire of their hearts" (v. 9).

OUTCOMES

Some of the greatest theological minds have wrestled with the problem of evil. Early Christian philosophers recognized the problem and were sure that Christ would somehow save all the righteous, but already the significance was lost of truths Peter and Paul had taught, leaving no certain answer to the question, "Shall those be wholly deprived of the kingdom of heaven who died before Christ's coming?"[5] Theologians scour the Bible for clues, acknowledging the problem and coming up with diverse solutions that tend to subtract or diminish one of the three truths. Perhaps God does not desire the salvation of all his children, some suggest. In the eighteenth century the great Jonathan Edwards longed to find a solution to the problem. One contemporary scholar finds in Edwards the seeds of a "dispositional soteriology," meaning a doctrine of salvation that requires only that one's disposition be redeemed by God through Christ. It does not require one to knowingly accept the Savior.[6] But John 3 declares otherwise, and thus the question persists, "What about those who never heard?"

The revealed, as compared to the philosophical, answer is not to subtract from the three known truths but to add one more that makes them all compatible and whole rather than problematic. That truth is contained in verses 8–9 of Doctrine and Covenants 137. "Thank God for Joseph Smith!" wrote David Paulsen, a philosopher who knows full well the pervasive problem and therefore appreciates the profound solution. His gratitude for Joseph is "not merely for being God's conduit in resolving one more thorny problem of evil, but for being the instrument through whom God restored the knowledge and priesthood powers that make the redemption of the dead possible. In an eternal perspective, the only evil is damnation, and by solving the problem of salvation for the dead, the Prophet removed the classical barriers encountered in the problem of soteriology."[7]

Joseph later revealed the ordinance of baptism for the dead that enables all mankind to make and keep the gospel covenants (see D&C 127–28). Joseph taught the doctrine to his father on his deathbed. In contrast to his reaction to Reverend Stockton's sermon, Father Smith "was delighted to hear" the truth and asked Joseph to attend to the ordinance of baptism on Alvin's behalf. Joseph and Hyrum fulfilled their father's dying wish. "I see Alvin," Father Smith said just a few minutes before his own passing.[8] Prophetically, section 137 solved a persistent problem faced by Joseph's family and many, many others.

Doctrine & Covenants 138

ORIGIN

Death haunted mankind in 1918. The Great War, known today as World War I, was in the process of claiming more than nine million lives. That staggering figure paled in comparison with the number of people slain in even less time by a global influenza pandemic. Worldwide the virus reaped a grim harvest of perhaps fifty million souls. It killed more than 195,000 Americans in October 1918, the deadliest month in American history, the month the Lord revealed Doctrine and Covenants 138.[1]

The "pervasiveness and ubiquity of death were overwhelming," yet it is hard to grasp for those of us who live distant from what witnesses themselves could hardly imagine and what cultural historians have described as creating a terrible, gnawing emptiness in tens of thousands of families mourning the losses of loved ones whose bodies were never recovered from the war's devastation or whose families were wiped out by disease.[2]

In the midst of the dead and dying was Joseph F. Smith, president of the Church. His life's experiences equipped him to grasp the enormity of death and its implications. His father, Hyrum, had been brutally shot to death when Joseph was five. Not many years later he lost his mother, "the sweetest soul that ever lived," he wrote, "when I was only a boy."[3] Death marked his life. His first child, Mercy Josephine, died at age two, leaving Joseph "vacant, lonely, desolate, deserted." His beloved eldest son died unexpectedly in January 1918, creating what President Smith called "my overwhelming burden of grief." Between these untimely deaths, President

Smith buried a wife and eleven other children.⁴ He tasted deeply the bitterness of death.

As general conference neared in October 1918, President Smith himself was less than two months from the end of his own mortality. Unwell, he surprised the Saints by appearing at conference on October 4. He spoke briefly, saying, "I have dwelt in the spirit of prayer, of supplication, of faith and of determination; and I have had my communications with the Spirit of the Lord continuously."⁵ Indeed he had. Just the day before, the Lord

Joseph F. Smith.

had given him the revelation recorded now in Doctrine and Covenants 138. After conference he dictated it to his son Joseph Fielding Smith.⁶

CONTENT

Doctrine and Covenants 138 is a Christ-centered text from beginning to end. "It is a document without parallel," said President Gordon B. Hinckley, adding, "there is nothing quite like it in all our sacred literature."⁷

It starts with President Joseph F. Smith pondering the atonement of Jesus Christ, continues with his witness of Christ's visit to the spirit world, proceeds with the gospel of Jesus Christ being preached to departed spirits, and concludes in the name of Jesus Christ. Section 138 is a testimony. President Smith's words emphasize his witness of Christ: "I saw" (v. 11), "I beheld" (vv. 15, 57), "I understood" (v. 25), "I perceived" (v. 29), "I observed" (v. 55), "I bear record, and I know that this record is true" (v. 60).

Section 138 begins with a recipe for revelation. President Smith used powerful verbs to describe what he did to receive the sublime series of visions. "I sat in my room *pondering* over the scriptures; and *reflecting* upon the great atoning sacrifice that was made by the Son of God, for the redemption of the world" (vv. 1–2; emphasis added). He intellectually engaged one of the deepest theological questions known to man as well as the most terrible questions of his time, a time in which "the sheer, overwhelming quantity of death awakened individual and communal grief on an unprecedented scale. With the loss came questions: What is the fate of the dead? Do they continue to exist? Is there life after death?"[8] He returned to relevant Bible passages he already knew well and "pondered over these things which are written" (v. 11).

Such a determined quest for light and knowledge results in revelation being given, and President Smith's revelation declares more than any previously recorded. He sees a gathering of the innumerable righteous dead, those who had been faithful in life. "I beheld that they were filled with joy and gladness, and were rejoicing together because the day of their deliverance was at hand" (v. 15). They were waiting for Christ to deliver them from the bondage of being disembodied, what verse 23 calls the "chains of hell" (see D&C 45:17; 93:33). The Savior arrived and preached the law of the gospel. He did not preach to the spirits of the ungodly or to those who in life had rejected the warnings of prophets.

This vision leads President Smith to marvel, to wonder and inquire further. Christ's three-year mortal ministry, full of miracles and power, resulted in precious few converts. How then could his comparatively short ministry among the dead be effective? What did Peter mean by writing that the Savior preached to the spirits in prison who had been disobedient in the days of Noah? These questions bring another revelation, a recognition "that the Lord went not in person among the wicked and disobedient" but sent messengers. In a sense he mustered an army to combat the effects of death and hell. He "organized his forces" and armed them "with power and authority, and commissioned them to go forth and carry the light of the gospel to them that were in darkness, even to all the spirits of men; and thus was the gospel preached to the dead" (v. 30).[9] Joseph Smith, Brigham Young, and Wilford Woodruff all taught that the Savior unlocked the spirit prison and provided for redemption of the dead.[10] But not until Joseph F. Smith's vision became public has mankind known how Christ "organized his forces," "appointed messengers," and "commissioned them to go forth" (v. 30). Section 138 spelled out the means by which the dead can be saved.[11]

It was news to Latter-day Saints in 1918, indeed to the world, that in the spirit world an army of missionaries taught the law of the gospel with the added dimension of "vicarious baptism for the remission of sins" (v. 33). The knowledge made it possible for the spirits to act for themselves, to be agents who were fully accountable for their new knowledge. The teaching fulfilled God's just plan of offering the same opportunities and blessings to all mankind, making each individual responsible to receive or reject "the sacrifice of the Son of God" (v. 35).

President Smith named many of the "great and mighty ones" whom the Lord taught personally "and gave them power to come forth, after his resurrection from the dead, to enter into his Father's kingdom, there to be crowned with immortality and eternal life" (vv. 38, 51). He saw faithful Saints from all dispensations, and surely he was moved deeply to see his own martyred father, Hyrum Smith, together with his brother Joseph and President Smith's own predecessors in the Church presidency "among the noble and great ones who were chosen in the beginning to be rulers in the Church of God" (v. 55). Likewise President Smith saw "our glorious Mother Eve, with many of her faithful daughters who had lived through the ages and worshiped the true and living God" (v. 39). And deeply comforting is his seeing that "the faithful elders of this dispensation, when they depart from mortal life, continue their labors in the preaching of the gospel of repentance and redemption, through the sacrifice of the Only Begotten Son of God, among those who are in darkness and under the bondage of sin in the great world of the spirits of the dead" (v. 57). As both an orphaned son and a grieving father, President Smith undoubtedly appreciated the vision's confirmation of "the redemption of the dead, and the sealing of the children to their parents" (v. 48).

OUTCOMES

Early Christians believed, as Doctrine and Covenants 138 declares in verse 58, that the dead could repent and be redeemed through exactly the same gospel of Jesus Christ that saves the repentant living. The determinant is not death but agency. Individuals are saved or damned based not on when they live or die but on what they decide to do with Christ's offer of salvation when they learn about it. But over the centuries, largely through the influence of Augustine, death had become "a firm boundary of salvation" in western Christianity.[12]

Despite so-called orthodox efforts to stamp it out, the tradition of Christ saving the repentant dead persisted. Based on the same Bible passages that President Smith pondered prior to his vision, many medieval Christians believed in what they called the "harrowing of hell," meaning Christ's disembodied descent into the spirit world between his crucifixion and resurrection to redeem the captives. A rich tradition of drama and art depict the Savior's mission of "deliverance" in which he declared "liberty to the captives who had been faithful" (D&C 138:18).[13] The earliest Christian creed, known as the Apostles Creed, declares that Christ "was crucified, died and was buried. He descended into hell. On the third day He rose again from the dead. He ascended into heaven."[14] Roman Catholics and some Protestant denominations still recite this thoroughly biblical doctrine, but many Christians have rejected the line that declares that Jesus descended into hell, or the spirit world. Influential reformers fought against the doctrine. John Calvin called it "nothing but a fable."[15] Martin Luther called it "figments of some stupid and bungling sophist."[16] By the 1600s the doctrine of Christ descending into the spirit world between his death and resurrection "had virtually disappeared" from Christian consciousness.[17]

Section 138 thus restored and expanded biblical doctrine. In doing so it reinforced the Bible's wholeness and truthfulness and its compatibility with the Book of Mormon and the Restoration. President Smith saw Adam and Eve and Old Testament patriarchs and prophets along with Book of Mormon prophets and Joseph Smith and others from the last dispensation all unified by the New Testament Savior and his unbounded gospel. The vision gives coherence to God's perfect plans for the redemption of his children, a wholeness that is lacking from most other theologies. Moreover, the revelation protects against false doctrines. The devastating toll of death at the time section 138 was received had people understandably looking into all kinds of hopeful but unsound teachings about the dead. Spiritualism thrived as people ached to commune with their departed loved ones. And a wide variety of alternative interpretations have been offered to the Bible passages President Smith pondered. None of them, in contrast to section 138, declares itself revelation.

A scarred survivor of the influenza pandemic wrote a powerful memoir that repeatedly asks, "Where are the dead?"[18] Latter-day Saint scholar George Tate wrote that section 138 answers this question and speaks to the "great, worldwide need" that underlies it. Indeed, as "the vision affirms the foundations of faith in a world where the faith of so many was shattered by the great calamities they witnessed and experienced, declaring to all the world through the mouth of the Lord's anointed that the Father and the Son live and are still earnestly engaged in the ongoing work of salvation for all God's children."[19]

On October 31, 1918, the ailing President Smith sent his son Joseph Fielding Smith to read the revelation to a meeting of the First Presidency and the Quorum of the Twelve Apostles. They "accepted and endorsed the revelation as the word of the Lord."[20] The *Deseret Evening News* published the revelation about a month later. In the meantime President Joseph F. Smith had passed from this life knowing perhaps more vividly than any other mortal what he could expect on arrival in the spirit world.

Official Declaration—1

ORIGIN

Under the leadership of President Brigham Young, the Saints sought refuge from their oppressors behind the formidable Wasatch Mountains in America's Great Basin. There the practice of plural marriage was announced at a conference in August 1852. Thomas Bullock read the revelation now recorded in Doctrine and Covenants 132. Apostle Orson Pratt announced the practice in the pattern of the biblical patriarchs. And President Brigham Young defended Joseph Smith and the history of the revelation. It was a bold, countercultural declaration that the Saints would obey revelation despite opposition.

The Saints had meanwhile applied to the United States government for statehood but were instead dealt a devastating blow when Utah was made a territory, not a state, as part of the Compromise of 1850. Citizens of a state could elect their own governor and appoint their own judges, but a territory was administered by the Congress from Washington, D.C. Thomas Kane, a friend and adviser to the Saints, had told them, "You are better off without any government from the hands of Congress than with a territorial government. The political intrigues of government officers will be against you. You can govern yourselves better than they can govern you." Kane predicted that "a strong political party" would rise in their midst "and against your interests."[1]

He was right. The federal government dictated Utah affairs throughout the 1850s, but the nation's primary concern was the sectional crisis over slavery. In 1854 the Republican party was formed and in 1856 ran its first candidate for president with the pledge that he would stop the spread of slavery and polygamy in the territories. Abraham Lincoln won the 1860 election, becoming the first Republican elected to the White House. The Southern states responded by seceding from the Union. In the subsequent turmoil of the Civil War, Congress passed the first of several anti-Mormon laws.

"Congress shall make no law . . . prohibiting the free exercise of religion," says the first amendment to the United States Constitution, but Congress did. The 1862 Morrill Act was intended "to punish and prevent the practice of polygamy in the territories of the United States" and to overrule Utah Territory's laws to the contrary.[2] The Morrill Act imposed fines for plural marriage and declared that the Church could not hold more than fifty thousand dollars' worth of assets. The Saints generally disregarded it, and the Civil War forestalled enforcement.

In the 1870s, however, an increasingly powerful anti-Mormon party formed in Utah, and the radical Republicans who dominated Congress worked to impose their will on the Saints. George Reynolds allowed himself to be used to test the constitutionality of the Morrill Act. In 1878 the United States Supreme Court unanimously ruled in *Reynolds v. United States* that the Morrill Act was indeed constitutional by making a distinction between belief and practice. Saints could believe in plural marriage, the Court said, but could not practice it. Emboldened by this ruling, Congress enacted even tougher laws in the 1880s, eliminating such basic rights as trial by jury for those who practiced plural marriage, removing Utah courts from local control, requiring test oaths for voters that kept many Saints from voting, and disenfranchising all women in Utah. The new laws lowered the standard of evidence required for conviction, leading federal officers to hunt Latter-day Saints and jail many of them, including Church leaders. An Idaho law prohibited Saints there from voting, and the Supreme Court unanimously upheld it in *Davis v. Beason* (1890), leading Utah's anti-Mormons to seek a similar law.

It is no overstatement to say that American culture in the second half of the nineteenth century was officially and almost completely anti-Mormon. The Saints defiantly endured the unprecedented assault on their religious and civil liberties. They tried every constitutional method to obtain their rights. They tried civil disobedience. In 1992, testifying before a congressional committee, Elder Dallin H. Oaks, himself an eminent jurist, declared, "I know of no other major religious group in America that has endured anything comparable to the officially sanctioned persecution that was imposed upon members of my church by federal, state, and local government officials. . . . Most of these denials of religious freedom received the express approval of the United States Supreme Court. It was a dark chapter in the history of religious freedom in this nation."[3] President Wilford Woodruff's last journal entry of 1889 says that "the nation has never been filled so full of lies against the Saints as today. 1890 will be an important year with the Latter Day Saints and the American nation."[4]

It was. On May 18, 1890, the Supreme Court ruled against the Church itself, dissolving its legal status and threatening to confiscate its property.[5] By August President Woodruff feared that the Church would lose control of the nearly completed Salt Lake Temple and the temples in St. George, Logan, and Manti, Utah. It became clear to him that the Church must choose between keeping plural marriage and having temple ordinances. He sought the Lord's will to know what to do.

Wilford Woodruff.

CONTENT

On September 24, 1890, President Woodruff met with his counselors and the apostles who were available. He solemnly told them "he had sought the will of the Lord, and it had been revealed to him that the Church must relinquish the practice of plural marriage."[6] A long discussion followed, resulting in a consensus to sustain the revelation. The Church leaders subsequently released to the press the statement that is now Official Declaration–1 in the Doctrine and Covenants. Replying to recent accusations that plural marriages were still being performed, it explains the Church's decision to not perform new plural marriages or to publicly advocate the doctrine. President Woodruff explained that he had even demolished the Endowment House, a building on Temple Square in which ordinances were performed while the Salt Lake Temple was constructed. He declared his intention to submit to the laws, however unconstitutional, and to urge Latter-day Saints to do likewise.

President Woodruff wrote in his journal entry the next day: "I have arrived at a point in the History of my life as the President of the Church of Jesus Christ of Latter Day Saints where I am under the necessity of acting for the Temporal Salvation of the Church. The United States Government has taken a Stand & passed Laws to destroy the Latter day Saints upon the Subject of polygamy or Patriarchal order of Marriage. And after Praying to the Lord & feeling inspired by his spirit I have issued the . . . Proclamation which is sustained by My counselors and the 12 Apostles."[7]

OUTCOMES

About two weeks later, at the October 1890 general conference of the Church, Lorenzo Snow, then president of the Quorum of the Twelve Apostles, presented the Manifesto, as he called it, to the Saints for a sustaining vote. Consent in that setting was unanimous, though not all Saints were enthusiastic about it. Many resented the government's oppressive measures that had led President Woodruff to seek the revelation. In a conference talk, President George Q. Cannon cited Doctrine and Covenants 124:49, in which the Lord explained that he would not require the Saints to keep a commandment any longer if they have diligently tried but their enemies "hinder them from performing that work."

Even so, after four decades of diligently striving to practice plural marriage, some Saints struggled to let it go. Those who were sealed in plural families could not simply stop being so. Government officials pushed President Woodruff toward an interpretation of the Manifesto that would have been devastating to families. He affirmed that the Manifesto curtailed future marriages but not earlier ones. "I did not, I could not, and would not promise that you would desert your wives and children," President Woodruff assured the Saints. "This you cannot do in honor."[8] Moreover, some Church leaders sanctioned selected plural marriages. Thus the practice of plural marriage ended gradually.

Speaking to the Saints in Brigham City a year after the Manifesto, President Woodruff said that the Lord had revealed to him that many Saints were disappointed by it. The Lord had told him to ask the Saints a question, he said, and to promise them an answer by the power of the Holy Ghost. "The question is this. Which was the wisest course for the Latter Day Saints to pursue, to continue to attempt to practice plural marriage with the laws of the nation against it and the opposition of 60,000,000 of people and at the cost of confiscation and loss of all the temples and the stopping of all the ordinances therein both for the living & the dead and the imprisonment of the First Presidency and Twelve and the leaders of heads of family in the Church and the confiscation of the personal property of the people (All of which of themselves would stop the practice)? . . . Or after doing and suffering what we have through our adherence to this principle to cease the practice and submit to the law and through doing so have the prophets, apostles, and fathers at home so they can instruct the people and attend to the duties of the Church, also leave the temples in the hands of the Saints so they can attend to the ordinances of the gospel both for the living & the dead?" President Woodruff assured the Saints that he and the apostles were led by revelation, and that the Lord would not permit them to lead the Saints astray. He promised that the Lord would confirm that truth to them if they would seek a testimony of it.[9]

Elder B. H. Roberts, a general authority at the time of the Manifesto, wrote poignantly about his response and the testimony that came to him on board a train:

"I was lingering about on the outside talking with the passengers, found the Salt Lake papers containing Pres. Woodruff's Manifesto. As soon as I entered the car, [Apostle John W. Taylor] called to me and showed me the papers containing the document, the headlines of which I read with astonishment. But no sooner had I read them, than like a flash of light all through my soul the Spirit said—'That is all right,' so it passed. Then I began to reflect upon the matter. I thought of all the Saints who had suffered to sustain that doctrine; I remembered my own exile, my own imprisonment; I thought of that of others. I remembered what sacrifices my wives had made for it; what others had made for it. We had preached it, sustained its divinity from the pulpit, in the press, from the lecture platform. Our community had endured every kind of reproach from the world for the sake of it—and was this to be the end? I had learned to expect that God would sustain both that principle and his Saints who carried it out, and to lay down like this was a kind of cowardly proceeding, so that the more I thought of it, the less I liked it. . . . . This matter continued to be a trial to me through the year 1891, and plagued me much, but I said but little about it; and by and by I began to remember the flash of light that first came to me when I first heard of it, and at last my feelings became reconciled to it. Perhaps I had transgressed in pushing from me the first testimony I received in relation to it, and allowing my own prejudices, and my own shortsighted, human reason to stand against the inspiration of God and the testimony it bore the manifesto was all right. When this fact began to dawn on my mind, I repented of my wrong and courted most earnestly the spirit of God for a testimony and gradually it came. I did not understand the purposes for which the Manifesto was issued . . . but sure I am that it is all right; that God has a purpose in it I feel assured, and in due time it will be manifest."[10]

President Woodruff worked with the Saints to help them become reconciled to the will of the Lord. Some excerpts of his teachings follow Official Declaration–1 in the Doctrine and Covenants. He emphasized two points. First, he testified that he had received revelation and would not have issued the Manifesto without the Lord's instruction to do so. Second, he explained a rationale for the revelation. Stopping the practice of plural marriage enabled the Saints to finish the Salt Lake Temple and maintain control of it for the performance of the ordinances of exaltation. "If you can understand that," said President Wilford Woodruff at the April 1893 dedication of the Salt Lake Temple, "that is a key to it."[11]

As hoped, the Manifesto defused persecution and enabled the Church to survive. Utah became a state in 1896, but the long-standing antagonisms and opposition did not end immediately or easily. Congress refused to seat Utah's elected representative B. H. Roberts. Congressional hearings over seating apostle Reed Smoot as senator, even though he was not a polygamist, led Church president Joseph F. Smith to issue a "Second Manifesto," which he read in general conference on April 6, 1904. It prohibited plural marriages and made Saints who presumed to enter into or officiate in them subject to excommunication. The Saints voted overwhelmingly to sustain President Smith's declaration. Two apostles dissented and were released from their callings. Apostate groups rejected the leadership of Wilford Woodruff. His promise remains in force, however. Elder Roberts proved its power by choosing to submit to the Holy Spirit and gaining a testimony that the Lord had ended the practice of plural marriage. All can do the same.

Official Declaration—2

ORIGIN

The first Africans brought to America were indentured servants who, like their European counterparts, were freed after their terms of servitude. When the number of such freedmen—both black Africans and white Europeans—grew to proportions that seemed threatening, Virginia landowners adopted laws that made the Africans slaves, meaning that their servant status became perpetual and inherited by their posterity. By the time the Church was organized in 1830, Africans and their descendants had been enslaved in the American colonies and later the United States for nearly two centuries.

The enslaving of Africans required an explanation, and on both sides of the Atlantic whites searched for and found in the Bible a justification. Genesis 9 records that Noah cursed his grandson Canaan to be a servant. Though the passage says nothing about race, some whites cited it as justification for enslaving Africans. As time wore on several other scriptures were used to justify race-based slavery. Anti-slavery advocates also found evidence for their position in the Bible. In a way, the Bible itself became a slave to the powerful cultural currents that emphasized white superiority over blacks.[1]

The Church emerged in the midst of this ongoing controversy. No other subject was more frequently in the news or engaged the passions of Joseph Smith's countrymen more than the race-based antagonisms that led finally to the Civil War, as Joseph had prophesied (see D&C 87). As in American culture generally, early Latter-day Saints possessed a variety of opinions, assumptions, and prejudices. Then, as now, these did not always align with the Lord's views. A major doctrinal theme of the Book of Mormon is that an individuals' decision to follow the Savior, nothing else, determines whether they will be saved by the atonement of Jesus Christ. He "denieth none that come unto him, black and white, bond and free, male and female; and he remembereth the heathen; and all are alike unto God, both Jew and Gentile" (2 Nephi 26:33). In October 1840, the First Presidency declared that soon "persons of all languages, and of every tongue, and of every color; . . . shall with us worship the Lord of Hosts in his holy temple."[2] A few free blacks joined the Church and were generally well received. At least one black man, Elijah Abel, received the priesthood in the 1830s, served multiple missions, and remained a faithful priesthood holder his entire life.[3]

Joseph generally reflected moderate views on race. He was not an abolitionist in the 1830s, but he believed in individual agency, welcomed blacks into his home, and taught that the inferior status of blacks was not inherent but based on lack of opportunity. "Change their situation with the white," Joseph said of blacks, "and they would be like them."[4] By the time he ran for president in 1844, Joseph's platform addressed the nation's most pressing problem by promising to "ameliorate the condition of all: black or white, bond or free; for the best of books says, 'God hath made of one blood all nations of men'" (Acts 17:26).[5]

At some point Church leaders decided that black men should not be ordained to the priesthood, at least not yet. Scholars have debated for decades when that decision was made and why. The evidence is inconclusive. It appears, though, that by 1849 black Latter-day Saint men were not being ordained to the priesthood. But the reasons for that decision and its timing are not clear.[6]

According to a prophecy of Enoch in the book of Moses in the Pearl of Great Price, Noah's grandson Canaan and his descendants were destined to live in a land cursed with excessive heat and therefore barrenness. Enoch also saw that their skin became black and they were hated (Moses 7:7–8). Enoch's prophecy does not state those things necessarily as cause and effect. Prophecies that are descriptive (things as they will be) are often misread as prescriptive (things as they should be), but it seems unlikely that God willed for Canaan's descendants to be "despised among all people" (Moses 7:8).

The book of Abraham suggests that the first pharaoh of Egypt was a son of Canaan and Egyptus, and thus a grandson of Ham and great-grandson of Noah. According to the book of Abraham, "Pharaoh, being a righteous man, established his kingdom and judged his people wisely and justly all his days, seeking earnestly to imitate" the patriarchal order of the priesthood (Abraham 1:26). Noah blessed him with wealth and wisdom "but cursed him as pertaining to the Priesthood" for reasons that are not specified (Abraham 1:26). The book of Abraham does not mention the race of the Canaanites, but readers have assumed a link between Enoch's prophecy in the book of Moses about Canaanites acquiring black skin and Abraham's description that Pharaoh could not have the priesthood as "a partaker of the blood of the Canaanites by birth" (Abraham 1:21).

Still, unanswered questions do remain. When was the link between the books of Moses and Abraham forged? How are those passages to be interpreted? Is there a genealogical link between the ancient Canaanites and modern Africans, or is such a link an unfounded assumption and a relatively recent creation by slavery proponents that was uncritically accepted? Were blacks denied the priesthood because of an inherited curse or because Latter-day Saints, conditioned by cultural prejudices, misinterpreted the Pearl of Great Price, or for some other reason?

Twentieth-century Church leaders considered such questions as the Church expanded in Brazil and other areas with large populations of Africans or descendants of Africans and as the civil rights movement advanced in the United States. Indeed, some wrestled earnestly with those questions, including Spencer W. Kimball. "Admittedly," he said, speaking as an apostle in 1963, "our direct and positive information is limited. I have wished the Lord had given us a little more clarity in the matter." He did not know whether to characterize the decision as "doctrine or policy," but acknowledged that it "has not varied in my memory." He continued, "I know it could. I know the Lord could change his policy and release the ban and forgive the possible error which brought about the deprivation. If the time comes, that he will do, I am sure."[7] Little did Elder Kimball know then how the Lord would implement change through him.

Meanwhile "a contradictory and confusing legacy of racist religious folklore" had grown up among the Saints to explain banning blacks from the priesthood.⁸ Concerned, the counselors in the First Presidency wrote to priesthood leaders in 1969, expressing their belief that the reasons for the ban were "known to God, but which He has not made fully known to man."⁹ More recently, Elder Dallin H. Oaks noted the danger of coming up with unrevealed reasons. "When we do we're on our own," he was quoted as saying. "Some people put reasons to the one we're talking about here, and they turned out to be spectacularly wrong." He declared that "the reasons turn out to be man-made to a great extent. The revelations are what we sustain as the will of the Lord and that's where the safety lies."¹⁰

Revelation came to Church president Spencer W. Kimball in 1978. His son and biographer wrote that "President Kimball was an old man when he set out to know with certainty for himself whether God wanted black men admitted to or excluded from the priesthood. Most would expect a man at his age to be firmly set in his ways, but instead he was able to reconsider the teachings of a lifetime and accept radical change."¹¹ President Kimball had spent years seeking answers. He had an intense desire to spread the gospel of Jesus Christ over the globe and invite every willing soul to partake of its blessings.

By the 1970s, thousands of black West Africans had accepted the gospel and waited with great faith for the day they could be baptized and the Church established in their homeland. Black Latter-day Saints from Salt Lake City to Rio de Janiero, Brazil, to Johannesburg, South Africa, similarly hoped and prayed for a revelation that would give the opportunity to all worthy men to hold the priesthood and thus make all the ordinances of the temple

Spencer W. Kimball.

available to every worthy Latter-day Saint. The revelation came to President Spencer W. Kimball and was confirmed to him and his counselors and the Quorum of the Twelve Apostles early in June 1978.

CONTENT

Following the pattern for revelation established by Doctrine and Covenants 9:8–9, President Kimball thoroughly studied the history of the policy. He sought the views of others and asked his brethren to similarly study the scriptures to seek understanding. For years he and his counselors and the apostles studied. In 1977, at President Kimball's request, some of the apostles submitted written analyses of the policy and their thoughts on the implications of making a change. Elder Bruce R. McConkie wrote that there was no scriptural reason that would prohibit a change. President Kimball spoke privately with each of his brethren to discern their candid views and convened several council meetings to discuss the issue exhaustively and freely. He could not let it rest. He said that he went to the temple alone day after day, seeking direction from the Lord.[12]

On March 9, 1978, after another discussion by the First Presidency and the Twelve in their weekly council meeting, they unanimously voted that a change would have to come by revelation to President Kimball. His son and biographer noted that "President Kimball agreed but also wanted them to learn the will of the Lord for themselves. He urged them to fast and pray individually over the question." Two weeks later President Kimball confided to his counselors that he felt impressed to lift the ban restricting black men from holding the priesthood. They agreed to sustain him and to discuss the issue again with the apostles before making a final decision. Concerned that his brethren know for themselves that President Kimball intended to do the Lord's will and not his own, he pleaded with the Lord to reveal His will to the apostles. Describing such experiences later to missionaries in South Africa, President Kimball said that "after everybody had gone out of the temple, I knelt and prayed. And I prayed with such fervency, I tell you! I knew that something was before us that was extremely important to many of the children of God. And I knew that we could receive the revelations of the Lord only by being worthy and ready for them and ready to accept them and to put them into place. Day after day I went and with great solemnity and seriousness, alone in the upper rooms of the Temple, and there I offered my soul and offered our efforts to go forward with the program and we wanted to do what he wanted."[13]

In late May, after more council meetings in which the issue was discussed, the First Presidency and the Twelve planned to come to their next meeting together fasting and praying for the Lord to manifest his will. Thus they met together in the temple on Thursday, June 1, 1978. After their regular routine of testifying and partaking of the sacrament, the prophets, seers, and revelators listened to President Spencer W. Kimball say: "Brethren, I have cancelled lunch for today. Would you be willing to remain in the temple with us? I would like you to continue to fast with me. I have been going to the temple almost daily for many weeks now, sometimes for hours, entreating the Lord for a clear answer. I have not been determined in advance what the answer should be. And I will be satisfied with a simple Yes or No, but I want to know. Whatever the Lord's decision is, I will defend it to the limits of my strength, even to death."[14]

President Kimball then described his tentative conclusion to lift the ban and the revelatory process that led him to it. He asked for the views of his brethren. Each of them spoke; each favored ending the restriction. Then, as they prepared to seek confirmation from the Lord for their decision, President Kimball asked, "Do you mind if I lead you in prayer?" They did not, and with remarkable unity carefully cultivated by their president and prophet, the men surrounded the temple altar and joined their faith. President Kimball prayed that they would be "cleansed and made free from sin so that we might receive the Lord's word."[15] He asked for a manifestation that they had arrived at the right decision to do the will of the Lord. The Lord answered. President Kimball testified that "this revelation and assurance came to me so clearly that there was no doubt about it."[16]

President Marion G. Romney, a counselor in the First Presidency, had prayed for a revelation for President Kimball, but he did not anticipate what came. In what he called a confession, President Romney described himself as "a stubborn man" who was "personally slow to accept change" and said he "would not have gone along without a witness" of his own. He testified, "From the experience we had in the temple I was sure that he had the answer. I got a witness in my own soul."[17]

Speaking nearly ten years later, President Gordon B. Hinckley bore his "personal witness of what occurred." He testified that "the Spirit of God was there. And by the power of the Holy Ghost there came to [President Kimball] an assurance that the thing for which he prayed was right, that the time had now come, and that now the wondrous blessings of the priesthood should be extended to worthy men everywhere regardless of lineage. Every man in that circle, by the power of the Holy Ghost, knew the same thing. It was a quiet and sublime occasion." The Lord had answered President Kimball's prayer for unity and certainty among the apostles. President Hinckley testified that "all of us knew that the time had come for a change and that the decision had come from the heavens. The answer was clear. There was perfect unity among us in our experience and in our understanding."[18]

In the ensuing week President Kimball spoke to the two apostles who had not been present at the temple meeting—one had been on assignment in South America and the other was too ill to attend. He received their sustaining support. He drafted a statement announcing the revelation. One week after the June 1 revelation the First Presidency presented it to the General Authorities assembled in the temple and received their sustaining vote. Then President Kimball put his hand on the knee of his counselor, President N. Eldon Tanner and said, "Go tell the world."[19] President Tanner released the statement to the press, and in minutes the word began to spread.

Part of the statement is canonized as Official Declaration–2. It is not a dictation of the words of Jesus Christ but rather a declaration by the First Presidency that the Lord had revealed his will. They described the context of the revelation as expanding missionary work and their great desire to extend the blessings of the priesthood and temple "to every worthy member of the Church." They explained that in light of prophecies made by their predecessors that the priesthood would someday be extended to those who had been denied, they had "pleaded long and earnestly" for that day to come. God had heard their prayers, they testified, "and by revelation . . . confirmed that the long-promised day has come when every faithful, worthy man in the Church may receive the holy priesthood, with power to exercise its divine authority, and enjoy with his loved ones every blessing that flows therefrom, including the blessings of the temple."

In their statement the First Presidency emphasized the revelation's theological consistency with Nephi's teachings that "all men are privileged the one like unto the other, and none are forbidden" and that the Lord "inviteth them all to come unto him and partake of his goodness; and he denieth none that come unto him, black and white, bond and free, male and female" (2 Nephi 26:28, 33). "We declare with soberness," they wrote, "that the Lord has now made known his will for the blessing of *all* his children throughout the earth who will hearken to the voice of his authorized servants" (Official Declaration–2; emphasis added). The Lord willed for all individuals to choose for themselves whether to obey the gospel and receive its blessings.

OUTCOMES

The revelation produced an electric effect both inside and outside the Church. President Gordon B. Hinckley remembered, "There was much weeping, with tears of gratitude not only on the part of those who previously had been denied the priesthood and who became the immediate beneficiaries of this announcement, but also by men and women of the Church across the world who had felt as we had felt concerning this matter."[20] Camilla Kimball, the prophet's wife, who had discerned his heavy burden, sat on her floor and wept with joy and relief when she heard the heavenly news.[21] President Hinckley testified that "not one of us . . . present on that occasion was ever quite the same after that. Nor has the Church been quite the same."[22]

The story headlined the nation's newspapers and television broadcasts. As President Kimball predicted, many of the news reports cast the decision as capitulation to American culture. But that was far too narrow an interpretation. Jan Shipps, a prominent scholar of Mormonism who is not a Latter-day Saint, emphasized the prophetic explanation for the revelation. It "will never be fully understood if it is regarded simply as a pragmatic doctrinal shift ultimately designed to bring Latter-day Saints into congruence with mainstream America," she wrote. "The timing and context, and even the wording of the revelation itself, indicate that the change has to do not with America so much as with the world."[23]

The recipients of the revelation refuted the idea of some who were not present that there was no real revelation. Elder David B. Haight, the most junior member of the Quorum of the Twelve when the revelation came, explained. "Just a few hours after the announcement was made to the press, I was assigned to attend a stake conference in Detroit, Michigan," he said. "When my plane landed in Chicago, I noticed an edition of the *Chicago Tribune* on the newsstand. The headline in the paper said, 'Mormons Give Blacks Priesthood.' And the subheading said, 'President Kimball Claims to Have Received a Revelation.' I bought a copy of the newspaper. I stared at one word in that subheading—*claims*. It stood out to me just like it was in red neon. As I walked along the hallway to make my plane connection, I thought, *Here I am now in Chicago walking through this busy airport, yet I was a witness to this revelation. I was there. I witnessed it. I felt that heavenly influence. I was part of it.* Little did the editor of that newspaper realize the truth of that revelation when he wrote, ' . . . Claims to Have Received a Revelation.' Little did he know, or the printer, or the man who put the ink on the press, or the one who delivered the newspaper—little did any of them know that it was truly a revelation from God. Little did they know what I knew because I was a witness to it."[24]

The revelation expanded the minds and opened the hearts of Latter-day Saints. Shortly after it came Elder Bruce R. McConkie spoke to nearly a thousand seminary teachers about 2 Nephi 26:33, the text declaring the Lord's universal and impartial invitation to come unto him. "These words have now taken on a new meaning," said Elder McConkie. "We have caught a new vision of their true significance. This also applies to a great number of other passages in the revelations. Since the Lord gave this revelation on the priesthood, our understanding of many passages has expanded. Many of us never imagined or supposed that they had the extensive and broad meaning that they do have." He went on to declare "the great significance that this event has in the Church, in the world . . . where the rolling forth of the great gospel is concerned." What about statements by earlier authorities to the contrary? Elder McConkie declared that in those cases "we spoke with a limited understanding and without the light and knowledge that has now come into the world."[25]

"Tremendous, eternal consequences for millions over the earth are flowing from that manifestation," according to President Hinckley. He described one Brazilian family who had joined the Church years before the revelation and served long and faithfully, including consecrating to the building of the temple in São Paulo, even though they anticipated that they could not partake of its sacred ordinances.[26] The First Presidency cited such faithfulness in their letter describing why the revelation was given. "Witnessing the faithfulness of those from whom the priesthood has been withheld," they wrote, "we have pleaded long and earnestly in [their] behalf" (Official Declaration–2).

Besides expanding the reach of priesthood and temple ordinances to this and other families in Brazil, the Caribbean, and other parts of the globe, the June 1978 revelation opened the vast continent of Africa for the spread of the gospel. Thousands of souls, long since converted, came into the Church overnight. Stakes and then temples followed in short order. Observers note that the African Saints are generally well educated and have no cultural inhibitions to sharing the gospel, and the retention rate of converts is excellent.[27] The Church and its most sacred ordinances are administered by "able and faithful" Saints who, according to President Hinckley, "honor and magnify the priesthood that they rightfully hold, having been called of God by prophecy and the laying on of hands by those in authority.

"This is but the beginning of greater things to come as the truth of the restored gospel covers the earth as the waters cover the mighty deep."[28]

Epilogue

I was seven years old when the Lord revealed that all worthy men could be ordained to the priesthood and thus all worthy women and men could receive the sacred temple ordinances. I have only a vague recollection that the June 1978 announcement was big news at our house. But that September I was baptized and, following a family tradition, attended general conference with my father in Salt Lake City. I remember that we rose very early to stand in line for a long time before being admitted to the Tabernacle. And I remember that the Saints spontaneously began singing "We Thank Thee, O God, for a Prophet" as President Spencer W. Kimball walked into the Tabernacle. During the singing I felt the overwhelming warmth of the Holy Spirit, duplicating an experience I had enjoyed when I was confirmed just a few days earlier. I knew President Kimball was a prophet, and I was thankful to God for that fact. I was present if

President Spencer W. Kimball shakes hands with children outside the Tabernacle between general conference sessions.

not perfectly attentive when President N. Eldon Tanner proposed that the Saints sustain the revelation that extended the blessings of the priesthood.[1]

Before a subsequent session of the conference, my father took my older brother and me to a spot outside the Tabernacle and instructed us to return there when the conference session ended. We obeyed and watched as ushers cordoned off an area and Presidents Kimball and Romney emerged and shook the hands of all the children, including me. A nearby photographer captured the moment and published it in the *Ensign* that reported the conference. It was many years before I understood the significance of those events. But now I recognize that the Lord gave me a personal and undeniable testimony of his chosen prophet on the very day the Saints sustained a momentous revelation to that prophet. One outcome of this personal witness is that I remain thankful to God for prophets and for revelations.

Notes

Preface
1. Gordon B. Hinckley, Conference Report (April 1966): 87.

A Brief History of the Doctrine & Covenants
1. Robert J. Woodford, "The Story of the Doctrine and Covenants," *Ensign* 14 (December 1984), 32.
2. Orson Pratt, *The Seer* 2, no. 3 (1854): 228; William McLellin, Journal, October 29–30, 1831, Church History Library, Salt Lake City; published in Jan Shipps and John W. Welch, eds., *The Journals of William E. McLellin, 1831–1836* (Urbana, Ill.: University of Illinois Press and Provo, Utah: BYU Studies, 1994), 45–47, 233–54.
3. Ezra Taft Benson, "The Gift of Modern Revelation," *Ensign* 16 (November 1986), 79.
4. Ibid.
5. David M. Robinson, ed., *The Spiritual Emerson: Essential Writings* (Boston: Beacon Press, 2003), 88–89.
6. Arthur M. Schlesinger, *The Age of Jackson* (Boston: Little, Brown, 1953), 129.
7. Andrew Delbanco, *The Death of Satan: How Americans Have Lost the Sense of Evil* (New York: Farrar, Straus, and Giroux, 1995), 105–6.
8. Far West Record, November 1, 1831, Church History Library, Salt Lake City.
9. Joseph Smith, *The Papers of Joseph Smith,* ed. Dean C. Jessee, 2 vols. (Salt Lake City: Deseret Book, 1989–92), 1:367.
10. Joseph Smith to William W. Phelps, November 27, 1832, in Joseph Smith, *Personal Writings of Joseph Smith,* ed. Dean C. Jessee, 2d ed. (Salt Lake City: Deseret Book and Provo, Utah: Brigham Young University Press, 2002), 287; punctuation standardized.
11. Smith, *Papers of Joseph Smith,* ed. Jessee, 1:367.
12. Richard Lyman Bushman, *Believing History: Latter-day Saint Essays,* ed. Reid L. Neilson and Jed Woodworth (New York: Columbia University Press, 2004), 258–59.
13. Far West Record, November 1–2, 1831.
14. Joseph Smith to William W. Phelps, November 27, 1832, in Smith, *Personal Writings of Joseph Smith,* ed. Jessee, 286–87. Melvin J. Peterson documented many examples of the editing in "Preparing Early Revelations for Publication," *Ensign* 15 (February 1985): 14–20.
15. Boyd K. Packer, Conference Report (April 1974): 137.

16. See, for example, Joseph Smith, *The Joseph Smith Papers*, ed. Dean C. Jessee, Ronald K. Esplin, and Richard Lyman Bushman (Salt Lake City: Church Historian's Press, 2008–), *Revelations and Translations* series, vol. 1, ed. Robin Scott Jensen, Robert J. Woodford, and Steven C. Harper (Salt Lake City: Church Historian's Press, 2009).
17. Robert J. Woodford documented these responses to the revelations. See "Joseph Smith and the Revelations: From Manuscripts to Publication," *Mormon Historical Studies* 6, no. 2 (Fall 2005): 135–44.
18. Richard Lyman Bushman, *Joseph Smith: Rough Stone Rolling* (New York: Knopf, 2005), 174.
19. Far West Record, November 8, 1831.
20. "Mormonism," in Joseph Smith Jr. et al., *History of The Church of Jesus Christ of Latter-day Saints*, ed. B. H. Roberts, 2d ed. rev., 7 vols. (Salt Lake City: Deseret Book, 1971), 1:397–98.
21. Kirtland Minute Book, August 17, 1835, Church History Library, Salt Lake City.
22. Ibid.
23. Bushman, *Rough Stone Rolling*, 282–85.
24. Kirtland Minute Book, August 17, 1835.
25. Woodford, "The Story of the Doctrine and Covenants," 32–39; "Doctrine and Covenants Editions," in *Encyclopedia of Mormonism*, ed. Daniel H. Ludlow et al., 4 vols. (New York: Macmillan, 1992), 1:425–27.
26. Woodford, "The Story of the Doctrine and Covenants," 32–39; "Doctrine and Covenants Editions," in Ludlow et al., *Encyclopedia of Mormonism*, 1:425–27.
27. Ralph Waldo Emerson, *The Complete Essays and Other Writings of Ralph Waldo Emerson*, ed. Brooks Atkinson (New York: Modern Library, 1950), 80.

Explanatory Introduction

1. Joseph Smith, *The Papers of Joseph Smith*, ed. Dean C. Jessee, 2 vols. (Salt Lake City: Deseret Book, 1989–92), 1:372.
2. Neal A. Maxwell, "The Doctrine and Covenants: The Voice of the Lord," *Ensign* 8 (December 1978): 4.
3. Richard Lyman Bushman, *Believing History: Latter-day Saint Essays*, ed. Reid L. Neilson and Jed Woodworth (New York: Columbia University Press, 2004), 253, 273.
4. E. Brooks Hollifield, *Theology in America: Christian Thought from the Age of the Puritans to the Civil War* (New Haven, Conn.: Yale University Press, 2003), 335.
5. Michael J. Preece, *Learning to Love the Doctrine and Covenants* (Salt Lake City: MJP Publishing, 1988), xi.
6. Hugh W. Nibley, *Approaching Zion*, ed. Don E. Norton (Salt Lake City: Deseret Book, 1989), 167, 174.
7. Gordon B. Hinckley, *Teachings of Gordon B. Hinckley* (Salt Lake City: Deseret Book, 1997), 639.
8. Neal A. Maxwell, "Consecrate Thy Performance," *Ensign* 32 (May 2002): 36.

Doctrine & Covenants 1

1. Far West Record, November 1–13, 1831, Church History Library, Salt Lake City; Joseph Smith to Dear Brethren, March 30, 1834, Church History Library, Salt Lake City. Oliver Cowdery Letterbook, 30–36, Huntington Library, San Marino, California.
2. Far West Record, November 12–13, 1831.

3. Joseph "dictated by the spirit the preface found in the Book of Doctrine and Covenants while sitting by a window in the room. Sidney Rigdon wrote it down. Joseph would deliver a few sentences and Sidney would write them down, then read them aloud, and if correct, then Joseph would proceed and deliver more, and by this process the preface was given." William Kelley to the editor, January 16, 1882, in *Saints' Herald* 29, no. 5 (March 1, 1882): 67.
4. Wilford Woodruff, *The Discourses of Wilford Woodruff: Fourth President of the Church of Jesus Christ of Latter-day Saints,* ed. G. Homer Durham (Salt Lake City: Bookcraft, 1946), 61.
5. John Whitmer understood the logic of Doctrine and Covenants 1 when he wrote in his Church history: "The Devil having great hold on the hearts of the children of men, the foolish traditions of our fathers is to be lamented, for they count themselves the children of wisdom, and great knowledge, in consequence of which, the fulness of the gospel finds its way to but few of the hearts of this generation. Although their hearts must be penetrated, whether they will hear or whether they will forbear." "History of John Whitmer," Community of Christ Archives, Independence, Missouri.
6. Nicholas Wolterstorff, *Divine Discourse: Philosophical Reflections on the Claim that God Speaks* (Cambridge: Cambridge University Press, 1995), 261.

Doctrine & Covenants 2
1. Joseph Smith, *The Papers of Joseph Smith,* ed. Dean C. Jessee, 2 vols. (Salt Lake City: Deseret Book, 1989–92), 1:127.
2. Smith, *Papers of Joseph Smith,* ed. Jessee, 1:278.
3. Russell M. Nelson, "The Atonement," *Ensign* 26 (November 1996): 35.

Doctrine & Covenants 3
1. Joseph Smith, *The Papers of Joseph Smith,* ed. Dean C. Jessee (Salt Lake City: Deseret Book, 1989), 1:9–10.
2. Lucy Mack Smith, *Lucy's Book: A Critical Edition of Lucy Mack Smith's Family Memoir,* ed. Lavina Fielding Anderson (Salt Lake City: Signature, 2001), 412–13.
3. Ibid., 415–17.
4. Ibid., 412–20; Steven C. Harper, *Joseph the Seer* (Provo, Utah: Harper Publishing, 2005), 51–53.
5. Richard Lyman Bushman, *Joseph Smith: Rough Stone Rolling* (New York: Knopf, 2005), 68.

Doctrine & Covenants 4
1. See Steven C. Harper, *Joseph the Seer* (Provo, Utah: Harper Publishing, 2005), 19–20.
2. Joseph Smith, *The Papers of Joseph Smith,* ed. Dean C. Jessee, 2 vols. (Salt Lake City: Deseret Book, 1989–92), 1:288.
3. Patriarchal Blessings Book, 1–2, Church History Library, Salt Lake City.
4. See Richard Lyman Bushman, *Joseph Smith: Rough Stone Rolling* (New York: Knopf, 2005), 114.

Doctrine & Covenants 5
1. Martin Harris, interview by Joel Tiffany, 1859, printed as "Mormonism—No. II," *Tiffany's Monthly* 5 (August 1859): 163–70.
2. Isaac Hale, "Mormonism," *Susquehanna Register and Northern Pennsylvanian* 9 (May 1, 1834): 1. Reprinted in *The [Utica] New York Baptist Register* 11 (June 13, 1834); E. D.

Howe, *Mormonism Unvailed* (Painesville, Ohio: E. D. Howe, 1834), 262–66; and Dan Vogel, *Early Mormon Documents,* 5 vols. (Salt Lake City: Signature, 1996), 4:287.

3. Joseph Smith, *The Papers of Joseph Smith,* ed. Dean C. Jessee, 2 vols. (Salt Lake City: Deseret Book, 1989–92), 1:235–38, 294–98.
4. Ibid.
5. Ibid.

Doctrine & Covenants 6

1. Joseph Smith, *The Papers of Joseph Smith,* ed. Dean C. Jessee, 2 vols. (Salt Lake City: Deseret Book, 1989–92), 1:10.
2. Lucy Mack Smith, *Lucy's Book: A Critical Edition of Lucy Mack Smith's Family Memoir,* ed. Lavina Fielding Anderson (Salt Lake City: Signature, 2001), 432–34; Joseph Smith Letterbook 1, 1–6, Church History Library, Salt Lake City. Smith, *Papers of Joseph Smith,* ed. Jessee, 1:10.
3. Richard Lyman Bushman, *Joseph Smith: Rough Stone Rolling* (New York: Knopf, 2005), 73.
4. Smith, *Papers of Joseph Smith,* ed. Jessee, 1:32–33.
5. See Noah Webster, *American Dictionary of the English Language* (1828), s.v. "mystery."
6. Smith, *Lucy's Book,* ed. Anderson, 438.
7. "Oliver Cowdery to the editor of *The Evening and the Morning Star,*" *Messenger and Advocate,* October 1834, 14.
8. Smith, *Papers of Joseph Smith,* ed. Jessee, 1:289.
9. "About the Book of Mormon," *Deseret News,* March 25, 1884, 2.
10. In his well-known 1741 sermon, "Sinners in the Hands of an Angry God," Jonathan Edwards described "the mere pleasure of God, I mean his sovereign pleasure, his arbitrary will, restrained by no obligation." John E. Smith, Harry S. Stout, and Kenneth P. Minkema, eds., *A Jonathan Edwards Reader* (New Haven, Conn.: Yale University Press, 1995), 90.

Doctrine & Covenants 7

1. Joseph Smith, *The Papers of Joseph Smith,* ed. Dean C. Jessee, 2 vols. (Salt Lake City: Deseret Book, 1989–92), 1:289.
2. Boyd K. Packer, *The Holy Temple* (Salt Lake City: Bookcraft, 1980), 83; Edward L. Kimball, *Lengthen Your Stride: The Presidency of Spencer W. Kimball* (Salt Lake City: Deseret Book, 2005), 108, 327.
3. A Book of Commandments for the Government of the Church of Christ (Independence, Mo.: W. W. Phelps, 1833), 19.
4. See Doctrine and Covenants 33:1 in 1835 edition.

Doctrine & Covenants 8

1. Joseph Smith, *The Papers of Joseph Smith,* ed. Dean C. Jessee, 2 vols. (Salt Lake City: Deseret Book, 1989–92), 1:289.
2. Robert J. Woodford, "The Historical Development of the Doctrine and Covenants" (Ph.D. dissertation, Brigham Young University, 1974), 2 vols., 1:185–89.

3. See 1 Nephi 16:29; Mosiah 8:15–18; Doctrine and Covenants 10:1; Joseph Smith–History 1:62.
4. A Book of Commandments for the Government of the Church of Christ (Independence, Mo.: W. W. Phelps, 1833), 19.

Doctrine & Covenants 9

1. "These were days never to be forgotten," Oliver wrote in 1834, "to sit under the sound of a voice dictated by the inspiration of heaven awakened the utmost gratitude of this bosom! Day after day I continued, uninterrupted, to write from his mouth, as he translated with the Urim and Thimmim, or, as the Nephites would have said, 'Interpreters,' the history or record called 'The Book of Mormon.'" *Messenger and Advocate,* October 1834, 14–16.

Doctrine & Covenants 10

1. See the preface to the 1830 edition of the Book of Mormon. The earliest manuscript of Doctrine and Covenants 10 is dated 1829. Assuming that section 10 fit better in the events of 1828, later historians revised the date to show a year earlier.

Doctrine & Covenants 11

1. Joseph Smith, *The Papers of Joseph Smith,* ed. Dean C. Jessee, 2 vols. (Salt Lake City: Deseret Book, 1989–92), 1:292.
2. Jan Shipps and John W. Welch, eds., *The Journals of William E. McLellin, 1831–1836* (Urbana, Ill.: University of Illinois Press and Provo, Utah: BYU Studies, 1994), 33–34.

Doctrine & Covenants 12

1. Joseph Smith, *The Papers of Joseph Smith,* ed. Dean C. Jessee, 2 vols. (Salt Lake City: Deseret Book, 1989–92), 1:293.
2. Ibid., 2:438.

Doctrine & Covenants 13

1. Joseph Smith, *The Papers of Joseph Smith,* ed. Dean C. Jessee, 2 vols. (Salt Lake City: Deseret Book, 1989–92), 1:30.
2. See also ibid., 1:30, 290.
3. See also ibid., 1:290.
4. See also ibid., 1:290–91.
5. See also ibid., 1:31.
6. See also ibid., 1:291.
7. Wilford Woodruff, Journal, June 27, 1839, Church History Library, Salt Lake City; Joseph Smith, Journal, as kept by Willard Richards, February 9, 1843, 170–72, Church History Library, Salt Lake City.

Doctrine & Covenants 14, 15, and 16

1. Joseph Smith, *The Papers of Joseph Smith,* ed. Dean C. Jessee, 2 vols. (Salt Lake City: Deseret Book, 1989–92), 1:294.
2. See Lyndon W. Cook, ed., *David Whitmer Interviews: A Restoration Witness* (Orem, Utah: Grandin Book, 1991).

3. Lyndon W. Cook, *The Revelations of the Prophet Joseph Smith* (Provo: Seventy's Mission Bookstore, 1981), 26.
4. Quoted in Richard Lloyd Anderson, *Investigating the Book of Mormon Witnesses* (Salt Lake City: Deseret Book, 1981), 131.

Doctrine & Covenants 17

1. Joseph Smith, *The Papers of Joseph Smith*, ed. Dean C. Jessee, 2 vols. (Salt Lake City: Deseret Book, 1989–92), 1:235–36; see also Steven C. Harper, *Joseph the Seer* (Provo, Utah: Harper Publishing, 2005), 63–65.
2. William Harrison Homer, "The Last Testimony of Martin Harris," affidavit, July 10, 1925, Church History Library, Salt Lake City. See also Harper, *Joseph the Seer,* 63–65.

Doctrine & Covenants 18

1. A Book of Commandments for the Government of the Church of Christ (Independence, Mo.: W. W. Phelps, 1833), 34. This volume was reprinted in 1972 by Herald House, the publishing division of the Reorganized Church of Jesus Christ of Latter Day Saints (now known as Community of Christ).
2. Truman G. Madsen, "The Savior, the Sacrament, and Self-Worth," in *The Arms of His Love* (Salt Lake City: Deseret Book, 2000), 248.
3. M. Russell Ballard, "The Atonement and the Value of One Soul," *Ensign* 34 (May 2004): 86–87.

Doctrine & Covenants 19

1. Pomeroy Tucker, *Origin, Rise, and Progress of Mormonism* (New York: D. Appleton, 1867), 41, 50.
2. Martin Harris, Mortgage to Egbert B. Grandin, August 25, 1829, Mortgages, Liber 3, 325, Wayne County Clerk's Office, Lyons, New York.
3. Joseph Knight, Manuscript History, Church History Library, Salt Lake City.
4. Ibid.
5. David B. Haight, "Our Lord and Savior," *Ensign* 18 (May 1988): 23; paragraphing altered.

Doctrine & Covenants 20

1. Scott H. Faulring, "An Examination of the 1829 'Articles of the Church of Christ' in Relation to Section 20 of the Doctrine and Covenants," *BYU Studies* 43, no. 4 (2004): 65–67.
2. Ibid., 69. There is some evidence that Oliver was reluctant to receive the new revelation, perhaps because it replaced his draft.
3. Richard Lloyd Anderson, "The Organization Revelations," in *Studies in Scripture: The Doctrine and Covenants,* ed. Robert L. Millet and Kent P. Jackson (Sandy, Utah: Randall Book, 1984), 112.
4. Oliver Cowdery, "Articles of the Church of Christ," Church History Library, Salt Lake City.
5. Joseph Smith, *The Papers of Joseph Smith*, ed. Dean C. Jessee, 2 vols. (Salt Lake City: Deseret Book, 1989–92), 1:260.
6. Ibid., 1:320.
7. Far West Record, September 26, 1830, Church History Library, Salt Lake City.
8. Ibid., June 9, 1830.

Doctrine & Covenants 21

1. Dean Jessee, "Joseph Knight's Recollection of Early Mormon History," *BYU Studies* 17, no. 1 (1976): 36–37; see also Joseph Smith, *The Papers of Joseph Smith,* ed. Dean C. Jessee, 2 vols. (Salt Lake City: Deseret Book, 1989–92), 1:302–3.
2. Nathan O. Hatch, *The Democratization of American Christianity* (New Haven, Conn.: Yale University Press, 1989), 17; Jeffrey R. Holland, "Prophets, Seers, and Revelators," *Ensign* 34 (November 2004): 6.
3. Quoted in I. Daniel Rupp, *He Pasa Ekklesia: An Original History of the Religious Denominations at Present Existing in the United States* (Philadelphia, Pa.: J.Y. Humphreys, 1844), in Smith, *Papers of Joseph Smith,* ed. Jessee, 1:448.
4. Smith, *Papers of Joseph Smith,* ed. Jessee, 1:303.
5. Jessee, "Joseph Knight's Recollection," 37.

Doctrine & Covenants 22

1. Joseph Smith, *The Papers of Joseph Smith,* ed. Dean C. Jessee, 2 vols. (Salt Lake City: Deseret Book, 1989–92), 1:304.
2. Orson Pratt, in *Journal of Discourses,* 26 vols. (Liverpool: F. D. Richards, 1855–86), 16:293, November 2, 1873.
3. Francis Wayland, *Notes on the Principles and Practices of Baptist Churches* (New York: Sheldon, Blakeman, 1857), 98.

Doctrine & Covenants 23

1. Joseph Smith, *The Papers of Joseph Smith,* ed. Dean C. Jessee, 2 vols. (Salt Lake City: Deseret Book, 1989–92), 1:304.
2. Dean Jessee, "Joseph Knight's Recollection of Early Mormon History," *BYU Studies* 17, no. 1 (1976): 37.

Doctrine & Covenants 24

1. Joseph Smith, *The Papers of Joseph Smith,* ed. Dean C. Jessee, 2 vols. (Salt Lake City: Deseret Book, 1989–92), 1:319.

Doctrine & Covenants 25

1. "Some of the Remarks of John S. Reed, Esq., as Delivered before the State Convention," *Times and Seasons* 5, no. 2 (June 1, 1844): 549–52.
2. Joseph Smith et al., Book of the Law of the Lord, August 16, 1842, 135, 164–65, quoted in Joseph Smith, *The Papers of Joseph Smith,* ed. Dean C. Jessee, 2 vols. (Salt Lake City: Deseret Book, 1989–92), 2:416; Joseph Smith Jr. et al., *History of The Church of Jesus Christ of Latter-day Saints,* ed. B. H. Roberts, 2d ed. rev., 7 vols. (Salt Lake City: Deseret Book, 1971), 5:106–7.
3. Carol Cornwall Madsen, "The 'Elect Lady' Revelation: The Historical and Doctrinal Context of Doctrine & Covenants 25," in *The Heavens Are Open: The 1992 Sperry Symposium on the Doctrine and Covenants and Church History,* ed. Byron R. Merrill et al. (Salt Lake City: Deseret Book, 1993), 211–18.

Doctrine & Covenants 26

1. Newel Knight, Autobiography and journal, 1846, Church History Library, Salt Lake City.
2. N. Eldon Tanner, "The Solemn Assembly," Conference Report (April 1974): 55.

Doctrine & Covenants 27

1. Joseph Smith, *The Papers of Joseph Smith,* ed. Dean C. Jessee, 2 vols. (Salt Lake City: Deseret Book, 1989–92), 2:321; "Newel Knight's Journal," in *Scraps of Biography* (Salt Lake City: Juvenile Instructor's Office, 1883), 62–63.
2. "Newel Knight's Journal," in *Scraps of Biography,* 62–63.
3. The stick of Ephraim is the Book of Mormon. See Ezekiel 37:16–17, to which 2 Nephi 3:17 refers. See also "The Book of Mormon," *The Evening and the Morning Star,* January 1833, 1.
4. See Ephesians 6:11–18.
5. "Newel Knight's Journal," in *Scraps of Biography,* 62–63.
6. Brigham Young, in *Journal of Discourses,* 26 vols. (Liverpool: F. D. Richards, 1855–86), 19:92, August 19, 1877. See also Heber C. Kimball, in *Journal of Discourses,* 10:245, July 19, 1863.
7. John Henry Smith, Diary, July 1906, Manuscripts Division, J. Willard Marriott Library, University of Utah, Salt Lake City.
8. This teaching is distinctive to Joseph Smith. He equated the archangel Michael with Adam, an idea apparently first documented in Oliver Cowdery's January 1, 1834, letter to John Whitmer. Oliver Cowdery Letterbook, 15, Huntington Library, San Marino, California. Similarly, Joseph interpreted references to the "Ancient of days" in the book of Daniel (7:9, 13, 22) as references to Adam. When Daniel "speaks of the Ancient of days," Joseph taught in 1839, "he means the oldest man, our Father Adam, Michael." Willard Richards, "Willard Richards Pocket Companion," 63, Church History Library, Salt Lake City.

Doctrine & Covenants 28

1. Joseph Smith, *The Papers of Joseph Smith,* ed. Dean C. Jessee, 2 vols. (Salt Lake City: Deseret Book, 1989–92), 1:263.
2. Newel Knight, Autobiography and journal, 1846, Church History Library, Salt Lake City.
3. Ibid.

Doctrine & Covenants 29

1. Neal A. Maxwell, "Hope through the Atonement of Jesus Christ," *Ensign* 28 (November 1998): 61.

Doctrine & Covenants 30

1. Joseph Smith, *The Papers of Joseph Smith,* ed. Dean C. Jessee, 2 vols. (Salt Lake City: Deseret Book, 1989–92), 1:324.
2. Peter Whitmer Jr., Journal, Historical Department Archives, The Church of Jesus Christ of Latter-day Saints, Salt Lake City.
3. *Western Courier* [Ravenna, Ohio], May 26, 1831. Levi Jackman wrote that "something like one hundred persons joined the Church from that place [Kirtland], with many other branches of the Church organized in adjoining towns and counties." Levi Jackman, Autobiography, L. Tom Perry Special Collections, Harold B. Lee Library, Brigham Young University, Provo, Utah.
4. Parley P. Pratt, *Autobiography of Parley P. Pratt,* ed. Scot Facer Proctor and Maurine Jensen Proctor (Salt Lake City: Deseret Book, 2000), 39; Samuel Smith, Journal, April 24, 1832, Church History Library, Salt Lake City.

Doctrine & Covenants 31

1. *Millennial Star* 26 (June 11, 1864): 375–76.
2. "History of Thos. Baldwin Marsh," *Deseret News,* March 24, 1858, 18.
3. Lucy Mack Smith, *The Revised and Enhanced History of Joseph Smith by His Mother,* ed. Scot Facer Proctor and Maurine Jensen Proctor (Salt Lake City: Bookcraft, 1996), 259–77.
4. Thomas B. Marsh to Heber C. Kimball, May 5, 1857, Church Archives, The Church of Jesus Christ of Latter-day Saints, Salt Lake City.

Doctrine & Covenants 32

1. Joseph Smith, *The Papers of Joseph Smith,* ed. Dean C. Jessee, 2 vols. (Salt Lake City: Deseret Book, 1989–92), 1:324–25.
2. "History of Parley P. Pratt," *Deseret News,* May 19, 1858.
3. Lucy Mack Smith, *Lucy's Book: A Critical Edition of Lucy Mack Smith's Family Memoir,* ed. Lavina Fielding Anderson (Salt Lake City: Signature, 2001), 502–3.
4. Ezra Booth to Rev. Ira Eddy, November 24, 1831, in *[Ravenna] Ohio Star,* December 8, 1831.
5. Smith, *Lucy's Book,* ed. Anderson, 503.
6. *Western Courier* [Ravenna, Ohio], May 26, 1831; Richard Lloyd Anderson, "The Impact of the First Preaching in Ohio," *BYU Studies* 11, no. 4 (1971): 478.
7. Anderson, "Impact of the First Preaching in Ohio," 496; Journal of Lyman Wight, as cited by Heman C. Smith, *History of the Reorganized Church of Jesus Christ of Latter Day Saints,* 4 vols. (1897–1903; reprint, Independence, Mo.: Herald House, 1951), 1:153.

Doctrine & Covenants 33

1. "Testimony of Brother E. Thayer Concerning the Latter Day Work," *Saints' Herald* 3 (October 1862): 79–80, 82–84.
2. Ibid.

Doctrine & Covenants 34

1. Elden J. Watson, comp., *The Orson Pratt Journals* (Salt Lake City: E. J. Watson, 1975), 9.
2. Orson Pratt, in *Journal of Discourses,* 26 vols. (Liverpool: F. D. Richards, 1855–86), 17:290, February 7, 1875.
3. Quoted in Breck England, *The Life and Thought of Orson Pratt* (Salt Lake City: University of Utah Press, 1985), xi.

Doctrine & Covenants 35

1. John Whitmer, "Book of John Whitmer," 1, Community of Christ Archives, Independence, Missouri.
2. Lucy Mack Smith, *Lucy's Book: A Critical Edition of Lucy Mack Smith's Family Memoir,* ed. Lavina Fielding Anderson (Salt Lake City: Signature, 2001), 504–5.
3. Whitmer, "Book of John Whitmer," 2.
4. Ibid., 4.
5. Ibid., 5.

Doctrine & Covenants 36

1. Richard Lloyd Anderson, "The Impact of the First Preaching in Ohio," *BYU Studies* 11, no. 4 (1971): 489.
2. History of Edward Partridge Jr., 5, quoted in Anderson, "Impact of the First Preaching in Ohio," 493.
3. Lucy Mack Smith, *Lucy's Book: A Critical Edition of Lucy Mack Smith's Family Memoir,* ed. Lavina Fielding Anderson (Salt Lake City: Signature, 2001), 504–5.
4. Joseph Smith, *The Papers of Joseph Smith,* ed. Dean C. Jessee, 2 vols. (Salt Lake City: Deseret Book, 1989–92), 2:66.

Doctrine & Covenants 37

1. John Whitmer, "Book of John Whitmer," 4, Community of Christ Archives, Independence, Missouri.
2. Lucy Mack Smith, *Lucy's Book: A Critical Edition of Lucy Mack Smith's Family Memoir,* ed. Lavina Fielding Anderson (Salt Lake City: Signature, 2001), 503–5.
3. Whitmer, "Book of John Whitmer," 5.
4. Ibid., 10.
5. Ibid., 5.

Doctrine & Covenants 38

1. Newel Knight, Autobiography and journal, 1846, Church History Library, Salt Lake City.
2. John Whitmer, "Book of John Whitmer," 6, Community of Christ Archives, Independence, Missouri.
3. Ibid., 5.
4. Ibid., 9.
5. William G. Hartley, *Stand by My Servant Joseph* (Salt Lake City: Deseret Book; Provo, Utah: Joseph Fielding Smith Institute for LDS History, 2003), 103.
6. Whitmer, "Book of John Whitmer," 9.
7. Knight, Autobiography and journal, 1846.
8. "Increased consecration is not so much a demand for more hours of Church work as it is for more awareness of Whose work this really is! For now, consecration may not require giving up worldly possessions so much as being less possessed by them." Neal A. Maxwell, "Settle This in Your Hearts," *Ensign* 22 (November 1992): 67.
9. "We tend to think of consecration only as yielding up, when divinely directed, our material possessions. But ultimate consecration is the yielding up of oneself to God." Neal A. Maxwell, "Consecrate Thy Performance," *Ensign* 32 (May 2002): 36.
10. Elder Jeffrey R. Holland taught the same principle in our time: "Pay your tithing as a declaration that possession of material goods and the accumulation of worldly wealth are *not* the uppermost goals of your existence. As one young husband and father, living on a student budget, recently told me, 'Perhaps our most pivotal moments as Latter-day Saints come when we have to swim directly against the current of the culture in which we live. Tithing provides just such a moment. Living in a world that emphasizes material acquisition and cultivates distrust for anyone or anything that has designs on our money, we shed that self-absorption to give freely, trustingly, and generously. By this act, we say—indeed—we are different, that we are God's peculiar people. In a society that tells us money is our most important asset, we declare emphatically it is not.'" Jeffrey R. Holland, "Like a Watered Garden," *Ensign* 31 (November 2001): 34.

11. Knight, Autobiography and journal, 1846.
12. Hartley, *Stand by My Servant Joseph,* 20–21; Richard Lloyd Anderson, *Investigating the Book of Mormon Witnesses* (Salt Lake City: Deseret Book, 1981), 124.
13. Hartley, *Stand by My Servant Joseph,* 103–5.
14. Lucy Mack Smith, *The Revised and Enhanced History of Joseph Smith by His Mother,* ed. Scot Facer Proctor and Maurine Jensen Proctor (Salt Lake City: Bookcraft, 1996), 259.
15. Ibid., 268.
16. Ibid., 266.
17. Ibid., 264–65.
18. Ibid., 269–70.
19. Knight, Autobiography and journal, 1846.
20. Quoted in Hartley, *Stand by My Servant Joseph,* 113.
21. Karl Ricks Anderson, *Joseph Smith's Kirtland: Eyewitness Accounts* (Salt Lake City: Deseret Book, 1989), 11–19.
22. Kirtland Township Trustees' Minutes and Poll Book, 1817–1838, Lake County Historical Society, Kirtland Hills, Ohio.
23. Anderson, *Joseph Smith's Kirtland,* 11–19.
24. Gordon B. Hinckley, *Teachings of Gordon B. Hinckley* (Salt Lake City: Deseret Book, 1997), 639. See Doctrine and Covenants 38:32; 42.
25. Revelation of January 12, 1838, Archives, The Church of Jesus Christ of Latter-day Saints, Salt Lake City.
26. Knight, Autobiography and journal, 1846.
27. Richard Lyman Bushman, *Believing History: Latter-day Saint Essays,* ed. Reid L. Neilson and Jed Woodworth (New York: Columbia University Press, 2004), 259.
28. Smith, *History of Joseph Smith,* ed. Proctor and Proctor, 268; Hartley, *Stand by My Servant Joseph,* 113.

Doctrine & Covenants 39 and 40

1. Joseph Smith, *The Papers of Joseph Smith,* ed. Dean C. Jessee, 2 vols. (Salt Lake City: Deseret Book, 1989–92), 1:346; or Doctrine and Covenants 40, headnote.
2. Smith, *Papers of Joseph Smith,* ed. Jessee, 1:346.
3. Payne Kenyon Kilbourne, *Sketches and Chronicles of the Town of Litchfield, Connecticut, Historical, Biographical, and Statistical: Together with a Complete Official Register of the Town* (Hartford, Conn.: Case, Lockwood and Company, 1859), 183.
4. Ibid.; Abel Stevens, *Memorials of the Introduction of Methodism into the Eastern States* (Boston, Mass.: Charles H. Pierce, 1848), 119; Stephen Parks, *Troy Conference Miscellany: Containing a Historical Sketch of Methodism within the Bounds of the Troy Conference of the Methodist Episcopal Church, with Reminiscences of Its Deceased, and Contributions by Its Living Ministers, with an Appendix* (Albany, N.Y.: J. Lord, 1854), 185; and *Vital Records of Marblehead, Massachusetts to the End of the Year 1849,* microform, 3 vols. (Salem, Mass.: Essex Institute, 1903–08,) 2:101, 177.
5. Parks, *Troy Conference Miscellany,* 185; Stevens, *Memorials of the Introduction of Methodism into the Eastern States,* 119, 185–86.
6. Smith, *Papers of Joseph Smith,* ed. Jessee, 1:346; Doctrine and Covenants 40, headnote.
7. Joseph Smith to William W. Phelps, January 11, 1833, Joseph Smith Letterbook 1, 18–20, Church History Library, Salt Lake City, in Dean C. Jessee, ed. and comp., *Personal*

Writings of Joseph Smith (1984; reprint, Salt Lake City: Deseret Book and Provo, Utah: Brigham Young University Press, 2002), 292–93.

8. Matthew L. Davis to Mrs. Matthew L. Davis, February 6, 1840, Church History Library, Salt Lake City.

Doctrine & Covenants 41

1. Edward Partridge Papers, May 26, 1839, Church History Library, Salt Lake City.
2. Richard Lloyd Anderson, "The Impact of the First Mormon Preaching in Ohio," *BYU Studies* 11, no. 4 (1971): 489.
3. History of Edward Partridge Jr., 5, quoted in Anderson, "Impact of the First Mormon Preaching in Ohio," 493; Lucy Mack Smith, *Lucy's Book: A Critical Edition of Lucy Mack Smith's Family Memoir,* ed. Lavina Fielding Anderson (Salt Lake City: Signature, 2001), 504–5.
4. Quoted in Scott H. Partridge, "Edward Partridge in Painesville, Ohio," *BYU Studies* 42, no. 1 (2003): 59.
5. B. H. Roberts, *A Comprehensive History of The Church of Jesus Christ of Latter-day Saints, Century One,* 6 vols. (Provo, Utah: Corporation of the President, The Church of Jesus Christ of Latter-day Saints, 1965), 1:244.
6. Eliza Maria Partridge Lyman, *Eliza Maria Partridge Journal,* ed. Scott H. Partridge (Provo, Utah: Grandin Book, 2003), 2–3.

Doctrine & Covenants 42

1. Joseph Smith, *The Papers of Joseph Smith,* ed. Dean C. Jessee, 2 vols. (Salt Lake City: Deseret Book, 1989–92), 1:347.
2. Ibid.
3. Quoted in Grant Underwood, "'The Laws of the Church of Christ' (D&C 42): A Textual and Historical Analysis," in *The Doctrine and Covenants: Revelations in Context* [2008 Sidney B. Sperry Symposium], ed. Andrew H. Hedges, J. Spencer Fluhman, and Alonzo L. Gaskill (Salt Lake City: Deseret Book and Provo: Brigham Young University, Religious Studies Center, 2008), 110.
4. Ibid., 112.
5. John Whitmer, "Book of John Whitmer," 17, Community of Christ Archives, Independence, Missouri.
6. Joseph Smith to Edward Partridge, June 25, 1833, Church History Library, Salt Lake City.
7. Joseph Smith to Edward Partridge, William Phelps, and other members of the United Firm, March 30, 1834, in Joseph Smith, *Personal Writings of Joseph Smith,* ed. Dean C. Jessee, 2d ed. (Salt Lake City: Deseret Book and Provo, Utah: Brigham Young University Press, 2002), 338–39. See also Deuteronomy 8:18.
8. Gordon B. Hinckley, *Teachings of Gordon B. Hinckley* (Salt Lake City: Deseret Book, 1997), 639.

Doctrine & Covenants 43

1. Thomas Müntzer, *Revelation and Revolution: Basic Writings of Thomas Müntzer,* ed. and trans. Michael G. Baylor (Bethlehem, Pa.: Lehigh University Press, 1993), 55.
2. Ibid.
3. Ibid., 54–55.

4. Richard Marius, *Martin Luther: The Christian between God and Death* (Cambridge: Harvard University Press, 1999), 406.
5. Ibid., 397.
6. Ibid., 398–400.
7. Quoted in Müntzer, *Revelation and Revolution,* 11.
8. Ralph Waldo Emerson, *The Complete Essays and Other Writings of Ralph Waldo Emerson,* ed. Brooks Atkinson (New York: Modern Library, 1950), 80.
9. John Whitmer, "Book of John Whitmer," 18, Community of Christ Archives, Independence, Missouri; Ezra Booth to Rev. Ira Eddy, November 29, 1831, in *[Ravenna] Ohio Star* (December 8, 1831); Joseph Smith, *The Papers of Joseph Smith,* ed. Dean C. Jessee, 2 vols. (Salt Lake City: Deseret Book, 1989–92), 1:349.
10. Whitmer, "Book of John Whitmer," 21.
11. Quoted in David Paulsen, "Joseph Smith Challenges the Theological World," *BYU Studies* 44, no. 4 (2005): 202.

Doctrine & Covenants 44

1. Joseph Smith, *The Papers of Joseph Smith,* ed. Dean C. Jessee, 2 vols. (Salt Lake City: Deseret Book, 1989–92), 1:349, 352–53.
2. "Act for the Incorporation of Religious Societies," in *Acts Passed at the First Session of the Seventeenth General Assembly of the State of Ohio,* Vol. XVII (Chillicothe, Ohio: Office of the Supporter, 1819), chapter LIV.

Doctrine & Covenants 45

1. Patricia T. Holland, "God's Covenant of Peace," in *The Arms of His Love* (Salt Lake City: Deseret Book, 2000), 375–76.

Doctrine & Covenants 46

1. John Whitmer, "Book of John Whitmer," 23, Community of Christ Archives, Independence, Missouri.
2. Ibid.
3. Joseph Smith, Journal, January 2, 1843, Church History Library, Salt Lake City.
4. Ibid.

Doctrine & Covenants 47

1. John Whitmer, "Book of John Whitmer," 24, Community of Christ Archives, Independence, Missouri.
2. Joseph Smith, *The Papers of Joseph Smith,* ed. Dean C. Jessee, 2 vols. (Salt Lake City: Deseret Book, 1989–92), 1:351.
3. Whitmer, "Book of John Whitmer," 1.
4. Richard L. Bushman, *Believing History: Latter-day Saint Essays,* ed. Reid L. Neilson and Jed Woodworth (New York: Columbia University Press, 2004), 258–59.

Doctrine & Covenants 48

1. John Whitmer, "Book of John Whitmer," 23, Community of Christ Archives, Independence, Missouri; see Joseph Smith, *The Papers of Joseph Smith,* ed. Dean C. Jessee, 2 vols. (Salt Lake City: Deseret Book, 1989–92), 1:351.

Doctrine & Covenants 49

1. F. W. Evans, *Shakers Compendium* (New York: D. Appleton, 1859), 1:26.
2. Lawrence R. Flake, "A Shaker View of a Mormon Mission," *BYU Studies* 20, no. 1 (1979): 94–99.
3. Evans, *Shakers Compendium,* 6:13; 4:16; 7:10; 11:64.
4. Ibid., 10:32–33.
5. Flake, "A Shaker View of a Mormon Mission," 96.
6. Joseph Smith, *The Papers of Joseph Smith,* ed. Dean C. Jessee, 2 vols. (Salt Lake City: Deseret Book, 1989–92), 1:351.
7. John Whitmer, "Book of John Whitmer," 26, Community of Christ Archives, Independence, Missouri.
8. Flake, "A Shaker View of a Mormon Mission," 97.
9. Ibid., 97–98.
10. Ibid., 98.
11. Ibid.
12. Parley P. Pratt, *Autobiography of Parley P. Pratt,* ed. Scot Facer Proctor and Maurine Jensen Proctor (Salt Lake City: Deseret Book, 2000), 70. John Whitmer added that the missionaries "went and proclaimed according to revelation given to them, but the Shakers hearkened not to their words, and received not the gospel that time; for they were bound up in tradition and priestcraft, and thus they are led away with foolish and vain imaginations." Whitmer, "Book of John Whitmer," 26.

Doctrine & Covenants 50

1. Autobiography of Levi Hancock, typescript, L. Tom Perry Special Collections, Harold B. Lee Library, Brigham Young University, Provo, Utah.
2. John Whitmer, "Book of John Whitmer," 26, Community of Christ Archives, Independence, Missouri.
3. Parley P. Pratt, *Autobiography of Parley P. Pratt,* ed. Scot Facer Proctor and Maurine Jensen Proctor (Salt Lake City: Deseret Book, 2000), 70–72.
4. See Steven C. Harper, *Joseph the Seer* (Provo, Utah: Harper Publishing, 2005), 27–28.
5. Philo Dibble, "Recollections of the Prophet Joseph Smith," *Juvenile Instructor* 27, no. 1 (January 1892): 22–23.
6. Whitmer, "Book of John Whitmer," 27.
7. Pratt, *Autobiography of Parley P. Pratt,* ed. Proctor and Proctor, 72.
8. Autobiography of Jared Carter, Church History Library, Salt Lake City.
9. Joseph Smith, Journal, January 2, 1843, Church History Library, Salt Lake City.
10. Pratt, *Autobiography of Parley P. Pratt,* ed. Proctor and Proctor, 79.

Doctrine & Covenants 51

1. William G. Hartley, *Stand by My Servant Joseph* (Salt Lake City: Deseret Book and Provo, Utah: Joseph Fielding Smith Institute for LDS History, 2003), 20–21; Richard Lloyd Anderson, *Investigating the Book of Mormon Witnesses* (Salt Lake City: Deseret Book, 1981), 124.
2. Newel Knight, Autobiography and journal, 1846, Church History Library, Salt Lake City.
3. Quoted in Hartley, *Stand by My Servant Joseph,* 113.

4. Geauga County Tax Records 1832, 230; Joseph Smith, *The Papers of Joseph Smith*, ed. Dean C. Jessee, 2 vols. (Salt Lake City: Deseret Book, 1989–92), 1:480; Dean Jessee, ed., "Joseph Knight's Recollection of Early Mormon History," *BYU Studies* 17, no. 1 (1976): 38–39.
5. Joseph Stringham to Leonor T. Alvarez, January 16, 2004. Copy in possession of the author.
6. Kirtland Revelation Book, 87–89, Church History Library, Salt Lake City.
7. Knight, Autobiography and journal, 1846; Jessee, "Joseph Knight's Recollection," 38–39.
8. "The Elders Stationed in Zion to the Churches Abroad," *The Evening and the Morning Star,* July 1833, 109.
9. *Painesville [Ohio] Telegraph,* April 26, 1833.
10. Joseph Smith to Edward Partridge, May 2, 1833, Joseph Smith Letterbook, Church History Library, Salt Lake City.
11. Ibid.

Doctrine & Covenants 52

1. John Whitmer called Doctrine and Covenants 52 a "revelation what to do." John Whitmer, "Book of John Whitmer," 29, Community of Christ Archives, Independence, Missouri.
2. Joseph Smith Jr. et al., *History of The Church of Jesus Christ of Latter-day Saints,* ed. B. H. Roberts, 2d ed. rev., 7 vols. (Salt Lake City: Deseret Book, 1971), 3:232; Rough Draft Notes of *History of the Church,* 1838, Church History Library, Salt Lake City; Joseph Smith, Manuscript History, Book C-1, 868–73, Church History Library, Salt Lake City.

Doctrine & Covenants 53

1. Joseph Smith, *The Papers of Joseph Smith,* ed. Dean C. Jessee, 2 vols. (Salt Lake City: Deseret Book, 1989–92), 1:353.

Doctrine & Covenants 54

1. Joseph Smith, *The Papers of Joseph Smith,* ed. Dean C. Jessee, 2 vols. (Salt Lake City: Deseret Book, 1989–92), 1:351; John Whitmer, "Book of John Whitmer," 26, Community of Christ Archives, Independence, Missouri.
2. Geauga County Tax Records 1832, 230; Smith, *Papers of Joseph Smith,* ed. Jessee, 1:480; Dean Jessee, ed., "Joseph Knight's Recollection of Early Mormon History," *BYU Studies* 17, no. 1 (1976): 29–39.
3. Newel Knight, Autobiography and journal, 30, 1846, Church History Library, Salt Lake City.
4. Kirtland Revelation Book, 87–89, Church History Library, Salt Lake City.
5. Jessee, "Joseph Knight's Recollection," 29–39.
6. Joseph Knight Jr., "Incidents of History 1827–1844," Church History Library, Salt Lake City.
7. Whitmer, "Book of John Whitmer," 29.
8. Smith, *Papers of Joseph Smith,* ed. Jessee, 1:353–54.

Doctrine & Covenants 55

1. Joseph Smith, *The Papers of Joseph Smith,* ed. Dean C. Jessee, 2 vols. (Salt Lake City: Deseret Book, 1989–92), 1:355.

Doctrine & Covenants 56

1. Kirtland Revelation Book, 91–92, Church History Library, Salt Lake City.
2. Joseph Smith, *The Papers of Joseph Smith,* ed. Dean C. Jessee, 2 vols. (Salt Lake City: Deseret Book, 1989–92), 1:356.
3. Kirtland Revelation Book, 91–92.
4. Thomas B. Marsh, "History of Thomas B. Marsh, Written by Himself," Church History Library, Salt Lake City.

Doctrine & Covenants 57

1. Joseph Smith, "To the elders of the church of Latter Day Saints," *Messenger and Advocate,* September 1835, 179–80.
2. Joseph Smith, *The Papers of Joseph Smith,* ed. Dean C. Jessee, 2 vols. (Salt Lake City: Deseret Book, 1989–92), 1:357.
3. Smith, "To the elders of the church of Latter Day Saints," 179–80.
4. Joseph Smith Letterbook 2, 54–55, Church History Library, Salt Lake City; Joseph Smith Jr. et al., *History of The Church of Jesus Christ of Latter-day Saints,* ed. B. H. Roberts, 2d ed. rev., 7 vols. (Salt Lake City: Deseret Book, 1971), 1:394.

Doctrine & Covenants 58

1. Joseph Smith, *The Papers of Joseph Smith,* ed. Dean C. Jessee, 2 vols. (Salt Lake City: Deseret Book, 1989–92), 1:357.
2. Richard Lyman Bushman, *Joseph Smith: Rough Stone Rolling* (New York: Knopf, 2005), 164.
3. Ezra Booth, *[Ravenna] Ohio Star,* November 24, 1831.
4. Ziba Peterson confessed at a conference held a few days later. Far West Record, August 4, 1831, Church History Library, Salt Lake City.
5. Bushman, *Rough Stone Rolling,* 164.
6. Booth, *[Ravenna] Ohio Star,* November 24, 1831.
7. Edward Partridge to Lydia Partridge, August 5, 1831, Emily Partridge Papers, Church History Library, Salt Lake City.
8. Quoted in Scott H. Partridge, "Edward Partridge in Painesville, Ohio," *BYU Studies* 42, no. 1 (2003): 64.
9. Quoted in ibid.
10. Orson Pratt, in *Journal of Discourses,* 26 vols. (Liverpool: F. D. Richards, 1855–86), 18:160–61, July 18, 1875.
11. Smith, *Papers of Joseph Smith,* ed. Jessee, 1:357.

Doctrine & Covenants 59

1. Joseph Smith, *The Papers of Joseph Smith,* ed. Dean C. Jessee, 2 vols. (Salt Lake City: Deseret Book, 1989–92), 1:361.
2. Ronald E. Romig, *Early Jackson County, Missouri: The "Mormon" Settlement on the Big Blue River* (Independence, Mo.: Missouri Mormon Frontier Foundation, 1996), iv–v. See also Smith, *Papers of Joseph Smith,* ed. Jessee, 1:361.
3. Gordon B. Hinckley, "Look to the Future," *Ensign* 27 (November 1997): 67.

4. Richard Lyman Bushman, *Joseph Smith: Rough Stone Rolling* (New York: Knopf, 2005), 163.
5. Smith, *Papers of Joseph Smith,* ed. Jessee, 1:359–60.

Doctrine & Covenants 60

1. Joseph Smith, *The Papers of Joseph Smith,* ed. Dean C. Jessee, 2 vols. (Salt Lake City: Deseret Book, 1989–92), 1:361.
2. *Times and Seasons* 5 (March 15, 1844): 464; Reynolds Cahoon, Journal, Church History Library, Salt Lake City.

Doctrine & Covenants 61

1. Joseph Smith, *The Papers of Joseph Smith,* ed. Dean C. Jessee, 2 vols. (Salt Lake City: Deseret Book, 1989–92), 1:361–62.
2. Ezra Booth to Edward Partridge, *[Ravenna] Ohio Star,* November 24, 1831.
3. Smith, *Papers of Joseph Smith,* ed. Jessee, 1:362; Richard Lyman Bushman, *Joseph Smith: Rough Stone Rolling* (New York: Knopf, 2005), 164.
4. Ezra Booth to Edward Partridge, September 20, 1831, *[Ravenna] Ohio Star,* November 24, 1831.
5. Smith, *Papers of Joseph Smith,* ed. Jessee, 1:362.
6. William Phelps, "The Way of Journeying for the Saints of the Church of Christ," *The Evening and the Morning Star,* December 1832, 52–53.
7. "Short History of WW Phelps' Stay in Missouri," Church History Library, Salt Lake City.

Doctrine & Covenants 62

1. Joseph Smith, *The Papers of Joseph Smith,* ed. Dean C. Jessee, 2 vols. (Salt Lake City: Deseret Book, 1989–92), 1:361–63.
2. Far West Record, August 24, 1831 [mistakenly dated August 2, 1831], Church History Library, Salt Lake City.

Doctrine & Covenants 63

1. John Whitmer, "Book of John Whitmer," 31, Community of Christ Archives, Independence, Missouri; Far West Record, October 1831, Church History Library, Salt Lake City.
2. Joseph Smith, *The Papers of Joseph Smith,* ed. Dean C. Jessee, 2 vols. (Salt Lake City: Deseret Book, 1989–92), 1:362–63.
3. Doctrine and Covenants 63:41. The Church History Library in Salt Lake City has an unpublished revelation in John Whitmer's handwriting, dated August 31, 1831, which says: "Behold thus saith the Lord by the voice of the spirit it is wisdom in me that my servent John Burk David Eliot Erastus Babit should take their Journey this fall to the land of Zion."
4. Joseph Smith, Manuscript History, Book A-1, 210, Church History Library, Salt Lake City.
5. Sidney Rigdon Papers, Church History Library, Salt Lake City; also in Lyndon W. Cook, *The Revelations of the Prophet Joseph Smith: A Historical and Biographical Commentary of the Doctrine and Covenants* (Provo, Utah: Seventy's Mission Bookstore, 1981), 99–101.
6. Whitmer, "Book of John Whitmer," 37.

Doctrine & Covenants 64

1. Joseph Smith, *The Papers of Joseph Smith,* ed. Dean C. Jessee, 2 vols. (Salt Lake City: Deseret Book, 1989–92), 1:363.
2. Ezra Booth, "Mormonism—No. V," *[Ravenna] Ohio Star,* November 10, 1831, 3.
3. Far West Record, September 6, 1831, Church History Library, Salt Lake City.
4. Ezra Booth, "Mormonism—No. VII," *[Ravenna] Ohio Star,* November 24, 1831, 1.

Doctrine & Covenants 65

1. Joseph Smith, *The Papers of Joseph Smith,* ed. Dean C. Jessee, 2 vols. (Salt Lake City: Deseret Book, 1989–92), 1:365–66.
2. See Jan Shipps and John W. Welch, eds., *The Journals of William E. McLellin, 1831–1836* (Urbana, Ill.: University of Illinois Press and Provo, Utah: BYU Studies, 1994), 243.
3. Henry William Bigler, Journal, February 1846–October 1899, Church History Library, Salt Lake City.
4. Parley P. Pratt, *Autobiography of Parley P. Pratt,* ed. Parley P. Pratt Jr., 4th ed. (Salt Lake City: Deseret Book, 1950), 211–12.
5. Andrew F. Ehat, "'It Seems like Heaven Began on Earth': Joseph Smith and the Constitution of the Kingdom of God," *BYU Studies* 20, no. 3 (1980): 253–79; italics removed.
6. Richard C. Galbraith, "Scriptural Index to the Journal of Discourses," published privately by the author, 21, copy in possession of Steven C. Harper; Richard C. Galbraith, "Scriptural Index to *Ensign* and General Conference Reports, April 1971–October 2000," published privately by the author, 8, copy in possession of Steven C. Harper.
7. Gordon B. Hinckley, "The State of the Church," *Ensign* 33 (November 2003): 7.
8. Smith, *Papers of Joseph Smith,* ed. Jessee, 1:540.

Doctrine & Covenants 66

1. Jan Shipps and John W. Welch, eds., *The Journals of William E. McLellin, 1831–1836* (Urbana, Ill.: University of Illinois Press and Provo, Utah: BYU Studies, 1994), 257–59.
2. Ibid., 46–47, 57.
3. Ibid., 87.
4. Joseph Smith, *Personal Writings of Joseph Smith,* ed. Dean C. Jessee, 2d ed. (Salt Lake City: Deseret Book and Provo, Utah: Brigham Young University Press, 2002), 265.
5. "The Scriptory Book of Joseph Smith Jr.," 40, Church History Library, Salt Lake City.

Doctrine & Covenants 67

1. Far West Record, November 1, 1831, Church History Library, Salt Lake City.
2. Ibid., November 1–13, 1831; JS to Dear Brethren, March 30, 1834, Oliver Cowdery Letterbook, 30–36, Huntington Library, San Marino, California.
3. Far West Record, November 12–13, 1831.
4. Richard Lyman Bushman, *Joseph Smith: Rough Stone Rolling* (New York: Knopf, 2005), 173–74.
5. Joseph Smith, *The Papers of Joseph Smith,* ed. Dean C. Jessee, 2 vols. (Salt Lake City: Deseret Book, 1989–92), 1:367.
6. Joseph Smith, Discourse, October 25, 1831, Far West Record.

7. Smith, *Papers of Joseph Smith,* ed. Jessee, 1:367; Jan Shipps and John W. Welch, eds., *The Journals of William E. McLellin, 1831–1836* (Urbana, Ill.: University of Illinois Press and Provo, Utah: BYU Studies, 1994), 251.
8. Smith, *Papers of Joseph Smith,* ed. Jessee, 1:367; Far West Record, November 1, 1831.
9. Joseph Smith to William W. Phelps, November 27, 1832, in Joseph Smith, *Personal Writings of Joseph Smith,* ed. Dean C. Jessee, 2d ed. (Salt Lake City: Deseret Book and Provo, Utah: Brigham Young University Press, 2002), 286; punctuation standardized.
10. Smith, *Papers of Joseph Smith,* ed. Jessee, 1:367.
11. Far West Record, November 1–2, 1831.

Doctrine & Covenants 68

1. Far West Record, October 25, 1831, November 2, 1831, Church History Library, Salt Lake City.
2. Careful students will notice this revelation's references to the First Presidency, which was not organized until 1832, after Doctrine and Covenants 68 was given. That is because section 68 includes revisions made after the First Presidency was organized. The revisions were incorporated in early manuscripts and then published in the 1835 Doctrine and Covenants.
3. "Resolved: that the mode and manner of regulating the Church of Christ, take effect from this time, according to a revelation received in Hiram, Portage County, Ohio, Nov. 11, 1831." Far West Record, July 3, 1832.
4. Ralph Waldo Emerson, *The Complete Essays and Other Writings of Ralph Waldo Emerson,* ed. Brooks Atkinson (New York: Modern Library, 1950), 80.

Doctrine & Covenants 69

1. John Whitmer, "Book of John Whitmer," 38, Community of Christ Archives, Independence, Missouri.
2. Joseph Smith, Remarks, Far West Record, November 12, 1831, Church History Library, Salt Lake City.
3. John wrote that he and Oliver left Ohio on November 20, 1831, and arrived safely in Independence, Missouri, on January 5, 1832. Whitmer, "Book of John Whitmer," 38.
4. Whitmer, "Book of John Whitmer."

Doctrine & Covenants 70

1. Far West Record, November 12–13, 1831, Church History Library, Salt Lake City.
2. Postscript, Joseph Smith to Edward Partridge and Others, March 30, 1834, in Joseph Smith, *Personal Writings of Joseph Smith,* ed. Dean C. Jessee, 2d ed. (Salt Lake City: Deseret Book and Provo, Utah: Brigham Young University Press, 2002), 338–39; spelling standardized.
3. Far West Record, November 8, 1831.
4. Richard Lyman Bushman, *Joseph Smith: Rough Stone Rolling* (New York: Knopf, 2005), 174.
5. Joseph Smith to William W. Phelps, November 27, 1832, in Smith, *Personal Writings of Joseph Smith,* ed. Jessee, 286; punctuation standardized.
6. Joseph Smith, Kirtland, Ohio, to Edward Partridge, William W. Phelps, and others, March 30, 1834, in Oliver Cowdery Letterbook, 30–36, in handwriting of Thomas Burdick, Huntington Library, San Marino, California. An accompanying letter from Oliver

Cowdery to William Phelps indicates that Oliver Cowdery wrote the original letter at Joseph Smith's dictation.

7. Joseph Smith, *The Papers of Joseph Smith*, ed. Dean C. Jessee, 2 vols. (Salt Lake City: Deseret Book, 1989–92), 1:367.
8. Far West Record, November 12–13, 1831.

Doctrine & Covenants 71

1. A. S. Hayden, *Early History of the Disciples in the Western Reserve, Ohio* (Cincinnati, Ohio: Chase and Hall, 1875), 250.
2. Joseph's history says that "about this time, Ezra Booth came out as an apostate. He came into the church upon seeing a person healed of an infirmity of many years standing. He had been a Methodist priest for some time previous to his embracing the fulness of the gospel, as developed in the book of Mormon, and upon his admission into the Church he was ordained an elder. . . . He went up to Missouri as a companion of Elder Morley; but when he actually learned that faith, humility, patience, and tribulation were before blessing. . . and when he was disappointed by his own evil heart, he turned away. And, as said before, became an apostate, and wrote a series of letters, which, by their coloring, falsity, and vain calculations to overthrow the work of the Lord, exposed his weakness, wickedness, and folly and left him a monument of his own shame for the world to wonder at." Joseph Smith, *The Papers of Joseph Smith*, ed. Dean C. Jessee, 2 vols. (Salt Lake City: Deseret Book, 1989–92), 1:363–64; punctuation and capitalization standardized.
3. George A. Smith, in *Journal of Discourses*, 26 vols. (Liverpool: F. D. Richards, 1855–86), 11:5, November 15, 1864.
4. Hayden, *Early History of the Disciples in the Western Reserve*, 250.
5. Wesley Perkins to Jacob Perkins, February 11, 1832, L. Tom Perry Special Collections, Harold B. Lee Library, Brigham Young University, Provo, Utah.
6. Smith, *The Papers of Joseph Smith*, ed. Jessee, 1:370.
7. Richard Lyman Bushman, *Joseph Smith: Rough Stone Rolling* (New York: Knopf, 2005), 599 n. 2; Richard S. Van Wagoner, *Sidney Rigdon: A Portrait of Religious Excess* (Salt Lake City: Signature, 1994), 111.
8. Smith, *Papers of Joseph Smith*, ed. Jessee, 1:370.

Doctrine & Covenants 72

1. Joseph Smith, *The Papers of Joseph Smith*, ed. Dean C. Jessee, 2 vols. (Salt Lake City: Deseret Book, 1989–92), 1:370.
2. Orson F. Whitney, "Newel K. Whitney," *Contributor* 6 (January 1885): 126; Larry Neil Poulsen, "The Life and Contributions of Newel Kimball Whitney" (master's thesis, Brigham Young University, 1966), 38; and "Aaronic Priesthood Minutes," March 3, 1877, Church History Library, Salt Lake City.
3. Elizabeth Ann Whitney, "A Leaf from an Autobiography, Continued," *Woman's Exponent* 7 (September 1, 1878): 71.
4. Joseph Smith to William Phelps, July 31, 1832, Church History Library, Salt Lake City, in Joseph Smith, *Personal Writings of Joseph Smith*, ed. Dean C. Jessee, 2d ed. (Salt Lake City: Deseret Book and Provo, Utah: Brigham Young University Press, 2002), 270.
5. "The Elders Stationed in Zion to the Churches Abroad, In Love, Greeting," *The Evening and the Morning Star*, July 1833, 111.

6. For examples, see Jan Shipps and John W. Welch, eds., *The Journals of William E. McLellin, 1831–1836* (Urbana, Ill.: University of Illinois Press and Provo, Utah: BYU Studies, 1994), 138.

Doctrine & Covenants 73

1. Joseph Smith, *The Papers of Joseph Smith,* ed. Dean C. Jessee, 2 vols. (Salt Lake City: Deseret Book, 1989–92), 1:371.

Doctrine & Covenants 74

1. Joseph Smith, *The Papers of Joseph Smith,* ed. Dean C. Jessee, 2 vols. (Salt Lake City: Deseret Book, 1989–92), 1:371.
2. LDS Bible Dictionary, "Circumcision," 646.

Doctrine & Covenants 75

1. Joseph Smith, *The Papers of Joseph Smith,* ed. Dean C. Jessee, 2 vols. (Salt Lake City: Deseret Book, 1989–92), 1:371.
2. Orson Pratt, *The Orson Pratt Journals,* comp. Elden J. Watson (Salt Lake City: E. J. Watson, 1975), January 25, 1832. Edson Barney statement reported in St. George, Utah, Stake General Minutes, December 23, 1860, Church History Library, Salt Lake City; manuscript copies of Doctrine and Covenants 75, Newel K. Whitney Collection, L. Tom Perry Special Collections, Harold B. Lee Library, Brigham Young University, Provo, Utah.
3. William McLellin to Beloved Relatives, August 4, 1832, typescript, Community of Christ Archives, Independence, Missouri; Jan Shipps and John W. Welch, eds., *The Journals of William E. McLellin, 1831–1836* (Urbana, Ill.: University of Illinois Press and Provo, Utah: BYU Studies, 1994), 33–34. See also Larry C. Porter, "The Odyssey of William E. McLellin: Man of Diversity," in Shipps and Welch, *Journals of William E. McLellin,* 301–2.
4. *Millennial Star* 26 (December 31, 1864): 835.
5. Orson Hyde, "History of Orson Hyde," *Millennial Star* 26 (December 3, 1864): 776.
6. "Events in the Life of Samuel Harrison Smith Including His Missionary Journal for the Year 1832," Church History Library, Salt Lake City.
7. Breck England, *The Life and Thought of Orson Pratt* (Salt Lake City: University of Utah Press, 1985), 29–31, 306.
8. *The Evening and the Morning Star,* February 1833, 69–70; March 1833, 84; May 1834, 156; Mark B. Nelson and Steven C. Harper, "The Imprisonment of Martin Harris in 1833," *BYU Studies* 45, no. 4 (2006): 113–15.
9. Hyrum Smith, Diary 1831–1835, 27, Church History Library, Salt Lake City.
10. *The Evening and the Morning Star,* June 1833, 100.
11. Sylvester Smith to Dear Brother, May 16, 1833, *The Evening and the Morning Star,* July 1833, 107.
12. Eden Smith, Journal, typescript, L. Tom Perry Special Collections, Harold B. Lee Library, Brigham Young University, Provo, Utah.

Doctrine & Covenants 76

1. John E. Smith, Harry S. Stout, and Kenneth P. Minkema, eds., *A Jonathan Edwards Reader* (New Haven, Conn.: Yale University Press, 2003), 90.
2. Joseph Smith to the Church and Bishop Partridge, March 20, 1839, Church History Library, Salt Lake City; spelling and capitalization modernized.

3. E. Brooks Holifield, *Theology in America: Christian Thought from the Age of the Puritans to the Civil War* (New Haven, Conn.: Yale University Press, 2003), 335. Richard Bushman calls such texts "exaltation revelations." Richard Lyman Bushman, *Joseph Smith: Rough Stone Rolling* (New York: Knopf, 2005), 195.
4. This phrase is from President Boyd K. Packer, who taught, "Save for the exception of the very few who defect to perdition, there is no habit, no addiction, no rebellion, no transgression, no apostasy, no crime exempted from the promise of complete forgiveness." Boyd K. Packer, "The Brilliant Morning of Forgiveness," *Ensign* 25 (November 1995): 18.
5. Weber Stake High Priests Quorum Minute Book 1896–1929, October 27, 1900, 110, Church History Library, Salt Lake City.
6. Charles L. Walker, *The Diary of Charles Lowell Walker*, ed. A. Karl Larson and Katherine M. Larson (Logan: Utah State University Press, 1980), 1:465–66.
7. *Times and Seasons* 5 (May 1, 1844): 522–26; Joseph Smith Jr. et al., *History of The Church of Jesus Christ of Latter-day Saints*, ed. B. H. Roberts, 2d ed. rev., 7 vols. (Salt Lake City: Deseret Book, 1971), 6:290.
8. Wilford Woodruff, "Remarks," *Deseret Weekly News*, September 5, 1891, 322.
9. Brigham Young, in *Journal of Discourses*, 26 vols. (Liverpool: F. D. Richards, 1855–86), 6:281, August 29, 1852.
10. Ibid., 16:42, May 18, 1873.
11. Joseph Smith, Diary, kept by Willard Richards, June 11, 1843, Church History Library, Salt Lake City; Joseph Smith, *An American Prophet's Record: The Diaries and Journals of Joseph Smith*, ed. Scott H. Faulring (Salt Lake City: Signature, 1989), 385. See 1 Corinthians 15.
12. First Presidency to Bishop Partridge, June 25, 1833, in Joseph Smith Letterbook 1, 44–50, Church History Library, Salt Lake City.
13. Joseph Smith, Manuscript History, Book A-1, 192–95, Church History Library, Salt Lake City, published first in *Times and Seasons* 5 (August 1, 1844) and later in Smith et al., *History of the Church*, 1:252–53. See also Bushman, *Rough Stone Rolling*, 195.

Doctrine & Covenants 77

1. Joseph Smith, *The Papers of Joseph Smith*, ed. Dean C. Jessee, 2 vols. (Salt Lake City: Deseret Book, 1989–92), 1:372; capitalization standardized.
2. Discourse, April 8, 1843, Nauvoo, Illinois, Church History Library, Salt Lake City; Andrew F. Ehat and Lyndon W. Cook, *The Words of Joseph Smith: The Contemporary Accounts of the Nauvoo Discourses of the Prophet Joseph*, Religious Studies Monograph Series, no. 6 (Provo, Utah: Religious Studies Center, Brigham Young University, 1980), 183–89; and Joseph Smith, *An American Prophet's Record: The Diaries and Journals of Joseph Smith*, ed. Scott H. Faulring (Salt Lake City: Signature, 1989), 355–57; punctuation standardized.
3. Discourse, April 8, 1843, Nauvoo, Illinois, Church History Library, Salt Lake City; Ehat and Cook, *Words of Joseph Smith*, 188.

Doctrine & Covenants 78

1. See Kirtland Revelation Book, 15–17, Church History Library, Salt Lake City; see also manuscript copy of Doctrine and Covenants 78, Newel K. Whitney Collection, Harold B. Lee Library, Brigham Young University, Provo, Utah: "& lo it must needs be that there be an organization of the Literary and Merchantile establishments of my church."
2. Orson Pratt, "Explanation of Substituted Names in the Covenants," *Millennial Star* 16 (March 18, 1854): 171–73, quoted in David J. Whittaker, "Substituted Names in the Published Revelations of Joseph Smith," *BYU Studies* 23, no. 1 (1983): 103–12.

3. Orson Pratt to Brigham Young, November 20, 1852, Church History Library, Salt Lake City, quoted in Whittaker, "Substituted Names in the Published Revelations of Joseph Smith," 103–12.

4. Whittaker, "Substituted Names in the Published Revelations of Joseph Smith," 103–12.

Doctrine & Covenants 79

1. Jared Carter, Autobiography, typescript, 9, Church History Library, Salt Lake City.
2. Carter, Autobiography, 7. Here Jared confused his first mission with his second. In both instances the Lord crowned him with sheaves as promised for his second mission in section 79.

Doctrine & Covenants 80

1. Eden Smith, Journal, Church History Library, Salt Lake City. Stephen Burnett had earlier preached with Eden Smith's father, John. See Lyndon W. Cook, *The Revelations of the Prophet Joseph Smith: A Historical and Biographical Commentary of the Doctrine and Covenants* (Provo, Utah: Seventy's Mission Bookstore, 1981), 170, 314.
2. Levi B. Wilder to the editor, February 15, 1835, *Messenger and Advocate*, February 1835, 75.
3. Joseph Smith, "Editorial," *Elders' Journal*, August 1838, 55–59.

Doctrine & Covenants 81

1. Kirtland Revelation Book, 10–11, Church History Library, Salt Lake City.

Doctrine & Covenants 82

1. Richard Lyman Bushman, *Joseph Smith: Rough Stone Rolling* (New York: Knopf, 2005), 179–80.
2. Joseph Smith, *The Papers of Joseph Smith*, ed. Dean C. Jessee, 2 vols. (Salt Lake City: Deseret Book, 1989–92), 1:379–81.
3. Max H. Parkin, "Joseph Smith and the United Firm," *BYU Studies* 46, no. 3 (2007): 5–6.
4. Far West Record, April 27, 1832, Church History Library, Salt Lake City.
5. Parkin, "Joseph Smith and the United Firm," 13.
6. Far West Record, April 30, 1832.
7. Parkin, "Joseph Smith and the United Firm," 15.
8. N. K. Whitney to S. F. Whitney, October 2 [year uncertain], Whitney Collection, L. Tom Perry Special Collections, Harold B. Lee Library, Brigham Young University, Provo, Utah.
9. Smith, *Papers of Joseph Smith*, ed. Jessee, 1:381.

Doctrine & Covenants 83

1. Joseph Smith, *The Papers of Joseph Smith*, ed. Dean C. Jessee, 2 vols. (Salt Lake City: Deseret Book, 1989–92), 1:381.

Doctrine & Covenants 84

1. Evan Greene, Journal, December 22, 1832, Church History Library, Salt Lake City; *Messenger and Advocate*, April 1836, 294.
2. Joseph Smith, *The Papers of Joseph Smith*, ed. Dean C. Jessee, 2 vols. (Salt Lake City: Deseret Book, 1989–92), 1:385.

3. Lula Greene Richards, "A Sketch of the Life of Evan M. Greene," typescript, in possession of the author.
4. Richards, "Sketch of the Life of Evan M. Greene," suggests that the revelation came in one sitting late on September 22 and early on September 23, but the evidence is inconclusive.
5. Ezra Taft Benson, "A New Witness for Christ," *Ensign* 14 (November 1984): 6.
6. Ezra Taft Benson, "Cleansing the Inner Vessel," *Ensign* 16 (May 1986): 5.
7. Joseph Smith Letterbook 1, 20–25, Church History Library, Salt Lake City; Kirtland Minute Book, January 13, 1833, Church History Library, Salt Lake City. See also Doctrine and Covenants 82.
8. Newel K. Whitney, undated statement, Newel K. Whitney Collection, L. Tom Perry Special Collections, Harold B. Lee Library, Brigham Young University, Provo, Utah; Samuel H. Smith, Journal, November 26, 1832, Church History Library, Salt Lake City; and Joseph Smith to Emma Smith, October 13, 1832, Community of Christ Archives, Independence, Missouri.
9. Richard Lyman Bushman, *Joseph Smith: Rough Stone Rolling* (New York: Knopf, 2005), 202–5.

Doctrine & Covenants 85

1. William E. McLellin to Beloved Relatives, August 4, 1832, typescript, Community of Christ Archives, Independence, Missouri.
2. Joseph Smith to William W. Phelps, November 27, 1832, Church History Library, Salt Lake City, in Joseph Smith, *Personal Writings of Joseph Smith,* ed. Dean C. Jessee, 2d ed. (Salt Lake City: Deseret Book and Provo, Utah: Brigham Young University Press, 2002), 285; spelling and punctuation standardized.
3. Joseph F. Smith et al., "One Mighty and Strong," *Deseret Evening News,* November 11, 1905, 4.
4. Oliver Cowdery to John Whitmer, January 1, 1834, Huntington Library, San Marino, California.
5. Smith, *Personal Writings of Joseph Smith,* ed. Jessee, 337.
6. Smith et al., "One Mighty and Strong," 4.
7. Joseph Smith, Book for Record, Church History Library, Salt Lake City, in Joseph Smith, *The Papers of Joseph Smith,* ed. Dean C. Jessee, 2 vols. (Salt Lake City: Deseret Book, 1989–92), 2:2; spelling standardized.
8. Joseph Smith et al., Book of the Law of the Lord, 26, Church History Library, Salt Lake City.
9. William Clayton, "History of the Nauvoo Temple," manuscript, Church History Library, Salt Lake City.
10. Smith et al., Book of the Law of the Lord, 164, 179.

Doctrine & Covenants 86

1. Joseph Smith, Book for Record, 4, Church History Library, Salt Lake City; spelling standardized.
2. Lorenzo Dow, *The Dealings of God, Man, and the Devil As Exemplified in the Life, Experience, and Travels of Lorenzo Dow* (Middletown, Ohio: Glasener and Marshall, 1849), 10.

Doctrine & Covenants 87

1. Richard Lyman Bushman, *Joseph Smith: Rough Stone Rolling* (New York: Knopf, 2005), 191.
2. Joseph Smith Jr. et al., *History of The Church of Jesus Christ of Latter-day Saints*, ed. B. H. Roberts, 2d ed. rev., 7 vols. (Salt Lake City: Deseret Book, 1971), 1:301; "Signs of the Times," *The Evening and the Morning Star* 1, no. 8, January 1833, 62.
3. Bushman, *Rough Stone Rolling*, 191.
4. Ibid., 192.
5. Ibid.; "A Mormon Prophecy," *Philadelphia Sunday Mercury,* May 5, 1861, reprinted in Robert J. Woodford, "Historical Development of the Doctrine and Covenants," 3 vols. (Ph.D. dissertation, Brigham Young University, 1974), 2:1110.
6. Abraham Lincoln, "Meditation on the Divine Will," in *Abraham Lincoln: His Speeches and Writings,* ed. Roy P. Basler (Cleveland, Ohio: World Publishing, 1946), 655.
7. Abraham Lincoln, "Second Inaugural Address," in ibid., 792–93.

Doctrine & Covenants 88

1. Kirtland Minute Book, December 27, 1832, Church History Library, Salt Lake City; Kirtland Revelation Book, 47–48, Church History Library, Salt Lake City.
2. Samuel H. Smith, Journal, Church History Library, Salt Lake City; spelling, punctuation, and capitalization standardized.
3. Jeffrey R. Holland, *Of Souls, Symbols, and Sacraments* (Salt Lake City: Deseret Book, 2001), 13.
4. Richard Lyman Bushman, *Joseph Smith: Rough Stone Rolling* (New York: Knopf, 2005), 206.
5. Margaret Barker, *On Earth As It Is in Heaven: Temple Symbolism in the New Testament* (Edinburgh: T & T Clark, 1995), 13.
6. Bushman, *Rough Stone Rolling,* 210–12.
7. Joseph Smith, Kirtland, Ohio, to William W. Phelps, Independence, Missouri, January 11, 1833, in Joseph Smith Letterbook 1, in handwriting of Frederick G. Williams, 18–20, Church History Library, Salt Lake City; some spelling standardized.
8. Ibid.; spelling and punctuation standardized.
9. Ibid.
10. Joseph Smith, Discourse, Kirtland, Ohio, November 12, 1835, Joseph Smith, Journal, Church History Library, Salt Lake City; Joseph Smith, *The Papers of Joseph Smith,* ed. Dean C. Jessee, 2 vols. (Salt Lake City: Deseret Book, 1989–92), 2:76.
11. Smith, Discourse, November 12, 1835; Smith, *Papers of Joseph Smith,* ed. Jessee, 2:76–77; spelling, capitalization, and punctuation standardized.
12. Smith, Discourse, November 12, 1835; Smith, *Papers of Joseph Smith,* ed. Jessee, 2:77; punctuation standardized.
13. Fulfillments of this prophecy are documented in Steven C. Harper, "'A Pentecost and Endowment Indeed': Six Eyewitness Accounts of the Kirtland Temple Experience," in *Opening the Heavens: Accounts of Divine Manifestations, 1820–1844,* ed. John W. Welch and Erick B. Carlson (Provo, Utah: Brigham Young University Press and Salt Lake City: Deseret Book, 2005), 327–71.

Doctrine & Covenants 89

1. *Saints Herald* (June 1, 1881): 163, 167.

2. *Western Farmer,* January 30, 1822; Steven C. Harper, *The Word of Wisdom* (Orem, Utah: Millennial Press, 2007), 27.
3. W. J. Rorabaugh, *The Alcoholic Republic: An American Tradition* (New York: Oxford University Press, 1979).
4. Richard Lyman Bushman, *Joseph Smith: Rough Stone Rolling* (New York: Knopf, 2005), 42.
5. Quoted in Rorabaugh, *Alcoholic Republic,* 216.
6. Brigham Young, in *Journal of Discourses,* 26 vols. (Liverpool: F. D. Richards, 1855–86), 12:158, February 8, 1868.
7. By 1800, the influential doctor Benjamin Rush had persuaded many authorities that all disease could be traced to overstimulation, and therefore all illness could be treated by so-called "heroic" methods of releasing the patient's excess energy. Joseph Smith's brother Alvin died in 1823 after a doctor's dose of mercurous chloride blocked rather than purged his digestive system. Joseph Smith and most Latter-day Saints had little confidence in the fledgling medical profession and its heroic practices until advances in medical science increased their confidence in professionals late in the nineteenth century. See Cecil O. Samuelson Jr., in *Encyclopedia of Mormonism,* ed. Daniel H. Ludlow et al., 4 vols. (New York: Macmillan, 1992), 2:875.
8. Lyndon W. Cook, ed., *David Whitmer Interviews: A Restoration Witness* (Orem, Utah: Grandin Book, 1991), 204.
9. See *The Tobacco Conspiracy,* DVD, directed by Nadia Collot (National Film Board of Canada and KUIV Productions, 2006); see also Richard Kluger, *Ashes to Ashes* (New York: Knopf, 1996).
10. Russell M. Nelson, "Addiction or Freedom," *Ensign* 18 (November 1988): 6.
11. Richard D. Hurt and Channing R. Robertson, "Prying Open the Door to the Tobacco Industry's Secrets about Nicotine," *Journal of the American Medical Association* 280, no. 13 (1998): 1173–74; *Tobacco Conspiracy,* DVD.
12. *Tobacco Conspiracy,* DVD.
13. Marlin K. Jensen, "May the Kingdom of God Go Forth," in *Out of Obscurity: The LDS Church in the Twentieth Century* [2000 Sidney B. Sperry Symposium], ed. Susan Easton Black et al., (Salt Lake City: Deseret Book, 2000), 9–10.
14. Ibid.
15. Gordon B. Hinckley, "Excerpts from Recent Addresses of President Gordon B. Hinckley," *Ensign* 26 (July 1996): 73.
16. Paul H. Peterson, "An Historical Analysis of the Word of Wisdom" (master's thesis, Brigham Young University, 1972), 101; Thomas G. Alexander, "The Word of Wisdom: From Principle to Requirement," *Dialogue: A Journal of Mormon Thought* 14, no. 3 (Autumn 1981): 84.
17. Young, in *Journal of Discourses,* 12:117, August 17, 1867.
18. Boyd K. Packer, "The Word of Wisdom: The Principle and the Promises," *Ensign* 26 (May 1996): 17; paragraphing altered.
19. Gordon B. Hinckley, "The Scourge of Illicit Drugs," *Ensign* 19 (November 1989): 50; Nelson, "Addiction or Freedom," 6–9.
20. John A. Widtsoe, *Evidences and Reconciliations,* 3 vols. (Salt Lake City: Bookcraft, 1951), 3:156.
21. Packer, "Word of Wisdom," 19.
22. Joel H. Johnson, *Voice from the Mountains* (Salt Lake City: Juvenile Instructor Office, 1881), 12.

23. Hyrum Smith, "The Word of Wisdom," *Times and Seasons* 3 (June 1, 1842): 799–801.
24. Peterson, "Historical Analysis of the Word of Wisdom," 22.
25. Lester E. Bush, "The Word of Wisdom in Early Nineteenth-Century Perspective," *Dialogue: A Journal of Mormon Thought* 14, no. 3 (Autumn 1981): 53, 63.
26. Kirtland Minute Book, February 20, 1834, Church History Library, Salt Lake City.
27. For a more detailed look at the Church's history regarding adherence to the Word of Wisdom, see Steven C. Harper, *The Word of Wisdom* (Orem, Utah: Millennial Press, 2007).
28. Quoted in Peterson, "Historical Analysis of the Word of Wisdom," 98.

Doctrine & Covenants 90

1. Revelation, January 5, 1834 [1833], Frederick G. Williams Papers, Church History Library, Salt Lake City.
2. Spelling and punctuation standardized.
3. William McLellin to Beloved Relatives, August 4, 1832, typescript, Community of Christ Archives, Independence, Missouri.
4. Kirtland Minute Book, March 18, 1833, Church History Library, Salt Lake City; Certificate, March 20, 1833, Frederick G. Williams Papers, Church History Library, Salt Lake City.

Doctrine & Covenants 91

1. Joseph Smith, Manuscript History, Book A-1, 279–80, Church History Library, Salt Lake City. This is the source for Joseph Smith Jr. et al., *History of The Church of Jesus Christ of Latter-day Saints,* ed. B. H. Roberts, 2d ed. rev., 7 vols. (Salt Lake City: Deseret Book, 1971), 1:331
2. The article on the Apocrypha in the LDS Bible Dictionary, pages 610–11, gives excellent information.
3. Isaac Newton, *An Historical Account of Two Notable Corruptions of Scripture* (London: R. Taylor, 1830).

Doctrine & Covenants 92

1. Max H. Parkin, "Joseph Smith and the United Firm," *BYU Studies* 46, no. 3 (2007): 13.
2. Revelation, January 22, 1833, Frederick G. Williams Papers, Church History Library, Salt Lake City.
3. Kirtland Minute Book, March 15, 1833, Church History Library, Salt Lake City.
4. Joseph Smith, *The Papers of Joseph Smith,* ed. Dean C. Jessee, 2 vols. (Salt Lake City: Deseret Book, 1989–92), 2:12–13.

Doctrine & Covenants 93

1. All editions of the Doctrine and Covenants since 1921 imply that these were the writings of John the Apostle. Orson Pratt believed they were writings of John the Baptist. See Orson Pratt, in *Journal of Discourses,* 26 vols. (Liverpool: F. D. Richards, 1855–86), 16:58, May 18, 1873. John Taylor believed the same. See John Taylor, *An Examination into and an Elucidation of the Great Principle of the Mediation and Atonement of Our Lord and Savior Jesus Christ* (Salt Lake City: Steven and Wallis, 1950), 55.
2. Richard Lyman Bushman, *Joseph Smith: Rough Stone Rolling* (New York: Knopf, 2005), 210.
3. Truman G. Madsen, *Joseph Smith the Prophet* (Salt Lake City: Bookcraft, 1989), 140–41.

Doctrine & Covenants 94
1. Kirtland Revelation Book, 64, Church History Library, Salt Lake City.
2. First Presidency in Kirtland, Ohio, to Church leaders in Missouri, August 6, 1833, Church History Library, Salt Lake City.
3. Ibid.

Doctrine & Covenants 95
1. Kirtland Minute Book, May 4, 1833, Church History Library, Salt Lake City.
2. Hyrum Smith, Reynolds Cahoon, Jared Carter to the Church of Christ, June 1, 1833, Joseph Smith Letterbook 1, 36–38, Church History Library, Salt Lake City.
3. Kirtland Minute Book, June 3, 1833; Truman Angell, Journal, typescript, L. Tom Perry Special Collections, Harold B. Lee Library, Brigham Young University, Provo, Utah; and Truman Angell to John Taylor, March 11, 1885, Church History Library, Salt Lake City.
4. Richard Lyman Bushman, *Joseph Smith: Rough Stone Rolling* (New York: Knopf, 2005), 217.
5. Joseph Smith to William W. Phelps, January 11, 1833, Kirtland, Ohio, Joseph Smith Letterbook 1, 18–20, Church History Library, Salt Lake City.
6. Bushman, *Rough Stone Rolling,* 218.

Doctrine & Covenants 96
1. Zebedee Coltrin, Journal, Church History Library, Salt Lake City.
2. Kirtland Minute Book, June 3 [4], 1833, Church History Library, Salt Lake City.
3. First Presidency to Brethren, June 25, 1833, Joseph Smith Letterbook 1, 44–50, Church History Library, Salt Lake City.

Doctrine & Covenants 97
1. Parley P. Pratt, *Autobiography of Parley P. Pratt,* ed. Scot Facer Proctor and Maurine Jensen Proctor (Salt Lake City: Deseret Book, 2000), 112–14.
2. Ibid. The First Presidency responded, "Having received br. Oliver's letter of July 9 as well as one from the breatheren composing the school in Zion according to your request we now answer them both in one letter as relates to the school in Zion according to your request we enquired of the Lord and send this letter the communication which we received from the Lord concerning the school in Zion. It was obtained August 2 and reads thus . . ." First Presidency to Beloved Brethren, August 6, 1833, Church History Library, Salt Lake City.
3. Pratt, *Autobiography of Parley P. Pratt,* ed. Proctor and Proctor, 114–16.

Doctrine & Covenants 98
1. Joseph Smith, Kirtland, Ohio, to William Phelps, John Whitmer, Edward Partridge, Isaac Morley, John Corrill, and Sidney Gilbert, Independence, Missouri, August 18, 1833, Church History Library, Salt Lake City.
2. Ibid.; spelling standardized.
3. Richard Lyman Bushman, *Joseph Smith: Rough Stone Rolling* (New York: Knopf, 2005), 226.
4. Joseph Smith, Manuscript History, Book A-1, 328–29, Church History Library, Salt Lake City.

Doctrine & Covenants 99

1. John Murdock, Autobiography, typescript, L. Tom Perry Special Collections, Brigham Young University, Provo, Utah.
2. Ibid.

Doctrine & Covenants 100

1. Joseph Smith, Kirtland, Ohio, to William Phelps, John Whitmer, Edward Partridge, Isaac Morley, John Corrill, and Sidney Gilbert, Independence, Missouri, August 18, 1833, Church History Library, Salt Lake City; capitalization and spelling standardized.
2. Richard Lyman Bushman, *Joseph Smith: Rough Stone Rolling* (New York: Knopf, 2005), 232.
3. Joseph Smith, Book for Record, 7, Church History Library, Salt Lake City; grammar standardized.
4. Smith to Phelps, Whitmer, Partridge, Morley, Corrill, and Gilbert, August 18, 1833.
5. Ibid.
6. Joseph Smith, Kirtland, Ohio, to Edward Partridge, William W. Phelps, John Whitmer, Algernon Sidney Gilbert, John Corrill, Isaac Morley and all Saints, Independence, Missouri, December 10, 1833, Joseph Smith Letterbook 1, in handwriting of Frederick G. Williams, 70–75, Church History Library, Salt Lake City; spelling and punctuation standardized.
7. Smith, Book for Record, 18.

Doctrine & Covenants 101

1. Joseph Smith, Kirtland, Ohio, to Edward Partridge, William W. Phelps, John Whitmer, Algernon Sidney Gilbert, John Corrill, Isaac Morley and all Saints, Independence, Missouri, December 10, 1833, Joseph Smith Letterbook 1, in handwriting of Frederick G. Williams, 70–75, Church History Library, Salt Lake City; spelling standardized.
2. Ibid.
3. Ira Ames, Journal and Autobiography, Church History Library, Salt Lake City, in Richard Lyman Bushman, *Joseph Smith: Rough Stone Rolling* (New York: Knopf, 2005), 229.
4. Bushman, *Rough Stone Rolling*, 229.
5. Smith to Partridge, Phelps, Whitmer, Gilbert, Corrill, Morley and all Saints, December 10, 1833.
6. Hugh Nibley, *The World and the Prophets* (Salt Lake City: Deseret Book, 1987), 182–90.

Doctrine & Covenants 102

1. Kirtland Minute Book, February 17–19, 1834, Church History Library, Salt Lake City.
2. Ibid.
3. Ibid.
4. Ibid.
5. Ibid.
6. Ibid.
7. Ibid.
8. Ibid.

Doctrine & Covenants 103

1. See Kenneth H. Winn, *Exiles in a Land of Liberty: Mormons in America, 1830–1846* (Chapel Hill: University of North Carolina Press, 1989).
2. William W. Phelps to Dear Brethren, December 15, 1833, *The Evening and the Morning Star,* January 1834, 127.
3. Peter Crawley and Richard L. Anderson, "The Political and Social Realities of Zion's Camp," *BYU Studies* 14, no. 4 (1974): 406–20.
4. Heber C. Kimball, Journal, 1834, Church History Library, Salt Lake City.

Doctrine & Covenants 104

1. Kirtland Minute Book, March 17, 1834, Church History Library, Salt Lake City.
2. Joseph Smith, Frederick G. Williams, Oliver Cowdery, Kirtland, Ohio, to Orson Hyde, New York, April 7, 1834, Church History Library, Salt Lake City; spelling standardized.
3. Ibid.; spelling standardized.
4. Joseph Smith, *The Papers of Joseph Smith,* ed. Dean C. Jessee, 2 vols. (Salt Lake City: Deseret Book, 1989–92), 2:29.
5. Kirtland Revelation Book, 100, Church History Library, Salt Lake City.
6. Ibid., 102; spelling standardized.
7. Neal A. Maxwell, *All These Things Shall Give Thee Experience* (Salt Lake City: Deseret Book, 1979), 2.
8. Kirtland Revelation Book, 100.
9. Max Parkin painstakingly documented each of these in "Joseph Smith and the United Firm," *BYU Studies* 46, no. 3 (2007): 5–66.
10. Frederick G. Williams Papers, Church History Library, Salt Lake City; Amt. of Balances due as of April 23, 1834, Newel K. Whitney Collection, L. Tom Perry Special Collections, Brigham Young University, Provo, Utah.
11. Smith, *Papers of Joseph Smith,* ed. Jessee, 2:32–35.
12. John Tanner, "Sketch of an Elder's Life," in *Scraps of Biography* (Salt Lake City: Juvenile Instructor's Office, 1883), 12.
13. Smith, *Papers of Joseph Smith,* ed. Jessee, 2:35.
14. Tanner, "Sketch of an Elder's Life," 12.

Doctrine & Covenants 105

1. Peter Crawley and Richard L. Anderson, "The Political and Social Realities of Zion's Camp," *BYU Studies* 14, no. 4 (1974): 406–20.
2. History of George Albert Smith, Church History Library, Salt Lake City; Crawley and Anderson, "Political and Social Realities of Zion's Camp," 406–20; Parley P. Pratt, *Autobiography of Parley P. Pratt,* ed. Parley P. Pratt Jr., 4th ed. (Salt Lake City: Deseret Book, 1950), 115.
3. Joseph Smith to Emma Smith, June 4, 1834, Church History Library, Salt Lake City.
4. John Whitmer, "Book of John Whitmer," 66–67, Community of Christ Archives, Independence, Missouri.
5. Letter from Cornelius Gilliam, Clay County, Missouri, June 21, 1834, and a statement by the Mormons, June 21, 1834, Church History Library, Salt Lake City. The two documents were pasted together and treated as one; *The Evening and the Morning Star,* July 1834, 8.
6. Kirtland Minute Book, February 14, 1835, Church History Library, Salt Lake City.

7. Joseph Smith to Lyman Wight, Edward Partridge, John Corrill, Isaac Morley, and others, Clay County, Missouri, August 16, 1834, copy in handwriting of Frederick G. Williams, Joseph Smith Letterbook 1, 84–87, Church History Library, Salt Lake City. See also Max H. Parkin, "A History of the Latter-day Saints in Clay County, Missouri, from 1833–1837" (Ph.D. dissertation, Brigham Young University, 1976), 159–66.
8. William W. Phelps, "A short history of W. W. Phelps' stay in Missouri," Church History Library, Salt Lake City.
9. Gordon B. Hinckley, *Teachings of Gordon B. Hinckley* (Salt Lake City: Deseret Book, 1997), 639.

Doctrine & Covenants 106

1. Joseph Smith, *The Papers of Joseph Smith*, ed. Dean C. Jessee, 2 vols. (Salt Lake City: Deseret Book, 1989–92), 2:24.
2. *Elders' Journal*, August 1838, 59; Joseph Smith, *Personal Writings of Joseph Smith*, ed. Dean C. Jessee, 2d ed. (Salt Lake City: Deseret Book and Provo, Utah: Brigham Young University Press, 2002), 667.

Doctrine & Covenants 107

1. William E. McLellin, "A Record of the Transactions of the Twelve," March 12, 1835, Church History Library, Salt Lake City.
2. Kirtland Minute Book, 198, Church History Library, Salt Lake City. The precise date of the apostles' request and the resulting revelation is problematic. It was almost certainly not on March 28, 1835. William McLellin's journals and corroborating evidence show that many of the apostles and most likely Joseph Smith were not in Kirtland on that date, which was probably entered in the minutes by mistake. The minutes actually say "March 28th, 1836," with the 6 crossed out and a 5 substituted. The revelation undoubtedly came in 1835; it was published in the 1835 edition of the Doctrine and Covenants, which is now the earliest known text. See *Messenger and Advocate*, August 1835, 161; Jan Shipps and John W. Welch, eds., *The Journals of William E. McLellin, 1831–1836* (Urbana, Ill.: University of Illinois Press and Provo, Utah: BYU Studies, 1994), 153, 167–68; William E. McLellin to Oliver Cowdery, Huntsburgh, Ohio, April 16, 1835, in *Messenger and Advocate*, June 1835, 102; Robert J. Woodford, "Historical Development of the Doctrine and Covenants," 3 vols. (Ph.D. dissertation, Brigham Young University, 1974), 3:1400–1401.

Church historian Willard Richards transferred revised minutes (dated March 28, 1835) into Joseph's manuscript history in 1843. See Howard C. Searle, "Willard Richards as Historian," *BYU Studies* 31, no. 2 (1991): 46, 55; Dean C. Jessee, "The Writing of Joseph Smith's History," *BYU Studies* 11, no. 4 (1971): 441. After entering the revised minutes into the manuscript history, Willard Richards added an undated statement in the voice of Joseph Smith, saying, "In compliance with the above request I enquired of the Lord and received for answer the following Revelation on Priesthood." Next, Richards recorded the full, amalgamated revelation "On Priesthood" into the manuscript history without dating or distinguishing between its component parts. See Joseph Smith, Manuscript History, Book B-1, 582–88, Church History Library, Salt Lake City; Joseph Smith Jr. et al., *History of The Church of Jesus Christ of Latter-day Saints*, ed. B. H. Roberts, 2d ed. rev., 7 vols. (Salt Lake City: Deseret Book, 1971), 2:209–17; Doctrine and Covenants 107:1–100; 1844 edition of the Doctrine and Covenants, 3:1–44. This part of Joseph's history was first published in the *Deseret News* by Willard Richards in 1852. "Life of Joseph Smith,"

Deseret News, January 24, 1852, 1; Howard C. Searle, "Authorship of the History of Joseph Smith: A Review Essay," *BYU Studies* 21, no. 1 (1981): 113.

When Orson Pratt prepared a new edition of the Doctrine and Covenants in 1876, he assigned the revised date of the minutes of the Twelve, March 28, 1835, to the revelation itself. Orson's heading for section 107 read: "A revelation through Joseph, the Prophet, given at Kirtland, Ohio, on Priesthood; the for[e] part, or the first fifty-eight verses, being given March 28th, 1835; the other items were revealed at sundry times." Historian's Office Journal, July 7, 1874, November 1875, Church History Library, Salt Lake City; Joseph Smith, Manuscript History, Book B-1, 581–82, Church History Library, Salt Lake City; see also Woodford, "Historical Development," 3:1398–1429.

It seems likely that the revelation was given between April 26 and April 28, 1835. All of the apostles had arrived in Kirtland by April 26 and were preparing to leave on their mission the following week. Their request for the revelation emphasizes that "the time when we are about to separate is near," and its March 28 date in their minutes may best be explained as being off by one month. Apparently none of the apostles individually documented the date of the revelation. See *Times and Seasons* 6 (April 15, 1845): 869; *Messenger and Advocate,* March 1835, 90; *Millennial Star* 27 (February 4, 1865): 87; Elden J. Watson, comp., *The Orson Pratt Journals* (Salt Lake City: E. J. Watson, 1975), 57; *Millennial Star* 26 (June 11, 1864): 391.

3. *Times and Seasons* 6 (April 15, 1845): 869.
4. Kirtland Revelation Book, 84–86, Church History Library, Salt Lake City.
5. See Doctrine and Covenants 107:1–58; Doctrine and Covenants, 1835 and 1844 editions, 3:1–30; Kirtland Revelation Book, 84–86. Before its 1835 publication, Joseph added amendments about the priesthood offices of priest, bishop, elder, and seventy to both of the main sections of section 107. Much of the new revelation mirrors verses 15–22 of section 68. The amendments to section 107 include much or all of what is now found as verses 61, 69–71, 73, 76–77, 88, 90, and 93–98.
6. Andrew F. Ehat and Lyndon W. Cook, *The Words of Joseph Smith: The Contemporary Accounts of the Nauvoo Discourses of the Prophet Joseph,* Religious Studies Monograph Series, no. 6 (Provo, Utah: Religious Studies Center, Brigham Young University, 1980), 59–60.
7. Richard Lyman Bushman, *Joseph Smith: Rough Stone Rolling* (New York: Knopf, 2005), 263.
8. Gordon B. Hinckley, "This Work Is Concerned with People," *Ensign* 25 (May 1995): 52.
9. See Douglas J. Davies, "World Religions: Dynamics and Constraints," *BYU Studies* 44, no. 4 (2005): 253–70.

Doctrine & Covenants 108

1. Joseph Smith, Journal, December 26, 1835, Church History Library, Salt Lake City, in Joseph Smith, *The Papers of Joseph Smith,* ed. Dean C. Jessee, 2 vols. (Salt Lake City: Deseret Book, 1989–92), 2:121–22.
2. Lyndon W. Cook, "Lyman Sherman—Man of God, Would-Be Apostle," *BYU Studies* 19, no. 1 (1978): 121–24.

Doctrine & Covenants 109

1. Joseph Smith, *The Papers of Joseph Smith,* ed. Dean C. Jessee, 2 vols. (Salt Lake City: Deseret Book, 1989–92), 2:191.
2. Oliver Cowdery, Sketchbook, March 26, 1836, Church History Library, Salt Lake City.

3. Steven C. Harper, "'A Pentecost and Endowment Indeed': Six Eyewitness Accounts of the Kirtland Temple Experience," in *Opening the Heavens: Accounts of Divine Manifestations, 1820–1844,* ed. John W. Welch and Erick B. Carlson (Provo, Utah: Brigham Young University Press and Salt Lake City: Deseret Book, 2005), 327–71.
4. Smith, *Papers of Joseph Smith,* ed. Jessee, 2:195.
5. Richard Lyman Bushman, *Joseph Smith: Rough Stone Rolling* (New York: Knopf, 2005), 317.
6. See Doctrine and Covenants 49:10, 23, for earlier usages in a different context.
7. Emphasis added. See Hugh Nibley, *A House of Glory* (Provo, Utah: Foundation for Ancient Research and Mormon Studies, 1993).

Doctrine & Covenants 110

1. John P. Pratt, "The Restoration of Priesthood Keys on Easter 1836, Part 2: Symbolism of Passover and of Elijah's Return," *Ensign* 15 (July 1985): 55.
2. Joseph Smith, *The Papers of Joseph Smith,* ed. Dean C. Jessee, 2 vols. (Salt Lake City: Deseret Book, 1989–92), 2:209.
3. Joseph Smith, Kirtland, Ohio, to William W. Phelps, Independence, Missouri, January 11, 1833, in Joseph Smith Letterbook 1, in handwriting of Frederick G. Williams, 18–20, Church History Library, Salt Lake City.
4. Stephen D. Ricks, "The Appearance of Elijah and Moses in the Kirtland Temple and the Jewish Passover," *BYU Studies* 23, no. 4 (1903): 483–86.
5. Ibid., 485.
6. Richard Lyman Bushman, *Joseph Smith: Rough Stone Rolling* (New York: Knopf, 2005), 320–21.

Doctrine & Covenants 111

1. On August 19, 1836, Joseph wrote to Emma, "My beloved Wife:-Bro. Hyrum is about to start for home before the rest of us, which seems wisdom in God, as our business here can not be determined as soon as we could wish to have it. I thought a line from me by him would be acceptable to you, even if it did not contain but little, that you may know that you and the children are much on my mind. With regard to the great object of our mission, you will be anxious to know. We have found the house since Bro. [William] Burgess left us, very luckily and providentially, as we had one spell been most discouraged. The house is occupied, and it will require much care and patience to rent or buy it. We think we shall be able to effect it; if not now within the course of a few months. We think we shall be at home about the middle of September. I can think of many things concerning our business, but can only pray that you may have wisdom to manage the concerns that involve on you, and want you should believe me that I am your sincere friend and husband. In haste. Yours &c., Joseph Smith, Jr." Joseph Smith, *Personal Writings of Joseph Smith,* ed. Dean C. Jessee, 2d ed. (Salt Lake City: Deseret Book and Provo, Utah: Brigham Young University Press, 2002), 389–90; Parley P. Pratt to Mary Ann Pratt, November 4, 1838, Church History Library, Salt Lake City.
2. See Noah Webster, *American Dictionary of the English Language* (1828), s.v. "follies."
3. David R. Proper, "Joseph Smith and Salem," *Essex Institute Historical Collections* 100 (April 1964): 93. On August 6, 1836, the day section 111 was revealed, the *Salem Observer* reprinted a *Long Island Star* article on rumors of treasure buried by Captain Kidd and unsuccessful efforts to find it.
4. *Salem Gazette,* December 7, 1841; *Salem Register,* June 2, 1842.

Doctrine & Covenants 112

1. Ronald K. Esplin, "The Emergence of Brigham Young and the Twelve to Mormon Leadership, 1830–1841" (Ph.D. dissertation, Brigham Young University, 1981), 287–92.
2. Wilford Woodruff, Journal, June 25, 1857, Church History Library, Salt Lake City.
3. Vilate Kimball to Heber C. Kimball, September 6, 1837, photocopy of original, Church History Library, Salt Lake City.
4. Esplin, "Emergence of Brigham Young," 285–87.
5. Kimball to Kimball, September 6, 1837.
6. Heber C. Kimball to Vilate Kimball, November 12, 1837, Church History Library, Salt Lake City.
7. George A. Smith, in *Journal of Discourses,* 26 vols. (Liverpool: F. D. Richards, 1855–86), 3:283–84, April 6, 1856.
8. Ibid.
9. Gordon B. Hinckley, "Small Acts Lead to Great Consequences," *Ensign* 14 (May 1984): 81–83; Brigham Young, in *Journal of Discourses,* 26 vols. (Liverpool: F. D. Richards, 1855–86), 5:206, September 6, 1857.
10. Thomas B. Marsh to Heber C. Kimball, May 5, 1857, Church History Library, Salt Lake City.

Doctrine & Covenants 113

1. The First Presidency consisted of Joseph Smith, Sidney Rigdon, and Hyrum Smith, who replaced Frederick G. Williams as second counselor in the First Presidency in November 1837. In addition to the three constituted First Presidency members, Joseph Smith Sr. and John Smith, the Prophet's uncle, had been sustained in September 1837 as assistant presidents. Oliver Cowdery, though not a member of the First Presidency per se, was assistant president. Taken together, these six men composed the presidency of the Church. With the exception of Cowdery, who was already in Missouri, the remaining five men and their families fled Kirtland and relocated in Missouri. Joseph Smith and Sidney Rigdon arrived in Far West, Missouri, on March 14, 1838, Hyrum Smith in May, John Smith in June, and Joseph Smith Sr. in late July or early August.
2. Although not specified here, the meaning was for the presidency to move to Far West, the headquarters of the Church in Missouri.
3. See Doctrine and Covenants 38:18. The Old Testament metaphor is from Exodus 3:8.
4. Revelation, Kirtland, Ohio, January 12, 1838; copy in Joseph Smith Journal, July 8, 1838, Church Historical Library, Salt Lake City, Utah; spelling and punctuation standardized.
5. Joseph Smith, *The Papers of Joseph Smith,* ed. Dean C. Jessee, 2 vols. (Salt Lake City: Deseret Book, 1989–92), 2:255.
6. Latter-day Saint Old Testament scholars interpret the "servant" who is a descendant of Jesse (David's father), of Joseph (of Egypt), and of Ephraim (Joseph's birthright son) to be none other than Joseph Smith. See Donald W. Parry, Jay A. Parry, and Tina M. Peterson, *Understanding Isaiah* (Salt Lake City: Deseret Book, 1998), 116–17.
7. Blessing, Joseph Smith Sr. to Joseph Smith Jr., Kirtland, Ohio, December 9, 1841, Patriarchal Blessings Book, Church History Library, Salt Lake City.

Doctrine & Covenants 114

1. Joseph Smith, *The Papers of Joseph Smith,* ed. Dean C. Jessee, 2 vols. (Salt Lake City: Deseret Book, 1989–92), 2:212–31.

Doctrine & Covenants 115

1. Far West Record, April 7, 1837, Church History Library, Salt Lake City; W. W. Phelps, letter dated July 7, 1837, *Messenger and Advocate,* July 1837, 529.
2. Far West Record, November 6, 1837.
3. Minutes, Kirtland, Ohio, Conference, Joseph Smith, May 3, 1834, in *The Evening and the Morning Star,* May 1834, 8.
4. Joseph Smith, Far West, Missouri, to the Church presidency, Kirtland, Ohio, March 29, 1838; copy in Joseph Smith, Journal, March 29, 1838, 23–26, Church History Library, Salt Lake City.
5. Thomas B. Marsh to Wilford Woodruff, April 30, 1838, Church History Library, Salt Lake City; spelling standardized.
6. Joseph Smith, *The Papers of Joseph Smith,* ed. Dean C. Jessee, 2 vols. (Salt Lake City: Deseret Book, 1989–92), 2:248; spelling standardized.
7. William A. Wood, "An Old Mormon City in Missouri," *American Magazine of History* 16 (1886): 98–99, in Leland Homer Gentry, "A History of the Latter-day Saints in Northern Missouri from 1836 to 1839" (Ph.D. dissertation, Brigham Young University, 1965), 64.
8. Smith, *Papers of Joseph Smith,* ed. Jessee, 2:243–48.
9. See "Conference Minutes," *Elders' Journal,* August 1838, 60–61.
10. Gustav Niebuhr, "Adapting 'Mormon' to Emphasize Christianity," *New York Times,* February 18, 2008. Elder Russell M. Nelson further emphasized the importance of using the Lord's given name for His Church: "Surely every word that proceeds from the mouth of the Lord is precious. So each word in this name must be important—divinely designated for a reason." Russell M. Nelson, "'Thus Shall My Church Be Called,'" *Ensign* 20 (May 1990): 16.

Doctrine & Covenants 116

1. *History of Caldwell and Livingston Counties* (St. Louis, Mo.: National Historical Company, 1886), 103–10.
2. *Elders' Journal,* November 1837, 28.
3. Jeffrey N. Walker, "Mormon Land Rights in Caldwell and Daviess Counties and the Mormon Conflict of 1838," *BYU Studies* 47, no. 1 (2008): 5–55.
4. Joseph Smith, *The Papers of Joseph Smith,* ed. Dean C. Jessee, 2 vols. (Salt Lake City: Deseret Book, 1989–92), 2:243.
5. Ibid., 2:244–45; spelling and capitalization standardized. See Daniel 7.
6. Bruce R. McConkie, *The Millennial Messiah: The Second Coming of the Son of Man* (Salt Lake City: Deseret Book, 1982), 578–79.
7. Robert J. Matthews, "Adam-ondi-Ahman," *BYU Studies* 13, no. 1 (1972): 27–35; Leland H. Gentry, "Adam-ondi-Ahman: A Brief Historical Survey," *BYU Studies* 13, no. 4 (1973): 553–76.
8. Walker, "Mormon Land Rights," 5–55.

Doctrine & Covenants 117

1. See Doctrine and Covenants 38:18. The Old Testament metaphor is from Exodus 3:8.
2. Revelation, Kirtland, Ohio, January 12, 1838, Church History Library, Salt Lake City, copied into Joseph Smith, Journal, July 8, 1838, Church History Library, Salt Lake City. See Joseph Smith, *The Papers of Joseph Smith,* ed. Dean C. Jessee, 2 vols. (Salt Lake City: Deseret Book, 1989–92), 2:255; spelling and punctuation standardized.

3. Mark L. Staker, "'Thou Art the Man': Newel K. Whitney in Ohio," *BYU Studies* 42, no. 1 (2003), 75–138, especially 113.
4. Joseph Smith, Journal, October 7, 1835; in Smith, *Papers of Joseph Smith*, ed. Jessee, 2:49.
5. Smith, *Papers of Joseph Smith*, ed. Jessee, 2:49–50.
6. Marvin R. Vincent, *Word Studies in the New Testament*, 4 vols. (Grand Rapids, Mich.: Eerdmans, 1976), 1:439.
7. Horace Kingsbury to all persons that are or may be interested, Painesville, Ohio, October 26, 1838, in Joseph Smith Letterbook 2, 40, Church History Library, Salt Lake City.
8. Boyd K. Packer, "The Least of These," *Ensign* 34 (November 2004): 86; Howard W. Hunter, "'No Less Serviceable,'" *Ensign* 22 (April 1992): 64.
9. Joseph Smith, Sidney Rigdon, Hyrum Smith, Commerce, Illinois, to all the Saints scattered abroad, May 13, 1839, Joseph Smith Letterbook 2, 45–46, Church History Library, Salt Lake City.
10. Joseph Smith, Sidney Rigdon, Hyrum Smith, Far West, Missouri, to Newel K. Whitney and Williams Marks, July 8, 1838, Church History Library, Salt Lake City.

Doctrine & Covenants 118

1. Joseph Smith, *The Papers of Joseph Smith*, ed. Dean C. Jessee, 2 vols. (Salt Lake City: Deseret Book, 1989–92), 2:256.
2. Wilford Woodruff, Journal, August 9, 1838, Church History Library, Salt Lake City; Thomas B. Marsh to Wilford Woodruff, July 14, 1838, Church History Library, Salt Lake City.
3. Wilford Woodruff, in *Journal of Discourses*, 26 vols. (Liverpool: F. D. Richards, 1855–86), 13:159, December 12, 1869.
4. Woodruff, Journal, April 1839.
5. Ibid., April 26, 1839; spelling, capitalization, and punctuation standardized.
6. William W. Phelps to Sally Phelps, May 1, 1839, Church History Library, Salt Lake City; spelling and capitalization standardized.
7. See James B. Allen, Ronald K. Esplin, and David J. Whittaker, *Men with a Mission, 1837–1841: The Quorum of the Twelve Apostles in the British Isles* (Salt Lake City: Deseret Book, 1992).

Doctrine & Covenants 119

1. Newel Whitney et al. to the Saints scattered abroad, September 18, 1837, *Messenger and Advocate*, September 1837, 561–64.
2. Far West Record, December 7, 1837, Church History Library, Salt Lake City.
3. Joseph Smith, *The Papers of Joseph Smith*, ed. Dean C. Jessee, 2 vols. (Salt Lake City: Deseret Book, 1989–92), 2:257.
4. Gordon B. Hinckley, *Teachings of Gordon B. Hinckley* (Salt Lake City: Deseret Book, 1997), 639.
5. Brigham Young, in *Journal of Discourses*, 26 vols. (Liverpool: F. D. Richards, 1855–86), 2:306, June 3, 1855.

Doctrine & Covenants 120

1. Joseph Smith, *The Papers of Joseph Smith*, ed. Dean C. Jessee, 2 vols. (Salt Lake City: Deseret Book, 1989–92), 2:259; spelling standardized.

2. Smith, *Papers of Joseph Smith*, ed. Jessee, 2:261; spelling, capitalization, and punctuation standardized.
3. Robert D. Hales, "Tithing: A Test of Faith with Eternal Blessings," *Ensign* 32 (November 2002): 28.

Doctrine & Covenants 121, 122, and 123

1. Quoted in Richard Lyman Bushman, *Joseph Smith: Rough Stone Rolling* (New York: Knopf, 2005), 368.
2. Joseph Smith to Emma Smith, November 12, 1838, Liberty, Missouri, in Joseph Smith, *Personal Writings of Joseph Smith*, ed. Dean C. Jessee, 2d ed. (Salt Lake City: Deseret Book and Provo, Utah: Brigham Young University Press, 2002), 406.
3. Joseph Smith, Liberty, Missouri, to Emma Smith, Far West, Missouri, December 1, 1838, Church History Library, Salt Lake City.
4. *Correspondence, Orders &c. in Relation to the Disturbances with the Mormons; and the Evidence* (Fayette, Mo.: Missouri General Assembly, 1841), 2.
5. Hyrum Smith, Affidavit before Nauvoo Municipal Court, July 1, 1843, in Joseph Smith Jr. et al., *History of The Church of Jesus Christ of Latter-day Saints*, ed. B. H. Roberts, 2d ed. rev., 7 vols. (Salt Lake City: Deseret Book, 1971), 3:420; also in Clark V. Johnson, ed., *Mormon Redress Petitions: Documents of the 1833–1838 Missouri Conflict* (Provo, Utah: Religious Studies Center, Brigham Young University, 1992), 632–35.
6. Gordon A. Madsen, "Joseph Smith and the Missouri Court of Inquiry: Austin A. King's Quest for Hostages," *BYU Studies* 43, no. 4 (2004): 93–136.
7. Smith et al., *History of the Church*, 3:215.
8. Bushman, *Rough Stone Rolling*, 379.
9. John Corrill, *A Brief History of the Church of Christ of Latter Day Saints* (St. Louis: Printed for the author, 1839), 48.
10. Bushman, *Rough Stone Rolling*, 379–80.
11. Dean C. Jessee and John W. Welch, eds., "Revelations in Context: Joseph Smith's Letter from Liberty Jail, March 20, 1839," *BYU Studies* 39, no. 3 (2000): 139.
12. Bushman, *Rough Stone Rolling*, 376.
13. The entire letter was published in Jessee and Welch, "Revelations in Context: Joseph Smith's Letter from Liberty Jail," 125–45; spelling and punctuation standardized.
14. Ibid., 134, 135; spelling and punctuation standardized.
15. Ibid., 137–38; spelling, punctuation, and capitalization standardized; emphasis added.
16. Ibid., 140; spelling, punctuation, and capitalization standardized.
17. Johnson, *Mormon Redress Petitions*.
18. Bushman, *Rough Stone Rolling*, 380.
19. B. H. Roberts, *A Comprehensive History of The Church of Jesus Christ of Latter-day Saints, Century One*, 6 vols. (Provo, Utah: The Church of Jesus Christ of Latter-day Saints, 1965), 1:526.
20. Bushman, *Rough Stone Rolling*, 380.
21. Joseph Smith to Presendia Huntington Buell, March 15, 1839, Liberty, Missouri, in Smith, *Personal Writings of Joseph Smith*, ed. Jessee, 427.
22. Joseph Smith to Emma Smith, March 21, 1839, Liberty, Missouri, in Smith, *Personal Writings of Joseph Smith*, ed. Jessee, 449; spelling standardized.

Doctrine & Covenants 124

1. Jeffrey Walker, "Mormon Land Rights in Caldwell and Daviess Counties and the Mormon Conflict of 1838," *BYU Studies* 47, no. 1 (2008): 5–55.
2. Transliterated, the Hebrew is equivalent to *NV*. The King James Version of the Bible renders the Hebrew of Isaiah 52:7 as "how beautiful upon the mountains . . ."
3. Glen M. Leonard, *Nauvoo: A Place of Peace, a People of Promise* (Salt Lake City: Deseret Book and Provo, Utah: Brigham Young University Press, 2002), 103.
4. Joseph Fielding Smith, quoted in Roy W. Doxey, *Latter-day Prophets and the Doctrine and Covenants,* 4 vols. (Salt Lake City: Deseret Book, 1978), 4:266.
5. Boyd K. Packer, *The Holy Temple* (Salt Lake City: Deseret Book, 2007), 177; paragraphing altered.
6. Andrew F. Ehat and Lyndon W. Cook, *The Words of Joseph Smith: The Contemporary Accounts of the Nauvoo Discourses of the Prophet Joseph,* Religious Studies Monograph Series, no. 6 (Provo, Utah: Religious Studies Center, Brigham Young University, 1980), 69.
7. Gordon B. Hinckley, "Of Missions, Temples, and Stewardship," *Ensign* 25 (November 1995): 53.

Doctrine & Covenants 125

1. Richard Lyman Bushman, *Joseph Smith: Rough Stone Rolling* (New York: Knopf, 2005), 382.
2. Joseph Smith to the Church, March 20, 1839, Liberty, Missouri, in Joseph Smith, *Personal Writings of Joseph Smith,* ed. Dean C. Jessee, 2d ed. (Salt Lake City: Deseret Book and Provo, Utah: Brigham Young University Press, 2002), 439.
3. General Conference, Minutes, October 6, 1839, Church History Library, Salt Lake City; Joseph Smith to the Church, May 27, 1839, Church History Library, Salt Lake City.
4. William Clayton, *An Intimate Chronicle: The Journals of William Clayton,* ed. George D. Smith (Salt Lake City: Signature, 1995), 86.
5. Alanson Ripley, in John Smith, Journal, March 6, 1841, Church History Library, Salt Lake City; spelling standardized.

Doctrine & Covenants 126

1. Leonard J. Arrington, *Brigham Young: American Moses* (New York: Knopf, 1985), 98.
2. Ibid., 99–100. Also see the consecration affidavits in the Brigham Young Collection, Church History Library, Salt Lake City.

Doctrine & Covenants 127 and 128

1. See Jeffrey A. Trumbower, *Rescue for the Dead: The Posthumous Salvation of Non-Christians in Early Christianity* (New York: Oxford University Press, 2001).
2. Hugh Nibley, "Baptism for the Dead in Ancient Times," in *Mormonism and Early Christianity* (Salt Lake City: Deseret Book and Provo, Utah: Foundation for Ancient Research and Mormon Studies, 1987), 148–49.
3. Simon Baker, in Journal History of the Church, August 15, 1840, Church History Library, Salt Lake City.
4. John Smith, Journal, October 15, 1840, Church History Library, Salt Lake City.
5. Vilate Kimball to Heber C. Kimball, October 11, 1840, Church History Library, Salt Lake City.

6. Minutes of the General Conference of the Church Held at Nauvoo, Elias Smith and Gustavus Hills, Rough Draft Notes of *History of the Church,* 1841, 17, Church History Library, Salt Lake City; Joseph Smith Jr. et al., *History of The Church of Jesus Christ of Latter-day Saints,* ed. B. H. Roberts, 2d ed. rev., 7 vols. (Salt Lake City: Deseret Book, 1971), 4:423–29.

7. Andrew F. Ehat and Lyndon W. Cook, *The Words of Joseph Smith: The Contemporary Accounts of the Nauvoo Discourses of the Prophet Joseph,* Religious Studies Monograph Series, no. 6 (Provo, Utah: Religious Studies Center, Brigham Young University, 1980), 129–31.

8. Boyd K. Packer, *The Holy Temple* (Salt Lake City: Bookcraft, 1980), 144–45.

9. See Gabriel Fackre, Ronald H. Nash, and John Sanders, *What about Those Who Have Never Heard?: Three Views on the Destiny of the Unevangelized,* ed. John Sanders (Downers Grove, Ill.: InterVarsity Press, 1995).

10. Wilford Woodruff, Journal, September 19, 1842, Church History Library, Salt Lake City.

11. Kimball to Kimball, October 11, 1840.

12. Reminiscences, December 29, 1897, in Brian H. Stuy, comp. and ed., *Collected Discourses,* 5 vols. (Burbank, Calif.: B.H.S. Publishing, 1987–92), 5:356.

13. Sally Carlisle Randall to Betty Carlisle, April 21, 1844, Harold B. Lee Library, Brigham Young University, Provo, Utah.

14. Nibley, "Baptism for the Dead in Ancient Times," 148–49.

Doctrine & Covenants 129

1. Wilford Woodruff, Journal, June 27, 1839, Church History Library, Salt Lake City.

2. Andrew F. Ehat and Lyndon W. Cook, *The Words of Joseph Smith: The Contemporary Accounts of the Nauvoo Discourses of the Prophet Joseph,* Religious Studies Monograph Series, no. 6 (Provo, Utah: Religious Studies Center, Brigham Young University, 1980), 44.

3. Joseph Smith, *The Papers of Joseph Smith,* ed. Dean C. Jessee, 2 vols. (Salt Lake City: Deseret Book, 1989–92), 2:379; punctuation standardized.

4. Heber Kimball to Parley Pratt, June 17, 1842, Pratt Papers, Church History Library, Salt Lake City; spelling standardized.

5. Joseph Smith, Journal, February 9, 1843, Church History Library, Salt Lake City.

6. Joseph Smith, Discourse, March 16, 1841, Nauvoo, Illinois, as recorded in William Patterson McIntire, Notebook 1840–1845, Church History Library, Salt Lake City.

7. Ibid.

Doctrine & Covenants 130

1. Joseph Smith, Journal, kept by Willard Richards, April 2, 1843, Church History Library, Salt Lake City.

2. Benjamin F. Johnson to President Anthon H. Lund, May 12, 1903, Church History Library, Salt Lake City.

3. Andrew F. Ehat and Lyndon W. Cook, *The Words of Joseph Smith: The Contemporary Accounts of the Nauvoo Discourses of the Prophet Joseph,* Religious Studies Monograph Series, no. 6 (Provo, Utah: Religious Studies Center, Brigham Young University, 1980), 170, 268–69.

4. Ibid.

5. Neal A. Maxwell, *If Thou Endure It Well* (Salt Lake City: Bookcraft, 1996), 27.

Doctrine & Covenants 131

1. Benjamin F. Johnson, *My Life's Review: The Autobiography of Benjamin F. Johnson*, ed. Lyndon W. Cook and Kevin V. Harker (Provo, Utah: Grandin Book, 1997), 85–86.
2. William Clayton, *An Intimate Chronicle: The Journals of William Clayton*, ed. George D. Smith (Salt Lake City: Signature, 1995), 102.
3. Ibid., 103; spelling standardized.
4. Andrew F. Ehat and Lyndon W. Cook, *The Words of Joseph Smith: The Contemporary Accounts of the Nauvoo Discourses of the Prophet Joseph*, Religious Studies Monograph Series, no. 6 (Provo, Utah: Religious Studies Center, Brigham Young University, 1980), 200–201.
5. Joseph Smith, *The Papers of Joseph Smith*, ed. Dean C. Jessee, 2 vols. (Salt Lake City: Deseret Book, 1989–92), 2:69; spelling standardized.
6. Ehat and Cook, *Words of Joseph Smith*, 202–4; Clayton, *Intimate Chronicle*, ed. Smith, 103–4.

Doctrine & Covenants 132

1. Richard Lyman Bushman, *Joseph Smith: Rough Stone Rolling* (New York: Knopf, 2005), 441.
2. Ibid., 437.
3. Ibid.
4. Helen Mar Whitney, *Woman's Exponent* 10 (November 1, 1881): 83.
5. Bushman, *Rough Stone Rolling*, 440.
6. Carol Cornwall Madsen, "'All Things Move in Order in the City': The Nauvoo Diary of Zina Diantha Huntington Jacobs," *BYU Studies* 19, no. 3 (1979): 291–92; spelling standardized.
7. Benjamin F. Johnson, *My Life's Review: The Autobiography of Benjamin F. Johnson*, ed. Lyndon W. Cook and Kevin V. Harker (Provo, Utah: Grandin Book, 1997), 83–84.
8. Lucy Walker Kimball, Autobiographical Sketch, Church History Library, Salt Lake City.
9. Helen Mar Whitney, *Woman's Exponent* 10 (October 15, 1881): 74.
10. Council of the Twelve Minutes, Book A, 11, Community of Christ Archives, Independence, Missouri.
11. William Clayton, Journal, July 12, 1843, William Clayton Letterbooks, Special Collections, J. Willard Marriott Library, University of Utah, Salt Lake City.
12. Joseph Smith, *An American Prophet's Record: The Diaries and Journals of Joseph Smith*, ed. Scott H. Faulring (Salt Lake City: Signature, 1989), September 28, 1843, 416; William Clayton, Journal, October 19, 1843, in William Clayton, *An Intimate Chronicle: The Journals of William Clayton*, ed. George D. Smith (Salt Lake City: Signature, 1995), 122.
13. Lucy M. Wright, "Emma Hale Smith," in *Woman's Exponent* 30, no. 8 (1901): 59.
14. Bushman, *Rough Stone Rolling*, 490.
15. Smith, *American Prophet's Record*, September 28, 1843, 416; Andrew F. Ehat, "Joseph Smith's Introduction of Temple Ordinances and the 1844 Mormon Succession Question" (master's thesis, Brigham Young University, 1981), 76–84; Clayton Journal, October 19, 1843, in Clayton, *Intimate Chronicle*, ed. Smith, 122.
16. Typescript copy of blessing, Church History Library, Salt Lake City; in Carol Cornwall Madsen, "The 'Elect Lady' Revelation: The Historical and Doctrinal Context of Doctrine and Covenants 25," in *The Heavens Are Open* (Salt Lake City: Deseret Book, 1993), 208.

Doctrine & Covenants 133

1. Joseph Smith, *The Papers of Joseph Smith*, ed. Dean C. Jessee, 2 vols. (Salt Lake City: Deseret Book, 1989–92), 1:368; spelling standardized.
2. *The Evening and the Morning Star*, May 1833, 89.

Doctrine & Covenants 134

1. Steven C. Harper, "'Dictated by Christ': Joseph Smith and the Politics of Revelation," *Journal of the Early Republic* 26 (Summer 2006): 275–304.
2. See "Free People of Color" and William W. Phelps's statement published later in the same issue, wherein he noted approvingly that much was being done "towards abolishing slavery," *The Evening and the Morning Star*, July 1833, 109, 111. The Church's political *Northern Times* newspaper printed on October 9, 1835, that the Church was "opposed to abolition, and whatever is calculated to disturb the peace and harmony of our Constitution and Country." See "Abolition," *Northern Times* (October 9, 1835). Joseph's views on race and blacks changed during his lifetime. See Richard Lyman Bushman, *Joseph Smith: Rough Stone Rolling* (New York: Knopf, 2005), 97–99, 288–89, 516–17. In 1836, Joseph Smith criticized the abolition movement and defended slavery as biblical. *Messenger and Advocate*, April 1836, 289–91. See also Warren Parrish, "For the Messenger and Advocate," *Messenger and Advocate* (April 1836): 295–96; and "The Abolitionists," *Messenger and Advocate* (April 1836): 299–301.
3. Minutes of General Assembly, August 17, 1835, Kirtland Minute Book, Church History Library, Salt Lake City.
4. *Messenger and Advocate* (April 1836): 239–41.

Doctrine & Covenants 135

1. *Times and Seasons* 5, no. 8 (April 15, 1844): 510.
2. David W. Kilbourne to Reverend Thomas Dent, June 29, 1844, Kilbourne Collection, State Historical Society of Iowa, Des Moines.
3. Dallin H. Oaks and Marvin S. Hill, *Carthage Conspiracy: The Trial of the Accused Assassins of Joseph Smith* (Urbana: University of Illinois Press, 1975), 6.
4. Josiah Quincy, *Figures of the Past, from the Leaves of Old Journals* (Boston, Mass.: Roberts Brothers, 1883), 337.
5. Ibid., 317.
6. Andrew F. Ehat and Lyndon W. Cook, *The Words of Joseph Smith: The Contemporary Accounts of the Nauvoo Discourses of the Prophet Joseph,* Religious Studies Monograph Series, no. 6 (Provo, Utah: Religious Studies Center, Brigham Young University, 1980), 341.

Doctrine & Covenants 136

1. Declaration of the apostles, circa September 1844 to March 1845, Church History Library, Salt Lake City.
2. Ibid.
3. Testimony written by Martha Tuttle Gardner, in possession of the author.
4. "At 4:30 PM the council adjourned. At seven, the Twelve met at Elder Benson's. President Young continued to dictate the word and will of the Lord. Council adjourned at ten P.M., when President Young retired with Dr. Richards to the Octagon and finished writing the same." Journal History of the Church, January 14, 1847, Church History Library, Salt Lake City.

5. Richard E. Bennett, *We'll Find the Place: The Mormon Exodus, 1846–1848* (Salt Lake City: Deseret Book, 1997), 70.
6. Ibid., 69.
7. Ibid.
8. Heber C. Kimball, Journal, January 19, 1847, Church History Library, Salt Lake City.
9. As quoted by Willard Richards, Journal, January 15, 1847, Church History Library, Salt Lake City.

Doctrine & Covenants 137

1. Joseph Smith, *The Papers of Joseph Smith*, ed. Dean C. Jessee, 2 vols. (Salt Lake City: Deseret Book, 1989–92), 2:440; spelling standardized.
2. According to Joseph's brother William Smith, cited in *Deseret News,* January 20, 1894; see Richard Lyman Bushman, *Joseph Smith: Rough Stone Rolling* (New York: Knopf, 2005), 110.
3. David L. Paulsen, "Joseph Smith and the Problem of Evil," *BYU Studies* 39, no. 1 (2000): 61.
4. Steven C. Harper, "'A Pentecost and Endowment Indeed': Six Eyewitness Accounts of the Kirtland Temple Experience," in *Opening the Heavens: Accounts of Divine Manifestations, 1820–1844,* ed. John W. Welch and Erick B. Carlson (Provo, Utah: Brigham Young University Press and Salt Lake City: Deseret Book, 2005), 338, 344.
5. Hugh Nibley, *Mormonism and Early Christianity* (Salt Lake City: Deseret Book and Provo, Utah: Foundation for Ancient Research and Mormon Studies, 1987), 101–3.
6. See Gerald R. McDermott, *Jonathan Edwards Confronts the Gods: Christian Theology, Enlightenment Religion, and Non-Christian Faiths* (New York: Oxford University Press, 1999). Leigh E. Schmidt, "The Edwards Revival; or, the Public Consequences of Exceedingly Careful Scholarship," *William and Mary Quarterly* 58, no. 2 (2001): 484–85.
7. Paulsen, "Joseph Smith and the Problem of Evil," 62.
8. Lucy Mack Smith, *Biographical Sketches of Joseph Smith, the Prophet, and His Progenitors for Many Generations* (London: published for Orson Pratt by S. W. Richards, 1853), 265–66, 270; Richard E. Turley Jr., "The Latter-day Saint Doctrine of Baptism for the Dead" (address given at BYU Family History Fireside, Brigham Young University, November 9, 2001), copy of unpublished manuscript in author's possession. Nauvoo baptismal records show that Alvin was baptized by proxy at the instance of his brother Hyrum. Nauvoo Temple, Baptisms for the Dead 1840–1845, Book A, 145,149, Church History Library, Salt Lake City.

Doctrine & Covenants 138

1. George S. Tate, "'The Great World of the Spirits of the Dead': Death, the Great War, and the 1918 Influenza Pandemic As Context for Doctrine and Covenants 138," *BYU Studies* 46, no. 1 (2007): 27, 33.
2. Ibid., 17–26.
3. Joseph F. Smith, "Status of Children in the Resurrection," in *Messages of the First Presidency,* comp. James R. Clark, 6 vols. (Salt Lake City: Bookcraft, 1965–75), 5:92.
4. Joseph Fielding Smith, *Life of Joseph F. Smith: Sixth President of The Church of Jesus Christ of Latter-day Saints* (Salt Lake City: Deseret News Press, 1938), 476.
5. Joseph F. Smith, Conference Report, October 1918, 2.
6. Smith, *Life of Joseph F. Smith,* 466.

7. Gordon B. Hinckley, "Remarks at the Dedication of the Joseph F. Smith Building at Brigham Young University" (address given at Brigham Young University, Provo, Utah, September 20, 2005), 4, copy of unpublished manuscript in possession of the author.
8. Tate, "'Great World of the Spirits of the Dead,'" 21.
9. This insight is from George S. Tate. See Tate, "Great World of the Spirits of the Dead," 34.
10. See Andrew F. Ehat and Lyndon W. Cook, *The Words of Joseph Smith: The Contemporary Accounts of the Nauvoo Discourses of the Prophet Joseph,* Religious Studies Monograph Series, no. 6 (Provo, Utah: Religious Studies Center, Brigham Young University, 1980), 370; Brigham Young, in *Journal of Discourses,* 26 vols. (Liverpool: F. D. Richards, 1855–86), 4:285, March 15, 1857; and Wilford Woodruff, *Wilford Woodruff's Journal, 1833–1898,* Typescript., ed. Scott G. Kenney, 9 vols. (Midvale, Utah: Signature, 1983–84), 6:390.
11. Douglas J. Davies, *The Mormon Culture of Salvation* (Burlington, Vt.: Ashgate, 2000), 98.
12. Jeffrey A. Trumbower, *Rescue for the Dead: The Posthumous Salvation of Non-Christians in Early Christianity* (New York: Oxford University Press, 2001), 3–9, 126–40.
13. The *Oxford English Dictionary* defines the verb "to harrow" as "to break up, crush, or pulverize with a harrow." K. M. Warren, "Harrowing of Hell," *The Catholic Encyclopedia,* 15 vols. (New York: Robert Appleton, 1910), vol. 7. See Karl Tamburr, *The Harrowing of Hell in Medieval England* (Woodbridge, Suffolk, England, and Rochester, New York: Boydell & Brewer, 2007).
14. Apostles Creed, available online at https://www.apuritansmind.com/creeds-and-confessions/the-apostles-creed/
15. John Calvin, *Institutes of the Christian Religion,* trans. Henry Beveridge, 2 vols. (Grand Rapids, Mich.: Eerdmans, 1957), 2:442.
16. Martin Luther, "First Lectures on the Psalms (Psalm 86)" in *Luther's Works II* (St. Louis, Mo.: Concordia, 1976), 175.
17. Heidi J. Hornik and Mikeal C. Parsons, "The Harrowing of Hell," *Bible Review* 19, no. 3 (2003): 50.
18. Katherine Anne Porter, *Pale Horse, Pale Rider: Three Short Novels* (New York: Harcourt Brace, 1939), 255, quoted in Tate, "'Great World of the Spirits of the Dead,'" 34.
19. Tate, "'Great World of the Spirits of the Dead,'" 40, 39–40.
20. James E. Talmage, Journal, October 31, 1918, Church History Library, Salt Lake City; Anthon H. Lund, Journal, October 31, 1918, Church History Library, Salt Lake City.

Official Declaration–1

1. Thomas Kane, quoted in Wilford Woodruff, Journal, November 26, 1849, Church History Library, Salt Lake City.
2. Morrill Act, 37th Congress, 2d session, July 1, 1862, chapter 126, page 501.
3. Reported in "Elder Oaks Testifies before U.S. Congressional Subcommittee," *Ensign* 22 (July 1992): 78, 79.
4. Wilford Woodruff, Journal, December 31, 1889, Church History Library, Salt Lake City.
5. Ibid., May 19, 1890.
6. James B. Allen and Glen M. Leonard, *The Story of the Latter-day Saints,* 2d ed. (Salt Lake City: Deseret Book, 1992), 414.
7. Wilford Woodruff, Journal, September 25, 1890, Church History Library, Salt Lake City; spelling standardized.
8. Wilford Woodruff, "Official Declaration," *Deseret Weekly,* October 4, 1980, 476.
9. Woodruff, Journal, October 25, 1891; spelling and capitalization standardized.

10. John Sillito, ed., *Historian's Apprentice: The Diaries of B. H. Roberts* (Salt Lake City: Signature, 2004), 225–27.
11. Doctrine and Covenants, page 293.

Official Declaration–2

1. Stephen R. Haynes, *Noah's Curse: The Biblical Justification of American Slavery* (New York: Oxford University Press, 2002).
2. "Report from the Presidency," *Times and Seasons* 1 (October 1840): 188.
3. Armand L. Mauss, *All Abraham's Children: Changing Mormon Conceptions of Race and Lineage* (Urbana: University of Illinois Press, 2003), 214–16.
4. Joseph Smith, *An American Prophet's Record: The Diaries and Journals of Joseph Smith*, ed. Scott H. Faulring (Salt Lake City: Signature, 1989), 269.
5. *Times and Seasons* 5 (May 15, 1844): 528.
6. Mauss, *All Abraham's Children*, 212–30.
7. Spencer W. Kimball, *The Teachings of Spencer W. Kimball*, ed. Edward L. Kimball (Salt Lake City: Bookcraft, 1982), 448–49. President David O. McKay called the priesthood ban a policy rather than a doctrine. See Edward L. Kimball, *Lengthen Your Stride: The Presidency of Spencer W. Kimball* (Salt Lake City: Deseret Book, 2005), 200–201.
8. Mauss, *All Abraham's Children*, 212.
9. Presidents Hugh B. Brown and Nathan Eldon Tanner to all the priesthood leaders in the Church, December 15, 1969, quoted in Lester E. Bush and Armand L. Mauss, eds., *Neither White Nor Black: Mormon Scholars Confront the Race Issue in a Universal Church* (Salt Lake City: Signature, 1984), 222–24.
10. Dallin H. Oaks, "Apostles Talk about Reasons for Lifting Ban," *Provo Daily Herald*, June 5, 1988, 21. LeGrand Richards, interview, Salt Lake City, Utah, August 16, 1978, L. Tom Perry Special Collections, Harold B. Lee Library, Brigham Young University, Provo, Utah.
11. Kimball, *Lengthen Your Stride*, 195.
12. Ibid., 216–17.
13. Ibid., 218–19.
14. Ibid., 220–21.
15. Bruce R. McConkie, *Doctrines of the Restoration: Sermons and Writings of Bruce R. McConkie*, ed. Mark L. McConkie (Salt Lake City: Bookcraft, 1989), 159.
16. Kimball, *Lengthen Your Stride*, 222–24.
17. Ibid., 228.
18. Gordon B. Hinckley, "Priesthood Restoration," *Ensign* 18 (October 1988): 69–72.
19. Kimball, *Lengthen Your Stride*, 228–29.
20. Hinckley, "Priesthood Restoration," 70.
21. Kimball, *Lengthen Your Stride*, 231.
22. Hinckley, "Priesthood Restoration," 70.
23. Jan Shipps, "The Mormons: Looking Forward and Outward," *Christian Century* (August 16–23, 1978): 761–66.
24. David B. Haight, "The Work Is True," *Ensign* 26 (May 1996): 22.
25. McConkie, *Doctrines of the Restoration*, 162, 165.
26. Hinckley, "Priesthood Restoration," 70; Helvecio Martins, *The Autobiography of Helvecio Martins* (Salt Lake City: Aspen Books, 1994).

27. E. Dale LeBaron, "The Church in Africa," in *Out of Obscurity: The Church in the Twentieth Century* (Salt Lake City: Deseret Book, 2000), 177–89.
28. Hinckley, "Priesthood Restoration," 71.

Epilogue
1. N. Eldon Tanner, "Revelation on Priesthood Accepted, Church Officers Sustained," *Ensign* 8 (November 1978): 16.

Index

Pages on which photographs appear are designated with italic type.

Aaron, gift of, 42–43
Aaronic Priesthood: restoration of, 56–58; mission guidelines for, 141; financial support for, 143; requirements for presiding over, 238, 397; Melchizedek Priesthood and, 296–97; oath and covenant of, 297; functions of, 396; presidencies of, 460
Abel, Elijah, 522
Accountability: agency and, 24–25, 99, 203, 458; for those who transgress, 100; stewardship and, 251; Word of Wisdom and, 328, 330–31, 333–35; agency and stewardship and, 383–84; for United Firm members, 387; consecration and, 501
Adam, 92–93, 99, 428
Adam-ondi-Ahman, 425, 428, 431
Addiction, 328–30
Adultery: Church discipline for, 143; Saints called to repent of, 219; William McLellin commanded to repent of, 230; plural marriage and, 487
Africans: enslavement of, 521; link between Canaanites and, 522–23; growth of Church amongst, 530. *See also* Black men
Agency: as theme in D&C, 14–15; definition of, 16; accountability and, 24–25, 203, 458; of Joseph Smith, 28; versus omnipotence and omniscience, 49–50;

views on salvation and, 97–98; gradual growth into, 99; teaching children, 100; covenants and, 134–35; law of God and, 144–45; Shakers' views on, 167; mission calls and, 198; Methodist views on, 262; salvation and, 271–72; Word of Wisdom and, 328, 333–35; Truman Madsen on, 349; freedom and, 373; stewardship and accountability and, 383–84; intelligence and, 475; consecration and, 501; in accepting gospel after death, 511–12
Alcohol, 30, 322–23, 332
American Civil War, 310–12, 475, 514–15, 521
American continent, Church to be built on, 47–48
American Revolution, 29
Amherst, Ohio, 179, 286
Anabaptists, 79–80
Anderson, Richard, on success of early missionaries, 109
Angel(s): shows plates to witnesses, 34, 62–64; restore Aaronic Priesthood, 56; gives revelation on sacrament, 92–94; teaches Joseph Smith how to discern spirits, 174–75; appears to Joseph Smith, 469; discerning, 473; time relativity and, 475
Angel Moroni, *22;* appears to Joseph Smith, 21; returns seer stones, 26, 28; teaches Joseph Smith prophecies of Isaiah, 419–20
Animals, wasting, 169, 170
Anointings, 458
Apocalypse, 315

579

Apocrypha, 340–42
Apostasy: section 1 prophesies of, 19; parable of wheat and tares and, 308–9; Thomas B. Marsh works against, 414–15; in Kirtland, Ohio, 418–19, 432; leadership vacancies due to, 422; effect on Twelve of, 435–39; persecution of Joseph Smith and, 495
Apostle(s): Spencer W. Kimball on, 41; taught to identify Satan, 58; revelation on calling, 66–67; as necessity for building Church, 73; Joseph Smith as, 93–94; Olivet discourse given to, 154–58; mission call of, 298–300, 414–15; rebel against Joseph Smith, 415; calling and ordination of new, 436; depart for Great Britain, 439; carry out temple ordinances, 461; Brigham Young as, 464–65. *See also* Quorum of the Seventy; Quorum of the Twelve Apostles
Apostles Creed, 512
Appearance, commandment on, 142
Area authorities, 399
Ark, steadying, 305
Arm, Joseph Smith heals, 247–48
Army, Joseph Smith to organize, 380
Articles and Covenants, 73–75
Ashley, Major N., 260
Assistant president, 459
Atonement: agency and, 14; Russell M. Nelson on, 23; brings salvation for souls, 65–67; described in revelation for Martin Harris, 70–71; children and, 256–57
Augustine, 466
Authority: as necessity for building Church, 73; of Jesus Christ, 138; of Joseph Smith, 163

Babbit, Almon, 459
Babcock, Phoebe Ann, 421
Babylon: choice between Zion and, 13, 14; restored Church as vehicle out of, 20; building Zion among, 208
Ballard, M. Russell, on value of souls, 67
Baptism: revelation on, 56–58; necessity of, 65; revelation on building Church and, 74–75; rebaptism, 79–80; of Joseph and Polly Peck Knight, 82; persecution incited by, 83; of Emma Smith, 86; of Thomas B. Marsh, 104; of Ezra Thayre and Northrup Sweet, 111; of Edward Partridge, 119–20; of Edward Partridge and Lydia Clisbee, 136; Shakers' views on, 167, 170; of Levi Hancock, 173; for children, 238; of Amasa M. Lyman, 260; resurrection and, 266; of Stephen Burnett, 284; of John the Baptist, 296
Baptism for the dead, 466–71, 506–7
Baptist Church, 79
Barker, Margaret, on light and presence of God, 315
Bassett, Heman, 173–74, 187
Bates (dissident who sues Church), 184–85
Bennett, John, 456–57
Benson, Ezra Taft: on promises made in D&C, 2; on neglect of Book of Mormon, 302
Bentine, Johan, 41
Bible: changes made to, 6; revelation on, 41; Sidney Rigdon called as scribe for, 117–18; revision of, 121–22, 154–58, 254, 307–9; Joseph Smith struggles to understand, 256; teachings on salvation in, 272; Apocrypha and, 340–42; plural marriage in, 480; justification for slavery in, 521
Billings, Titus, 220, 221
Bishop(s): Edward Partridge called as, 136–38; role in consecration of, 141, 145, 183; cultivate spiritual gifts, 161; requirements for calling, 238; role in Church discipline, 239; appointment and duties of, 250–53; office of, 296; role in priesthood hierarchy of, 397; disposition of tithing and, 444–45
Black men: acceptance in Church of, 522; link between Canaanites and, 522–23; priesthood withheld from, 523–24; priesthood made available to worthy, 524–30
Blessing(s): requirements for receiving, 14–16; of priesthood holders, 298; of Word of Wisdom, 329, 330–31; of high councilors, 376–77; of tithing, 442–43; Emma Smith writes, 489
Body: soul and, 314; Word of Wisdom and, 327–28
Boggs, Lilburn, 428–29, 467
Book of Commandments, *8:* publication of, 1–2, 6–10, 18, 233–36, 241–42, 490; testimony of, 5; Oliver Cowdery and John Whitmer to carry, 241–42;

financial support for those who oversee, 243–46; bishops are to support publication of, 253; financial support for publication of, 281. *See also* Doctrine and Covenants

Book of Mormon: understanding revelations in, xviii; first printing of, 4; translation of, 19, 59; Martin Harris loses pages of, 24–26; Joseph Smith chosen to translate, 27; promises made to engravers of, 28; Martin Harris to help with, 31; three witnesses for, 33–34, 62–64; Oliver Cowdery as scribe for, 36–37; retranslating lost pages of, 46–50; Hyrum Smith studies, 52–53; building Church of Christ through, 65–67; Martin Harris mortgages land to publish, 68–72; organization of Church to come through, 73–75; Lamanites and, 101; conversion success with, 103; Thomas B. Marsh learns of, 104; Ezra Thayre buys, 110–11; counsel for meetings in, 159–60; remembering, 297–98; neglect of, 301–2. *See also* Gold plates

Book of the Law of the Lord, 460–61, 504

Book of Wealth, The, 3

Booth, Ezra: arrives in Missouri, 202; leaves Church, 224; speaks against Joseph Smith, 247–48, 249, 254

Boynton, John, 415

Breastplate, witnesses of, 62–64

Brother of Jared, 234

Brown, Pelatiah, 276

Brunson, Seymour, 260, 261, 466

Buffalo, New York, 106, 128–29

Building committee, 351, 352

Bullock, Thomas, 514

Burgess (Church convert), 412

Burnett, Stephen, 261, 284–85

Burroughs, Philip, 103

Bushman, Richard: on revelations of Joseph Smith, 11; on Lord's rebuking Joseph Smith, 27; on section 88 of D&C, 314–15; on School of the Prophets, 316–17; on Joseph Smith and temple construction, 354; on Joseph Smith and politics, 363; on effect of priesthood on fathers, 398; on dissent among Saints, 448; on plural marriages of Joseph Smith, 481; on plural marriage as trial, 488

Caffeine, 328–29

Cahoon, Reynolds: mission call of, 214, 260; as building committee member, 351, 352

Caldwell County, Missouri: John Whitmer acquires land in, 61; establishment of, 423, 427

Callings, Word of Wisdom and, 333–34

Calvin, John, on Jesus Christ descending into spirit world, 512

Calvinism, 74, 97, 262

Camisards, 166

Canaanites, 522–23

Canals, 213–14

Cannon, George Q., on relinquishing plural marriage, 517

Carlisle, Sally, on baptism for the dead, 470–71

Carter, Gideon, 261

Carter, Jared: discerns false spirit, 179; to be ordained as priest, 187; mission call of, 282–83; as building committee member, 351, 352; called as high councilor, 375

Carter, John S., 375

Carter, Phoebe, 130

Carter, Simeon, 260

Carthage Jail, 227, 495–96

Celestial kingdom: vision of, 267, 268–69; earth as, 475; vision of Alvin Smith and, 504–7

Chamberlain, Esquire, 128

Charters, 455

Children: raising, 13; turning hearts of, toward fathers, 22–23; teaching, 100; parents are required to teach gospel to, 238–40; circumcision and, 255–57; brethren compared to, 280; fathers are required to provide for, 292–93

Cholera, 214

Christianity: redemption of, 48–49; circumcision and, 255–57; views on afterlife in, 270–71

Church leaders (Missouri): disagreements among, 288–89; Joseph Smith rebukes, 302, 318–19, 339; letter from Joseph Smith to, 362; letters to Joseph Smith from, 370

Church meetings, conducting, with Holy Ghost, 159–61

Church of Jesus Christ of Latter-day Saints: fiftieth anniversary of, 9; revelations on organization of, 17; Wilford Woodruff on revelation and, 19; as vehicle out of Babylon, 20; Joseph Knight's role in restoration of, 55; revelation on building, 65–67, 73–75; organization of, 76–78; to be run by common consent, 90; receiving revelation for, 95–96, 149–51; law of, 139–46; discipline, 143–44, 239; legal requirements for organization of, 153; keeping records and history of, 162–63, 241, 242; constitution of, 238; Word of Wisdom and callings in, 333–34; counsel on finances of, 336–39; council for administration and discipline of, 375–78; organization and growth of, 398–99; seventh anniversary of, 423; name of, 423, 425–26; reorganization of quorums in, 460; attitude toward government of, 493–94; Brigham Young leads, 499–500; governmental persecution against, 514–16, 519–20; subjects itself to laws, 516–17; views on slavery and race of, 521–22

Cincinnati, Ohio, 210, 213–14

Circumcision, 255–57

Civil War, 310–12, 475, 514–15, 521

Clay County, Missouri, Zion's Camp arrives in, 389

Clayton, William: called as temple recorder, 306; learns to discern false spirits, 472; attends stake conference, 474–75; sealing of, 477–78; on knowledge and power, 478; as journal scribe, 485

Clisbee, Lydia, 119, 136

Clothing: for missionaries, 107–8; commandment on, 142

Coburn, Emily, 83

Coca-Cola, 328–29

Coe, Joseph: learns will of God, 194–95; called as high councilor, 375; participates in high council trial, 377

Coffee, 324, 333

Colesville, New York: Knight family lives in, 54; persecution in, 83, 90–91; strengthening Saints in, 122; plan revealed to Saints in, 123–31; Polly and Joseph Knight leave, 181

Coltrin, Zebedee, 387

Columbus, Christopher, 323

Comma Johanneum, 341

Commandment(s): for Hyrum Smith, 51–52; keeping, 208; Word of Wisdom as, 334–35; power to build temple comes through obeying, 353; Zion will prosper through obedience to, 358

Commerce, Illinois, 455

Common consent, 90, 91

Conference: activities to prepare for, 90–91; September 1830, 97, 101, 107; in Fayette, New York, 104, 123; for elders, 152–53, 186–89; commandment to hold, 204; high priests gather at, 237–40; January 1832, 258; in Amherst, Ohio, 286; in Hiram, Ohio, 490

Confirmation: of Emma Smith and Sally Knight, 92; of Edward Partridge, 120; of children, 238

Congregationalism, 29

Consecration: as theme of D&C, 17; God gives law of, 130, 139, 141–42; practicing law of, 144–46, 181–85; Saints cursed over, 196–98; Edward Partridge commanded to implement law of, 203; two commandments of, 207; specific instructions on, 223; William McLellin breaks law of, 231; stewardship and, 243–46; role of bishop in, 251–52, 253; storehouse and, 279–81; United Firm and, 289–91, 382–83; counsel for keeping law of, 292–93, 297; for missionaries, 300; temple building and, 301–2; keeping records of, 304–6; of Vienna Jaques, 337–38; purchasing land and, 372; acknowledging Lord in, 386; Zion to be built by obedience to law of, 392; tithing and, 440–43; Joseph Smith on importance of, 449–50; for construction of Nauvoo Temple, 457–58; for Zion, 501. *See also* United Firm

Conspiracy, of tobacco companies, 325–27

Constitution of the United States: Church members uphold, 360, 362–63; freedom and, 373

Constitution of the Church, 238

Contention, among elders on Missouri River, 212–15

Copley, Leman: conversion of, 136; called to preach to Shakers, 168, 170–71; offers land to Saints, 181; refuses to consecrate land, 184, 192–93

Cornerstone, 436–39

Corrill, John, 178, 186
Council, for Church administration and discipline, 375–78
Council of Trent, 340
Council on the Disposition of the Tithes, 444–45
Court proceedings of Joseph Smith, 83–84, 446–47
Covel, James, 132–33
Covenant(s): revelations on blessings and, 15–16; James Covill breaks, 134–35; resurrection and, 266; consecration as, 383–84, 442; marriage as, 486. *See also* New and everlasting covenant
Covill, James, 132–35
Cowdery, Oliver, *37;* attends meeting on publication of D&C, 4, 18; assists in publication of revelations, 6; asks consent for publication, 7; as witness, 33–34, 62–64; as scribe, 36–37, 51, 69; revelation given to, 37–38, 40–41; faith of, 38–39; seeks gift of translation, 42–43; learns to receive revelation, 44–45; ordained to Aaronic Priesthood, 56–58, *57;* seeks revelation on building Church, 65–67; to write Articles and Covenants, 73–75; demands change to revelation on baptism, 74–75; to preside over Saints, 77; Lord's will for, 81–82; faces persecution with Joseph Smith, 84; counsel on missionary work and persecution given to, 84–85; Emma Smith to help with scribal duties of, 87; to prepare for conference, 90–91; to teach for Joseph Smith, 95–96; called to mission to Lamanites, 101, 107–9; Peter Whitmer serves with, 102–3; delivers revelation to Ezra Thayre, 111; ordains Sidney Rigdon as elder, 116; teaches Edward Partridge, 119, 136; departs for west, 121; mentioned, 132; assumes record keeping responsibilities, 162, 163; teachers Shakers, 168; bears testimony, 173; leads missionaries to Missouri, 174; William W. Phelps called to assist, 194; called to help with printing, 200; called to Cincinnati, Ohio, 210, 213–14; rebukes elders over contention, 212; commanded to visit branches in Missouri, 220–21; raises funds to buy land in Missouri, 221–22; commanded to carry Book of Commandments, 239, 241–42, 243, 490; as steward of Book of Commandments, 244–46; brings news of persecution in Missouri, 362; converts John Murdock, 364; suggests Saints move location, 368; announces revelation, 371; called as high councilor, 375; takes meeting minutes, 375; participates in high council trial, 377; prays for financial help, 387–88; helps write dedicatory prayer, 402; Jesus Christ appears to, 407–9; travels to Salem, Massachusetts, 412–13; Church discipline of, 421; as assistant president, 459; statement on Church and government of, 493–94; on vision of celestial kingdom, 505
Cowdery, Warren, 393–94
Creation: as process, 98–99; appreciation for, 208–9; of universe, 314–15; Truman Madsen on, 348
Crosby, Caroline, on gathering in Ohio, 129–30
Cutler, Alpheus, 438

Daniel, prophecy of, 227–28
Daviess County, Missouri, 425, 427–28
Davis v. Beason (1890), 515
Deacon, office of, 296
Dead: redemption for, 504–7; missionary work for, 508–13
Dead works, 79–80
Death: of Joseph Smith, 8, 227, 461, 495–98, 502; healing and, 142; second, 219; fear of, 268; of David W. Patten, 422, 437; of Hyrum Smith, 495–98; accepting gospel after, 508–13
Debt: righteous borrowing and, 224; of United Firm, 382–83, 386–87; Joseph Smith takes drastic measures to pay, 412–13; for temple in Far West, Missouri, 424; Oliver Granger settles First Presidency's, 432–33
Deception: gifts of Spirit and, 159–61; of false spirits, 172–80; pattern to avoid, 187
Degrees of glory, 267–69, 314–15. *See also* Celestial kingdom; Telestial kingdom; Terrestrial kingdom
Destroyer, 212, 213
de Tocqueville, Alexis, 3

Dibble, Philo, on false spirits in Ohio, 175
Discernment, of false spirits, 172–80, 188, 472–73
Discipline: for various sins, 143–44; role of bishops in, 239; council for, 375–78; of apostles, 421; righteous dominion and, 450
Dissent. *See* Apostasy
Dives, 384
Divine potential, 346–47, 348, 405–6, 453–54
Divining rod, 42, 43
Divorce, 143
Doctrine, as necessity for building Church, 74
Doctrine and Covenants: history of, 1–10; Explanatory Introduction of, 11–17; pseudonyms in, 277–79. *See also* Book of Commandments
Dodds, Asa, 260
Doniphan, Alexander, 446
Dreams, of Joseph Smith Sr., 29
Drugs, 329
Dualism, 13–14
Dunklin, Daniel, 374, 379, 389

Eames, Ruggles, 261
Earth: salvation for, 23; David Whitmer's concern with, 102; appreciation for, 208–9
Easter Sunday, 407–9
East India Marine Society Museum, 413
Editing: of Book of Commandments, 5–6, 245–46; Orson Pratt and, 9
Education: School of the Prophets and, 316–17; tobacco use and, 323–24
Edwards, Jonathan, 506
Elders: mission guidelines for, 141; commanded to prepare for missionary work, 149–50; commanded to gather in conference, 152–53; revelation on false spirits given to, 176–78; counsel given to, 186–89, 223–25; callings of, 203–4; commanded to preach gospel, 210–11; contention among, 212–15; commanded to preach repentance in Ohio, 214; travel to Missouri, 216–17; are accountable to bishops, 251, 252; called to continue missionary work, 254; Lord's will for, 258–61; office of, 296; pray for revelation, 313–14; tobacco use and, 323–24; quorum presidency of, 460
Elders' Journal, 415
Elders school, 357–59
Elect: agency and, 14, 97–98; salvation and, 74; gathering of, 98–99, 111
Elections: common consent in, 91; persecution and, 515
Elias: prophecy on sacrament with, 92–93; restores priesthood keys, 409
Elijah: prophecy of, 21–23; prophecy on sacrament with, 92–93; restores priesthood keys, 409; fulfillment of prophecy on, 409–10
Emerson, Ralph Waldo, 3, 148, 239
Emigration, 500–503
End of the world, 315
Endowment House, 517
Endowment with power: agency and, 98–99; promise of, 124; Saints participate in, 130–31; priesthood and, 296, 409–10; preparation for, 319–20; Zion postponed for, 390, 391; taken in Kirtland temple, 391–92; in Liberty Jail, 453
Enduring, David Whitmer and, 60
England, D&C published in, 9. *See also* Great Britain
Enoch: prophecy of, 121–22, 522–23; people of, 155, 158
Eternal life: Russell M. Nelson on, 23; promised to Joseph Smith, 32–33
Eternal marriage, 486–87
Eve, 99, 511
Evil: knowledge of good and, 144; false spirits and, 172–80; mortals and, 256–57; escaping, through Word of Wisdom, 325
Exaltation: requirements for, 16; divine potential and, 345–49; marriage and, 485–88; of Emma and Joseph Smith, 488–89
Excommunication: of David Whitmer, 60; of John Whitmer, 61; of adulterers, 141, 143; for breaking law of consecration, 142; of stewards, 183; of William McLellin, 232; of Philastus Hurlbut, 367; of Thomas B. Marsh, 416, 436; of dissident Saints, 418; of apostles, 421, 435
Explanatory Introduction, 11–17

Expositor, The, 495
Extermination order, 415–16, 425, 428–29, 436, 446

Faith: lectures on, 8, 9; of Martin Harris, 31; of Oliver Cowdery, 38–39, 42–43; of Lucy Mack Smith, 129; precedes miracles, 219; of Zion's Camp, 381
Fall, 99, 256–57
False Christs, 169, 170
False prophets, 148–49
False spirits, 172–80, 472–73
Family: sealing, 23; Joseph Smith will be able to care for, 84–85; financial support for missionaries,' 142–43, 259, 299–300; husbands required to provide for, 292–93; First Presidency rebuked for neglecting care of, 347; Joseph Smith worries over safety of, 367–69; of Brigham Young, 464–65
Farms, purchased in Kirtland, Ohio, 355–56
Farr, Lorin, on telestial kingdom, 267–68
Farr, Olive, 260
Far West, Missouri: Joseph Smith and family move to, 418–19; named as county seat, 423; as gathering place for Church, 430–31; persecution in, 437, 446
Far West Temple, 423–26, 436–39
Fasting, 207–9
Father(s): turning hearts of, toward children, 22–23; should pattern parenting after God, 100; are required to provide for children, 292–93; God as loving, 349; priesthood exalts, 397–98
Fault finding, among brethren, 320
Fayette, New York: Book of Mormon translated in, 59; Joseph Smith travels with Joseph Knight to, 76; conference held in, 97, 101, 104
Fear: of restored Church, 48–49; of Second Coming, 156; Saints unable to rend veil due to, 234; of death, 268
Feast, 202–3
Fig tree, parable of, 156–57
Finances: counsel on, 336–39; for construction of Kirtland temple, 354; for United Firm, 382–83, 387–88
Financial support: Martin Harris concerned with, 68–72; revelation on, 84–85; of Emma Smith, 86; for families of missionaries, 142–43, 259; for those who oversee Book of Commandments, 243–46; to purchase land and fund publication of scriptures, 277–81; for missionaries and families, 299–300
First Presidency: oversees new edition of D&C, 9–10; revelation given to, 13; will select bishops, 238; organization of, 286–87; visits Missouri Church leaders, 288–89; on steadying the ark, 305; given day-to-day responsibilities, 337; rebuked for neglecting care of families, 347; commandment to build office for, 350; functions of, 396; Oliver Granger settles debts of, 432–33; letter to Newel K. Whitney and William Marks from, 433–34; disposition of tithing and, 444–45; William Law called to, 459; reorganization of, 460; blesses Joseph Smith Sr., 505
Foot washing (ordinance), 319
Foot washing (symbol of accountability): commandment for, 211, 259, 299; John Murdock commanded to, 365, 366
Ford, Thomas, 495–96
Foreknowing, 135
Foreordination, 135
Forgiveness: Joseph Smith prays for, 26–28; law of just war and, 361–62
Fox, George, 167
Freedom: for American continent, 47–48; preserving, 360; agency and, 373
Freedom, New York, 393–94
French, Peter, 130, 355–56
French farm, 355–56
Fruits, 333
Fuller, Edson, 173–74
Fulness, 345
Fulness of times, 469
Funeral: of Polly Knight, 207; of Alvin Smith, 504

Galland, Isaac, 462
Gardner, Martha Tuttle, on Brigham Young as Church leader, 500
Garment, 458
Gathering: in Ohio, 123–31; administering to needs of Saints and, 140; in Zion, 295; in Caldwell County, Missouri, 423; in Nauvoo, Illinois, 459–60, 463;

missionary work and, 490–92; in West, 500–503; of righteous dead, 510

Gause, Jesse, 286–89

Gift(s): of knowing mysteries, 37–38; of translation, 42–43; of Hyrum Smith, 52; spiritual, 160–61

Gilbert, Elizabeth, 191, 202

Gilbert, Sidney: revelation for, 190–91; buys land in Missouri, 199, 200; establishes store, 201, 225; arrives in Missouri, 202; commanded to travel on Missouri River, 213; handles money to buy land, 222; establishes storehouse, 224–25; is not exempt from consecration, 244; pseudonym for, 279; role in United Firm of, 290

Glory of God: intelligence as, 13, 345

God: relying on, 3–4; putting trust in, 26–27; nature of, 217; requirements for seeing, 234–35; Satan rebels against, 265; Sidney Rigdon sees and testifies of, 270; Abraham Lincoln on Civil War and, 312; worshipping and drawing unto, 345–49; gives Saints trials, 371; gives agency, 373; becoming like, 405–6; time relativity and, 475

Godhead: controversy over, 341; nature of, 475

Gold plates: covenant over, 32; witnesses of, 33–34, 62–64; Joseph Smith cannot obtain, 174. *See also* Book of Mormon

Good, knowledge of evil and, 144

Gospel: restoration of, 19, 47–48; revelation on restoring full, 65–67; parents required to teach children, 238–40; parable of wheat and tares and, 308–9

Gould, Sarah, 132

Government: prayer for, 226–28; Church members are subject to, 362–63; Saints to seek redress from, 372; of Nauvoo, Illinois, 455–56; proclamation written to leaders of, 456; Church's attitude toward, 493–94; of Utah Territory, 514–15

Grace, salvation comes through, 74

Graham, Sylvester, 333

Grandin, Egbert, 68, 154

Granger, Oliver, 432–33

Grant, Heber J.: oversees new edition of D&C, 9; opinion on Coca-Cola of, 329; on obeying commandments, 335

Grant, Jedediah, on revelation given through Brigham Young, 502–3

Great Britain: D&C published in, 9; Heber C. Kimball called to, 410; Thomas B. Marsh to oversee missionary work in, 414–15; apostles called to, 421, 435–36; apostles depart for, 439; Brigham Young serves in, 464–65

Greene, Evan, 294, 302

Griffin, Selah, 196–97

Habit-forming substances, 328–30

Haight, David B.: on putting off repentance, 71–72; on revelation on priesthood, 529

Hale, Isaac: on revelation given to Martin Harris, 31; Joseph Smith lives on property of, 36

Hales, Robert D., on disposition of tithes, 445

Hancock, Alvah, 172

Hancock, Levi, 172–74, 180

Hansen, W. Eugene, 326

Harmony, Pennsylvania: Martin Harris travels to, 24; Joseph Smith Sr. visits Joseph Smith in, 29; Martin Harris visits Joseph Smith in, 31; Hyrum Smith visits Joseph Smith in, 51; Joseph Smith returns to, 83–84

Harris, Emer, 260

Harris, George, 419

Harris, Lucinda, 419

Harris, Lucy, 24

Harris, Martin, *32;* approaches Lord with demands, 16; loses Book of Mormon pages, 24–26; seeks greater witness, 31–35; retranslating Book of Mormon pages lost by, 46–50; as witness, 62–64; revelation for, 68–72; Thomas B. Marsh seeks out, 104; bears testimony of Book of Mormon to Ezra Thayre, 110; moves to Ohio, 127–28; commanded to consecrate property, 203, 205; as Book of Mormon scribe, 243; as steward of Book of Commandments, 244–46; called as high councilor, 375

Harrison, William, 456

Haun's Mill, 448

Haws, Peter, 457

Hawthorne, Nathaniel, 413

Healing: of Electa Peck, 127;

commandment on, 142; of Elsa Johnson, 247–48; of Olive Farr, 260
Hearts, turning, of fathers and children, 22–23
Heaven, 270–71. *See also* Degrees of glory
Heavenly messengers, 469, 473
Heavenly Mother, 167–68
Hell, 270–71, 512
Higbee, Elias, 419
High council: rules on Word of Wisdom transgression and Church offices, 333–34; Church discipline and, 375; of Nauvoo Stake, 460
High councilors, Joseph Smith blesses, 376–77
High priests: will of God concerning, 237–40; bishops to be selected from, 238; mission call of, 298–300; pray for revelation, 313–14; acquire farms in Kirtland, Ohio, 355–56; chosen to serve on high council, 375–76; quorum of, 460
Hinckley, Gordon B.: on personal scripture study, xix; on law of consecration, 17, 146, 392, 442; on keeping Sabbath day holy, 208; on kingdom of heaven, 227–28; on applying common sense to Word of Wisdom, 329; on area authorities, 399; on repentance of Thomas B. Marsh, 416–17; on temples, 461; on section 138, 509; on revelation on priesthood, 527; on reaction to revelation on priesthood, 528, 530
Hiram, Ohio: home of John and Elsa Johnson in, 1–2, 4, 18, 233; Joseph Smith and Sidney Rigdon move to, 222; Joseph Smith moves to, 223, 226; conference in, 490
Hodges, Curtis, 377–78
Holland, Jeffrey R.: on Second Coming, 156; on souls, 314
Holland, Patricia, 156
Holy Ghost: revelation through, 42, 269–70, commandment to teach by, 141; conducting meetings with, 159–61; discerning between false spirits and, 172–80; as necessary element for seeing God, 234–35; missionaries are to preach with, 237–38; resurrection and, 266; telestial kingdom and, 268; nature of, 475

Holy places, 311
Hot drinks, 333
Howe, Eber, 152
Hubble (false prophetess), 148–49
Humility: of Martin Harris, 34–35; of Oliver Cowdery, 82
Humphrey, Solomon, 187
Huntington, Oliver, 130
Huntington, Zina, on plural marriage, 482
Hurlbut, Philastus, 367
Husbands, are required to provide for families, 292–93
Hyde, Orson: copies transcription, 5; mission call of, 237, 259, 260, 414; called as apostle, 239; rebukes Missouri Church leaders, 302; called as high councilor, 375; takes meeting minutes, 375; reports on Daniel Dunklin's broken promise, 389; success in Great Britain of, 421; rebels against Joseph Smith, 447; speaks on Second Coming, 474–75
Hymn, sung at judgment, 300
Hymnal, 87, 88

I Am, 407
Illinois, Saints move to, 436. *See also* Specific locations
Independence, Missouri: revelations to be published in, 2; established as Zion, 199–201; building up, 202–6, 218–22; authorized travel routes to, 213–14; elders travel to, 216–17; teaching children gospel in, 238–39; Book of Commandments carried to, 241–42; temple to be built in, 294–98; Saints fail to build temple in, 301–2; counsel on reacting to persecution in, 360–63; Joseph Smith worries about, 368
Indians, selling supplies to, 200. *See also* Lamanites
Individualism, 3–4
Influenza pandemic, 508
Intelligence: as glory of God, 13, 345; obtaining, 347; Truman Madsen on, 348; agency and, 475
Isaiah (book): fulfillment of declaration in, 226–27; clarification of, 419–20

Jackman, Levi, on D&C, 7
Jackson, Andrew, 310
Jackson County, Missouri: persecution in,

6–7, 357–59; Joseph Smith visits Saints in, 292; Saints driven from, 370–74; returning persecuted Saints to, 379–81; Zion postponed in, 390–91; land purchased in, 392
James (apostle): priesthood keys and, 40–41; prophecy on sacrament with, 92–94
James, George, 187
Jaques, Vienna, 88, 337–38
Jensen, Marlin K., 326–27
Jesse, stem of, 419–20
Jesuits, 349
Jesus Christ: D&C as book of, 2; relying on, 3–4; revelations and words of, 11–12; will save all, 14; sets conditions for covenants, 15–16; omniscience and omnipotence of, 49–50; teaches ordinance of baptism, 56; suffered for salvation of souls, 65–67; judgment and punishments of, 69–70; listening to, 97; receiving, 133; authority of, 138; law of, 139–46; false impersonators of, 169, 170; nature of, 217; taking name of, in vain, 221; vision of, 264–67; as Savior, 265–66; divine development of, 346–47; Truman Madsen on divinity of, 348; appears to Joseph Smith and Oliver Cowdery, 407–9; journal entry on vision of, *408;* as Passover lamb, 410; teaches spirits in spirit world, 508–13; salvation comes through accepting, 522. *See also* Second coming
Joan of Arc, 147
Johnson, Almira, 482–83
Johnson, Benjamin, 477–78, 482–83
Johnson, Elsa, 2; council convened in home of, 1–2, 4, 18, 233; Joseph Smith and Sidney Rigdon live with, 222, 226; Joseph Smith heals, 247–48
Johnson, John, 2; council convened in home of, 1–2, 4, 18, 233; Joseph Smith and Sidney Rigdon live with, 222, 226; called as apostle, 239; Ezra Booth visits home of, 247–48; joins United Firm, 356; called as high councilor, 375
Johnson, Luke: called as apostle, 239; mission of, 258–59, 260, 261; called as high councilor, 376; rebels against Joseph Smith, 415
Johnson, Lyman, 260, 415
Johnson, Melissa, 477–78

John the Baptist, *57;* visits Joseph Smith and Oliver Cowdery, 57–58; prophecy on sacrament with, 92–93; baptism and ordination of, 296; section 93 and, 346
John the Revelator: revelation on, 40–41; prophecy on sacrament with, 92–94; explanations of revelations of, 273–76; section 93 and, 346
Journal: of Joseph Smith, 305–6; vision of Jesus Christ recorded in, *408*
Judaism: circumcision and, 255–57; parallels between Mormonism and, 409–10
Judge, unjust, 372
Judgment, 69–70, 196–97, 315

Kane, Thomas, 514
Keys: sealing, 16; given to Joseph Smith, 23; apostles to keep priesthood, 40–41; identifying Satan using, 58; prophecy on restoration of, 92–94; faith of Joseph Smith and, 117; equality of Presidency over, 336–37, 339; restoration of, 409–10; discerning false spirits through, 472–73; conferred upon apostles, 499
Kimball, Camilla, 528
Kimball, Heber C.: on mission to help displaced Saints, 380–81; on revelation for Twelve Apostles, 395; mission call to Great Britain of, 410, 414; success in Great Britain of, 415, 421; letter from Thomas B. Marsh to, 417; lays cornerstone of Far West temple, 438; on discerning false spirits, 472; commanded to participate in plural marriage, 483–84; on revelation given through Brigham Young, 502
Kimball, Helen: on Joseph Smith's views on plural marriage, 481; on plural marriage, 483–84
Kimball, Spencer W., *524, 531;* on holding priesthood keys, 41; on withholding priesthood from black men, 523; receives revelation on priesthood, 524–30
Kimball, Vilate: Thomas B. Marsh speaks with, 415; on baptism for the dead, 470; receives revelation on plural marriage, 483–84
King, Austin A., 227, 446–47
Kingdom of God, 226–28
Kirtland, Ohio: printing press established in, 7; persecution in, 130, 367; blessings

fulfilled in, 130–31; commandment to leave, 131, 189; Saints commanded to stay in, 220; building construction in, 350–51; farms purchased in, 355–56; materialism of Saints in, 361; stake established in, 377; Joseph Smith and family leave, 418–19, 430–31; apostasy in, 432; Oliver Granger settles First Presidency's debts in, 432–33; Newel K. Whitney and William Marks commanded to leave, 433–34

Kirtland Revelation Book. *See* Revelation Book 2

Kirtland Safety Society, 418

Kirtland Temple, *406;* dedicatory prayer for, 16, 402–6, *403;* French farm and, 130; construction of, 318, 319; dedication of, 320; commandment to build, 350–51; Saints rebuked for not building, 352–54; Saints consecrate money for, 387–88; construction and completion of, 391–92; Jesus Christ appears in, 407–9

Kitchell, Ashbel, 168, 170–71

Knight, Joseph: revelation for, 54–55; travels to Fayette, New York, 76; on organization of Church, 78; Lord's will for, 81–82; sacrifices to gather in Ohio, 127; moves to Ohio, 181; on leaving Leman Copley's land, 192

Knight, Newel: testifies for Joseph Smith, 83; on comfort from persecution, 90–91; on revelation on sacrament, 92; on sacrament, 93; on revelations of Hiram Page, 95; on revelation to gather Saints, 123; on sacrifices of gathering, 126, 127; moves to Ohio, 127; leads Colesville Saints, 192–93; mission call of, 196

Knight, Polly Peck: baptism of, 82; sacrifices to gather in Ohio, 127; moves to Ohio, 181; death of, 207

Knight, Sally, 92

Knowledge, salvation and, 478–79

Laban's sword, 62–64

Lamanites: Church to be restored to, 47–48; Oliver Cowdery to teach, 95–96; missionary work to, 101–3, 107–9. *See also* Indians

Lamb, 331, 410

Land: purchasing, 157–58, 199–201, 392; Saints commanded to share, 164–65; organizing, for Saints in Ohio, 181–85; purchasing and consecrating, 204, 372; left in Ohio, 218; commandment to buy, 219–20, 390; raising funds for, 220–22, 277–81; pseudonyms for revelations on purchasing, 278; for apostate Saints, 292; farms purchased in Kirtland, Ohio, 355–56; Saints should not sell, 372–73; preemption laws and, 427–28; Isaac Galland offers to sell, 462. *See also* Property

Language, simple, 233–36

Last days, preparing for, 98–99

Last dispensation, 19, 469

Law: of Jesus Christ, 139–46; Church commanded to follow, 153, 516–17; of just war, 361–62

Law, William, 458–59, 460

Law of Moses, 256

Lazarus, 384

Leadership, in Ohio, 121–22, 174

Lectures on faith, 8, 9

Lee, Ann, 166–67, 170

Leg operation, 322

Lehi (book), 46–50, 49

Letter(s): of Ezra Booth, 247–48, 254; from Joseph Smith to William Phelps, 304–6; from Joseph Smith to Vienna Jaques, 337–38; from building committee, 352; from Joseph Smith to Church leaders in Missouri, 362; from Missouri Church leaders to Joseph Smith, 370; from Thomas B. Marsh to Heber C. Kimball, 417; from Thomas B. Marsh to Wilford Woodruff, 424; from First Presidency to Newel K. Whitney and William Marks, 433–34; from Liberty Jail, 446–54; to Joseph Smith in Liberty Jail, 449; from Joseph Smith to Edward Partridge, 462; from Joseph Smith on temple ordinances, 467–68; from Heber C. Kimball to Parley P. Pratt, 472

Liahona, witnesses of, 62–64

Liberty Jail, 227, 262, 446–54, *447*

Life, purpose of, 453–54

Light, truth and, 315

Lincoln, Abraham, 514–15; on Civil War, 312

Literary Firm: organization of, 243–46; bishops are to support, 253; responsibilities of Joseph Smith in, 277;

financial support for, 281; Kirtland farms and, 356; stewardships of, 386
Little season, 392
Love, of Jesus Christ, 71–72
Lucas, Samuel, 446
Luther, Martin, 147; on Jesus Christ descending into spirit world, 512
Lying, 144
Lyman, Amasa, 130, 260

Madsen, Truman, 348–49; on value of souls, 66–67
Malaria, 459
Malichi, prophecy of, 21–23
Marks, William, 431–34
Marriage: Shakers' views on, 167, 170; divinity of, 169; of William McLellin and Emiline Miller, 231, 260; between Christians and Jews, 255–57; sealing and, 477–78; exaltation and, 485–88. *See also* Plural marriage; Sealing
Marsh, Elizabeth, 104
Marsh, Thomas B.: conversion and revelation for, 104–6; moves to Ohio, 127; mission of, 196–98, 260; fights against apostasy among Twelve, 414–15; apostasy and repentance of, 415–17; as president of Twelve Apostles, 421; on revelation on Far West, Missouri, 424; seeks revelation on Twelve, 435; calls new apostles, 436; George A. Smith replaces, 438; rebels against Joseph Smith, 447
Marvelous work, 30, 51, 54, 59
Materialism: of David Whitmer, 102; of Isaac Morley, 225; of children, 238; of Stephen Burnett, 285; of Kirtland Saints, 361; of Newel K. Whitney and William Marks, 432; Joseph Smith on, 449–50
Matthews, Dr., 366
Maxwell, Neal A.: on hearing voice of Jesus Christ in scriptures, 11; on law of consecration, 17; on timing of Second Coming, 98; on becoming less possessed, 126; on God and time, 476
McConkie, Bruce R.: researches priesthood, 525; on revelation on priesthood, 529–30
McLellin, William, *231;* author understands, xvii; assessing promises and blessings given to, xix; fails to write revelation, 4–5, 235–36; conversion of, 53; revelation for, 229–32; journal of, *230;* called as apostle, 239; rebuke and mission call of, 258–59; leaves mission, 260; refuses to consecrate property, 304; rebuke of, 339; rebels against Joseph Smith, 415, 448
Meat, 167, 169, 170, 333
Melchizedek Priesthood: financial support for, 143; presides over Aaronic Priesthood, 238; taken from earth, 296; oath and covenant of, 297; functions of, 396; duties of presiding in quorums of, 397
Men, effect of priesthood on, 397–98
Mercy, through repentance, 27, 28
Methodism, 262
Millennium: description of, 157; transfiguration of earth and, 219; telestial glory and, 268, 269; Civil War as sign of, 310–12; prophecy on, 371
Miller, Emiline, 231, 260
Miller, George, 457
Miller, William, 474
Miracles: instructions for, 84; faith precedes, 219; will follow missionaries, 299
Missionary work: making revelations available for, 1; printing revelations for, 18; section 1 calls for, 19–20; of Joseph Smith Sr., 30; of Hyrum Smith, 52–53; of John and Peter Whitmer, 60–61; of Hyrum Smith, Samuel Smith, Joseph Smith Sr., and Joseph Knight, 81–82; of Joseph Smith and Oliver Cowdery, 84–85; of Oliver Cowdery, 95–96; among Lamanites, 101–3, 107–9; of Thomas B. Marsh, 105–6, 196–98; of Edward Partridge, 120; James Covill called to, 133; companionships formed for, 140; guidelines for, 141; financial support for, 142–43, 299–300; elders commanded to prepare for, 149–50; among Shakers, 168–71; in Missouri, 187; of elders traveling to Ohio, 210–11; William McLellin called to, 230–31; high priests called to, 237–38; record keeping and, 241, 259; Joseph Smith and Sidney Rigdon called to, 248–49; elders called to continue, 254; Lord's will for, 258–61; Jared Carter called to, 282–83; Stephen Burnett called to,

284–85; of Evan Greene, 294, 302; brethren called to, 298–300; parable of wheat and tares and, 308–9; School of the Prophets and, 316–17; endowment and, 320; John Murdock called to, 365–66; of Joseph Smith and Sidney Rigdon, 367–69; of apostles, 395, 396–97; in Great Britain, 410, 414–15, 435–36; in Salem, Massachusetts, 412–13; Twelve called to, 421–22; of Brigham Young, 464–65; preparing for Second Coming and, 490–92; in spirit world, 508–13

Missouri: consecration in, 184–85; elders called to, 186–87; revealed as Zion, 188–89; Sidney Gilbert to travel to, 190–91; Colesville Saints relocate to, 192–93; William W. Phelps and Joseph Coe commanded to go to, 194–95; Joseph Smith travels to, 199; counsel given to elders returning to, 223–25; William McLellin moves to, 231; teaching children gospel in, 238–39; Satan turns away Church leaders in, 279–81; First Presidency visits Church leaders in, 288–89; rebuke of Church leaders in, 302; record keeping and gathering in, 304–6; Joseph Smith rebukes Saints and Church leaders in, 318–19; building construction in, 350–51; promises made to Saints in, 357–59; Joseph Smith plans trip to, 382–83; Newel K. Whitney and William Marks commanded to move to, 431–34; order given to drive Saints from, 415–16, 425, 428–29, 436, 446. *See also* specific locations

Missouri River, 212–15

Moore, Michael, 326

Morley, Isaac: arrives in Missouri, 202; farm of, 218, 220, 221, 225; repents and receives forgiveness, 224

Mormonism, parallels between Judaism and, 409–10

Moroni. *See* Angel Moroni

Morrill Act (1862), 515

Mortgage, 68–72

Moses (book): revelation on, 121–22; revision of, 154

Moses (prophet): spirit of revelation of, 42; priesthood authority and, 295; reveals instructions to save Israelite children, 331; restores priesthood keys, 409; prophecy on Elijah and, 410

Mount of Transfiguration, 410

Müntzer, Thomas, 147–48

Murder, 144

Murdock, John: faces persecution, 159; asks for revelation on false spirits, 175; called to Missouri, 186–87; meets Missouri River elders, 216–17; baptizes Stephen Burnett, 284; conversion and family of, 364–65; mission call of, 365–66

Murdock, Joseph, 288, 365

Murdock, Julia, 364

Myers, Jacob, 387

Mysteries, gift of knowing, 37–38

Name: of Jesus Christ, 221; of Church, 423–26

Nashville, Iowa, 463

Native Americans selling supplies to, 200. *See also* Lamanites

Nauvoo, Illinois: Newel K. Whitney serves as bishop in, 434; establishment of, 455–56; growth of, 460–61; Saints to gather in areas around, 462–63; Brigham Young's responsibilities in, 464–65

Nauvoo House, 458

Nauvoo House Association, 457

Nauvoo Neighbor, 8

Nauvoo Stake high council, 460

Nauvoo Temple, *457;* construction and ordinances of, 457–58; ordinances performed in, 461, 467–71

Nelson, Russell M., on eternal life, 23

Nephi: translation of book of, 47–48; small plates of, 49

Nephites, learn baptismal ordinance, 56

New and everlasting covenant, 79–80, 155, 169

Newell, Grandison, 152

New Jerusalem. *See* Zion

Newton, Isaac, on controversy over trinity, 341

New York: Edward Partridge accommodates needs of Saints in, 164–65; Joseph Smith seeks financial support in, 382–83

New York Times, 425

Nibley, Hugh: on law of consecration in D&C, 17; on revelation on baptism for the dead, 471

Nicolaitane, 432

592 — Index

Nobleman, 372
North Union, Ohio, 167, 170–71

Oaks, Dallin H.: on name of Church, 425–26; on persecution of Church, 516; on reasons for withholding priesthood from blacks, 524
Obedience: of Joseph Smith, 19; agency and, 198; of Edward Partridge, 204–5; of William McLellin, 229–32; eternal advancement through, 314–15; Heber J. Grant on, 335; power to build temple comes through, 353; Zion will prosper through, 358
Official Declaration–1: added to D&C, 9; origin, 514–16; content, 516–17; outcomes, 517–20
Official Declaration–2: obliterates artificial barriers, 14; temple covenants in, 16; origin, 521–25; content, 525–28; outcomes, 528–30
Ohio: mission success in, 103, 109; leadership in, 121–22, 174; Saints commanded to gather in, 123–31; Saints commanded to stay in, 164–65; organizing Saints in, 181–85; Joseph Smith, Sidney Rigdon, and Oliver Cowdery to return to, 204; elders return to, 210–11; elders face contention while traveling to, 212–15; elders to preach repentance in, 214; dealing with property left in, 218; bishop appointed over Saints in, 250–53. *See also* Kirtland, Ohio
Ohio Star, 249
Olive Leaf revelation, 316–17
Olivet discourse, 154–58
Omnipotence, 49–50
Omniscience, 49–50
Ontario Phoenix, 194
Optimism, 156
Ordain, 468–69
Order: for revelation, 96, 149–51; for ordinances, 468–69
Ordinances: as theme in D&C, 16; building Church and, 74–75; temple, 410–11; in Nauvoo Temple, 457–58, 461; proper order for, 466–71
Ordinations: to Aaronic Priesthood, 56–58; missionary work and, 140–41

Original sin, 256–57
Orphans, 292

Pack, Frederick, 328–29
Packer, Boyd K.: on corrections made to revelations, 6; on Spencer W. Kimball in Denmark, 41; on Word of Wisdom, 329, 332; on efforts of Oliver Granger, 433; on temple ordinances, 458; on definitions of order, ordinance, and ordained, 468
Page, Hiram, 95–96, 102
Page, John E., 438
Painesville [Ohio] Telegraph, 129
Parable: of fig tree, 156–57; of wheat and tares, 307–9; of nobleman and vineyard, 372; of unjust judge, 372
Parenting, 100, 238–40, 347
Parrish, Warren, 284–85
Partridge, Edward, *137;* seeks out Joseph Smith, 116; conversion and revelation for, 119–20; called as bishop, 136–38; role in consecration of, 141, 145; seeks to accommodate needs of New York Saints, 164–65; promised forgiveness, 178; consecration instructions given to, 181–85; buys land in Missouri, 199, 200–201; arrives in Missouri, 202; commanded to repent of skepticism and move to Missouri, 203; to preside at conference, 204; faith and obedience of, 204–5; handles money to purchase land, 222; repents and receives forgiveness, 224; to discipline disobedient Saints, 239; commanded to buy land, 242, 250, 281; is not exempt from consecration, 244; pseudonym for, 279; Joseph Smith on, 288; disagreement with Sidney Rigdon of, 289; persecution of, 290, 337, 360; to handle consecrated items for missionaries, 300; William McLellin refuses to meet with, 304; repents of steadying ark, 305; cares for children of John Murdock, 365–66; is with Lord, 457; Joseph Smith writes to, 462
Partridge, Lydia, 205
Passover, 331, 409–10
Patriarch: calling, 397; Hyrum Smith called as, 459
Patriarchal blessing, of Joseph Smith, 420
Patten, David W.: rebels against Joseph

Smith, 415; revelation given for, 421–22; death of, 437; is with Lord, 457
Patten, Phoebe Ann Babcock, 421
Paul (apostle), 347–48
Paulsen, David, on redemption for dead, 506
Peace, Saints to sue for, 391
Pearl of Great Price, 154
Peck, Electa, 127
Perfection, in revelations, 6
Persecution: printing impeded by, 6–7; of Joseph Smith, 83–84, 470, 495–96; using law for, 85; effect on Emma Smith of, 86; in New York, 90, 106; gathering will prevent, 123–24; en route to Ohio, 127; in Kirtland, Ohio, 130, 367; commandment to gather against, 152–53; deception and, 159–61; in Independence, Missouri, 201; revelation foretelling, in Missouri, 202; purchasing lands to avoid, 219–20; destruction of printing press as, 246, 350–51; Joseph Smith and Sidney Rigdon suffer, 288; of United Firm interests, 290; of Edward Partridge, 337; in Jackson County, Missouri, 357–59, 370–74; counsel on reacting to, 360–63; Saints to seek redress over, 372; Zion's Camp incites, 389; Thomas B. Marsh incites, 415–16; Joseph Smith leaves Kirtland, Ohio due to, 418–19, 430–31; in Adam-ondi-Ahman, 428–29; in Far West, Missouri, 437; letter from Liberty Jail on, 446–54; Saints commanded to document, 451–52; Joseph Smith faces false accusations and, 467; of Church in Utah, 514–16, 519–20
Perseverance of the Saints, 74
Personal revelation, 151
Peter (apostle), 40–41, 93–94
Peterson, Ziba: missionary work of, 107–9; loses preaching license, 203; confesses sins, 205
Phelps, Morris, 437
Phelps, William W.: called as printer, 2, 18, 200; establishes printing office, 6–7, 201; on D&C, 7; as steward of printing press, 145, 245; learns will of God, 194–95; called to repentance, 203; sees Destroyer, 212; commanded to travel on Missouri River, 213; warns of dangers of traveling on Missouri River, 214–15; to counsel and assist John Whitmer, 241; publishes Book of Commandments, 242, 243, 490; as steward of Book of Commandments, 244–46; on recommends, 253; identifies real names of pseudonyms, 278–79; letter from Joseph Smith to, 304–6; letter on government support for displaced Saints, 379; on laying of Far West temple cornerstone, 438–39; controversial statements of, 493
Plan of salvation: as fundamental doctrine, 74; endowment with power and, 99; Joseph Smith and Sidney Rigdon understand, 264–65; rejoicing in, 266
Plates. *See* Gold plates
Plato, 348–49
Plural marriage: official declaration on, 9; commandment and practice of, 480–85; revelation on, 485–88; as trial, 488; Saints face governmental persecution over, 514–16; revelation on relinquishing, 516–17; outcomes of relinquishing, 517–20
Politics, Joseph Smith and, 363, 495, 522
Polygamy. *See* Plural marriage
Polygyny, 480
Poor, consecrating goods for, 184–85
Pratt, Orson, *114;* makes changes to D&C, 9; on rebaptism, 79; called to preach repentance, 113–15; on Martin Harris's consecrating property, 205; mission of, 260; on pseudonyms, 278; publicizes names and reasons for pseudonyms, 278; rebels against Joseph Smith, 415; on Adam-ondi-Ahman, 428; lays cornerstone of Far West temple, 438; announces revelation on plural marriage, 514
Pratt, Parley P., *108;* taught to identify Satan, 58; missionary work of, 107–9; baptizes Ezra Thayre and Northrup Sweet, 111; converts Sidney Rigdon, 116; teaches Edward Partridge, 119; baptizes Lydia Clisbee, 136; called to preach to Shakers, 168, 170–71; converts Levi Hancock, 172–73; on revelation on false spirits, 175–76; called to visit branches, 178; on visiting branches, 180; on treason charge, 227; on Elders school,

357–58, 359; seeks counsel for displaced Saints, 379; called to gather army, 380; reports on Daniel Dunklin's broken promise, 389; rebels against Joseph Smith, 415; imprisonment of, 437; Heber C. Kimball writes to, 472

Prayer(s): to dedicate Kirtland temple, 16, 402–6, *403;* Oliver Cowdery receives answers to, 36, 38–39; for payment on French farm, 130; revelation on Sabbath and, 207–9; for ideal government, 226–28; to rend veil, 233–36; of gathered high priests for revelation, 313–14

Preemption laws, 427–28

Premortal existence: Satan leads souls away in, 99; Satan rebels in, 265

Presidential campaign of Joseph Smith, 495, 522

Pride: of self, 3; Martin Harris struggles with, 34–35; of Oliver Cowdery, 82; Emma Smith and, 87; clothing and, 142

Priesthood: restoration of, 16, 17, 23; prophecy of Elijah and, 21–23; keys, 40–41, 409–10; duties of, 74–75; prophecy on restoration of, 92–94; elders are to lead with, 177–78; temple ordinances and, 295–98; government and function of, 395–99; stem of Jesse and, 419–20; righteous dominion and, 450; reorganization of quorums of, 460; order for temple ordinances and, 468–69; discerning false spirits through, 472–73; authority conferred to Apostles, 499; for black men, 522; withheld from black men, 523–24; made available to all worthy men, 524–30

Printing, increase in, 18

Printing office: William Phelps establishes, 6–7, 201; William Phelps called to establish, 194–95, 200; commandment to build, 350–51

Printing press: William Phelps as steward over, 145, 245; destruction of, 246, 290, 360

Prior, Samuel, 479

Proclamation, Joseph Smith commanded to write, 456

Proof, 219

Property: Saints commanded to leave, 124; insignificance of, 125–26; purchasing, 157–58; organizing, for Saints in Ohio, 181–85; left in Ohio, 218; instructions on consecration of, 223. *See also* Land

Prophet(s): Joseph Smith as, 28; false, 148–49; author's testimony of, 531–32

Pseudonyms, 277–79

Punishment, 69–70

Quakerism, 167

Quincy, Josiah, on Joseph Smith, 497

Quorum of the Seventy: mission calls of, 396; reorganization of, 460. *See also* Apostles

Quorum of the Twelve Apostles: testimony of, 8; establishment and responsibilities of, 395–99; Thomas B. Marsh fights apostasy amongst, 414–15; mission calls of, 421–22; fill vacancies and lay cornerstone of Far West temple, 435–39; reorganization of, 460; priesthood keys conferred to, 499. *See also* Apostles

Race, 521–22

[Ravenna] Ohio Star, 249

Rebaptism, 79–80

Recommends, 252, 253

Record keeping: commandment on, 76–78; John Whitmer called to, 162–63; Church history and, 241, 242; missionary work and, 259; consecration and, 304–6; for redress for persecution, 451–52; baptisms for the dead and, 466–71

Redress: commandment to seek, 372, 390; documenting persecution for, 451–52

Relief Society, learns to discern false spirits, 472

Repentance: receiving mercy through, 27, 28; Joseph Smith called to, 32–33; John and Peter Whitmer to declare, 60–61; importance of, 65–67; Martin Harris called to, 68–72; David B. Haight on, 71–72; precedes baptism, 74–75; agency and, 98; Ezra Thayre and Northrup Sweet to preach, 111–12; Orson Pratt called to preach, 113–15; elders commanded to preach, 150, 152, 214; preparing for Second Coming and, 168–69; Saints called unto, 197; William Phelps called to, 203; for adultery, 219; calling sinners unto, 221; law of just war and, 361–62; after death, 511–12

Restoration: of Church, 17; of gospel, 19; fear of, 48–49; Joseph Knight's role in, 55; of priesthood keys, 92–94, 409–10

Resurrection: of apostles and righteous, 157; Shakers' views on, 167; Joseph Smith and Sidney Rigdon understand, 264–67; degrees of, 270–71; sealing and, 478; marriage after, 486

Revelation(s): difficulty in understanding, xvii–xviii; understanding context of, xviii–xix, 12; compared to works of art, xix–xx; testimony of, 4–5; editing, 5–6; locations of (map), *10;* strategic and tactical, 12–13; Wilford Woodruff on Church and, 19; on John the apostle, 40–41; Oliver Cowdery learns to receive, 44–45; Church-wide, 95–96, 149–51; challenges of, 147–49; Saints' willingness to follow, 163; sacredness of, 221; prayer for confirmation of, 233–36; spelling and punctuation in, 245–46; using pseudonyms in, 277–79; expand on Bible, 309; high priests pray for, 313–14; order for, 400–401

Revelation Book 2, *263,* 384, *385*

Reynolds, George, 515

Reynolds v. United States, 515

Richards, Willard: called as clerk, 306; called as apostle, 436; as journal scribe, 474; accompanies Hyrum and Joseph Smith to Carthage Jail, 496

Rich man, 384

Rigdon, Sidney: writes revelations, 2, 5; transcribes section 1, 18; revelation given for, 116–18; Edward Partridge travels with, 119; confirms Edward Partridge, 120; as scribe, 121–22, 243; revelation on James Covill given to, 132; invited to live with Leman Copley, 136; commandment for elders to gather given to, 152–53; called to preach to Shakers, 168, 170–71; bears testimony, 173; called to Missouri, 186; Sidney Gilbert to travel with, 190; dedicates Independence, Missouri, 200; arrives in Missouri, 202; to describe land and declare word of God, 204, 218; dedicates and describes land of Zion, 205; called to Cincinnati, Ohio, 210, 213–14; commanded to find new home, 221; Lord rejects land description of, 221; moves to Hiram, Ohio, 222; as steward of Book of Commandments, 244–46; called to preach gospel to neighbors, 248–49; to continue revising Bible, 254; receives vision of Jesus Christ, 264–67; on vision of God, 270; pseudonym for, 278; commanded to counsel with Missouri Church leaders, 280; called as counselor to Joseph Smith, 286, 460; suffers persecution, 288, 448; visits Missouri Church leaders, 288–89; repentance and forgiveness of, 336–37; ordination of, 339; mission with Joseph Smith of, 367–69; as member of council presidency, 375; called to teach eastern Saints, 380; travels to Salem, Massachusetts, 412–13; calls Willard Richards as apostle, 436; health promised to, 459–60; presents statement on Church and government, 493

Riggs, Burr, 173–74, 260

Righteous dominion, 450

Ripley, Alanson, on moving to Zarahemla, Iowa, 463

Roberts, B. H.: on calling of bishops, 138; on Liberty Jail, 453; on relinquishing plural marriage, 518–19

Robinson, George: on building Far West Temple, 425; as journal scribe, 428

Roll of paper, 110, 111–12

Romney, Marion G., on revelation on priesthood, 526–27

Ryder, Simonds, 187

Sabbath day, 207–9, 238

Sacrament: revelation on building Church and, 74–75; with Jesus Christ and prophets, 92–94; false spirit disrupts, 179

Saint Teresa of Avila, 147

"Saith the Lord," 431–32

Salem, Massachusetts, 412–13

Salem Gazette, 413

Salem Register, 413

Salt Lake Temple, 519

Salvation: for all, 14; at Second Coming, 20; for earth, 23; apostles and keys required for, 41; idea of elect and, 74; Joseph Smith and Sidney Rigdon receive revelation on, 262–66; degrees of, 270–

71; agency and, 271–72; knowledge and, 478–79; for dead, 504–7; race and, 522

Satan: revelations on, 16–17; servants of, 46–47; God uses omniscience against, 50; identifying, 58; agency and, 99; limited powers of, 99; false spirits and, 172–80; pattern to avoid deception by, 187; discerning, 188, 472–73; William Phelps sees, 212; hates Zion, 218; rebellion and attack on Saints of, 265; destiny of, 272; turns away Church leaders in Missouri, 279–81; battle with, 315

School of elders, 357–59

School of the Prophets, 316–17, 352, 353, 354

Scribe(s): for revelations, 5; Oliver Cowdery as, 36, 38–39, 44–45; Emma Smith as, 87; Sidney Rigdon as, 117–18; of Book of Mormon and revelations, 243

Scriptures: D&C accepted as, 7–8; hearing voice of Jesus Christ in, 11–12; definition of term, 239; Joseph Smith studies, 273; patterns for studying, 276; financial support for publishing, 277–81; Apocrypha and, 340–42; treasury for publication of, 386

Sealing: revelation on, 16, 477–78; Russell M. Nelson on, 23

Second coming: section 1 prophesies of, 19; salvation or damnation at, 20; preparing for, 98–99, 123, 155–58, 168–69, 226, 490–92; consecration and, 223–24; description of, 315; timing of, 474–76

Second death, 219

Seer stone(s): Moroni returns, 26, 28; earth will become, 475

Self-reliance, 3–4

Servants of Satan, 46–47

Shakers, 166–71

Sherer, John, 83

Sherman, Lyman, 400–401

Shipps, Jan, on revelation on priesthood, 528–29

Sick, healing, 142

Sign seeking, 219

Sin: of Joseph Smith, 84; Saints commanded to repent of, 197; ignoring priesthood as, 297–98; as cause of Saints' persecution, 371

Slavery, 310–12, 521–22

Smith, Alvin, 25, 504–7

Smith, Asael, 262

Smith, Eden, 261, 284

Smith, Emma Hale, *88;* gives birth to Alvin Smith, 25; as Book of Mormon scribe, 36; baptism of, 83; counsel and promises given to, 86–89; confirmation of, 92; works to prepare missionaries, 107–8; on missionaries to Lamanites, 109; sacrifices to gather in Ohio, 127; Joseph Smith records tribute to, 306; complains over spit-covered floor, 323; adopts twins of John Murdock, 365; moves to Far West, Missouri, 419; friendship with Elizabeth Ann Whitney, 432; mentioned, 446; reads letter from Liberty Jail, 452; sealing of, 478; plural marriage and, 481, 484–85; commanded to accept plural marriage, 487–88; exaltation of, 488–89; writes blessing, 489

Smith, Frederick, 419

Smith, George A.: on Ezra Booth, 248; ordained apostle, 438

Smith, Hyrum, *459;* eats breakfast with Martin Harris, 26; revelation for, 51–53; Lord's will for, 81–82; Ezra Thayre attends preaching meeting of, 110; moves to Ohio, 127; called to Missouri, 186–87; meets Missouri River elders, 216–17; mission of, 260–61; rebukes Missouri Church leaders, 302; Joseph Smith records tribute to, 306; on hot drinks, 333; as building committee member, 351, 352; travels to Salem, Massachusetts, 412–13; on persecution of Mormons, 447; love of God for, 456; called as assistant president and patriarch, 459; accepts revelation on plural marriage, 484–85; death of, 496, 508; confers priesthood keys on apostles, 499; Joseph F. Smith sees, 511

Smith, John, 375

Smith, Joseph

Dissent and persecution

Persecution of, 83–84, 288, 367, 467, 470; Saints find fault with, 284–85; on fault finding, 320; reacts to persecution in Missouri, 362–63, 379–81; called to organize army, 380; apostles rebel against, 415; Saints rebel against, 447–

48; suffering of, 450–51, 453–54; seeks redress for Missouri losses, 451–52

Life and family
Death of, 8, 227, 461, 495–98, 502; William Whittaker portrait of, *19;* Joseph Knight provides food and supplies to, 54, 55; Sidney Rigdon's friendship with, 117–18; invited to live with Leman Copley, 136; location for home of, 218; commanded to find new home, 221; moves to Hiram, Ohio, 222, 223, 226; religious background of, 262; leg operation of, 322; adopts twins of John Murdock, 365; Newel K. Whitney's friendship with, 432; practices plural marriage, 480–85; views on race of, 522

Prophet and Church leader
divine calling of, 12; priesthood keys restored to, 16, 23; called as prophet, 19; ordained to Aaronic Priesthood, 56–58, *57;* organizes Church, 76–78; to prepare for conference, 90–91; as apostle, 93–94; strengthens New York Saints, 121–22; Saints follow voice of, 131, 163; on foreknowing and foreordination, 135; chastens William Phelps, 145, 245; on consecration, 145, 291; as prophet of Church, 149, 150–51; on spiritual gifts, 161; learns to discern spirits, 174–75; on deception of Satan, 180; counsels Edward Partridge on consecration, 184–85; called to Missouri, 186; Sidney Gilbert to travel with, 190; on traveling to Missouri, 199; arrives in Missouri, 202; exhorts Saints to obey commandments, 205–6; called to Cincinnati, Ohio, 210, 213–14; leads elders at Missouri River, 212; commanded to visit branches in Missouri, 220–21; answers questions of William McLellin, 229; William McLellin's testimony of, 231; heals Elsa Johnson, 247–48; called to preach gospel to neighbors, 248–49; on fear of death, 268; commanded to counsel with Missouri Church leaders, 280; called as president of High Priesthood, 286; visits Missouri Church leaders, 288–89; visits Saints in Jackson County, Missouri, 292; rebukes Saints and Church leaders in Missouri, 318–19; on preparing for solemn assembly, 319–20; dedicates Kirtland temple, 320, 402; letter to Vienna Jaques from, 337–38; uncertainty on building Zion of, 339; Frederick G. Williams called as counselor to, 343–44; Truman Madsen on, 348–49; raises funds for Kirtland temple construction, 354; mission with Sidney Rigdon of, 367–69; letters from Missouri Church leaders to, 370; as member of council presidency, 375; role in council of, 376; blesses high councilors, 376–77; seeks financial support in Missouri, 382–83; prays for financial help, 387–88; uses priesthood keys, 410–11; travels to Salem, Massachusetts, 412–13; as stem of Jesse, 419–20; First Presidency calling of, 460; teaches redemption for dead, 466–67, 510; corrects Orson Hyde's teachings on Second Coming, 474–75; seals Melissa and Benjamin Johnson, 477–78; exaltation of, 488–89; significance of, 497–98; confers priesthood keys on apostles, 499

Revelations, visions, and visitations
dictates revelations, 2, 5, 6; challenges Church leaders to gain testimony of revelations, 4–5; on revelations, 11, 236; Angel Moroni appears to, 21; seeks revelation on building Church, 65–67; defends revelation on baptism, 74–75; on stone in Daniel's prophecy, 227; defends revelations, 245–46; receives vision of Jesus Christ, 264–67; on vision of degrees of glory, 272; on understanding revelations of John, 276; Jesus Christ appears to, 407–9; heavenly messengers seen by, 469; Joseph F. Smith sees, 511

Scriptures and publications
holds meeting on publishing revelations, 1–2, 18; to head publication committee, 7; gives Martin Harris Book of Mormon manuscript pages, 24–26; prays for forgiveness over lost pages, 26–28; as mediator between Martin Harris and Jesus Christ, 32–33; three witnesses testify of, 33–34, 62–64; Olivery Cowdery becomes scribe for, 36–37; gift of translation of, 44–46; revises

Bible, 154–58, 254, 307–9; simple language of, 233–36; writes history of Church, 242; as steward of Book of Commandments, 244–46; struggles to understand Bible, 256; studies scriptures, 273; responsibilities in Literary Firm of, 277; pseudonym for, 278; begins record keeping, 305–6

Smith, Joseph F., 508–13, *509*

Smith, Joseph Fielding: on Nauvoo Temple ordinances, 457–58; Joseph F. Smith dictates revelation to, 509; reads revelation to Church leaders, 513

Smith, Joseph III, 419, 446

Smith, Joseph Sr.: dreams and purpose of, 29; revelation given to, 30, 51; Lord's will for, 81–82; moves to Ohio, 127; asks Oliver Huntington to move to Ohio, 130; religious affiliations of, 262; alcohol habits of, 322; financial counsel given to, 337; called as high councilor, 375; gives Joseph Smith patriarchal blessing, 420; sits at Lord's right hand, 457; replaced as patriarch, 459; blesses Joseph Smith, 505; learns doctrine of baptism for the dead, 506–7

Smith, Julia, 419

Smith, Lucy Mack, *128;* on breakfast with Martin Harris, 25–26; argues with Thomas B. Marsh, 106; on work ethic of Emma Smith, 107–8; on Edward Partridge, 119–20; on section 37, 121; leads Saints to Ohio, 128–29; on leg operation of Joseph Smith, 322

Smith, Mercy Josephine, 508

Smith, Samuel: brings Oliver Cowdery to home of Emma and Joseph Smith, 36; baptism of, 51, 58; Lord's will for, 81–82; commanded to preach with Reynolds Cahoon, 214; William McLellin serves mission with, 231; mission of, 259, 260; on revelations given in section 88, 313–14; called as high councilor, 375

Smith, Sylvester, 261, 376

Smoot, Reed, 520

Snider, John, 457

Snow, Erastus, 413

Snow, Lorenzo, 517

Solemn assembly: lectures on faith for, 9; preparation for, 319–20; held in Kirtland temple, 391–92; Lyman Sherman to wait for, 400–401

Soteriology, 262

Soul: worth of, 65–67, 125–26; as combination of spirit and body, 314; Word of Wisdom and, 327–28

Spirits: false, 172–80, 472–73; soul and, 314

Spiritual gifts, 160–61

Spirit world, missionary work in, 508–13

Spring Hill, Missouri, 425, 427, 428

St. Louis, Missouri, 210–11

Stakes, Joseph Smith to establish new, 425, 427–28

Stanton, Daniel, 261

Statehood, 514

Steadying the ark, 305

Stealing, 144

Stem of Jesse, 419–20

Stewardship: consecration and, 144–46, 243–46, 501; for Ohio Saints, 182–83; accountability and, 251; Word of Wisdom and, 328, 330; over French farm, 355–56; of United Firm, 382–88

Stockton, Benjamin, 504

Stone, 227

Storehouse: commandment to establish, 141–42; of Sidney Gilbert, 224–25; as stewardship of bishops, 251; of Newel K. Whitney, 277; United Firm organized for, 279–81; joining of printing operations and, 290; widows, orphans, and children have access to, 292

Stowell, Josiah, 83

Suffering: of Joseph Smith, 450–51; purpose of, 453–54

Suicide, 267–68

Sweet, Northrup, 111–12

Sword of Laban, 62–64

Talents, 289

Tanner, John, 130, 388

Tanner, N. Eldon, 527, 531–32

Tares, 307–9

Tate, George, on vision of missionary work in spirit world, 513

Taylor, John: wounded in Liberty Jail, 8, 496; Word of Wisdom and, 334; called as apostle, 422; lays cornerstone of Far West temple, 438

Tea, 324, 333

Teacher, office of, 296
Telestial kingdom, 267–69
Temperance movement, 322–23
Temple: commandment to build, 16, 350–51, 357–59; sealing families in, 23; Jesus Christ prophesies destruction of, 155; Independence, Missouri site for, 200; Joseph Smith dedicates site for, 200; priesthood and, 295–98, 302–3; consecration and construction of, 301–2; preparation for attending, 316–17; Joseph Smith emphasizes importance of, 318–19; obedience to Word of Wisdom and, 335; Saints rebuked for not building, 352–54; ordinances, 410–11; Gordon B. Hinckley on, 461. *See also* Far West Temple; Kirtland Temple; Nauvoo Temple
Temptation, limited, 99
Ten Commandments, 141, 207
Teresa of Avila, Saint, 147
Terrestrial kingdom, 267, 268–69
Testimony: of revelations, 4–5, 234, 235; of D&C, 7–8; of prophets, 531–32
Thayre, Ezra: conversion and revelation for, 110–12; mission of, 196, 260; commanded to repent, 197; actions of, 198; brings charges against Curtis Hodges, 377–78
Thompson, Ohio, 192–93
Thompson, Robert, 456
Three witnesses, 33–34, 60, 62–64
Time, relativity of, 474, 475
Tithing: resurrection and, 223; beginning of, 440–43; disposition of, 444–45
Tobacco, 323–27, 332–33
Tocqueville, Alexis de, 3
Translation: gift of, 42–43; Oliver Cowdery loses gift of, 44–45; Joseph Smith regains gift of, 46
Treason, Joseph Smith charged with, 227, 415–16
Treasure hunting, 412–13
Treasury, commandment to establish, 386
Trials (adversity): revelation foretelling, 202; purpose of, 371, 453–54; plural marriage as, 488
Trials (legal proceedings), of Joseph Smith, 83–84, 446–47
Trinity, controversy over, 341
Trumpet, 110, 111–12

Truth: in revelations, 6; light and, 315; Truman Madsen on, 349

United Firm: organization of, 278–81, 289–91; covenant of, 337, 442; Frederick G. Williams joins, 343–44; Kirtland farms and, 356; dissolution of, 382–88; role of Newel K. Whitney in, 432
United order. *See* United Firm
United Society of Believers in Christ's Second Appearing, 166–71
Universalism, 262
Unjust judge, 372
Urim and Thummim: Joseph Smith loses, 46; revelation received through, 51, 59; witnesses of, 62–64
Utah, government of, 514–15

Van Buren, Martin, 451–52
Vegetables, 333
Vegetarianism, 167, 169
Veil, prayer to rend, 233–36
Vineyard, 372
Vision: of Ezra Thayre, 110; of Levi Hancock, 173; of Jesus Christ and resurrection, 264–67; of degrees of glory, 267–69; comes through power of Holy Ghost, 269–70; of God, 270; of Kirtland temple, 353–54; of ancient church council, 376; of Jesus Christ in Kirtland Temple, 407–9; of Alvin Smith and celestial kingdom, 504–7; of missionary work in spirit world, 508–13
Voice of God, as scripture, 239
Voting: common consent in, 91; as means for persecution, 515

Wakefield, Joseph, 178, 180, 187
Walker, Charles Lowell, on telestial kingdom, 268
Walker, Lucy, 483
Wants, 182–83
War: American Civil War, 310–12, 475, 514–15, 521; law of just, 361–62; World War I, 508
Washing of feet (ordinance), 319
Washing of feet (symbol of accountability): commandment for, 211, 259, 299; John Murdock commanded to, 365, 366
Washings, 458

Water(s): Brigham Young on sacrament and, 93; dangers upon, 213
Wayland, Francis, on baptism, 80
Wealth: obsession with, 3–4; worldly versus spiritual, 124, 125–26
Welton, Micah, 261
"We Thank Thee, O God, for a Prophet," 531
Wheat and tares, 307–9
Whitlock, Harvey, 216–17
Whitmer, David: as witness, 33–34, 62–64; Oliver Cowdery writes to, 39; revelation for, 59–60; seeks revelation on building Church, 65–67; Lord chastens, 101–2; meets Missouri River elders, 216–17; Church discipline of, 421
Whitmer, John, *163;* copies transcription, 5; assists in publication of revelations, 6; on D&C, 7; revelation for, 59, 60–61; to prepare for conference, 90–91; missionary work of, 103; as scribe, 114; on revelation for Sidney Rigdon, 116–17, 118; letter from, 121; on section 37, 121, 122; on revelation to gather Saints, 123, 126; on evil surrounding New York Saints, 125; mentioned, 132; on law of Church of Jesus Christ, 144; on revelation on revelatory authority, 150; on revelation on Church meetings, 159; called to write Church history, 162–63; on missionary work among Shakers, 168; called to preside over Ohio, 174; on false spirits, 175; on conference of elders, 186; raises funds to buy land in Missouri, 222; as steward of Book of Commandments, 241–42, 243, 244–46; pseudonym for, 279
Whitmer, Peter: revelation for, 59, 60–61; missionary work of, 102–3, 107–9
Whitney, Elizabeth Ann, 130, 432
Whitney, Newel K., *251;* on D&C, 7; revelation given to, 13; Emma and Joseph Smith stay with, 130; mentioned, 190; called to buy land in Missouri, 204; commanded to stay in Kirtland, Ohio, 220; raises funds to buy land in Missouri, 221–22; consecrates land, 222; keeps store, 225; called as bishop over Ohio, 251–52; responsibilities of, 277; pseudonym for, 278; commanded to counsel with Missouri Church leaders, 280; role in United Firm of, 290; to handle consecrated items for missionaries, 300; called to visit Church branches, 301; Joseph Smith records tribute to, 306; classes held in store of, 323; rebuked for neglecting care of family, 347; called as steward of French farm, 355–56; commanded to move to Far West, Missouri, 431–34; encourages tithing, 440
Whittaker, David, 278–79
Whittaker, William, 19
Widows, 292
Wight, Lyman: called to Missouri, 186; to beware Satan, 187; seeks counsel for displaced Saints, 379; called to gather army, 380; home of, 425; land purchases of, 427; called as member of Nauvoo House Association, 457
Williams, Frederick G.: transcribes revelations, 5; farm of, 197, 218; consecrates land, 222, 225; called as counselor to Joseph Smith, 287; as scribe, 304–6; repentance and forgiveness of, 336–37; ordination of, 339; joins United Firm, 343–44; as member of council presidency, 375
Will of God, agency and, 328
Wilson, Calves, 260
Winchester, Benjamin, 413
Wine, 92–94
Witnesses: of gold plates, 33–34, 62–64; David Whitmer as, 60; of Book of Commandments, 236
Woodford, Robert, on D&C, 1
Woodruff, Wilford, *516;* publishes D&C in Great Britain, 9; on revelation, 19; on telestial kingdom, 268; on learning about salvation, 271; called as apostle, 422, 436; letter from Thomas B. Marsh to, 424; lays cornerstone of Far West temple, 436–39; on baptism for the dead, 470; on persecution of Joseph Smith, 470; on discerning false spirits, 472; teaches redemption for dead, 510; on persecution of Church, 516; receives revelation relinquishing plural marriage, 516–17; on relinquishing plural marriage, 517–18
Word of Wisdom: origin, 322–24; content, 324–32; outcomes, 332–35

Works, 345–46
Worldliness. *See* Materialism
World War I, 508
Worship, 345–49

Young, Brigham, *500;* makes changes to D&C, 9; on sacrament water, 93; on Satan and agency, 99; on Orson Pratt, 115; moves to Ohio, 130; on vision of degrees of glory, 271–72; publicizes names and reasons for pseudonyms, 278; on origin of Word of Wisdom, 323–24; on applying common sense to Word of Wisdom, 329; tobacco use of, 334; Thomas B. Marsh consults with, 414; forgives Thomas B. Marsh, 416–17; ordains Willard Richards as apostle, 436; lays cornerstone of Far West temple, 436–39; collects tithes, 442; as president of Twelve Apostles, 460; family and callings of, 464–65; blamed for plural marriage, 489; leads Church, 499–500; leads emigration of Saints, 500–503; teaches redemption for dead, 510; announces revelation on plural marriage, 514

Zarahemla, Iowa, 462–63
Zion: as contrast to individualism, 4; choice between Babylon and, 13, 14; location of, 96, 164–65; commandment to buy land for, 157–58; Missouri revealed as, 188–89; Independence, Missouri established as, 199–201; amongst Babylon, 208; Satan's hate for, 218; building, 224; organizing storehouses for, 279–81; problems in building, 290; Saints to gather in, 295; Joseph Smith's uncertainty in building, 339; Joseph Smith worries about, 368; to be built in Jackson County, Missouri, 371; redemption of, 374, 379–81; postponed in Missouri, 390–91; little season preceding, 392; consecration for, 501. *See also* Independence, Missouri; Nauvoo, Illinois
Zion's Camp: gathering of, 379–81; arrives in Clay County, Missouri, 389; commanded to retreat, 390–91

About the Author

STEVEN C. HARPER is a professor of Church history and doctrine at Brigham Young University. In 2012 Steve was appointed as the managing historian and a general editor of *Saints: The Story of the Church of Jesus Christ in the Latter Days*. He was named editor in chief of *BYU Studies Quarterly* in September 2018. He earned a bachelor's degree from BYU, an MA in American history from Utah State University, and a PhD in early American history from Lehigh University in Bethlehem, Pennsylvania. He began teaching courses in religion and history at BYU Hawaii in 2000 and joined the Religious Education faculty at BYU in 2002. That year he also became a volume editor of *The Joseph Smith Papers* and the document editor for *BYU Studies*. He taught at the BYU Jerusalem Center for Near Eastern Studies in 2011–2012. He is also the author of several books, including *Joseph Smith's First Vision: A Guide to the Historical Accounts* and *First Vision: Memory and Mormon Origins*, along with dozens of articles. He and his wife, Jennifer Sebring Harper, live in Utah.